Coroners' Investigations and

While every care has been taken to ensure the accuracy of this work, no responsibility for loss or damage occasioned to any person acting or refraining from action as a result of any statement in it can be accepted by the authors, editors or publishers.

Coroners' Investigations and Inquests

General Editors

Richard Baker

Rose Harvey-Sullivan

James Robottom

James Weston

Barristers at 7BR

LexisNexis® UK & Worldwide

United Kingdom	RELX (UK) Limited trading as LexisNexis®, 1–3 Strand, London WC2N 5JR
LNUK Global Partners	LexisNexis® encompasses authoritative legal publishing brands dating back to the 19th century including: Butterworths® in the United Kingdom, Canada and the Asia-Pacific region; Les Editions du Juris Classeur in France; and Matthew Bender® worldwide. Details of LexisNexis® locations worldwide can be found at www.lexisnexis.com

© 2021 RELX (UK) Ltd.
Published by LexisNexis®

All rights reserved. No part of this publication may be reproduced in any material form (including photocopying or storing it in any medium by electronic means and whether or not transiently or incidentally to some other use of this publication) without the written permission of the copyright owner except in accordance with the provisions of the Copyright, Designs and Patents Act 1988 or under the terms of a licence issued by the Copyright Licensing Agency Ltd, 5th Floor, Shackleton House, 4 Battlebridge Lane, London, SE1 2HX. Applications for the copyright owner's written permission to reproduce any part of this publication should be addressed to the publisher.
Warning: The doing of an unauthorised act in relation to a copyright work may result in both a civil claim for damages and criminal prosecution.

Crown copyright material is reproduced with the permission of the Controller of HMSO and the Queen's Printer for Scotland. Parliamentary copyright material is reproduced with the permission of the Controller of Her Majesty's Stationery Office on behalf of Parliament. Any European material in this work which has been reproduced from EUR-lex, the official European Communities legislation website, is European Communities copyright.

LexisNexis® and the Knowledge Burst logo are registered trademarks of RELX Group plc, used under license. Butterworths® and Tolley® are registered trademarks of RELX (UK) Ltd. Matthew Bender® is a registered trademark of Matthew Bender & Company Inc. Other products and services may be trademarks or registered trademarks of their respective companies.
A CIP Catalogue record for this book is available from the British Library.

ISBN 978-1-4743-1753-5

ISBN for this volume: 9781474317535

Printed and bound by Hobbs the Printers, Hampshire SO40 3WX

Visit LexisNexis at http://www.lexisnexis.co.uk

Foreword

When someone dies unnaturally, it is incumbent on the justice system to provide a proper framework in order to understand what has happened and to seek to prevent its recurrence. The most common way in which it does so is by holding an inquest. The law relating to inquests, which must encompass both catastrophic events such as the Hillsborough Disaster and those on a lesser scale (albeit equally distressing to those who have lost loved ones) is by no means straightforward. Many of us think it ripe for comprehensive reform (as the recent Justice report, 'When Things Go Wrong: the response of the justice system' suggests).

In the meantime I welcome wholeheartedly this new publication dealing with the coronial system. Richard Baker, Rose Harvey-Sullivan, James Robottom and James Weston are to be congratulated on editing so readable and practical a publication. Its breadth is admirable. Every aspect of inquests is covered, from the investigation, to the hearing, to the conclusions and consequential events. Even the important topic of funding and costs is not omitted. The often difficult issue of the relationship between inquests and other proceedings, such as prosecutions, civil proceedings, and in cases of catastrophic events, public inquiries is also comprehensively dealt with.

What any busy practitioner will particularly welcome are the practical guides dealing with particular types of inquest, which feature at Chapters 13 to 20.

While obviously written with the practitioner in mind, anyone who has to give evidence will also find it helpful reading in order to understand their role in context.

In short, this is a new important reference source for any practitioner in this area of the law. It should be on the shelf of all those whose work involves inquests.

The Right Honourable Sir John Goldring

Preface to the First Edition

The role of a coroner is unique within the sphere of the British judiciary. This book focuses on their obligation to investigate violent and unnatural deaths and is intended to be read primarily by practitioners, whether they are representing families, individuals or organisations. It was written as a practical and, we hope, accessible guide to the law, practice and procedure of coroners' courts. Our aim has been to write a text that not only serves as a reference point on the law and a guide as to the issues that arise at each stage of the investigation process, but also one which considers specific types of inquest in more specialised fields. These practical guides, found at Chapters 13 to 20, should offer clear guidance to those who are unfamiliar with the particular sub-speciality, and act as a resource for those who are more experienced.

This book has been produced as a collaborative effort by the authors listed overleaf. Writing the first edition of any book is a difficult and time-consuming exercise and we would like to thank them for their contributions and their patience with us.

When we began to write this book, we could not have predicted the impact of the COVID-19 pandemic on society and on the courts. Coroners' courts, in particular, have come under unprecedented pressure during 2020. Thousands of families have tragically been bereaved. At the time of writing, it remains to be seen what role coroners' courts will take in investigating COVID-related deaths. We have been able to incorporate the Chief Coroner's initial guidance to coroners during the pandemic. We hope that this guidance soon becomes obsolete.

Richard Baker
Rose Harvey-Sullivan
James Robottom
James Weston
February 2021

Contributors

General Editors

Richard Baker, Rose Harvey-Sullivan, James Robottom and James Weston, Barristers at 7BR

Contributors

Richard Baker, Barrister at 7BR

Chapter 4, Preliminary Issues and the Pre-Inquest Review

Chapter 5, The Inquest Hearing

Chapter 10, Representing Families at Inquests

Chapter 13, Clinical Inquests

Ross Beaton, Barrister at 7BR

Chapter 2, The Investigation

Chapter 19, Military Inquests

Conor Dufficy, Barrister at 7BR

Chapter 4, Preliminary Issues and the Pre-Inquest Review

Chapter 12, Press and Publicity at Inquests

Chapter 18, Product-related Deaths

Sarah Edwards, Barrister at 7BR

Chapter 6, Conclusions and Records of Inquests

Chapter 22, Inquests and Family Proceedings

Rose Harvey-Sullivan, Barrister at 7BR

Chapter 1, The Role of the Coroner

Chapter 6, Conclusions and Records of Inquests

Chapter 7, Reports to Prevent Future Deaths

Chapter 8, Challenging Coronial Decisions: Judicial Review and Statutory Review

Contributors

Chapter 12, Press and Publicity at Inquests

Chapter 15, Mental Health and Mental Capacity

Chapter 20, Inquests and COVID-19

Tom Jervis, Solicitor at Leigh Day

Chapter 12, Press and Publicity at Inquests

Chapter 18, Product-related Deaths

Adam Korn, Barrister at 7BR

Chapter 5, The Inquest Hearing

Chapter 17, Road Traffic Collision Deaths

Chapter 23, Inquests and Civil Proceedings

Kate Lumbers, Barrister at 7BR

Chapter 6, Conclusions and Records of Inquests

Chapter 13, Clinical Inquests

James Macdonald, Barrister at 7BR

Chapter 3, Scope and Article 2 ECHR

Chapter 17, Road Traffic Collision Deaths

Chapter 24, Inquests and Public Inquiries

David Matthew, Barrister at 7BR

Chapter 21, Inquests and Criminal Proceedings

Claire Moore, Solicitor at DAC Beachcroft

Chapter 16, Workplace Deaths

Jill Paterson, Solicitor at Leigh Day

Chapter 12, Press and Publicity at Inquests

Chapter 18, Product-related Deaths

Lynda Reynolds, Solicitor at Hugh James

Chapter 9, Funding and Costs

Chapter 10, Representing Families at Inquests

James Robottom, Barrister at 7BR

Chapter 2, The Investigation

Chapter 3, Scope and Article 2 ECHR

Chapter 6, Conclusions and Records of Inquests

Chapter 8, Challenging Coronial Decisions: Judicial Review and Statutory Review

Chapter 15, Mental Health and Mental Capacity

Chapter 20, Inquests and COVID-19

Kate Temple-Mabe, Barrister at 7BR

Chapter 1, The Role of the Coroner

Chapter 5, The Inquest Hearing

Chapter 23, Inquests and Civil Proceedings

James Weston, Barrister at 7BR

Chapter 9, Funding and Costs

Chapter 11, Representing Organisations at Inquests

Chapter 12, Press and Publicity at Inquests

Chapter 14, Deaths in Custody

Contents

Foreword	v
Preface to the First Edition	vii
Contributors	ix
Table of Statutes	xxvii
Table of Statutory Instruments	xxxi
Table of Cases	xxxiii

Chapter 1 The Role of the Coroner

What is a coroner?	1.1
Purpose of an inquest	1.5
Inquests are inquisitorial, not adversarial	1.9
Categories of coroner	1.15
(a) The Chief Coroner	1.16
(b) Senior coroners	1.20
(c) Area and assistant coroners	1.23
(d) Coroners' officers	1.26

Chapter 2 The Investigation

Introduction to coroners' investigations	2.1
Body in the coroner's area – standard notification of deaths	
Certification and notification of deaths by medical practitioners	2.4
Medical examiners	2.12
Notification of deaths by registrars	2.13
Other notifications where the body is present	2.17
The investigation	2.22
Coroner's decision that no post mortem or investigation is required	2.31
Disputes around the end of life	2.33

Contents

Stillbirths	2.35
Opening an investigation	2.38
Interim death certificate	2.44
Investigations without a body	2.46
Post-mortem examinations	2.53
Organ donation and tissue retention	2.56
Exhumation	2.61
Requests for expedited post mortems	2.65
Arrangements for post mortem	2.67
Non-invasive post mortems	2.70
Conduct of the post mortem	2.75
Second post mortems	2.83
Discontinuance where the post mortem reveals the cause of death	2.86
Release of the body following post mortem	2.89
Transfer of jurisdiction	2.91
Coroner's investigation – practical steps to gather evidence	2.98
Fast track and documentary inquests	2.104
Conclusion following fast track or documentary inquest	2.111
Suspension of investigation	
Duty to suspend	2.113
Suspension due to public inquiry	2.119
Discretion to suspend	2.122
Consequences of suspension	2.123
Resumption of investigation or inquest	2.126
Chapter 3 Scope and Article 2 ECHR	
Scope	
Introduction	3.2
Statutory provisions	3.3
Jamieson inquests and *Middleton* inquests	3.10
The coroner's discretion as to scope	3.22
The determination of scope in practice	3.29
The European Convention on Human Rights	3.35
The structure of the substantive ECHR rights	3.39

The Human Rights Act 1998	3.40
The relevance of the HRA 1998 to inquests	3.42
The ECHR and inquests	
Scope of Art 2 inquests	3.51
Article 2 ECHR – The Right to Life	3.55
The negative duty	3.61
The positive substantive duties	
The systemic duty	3.70
(a) Dangerous activities and natural hazards	3.72
(b) Certain mental health patients	3.79
(c) Prisoners and detainees	3.80
(d) Military operations	3.81
(e) Systemic disfunction in general clinical care	3.83
The operational duty	3.88
Features of the operational duty	3.93
The investigative duty	3.98
Engagement of the investigative duty	3.102
Criteria for compliance with the investigative duty	3.104
Chapter 4 Preliminary Issues and the Pre-inquest Review (PIR)	
The pre-inquest review	4.1
Properly interested persons	4.11
Interested person status	4.13
The rights of interested persons	4.24
Scope and Art 2	4.32
Witness evidence	
Coroner's discretion	4.33
Power to compel	4.35
Protective measures	4.36
Rule 23 and the use of documentary evidence at the inquest	4.42
Disclosure	
Introduction	4.48
Disclosure of material to the coroner	4.51
Public interest immunity	4.58

Contents

Notices and summonses	4.61
Disclosure by the coroner to interested persons	4.66
Medical records	4.83
Requirement for a jury	4.86
Deaths in state detention	4.93
Death by act or omission of a police officer	4.100
Deaths caused by a notifiable accident, poisoning or disease	4.101
Validity of proceedings where a jury is not summoned	4.108
Discretion to summon a jury	4.109
Experts	4.114
Coroner's discretion	4.115
Experts' duties and fees	4.125

Chapter 5 The Inquest Hearing

Coroner's introduction	5.1
Order of evidence	5.2
Calling and questioning witnesses	5.4
Admissibility of evidence at inquests	5.13
Hearsay	5.14
Duty to act fairly	5.21
Privilege against self-incrimination	5.25
Closing submissions	5.30
The jury at the inquest hearing	5.34
Jury questionnaires	5.45

Chapter 6 Conclusions and Records of Inquests

A – The Record of Inquest	6.7
Box 1: name of deceased	6.9
Box 2: medical cause of death	6.10
Box 3: how, when and where the deceased came about their death	6.13
Box 3 and Art 2: in what circumstances did the deceased come about their death?	6.15
Box 4: conclusion as to the death	6.22
Box 5: further particulars	6.25
Attestation	6.27

Caption	6.28
B – Conclusions: practicalities	
Making submissions	6.29
Reasons	6.30
Conclusions in jury inquests	6.34
Conclusions in cases where there have been related criminal proceedings	6.42
Admissions by an interested person	6.43
C – Short-form conclusions	
Overview	6.49
I. Accident or misadventure	6.55
II. Alcohol/drug related	6.59
III. Industrial disease	6.61
IV. Lawful killing/unlawful killing	6.62
Lawful killing	6.68
Unlawful killing	6.69
Parties and causation	6.110
Standard of proof	6.111
Directions to the jury	6.112
V. Natural causes	6.117
VI. Open conclusion	6.119
VII. Road traffic collision	6.126
VIII. Stillbirth	6.128
IX. Suicide	6.134
D – Neglect	6.142
Definition of neglect	6.143
Failure v 'gross' failure	6.149
Neglect as a series of acts or omissions	6.151
Neglect in cases involving self-harm and accidents	6.158
E – Narrative conclusions	
What is a narrative conclusion?	6.160
The content of a narrative conclusion	
Article 2 inquests	6.164

Contents

Non-Article 2 inquests	6.170
F – Standard of proof	6.172
G – Causation	6.174
Causation and neglect	6.181
Article 2 and causation	6.186
Causation, conclusions and Art 2 in jury inquests	6.188
Galbraith Plus – leaving decisions to the jury	6.198

Chapter 7   Reports to Prevent Future Deaths

When are PFD reports required?	7.3
Submissions/evidence regarding PFD reports	7.5
PFD reports in cases involving juries	7.8
Timing	
(a) When should the PFD report be produced?	7.10
(b) When should the PFD report be sent?	7.12
Content of a PFD report	7.13
(a) What can form the basis for the coroner's concerns?	7.15
(b) How should the concerns be expressed?	7.18
(c) What should the coroner avoid in a PFD report?	7.21
What happens to the report?	7.24
Letter instead of report	7.27
Relationship between PFD reports and Art 2	7.29
Challenging a PFD report	7.30

Chapter 8   Challenging Coronial Decisions: Judicial Review and Statutory Review

Introduction to challenging a coroner's decision	8.1
Statutory review: the statutory power to order a (new) inquest or investigation	8.2
Practical matters	
Who can make an application under s 13?	8.4
The Attorney General must authorise any application under s 13 CA 1988	8.6
Making the application	8.9
A coroner must have jurisdiction over the death for s 13 CA 1988 to bite	8.10

Power to order an investigation where the coroner has refused or neglected to do so (s 13(1)(a) CA 1988)	8.11
Jurisdiction (s 1(4) CJA 2009)	8.13
Section 1(2) CJA 2009 – duty to investigate because of the nature of the death	8.14
Power to quash the findings made at an inquest and order a new investigation (s 13(1)(b) CA 1988)	8.16
What makes it necessary or desirable in the interests of justice to conduct another investigation or inquest?	8.19
New evidence	8.24
Fraud	8.32
Material irregularities or errors	8.33
Judicial review	
Practical matters	
Who can make an application for judicial review of coronial decisions?	8.36
Procedure – s 31 SCA 1981, CPR Pt 54	8.39
Coronial decisions susceptible to judicial review	8.46
Timing of challenge	8.48
Grounds of review	
Common law	8.50
Article 2 ECHR	8.58
Remedies	8.60
Costs	8.65
Statutory review or judicial review?	8.67

Chapter 9   Funding and Costs

Funding	
Inquest funding	9.1
The role of legal representatives	9.7
Legal aid	9.9
Means test	9.13
Merits test	9.16
Legal help	9.20
Legal representation	9.24
Conditional fee agreements	9.29

Contents

Before the event insurance and union membership	9.34
Privately funded retainer	9.36
Charitable assistance	9.38
Costs recovery	9.41
General principles of costs recovery	9.42
Relevance	9.44
Proportionality	9.47
Examples and authorities in practice	9.52
Chapter 10 Representing Families at Inquests	
Immediately after the death	10.3
The post mortem and post-mortem report	10.12
The post-mortem report	10.14
Oral evidence	10.17
First contact with a solicitor	10.19
Client care throughout the process	10.28
Client care at pre-inquest review hearings	10.34
Disclosure	10.38
Witness statements	
Statements from members of the family	10.43
Statements from other witnesses	10.48
Inquest hearing	10.49
Giving evidence at the inquest	10.58
Expert evidence	10.63
Medical cause of death	10.67
Conclusions	10.71
Prevention of future deaths	10.78
After the inquest	10.80
Chapter 11 Representing Organisations at Inquests	
First involvement	11.2
Conflicts of interest	11.5
Previous reports and investigations	11.6
Media	11.7
Pre-inquest review hearing	11.8

Preparing for the inquest	11.9
The inquest hearing	11.12
After the inquest	11.15

Chapter 12   Press and Publicity at Inquests

Applications by the media for disclosure of documents	12.4
Attendance at inquests	12.9
Reporting restrictions	12.10
Live communications/publications during a hearing	12.13
Anonymity	12.14
Children in coronial proceedings	
(a) Child witnesses	12.17
(b) Deceased children	12.19
Challenges to a coroner's decision regarding media access	12.21
Families and the media	12.22
Organisations and the media	12.31

Chapter 13   Clinical Inquests

Representing families at clinical inquests	13.2
Clinical negligence	13.3
Jurisdiction	13.6
Scope and Art 2 of the ECHR	13.15
Clinical negligence and the operational duty	13.20
Disclosure and medical records	13.26
Serious untoward incident reports and the duty of candour	13.31
Expert evidence	13.33
Impact of clinical negligence on conclusions	13.38

Chapter 14   Deaths in Custody

Suicide and self-inflicted deaths	14.8
Excessive force	14.16
Medical care	14.18
Disclosure	14.19
Parallel state investigations	14.20
Expert evidence	14.21
Client care	14.23

Contents

Chapter 15 Mental Health and Mental Capacity

Introduction	15.1
Mental health	
Representing clients at mental health inquests	15.3
Inquest law and mental healthcare	
Jurisdiction	15.6
Scope, determinations and Art 2 ECHR	15.9
Suicide conclusions	15.16
Neglect conclusions	15.17
Juries	15.18
Mental healthcare	
Mental health trusts and service providers	15.19
Inpatient and tertiary mental health services	15.21
The Mental Health Act 1983	15.22
Community mental health services	15.26
The Care Programme Approach	15.27
Experts and elements of mental healthcare	15.33
Witnesses and disclosure	15.39
Mental capacity	15.41
Basic principles of mental capacity	
What is the test for lacking capacity?	15.43
What does it mean if someone is deprived of their liberty?	15.47
When is it legal to deprive someone of their liberty? What is a DoLS?	15.49
DoLS authorisations by the relevant local authority	15.50
Orders issued by the Court of Protection	15.51
Jurisdiction and 'state detention' for the purposes of an inquest	
What does the CJA 2009 mean by 'state detention'?	15.53
Deaths after 3 April 2017	15.57
Deaths prior to 3 April 2017	15.60
When is a jury required?	15.62

When is Art 2 ECHR engaged in cases involving the death of someone deprived of their liberty?	**15.64**
Maguire and the Art 2 ECHR operational duty	**15.69**
Maguire and the general Art 2 ECHR duty to put in place a regulatory framework sufficient to protect life	**15.71**
How does the judgment in *Maguire* square with other existing decisions?	**15.72**
Suicide conclusions	**15.75**

Chapter 16   Workplace Deaths

Introduction to workplace deaths	**16.1**
Interplay with regulatory proceedings	**16.5**
Homicide offences	**16.7**
Other offences	**16.10**
Memorandum of understanding between the Chief Coroner and HSE	**16.13**
Timeline of proceedings	**16.15**
Preparing for an inquest	**16.23**
Interested persons	**16.30**
Family members	**16.31**
The deceased's employer	**16.32**
Other organisations	**16.34**
Trade union representative	**16.37**
Individuals	**16.38**
Enforcing authority	**16.39**
Disclosure	**16.41**
Jury inquest	**16.44**
Witnesses	**16.45**
Inquest conclusions	**16.51**
Report to prevent future deaths	**16.54**

Chapter 17   Road Traffic Collision Deaths

Do all road traffic collision deaths require an inquest?	**17.3**
Identification of interested persons	**17.6**
Pre-inquest review and conduct of the inquest	**17.8**
Criminal proceedings	**17.14**
Conclusions: short-form and narrative	**17.21**

Contents

Prevention of future deaths	17.26
Chapter 18 Product-related Deaths	
Which 'products'?	18.2
Interested persons	18.3
Further information	18.14
Disclosure and regulatory issues	18.15
Factual and expert evidence	18.20
Media	18.25
Chapter 19 Military Inquests	
Organisation of military inquests	19.4
Legal and practical assistance for families	19.11
Representation and attendance at inquests	19.15
Disclosure	19.19
Internal military investigations	19.30
Deaths in combat	19.36
Combat and Crown immunity	19.40
Practical examples	
Brecon Beacons SAS training	19.42
Jason Smith (Iraq)	19.47
Deepcut	19.49
Chapter 20 Inquests and COVID-19	
The Coronavirus Act 2020	20.4
Guidance No 34 – Chief Coroner's Guidance for coroners on COVID-19	20.5
(a) COVID-19 as a natural cause of death	20.6
(b) COVID-19 and post-mortems	20.13
(c) COVID-19 and deaths occurring in prison or otherwise in state detention	20.14
Guidance No 36 – Summary of the Coronavirus Act 2020, provisions relevant to coroners	20.15
(a) COVID-19 and Medical Certificates of Cause of Death (MCCD)	20.16
(b) Documentation required for cremations during the coronavirus pandemic	20.19
(c) Jury inquests and COVID-19 deaths	20.20

Guidance No 37 – COVID-19 deaths and possible exposure in the workplace	20.22
(a) What does the Guidance say, and when should a COVID-19-related death be referred to the coroner?	20.23
(b) Can/should coroners consider any COVID-19 deaths involving PPE issues or matters of public policy?	20.26

Chapter 21 Inquests and Criminal Proceedings

Initial jurisdiction	21.2
Rules for precedence	21.3
Coroner's duty to suspend; cases where a person may be charged	21.5
Coroner's duty to suspend; cases where a person has been charged	21.10
Discretionary suspensions	21.15
Effect of suspension of investigation, good practice on suspension	21.17
Exceptions to compulsory suspension	21.19
Compulsory adjournment under the Coroners Rules	21.22
Disclosure	
Disclosure of material from criminal process to parties at resumed inquest	21.24
Disclosure and use of material limited by statutory or legal prohibition on disclosure	21.26
The coroner's discretion on disclosure	21.28
Documents publicly available	21.30
Material generated by a police criminal investigation	21.34
Disclosure in criminal proceedings – 'relevant', 'sensitive' and 'non-sensitive' material'	21.35
Practical guidance on material to look for in criminal disclosure	21.37
Other criminal process material	21.39
Resumption of investigation or inquest	
Later resumption of the investigation	21.40
Sufficient reason	21.43
Resumption under Art 2	21.49
Inquest findings must be consistent with the result of the criminal process	21.52

Contents

Criminal proceedings initiated following inquest verdict	21.53
Victim's right of review	21.57
Criminal trial not bound by inquest verdict	21.58

Chapter 22 Inquests and Family Proceedings

Reporting restrictions in respect of children involved in or affected by an inquest	22.12

Chapter 23 Inquests and Civil Proceedings

Types of civil proceedings that may follow an inquest	23.5
Is the conclusion of an inquest binding or admissible in subsequent civil proceedings?	23.7

Chapter 24 Inquests and Public Inquiries

What is a public inquiry?	24.3
Similarities and differences	24.21
Why a public inquiry rather than an inquest?	24.25
Reasons of scope	24.29
Practical, procedural and evidential differences between an inquest and inquiry	24.44

Appendix 1 Statutory Material

Coroners and Justice Act 2009 (extracts only)	A1.1
Coroners (Inquests) Rules 2013, SI 2013/1616	A1.2
Coroners (Investigations) Regulations 2013, SI 2013/1629	A1.3
Index	417

Table of Statutes

References in the right-hand column are to paragraph number. Where the paragraph number is set in **bold**, this indicates that the legislation is set out in part or in full

A

Access to Health Records Act 1990
  s 3 .... 4.84, 4.85, 13.29

B

Births and Deaths Registration Act 1926
  s 4 .... 2.21
Births and Deaths Registration Act 1953
  .... 1.5, 3.6, 6.8
  s 16, 17 .... 2.13
  s 19 .... 2.14
  s 22 .... 2.9
  s 27 .... 6.34
  s 36(a)–(e) 2.14
  s 41 .... 2.35, 2.128
  Sch 2
    Form 14 .... 2.4

C

Care Act 2014
  s 73 .... 15.20
  s 73(1), (2) **15.55**
  s 74(3) 15.56
Children Act 1989
  .... 22.4
  s 17 .... 3.97
  s 31 .... 22.1
  s 33 .... 22.1
  s 35 .... 22.1
Children and Young Person's Act 1933
  s 39 .... 12.17, 12.18, 22.12
Civil Evidence Act 1995
  s 1(1) 23.9
  s 4 .... 5.17
Civil Partnerships, Marriages and Deaths (Registration) Act 2019
  .... 2.35
Constitutional Reform Act 2005
  .... 24.7
Consumer Protection Act 1987
  .... 18.6, 18.13
  s 2 .... 18.7, 18.8
  s 3 .... 18.11
  s 4(e) 18.12
  s 5 .... 18.10
Contempt of Court Act 1981
  .... 12.3
  s 4(2) 12.12, 21.27
  s 8 .... 6.38
Coronavirus Act 2020
  .... 2.10, 20.15, 20.21

Coronavirus Act 2020 – *cont.*
  s 19 .... 20.19
  s 30 .... 20.4, 20.20
  s 30(1), (2) 4.107
  Sch 13
    para 7(1) 20.18
Coroner (Amendment) Act 1926
Coroners Act 1887
  s 6 .... 8.2
Coroners Act 1988
  .... 2.23, 4.92, 4.95, 4.97
  s 8 .... 8.52
  s 8(1)(a) 13.11, 13.13
  s 8(3) 4.91
  s 11(2) 4.33
  s 11(5) 3.13
  s 11(5)(b)(ii) 3.14
  s 13 ...... 8.1, 8.2, 8.4, 8.5, 8.10, 8.73
  s 13(1) 8.6
  s 13(1)(a) 8.11, 8.72
  s 13(1)(b) 8.16, 8.17, 8.23, 8.33
  s 15 .... 8.15
  s 30 .... 1.2
Coroners and Justice Act 2009
  .... 2.3, 2.26, 2.97, 3.2, 3.26, 3.99,
    3.100, 4.33, 4.43, 4.49, 4.50, 4.51,
    4.94, 4.110, 6.30, 6.73, 8.52, 8.67,
    10.24, 18.20, 19.6, 20.7, 20.31, 24.27
  s 1 . 2.2, 2.28, 4.91, 6.118, 6.127, 8.10,
    8.47, 20.10, 21.2, 24.25, 24.43
  s 1(1) 2.22, 2.51, 5.4, **8.11**, 17.3
  s 1(1)(b) 13.26
  s 1(2) 1.1, **2.22**, 6.130, **8.11**, 8.14,
    13.6, 14.5, 15.6, 15.7, 15.61, 21.1
  s 1(2)(a) 17.3
  s 1(2)(b) 13.26
  s 1(2)(c) 4.93, 15.53, 15.59
  s 1(4) 2.46, 2.48, 2.50, 2.52, 8.13,
    8.15
  s 1(7) 2.29, 2.31
  s 2 .... 2.92
  s 2(1) 3.56
  s 3 .... 2.92
  s 4 .... 2.2, 2.86, 2.88, 15.6
  s 4(1) 2.39
  s 4(2) 2.40
  s 4(2)(a) 17.5
  s 4(4) 4.29
  s 5 .. 1.8, 3.1, 3.3, **3.4**, 3.9, 3.27, 8.55,
    13.16, 13.38, 15.65, 24.22, 24.29,
    24.33, 24.36, 24.41, 24.57
  s 5(1) 1.5, 1.7, 3.13, 3.31, 6.48,
    17.11, 17.12, 17.15, 17.25
  s 5(1)(b) 1.6, 6.44

xxvii

Table of Statutes

Coroners and Justice Act 2009 – *cont.*
    s 5(2) ... 1.6, 1.7, 3.6, 3.11, 3.19, 3.21, 3.22, 3.25, 3.31, 3.51, 3.53, 6.2, 6.8, 6.16, 5.44, 13.18, 17.11, 17.12, 17.23, 17.25, 24.31
    s 5(3) 1.7, 3.7, 5.35, 17.25
    s 6 ... 2.2, 2.38, 2.39, 2.41, 8.16, 17.5, 24.44
    s 7 .... 2.23, 15.62, 15.63
    s 7(1) 4.87, 4.109
    s 7(2) .. 4.87, 4.91, 4.109, 4.113, 14.6, 15.18, 20.4
    s 7(2)(a) 4.90, 17.13
    s 7(2)(b) 4.90
    s 7(2)(c) 2.11, 4.90, 4.101, 4.107, 16.44
    s 7(3) 4.87, 4.109, 4.113, 21.47
    s 7(4) 4.101
    s 8(1) 5.35, 5.39
    s 8(4) 4.88, 5.35
    s 9 .... 6.39
    s 9(3) 6.40
    s 10 ...... 3.1, 3.3, 3.5, 6.3, 6.39, 8.53, 10.23, 15.65, 24.22
    s 10(1) **6.1**
    s 10(1)(a) 3.11
    s 10(2) 1.11, 3.8, 5.35, 6.24, 6.113, 6.170, 13.17, 13.39, 17.25, 23.3
    s 10(2)(a) 6.62
    s 11 .... 2.115
    s 12, 13 .... 2.20
    s 14 . 2.39, 2.53, 2.62, 2.69, 2.70, 2.81, 21.2
    s 15 .... 2.54, 21.2
    s 16 .... 19.21
    Pt 1, Ch 4 (ss 25–31)
         .... 1.1
    s 32 .... 4.52, 4.54
    s 40 .... 8.1
    s 47 .... 4.13, 4.22, 4.23, 8.38
    s 47(2) 17.6
    s 47(2)(a) 4.17, 24.48
    s 47(2)(b)–(e) 4.17
    s 47(2)(f) 4.17, 4.18
    s 47(2)(g) 4.17, 16.37
    s 47(2)(h) 4.17, 16.39
    s 47(2)(i)–(l) 4.17
    s 47(2)(m) 4.16
    s 47(7) 4.14
    s 48 .... 21.5
    s 48(1) 4.52
    s 48(2) 4.93, 15.54, 15.59
    s 48(2A) 15.57, 15.59, 15.60
    Sch 1 .... 3.104, 17.17, 17.19, 21.3, 21.22, 24.34, 24.36
        para 1 .. 2.114, 2.117, 2.118, 2.126, 21.5, 21.40
        para 1(1) 21.10
        para 1(2) 16.7
        para 1(4), (5) 21.8
        para 1(6) 2.115, 17.15, 21.6
        para 1(7) 21.8

Coroners and Justice Act 2009 – *cont.*
    para 2 .. 2.116–2.118, 17.15, 21.10
    para 2(3), (4) 21.12
    para 2(5) 21.12, 21.19
    para 2(6)(c) 2.117
    para 2(7)(d) 21.41
    para 3 .. 2.119, 17.15, 21.14, 24.31, 24.38, 24.39, 24.57
    para 3(1) **24.30**
    para 3(2) **24.30**
    para 4 .. 2.119, 17.15, 21.14, 24.33, 24.57
    para 4(2) **24.31**
    para 5 ... 2.122, 16.16, 17.15, 21.4, 21.15, 21.23, 21.42, 24.39
    para 6 .... 2.123, 21.17
    para 7 .... 2.118, 21.40
    para 8 .... 2.128, 17.15
    para 8(1) 21.41
    para 8(2) 21.20
    para 8(3) 21.41
    para 8(5) 21.20, 21.52, 21.58
    para 9 .... 24.32, 24.37
    para 9(11) 6.42, 21.52, 24.33
    para 10 .... 21.42
    Sch 2 .... 1.1
    Sch 3 .... 1.15
        para 2(1) 1.23
        para 3 .... 1.21, 1.25
        para 8 .... 1.23
        para 8(2) 1.25
    Sch 4 .... 1.15
    Sch 5 ...... 2.61, 4.61, 4.64, 4.65, 5.4, 13.26
        para 1 .... 4.35, 4.120
        para 1(1) 4.54
        para 1(2) 4.52, 18.18
        para 1(3) 4.62, 4.63
        para 1(4), (5) 4.63
        para 1(6) 4.52
        para 1(7) 4.56
        para 2(1) 4.57
        para 2(2) 4.35, 4.57
        para 3 .... 4.35
        para 5 .... 4.120
        para 7 .... 1.7, 3.9, 7.1, 7.9, 17.25, 18.16
        para 7(1)(b) 7.3, 7.15
        para 7(1)(c) 7.24
        para 7(2) 7.31
        para 7(3) 7.26
    Sch 6
        Pt 2 .... 4.35
        para 6, 7 .... 4.62
    Sch 8
        para 1 .... 1.16
    Sch 10 .... 24.55, 24.56
Corporate Manslaughter and Corporate Homicide Act 2007
    s 1 .... 6.97, 16.7
    s 1(1) 6.94
    s 1(2) 6.95

Table of Statutes

Corporate Manslaughter and Corporate Homicide Act 2007 – *cont.*
s 1(3) 6.96
s 2(1) 6.97
s 2(1)(a)–(c) 6.39
s 2(2) 6.97
s 2(3) 6.97, 6.98
s 2(4)–(6) 6.97
s 3 .... 6.98
s 4 .... 6.98
s 4(1)(a) 6.99
s 4(1)(c) 6.99
s 4(2), (3) 6.99
s 5 .... 6.98
s 5(1)(a)–(c) 6.99
s 5(2) 6.99
s 6 .... 6.98
s 6(1) 6.99
s 6(3)(a), (b) 6.99
s 6(4) 6.99
s 8(1)–(3) 6.100
s 8(4) 6.99, 6.101
s 18 .... 6.95
s 20 .... 6.93
Sch 1 .... 6.95
Crime and Disorder Act 1998
s 51, 52 .... 21.11
Criminal Justice Act 1977
s 56(1) 6.62
Criminal Justice Act 2003
.... 4.88
Criminal Justice and Immigration Act 2008
s 76 .... 6.106
s 76(3)–(8) 6.109
Criminal Law Act 1967
s 3 .... 6.106
Criminal Procedure and Investigations Act 1996
s 5–6A 21.35
s 17, 18 .... 21.27

H

Health and Safety at Work etc. Act 1974
.. 6.66, 6.102, 16.10, 16.11, 16.12, 16.52
s 19 .... 4.101
Health and Social Care Act 2008
.... 13.32
Health and Social Care Act 2012
.... 13.32
Homicide Act 1957
s 2 .... 6.73
s 3 .... 6.73, 6.74
s 4 .... 6.73
Human Rights Act 1998
. 1.6, 3.16, 3.35, 3.50, 3.81, 3.100, 4.66, 4.91, 4.94, 9.46, 9.48, 15.2, 15.47
s 1(2) 3.40
s 2(1) 3.45

Human Rights Act 1998 – *cont.*
s 3 .... 8.58
s 4 .... 3.40, 8.58
s 6 . 3.40, 3.41, 3.44, 4.93, 8.58, 15.20, 15.54
s 6(2) 3.42
s 6(3)(a) 3.42
s 6(3)(b) 3.43, 15.55
s 7 .... 3.41, 3.58
s 8 .... 3.41
s 8(1) 8.63
Sch 1 .... 3.37, 3.40
Human Tissue Act 2004
s 11 .... 2.56, 21.2
Human Transplantation (Wales) Act 2013
.... 2.57

I

Infanticide Act 1938
s 1 .... 6.103
Inquiries Act 2005
.. 2.119, 2.120, 3.51, 17.15, 19.28, 24.17, 24.19, 24.20, 24.22, 24.23, 24.30, 24.40, 24.43, 24.56, 24.57, 24.58, 24.59
s 1(1) 24.5
s 2 .... 24.5
s 2(2) 24.8
s 3 .... 24.5
s 4(3) 24.6
s 5(1) 24.5
s 5(3) 24.6
s 5(6) 24.6
s 10 .... 24.7
s 14 .... 24.46
s 14(4) 24.15
s 15 .... 24.16
s 17 .... 24.9, 24.11
s 18 .... 24.9, 24.10, 24.11
s 19 .... 24.9, 24.47
s 19(3)(b) 24.10
s 19(4) 24.10
s 20 .... 24.9, 24.47
s 21–23 .... 24.9
s 25(3)–(5) 24.13
s 35 .... 24.9
s 40 .... 24.49
Investigatory Powers Act 2016
.... 24.55

J

Juries Act 1974 .... 5.35, 5.36
s 1 .... 4.88
Sch 1 .... 4.88

L

Legal Aid Sentencing and Punishment of Offenders Act 2012
.... 3.104

xxix

Table of Statutes

Limitation Act 1980
 s 11A 18.13

M

Mental Capacity Act 2005
 ..... 3.92, 5.36, 15.1, 15.11, 15.41, 15.47
 s 1(2), (3) 15.44
 s 2(1), (2) 15.43
 s 2(4) 15.44
 s 4 .... 15.45
 s 4A(3) 4.93, 15.57
 s 4A(5) 4.93, 15.57
 s 4B 4.93, 15.57
 s 21A 15.51
 Sch A1 .... 15.49, 15.68
Mental Health Act 1983
 ... 4.95, 5.36, 6.139, 13.20, 13.25, 15.1, 15.9, 15.13, 15.18, 15.22, 15.24, 15.38, 17.13
 s 1(2) 15.23
 s 2, 3 ... 4.96, 15.6, 15.8, 15.21, 15.23
 s 17 .... 4.96
 s 26 .... 15.25
 Pt III (ss 35–55) 15.21, 15.23
 s 37 .... 4.96
 s 41 .... 4.96

N

National Assistance Act 1948
 .... 3.44

O

Offences Against the Person Act 1861
 s 9 .... 6.75
Organ Donation (Deemed Consent) Act 2019 .... 2.57

P

Police Reform Act 2002
 .... 4.13
Policing and Crime Act 2017
 s 178(4) 4.93

Prosecution of Offences Act 1985
 s 1(7) 21.5
Public Health (Control of Disease) Act 1984 .... 4.107

R

Road Traffic Act 1988
 s 1 .... 17.17
 s 2 .... 17.20
 s 2B 17.17, 21.11
 s 3ZB 17.17, 21.11
 s 3ZC 17.17
 s 3A 17.17
 s 192(1) 6.127

S

Senior Courts Act 1981
 s 31 .... 8.39, 8.45
 s 31(1) 8.60
 s 31(3) 8.36
 s 31(5A) 8.64
 s 51 .... 9.42, 9.43, 9.52
Sexual Offences (Amendment) Act 1992
 s 1–4 .... 21.27
Social Security Contributions and Benefits Act 1992 .... 4.13

T

Treasure Act 1996 .... 1.2
Tribunal of Inquiry (Evidence) Act 1921
 .... 24.4, 24.11, 24.35

V

Visiting Forces Act 1952
 .... 2.121

Y

Youth Justice and Criminal Evidence Act 1999
 s 45–46 .... 21.27

Table of Statutory Instruments

References in the right-hand column are to paragraph number. Where the paragraph number is set in **bold**, this indicates that the legislation is set out in part or in full

C

Civil Aviation (Investigation of Air Accidents and Incidents) Regulations 1996, SI 1996/2798 .... 4.56, 4.65
Civil Procedure Rules 1998, SI 1998/3132
  Pt 3
    r 3.1(2)(a) 8.43
  Pt 8 .... 8.9, 8.39
    r 8.2 .... 8.44
    PD 8A 8.9
  Pt 14
    r 14.1A 9.46, 11.10
  Pt 35 .... 4.125
  PD 35
    Section 2, 3 .... 4.125
  Pt 44
    r 44.3(2) 9.47
      (5) 9.48
    44.4(3) 9.48
  Pt 45
    r 45.9(4) 6.127
  Pt 52
    r 52.8 .... 8.45
  Pt 54
    r 54.4 .... 8.45
      54.5(1), (2) **8.41**
      54.6 .... 8.44
      54.8 .... 8.39
    PD 54A 8.44
      para 8.4 .... 8.45
        8.6 .... 8.66
  Pre-Action Protocols
  Pre-Action Protocol for Judicial Review 8.40
Coroners Allowances, Fees and Expenses Regulations 2013, SI 2013/1615
  reg 9, 10 .... 4.126
    12 .... 4.72
Coroners (Amendment) Rules 2004, SI 2004/921
  r 1 .... 4.88
Coroners (Inquests) Rules 2013, SI 2013/1616 ... 4.49, 4.50, 4.82, 6.119, 6.126, 6.170
  r 2 .... 4.67
    (1) 4.52
    9, 10 .... 4.29
    11 .... 12.1, 12.3
      (2) 12.9
      (3) 4.3, 12.9

Coroners (Inquests) Rules 2013, SI 2013/1616 – *cont.*
  r 11(4) 12.9
    (5) 4.3, 12.9
  Pt 3 (rr 12–15) 4.66
  r 12 .... 4.69, 21.2, 21.25
    13 .... 4.27, 21.25
      (1) 4.68, 10.14, 13.27
      (2)(a) 4.26, 10.14
    14 .... 4.71, 21.25
    15 .... 2.82, 4.76, 21.25
      (d) 21.28
    16 .... 4.72, 21.25
    17 .... 4.39
    18 .... 12.16
      (1), (2) 4.39
      (3) 4.39
        (b), (c) 4.38
      (4) 4.39
    19(1) 4.29, 4.34, 24.48
      (2) 1.8, 5.8, 24.48
    20(1), (2) 5.6
    21(c) 5.3
    22 .... 4.57, 16.38, 16.46
      (1), (2) 5.25
    23 .... 2.107, 2.108, 4.29, 4.43, 4.46, 5.5, 8.33, 20.11
      (3) 4.45
    25 .... 4.29, 6.62, 6.67
      (1) 21.17
      (3) 2.133
      (4) 3.104, **21.22**
    27 .... 5.1, 5.30, 6.8
    30 .... 5.34
    32 .... 4.108
    33 .... 5.35
    34 .... 6.3, 6.8
  Sch 1
    para 1 .... 17.21
Coroners (Investigations) Regulations 2013, SI 2013/1629 .... 12.4
  reg 2 .... 2.32
    5(1), (2) 2.41
    8 .... 2.42
    10 .... 4.29
    11 .... 2.55, 4.41
      (2) 2.41
    12 .... 2.79
    13 .... 2.67, 4.25
    14 .... 2.80
      (5), (6) 10.18
    16 .... 2.81
    17 .... 4.29
    18 .... 2.93, 4.29

xxxi

Table of Statutory Instruments

Coroners (Investigations) Regulations 2013, SI 2013/1629 – *cont.*
 reg 19 .... 2.94
 20 .... 2.55, 4.26
 21 .... 2.89
 23 .. 4.26, 4.42, 4.44, 10.14, 10.60
 25 .... 1.16
 reg 27(2) 18.14
 28 ...... 3.31, 3.80, 7.1, 7.15, 7.23,
  11.1, 11.4, 11.11, 21.45
 (3) 7.3
 29 .... 7.1
Coroners Rules 1984, SI 1984/552
 .... 4.44, 6.3, 6.119, 23.4
 r 20(2)(g) 4.22
 36(1)(b) 3.14, 6.170
 37 .... 5.19
 43 .... 3.80, 6.193
 (1) 7.15
Cremation (England and Wales) Regulations 2008, SI 2008/2841
 reg 18 .... 2.90
Criminal Procedure Rules 2020, SI 2020/759
 Pt 5
 r 5.5(2) 21.33
 5.7 .... 21.30
 5.8 .... 21.30
 (7) 21.32
 5.9 .... 21.30
 PD 5B.1–5 .... 21.30
 5B.6 .... 21.30, 21.31
 5B.7–30 .... 21.30

F

Family Procedure Rules 2010, SI 2010/2955
 .... 22.11

H

Health and Safety (Enforcing Authority) Regulations 1998, SI 1998/494
 .... 16.6
Health and Social Care Act 2008 (Regulated Activities) Regulations 2014, SI 2014/2936
 reg 20(1)–(4) 13.31
 (8) 13.31, 13.32

Health Protection (Notification) Regulations 2010, SI 2010/659
 .... 20.4, 20.7, 20.20
 Sch 1 .... 2.11, 4.107

I

Inquiry Rules 2006, SI 2006/1838
 .... 24.9, 24.49
 r 10 .... 24.48
 11 .... 24.24, 24.48
 13–16 .... 24.14
 17 .... 24.24, 24.48

N

Notification of Deaths Regulations 2019, SI 2019/1112 .... 2.6, 20.8, 20.23
 reg 3(1)(a) 16.3
 (e), (f) 20.18
 24 .... 20.6

R

Registration of Births and Deaths Regulations 1987, SI 1981/2088
 reg 41 .... 2.15
Removal of Bodies Regulations 1954, SI 1954/448 .... 2.21
Removal of Bodies (Amendment) Regulations 1971, SI 1971/1354
 .... 2.21
Reporting of Injuries, Diseases and Dangerous Occurrences Regulations 2013, SI 2013/1471
 .... 4.104, 16.3
 reg 2(2) 4.102
 6(1) 4.102, 16.44
 11 .... 4.106
 14(1), (2) 4.102, 4.103
 (3) 4.103

S

Social Security (Industrial Injuries) Prescribed Disease Regulations 1985, SI 1985/967 .... 6.61

Table of Cases

A

A (A Child) (withdrawal of life support), Re [2015] EWHC 443 (Fam), [2016] 1 FLR 241, [2015] 2 FCR 489, [2015] Fam Law 527, 143 BMLR 192, [2015] All ER (D) 122 (Mar) 2.33, 2.34
A v HM Coroner For Central & North West London [2014] EWHC 2676 (Admin) 22.8
A Local Authority v AF [2015] EWFC 74, 165 NLJ 7667, [2015] All ER (D) 23 (Sep) 2.77, 6.106
AXA General Insurance Ltd v Lord Advocate (Scotland) [2011] UKSC 46, [2012] 1 AC 868, [2011] 3 WLR 871, 122 BMLR 149, (2011) Times, 19 October, 2012 SC (UKSC) 122, 2011 SLT 1061, [2011] All ER (D) 101 (Oct), 2011 Scot (D) 14/10, SC 8.37
Airedale NHS Trust v Bland [1993] AC 789, [1993] 1 All ER 821, [1993] 2 WLR 316, [1993] 3 LRC 340, [1993] 1 FLR 1026, [1994] 1 FCR 485, [1993] Fam Law 473, [1993] Crim LR 877, [1993] 4 Med LR 39, 12 BMLR 64, [1993] NLJR 199, (1993) Times, 5 February, HL 2.33, 6.72
Al-Rawas v Hassan Khan & Co (a firm) [2017] EWCA Civ 42, [2017] 1 WLR 2301, [2017] All ER (D) 66 (Feb) 6.108
Al-Skeini v UK (2011) 53 EHRR 18 .... 3.38, 19.37
Allman v HM Coroner for West Sussex [2012] EWHC 534 (Admin), 176 JP 285 ..... 4.19
Andonicou and Constantinou v Cyprus (1998) 25 EHRR 20 .... 3.65
Anguelova v Bulgaria (2004) EHRR 31 .... 13.22
Anusca v Moldova (App No 24034/07) (18 May 2010, unreported) 3.104
Ashley v Chief Constable of Sussex Police [2008] UKHL 25, [2008] 1 AC 962, [2008] 3 All ER 573, [2008] 2 WLR 975, [2009] 1 LRC 585, [2008] NLJR 632, (2008) Times, 24 April, [2008] All ER (D) 326 (Apr), HL 3.68
Associated Provincial Picture Houses Ltd v Wednesbury Corpn [1948] 1 KB 223, [1947] 2 All ER 680, 45 LGR 635, 112 JP 55, [1948] LJR 190, 92 Sol Jo 26, 177 LT 641, 63 TLR 623, CA 8.52
Aston Cantlow and Wilmcote with Billesley Parochial Church Council v Wallbank [2003] UKHL 37, [2004] 1 AC 546, [2003] 3 All ER 1213, [2003] 3 WLR 283, [2003] 33 LS Gaz R 28, [2003] NLJR 1030, (2003) Times, 27 June, 147 Sol Jo LB 812, [2003] All ER (D) 360 (Jun), HL 3.43
A-G v HM Coroner of South Yorkshire (West) [2012] EWHC 3783 (Admin), 177 CL&J 46, [2012] All ER (D) 175 (Dec), DC 8.20, 8.21, 8.24, 8.25, 8.29, 8.33, 24.35
A-G v Leveller Magazine Ltd [1979] AC 440, [1979] 1 All ER 745, [1979] 2 WLR 247, 68 Cr App Rep 342, 143 JP 260, 123 Sol Jo 129, HL 4.36, 4.38
A-G's Reference (No 2 of 1999) [2000] QB 796, [2000] 3 All ER 182, [2000] 3 WLR 195, [2000] 2 BCLC 257, [2000] 2 Cr App Rep 207, [2000] IRLR 417, [2000] Crim LR 475, [2001] BCC 210, [2000] 09 LS Gaz R 39, (2000) Times, 29 February, [2000] Lexis Citation 2652, [2000] All ER (D) 178 .... 6.92
A-G's Reference (No 3 of 1994) [1998] AC 245, [1997] 3 All ER 936, [1997] 3 WLR 421, [1998] 1 LRC 558, [1998] 1 Cr App Rep 91, [1997] Crim LR 829, [1997] 36 LS Gaz R 44, [1997] NLJR 1185, (1997) Times, 25 July, HL 6.71, 6.129
Aydin v Turkey (App No 23178/94) (1997) 25 EHRR 251, 3 BHRC 300, [1997] ECHR 23178/94, EctHR 3.39

B

Banel v Lithuania (App No 14326/11) [2013] ECHR 14326/11, EctHR 3.78
Beresford, Re (1952) 36 Cr App Rep 1 .... 17.20
Binisan v Romania (App No 39438/05) [2014] ECHR 39438/05, EctHR 3.78
Bird v Keep [1918] 2 KB 692, 87 LJKB 1199, 11 BWCC 133, 62 Sol Jo 666, 118 LT 633, 34 TLR 513, CA 23.8
Brincat v Malta (App No 60908/11), (24 October 2014, unreported) 3.92
Bithell, Re (1986) 150 JP 273 .... 5.11
Bithell, Re [1986] 1 WLUK 114 .... 8.69
Boyle v Wiseman (1855) 10 Ex 647 .... 4.35, 5.26

Table of Cases

Brincat v Malta (App Nos 60908/11, 62110/11, 62129/11, 62312/11 and 62338/11) [2014] ECHR 60908/11, EctHR 3.78
Brown v Bennett [2002] 2 All ER 273, [2002] 1 WLR 713, [2002] 02 LS Gaz R 27, [2001] NLJR 1733, (2001) Times, 21 November, 145 Sol Jo LB 267, [2001] All ER (D) 247 (Nov) 4.61
Brown v Norfolk Coroner [2014] EWHC 187 (Admin), [2014] 1 WLR 3191, 178 JP 462 .... 4.8, 4.75
Budayeva v Russia (App Nos 15339/02, 21166/02, 20058/02 and 15343/02) (2008) 59 EHRR 59, [2008] ECHR 15339/02, EctHR 3.75, 3.76, 3.92

C

CM v Executor of the Estate of EJ (deceased) [2013] EWHC 1680 (Fam), [2013] 2 FLR 1410, [2013] Fam Law 964, 133 BMLR 203, [2013] NLJR 20, [2013] All ER (D) 148 (Jun) 2.56
CP (A Child) v First-tier Tribunal (Criminal Injuries Compensation) (British Pregnancy Advisory Service/Birthrights and another intervening) [2014] EWCA Civ 1554, [2015] QB 459, [2015] 4 All ER 60, [2015] 2 WLR 463, [2015] 1 Cr App Rep 246, [2015] 2 FLR 1163, [2015] Fam Law 123, 142 BMLR 18, [2015] PIQR P179, (2015) Times, 14 January, [2014] All ER (D) 48 (Dec) 6.70
Câmpeanu v Romania (App No 47848/08), (17 July 2014, unreported) 3.92
Canning v County of Northampton Coroner [2006] EWCA Civ 1225, [2006] All ER (D) 187 (Nov) 2.23
Chambers v HM Coroner for Preston and West Lancashire [2015] EWHC 31 (Admin), [2015] All ER (D) 57 (Jan) 6.124, 8.30, 8.34
Chief Constable of West Yorkshire Police and Officers B and E v Dyer. See R (on the application of Dyer) v HM Assistant Coroner for West Yorkshire (Western)
Clayton v South Yorkshire (East District) Coroner [2005] EWHC 1196 (Admin), [2005] All ER (D) 108 (Jun), DC 6.38, 6.40, 8.33
Connah v Plymouth Hospitals NHS Trust [2010] EWHC 1727 (Admin), [2010] All ER (D) 130 (Jul), DC 2.48, 8.10, 8.15
Coroner for Southern District of Manchester v Stockport Nhs Foundation Trust [2015] EWHC 2675 (Admin) 8.26
Criminal Practice Direction 2015 [2015] EWCA Crim 1567, [2015] All ER (D) 134 (Sep) 21.30

D

Daniel v St George's Healthcare NHS Trust [2016] EWHC 23 (QB), [2016] 4 WLR 32, [2016] All ER (D) 197 (Jan) 3.92, 13.24, 14.18, 15.73
Da Silva v United Kingdom (App No 5878/08) (2016) 63 EHRR 12, 30 March 2016 .... 3.67, 3.68, 6.108
Davis, Re [1968] 1 QB 72, [1967] 1 All ER 688, [1967] 2 WLR 1089, 111 Sol Jo 115 .... 6.136
Dawson, Re (1985) 81 CAR 150 .... 6.90
DPP v Majewski [1977] AC 443, [1976] 2 All ER 142, [1976] 2 WLR 623, 62 Cr App Rep 262, 140 JP 315, [1976] Crim LR 374, 120 Sol Jo 299, HL 6.106
DPP v Morgan [1976] AC 182, [1975] 2 All ER 347, [1975] 2 WLR 913, 61 Cr App Rep 136, 139 JP 476, 119 Sol Jo 319, HL 6.106
DPP v Newbury; DPP v Jones [1977] AC 500, [1976] 2 All ER 365, [1976] 2 WLR 918, 62 Cr App Rep 291, 140 JP 370, 120 Sol Jo 402, HL 6.80
Douglas v Ministry of Justice [2018] Inquest LR 71 .... 9.45, 9.46, 9.54, 9.55
Dowler v Hornsey Coroners Court [2009] EWHC 3300 (Admin), 111 BMLR 124, [2009] All ER (D) 86 (Nov) 4.15
Dumpe v Latvia (App No 71506/13) (16 October 2018, unreported) 15.72

E

Edwards v United Kingdom (2002) 35 EHRR 19 .... 3.92

Table of Cases

F

Fernandes Oliveira v Portugal (2019) 69 EHRR 8, [2019] ECHR 106 .... 3.92, 3.94, 15.9, 15.10, 15.14, 15.71, 15.72
Finucane's application for judicial review (Northern Ireland), Re [2019] UKSC 7, [2019] NI 292, [2019] 3 All ER 191, [2019] 4 LRC 73, [2019] All ER (D) 147 (Feb), SC 3.50
Flower v Coroner for the County of Devon, Plymouth, Torbay and South Devon [2015] EWHC 3666 (Admin), [2016] 1 WLR 2221, 180 JP 141, [2015] All ER (D) 160 (Dec) 2.125, 8.16
Frost v Her Majesty's Coroner for West Yorkshire (Eastern District), Re [2019] EWHC 1100 (Admin), [2019] All ER (D) 60 (May) 8.22, 8.28
Fullick v Metropolitan Police Commissioner [2019] EWHC 1941 (QB), [2019] Costs LR 1231 .... 9.41, 9.43, 9.44, 9.45, 9.48, 9.49, 9.50, 9.52, 9.53, 9.54

G

G4S Care and Justice Services Ltd v Luke (suing on behalf of and as administrator of the estate of Dean Boland) [2019] EWHC 1648 (QB), 169 NLJ 7848 .... 3.90
Ghaidan v Godin-Mendoza [2004] UKHL 30, [2004] 2 AC 557, [2004] 3 WLR 113, [2004] 2 FLR 600, [2004] 2 FCR 481, [2004] Fam Law 641, [2004] HLR 827, [2004] 2 EGLR 132, [2004] 27 LS Gaz R 30, [2004] NLJR 1013, (2004) Times, 24 June, 148 Sol Jo LB 792, 16 BHRC 671, [2004] All ER (D) 210 (Jun), sub nom Ghaidan v Mendoza [2004] 3 All ER 411, [2005] 1 LRC 449, HL 8.58
Gray v HM Coroner for Surrey [2017] EWHC 3648 (Admin) 19.49

H

Hammersmith and Fulham London Borough Council v Secretary of State for the Environment. See R v Secretary of State for the Environment, ex p Hammersmith and Fulham London Borough Council
Handley v HM Coroner for Birmingham [2011] EWHC 3337 (Admin) 4.91
Her Majestys Senior Coroner for North West Wales [2017] EWHC 2557 (Admin) 8.5, 8.26
HM Senior Coroner for Birmingham and Solihull, Re [2018] EWHC 3443 (Admin) 8.5, 8.21, 8.26
HM Senior Coroner For The County Of Cumbria v Ian Smith Her Majesty's Former Senior Coroner For South & East Cumbria [2015] EWHC 2465 (Admin) 22.8
HM Senior Coroner For The Eastern Area Of Greater London v Whitworth (deceased) [2017] EWHC 3201 (Admin), 182 JP 129 .... 8.5, 8.26
Hollington v F Hewthorn & Co Ltd [1943] KB 587, [1943] 2 All ER 35, 112 LJKB 463, 87 Sol Jo 247, 169 LT 21, 59 TLR 321 .... 22.4
Hopkins v HM Coroner For Swansea And Neath And Port Talbot [2018] EWHC 1604 (Admin) 8.31
Howlett v Coroner for the County of Devon [2006] EWHC 2570 (Admin), [2006] All ER (D) 46 (Oct), DC 2.74

I

Inner West London Coroner v Channel 4 Television Corpn [2007] EWHC 2513 (QB), [2008] 1 WLR 945, 100 BMLR 44, (2007) Times, 11 December, [2007] All ER (D) 467 (Oct) 4.70

J

JC and RT v Central Criminal Court [2014] EWHC 1041 (QB) 12.18
JS, Re [2012] EWHC 1379 (Fam) 22.1
Jacobs Application for Judicial Review, Re (1999) 53 BMLR 21, CA 8.72
James v Her Majesty's Coroner For Surrey [2014] EWHC 2585 (Admin) 19.49
Janowiec v Russia (App Nos 55508/07 and 29520/09) [2013] ECHR 55508/07, EctHR 3.50
Jenkins v HM Coroner For Bridgend And Glamorgan Valleys [2012] EWHC 3175 (Admin) 6.137

Table of Cases

Jones v Gwent Coroner [2015] EWHC 2178 (Admin) 8.73
Jordan's Application, Re (29 June 1996, unreported) 4.36
Jordan v United Kingdom (2003) 37 EHRR 2 ..... 3.98, 3.103, 3.104, 3.105, 3.107, 6.160

K

Kats v Ukraine (App No 29971/04) (2008) 51 EHRR 1066, [2008] ECHR 29971/04,
    EctHR 3.92, 14.18
Keenan v United Kingdom (2002) 35 EHRR 487 .... 3.92
Kelly (Captain Christopher John), matter of (1996) 161 JP 417, DC 7.1
Ketcher's Application for Judicial Review, Re [2020] 6 WLUK 195 .... 13.33
Ketcher, Re [2020] NICA 31, NICA 6.119
Kiliinç v Turkey (App No 40145/98) (7 June 2005, unreported) 3.92
Kolyadenko v Russia (App Nos 17423/05, 20534/05, 20678/05, 23263/05, 24283/05
    and 35673/05) (2012) 33 BHRC 159, [2012] ECHR 17423/05, EctHR 3.73

L

Land Securities plc v Westminster City Council [1993] 4 All ER 124, [1993] 1 WLR 286,
    65 P & CR 387, [1992] 2 EGLR 15, [1993] 5 LS Gaz R 42, [1992] 44 EG 153 ...... 23.8
Lavelle (by their mother and litigation friend, Michelle Lavelle) v Noble [2011] EWCA
    Civ 441, [2011] All ER (D) 179 (Apr) 23.9
Lopes de Sousa Fernandes v Portugal (App No 56080/13) (2018) 66 EHRR 28,
    ECtHR 3.84, 3.85, 3.87, 13.18
Lynch v Chief Constable of Warwickshire [2014] Inquest LR 247, [2014] 11 WLUK
    332 .... 9.45, 9.49, 9.51, 9.54, 9.55, 13.4

M

M Özel v Turkey (App No 14350/05) (2 May 2016, unreported) 3.92
MB (an adult: medical treatment), Re [1997] 2 FLR 426, [1997] 2 FCR 541, [1997] Fam
    Law 542, [1997] 8 Med LR 217, 38 BMLR 175, [1997] NLJR 600, (1997) Times,
    18 April 6.130
McCann v United Kingdom (App No 18984/91) (1995) 21 EHRR 97, (1995) Times,
    9 October, [1995] ECHR 18984/91, EctHR 3.65, 3.66
McDonnell v HM Assistant Coroner for West London [2016] EWHC 3078 (Admin),
    154 BMLR 188, [2016] All ER (D) 71 (Dec) 3.23, 6.55
McGhee v National Coal Board [1972] 3 All ER 1008, [1973] 1 WLR 1, 13 KIR 471,
    116 Sol Jo 967, 1973 SC (HL) 37, HL 13.10
McKerr, Re [2004] UKHL 12, [2004] NI 212, [2004] 2 All ER 409, [2004] 1 WLR 807,
    (2004) Times, 12 March, 148 Sol Jo LB 355, 17 BHRC 68, [2004] All ER (D) 210
    (Mar), HL 3.50
McKerr's Application (No 2), Re [1993] NI 249, NICA 5.21
Medical Defence Union v Bascombe Sinclair [1990] 1 Med LR 359 .... 8.38
Moohan v Lord Advocate [2014] UKSC 67, [2015] AC 901, [2015] 2 All ER 361,
    [2015] 2 WLR 141, [2015] 4 LRC 379, 165 NLJ 7636, (2014) Times, 30 December,
    2015 SC (UKSC) 1, 2015 SLT 2, [2014] All ER (D) 186 (Dec), 2014 Scot (D) 14/12,
    SC 3.48
Mueller v Her Majesty's Area Coroner for Manchester West [2017] EWHC 3000
    (Admin) 2.110, 4.45, 5.7

N

N (a child) v HM Coroner for Liverpool [2001] EWHC 922 (Admin) . 4.116, 4.122, 13.36
Nachova v Bulgaria (2006) 42 EHRR 43 .... 3.104
Nencheva v Bulgaria (App No 48606/06) (18 June 2013, unreported) 3.92
Nicholls v HM Coroner for Liverpool [2002] AC 89 .... 6.182

O

O'Callaghan, Re (1899) VLR 957 .... 5.28
O'Keefe v Ireland [2014] 59 EHRR 15 .... 6.186

Oneryildiz v Turkey (App No 48939/99) (2004) 41 EHRR 325, 18 BHRC 145, [2005] 41 EHRR 20, [2004] ECHR 48939/99, EctHR 3.70, 3.72, 3.92, 3.104
Orde van Vlaamse Balies v Ministerraad C-667/18 (14 May 2020, unreported) 9.35
Osman v United Kingdom (App No 23452/94) (1998) 29 EHRR 245, [1999] 1 FLR 193, [1999] Fam Law 86, [1999] Crim LR 82, (1998) Times, 5 November, 5 BHRC 293, [1998] ECHR 23452/94, EctHR 3.59, 3.88

P

Palmer v R [1971] AC 814, [1971] 1 All ER 1077, [1971] 2 WLR 831, 16 WIR 499, 55 Cr App Rep 223, 115 Sol Jo 264, PC 6.109
Peacock v London Weekend Television (1985) 150 JP 71 .... 4.35
Polanski v Condé Nast Publications Ltd [2005] UKHL 10, [2005] 1 All ER 945, [2005] 1 WLR 637, [2005] NLJR 245, (2005) Times, 11 February, 149 Sol Jo LB 233, [2005] EMLR 287, [2005] All ER (D) 139 (Feb), HL 5.14
Poplar Housing and Regeneration Community Association Ltd v Donoghue [2001] EWCA Civ 595, [2001] Fam Law 588, [2002] QB 48, [2001] 4 All ER 604, [2001] 3 WLR 183, [2001] LGR 489, [2001] 2 FLR 284, [2001] 3 FCR 74, 33 HLR 823, [2001] 19 LS Gaz R 38, [2001] 19 EGCS 141, (2001) Times, 21 June, 145 Sol Jo LB 122, [2001] All ER (D) 210 (Apr) 3.43
Powell v The Chief Constable of West Midlands Police [2018] EWHC B12 (Costs) [2018] EWHC B12 (Costs) 13.4
Powell v UK (App No 45305/99) [2000] ECHR 703, 30 EHRR CD 362 .... 3.83

R

R v Adomako [1995] 1 AC 171, [1994] 3 All ER 79, [1994] 3 WLR 288, [1994] 2 LRC 800, 158 JP 653, [1994] Crim LR 757, [1994] 5 Med LR 277, 19 BMLR 56, [1994] NLJR 936, (1994) Times, 4 July, HL 6.81
R (Dr Siddiqi and Dr Paeprer-Rohricht) v Assistant Coroner for East London CO/2892/2017 (28 September 2017, unreported) 7.30
R (on the application of Maguire) v Assistant Coroner for West Yorkshire (Eastern Area) [2017] EWHC 2039 (Admin), 167 NLJ 7760, [2017] All ER (D) 59 (Aug); affd sub nom R (on the application of Maguire) v Assistant Coroner For West Yorkshire (Eastern Area) [2018] EWCA Civ 6, [2018] All ER (D) 70 (Jan) 4.34, 8.47, 8.56, 8.57
R (on the application of the Secretary of State for the Home Department) v Assistant Deputy Coroner for Inner West London [2010] EWHC 3098 (Admin), [2011] 3 All ER 1001, [2011] 1 WLR 2564, 174 JP 593, [2010] 48 LS Gaz R 14, [2010] NLJR 1717, (2011) Times, 12 January, [2010] All ER (D) 303 (Nov) 4.23
R (on the application of Duggan) v Assistant Deputy Coroner for the Northern District of Greater London [2017] EWCA Civ 142, [2017] 4 All ER 104, [2017] 1 WLR 2199, 167 NLJ 7741, [2017] All ER (D) 179 (Mar) 3.68, 3.69
R v Avon Deputy Coroner, ex parte Lambourne (29 July 2002, unreported), DC 8.47
R v Bateman (1925) 19 Cr App Rep 8, 89 JP 162, 94 LJKB 791, 28 Cox CC 33, [1925] All ER Rep 45, 69 Sol Jo 622, 133 LT 730, 41 TLR 557, NICrCA 6.84
R (on the application of Goodson) v Bedfordshire and Luton Coroner (Luton and Dunstable Hospital NHS Trust, interested party) [2004] EWHC 2931 (Admin), [2005] 2 All ER 791, [2006] 1 WLR 432, 84 BMLR 72, [2004] All ER (D) 298 (Dec) 6.116, 6.117, 13.34
R v Bedfordshire Coroner Ex Parte Local Sunday Newspapers Ltd (1999) 164 JP 283, [1999] Lexis Citation 4130 .... 4.36, 8.35
R (on the application of Davies) v Birmingham Deputy Coroner [2003] EWCA Civ 1739, 147 Sol Jo LB 1426, [2003] All ER (D) 40 (Dec) 6.154
R (on the application of Davies) v Birmingham Deputy Coroner [2004] EWCA Civ 207, [2004] 3 All ER 543, [2004] 1 WLR 2739, 80 BMLR 48, (2004) Times, 10 March, 148 Sol Jo LB 297, [2004] 4 Costs LR 545, [2004] All ER (D) 455 (Feb) 8.65
R (Syed) v Bradford Council (4 December 2001, unreported) 5.31
R (on the application of Aineto) v Brighton and Hove District Coroner; Aineto v Brighton and Hove District Coroner [2003] EWHC 1896 (Admin), [2003] All ER (D) 353 (Jul), DC 4.104, 4.108, 8.61
R v Bristol Coroner, ex p Kerr [1974] QB 652, [1974] 2 All ER 719, [1974] 2 WLR 816, 138 JP 562, 118 Sol Jo 332, DC 2.54, 8.38, 21.2

Table of Cases

R v Cardiff Coroner, ex p Thomas [1970] 3 All ER 469, [1970] 1 WLR 1475, 134 JP 673, 114 Sol Jo 788, DC 6.134, 6.136

R (on the application of Antoniou) v Central and North West London NHS Foundation Trust [2013] EWHC 3055 (Admin), [2015] 1 WLR 4459, 135 BMLR 89, [2013] All ER (D) 126 (Oct), DC 2.103, 3.104

R v Chief Constable of the West Midlands Police, ex parte Wiley; R v Chief Constable of the Nottinghamshire Constabulary, ex parte Sunderland [1995] 1 AC 274, [1994] 3 All ER 420, [1994] 3 WLR 433, [1994] 3 LRC 162, 159 LG Rev 181, [1994] 40 LS Gaz R 35, [1994] NLJR 1008, (1994) Times, 15 July, 138 Sol Jo LB 156, HL 4.60

R (on the application of Guardian News and Media Ltd) v City of Westminster Magistrates' Court [2012] EWCA Civ 420, [2013] QB 618, [2012] 3 All ER 551, [2012] 3 WLR 1343, [2012] IP & T 699, [2012] NLJR 619, (2012) Times, 12 July, [2012] All ER (D) 18 (Apr) 12.7, 21.30

R v Coley [2013] EWCA Crim 223, [2013] All ER (D) 06 (Apr) 6.106

R v Coroner for Birmingham and Solihull, ex p Benton (1997) 162 JP 807, [1997] 8 Med LR 362 .... 2.28, 6.58, 6.118, 6.152, 13.17, 13.38, 23.4

R (on the application of Hambleton) v Coroner for the Birmingham Inquests (1974) [2018] EWCA Civ 2081, [2019] 2 All ER 251, [2019] 1 WLR 3417, 168 NLJ 7811, [2018] All ER (D) 62 (Sep) 3.2, 3.6, 3.25, 8.47, 8.55

R (Nicholls) v Coroner for City of Liverpool [2001] EWHC 922 (Admin) 6.149, 6.155

R v Cotswold Geotechnical (Holdings) Ltd [2011] EWCA Crim 1337, [2012] 1 Cr App Rep (S) 153, (2011) Times, 20 July, [2011] All ER (D) 100 (May) 6.102

R (on the application of Mullholland) v Coroner for St Pancras, Mullholland v Coroner for St Pancras [2003] EWHC 2612 (Admin), 78 BMLR 75, [2003] All ER (D) 108 (Nov) 6.116

R v Coroner for Southern District of Greater London ex p Driscoll (1993) JP 45 DC 4.16, 4.17

R (on the application of Lagos) v Coroner for the City of London [2013] EWHC 423 (Admin), 177 CL&J 226, [2013] All ER (D) 203 (Mar) 4.77, 11.6

R (on the application of P) v Coroner for the District of Avon [2009] EWCA Civ 1367, 112 BMLR 77, [2009] All ER (D) 185 (Dec) 17.24

R (on the application of Brown) v County Borough of Neath & Port Talbot Coroner [2006] EWHC 2019 (Admin), [2006] All ER (D) 204 (Jun) 6.114, 6.115

R (on the application of Bodycote HIP Ltd) v County of Herefordshire Coroner [2008] EWHC 164 (Admin), [2008] All ER (D) 07 (Jan) 6.170

R (on the application of Cash) v County of Northamptonshire Coroner [2007] EWHC 1354 (Admin), [2007] 4 All ER 903, [2007] NLJR 895, [2007] All ER (D) 71 (Jun) 6.23, 8.47

R v Dawson, R v Nolan, R v Walmsley (1985) 81 Cr App Rep 150, 149 JP 513, [1985] Crim LR 383, [1985] LS Gaz R 1562, CA 6.80

R v Derby Magistrates' Court, ex p B [1996] AC 487, [1995] 4 All ER 526, [1995] 3 WLR 681, [1996] 1 Cr App Rep 385, [1996] 1 FLR 513, [1996] Fam Law 210, 159 JP 785, [1996] Crim LR 190, [1995] NLJR 1575, (1995) Times, 25 October, 139 Sol Jo LB 219, HL 5.29

R v Derby and South Derbyshire Coroner ex p Hart [2000] 164 JP 429 .... 4.22

R (on the application of RJ) v Director of Legal Aid Casework [2016] EWHC 645 (Admin), [2016] All ER (D) 56 (Apr) 23.8

R (on the application of Oliver) v Director of Public Prosecution [2016] EWHC 1771 (Admin), [2016] All ER (D) 192 (Jul) 6.87

R v Divine, ex p Walton [1930] 2 KB 29, 28 LGR 283, 94 JP 129, 99 LJKB 433, [1930] All ER Rep 302, 143 LT 235, 46 TLR 321, DC 5.13, 8.19

R (on the application of Paul) v Deputy Coroner of the Queen's Household and Assistant Deputy Coroner for Surrey; R (on the application of Al Fayed) v same [2007] EWHC 408 (Admin), [2008] QB 172, [2007] 2 All ER 509, [2007] 3 WLR 503, 95 BMLR 137, [2007] NLJR 366, (2007) Times, 12 March, [2007] All ER (D) 31 (Mar), DC 4.86, 6.113

R (on the application of O'Connor) v District of Avon Coroner [2009] EWHC 854 (Admin), [2011] QB 106, [2009] 4 All ER 1020, [2010] 2 WLR 1299, [2009] All ER (D) 49 (May), DC 8.64

R v Durham Coroner ex p Attorney General, The Times, 29 June 1978 .... 6.69

Table of Cases

R v East Sussex Coroner, ex p Healy [1989] 1 All ER 30, [1988] 1 WLR 1194, 153 JP 1, (1988) Times, 1 June 2.47, 2.51
R v East Sussex Coroner ex p Homberg [1994] 158 JP 357 DC 5.20
R v Felixstowe Justices, ex p Leigh [1987] QB 582, [1987] 1 All ER 551, [1987] 2 WLR 380, 84 Cr App Rep 327, 151 JP 65, [1987] Crim LR 125, 130 Sol Jo 767, [1987] LS Gaz R 901, [1986] NLJ Rep 988, DC 8.38
R v Fitzgerald ex p O'Brien and Bourchier (1883) 17 IRLT 34 .... 6.13
R v Galbraith [1981] 1 WLR 1039, (1981) 73 Cr App 124, CA 6.190, 6.198
R v Goodfellow (1986) 83 Cr App Rep 23, [1986] Crim LR 468, CA 6.77
R v Gore [2007] EWCA Crim 2789, [2008] Crim LR 388, CA 6.105
R v Greater London Coroner, ex p Ridley [1986] 1 All ER 37, 149 JP 657, 129 Sol Jo 871, [1986] LS Gaz R 3533, sub nom R v HM Coroner for Greater London (Southern District), ex p Ridley [1985] 1 WLR 1347 .... 8.47
R v Greater Manchester Coroner, ex p Tal [1985] QB 67, [1984] 3 All ER 240, [1984] 3 WLR 643, 128 Sol Jo 500, DC 5.13, 8.46
R (on the application of Wilkinson) v Greater Manchester South District Coroner [2012] EWHC 2755 (Admin), 176 JP 665, [2012] All ER (D) 117 (Oct) 6.66, 8.62
R v Hasan [2005] UKHL 22, [2005] 4 All ER 685, [2005] 2 Cr App Rep 314, [2006] Crim LR 142, (2005) Times, 21 March, 149 Sol Jo LB 360, [2005] All ER (D) 299 (Mar), sub nom R v Z [2005] 2 AC 467, [2005] 2 WLR 709, HL 6.106
R (on the application of Hamilton-Jackson) v HM Assistant Coroner for Mid Kent and Medway [2016] EWHC 1796 (Admin), [2016] All ER (D) 161 (Jul) 5.46
R (on the application of Smith) v HM Assistant Coroner for North West Wales [2020] EWHC 781 (Admin), 174 BMLR 142 . 6.32, 6.46, 6.110, 6.121, 6.159, 6.167, 6.196, 11.10
R (on the application of Lee) v HM Assistant Coroner for the City of Sunderland [2019] EWHC 3227 (Admin), [2019] All ER (D) 94 (Sep) 3.97, 4.98, 15.13
R (on the application of Dyer) v HM Assistant Coroner for West Yorkshire (Western) [2019] EWHC 2897 (Admin), [2019] All ER (D) 213 (Oct); revsd sub nom Chief Constable of West Yorkshire Police and Officers B and E v Dyer [2020] EWCA Civ 1375, [2020] All ER (D) 24 (Nov) 4.41
R (on the application of LePage) v HM Assistant Deputy Coroner for Inner South London [2012] EWHC 1485 (Admin), [2012] All ER (D) 17 (Jun), DC 6.115, 6.117, 13.35
R (on the application of Shaw) v HM Coroner [2013] EWHC 386 (Admin), [2013] All ER (D) 240 (Mar) 8.47, 8.54
R v HM Coroner at Hammersmith, ex p Peach (Nos 1 and 2) [1980] QB 211, [1980] 2 All ER 7, [1980] 2 WLR 496, 144 JP 277, [1980] Crim LR 238, 124 Sol Jo 17 .... 4.66, 4.79
R (Longfield Care Homes) v HM Coroner for Blackburn [2004] EWHC 2467 (Admin) 6.143, 6.158, 6.202, 8.62
R (on the application of Mack) v HM Coroner for Birmingham and Solihull [2011] EWCA Civ 712 .... 4.34, 4.33, 18.20, 18.22
R v HM Coroner for Birmingham and Solihill, ex p Cotton (1995) 160 JP 123, [1995] Lexis Citation 3486 .... 13.3
R v HM Coroner for City of London, ex p Barber [1975] 3 All ER 538, sub nom R v City of London Coroner, ex p Barber [1975] 1 WLR 1310, [1975] Crim LR 515, 119 Sol Jo 697, DC 6.122, 6.136
R v HM Coroner for Derbyshire (Scarsdale) ex parte Fletcher [1992] 1 WLUK 273 .... 8.25
R v HM Coroner for East Berkshire, ex p Buckley (1992) 157 JP 425, (1992) Times, 1 December 5.32, 6.37
R (Dawson) v HM Coroner for East Riding and Kingston upon Hull Coroners District [2001] EWHC Admin 352; [2001] Inquest LR 233 .... 6.175
R v HM Coroner for Exeter and East Devon ex p Palmer (10 December 1997, unreported) 6.202
R (on the application of Goldstein) v HM Coroner For Inner London District Greater London [2014] EWHC 3889 (Admin) 2.73
R (on the application of Allen) v HM Coroner for Inner North London [2009] EWCA Civ 623, [2009] All ER (D) 287 (Jun) 6.23
R v HM Coroner for Inner North London, ex p Cohen (1993) 158 JP 644, DC 4.81
R v HM Coroner for Inner North London, ex p Linnane [1989] 2 All ER 254, [1989] 1 WLR 395 .... 14.5

xxxix

Table of Cases

R v HM Coroner for Inner North London, ex p Linnane (No 2) (1990) 155 JP 343, (1990) Times, 6 August, DC 6.114, 8.62, 13.34
R (Collins) v HM Coroner for Inner South London [2004] EWHC 2421 (Admin) 4.110
R (on the application of Kent County Council) v HM Coroner for Kent [2012] EWHC 2768 (Admin), 177 JP 82, [2012] All ER (D) 125 (Oct) 3.90, 3.97
R (Hay) v HM Coroner for Lincolnshire (19 February 1999, unreported) 4.66
R (on the application of Cooper) v HM Coroner for North East Kent [2014] EWHC 586 (Admin), 178 JP 505, [2014] All ER (D) 282 (Feb) 8.48
R v HM Coroner for North Humberside and Scunthorpe, ex p Jamieson [1995] QB 1, [1994] 3 All ER 972, [1994] 3 WLR 82, 158 JP 1011, 19 BMLR 35, (1994) Times, 28 April 1.4, 3.12, 3.18, 4.50, 5.12, 6.14, 6.142, 6.144, 6.158, 15.35
R (on the application of Mcleish) v HM Coroner for the Northern District of Greater London [2010] EWHC 3624 (Admin), [2010] All ER (D) 211 (Nov) 4.31, 4.73
R v HM Coroner for Portsmouth, ex p Keane (1989) 153 JP 658, (1989) Times, 5 July 8.47
R v HM Coroner for South Glamorgan, ex p BP Chemicals Ltd (1987) 151 JP 799 .... 6.61
R v HM Coroner for Southwark, ex p Fields (1998) 162 JP 411 .... 5.10
R (on the application of Hair) v HM Coroner for Staffordshire (South) [2010] EWHC 2580 (Admin), [2010] All ER (D) 172 (Oct) 4.33, 5.30
R v HM Coroner for Surrey, ex p Wright [1997] QB 786, [1997] 1 All ER 823, [1997] 2 WLR 16, 160 JP 581, 33 BMLR 90, (1996) Times, 15 July, [1996] Lexis Citation 1212; affd (1996) 35 BMLR 57 .... 6.152, 6.157
R v HM Coroner for Western District of East Sussex, ex p Homber, Roberts and Manners (1994) 158 JP 357 .... 3.28, 5.43, 8.22, 13.11, 13.17
R v HM Coroner for Wiltshire, ex p Clegg (1996) 161 JP 521, [1996] Lexis Citation 3287 .... 6.151
R (on the application of Duffy) v HM Deputy Coroner for the County of Worcestershire [2013] EWHC 1654 (Admin), 134 BMLR 86, [2013] All ER (D) 195 (Jun) 6.123
R (Bentley) v HM Coroner in the District of Avon [2001] EWHC 170 (Admin), (2001) 74 BMCRI 4.31, 4.50, 4.75, 5.22
R (on the application of LF) v HM Senior Coroner for Inner South London [2017] EWCA Civ 31, [2018] QB 487, [2017] 3 WLR 382, [2017] COPLR 172, [2017] All ER (D) 99 (Jan) 4.91, 4.99, 15.59
R (on the application of Iroko) v HM Senior Coroner for Inner London South [2020] EWHC 1753 (Admin), 176 BMLR 81, [2020] All ER (D) 20 (Jul) 13.18, 13.19
R (on the application of Adath Yisroel Burial Society) v HM Senior Coroner for Inner North London [2018] EWHC 969 (Admin), [2019] QB 251, [2018] 3 All ER 1088, [2018] 3 WLR 1354, 162 BMLR 217, 168 NLJ 7792, (2018) Times, 15 May, [2018] All ER (D) 128 (Apr) 2.65, 8.38, 8.47, 8.54
R (on the application of Fullick) v HM Senior Coroner For Inner North London [2015] EWHC 3522 (Admin), [2015] All ER (D) 37 (Dec) 4.91, 4.100, 4.109, 6.113
R (on the application of Parkinson) v HM Senior Coroner for Kent [2018] EWHC 1501 (Admin), [2018] 4 All ER 517, [2018] 4 WLR 106, 169 BMLR 74, [2018] All ER (D) 78 (Jun) 3.83, 8.47, 8.66, 13.18, 13.19
R (on the application of Carwyn Jones) v HM Senior Coroner for North Wales (East and Central) [2019] EWHC 1494 (Admin), [2019] All ER (D) 149 (May) 4.34
R (on the application of Tainton) v HM Senior Coroner for Preston and West Lancashire [2016] EWHC 1396 (Admin), [2016] 4 WLR 157, 166 NLJ 7704, [2016] All ER (D) 98 (Jun) 6.44, 6.45, 6.175, 6.190, 6.191, 6.193, 6.203, 8.62, 11.10
R (on the application of Worthington) v HM Senior Coroner for the County of Cumbria [2018] EWHC 3386 (Admin), [2018] All ER (D) 43 (Dec) 3.24, 3.28, 6.48
R (on the application of T) v HM Senior Coroner for the County of west Yorkshire (West Area) [2017] EWCA Civ 318, [2018] 2 WLR 211, 182 JP 16, [2017] All ER (D) 07 (May) 6.130, 8.47, 8.48, 12.14, 12.15
R (on the application of Chidlow) v HM Senior Coroner for Blackpool and Fylde [2019] EWHC 581 (Admin), [2019] All ER (D) 73 (Mar) 6.177
R (on the application of Khan) v Her Majesty's Coroner for West Hertfordshire [2002] EWHC 302 (Admin), [2002] All ER (D) 68 (Mar) 6.182, 6.183, 8.48
R (on the application of GS, a child (by her grandfather and litigation friend)) v HM Senior Coroner for Wiltshire and Swindon [2020] EWHC 2007 (Admin), [2020] 1 WLR 4889 .... 8.47, 8.48, 8.53

Table of Cases

R (on the application of Palmer) v Her Majesty's Coroner for the County of Worcestershire [2011] EWHC 1453 (Admin), [2011] LGR 952, [2011] All ER (D) 196 (Jun) 3.102
R (on the application of Rotsztein) v Her Majesty's Senior Coroner for Inner North London [2015] EWHC 2764 (Admin), [2015] All ER (D) 382 (Jul) 2.72
R (on the application of Maguire) v Her Majesty's Senior Coroner for Blackpool and Fylde [2020] EWCA Civ 738, [2020] 3 WLR 1268, [2020] COPLR 654, 176 BMLR 50, [2020] All ER (D) 53 (Jun) ... 3.20, 3.92, 3.93, 4.93, 4.94, 13.18, 15.11, 15.68, 15.69, 15.70, 15.72
R (on the application of the Secretary of State) v Her Majesty's Senior Coroner for Norfolk [2016] EWHC 2279 (Admin), 181 JP 59, 166 NLJ 7718, [2016] All ER (D) 02 (Oct) 4.57, 4.65, 19.33
R (on the application of Silvera) v Her Majesty's Senior Coroner for Oxfordshire [2017] EWHC 2499 (Admin), [2017] All ER (D) 107 (Oct) 21.49
R (on the application of Maughan) v Her Majesty's Senior Coroner for Oxfordshire [2020] UKSC 46, [2020] 3 WLR 1298, [2020] All ER (D) 73 (Nov), SC ... 1.13, 6.8, 6.53, 6.62, 6.136, 6.140, 6.172, 15.4, 15.16
R (on the application of Ahmed) v Her Majesty's South & East Cumbria [2009] EWHC 1653 (Admin) 18.20
R v Howen [1987] AC 417, [1987] 1 All ER 771, [1987] 2 WLR 568, [1987] LRC (Crim) 413, 85 Cr App Rep 32, 151 JP 265, [1987] Crim LR 480, 131 Sol Jo 258, [1987] LS Gaz R 900, [1987] NLJ Rep 197, (1987) Times, 20 February, HL 6.106
R v Inglis [2010] EWCA Crim 2637, [2011] 1 WLR 1110, [2011] 2 Cr App Rep (S) 66, [2011] Crim LR 243, 117 BMLR 65, 174 CL&J 734, (2010) Times, 22 November, 154 Sol Jo (no 44) 30, [2010] All ER (D) 140 (Nov) 6.72
R v Inner West London Coroner, ex p Dallaglio [1994] 4 All ER 139   ..... 1.3, 3.28, 21.45
R v Inner South London Coroner, ex p Douglas-Williams [1999] 1 All ER 344, 162 JP 751, (1998) Times, 4 September, [1998] Lexis Citation 2986, [1998] All ER (D) 390 .... 5.21, 6.185, 8.47, 8.71
R v Inner South London Coroner, ex p Kendall [1989] 1 All ER 72, [1988] 1 WLR 1186, 132 Sol Jo 1460, [1989] 2 LS Gaz R 38, (1988) Times, 8 June, sub nom R v Southwark Coroners' Court, ex p Kendall 153 JP 117 .... 6.53, 6.56, 6.60
R v Inner London North District Coroner, ex p Linnane [1989] 2 All ER 254, [1989] 1 WLR 395, 133 Sol Jo 389, [1989] 15 LS Gaz R 40, DC 4.91, 4.97, 14.5
R v Institute of Chartered Accountants in England and Wales, ex p Andreou [1996] COD 489, [1996] Lexis Citation 1225, 8 Admin LR 557, CA 8.43
R (on the application of Touche) v Inner London North Coroner [2001] EWCA Civ 383, [2001] QB 1206, [2001] 2 All ER 752, [2001] 3 WLR 148, 165 JP 526, 60 BMLR 170, [2001] 20 LS Gaz R 40, (2001) Times, 30 March, [2001] All ER (D) 242 (Mar) 6.118, 6.156, 8.47, 8.52, 8.72, 13.12, 13.13, 20.25
R (on the application of Takoushis) v Inner London North Coroner [2005] EWCA Civ 1440, [2006] 1 WLR 461, 87 BMLR 149, (2005) Times, 8 December, 149 Sol Jo LB 1489, [2005] All ER (D) 416 (Nov) 3.79, 3.86, 3.104, 6.116, 6.118
R (on the application of Anderson) v Inner North Greater London Coroner [2004] EWHC 2729 (Admin), [2004] All ER (D) 410 (Nov) 5.33
R (on the application of Stanley) v Inner North London Coroner [2003] EWHC 1180 (Admin), (2003) Times, 12 June, [2003] All ER (D) 351 (Apr) ... 5.10, 6.116, 6.124, 11.6, 13.35
R (on the application of Coker) v Inner South London Coroner [2006] EWHC 614 (Admin), [2006] All ER (D) 405 (Mar) 4.5
R (on the application of Paul) v Inner West London Assistant Deputy Coroner [2007] EWCA Civ 1259, [2008] 1 All ER 981, [2008] 1 WLR 1335, (2007) Times, 11 December, [2007] All ER (D) 435 (Nov) 4.46, 4.47
R v Jogee [2016] UKSC 8, [2017] AC 387, [2016] 2 All ER 1, 87 WIR 439, [2016] 2 LRC 684, [2016] 1 Cr App Rep 485, 180 JP 313, (2016) Times, 02 March, [2016] All ER (D) 167 (Feb), SC 6.110
R v Killick [2011] EWCA Crim 1608, [2012] 1 Cr App Rep 121, [2011] All ER (D) 237 (Jun) 21.57
R v Lamb [1967] 2 QB 981, [1967] 2 All ER 1282, [1967] 3 WLR 888, 51 Cr App Rep 417, 131 JP 456, 111 Sol Jo 541 .... 6.106
R v Legal Aid Board ex parte Hughes (1992) 5 Admin L Rep 623   .... 8.45

Table of Cases

R (on the application of Humberstone) v Legal Services Commission (The Lord Chancellor intervening) [2010] EWCA Civ 1479, [2011] 1 WLR 1460, 118 BMLR 79, [2011] NLJR 27, (2011) Times, 16 February, [2011] 5 Costs LR 701, [2010] All ER (D) 255 (Dec) 3.84, 3.104

R v Lincoln Coroner, ex p Hay [2000] Lloyd's Rep Med 264, (1999) Times, 30 March, [1999] Lexis Citation 2313, (1999) 163 JP 666, [1999] All ER (D) 173 ... 4.34, 4.34, 5.13, 5.26

R (Revenue and Customs Comrs) v Liverpool Coroner (Associated of Personal Injury Lawyers intervening) [2014] EWHC 1586 (Admin), [2015] QB 481, [2014] 3 WLR 1660, 179 JP 343 .... 4.50, 4.56

R (on the application of Letts) v Lord Chancellor (Equality & Human Rights Commission intervening) [2015] EWHC 402 (Admin), [2016] 2 All ER 968, [2015] 1 WLR 4497, 165 NLJ 7643, [2015] 2 Costs LR 217, [2015] All ER (D) 230 (Feb) 14.5

R v Mark [2004] EWCA Crim 2490, [2004] All ER (D) 35 (Oct) 6.92

R (on the application of Lewis) v Mid and North Division of Shropshire Coroner [2009] EWCA Civ 1403, [2010] 3 All ER 858, [2010] 1 WLR 1836, 174 JP 49, 112 BMLR 90, [2010] 2 LS Gaz R 17, (2010) Times, 11 January, [2009] All ER (D) 199 (Dec) 3.80, 6.47, 6.166, 6.189, 7.29

R (on the application of Nicklinson) v Ministry of Justice; R (on the application of AM) v DPP [2013] EWCA Civ 961, [2015] AC 657, [2014] 2 All ER 32, [2014] 3 WLR 200, [2014] 3 LRC 264, [2014] 1 FCR 316, 133 BMLR 46, (2013) Times, 08 October, [2013] All ER (D) 392 (Jul); [2014] UKSC 38, [2015] AC 657, [2014] 3 All ER 843, [2014] 3 WLR 200, [2015] 1 LRC 414, [2014] 3 FCR 1, 139 BMLR 1, (2014) Times, 26 June, 36 BHRC 465, [2014] All ER (D) 195 (Jun), SC 6.76

R v Misra [2004] EWCA Crim 2375, [2005] 1 Cr App Rep 328, (2004) Times, 13 October, 148 Sol Jo LB 1213, [2004] All ER (D) 107 (Oct) 6.86, 6.87

R (on the application of Warren) v Northamptonshire Assistant Deputy Coroner [2008] EWHC 966 (Admin), [2008] All ER (D) 393 (Apr) 6.116, 6.124, 13.35

R (on the application of Hurst) v Northern District of London Coroner [2007] UKHL 13, [2007] 2 AC 189, [2007] 2 All ER 1025, [2007] 2 WLR 726, [2007] NLJR 519, (2007) Times, 29 March, [2007] All ER (D) 470 (Mar), HL . 3.20, 3.28, 3.99, 3.100, 3.102, 8.47, 13.17

R v Nedrick [1986] 3 All ER 1, [1986] 1 WLR 1025, [1986] LRC (Crim) 773, 83 Cr App Rep 267, 8 Cr App Rep (S) 179, 150 JP 589, [1986] Crim LR 792, 130 Sol Jo 572, [1986] LS Gaz R 2755 .... 6.72

R (on the application of Moss) v North and South Districts of Durham and Darlington Coroner [2008] EWHC 2940 (Admin), 173 JP 65, [2008] All ER (D) 292 (Nov) 3.102

R v North Humberside Coroner, Ex p Jamieson [1995] 1 QB 124 .... 1.11

R v Osman [2015] EWCA Crim 167, [2015] 2 Cr App Rep (S) 36 .... 6.77

R (on the application of A) v Partnerships in Care Ltd [2002] EWHC 529 (Admin), [2002] 1 WLR 2610, (2002) Times, 23 April, [2002] All ER (D) 23 (Apr) 3.44, 15.20

R (on the application of Andrew Campbell) v Parliamentary Ombudsman [2017] EWHC 3729 (Admin), [2017] All ER (D) 229 (Mar) 8.48, 8.49

R v Poplar Coroner, ex p Thomas [1993] QB 610, [1993] 2 All ER 381, [1993] 2 WLR 547, 11 BMLR 37, (1992) Times, 23 December 6.118, 13.9

R v Portsmouth Coroner, ex p Anderson [1988] 2 All ER 604, [1987] 1 WLR 1640, 152 JP 56, 131 Sol Jo 1455, [1987] LS Gaz R 3254, (1987) Times, 6 August, DC 6.56

R (on the application of Gentle) v Prime Minister [2008] UKHL 20, [2008] 1 AC 1356, [2008] 3 All ER 1, [2008] 2 WLR 879, (2008) Times, 10 April, 27 BHRC 1, [2008] All ER (D) 111 (Apr), HL 3.79, 24.43

R (on the application of Al-Skeini) v Secretary of State for Defence [2007] UKHL 26, [2008] 1 AC 153, [2007] 3 All ER 685, [2007] 3 WLR 33, [2008] 1 LRC 618, [2007] NLJR 894, (2007) Times, 14 June, 22 BHRC 518, [2007] All ER (D) 106 (Jun), HL 3.46

R (on the application of Long) v Secretary of State for Defence [2014] EWHC 2391 (Admin), [2014] All ER (D) 144 (Jul), DC; affd on other grounds [2015] EWCA Civ 770, [2015] 1 WLR 5006, (2015) Times, 12 August, [2015] All ER (D) 206 (Jul) 3.82, 19.38

R (on the application of Mousa) v Secretary of State for Defence (No 2) [2013] EWHC 1412 (Admin), [2013] All ER (D) 302 (May), DC 3.104, 19.3

Table of Cases

R (on the application of Smith) v Secretary of State for Defence [2010] UKSC 29, [2011] 1 AC 1, [2010] 3 All ER 1067, [2010] 3 WLR 223, [2010] 5 LRC 558, [2010] 28 LS Gaz R 17, [2010] NLJR 973, (2010) Times, 08 July, 154 Sol Jo (no 26) 28, 29 BHRC 497, [2010] All ER (D) 261 (Jun), SC 3.104, 4.71, 4.73, 19.36, 19.47

R (on the application of Sustainable Development Capital LLP) v Secretary of State for Business, Energy and Industrial Strategy [2017] EWHC 771 (Admin) 8.42

R (on the application of Bancoult) v Secretary of State for Foreign and Commonwealth Affairs [2007] EWCA Civ 498, [2008] QB 365, [2007] 3 WLR 768, [2007] 3 LRC 836, (2007) Times, 31 May, 151 Sol Jo LB 707, [2007] All ER (D) 399 (May); revsd [2008] UKHL 61, [2009] AC 453, [2008] 4 All ER 1055, [2008] 3 WLR 955, [2008] 5 LRC 769, [2008] NLJR 1530, (2008) Times, 23 October, 152 Sol Jo (no 41) 29, [2008] All ER (D) 219 (Oct), HL; affd sub nom R (on the application of Bancoult (No2) v Secretary of State for Foreign and Commonwealth Affairs [2016] UKSC 35, [2017] AC 300, [2017] 1 All ER 403, [2016] 3 WLR 157, [2017] 1 LRC 65, 167 NLJ 7706, [2016] All ER (D) 173 (Jun), SC 8.37

R (on the application of Mohamed) v Secretary of State for Foreign and Commonwealth Affairs [2009] EWHC 2549 (Admin), [2009] 1 WLR 2653, [2009] All ER (D) 185 (Oct), DC; affd [2010] EWCA Civ 65, [2011] QB 218, [2010] 4 All ER 91, [2010] 3 WLR 554, (2010) Times, 16 February, [2010] All ER (D) 118 (Feb) 4.60

R (on the application of Khan) v Secretary of State for Health [2003] EWCA Civ 1129, [2003] 4 All ER 1239, [2004] 1 WLR 971, [2003] 3 FCR 341, 76 BMLR 118, [2003] 44 LS Gaz R 30, (2003) Times, 15 October, 147 Sol Jo LB 1207, [2003] All ER (D) 191 (Oct) 3.86, 3.101, 3.107

R (on the application of HM Coroner for the Eastern District of London) v Secretary of State for Justice [2009] EWHC 1974 (Admin), [2009] All ER (D) 353 (Jul), DC 2.64

R v Secretary of State for the Environment, ex p Hammersmith and Fulham London Borough Council [1991] 1 AC 521, [1990] 3 WLR 898, 89 LGR 129, [1990] NLJR 1422, [1990] RVR 188, (1990) Times, 5 October, sub nom Hammersmith and Fulham London Borough Council v Secretary of State for the Environment [1990] 3 All ER 589, 134 Sol Jo 1226, HL 4.31

R (on the application of Amin) v Secretary of State for the Home Department [2003] UKHL 51, [2004] 1 AC 653, [2003] 4 All ER 1264, [2003] 3 WLR 1169, [2004] 3 LRC 746, 76 BMLR 143, [2003] 44 LS Gaz R 32, [2003] NLJR 1600, (2003) Times, 17 October, 15 BHRC 362, [2003] All ER (D) 256 (Oct), HLsub nom R (on the application of Middleton) v West Somerset Coroner [2004] UKHL 10, [2004] 2 AC 182, [2004] 2 All ER 465, [2004] 2 WLR 800, 168 JP 329, 79 BMLR 51, [2004] NLJR 417, (2004) Times, 12 March, 148 Sol Jo LB 354, 17 BHRC 49, [2004] All ER (D) 218 (Mar), HL . 3.16, 3.17, 3.18, 3.51, 3.71, 3.99, 3.100, 3.104, 5.12, 6.16, 6.17, 6.18, 6.24, 6.115, 6.124, 6.143, 6.164, 6.166, 8.47, 8.58, 8.63, 17.11, 21.51, 23.4

R (on the application of D) v Secretary of State for the Home Department (Inquest intervening) [2006] EWCA Civ 143, [2006] 3 All ER 946, (2006) Times, 21 March, [2006] All ER (D) 403 (Feb) 4.4

R (on the application of JL) v Secretary of State for the Home Department [2008] UKHL 68, [2009] AC 588, [2009] 2 All ER 521, [2008] 3 WLR 1325, [2008] NLJR 1719, (2008) Times, 2 December, 152 Sol Jo (no 46) 31, 27 BHRC 24, [2008] All ER (D) 256 (Nov), HL 3.80, 3.104, 24.42

R (on the application of Kigen) v Secretary of State for the Home Department [2015] EWCA Civ 1286, [2016] 1 WLR 723, [2016] INLR 645, 166 NLJ 7683, [2015] All ER (D) 132 (Dec) 8.43

R (on the application of Litvinenko) v Secretary Of State for the Home Department [2014] EWHC 194 (Admin), [2014] All ER (D) 113 (Feb), DC 3.104, 24.58

R (on the application of Sathivel) v Secretary of State for the Home Department; [2018] EWHC 913 (Admin), [2018] 3 All ER 79, [2018] 4 WLR 89, 168 NLJ 7794, [2018] All ER (D) 11 (May) 8.45

R (Wright) v Secretary of State for the Home Department [2001] EWHC 520 (Admin) 2.27, 4.124, 13.35

R v Secretary of State for the Home Department ex parte Weatherhead [1995] 12 WLUK 254. .... 2.49

R (on the application of Lin) v Secretary of State for Transport [2006] EWHC 2575 (Admin), [2006] All ER (D) 472 (Jul) 5.9

R (Trivedi) v Southwark Coroner [2016] EWHC 2764 (Admin) 8.47

Table of Cases

R (on the application of Platts) v South Yorkshire Coroner [2008] EWHC 2502 (Admin), 172 JP 632, [2008] All ER (D) 244 (Oct) 4.14

R (on the application of Ullah) v Special Adjudicator; Do v Secretary of State for the Home Department [2004] UKHL 26, [2004] 2 AC 323, [2004] 3 All ER 785, [2004] 3 WLR 23, [2005] 1 LRC 740, [2004] INLR 381, [2004] 28 LS Gaz R 33, [2004] NLJR 985, (2004) Times, 18 June, 148 Sol Jo LB 762, [2004] All ER (D) 153 (Jun), HL 3.45

R v Sellu [2016] EWCA Crim 1716, [2017] 4 WLR 64, [2017] 1 Cr App Rep 349, [2017] Crim LR 799, [2016] All ER (D) 114 (Nov) 6.88, 6.90

R (on the application of Hicks) v Senior Coroner for Inner North London [2016] EWHC 1726 (Admin), 181 JP 1, [2016] All ER (D) 81 (Jul) 4.40

R (on the application of Lewis) v Senior Coroner For North West Kent [2020] EWHC 471 (Admin), 174 BMLR 160, [2020] All ER (D) 42 (Mar) 5.45, 6.150

R (on the application of Skelton) v Senior Coroner for West Sussex [2020] EWHC 2813 (Admin), 177 BMLR 167, [2020] All ER (D) 134 (Oct) 3.51, 3.90, 3.91, 8.59

R v Shrewsbury Coroner's Court, ex p British Parachute Association (1987) 152 JP 123, (1987) Times, 21 September, DC 7.18

R v Singh (Gurphal) [1999] Crim LR 582, (1999) Times, 17 April, [1999] Lexis Citation 2039, [1999] All ER (D) 179, CA 6.92

R v Solomon [1958] 1 QB 203, [1957] 3 All ER 497, [1957] 3 WLR 915, 42 Cr App Rep 9, 122 JP 28, 101 Sol Jo 921, NICrCA 5.34

R v South London Coroner, ex p Thompson (1982) 126 Sol Jo 625, (1982) Times, 9 July, [1982] Lexis Citation 1288, DC 1.10, 3.26, 6.6, 6.160, 20.31

R v Southwark Coroner, ex p Hicks [1987] 2 All ER 140, [1987] 1 WLR 1624, 151 JP 441, 131 Sol Jo 1590, [1987] LS Gaz R 3657, (1987) Times, 27 January .. 4.79, 5.31, 6.38

R v Spratt [1991] 2 All ER 210, [1990] 1 WLR 1073, 91 Cr App Rep 362, 154 JP 884, [1990] Crim LR 797, 134 Sol Jo 860, [1990] 26 LS Gaz R 38, (1990) Times, 14 May, [1990] Lexis Citation 3233 .... 6.78

R v Stratford-on-Avon District Council, ex p Jackson [1985] 3 All ER 769, [1985] 1 WLR 1319, 84 LGR 287, 51 P & CR 76, 129 Sol Jo 854, [1985] LS Gaz R 3533 .... 8.43

R (Maguire) v The Assistant Coroner for West Yorkshire (Eastern Area) [2018] EWCA Civ 6 .... 4.33

R v Tunstill [2018] EWCA Crim 1696, [2019] 1 WLR 416, [2018] 2 Cr App Rep 499, [2019] Crim LR 163, [2018] All ER (D) 26 (Aug) 6.104

R (on the application of Hall) v University College London Hospitals NHS Foundation Trust [2013] EWHC 198 (Admin), [2013] NLJR 208, [2013] All ER (D) 119 (Feb), DC 13.23

R (on the application of Middleton) v West Somerset Coroner. See R (on the application of Amin) v Secretary of State for the Home Department

R (on the application of Sacker) v West Yorkshire Coroner [2004] UKHL 11, [2004] 2 All ER 487, [2004] 1 WLR 796, 79 BMLR 40, (2004) Times, 12 March, 148 Sol Jo LB 354, [2004] All ER (D) 225 (Mar), HL 3.80, 3.100, 3.104, 14.8

R v Watson [1989] 2 All ER 865, [1989] 1 WLR 684, [1990] LRC (Crim) 430, 89 Cr App Rep 211, [1989] Crim LR 733, 133 Sol Jo 876, [1989] 28 LS Gaz R 39, [1989] NLJR 866, (1989) Times, 29 May 6.77

R v Watson [1988] QB 690, [1988] 1 All ER 897, [1988] 2 WLR 1156, 87 Cr App Rep 1, [1988] Crim LR 464, 132 Sol Jo 564, [1988] 15 LS Gaz R 35, [1988] NLJR 77, (1988) Times, 10 March 6.40

R (Southall Black Sisters) v West Yorkshire Coroner [2002] EWHC 1914 (Admin) 8.38

R v West Yorkshire Coroner ex p National Union of Mineworkers (Yorkshire Area) [1986] CLY 448 .... 6.111

R v West Yorkshire Coroner, ex p Smith [1983] QB 335, [1982] 3 All ER 1098, [1982] 3 WLR 920, 126 Sol Jo 728 .... 2.20, 19.5

R v West Yorkshire Coroner, ex p Smith (No 2) [1985] QB 1096, [1985] 1 All ER 100, [1985] 2 WLR 332, 149 JP 97, 129 Sol Jo 131, DC 4.35, 8.38

R v Williams (Gladstone) [1987] 3 All ER 411, 78 Cr App Rep 276, [1984] Crim LR 163, [1984] LS Gaz R 278 .... 6.108

R (on the application of Craik) v Wiltshire & Swindon Coroner [2004] EWHC 2653 (Admin), [2004] All ER (D) 347 (Nov) 8.48

Table of Cases

R v Wolverhampton Coroner, ex p McCurbin [1990] 2 All ER 759, [1990] 1 WLR 719, 155 JP 33, (1990) Times, 24 April 6.112, 8.61
R v York City Coroner (1863) 28 JP 9, 9 Cox CC 373, 3 New Rep 165, 9 LT 424 .... 5.39
Rabone v Pennine Care NHS Foundation Trust [2012] UKSC 2, [2012] 2 AC 72, [2012] 2 All ER 381, [2012] 2 WLR 381, [2012] 5 LRC 465, [2012] PTSR 497, 156 Sol Jo (no 6) 31, 124 BMLR 148, [2012] 08 LS Gaz R 19, [2012] NLJR 261, (2012) Times, 20 February, 33 BHRC 208, [2012] All ER (D) 59 (Feb), SC . 3.48, 3.92, 3.96, 4.98, 13.20, 13.25, 14.5, 15.9, 15.10
Ramsahai v The Netherlands (2008) 46 EHRR 43 .... 3.104
Rantsev v Cyprus and Russia (App No 25965/04) (2010) 51 EHRR 1, 28 BHRC 313, [2010] ECHR 25965/04, EctHR 3.39
Rapier, Re [1988] QB 26, [1986] 3 All ER 726, [1986] 3 WLR 830, 150 JP 481, 130 Sol Jo 714, [1986] LS Gaz R 2654 .... 8.4
Roach v Home Office; Matthews v Home Office [2009] EWHC 312 (QB), [2010] QB 256, [2009] 3 All ER 510, [2010] 2 WLR 746, [2009] NLJR 474, [2009] 2 Costs LR 287, [2009] All ER (D) 164 (Mar) 9.41, 9.43, 9.47, 9.49, 9.52, 9.53, 9.54, 13.4
Rogers v Hoyle [2014] EWCA Civ 257, [2015] QB 265, [2014] 3 All ER 550, [2014] 3 WLR 148, [2014] All ER (D) 131 (Mar) 23.8
Ross v Bowbelle (Owners) [1997] 1 WLR 1159, [1997] 2 Lloyd's Rep 196, (1997) Times, 8 April, [1997] Lexis Citation 2008, [1998] 1 Costs LR 32, CA 9.46
Royal Bank of Scotland plc v Highland Financial Partners LP [2013] EWCA Civ 328, [2013] All ER (D) 65 (Apr) 8.32
Rushbrooke v HM Coroner for West London [2020] EWHC 1612 (Admin), 176 BMLR 99, [2020] All ER (D) 154 (Jun) 8.35

S

Sarjantson v Humberside Police Chief Constable [2013] EWCA Civ 1252, [2014] QB 411, [2014] 1 All ER 960, [2013] 3 WLR 1540, [2013] All ER (D) 205 (Oct) 6.187
Savage v South Essex Partnership NHS Foundation Trust [2008] UKHL 74, [2009] AC 681, [2009] 1 All ER 1053, [2009] 2 WLR 115, [2009] PTSR 469, 105 BMLR 180, (2008) Times, 11 December, 153 Sol Jo (no 1) 34, 27 BHRC 57, [2008] All ER (D) 104 (Dec), HL 3.83, 3.90, 3.91, 3.92, 13.20, 15.9
Scott v HM Coroner for Inner West London [2001] EWHC 105 (Admin), 62 BMLR 222 .... 6.146, 6.151, 6.153
Secretary of State for Justice v HM Deputy Coroner Eastern District of West Yorkshire [2012] EWHC 1634 (Admin), 176 CL&J 545, [2012] All ER (D) 10 (Sep) 6.83, 6.200
Secretary of State for the Home Department v Her Majesty's Senior Coroner for Surrey [2016] EWHC 3001 (Admin), [2017] 3 All ER 764, [2017] 4 WLR 191, 181 JP 157, 166 NLJ 7725, 166 NLJ 7726, [2016] All ER (D) 144 (Nov) 19.28
Shafi v HM Senior Coroner For East London [2015] EWHC 2106 (Admin), [2016] 1 WLR 640, 179 JP 439, [2015] All ER (D) 207 (Jul) 2.102, 4.94, 8.33, 14.5
Siberry's Application for Judicial Review, Re [2008] NIQB 147 .... 11.6, 15.37
Silih v Slovenia (App No 71463/01) (2009) 49 EHRR 996, [2009] ECHR 71463/01, EctHR 3.50
Smith v DPP [2000] RTR 36, 164 JP 96, [1999] 32 LS Gaz R 34, [1999] 34 LS Gaz R 34, (1999) Times, 28 July, [1999] Lexis Citation 2983, DC 17.20
Smith v Ministry of Defence; Ellis v Ministry of Defence; Allbutt v Ministry of Defence [2013] UKSC 41, [2014] AC 52, [2013] 4 All ER 794, [2013] 3 WLR 69, [2014] 1 LRC 663, [2013] NLJR 18, (2013) Times, 24 July, 35 BHRC 711, [2013] All ER (D) 167 (Jun), SC 3.38, 3.81, 3.82, 3.92, 19.37, 19.40
Stobart v Nottingham Health Authority [1992] 3 Med LR 284, [1993] PIQR P 259, [1991] Lexis Citation 2518 .... 4.85, 13.29
Stoyanovi v Bulgaria (App No 42980/04), (9 November 2010, unreported) 3.74
Surrey County Council v P (Equality and Human Rights Commission intervening) [2014] UKSC 19, [2014] AC 896, [2014] 2 All ER 585, [2014] 2 WLR 642, [2014] 5 LRC 428, [2014] PTSR 460, [2014] 2 FCR 71, [2014] COPLR 313, 137 BMLR 16, (2014) Times, 01 April, [2014] All ER (D) 185 (Mar), SC 4.93, 15.48

Table of Cases

T

Tabarn, Re [1998] EWHC 8 (Admin), [2000] Inquest LR 52 .... 6.120
Takhar v Gracefield Developments Ltd [2019] UKSC 13, [2020] AC 450, [2019] 3 All ER 283, [2019] 2 WLR 984, [2019] 3 LRC 501, [2019] EGLR 19, [2019] PLSCS 54, 169 NLJ 7834, [2019] All ER (D) 94 (Mar), SC 8.32
Tarariyeva v Russia (2009) 48 EHRR 26 .... 3.92, 3.59, 14.18
Terry v East Sussex Coroner [2001] EWCA Civ 1094, [2002] QB 312, [2002] 2 All ER 141, [2001] 3 WLR 605, 62 BMLR 60, [2001] 34 LS Gaz R 37, (2001) Times, 26 July, 145 Sol Jo LB 190, [2001] All ER (D) 139 (Jul) 8.72
Thompson v HM Assistant Coroner For County Durham & Darlington [2015] EWHC 1781 (Admin) 6.123, 8.33
Three Rivers District Council v Bank of England [2003] 2 AC 1, [2000] 3 All ER 1, [2000] 2 WLR 1220, [2000] 3 CMLR 205, [2000] Lloyd's Rep Bank 235, [2000] NLJR 769, (2000) Times, 19 May, [2000] Lexis Citation 3004, [2000] All ER (D) 690, HL[2001] UKHL 16, [2001] 2 All ER 513, [2001] Lloyd's Rep Bank 125, (2001) Times, 23 March, [2001] All ER (D) 269 (Mar), HL 23.8
Trubnikov v Russia (App No 49790/99), (5 July 2005, unreported) 3.104
Tyrrell v HM Senior Coroner County Durham and Darlington [2016] EWHC 1892 (Admin), 153 BMLR 208, [2016] All ER (D) 155 (Jul) 3.92, 3.103, 14.5, 15.15, 15.73

V

Van Colle v Chief Constable of Hertfordshire Police; Smith v Chief Constable of Sussex Police [2008] UKHL 50, [2009] AC 225, [2008] 3 All ER 977, [2008] 3 WLR 593, [2009] 3 LRC 272, [2009] 1 Cr App Rep 146, [2009] PIQR P9, (2008) Times, 4 August, (2008) Times, 1 August, 152 Sol Jo (no 32) 31, [2008] All ER (D) 408 (Jul), HL 3.89, 3.95

W

Waddle v Wallsend Shipping Co Ltd [1952] 2 Lloyd's Rep 105 .... 23.8
Wakley v Crooke (1847) 4 Ex 511 .... 4.35, 5.26
Watts v United Kingdom (2010) 51 EHRR SE 66 .... 3.92
Wilson v HM Senior Coroner for Birmingham and Solihull [2015] EWHC 2561 (Admin), 165 NLJ 7668, [2015] All ER (D) 38 (Sep) 4.50
Worcestershire County Council v HM Coroner for the County of Worcestershire [2013] EWHC 1711 (QB), [2013] PTSR D41, [2013] All ER (D) 203 (Jun) 4.51, 4.58, 16.42

Y

YL v Birmingham City Council [2007] UKHL 27, [2008] 1 AC 95, [2007] 3 All ER 957, [2007] 3 WLR 112, [2008] LGR 273, [2007] HLR 651, 96 BMLR 1, [2007] NLJR 938, 151 Sol Jo LB 860, [2007] All ER (D) 207 (Jun), HL 3.44

Z

Z v United Kingdom (App No 29392/95) (2001) 34 EHRR 97, [2001] 2 FLR 612, [2001] 2 FCR 246, [2001] Fam Law 583, (2001) Times, 31 May, 10 BHRC 384, [2001] ECHR 29392/95, EctHR 3.96, 15.10

Chapter 1

THE ROLE OF THE CORONER

WHAT IS A CORONER?

1.1 The role of the coroner has existed since at least 1194. Throughout their history, coroners have held various powers and responsibilities. In modern times the coroner is an independent officer with judicial and executive functions whose usual role is to explore the circumstances of sudden, violent or unnatural deaths, and deaths in custody or state detention[1]. They achieve this by conducting investigations and, if necessary, inquests – hearings in which they listen to and read evidence relating to the deceased's death[2]. Coroners are appointed to local areas and are funded by local authorities[3]. There are 96 separate coroners' jurisdictions across England and Wales[4].

[1] CJA 2009, s 1(2).
[2] Coroners have powers to conduct investigations and inquests in respect of treasure as well as deaths but this text does not address this function (see CJA 2009, Pt 1, Ch 4).
[3] CJA 2009, Sch 2; Chief Coroner's Guidance No 6, The Appointment of Coroners (revised March 2020), paras 1–4 and 7–8.
[4] 'How to become a coroner: introductory pack' p 2 (24 February 2014).

1.2 This book is directed towards the coroner's role in investigating sudden, violent or unnatural deaths. But that is not the limit of the coroner's responsibility. They also continue to have jurisdiction over treasure found in their area. Pursuant to s 30 of the Coroners Act 1988 they are obliged to inquire into found objects and determine whether it is treasure within the meaning of the Treasure Act 1996. This aspect of a coroner's role is not dealt with in this text.

1.3 Coroners must remain independent, impartial and fair. This responsibility was emphasised by Bingham LJ (as he then was) in *R v Inner West London Coroner ex parte Dallagio and Lockwood Croft*[1]:

> 'There is . . . nothing in the coroner's role which indicates that he is, or should be subject to any lower standard of impartiality than other judicial decision makers: if anything, his central and dominant role in the conduct of an inquest might be said to call for a higher standard since those interested in the proceedings are, to an unusual extent, dependent on his sense of fairness.'

[1] [1994] 4 All ER 139.

1.4 Lord Bingham MR then went on, in *R v North Humberside Coroner, ex parte Jamieson*[1] to observe that a coroner must 'ensure that the relevant facts are fully, fairly and fearlessly investigated . . . he fails in his duty if his investigation is superficial, slipshod or perfunctory'².

[1] [1995] QB 1.
[2] [1995] QB 1 at p 26.

PURPOSE OF AN INQUEST

1.5 The purpose of an inquest, as set out in s 5(1) of the Coroners and Justice Act 2009 (CJA 2009) is to ascertain:

(a) who the deceased was;
(b) how, when and where the deceased came by their death; and
(c) any particulars required to be registered under the Births and Deaths Registration Act 1953 (BDRA 1953).

1.6 Under s 5(2), where it is necessary in order to avoid a breach of any Convention rights protected by the Human Rights Act 1998 (HRA 1998), the purpose set out at s 5(1)(b) must be read as 'including the purpose of ascertaining in what circumstances the deceased came by his or her death'[1].

[1] For more on the circumstances which trigger s 5(2), see CHAPTER 3.

1.7 It is at face value a neutral task, and the coroner and jury are prevented by s 5(3) from expressing an opinion on any matters other than those set out in s 5(1) and, where appropriate, s 5(2). However, if the inquest gives rise to a concern that circumstances exist, or will continue to exist, which create a risk of other deaths in the future, and in the coroner is of the opinion that preventative action should be taken, then the coroner has a duty to report the matter to a person who may have power to take such action[1].

[1] CJA 2009, Sch 5, para 7; see also CHAPTER 5.

1.8 In arriving at a conclusion on the matters required by s 5, the coroner embarks on an investigative task. The evidence called is limited to that which is relevant to ascertaining the matters in s 5, but in general any evidence is admissible. In oral evidence, the coroner must limit the questions which may be asked of a witness to those which are focused on the relevant matters[1]. In this manner, the proceedings should remain narrowly focused on answering the required questions.

[1] Coroners (Inquests) Rules 2013, SI 2013/1616, r 19(2).

INQUESTS ARE INQUISITORIAL, NOT ADVERSARIAL

1.9 Unlike many other courts, coroners' courts are 'inquisitorial', as opposed to 'adversarial'. This means there are no prosecutors or defendants; rather, the coroner, sometimes assisted by experts or legal representatives for the interested persons, investigates the circumstances of a death and decides what the facts of the case are.

1.10 The difference between adversarial and inquisitorial hearings was set out by Lord Lane CJ in *R v South London Coroner Ex p Thompson*[1], in which it

Inquests are inquisitorial, not adversarial **1.14**

is reiterated that an inquest 'is an inquisitorial process, a process of investigation quite unlike a trial where the prosecutor accuses and the accused defends, the judge holding the balance or the ring, whichever metaphor one chooses to use'. Lord Lane also observed that 'the procedure and rules of evidence which are suitable for [trials] are unsuitable for inquests'[2].

[1] (1982) 126 SJ 625, DC.
[2] *R v South London Coroner Ex p Thompson* (1982) 126 SJ 625, DC.

1.11 It is worth bearing in mind that 'it is not the function of a coroner or their jury to determine, or appear to determine, any question of criminal or civil liability, to apportion guilt or attribute blame'[1]. Indeed, the coroner's court is not able to offer any 'remedy' to any interested party, and the coroner is expressly forbidden from reaching a conclusion that appears to determine any questions of criminal or civil liability[2].

[1] *R v North Humberside Coroner, Ex p Jamieson* [1995] 1 QB 124.
[2] CJA 2009, s 10(2).

1.12 Traditionally the role of the coroner has been entwined with the criminal justice system; at times this led to tensions between the fact that inquests ought to be inquisitorial and non-blame oriented, and their often contentious subject matter – particularly in cases involving potential conclusions of unlawful killing (where there may be linked criminal proceedings) or suicide (which has historically attracted a great deal of stigma). This was reflected in the fact that until 2020, both these conclusions required the coroner or jury to apply the criminal standard of proof to the facts, rather than the civil standard, as was the case for all other types of coronial conclusion.

1.13 This tension was considered by the Supreme Court in *R (on the application of Maughan) v HM Senior Coroner for Oxfordshire*[1]. The Court determined that going forward, the civil standard of proof should be applied for all types of conclusion, including unlawful killing and suicide. A key part of the reason for this decision was the changing role of inquests.

[1] [2020] UKSC 46.

1.14 As emphasised by both Lady Arden and Lord Kerr, the strong links between inquests and the criminal process are now matters of historical fact only. Lady Arden observed that instead, 'inquests are concerned today not with criminal justice . . . They take a new and different purpose in a case such as this'[1] ie to 'identify lessons to be learnt for the future'[2] and prevent future deaths. Key ways in which this is increasingly achieved in inquests are through the requirements of Art 2 of the European Convention on Human Rights in appropriate cases[3], and in coroners issuing reports to prevent future deaths[4].

[1] At [81].
[2] At [8].
[3] See CHAPTER 3.
[4] See CHAPTER 7.

1.15 *The Role of the Coroner*

CATEGORIES OF CORONER

1.15 Since 2013, and as a result of the CJA 2009, the various coronial roles have been defined as follows[1]:

(a)   The Chief Coroner;
(b)   Senior coroners;
(c)   Area coroners;
(d)   Assistant coroners.

[1] CJA 2009, Schs 3 and 4.

(a) The Chief Coroner

1.16 A Chief Coroner, who must be a judge of the High Court or a circuit judge, and under the age of 70[1], coordinates and supervises the coronial system, aiming to improve the quality of performance and to standardise procedure and training. Whilst there is no formal right of appeal against a coroner's decision to the Chief Coroner, the Chief Coroner may request information from a coroner in relation to an inquest and the coroner concerned must respond[2]. Therefore, it may well be worthwhile making representations to the Chief Coroner if communication with a coroner about a particular inquest falls on deaf ears. A formal legal challenge to such a coroner's decision, however, can only be made by way of judicial review proceedings[3].

[1] CJA 2009, Sch 8, para 1.
[2] Coroners (Investigations) Regulations 2013, SI 2013/1629, reg 25.
[3] See CHAPTER 8.

1.17 The Chief Coroner regularly issues 'guidance' in the form of documents dealing with specific procedural aspects of inquests eg 'Conclusions: Short-form and Narrative' (Chief Coroner's Guidance No 17), or 'Coroners and the Media' (Chief Coroner's Guidance No 25). These are not legally binding on coroners but for obvious reasons they are highly persuasive and have significant impact on the way in which coroners interpret existing legislation and case law.

1.18 The Chief Coroner also issues law sheets. These are similar to the guidance but are generally centred around a specific legal point eg 'Galbraith plus' (Law Sheet No 2) or 'hearsay evidence' (Law Sheet No 4).

1.19 The law sheets and guidance documents are designed to assist coroners in carrying out their duties; they are generally very practical in tone, and are often a helpful starting point for practitioners when considering a particular aspect of coronial law or procedure.

(b) Senior coroners

1.20 Each of the 96 'areas' or jurisdictions across England and Wales has a senior coroner who has overall responsibility for dealing with any death reported to them that occurred within their jurisdiction. They are expected to directly oversee any significant cases in their area, and to manage the caseload of assistant/area coroners and coroners' officers working under them.

1.21 Senior coroners must meet the five-year judicial eligibility qualification (ie must have five years' legal experience) and must be under the age of 70[1]. Ideally, they will also have medical knowledge. Coroners are members of the judiciary (though their work is funded by the relevant local authority for the area in which they sit).

[1] CJA 2009, Sch 3, para 3.

1.22 In practical terms, it is the senior coroners, area coroners and assistant coroners who hear cases on a day to day basis.

(c) Area and assistant coroners

1.23 Senior coroners are required to appoint a specified number of area and/or assistant coroners as directed by the Lord Chancellor[1]. The purpose of the assistant and area coroners is to assist the senior coroner in carrying out their duties[2].

[1] CJA 2009, Sch 3, para 2(1).
[2] CJA 2009, Sch 3, para 8.

1.24 For complex or very high-profile cases, coroners may sometimes appoint a serving judge as an assistant coroner in order for them to preside over that particular case.

1.25 Like the senior coroner, area and assistant coroners sit within one of the 96 areas nationwide. They are required to have the same qualifications as a senior coroner[1], but often sit part time whilst continuing to practice in their existing field (usually as a solicitor or barrister, or as a doctor). They have the same powers as a senior coroner in investigating a death and holding an inquest[2]. Also, like senior coroners, area and assistant coroners are members of the judiciary.

[1] CJA 2009, Sch 3, para 3.
[2] CJA 2009, Sch 3, para 8(2).

(d) Coroners' officers

1.26 This is not a 'type' of coroner. Rather, the coroner's officer is an individual employed to assist the coroner in managing their position/responsibilities. The coroner's officer plays an important role in inquests. They assist the coroner in obtaining relevant evidence during the investigation, deal with correspondence between the coroner's office and interested persons, manage hearing bundles and perform a myriad of tasks to ensure the smooth running of hearings. For families, they are often the person with whom they have the most communication in advance of an inquest. Similarly, they regularly liaise with legal representatives for both families and organisations. If a firm or organisation is one that is routinely involved with inquests, it is worth them getting to know the coroner's officer in the relevant

1.26 *The Role of the Coroner*

court and understanding their way of working so they can best engage with and assist the coronial process.

Chapter 2
THE INVESTIGATION

INTRODUCTION TO CORONERS' INVESTIGATIONS

2.1 In 2019, there were 530,841 deaths registered in England and Wales. Of these, 210,900 were reported to a coroner, the lowest level since 1998. A total of 82,100 post-mortem examinations were conducted. 30,000 inquests were opened as a result, and 31,300 concluded.

2.2 The Coroners and Justice Act 2009 (CJA 2009) introduced a distinction between an 'investigation'[1], which covers the whole process of investigation of a death under the Act, and an 'inquest' which is the legal hearing or hearings which investigate the death. Once an investigation is opened, a coroner is under a duty to hold an inquest into the death other than in certain specified circumstances[2].

[1] Section 1 CJA 2009.
[2] Section 6 and s 4 CJA 2009.

2.3 This chapter will cover the mechanisms by which coroners become aware that a death has occurred which may require investigation, the jurisdiction under the CJA 2009 and the opening of an investigation, and the preliminary steps once an investigation is underway, including the post-mortem stage and other investigative steps which the coroner may take to secure evidence for the inquest. Finally, it will cover the circumstances in which a coroner must or may suspend or discontinue an investigation which has been commenced, and the process for resuming such an investigation thereafter.

BODY IN THE CORONER'S AREA – STANDARD NOTIFICATION OF DEATHS

Certification and notification of deaths by medical practitioners

2.4 When a person dies, the fact of their death can be confirmed by various health professionals, including unregistered medical practitioners such as paramedics. Other than in relatively unusual circumstances, a medical practitioner will be asked to certify the *cause* of every death shortly after it occurs. For deaths in hospital, this may be a treating physician, whereas for deaths in the community, it is likely to be a general practitioner who attended the deceased in their last illness. The medical certificate requires the practitioner to state the cause of death to the best of their knowledge and belief[1]. The doctor signing the certificate is not required to be *sure* of the cause of death or even

2.4 *The Investigation*

necessarily satisfied on the balance of probabilities[2]. Coroners should therefore exercise a degree of care when approaching the medical cause of death on medical certificates.

[1] BDRA 1953, Sch 2, Form 14.
[2] Guidance for doctors completing Medical Certificates of Cause of Death in England and Wales, Office for National Statistics, September 2018.

2.5 The rules for the certification of the cause of death were subject to relaxation during the COVID-19 pandemic to allow any doctor, including a medical examiner or recently retired doctor returning to work, to complete the medical certificate of cause of death, and not necessarily the attending doctor[1]. The guidance nonetheless retains the obligation for death to be certified based upon the conclusions of doctors who attended the deceased within 28 days of death. If no doctor had seen the deceased within that period before death, either in person or by video, the registrar remains obliged to refer the death to the coroner. The Office for National Statistics produces guidance for doctors on their obligation to notify coroners ('Guidance for doctors completing Medical Certificates of Cause of Death in England and Wales'), which is freely available online. See CHAPTER 20 for further details of changes to procedures as a result of the coronavirus pandemic.

[1] Chief Coroner's Guidance No 34, Covid-19, para 22.

2.6 Notifications to coroners are required by the medical practitioner who completed the certificate of cause of death under the Notification of Deaths Regulations 2019[1] if they have reasonable (more than minimal, negligible or trivial) cause to suspect that the death was due to:

- poisoning, including by an otherwise benign substance (though the guidance comments that in the case of alcohol and smoking related deaths, only those caused by acute poisoning rather than long standing consumption should be notified);
- exposure to or contact with a toxic substance;
- the use of a medicinal product, controlled drug or psychoactive substance;
- violence;
- trauma or injury;
- self-harm;
- neglect, including self-neglect;
- the person undergoing a treatment or procedure of a medical or similar nature;
- an injury or disease attributable to any employment held by the person during the person's lifetime; or
- another cause which is not natural.

[1] SI 2019/1112.

2.7 Notification is also required if:

- the deceased had not been attended by a registered medical practitioner during their last illness (this term is not defined within primary legislation but guidance provided to doctors suggests that attendance should be within 14 days of death or within 28 days in exceptional

Standard notification of deaths **2.12**

circumstances, such as the COVID-19 pandemic)[1], or a doctor had not attended after death;
- having taken reasonable steps, the medical practitioner is unable to ascertain the cause of the deceased's death;
- having taken reasonable steps, they are unable to ascertain the deceased's identity; or
- the person died in custody or other state detention.

[1] The medical practitioner can certify based upon attending the deceased prior to their death or seeing their body after death. There is, however, no requirement that the medical practitioner inspect or even see the body of the deceased prior to certifying their death.

2.8 Even where members of the public, such as family members, have reported a death to a coroner, there is still an obligation for the medical professional to do it themselves.

2.9 Under s 22 of the Births and Deaths Registration Act 1953 (BDRA 1953), if the registered medical practitioner signing the medical certificate of the cause of death 'attended the deceased during his last illness', that medical practitioner is also required to give notice, in writing, to 'some qualified informant', which will usually mean the next of kin, if known, that they have signed the certificate.

2.10 In exceptional circumstances, rules governing the certification of the cause of deaths are amended. For instance, as above at **2.5**, the rules were subject to relaxation during the COVID-19 pandemic to allow any doctor, including a medical examiner or recently retired doctor returning to work, to complete the medical certificate of cause of death, and not necessarily the attending doctor[1].

[1] Guidance for doctors completing Medical Certificates of Cause of Death in England and Wales, Office for National Statistics, revised April 2020 in accordance with the Coronavirus Act 2020.

2.11 There is an important distinction between a 'notifiable disease', which is required to be notified to Public Health England pursuant to the Health Protection (Notification) Regulations 2010[1], and the requirement to notify a death to a coroner. Notifiable diseases are those listed in Sch 1 to the 2010 Regulations. The Regulations were amended in 2020 to make COVID-19 a notifiable disease. The notifiable status of a disease itself does not form part of the test for jurisdiction under the CJA 2009. However, it is relevant to the question whether an inquest must sit with a jury[2].

[1] SI 2010/659.
[2] Section 7(2)(c) CJA 2009, see Chapter 5 on juries.

Medical examiners

2.12 In 2019 National Medical Examiners (NME) were introduced across England and Wales. Where such examiners are in place, they are expected to take the lead and set out consistent approaches to matters including the certification of cause of death, initially in hospitals and, as their capacity increases, in the community. In practical terms, though, the NME is likely to

2.12 *The Investigation*

remain focused on deaths in a small number of hospitals for the foreseeable future.

Notification of deaths by registrars

2.13 Irrespective of whether the coroner is notified of a death, there is an obligation to report a death occurring in England and Wales to a registrar of births and deaths. That notification can be made by a wide variety of individuals, including the deceased person's nearest relatives and extending to any person who was present at the death or who found and took charge of the body[1].

[1] BDRA 1953, ss 16 and 17.

2.14 The registrar has the power to request the information required to register the death from a qualified informant and require their attendance at the registrar's office to provide information and sign the register[1]. The willful failure on the part of a qualified informant to comply with the registrar's requests and questions can amount to criminal offences[2].

[1] BDRA 1953, s 19.
[2] BDRA 1953, s 36(a)–(e).

2.15 If the coroner has not been informed of the death, the registrar may not issue a certificate permitting disposal of a body unless they are satisfied that the case is not one that should be notified to the coroner[1].

[1] Registration of Births and Deaths Regulations 1987, SI 1981/2088, reg 41.

2.16 The registrar's obligations to notify the coroner are largely residual to those of registered medical professionals. The registrar effectively acts as a second line of defence in ensuring that all cases which should have been notified by medical professionals when certifying the death are notified, as well as ensuring that in any case where, for some reason, an attempt was made to register a death without an appropriate medical certificate of the cause of death, the coroner is notified as required (the cause of death being unknown).

Other notifications where the body is present

2.17 In some cases, notifications will be made by police forces, by the governors of custody facilities, or by other professionals. Given the notification requirements on registered medical professionals and on registrars, any such notifications will normally only serve to tell the coroner about a death of which they are already aware.

2.18 There may be cases where family members have concerns of their own, for instance about the quality of medical care, and think that the coroner should investigate. The mere fact that they raise concerns does not mean that a coroner's investigation will necessarily follow. However, where there are such concerns it is helpful if they are raised at an early stage. In practical terms, the simplest way for family members to raise any concerns may be by inquiring with the registrar at the office when they go to register the death. Otherwise, coroner's offices often have online systems for notifications (separate from those for use by medical professionals). If, for some reason, neither of these means is possible, the family will need to make contact with the coroner's office directly. For obvious reasons, it is important for such concerns to be raised before the body is either buried or disposed of (for instance by cremation), otherwise any forensic investigations are likely to become significantly more difficult if not impossible.

2.19 In cases where a death occurs abroad and the body is repatriated, the family (or the professionals dealing with the funeral arrangements) should inform their local coroner if the death was violent or unnatural. Normally, if family members want an inquest to take place, the body should be repatriated (as opposed to being cremated abroad and the ashes being repatriated) so that it is available for post-mortem examination in the UK if required. The coroner for the area where the body enters the United Kingdom (if in England or Wales) has jurisdiction but will usually transfer jurisdiction to the area where the burial is to occur. This rule will not usually apply in cases of mass casualty incidents occurring outside of the United Kingdom, where the coroner for the point of entry, usually the West London Coroner with jurisdiction over Heathrow Airport, will retain jurisdiction. Deaths of military personnel serving overseas are the subject of special procedures, set out in CHAPTER **19**.

2.20 Coroners are under a duty to conduct an investigation into any death abroad where the body is returned to their area and the circumstances are such that an investigation would have been mandated if the death had occurred in England or Wales[1].

[1] *R v West Yorkshire Coroner ex parte Smith* [1983] QB 335. See also ss 12 and 13 CJA 2009.

2.21 Once a body is in England or Wales, anyone who wishes to move it out of the jurisdiction (including to Scotland or Northern Ireland) is required to notify the local senior coroner[1]. The coroner will normally then issue an Out of England and Wales Order granting permission[2].

[1] Births and Deaths Registration Act 1926, s 4.
[2] See also the Removal of Bodies Regulations 1954, SI 1954/448 and the Removal of Bodies (Amendment) Regulations 1971, SI 1987/1354.

THE INVESTIGATION

2.22 Jurisdiction to open a coronial investigation is established by s 1 of the CJA 2009, sub-ss (1) and (2) of which set out as follows:

'**1 Duty to investigate certain deaths**
(1) A senior coroner who is made aware that the body of a deceased person is within that coroner's area must as soon as practicable conduct an investigation into the person's death if subsection (2) applies.
(2) This subsection applies if the coroner has reason to suspect that—
    (a) the deceased died a violent or unnatural death,
    (b) the cause of death is unknown, or
    (c) the deceased died while in custody or otherwise in state detention.'

2.23 The 'reason to suspect' test carries a low threshold and is objective in nature. The standard does not equate to prima facie proof, which requires

2.23 *The Investigation*

admissible evidence, whereas reasonable suspicion can include matters which may not be adduced in evidence[1].

[1] *R (Fullick) v HM Senior Coroner for Inner London North* [2012] EWHC 3522 (Admin), a case concerning the identical language in s 7 CJA 2009. See also *R (Canning) v Northampton Coroner* [2006] EWCA Civ 1225 on the reasonable cause test under the Coroners Act 1988.

2.24 If it is suspected that the death was violent or unnatural, or the cause is unknown, a post mortem will usually be necessary as a preliminary step, before deciding whether or not to proceed to a full investigation.

2.25 'Violent' deaths include suicides and death caused by injury, including road traffic accidents. These are often easier to identify at the preliminary stages.

2.26 However, the term 'unnatural' is more problematic. It is not defined in the CJA 2009 or under previous statutes.

2.27 *R v HM Coroner for Inner North London Ex p Touche* concerned the death of a woman from a cerebral haemorrhage following the birth of twins. It was thought that her death was related to eclampsia, a condition that could have been identified and treated if her blood pressure had been monitored. The coroner declined to hold an inquest on the basis that the death was caused by a natural process. The hearing before the Divisional Court and Court of Appeal was concerned amongst other things as to whether there was a conflict between the judgment of Dillon LJ and Simon Brown LJ in *Ex p Thomas*. Having determined that an inquest should be held given the possibility that the coroner might add a rider of 'neglect' to a conclusion that the death was due to natural causes, Simon Brown LJ added (1219):

> 'But undoubtedly there will be cases which fall outside the category of "neglect" and yet appear to call for an inquest on the basis already indicated, namely, cases involving a wholly unexpected death from natural causes which would not have occurred but for some culpable human failure . . . It is the combination of their unexpectedness and the culpable human failing that allowed them to happen which to my mind makes such deaths unnatural. Deaths by natural causes though undoubtedly they are, they should plainly never have happened and in that sense are unnatural.'

2.28 An 'unnatural' death for the purposes of establishing jurisdiction under s 1 does not, therefore, carry obverse meaning to a 'natural causes' conclusion. The concept of 'unnatural death' at the jurisdiction stage is wider. A culpable omission to treat a medical patient would render a death unnatural for the purposes of s 1 as in *Touche*, but such a death would nevertheless be likely to result in a 'natural causes' conclusion (whether in conjunction with other conclusions, or a finding of neglect, or not at the end of an inquest)[1]. See CHAPTER 6 for 'natural causes' as a conclusion.

[1] *R v Birmingham and Solihull Coroner ex p Benton* (1997) 1962 JP 807, 8 Med LR 362.

2.29 The coroner has a broad power under s 1(7) CJA 2009 to conduct 'whatever [preliminary] enquiries seem necessary' to decide whether the duty to conduct a full investigation applies, and that includes ordering a post-mortem examination if such an examination is deemed necessary.

2.30 The definition of a death 'in custody or otherwise in state detention', is covered in CHAPTER **14**.

Coroner's decision that no post mortem or investigation is required

2.31 If a coroner decides, either on the basis of the information available at the time of the notification of death alone, or on the basis of some preliminary enquiries (made under s 1(7) CJA 2009), that it is not necessary to open any investigation, and no post mortem is required, they will normally issue a Form 100A, which essentially informs the registrar that they do not intend to investigate further and that the body may be buried, cremated, or otherwise disposed of.

2.32 The senior coroner for an area is required to keep a register of all deaths 'reported' in their area, including the date on which the death was reported to them and (if known) the deceased's name, age, gender and address, any other identifying information, and the place of death or the place where the body was found[1]. This duty applies regardless of whether or not the death is investigated.

[1] Coroners (Investigations) Regulations 2013, SI 2013/1629, reg 2.

Disputes around the end of life

2.33 In a small number of cases disputes have arisen over whether the body of the individual in question is living or dead. There is no statutory definition of death in English law[1]. The absence of brain stem function is sufficient to indicate death, even where a body is still ventilated[2]. The presence of a heartbeat and breathing, whilst enough to prove that a person lived, does not mean that they are alive if those functions are maintained by mechanical means.

[1] *Re A (A Child)* [2015] EWHC 443 (Fam) at [12].
[2] *Airedale NHS v Bland* [1993] AC 789.

2.34 In the case of *Re A (a child)*[1], a dispute arose where the child of a Saudi family suffered brain stem death in an English hospital but continued to be supported on a ventilator. His father wished to attempt to transport the child to Saudi Arabia in the hope that he would continue to be supported indefinitely on a ventilator there. The local coroner became involved and purported to assert authority over the case on the basis that the child was deceased and proposed to issue an Out of England certificate so that the body could be repatriated to Saudi Arabia. The matter came before Hayden J, President of the Family Division, who was critical of the coroner's decision to become involved and made it clear that disputes of this nature were to be determined, if necessary, in the Family Division of the High Court, and not under coronial powers.

[1] [2015] EWHC 443 (Fam).

2.35 The Investigation

STILLBIRTHS

2.35 A stillbirth occurs where a baby is dead before it has lived independently from its mother. The common law test for being born alive is whether the baby breathed or was otherwise alive having been fully expelled from its mother – *R v Poulton*[1]. This is reflected in the definition of a stillbirth under s 41 of the BDRA 1953, which is of 'a child which has issued forth from its mother after the twenty-fourth week of pregnancy and which did not at any time after being completely expelled from its mother breathe or show any other signs of life'. It follows that under the present law a coroner would not have jurisdiction to investigate a stillbirth, there being no life in the legal sense, and therefore no death. Proposals have been made to change this position, with the Civil Partnerships, Marriages and Deaths (Registration) Act 2019 (which began life as a Private Member's Bill) mandating the government to undertake a consultation on extending coroners' jurisdiction to cover stillbirths. That consultation took place in 2019, but as at December 2020, no further legislation had been proposed on this point.

[1] (1832) 172 ER 997.

2.36 As a baby might live for a very short time after it is born or it might be unclear whether the baby ever lived independently, it is not uncommon for coroners to carry out investigations in order to answer such issues. If there is a reasonable basis for believing that a child was born alive, a coroner may conduct a preliminary investigation (which, in practice, will usually mean directing a post mortem by an appropriate paediatric pathologist). If, following that preliminary investigation, the coroner continues to have a reasonable basis for thinking the child was born alive, a further investigation, and potentially a full inquest, may follow. One of the key issues at such an inquest is likely to be whether or not the child was in fact born alive. 'Stillbirth' is an available conclusion for an inquest for this reason. See CHAPTER 6 for stillbirth as a conclusion and the completion of the Record of Inquest.

2.37 In *R (T) v West Yorkshire (Western Area) Senior Coroner*[1], the Court of Appeal dismissed an application for judicial review which had sought to quash a coroner's decision to hold an inquest in circumstances where a mother had given birth in secret at home, in circumstances where it could not be established that the baby was born alive. The Court of Appeal held that the coroner did not have to be satisfied, on the balance of probabilities, that the child had been born alive. It was enough for the coroner to suspect that there may have been a live birth followed by foul play.

[1] [2018] 2 WLR 211.

OPENING AN INVESTIGATION

2.38 Once a coroner determines that they are under a duty to investigate, they are obliged to attempt to identify the deceased's next of kin or personal representative and to inform them of their decision to commence an investigation[1]. Note that there is no such duty while the coroner is conducting preliminary enquiries, although there is a duty to attempt to contact the next of kin ahead of a post mortem (see below).

[1] Coroners (Investigations) Regulations 2013, SI 2013/1629, reg 6.

2.39 Once an investigation is opened it must proceed to inquest (s 6 CJA 2009) unless the criteria for discontinuance of an investigation under s 4 are satisfied. Those criteria are where: (i) a post-mortem examination under s 14 has revealed the cause of death before the coroner has begun holding an inquest; and (ii) the coroner thinks it is not necessary to hold an investigation (s 4(1)).

2.40 That discontinuance power does not arise in cases where the coroner retains reason to suspect that the deceased died a violent or unnatural death or died in custody or otherwise in state detention (s 4(2)). Where an investigation is discontinued no inquest may take place. The coroner must give a written explanation as to why the investigation was discontinued if asked to do so by any interested person.

2.41 A coroner must open an inquest into a death as soon as practicable after the date on which they consider the duty to hold an inquest under s 6 CJA 2009 applies[1]. The inquest should be opened at a public hearing (although it is acceptable to open it in private if no court room is available at the time, and to announce that fact in public at the next hearing)[2]. Where possible the coroner is required to set the dates for any subsequent hearings when opening the inquest[3]. Inquests must be held on working days unless there is some urgent reason to do otherwise.

[1] Coroners (Inquests) Rules 2013, SI 2013/1616, r 5(1).
[2] Coroners (Inquests) Rules 2013, SI 2013/1616, r 11(2).
[3] Coroners (Inquests) Rules 2013, SI 2013/1616, r 5(2).

2.42 The coroner should aim to complete the inquest within six months[1]. In practical terms, relatively straightforward matters will be opened and then listed for a short hearing for the next available date in the coroner's diary after allowing one or two months to gather any documentary evidence which may be required. More complex matters may have a notional inquest listing for several months' time, but a pre-inquest review is likely to be listed at which interested parties can make submissions about the scope of the inquest, any investigation which may be required, and arrangements for the final hearing, including suggested time estimates.

[1] Coroners (Inquests) Rules 2013, SI 2013/1616, r 8.

2.43 It is common for the coroner to take some evidence at the time of opening the inquest, usually the evidence relating to the identification of the deceased person and the information needed for registering the death. The opening of the inquest is also commonly the time when the coroner will hear any outstanding applications relating to the release of the body. If the case involves a suspected homicide a police officer may attend and provide an update on the progress of any police enquiries.

2.44 *The Investigation*

Interim death certificate

2.44 In cases where the coroner determines that no investigation is required and releases the body, the death certificate will be issued in the usual way by the registrar (based on the information provided by the coroner using Form 100A). In cases where the coroner discontinues an investigation following a post mortem because the cause of death has been ascertained, the death certificate will again be issued by the registrar based on Form 100B.

2.45 In cases where the investigation continues and an inquest is opened, the next of kin will not be able to obtain a death certificate until the inquest has concluded. This can pose practical problems. In such cases, the coroner may provide the deceased's next of kin or personal representative with a 'certificate of the fact of death', also known as an interim death certificate, using Form 1.

INVESTIGATIONS WITHOUT A BODY

2.46 It is sadly not unknown for bodies to be destroyed or lost, due to the effects of fire or explosions or because of deliberate concealment or loss at sea. Under s 1(4) of the CJA 2009, a senior coroner has the power to report to the Chief Coroner where they have reason to believe that:

(a) a death has or occurred in or near their area;
(b) the circumstances of the death are such that there should be an investigation into it; *and*
(c) the body has been destroyed, or lost, or is otherwise absent.

The s 1(4) power does not give the Chief Coroner any general discretion to order investigations into matters which would not otherwise fall within a coroner's jurisdiction. It only applies where there is reason to believe that the death occurred in or near the coroner's area. It will therefore not apply to deaths abroad (where the coroner's jurisdiction is only established by the remains being brought back to England or Wales).

2.47 The meaning of 'near' is not defined, and there is limited case law on the point. In *R v HM Coroner for East Sussex ex parte Healy*[1], the death of a diver who had been exploring a wreck some eight or nine miles off the Sussex coast and whose body was never recovered was found not to be near enough to trigger the equivalent provision of previous legislation on this point. The Chief Coroner's Guidance No 18[2] suggests that in a more recent case (not identified in the note), a coroner was correct not to refer a case where an elderly man was presumed to have gone overboard in a seagoing fishing boat, the location of which at the time of the death was unknown but which was found 14 miles off shore.

[1] [1988] 1 WLR 1194.
[2] Chief Coroner's Guidance No 18, Section 1(4) Reports: Investigation Without a Body (revised 14 January 2016).

2.48 In *Connah v Plymouth Hospitals NHS Trust*[1] the court considered various aspects of s 1(4). The applicant argued that the former Coroner for Plymouth, the current Coroner for Plymouth, and the current Coroner for Cornwall were all at fault for having failed to commence an investigation and inquest into the death of his wife. Not only were the two Plymouth Coroners not required to hold inquests because the deceased's body had never lain in their district (ie not within their physical jurisdiction), but the court also determined that the Cornwall Coroner had not improperly refused to hold an investigation, since she had not been coroner at the time when the deceased's body had lain in her district. By the time she had become coroner the body had been cremated, and so the question of the duty under s 1 CJA 2009 for the **current** coroner did not arise.

[1] [2010] EWHC 1727 (Admin).

2.49 There must be reason to believe that a death has actually occurred, as opposed to the person simply being missing. The coroner will have to consider the balance of the available evidence as to whether or not there is reason to believe that a death occurred. The Chief Coroner's Guidance No 18 suggests that the person's car being found near a well-known location for suicide would tend to give a coroner reason to believe that there had been a death. Certainty is not required, as confirmed in *R v Secretary of State for the Home Department ex parte Weatherhead*[1].

[1] [1995] 12 WLUK 254.

2.50 If the first and third limbs of s 1(4) are satisfied (see above), the coroner must consider the second limb ie whether or not the circumstances of the death are such that there should be an investigation into it. The power to refer a case to the Chief Coroner is a discretion which must be exercised fairly, taking account of all the relevant circumstances and the evidence which is available, or which would be available if the coroner undertook reasonable enquiries. The exercise of this discretion is susceptible to judicial review, although there are very few cases where this has arisen.

2.51 A coroner would probably conclude that there should be an investigation into the death if it appears to have occurred in circumstances where the s 1(1) duty to investigate would have been engaged if the body had been found. There could, however, be circumstances where the coroner might reasonably decline to refer a case to the Chief Coroner, even where one of those criteria was engaged. A coroner might decline to exercise their discretion to refer if there had already been an adequate inquiry into the deaths, for instance by way of a public inquiry or by some other means[1].

[1] *Ex Parte Healy* [1988] 1 WLR 1194.

2.52 A subsequent decision by the Chief Coroner to direct that an investigation be held, or a refusal to make such a direction, following a report from a coroner under s 1(4), would of course also be susceptible to judicial review.

POST-MORTEM EXAMINATIONS

2.53 Section 14 of the CJA 2009 provides that a post-mortem examination may be conducted either where the coroner is conducting an investigation or where the coroner considers that such an examination is necessary in order to determine whether or not an investigation is required. For instance, there will

2.53 *The Investigation*

be many cases where a post-mortem examination makes it clear what the cause of death was, and that it was not unnatural or violent. In such cases, the coroner will not need to conduct any investigation.

2.54 Once a coroner determines that they have a duty to investigate they take control of the body and retain such control until either a decision is made to release it for burial or cremation or the inquest has concluded[1]. The coroner has power under s 15 of the CJA 2009 to have the body removed to any suitable location for the purposes of the post mortem.

[1] *R v Bristol Coroner ex parte Kerr* [1974] 2 WLR 816.

2.55 Coroners are required, by reg 11 of the Coroners (Investigations) Regulations 2013[1], to avoid delay in post-mortem examinations and to carry these out as soon as reasonably practicable. The coroner is also required, by reg 20 of the Coroners (Investigations) Regulations 2013, to release the body for burial or cremation as soon as is reasonably practicable, and to inform the deceased's next of kin or personal representative of the reason for any delay beyond 28 days in releasing the body.

[1] SI 2013/1629.

Organ donation and tissue retention

2.56 Under s 11 Human Tissue Act 2004, the coroner's consent is required before removing or dealing with any tissues or other material from the body of a deceased person which is, or may be, required for coronial purposes. If there is no reason to think that the death will require investigation by a coroner (it being relevant to note that a large number of deaths are never even notified to a coroner), then the coroner will have no role to play and would not have jurisdiction to object. Where there is a requirement for material to be taken for some reason other than coronial purposes and relevant consent cannot be obtained from next of kin for any reason, an application to the High Court is likely to be required[1].

[1] *CM v Executor of the estate of EJ (deceased), HM Coroner for the Southern District of London* [2013] EWHC 1680 (Fam).

2.57 The full details of the law around organ donation are beyond the scope of this book. However, it is relevant to note that, for most cases involving the death of an adult in Wales, consent to donate organs for transplantation purposes is assumed to have been given since 1 December 2015 under the Human Transplantation (Wales) Act 2013, unless displaced by some evidence of the deceased's actual intentions. The position is similar in England since May 2020 under the Organ Donation (Deemed Consent) Act 2019. The number of requests for permission to take organs or other material in cases where the coroner's consent is required is therefore likely to rise rapidly.

2.58 The Chief Coroner issued Guidance No 26 on Organ Donation on 1 December 2017. It is explicitly premised on the basis that allowing organ and tissue donation to go ahead where possible is in the wider public interest. It reminds coroners that:

(a) they must make decisions about consent to removal of tissue for transplantation themselves, not purport to delegate these decisions to their officials;

(b) when consulted about an imminent death, they should give an initial indication prior to the death as to whether or not they intend to object to tissue being taken for transplantation;

(c) they should ensure that at least one coroner in an area is available at all times to address urgent out of hours requests relating to organ or tissue donation.

2.59 As with most coronial decisions, a decision either to object or not to object to organ harvesting is susceptible to judicial review (including potentially by the police force investigating a suspected homicide).

2.60 Where coroners consent to organ removal and donation, they may wish to explore with the family whether or not they would wish to have information about the recipients of any of the organs in the public domain. If they would be happy for such information to be public, the coroner may wish to invite the relevant transplant coordinator to write to them about the use made of the donated organs.

Exhumation

2.61 The coroner's powers to order exhumation are set out in Sch 5 to the CJA 2009. They arise in two different circumstances (and are only available to senior coroners).

2.62 The first is when the body is buried anywhere within England or Wales (including outside the coroner's own area) and the coroner thinks it is necessary for the body to be examined under s 14 CJA 2009. The explanatory notes to the CJA 2009 suggest that, because a coroner will normally only have jurisdiction to investigate a death on the basis that the body lies within their area, the power will generally only be exercised within that area. The limited exceptions to this would be where, for instance, a fresh inquest is taking place before another coroner, who may be from another area. There is no power for the coroner to order the exhumation of a body other than for the person into whose death they are considering and they think it necessary that an investigation may be required.

2.63 The second set of circumstances are where the body is buried within the coroner's own area and the coroner thinks it is necessary for that body to be examined for the purposes of actual or contemplated criminal proceedings concerning the death of either that person themselves or another person who died in connected circumstances.

2.64 In either circumstance, the coroner's power must be exercised insofar as possible without trespassing on the established rights of others, and it does not give the coroner an automatic right to override other requirements, for

2.64 *The Investigation*

instance to obtain permission from church authorities to excavate on consecrated ground[1].

[1] *R (HM Coroner for East London) v Secretary of State for Justice* [2009] EWHC 1974 (Admin).

Requests for expedited post mortems

2.65 In some jurisdictions, the coroner will have a policy on how to prioritise requests for expedited post mortems, which may either be published or available on request. Even if there is a written policy in place, however, it must still be applied flexibly and with due regard to the particular circumstances of the request in question. In *R (Adath Yisroel Burial Society) v HM Senior Coroner for Inner North London*[1], the Divisional Court stated that:

- a coroner cannot lawfully refuse to take account of religious reasons for seeking expedition of decisions, including to release a body for burial;
- a coroner is entitled to prioritise cases, even though this may mean that one family waits longer for the release of a body as a result of another family's request for expedition;
- any policy must be flexible and enable all relevant considerations to be taken into account;
- limitations on resources cannot justify discrimination;
- a coroner should not impose a rule of automatic priority for cases where expedition is sought for religious reasons;
- in cases where the coroner has taken all relevant considerations into account when dealing with a request for expedition, they will be taken to have a margin of appreciation within which the court would be slow to intervene.

[1] [2018] EWHC 969 (Admin), [2019] QB 251, [2018] 3 All ER 1088.

2.66 Following *Adath Yisroel*, the Chief Coroner issued Guidance No 28[1]. It emphasised that decisions about expedition are judicial decisions, which must be taken by a coroner rather than by an official and which are subject to judicial review in the High Court (and not to any control by the Chief Coroner himself). It did not require coroners' areas to issue written policies on dealing with requests for expedition and noted that the approach might differ quite properly from one area of the country to another because of the different characteristics of different areas.

[1] Chief Coroner's Guidance No 28, Report of Death to the Coroner: Decision Making and Expedited Decisions (17 May 2018).

Arrangements for post mortem

2.67 Once the coroner has made a decision to direct a post mortem, they must (under reg 13 of the Coroners (Investigations) Regulations 2013[1]) notify certain individuals of the date, time and place of that post mortem, unless to do so is impracticable or would cause the post mortem to be unreasonably delayed (in this respect, it is considered best practice for post mortems to take place within 24 hours of death):

- next of kin/personal representative of the deceased;
- any other person who has indicated their desire to be represented at the post mortem to the coroner;
- the hospital (if the deceased died in hospital);
- an appropriate enforcing authority eg the HSE, if the death was as a result of a notifiable accident or disease;
- any government department which has indicated its desire to be represented to the coroner;
- any chief officer of police who has indicated their desire to be represented to the coroner.

[1] SI 2013/1629.

2.68 Any of the above may appoint a medical practitioner to attend the post mortem or, if they are a medical practitioner, they may attend themselves. The police force may appoint an officer to attend. Otherwise, anyone who wishes to attend requires the coroner's consent.

2.69 Under s 14 of the CJA 2009, where any person informs the coroner in advance of a post mortem that they believe the death was caused wholly or in part by improper or negligent treatment provided by a medical practitioner, that practitioner should not themselves attend the post mortem, although they are entitled to be represented by another medical practitioner instead. This provision does not invalidate the results of a post mortem which was attended by such a practitioner before the coroner was informed of the allegation.

Non-invasive post mortems

2.70 Section 14 of the CJA 2009 provides that the coroner directing the post mortem may specify 'the kind of examination to be made' and that the examination may be performed either by a registered medical practitioner or, where 'a particular kind of examination is requested', by 'a practitioner of a description designated by the Chief Coroner as suitable to make examinations of that kind'.

2.71 At the time of writing, the Chief Coroner's Guidance No 1 regarding the use of post mortem imagery (ie use of technology as opposed to invasive post mortem techniques) was last updated in early 2016. As medical technology continues to advance, coroners should have regard to the technological position as at the date of their decision. For instance, in 2017, a major study was conducted of post mortems in adult cases considered by coroners in Leicestershire over a number of years. It concluded that post mortem CT scanning with the addition of targeted coronary angiography (PMCTA), if used before conventional autopsies in the first instance, could avoid the need for a conventional autopsy in up to 92 per cent of cases, although it had recognised weaknesses for instance in diagnosing pulmonary thromboembolism and PMCTA followed by a full conventional autopsy should be seen as the gold standard[1].

[1] Rutty et al 'Diagnostic accuracy of post-mortem CT with targeted coronary angiography versus autopsy for coroner-requested post-mortem investigations: a prospective, masked, comparison study' *The Lancet* [2017] Jul 8; 390(10090), pp 145–154 – available without charge at thelancet.com.

2.72 The Investigation

2.72 In R (Rotsztein) v HM Senior Coroner for Inner North London[1], the High Court considered a challenge by a Jewish family to a decision by a coroner to direct that an invasive autopsy be conducted. Mitting J considered that, where an objection to an invasive autopsy was made on religious grounds about which the deceased's family had a unity of view, the coroner should approach the matter by asking the following questions:

- Is there an established religious tenet that invasive autopsy is to be avoided? If not, Art 9 of the European Convention on Human Rights (ECHR) would not be engaged.
- Is there a realistic possibility (which may fall well short of a 50 per cent chance) that a non-invasive procedure will establish the cause of death?
- Can the autopsy and other examinations be undertaken without undue delay? Would, therefore, the use of the proposed non-invasive procedure have the effect of causing undue delay?
- Will the proposed non-invasive procedure, if attempted, impair the effectiveness of a conventional autopsy if one turns out to be required?
- Is there any countervailing need for an immediate invasive autopsy? In a case of suspected homicide, for instance, there might be a strong interest in proceeding to an invasive autopsy forthwith rather than risking delay to the investigation, and that interest might outweigh the family's interest in avoiding one.
- Is it possible to perform the non-invasive procedure without imposing an additional cost burden on the coroner? For instance, if the family propose to pay for the non-invasive procedure themselves.

[1] [2015] EWHC 2764 (Admin).

2.73 Where a coroner determines that an invasive post mortem is required and the family disagree, that decision is subject to judicial review, and may also be the subject of injunctive relief pending a substantive hearing. There is little judicial guidance on how to approach this. In R (Goldstein) v HM Coroner for Inner London[1], the Divisional Court (Mitting J sitting with the Chief Coroner) considered such an application and ordered a step by step approach by the pathologist, namely that non-invasive procedures would be employed in the first instance; followed by minimally invasive procedures if they had not been able to establish the cause of death at the first step; followed by a fully invasive procedure should they consider that necessary. All of those steps were to be at the family's expense (the family wishing to have the matter expedited so that the body could be taken to Israel for burial as soon as possible).

[1] [2014] EWHC 3889 (Admin).

2.74 It is important to note that a decision by the coroner *not* to conduct a post mortem is also capable of challenge[1].

[1] Howlett v HM Coroner for the County of Devon [2006] EWHC 2570 (Admin).

Conduct of the post mortem

2.75 The Chief Coroner's Guidance No 32 deals with post-mortem examinations[1]. It confirms that pathologists instructed to conduct post mortems will normally be consultant histopathologists, working for NHS trusts, or Home

Office registered forensic pathologists. Their duty is to the court, as independent experts, regardless of who has paid for the examination. It may be necessary for experts in particular disciplines to be instructed, such as specialists in osteology, anthropology, odontology and even archaeology. The pathologist may require the input of other experts, such as toxicologists, or experts in the pathology of the brain or other organs before completing their report. In cases involving children it will be necessary to instruct a paediatric pathologist.

[1] Chief Coroner's Guidance No 32, Post-Mortem Examinations including Second Post-Mortem Examinations (23 September 2019).

2.76 In practice, 95 per cent of post-mortem examinations are so-called 'standard' examinations, for which the pathologist is paid a fixed, relatively low, fee. These are normally conducted by hospital-based histopathologists. In slightly more complex cases, where 'additional skills' are required, a fixed additional fee applies. This may include cases of young children, for instance, where the anatomy differs significantly from that of adults and where it may be advisable to have a pathologist with particular specialist expertise, or to have medical professionals from more than one discipline present to assist.

2.77 In the case of sudden unexplained deaths of infants, the post mortem should take place within 48 hours, for reasons set out in *A Local Authority v AF*[1].

[1] [2015] EWFC 74.

2.78 The Chief Coroner's Guidance No 32 suggests, in line with the Forensic Science Regulator's Code of Practice and Performance Standards, that a full forensic standard examination should be ordered in the case of any death where a crime is reasonably suspected.

2.79 In cases where homicide is suspected, the coroner is obliged to consult with the police about who should conduct the post mortem[1]. In almost all cases, this will be conducted by a Home Office registered forensic pathologist, instructed in conjunction with the police. In addition to their duties to the coroner, the pathologist will advise the police as to any items which should be retained for their investigation. The body will be examined to ascertain not only the deceased's identity and the cause of death, but also for anything which might be evidence of the perpetrator, such as traces of blood. Multiple specialists may need to be involved. Around 2,000 forensic post mortems are undertaken each year in England and Wales[2].

[1] Coroners (Investigations) Regulations 2013, r 12.
[2] Chief Coroner's Guidance No 32, Post-Mortem Examinations, para 40.

2.80 When any material, including blood samples, is taken from the body as part of the post mortem, it may be preserved or retained by the pathologist if it relates to the cause of death or identity of the deceased. If any such material is retained, the pathologist must give the coroner written notification of what material they have retained and why[1]. The coroner must then specify how long that material is to be retained and must notify the deceased's next of kin or personal representative and any other relative who was represented at the post

2.80 *The Investigation*

mortem of the position. Once the material is no longer required, it may be returned to a relative, buried/cremated, or used for medical research purposes if the family consent.

[1] Coroners (Investigations) Regulations 2013, SI 2013/1629, reg 14.

2.81 Following the post mortem, the person appointed by the coroner to carry it out must provide the coroner with the post-mortem report as soon as practicable[1] but must not provide any other person with a copy of that report unless authorised in writing by the coroner to do so[2]. If multiple professionals have been involved in the post mortem and there is a divergence of view about various signs noted at post mortem, this must be fully recorded and summarised in the final report. In non-homicide cases, the pathologist must give their view, on the balance of probabilities, as to the cause of death. The Chief Coroner's Guidance No 32 indicates that pathologists' reports should be provided to coroners within three to four weeks, unless further reports are required from other experts.

[1] CJA 2009, s 14.
[2] Coroners (Investigations) Regulations 2013, SI 2013/1629, reg 16.

2.82 The coroner will normally be expected to disclose that report to any properly interested persons on request although in potential homicide cases, the coroner should consult the police and/or the CPS prior to such disclosure as there may be cases where some aspects should be withheld as relating to potential criminal proceedings[1]. Where family members are not legally represented, many coroners adopt a practice of providing the report itself (which will often contain distressing imagery and details) to the individual's GP and notifying them by letter so that they can consult their GP about it, in order to avoid shock and upset which may arise from receiving the report directly.

[1] Coroners (Inquests) Rules 2013, SI 2013/1616, r 15.

Second post mortems

2.83 The Chief Coroner's view, as set out in Guidance No 32[1], is that there is no automatic right to a second post mortem, even when requested by a defendant in a homicide case. Each request must be made to the coroner, who has control of the body until it is released and must be reviewed on its merits. In such cases, it is imperative that the pathologist should produce at least a summary report to the coroner as soon as possible so that the coroner can make this available to any defendant considering seeking a second post mortem. This should avoid the position where defendants wish to commission a second post mortem urgently without knowing the results of the first.

[1] Chief Coroner's Guidance No 32, Post-Mortem Examinations, Pt 3.

2.84 The guidance suggests that, in homicide cases, the coroner should give suspects or defendants a period of notice of around five days before they intend to release the body, so that they can make a request for a second post mortem if they wish. Such requests should be reasoned and in writing. If the coroner refuses permission, this refusal should also be reasoned and in writing, and a period of around five days should follow before the coroner releases the body so that the defendant can seek injunctive relief from the High Court or such

Post-mortem examinations **2.90**

other remedy as they see fit[1]. The guidance explicitly states that the previous position, as set out in Home Office Circular 30/1999, no longer applies. It comments that second post mortems will very rarely be appropriate following road traffic collisions[2].

[1] Chief Coroner's Guidance No 32, Post-Mortem Examinations, para 53.
[2] Chief Coroner's Guidance No 32, Post-Mortem Examinations, para 78.

2.85 In most cases, once the coroner has released the body, it will be released to the control of the next of kin or personal representative. They will therefore be in a position to conduct a second post mortem if they so wish once the body has been released to them.

Discontinuance where the post mortem reveals the cause of death

2.86 Under s 4 of the CJA 2009, the coroner must discontinue any investigation if the post mortem reveals the cause of death before the inquest has begun, and the coroner thinks that it is not necessary to continue the investigation. The provision does not apply to violent or unnatural deaths, or to deaths in custody or other state detention. A coroner who discontinues an investigation under s 4 must give written reasons for that decision to any interested person who requests them[1].

[1] Coroners (Investigations) Regulations 2013, reg 17.

2.87 A decision to discontinue is susceptible to judicial review. The coroner would be required to continue the investigation if there were other reasons to think that it was 'necessary' to do so, for instance because there was an argument that the level of care had constituted neglect.

2.88 Where a case is discontinued under s 4 CJA 2009, the coroner must simply record the cause of death, complete Form 100B to notify the registrar, and notify the deceased's next of kin or personal representative using Form 2. The coroner must not make any other findings. The coroner would not, however, be prevented from opening a fresh investigation into the death if there was good reason to do so (for instance, if new evidence came to light).

Release of the body following post mortem

2.89 Once it has been determined that it is not necessary for the coroner to retain control of the body, the coroner will release the body to the next of kin or personal representative. Under reg 21 of the Coroners (Investigations) Regulations 2013[1], the coroner may only issue an order authorising burial or cremation where the coroner 'no longer needs to retain the body for the purposes of the investigation'. The coroner will use Form 3 when issuing an order permitting burial of the body.

[1] SI 2013/1629.

2.90 If the body is to be cremated rather than buried, the coroner must also, under reg 18 of the Cremation (England and Wales) Regulations 2008[1], complete a Cremation 6 form, which certifies either that a post mortem has

2.90 *The Investigation*

been done and as a result no inquest is necessary; or that an inquest has been opened; or that the death took place outside the UK and that no post mortem or inquest is necessary. In any event, where the coroner is releasing the body for cremation, they must certify that there is no need for any further examination of the body.

[1] SI 2008/2841.

TRANSFER OF JURISDICTION

2.91 In some cases, a coroner may determine that the duty to investigate is engaged, but may consider that the investigation and inquest should be undertaken by another coroner. It is very common for cases to be assigned by a senior coroner to an assistant coroner within the same area. Such decisions are made on a local basis to expedite matters and do not raise any issues of jurisdiction. There is no requirement for cases to be transferred at the start of an investigation, but in practical terms this will normally be the best approach.

2.92 The Chief Coroner's Guidance No 24 covers transfers of jurisdiction and related matters[1]. Under s 2 of the CJA 2009, where any senior coroner requests another senior coroner to conduct an investigation, that request must be notified to the Chief Coroner, along with confirmation of whether or not the other senior coroner agrees. The Chief Coroner also has power, under s 3 of the CJA 2009, to direct a particular senior coroner to conduct an investigation which would otherwise have fallen into a different senior coroner's jurisdiction. The vast majority of transfers are by agreement. If there is any difficulty in reaching agreement, it is the Chief Coroner's practice to host a telephone conference and to attempt to reach agreement, rather than issuing a direction.

[1] Chief Coroner's Guidance No 24, Transfers (revised 1 April 2019).

2.93 The senior coroner taking conduct of the investigation must begin, or continue, the investigation as soon as practicable. Under reg 18 of the Coroners (Investigations) Regulations 2013[1], the coroner relinquishing jurisdiction must provide all relevant evidence, documents and other information to the coroner taking up the investigation within five working days of the transfer being agreed or directed, unless there are exceptional circumstances. The coroner taking up the investigation must inform the next of kin/personal representative, and any other interested persons who are already known, within the same timescale.

[1] SI 2013/1629.

2.94 Regulation 19 of the Coroners (Investigations) Regulations 2013[1] provides that the costs associated with the investigation, from the point at which it is transferred onwards, are borne by the receiving coroner's local authority in cases of transfer by agreement. Such costs are however borne by the originating coroner's local authority in cases where the Chief Coroner has issued a direction, unless the Chief Coroner directs otherwise.

[1] SI 2019/1629.

2.95 In cases where a body is being repatriated from overseas and an inquest is expected, families should normally make contact with the coroner for the area of intended burial in advance of the repatriation. The coroner for that area will normally take jurisdiction and arrangements will then be made with the coroner for the relevant port of arrival to treat the body as being in transit. That will normally avoid any need for a formal transfer request[1].

[1] Chief Coroner's Guidance No 24, Transfers, para 23.

2.96 The Chief Coroner's Guidance No 24[1] suggests that, where families ask for a transfer, that will normally be good reason for this to occur. In cases of mass fatalities, the Chief Coroner will make arrangements for a single hearing to be held before a single coroner (who may be a High Court judge or, as in the Westminster Bridge Inquests, the Chief Coroner himself), and transfers will be made either by agreement or direction as required.

[1] Chief Coroner's Guidance No 24, Transfers.

2.97 Like any judicial decision by a coroner, decisions around transfer of jurisdiction are susceptible, in principle, to judicial review. At the time of writing, there has been no reported case of such a judicial review having been taken on this issue since the entry into force of CJA 2009. In light of the Chief Coroner's Guidance, it would be unreasonable not to take account of the views of family members. However, the guidance also makes clear that such views are not necessarily decisive if there is some good reason not to follow them. The location of the Hillsborough Inquests was contested and was the subject of a ruling by Goldring LJ, who commented that 'in the ordinary course of events, inquests can be expected to take place at a location which is most convenient to the bereaved and other interested persons and witnesses'[1].

[1] Hillsborough Inquests, Ruling of Goldring LJ, 2 May 2013. At the time of writing the Hillsborough Inquests website has been temporarily taken down due to legal proceedings.

CORONER'S INVESTIGATION – PRACTICAL STEPS TO GATHER EVIDENCE

2.98 Once the coroner has determined that an investigation is required, the inquest has been opened, and (in many cases) the post mortem undertaken, a period of time will follow during which the coroner's investigation will take place. In some high-profile inquests, the police may provide a high degree of support – for instance, in the In Amenas Inquests concerning the deaths of British nationals following a major terrorist attack on industrial facilities in Algeria, the Metropolitan Police assigned a team of specialist investigators to assist the coroner. In such cases, the coroner may also appoint counsel to the inquest (CTI) to assist in the investigation. In the vast majority of cases, however, the coroner will have to take the initiative in obtaining documentary disclosure from other agencies, assisted by a single coroner's officer (often a serving or former police officer) and limited support staff.

2.99 The sources of information that the coroner might obtain are various. In clinical cases the coroner will usually exercise their power to obtain copies of the deceased's medical records. Where emergency ambulance calls are involved, it may be possible to obtain the actual call recording from the

2.99 *The Investigation*

ambulance service in question, as well as the contemporaneous note. The manner in which matters were communicated can in itself be significant evidence.

2.100 It may be possible to obtain CCTV evidence from the location of a relevant incident. Again, there is no uniformity to how and where CCTV material is recorded, often by private operators, and the only useful rule of thumb is that if such material is thought to be relevant, it should be sought at as early a stage as possible because it is often not stored for a long time.

2.101 In cases involving deaths in police custody, the police custody records, including any interview notes or tapes, should be obtained. The Independent Police Complaints Commission would be expected to be involved from a very early stage and will be able to assist with securing all time-sensitive evidence. For deaths in prison, the Prisons and Probation Ombudsman will play a similar role.

2.102 When a death occurs abroad, the coroner will usually be more limited in their ability to investigate. They will not have jurisdiction to compel evidence from foreign witnesses, organisations or state authorities. In *Shafi v HM Senior Coroner for East London*[1], the Divisional Court considered a challenge to a coroner's approach to investigating a death in custody in Dubai. He had relied on the Foreign Office to request a variety of material from the Dubai authorities, including CCTV footage. While it appears that some of the material, such as the autopsy and toxicology reports, was provided, the CCTV footage was not. The Dubai authorities stated that they had no such footage. The Divisional Court held that the coroner, by making the request via the FCO, had done enough to comply with his legal duties, notwithstanding the family's dissatisfaction. It commented that the coroner will make all reasonable efforts to obtain sufficient relevant evidence, with a view to holding a full inquiry, but that it is not desirable to wait indefinitely and that the coroner must ultimately proceed with the inquest on the basis of the material available, provided that it is in the interests of justice to do so. It said that 'in the inquest itself there must always be sufficient inquiry by the coroner, but what is sufficient will depend on the circumstances of the individual case'. However, while *Shafi* gives useful guidance as to the approach which the Divisional Court would take in future, the inquest itself was quashed for other reasons, so the remarks on the coroner's duties around seeking evidence from abroad are obiter.

[1] [2015] EWHC 2106 (Admin).

2.103 Where there are investigations by bodies such as the Independent Police Complaints Commission (IPCC), Prisons and Probation Ombudsman (PPO), Health and Safety Executive (HSE), Care Quality Commission (CQC), Rail Accident Investigation Branch (RAIB) or similar, those will often gather a large volume of material, including witness statements, produced for the purposes of those inquiries. For unexpected deaths in hospital, there are often internal investigations, resulting in serious untoward incident reports. It is important to note that these reports are not considered independent. As set out for instance in *R (Antoniou) v CNWL NHST*[1], there is no obligation for investigations other than the coroner's investigation to be independent. It is therefore all the more important that the coroner does not simply rely on the scope, approach and conclusions of such reports and instead makes a truly independent assessment. Note that statements are often taken by the makers of those reports on the basis of assurances that they will not be disclosed. Such assurances do not provide any legal basis for resisting disclosure to the coroner (which should be made clear when they are taken, though often this is not done), but they may well provide a basis for resisting further disclosure on *Worcestershire*[2] principles. Note that, in a number of cases, these investigatory bodies now have specific Memoranda of Understanding with the Chief Coroner or, in some cases, with the Coroner's Society of England and Wales (the latter being likely to carry less weight than the former if any dispute as to their application were to arise).

[1] [2013] EWHC 3055 (Admin).
[2] *Worcestershire County Council and Anor v HM Coroner for the County of Worcestershire* [2013] EWHC 1711 (QB).

FAST TRACK AND DOCUMENTARY INQUESTS

2.104 In some cases, very little information will be required to reach a conclusion, and it may be possible to open the inquest and conclude it on the same occasion. Given the requirement to open an inquest as soon as reasonably practicable once it appears that the duty to investigate arises, however, there are likely to be many more cases where an inquest is opened but very little further investigation is actually required, so that it is possible to conclude it very shortly thereafter on the documents alone (but not to conclude it at the same occasion as it is opened).

2.105 The Chief Coroner's Guidance No 29[1] sets out various considerations which apply to such inquests. It makes clear that, in any case where concerns are raised by family members or any other agency, fast track or documentary inquests will not be appropriate. Their advantage is to allow the process to be completed swiftly where there are no real concerns requiring investigation.

[1] Chief Coroner's Guidance No 29, Documentary Inquests (20 November 2018).

2.106 The guidance suggests that a fast track inquest ie opened and closed on the same occasion could be suitable in cases where the death arises from industrial disease, the cause of which had already been established during life – so that a full inquest would add nothing to what was already known – or from drug use where the cause was clear from post-mortem toxicology and there was no suggestion of suicide and no other family concerns. It also suggests that, where the medical cause of death remains unknown following the post mortem, but there is no suggestion that it was unnatural and no other reason (such as the death having occurred in custody) to hold a full inquest, it may be appropriate to adopt the fast track procedure. In such a case, the coroner would be likely to open the inquest, read the post-mortem report and some comment on the circumstances of the death, and reach an open conclusion.

2.107 Where some further investigation is required after the initial opening of the inquest, but that investigation does not reveal any cause for concern or

2.107 *The Investigation*

controversy about the death, the coroner may proceed to a documentary inquest (also known as a short form or rule 23 inquest). The guidance gives the example of a suicide in the community where there is a clear suicide note and no other cause for concern. It stresses that the coroner must take care not to give the family any impression that they are obliged to accept this form of an inquest, and to ensure that if they do raise concerns which require further investigation, these are addressed.

2.108 A documentary inquest will proceed with all evidence being admitted under r 23 of the Coroners (Inquests) Rules 2013[1] ie read into the record without the witness being called to give oral evidence. The key requirements in the case of a documentary inquest, which will often be held with nobody other than the coroner and their staff present, are that documentary evidence can only be admitted under r 23 if:

(a) that written evidence is unlikely to be disputed;
(b) it is made clear in advance that any interested person may object to its admission; and
(c) it is also made clear in advance that any interested person may see a copy of that evidence if they so wish.

[1] SI 2013/1616.

2.109 In practical terms, this means that, prior to holding any documentary inquest, the coroner must give the next of kin or personal representative, and any other interested persons, notice that they consider the case suitable for a documentary inquest, and give them an opportunity to consent or object.

2.110 The Divisional Court considered the correct approach to documentary inquests in *Simon Mueller v HM Area Coroner for Manchester West*[1]. In that case, the coroner had given disclosure of the documentary evidence on which they intended to rely and obtained consent for a documentary inquest to be held in a case where there was a suicide note. However, the coroner apparently read out a summary of the note which gave an inaccurate impression of the deceased's husband. That summary was subsequently reported in the press, causing distress. The Divisional Court said that:

> 'it is to be welcomed that . . . the coroner engaged with the family to seek to deal with this inquest without the need for the attendance of the family or witnesses. When appropriate, such an approach can entirely properly lessen the impact of an inquest on the family of the deceased. In those circumstances, however, it is particularly important to consider with care what is to be read into the record of the inquest . . . [before any documentary inquest is held] it is equally important to explain to all concerned, in advance, exactly what that will mean. The coroner should indicate which statements and documents are likely to be read or summarised at the public hearing, and which parts (if any) of the statements or documents are not to be read . . .'

[1] [2017] EWHC 3000 (Admin).

Conclusion following fast track or documentary inquest

2.111 Given that fast track or documentary inquests will only be appropriate for deaths which do not raise any complex or controversial issues, the conclusions should be straightforward. The coroner will record the conclusion using Form 2, recording how, when and where the deceased came by their death and, in almost all cases suitable for a documentary inquest, a short form conclusion.

2.112 The coroner will then also complete Form 99, which is sent to the registrar, allowing the death to be registered. The body can then be buried or cremated, if this had not already been released during the course of the investigation.

SUSPENSION OF INVESTIGATION

Duty to suspend

2.113 In some circumstances, it may be necessary for an investigation which is underway to be suspended. This can arise even while the inquest is in progress and evidence is being heard (strictly speaking, the inquest is the final part of the overall investigation). The Chief Coroner's Guidance No 33[1] on the suspension, adjournment and resumption of inquests comments that the underlying premise of the law in this area is that investigations into deaths should not be duplicated.

[1] Published 7 October 2019.

2.114 The coroner is required, under para 1 of Sch 1 to the CJA 2009, to suspend an investigation if they are requested to do so by a prosecuting authority on the basis that someone may be charged with a homicide offence involving the death of the deceased, or any offence alleged to be a related offence. This includes equivalent service offences where the prosecution would be before a military court and the request comes from the appropriate military prosecutor.

2.115 A 'homicide offence' is defined as any of the following[1]:

(a) murder;
(b) manslaughter;
(c) corporate manslaughter;
(d) infanticide;
(e) road traffic offences of causing death by:
    (i) dangerous driving;
    (ii) careless or inconsiderate driving;
    (iii) careless driving while under the influence of drink or drugs;
    (iv) driving when unlicensed, disqualified or uninsured;
(f) encouraging or assisting suicide;
(g) causing or allowing the death of a child or vulnerable adult.

A 'related offence' means an offence which involves the death of the deceased, or of a person other than the deceased where it is committed in circumstances connected with the death of the deceased[2].

[1] CJA 2009, s 11, Sch 1, para 1(6).
[2] CJA 2009, s 11, Sch 1, para 1(6).

2.116 *The Investigation*

2.116 The coroner is also required, under the CJA 2009, Sch 1, para 2 to suspend an investigation if they become aware that a person has in fact been charged with a homicide offence relating to the death of the deceased, unless the relevant prosecuting authority indicates that it has no objection to the coroner's investigation continuing. Where any person is charged with a related offence, the burden is on the prosecuting authority to inform the coroner that the person has been charged, that it considers the offence to be a related one, and that it seeks a suspension of the coroner's investigation.

2.117 Under Sch 1, para 2, which applies to cases where someone has been charged, the coroner has the power to continue notwithstanding the objections of a prosecuting authority, pursuant to Sch 1, para 2(6)(c), if there is an 'exceptional reason' for not suspending the investigation. That wording is not replicated in Sch 1, para 1, which relates to cases where a suspension is requested on the basis that someone may be charged.

2.118 Any suspension under either paragraph should be dealt with publicly in court, with a review date being set when the investigation is suspended. A suspension under Sch 1, para 1 must be for at least 28 days, although it may be longer. It may be extended at the request of the relevant prosecuting authority and can be extended more than once. If an investigation has been suspended under para 1, because someone may be charged, and charges are in fact brought, that suspension will continue under Sch 1, para 2. This is important because the coroner has a duty, under Sch 1, para 7, to resume any investigation suspended under para 1 once the period of suspension has ended, but the position is different for an investigation suspended under Sch 1, para 2.

See CHAPTER 21 for further detail of the interplay between inquests and criminal proceedings.

Suspension due to public inquiry

2.119 Under para 3 of Sch 1 of the CJA 2009, the coroner must suspend an investigation if requested to do so by the Lord Chancellor on the basis that the cause of death is likely to be adequately investigated by an inquiry which either has been or will be established under the Inquiries Act 2005. However, the coroner need not suspend the investigation if there is an exceptional reason for not doing so. Furthermore, Sch 1, para 3 only applies if the inquiry has actually had a judge of the High Court, Court of Appeal or Supreme Court appointed to lead it. Sch 1, para 4 also sets out a requirement that the terms of reference of the inquiry must be such that it has among its purposes to ascertain those matters which an inquest would be required to investigate ie who, where, when, by what means and, where appropriate, in what circumstances the deceased came by their death. See CHAPTER 24 for further detail of the interplay between inquests and inquiries.

2.120 There are high profile instances of inquests being suspended for an Inquiries Act inquiry to be held, perhaps most obviously in the case of the Litvinenko Inquiry. That was set up on 31 July 2014, with the senior judge who had previously been appointed as coroner to hold an inquest into the death, Sir Robert Owen, being appointed to lead the inquiry. He held a short hearing at which he suspended the inquest and commenced the inquiry.

2.121 The Visiting Forces Act 1952 (as amended) further provides that, in a case of the death of someone who has a 'relevant association' with a member of a 'visiting force' ie foreign military personnel based in or visiting the UK, foreign civilian staff associated with that force, and their dependents, the coroner shall not commence an investigation or, if commenced, shall suspend it. Such investigations may not continue without the consent of the Lord Chancellor.

Discretion to suspend

2.122 The coroner also has a general discretion, under the CJA 2009, Sch 1, para 5, to suspend an investigation if it appears 'that it would be appropriate to do so'. Examples given in Guidance No 33 include where there is an investigation by another body, such as the Health and Safety Executive, or in another jurisdiction (as may be the case with deaths abroad).

Consequences of suspension

2.123 When a coroner suspends an investigation and an inquest is already underway, the inquest is also suspended. If a jury has been empanelled, the coroner has a discretion under the CJA 2009, Sch 1, para 6 to discharge them. If the jury is not discharged, then if the inquest is later resumed and at least seven of the jurors are still available to serve, the resumed inquest must be held with that jury (if a jury is required at all).

2.124 When suspending an investigation, the coroner must provide the registrar with the particulars required to register the death. This is done using Form 120. The coroner must first have opened an inquest to take evidence of identification.

2.125 If an investigation is suspended and not concluded, even if the coroner makes a formal decision not to resume (see below at **2.132**), the coroner can (indeed must) resume the investigation if there is sufficient reason to do so[1]. In such cases, the appropriate approach for anyone seeking further investigation is to ask the original coroner to resume the investigation (and potentially judicially review any refusal) rather than applying to the High Court to have the findings of the original inquest quashed. See CHAPTER 8 for further detail on challenging coronial decisions.

[1] *Flower v HM Coroner for Devon* [2015] EWHC 3666 (Admin).

RESUMPTION OF INVESTIGATION OR INQUEST

2.126 When an investigation has been suspended because someone may be charged with a relevant offence, the coroner must resume it once the specified

2.126 *The Investigation*

period of suspension has expired (bearing in mind that this period can be extended on more than one occasion if necessary)[1].

[1] CJA 2009 Sch 1, para 1; Chief Coroner's Guidance No 33 Suspension, Adjournment and Resumption of Investigations and Inquests, para 5.

2.127 When an investigation has been suspended because someone has in fact been charged with a relevant offence, the investigation must remain suspended until the conclusion of those criminal proceedings. The coroner must then consider whether or not there is 'sufficient reason' to resume the investigation. If there is, it is mandatory to resume, and if not, there is no discretion to do so. However, any conclusions must be consistent with the verdicts of the criminal proceedings[1].

[1] CJA 2009, Sch 1, para 8(1); Chief Coroner's Guidance No 33 Suspension, Adjournment and Resumption of Investigations and Inquests, para 23.

2.128 When an investigation has been suspended in order for a public inquiry to take place, the coroner must wait at least 28 days from the conclusion of the inquiry. The investigation must remain suspended pending any criminal proceedings for homicide or related offences concerning the deceased's death, save with the consent of the relevant prosecuting authority. The coroner must then consider whether or not there is 'sufficient reason' to resume the investigation. If there is, it is mandatory to resume, and if not, there is no discretion to do so. However, any conclusions must be consistent with the findings of the inquiry and the verdicts in any resulting criminal proceedings[1].

[1] CJA 2009, Sch 1, para 8.

2.129 It is not mandatory to hold a resumed inquest with a jury. As will be clear from the above, there will be many cases where the inquest conclusion will be dictated by the result of the inquiry or criminal trials for which the investigation was suspended, so that empanelling or recalling a jury would serve no useful purpose.

2.130 When the coroner has suspended an investigation for discretionary reasons, they may resume it at any time if they 'think that there is sufficient reason for resuming it'. This is a very wide discretion. In exercising it, the coroner will normally be expected to have regard to the extent to which the facts surrounding the death have already been sufficiently established in other proceedings, in such a manner that the public interest is adequately served. The requirements of Art 2 are relevant, as are the facts that an inquest is a public forum in which the deceased's family can participate, and that the coroner is under a duty to write a report to prevent future deaths if there is cause to do so, which is not usually the case in other fora.

2.131 Guidance No 33 refers to a trend for attempts to resume inquests after a significant period of time has elapsed. It asks coroners to inform the Chief Coroner when dealing with such cases, and notes that consideration should be given to the length of time which has elapsed since the events in question.

2.132 If the coroner reaches a positive decision not to resume an investigation, they should provide a certificate of this to the registrar using Form 121. Note that, as discussed at **2.125** above, this does not prevent the investigation from being resumed if there is sufficient reason to do so in light of information which becomes available at a future date.

2.133 Before resuming any inquest, the coroner is required to inform all the interested persons of the details of the resumed hearing. While there is no equivalent mandatory requirement for resuming investigations, which have not yet reached the stage of a final inquest hearing, it would plainly be good practice to adopt the same approach[1].

[1] Coroners (Inquests) Rules 2013, r 25(3).

Chapter 3

SCOPE AND ARTICLE 2 ECHR

3.1 This chapter will consider the scope of an inquest, as determined by ss 5 and 10 of the Coroners and Justice Act 2009 (CJA 2009), and the requirements of Art 2 of the European Convention on Human Rights (ECHR), as fulfilled in England and Wales through the investigation and inquest process.

SCOPE

Introduction

3.2 In *R (Hambleton) v Coroner for the Birmingham Inquests*[1], Lord Burnett CJ[2] endorsed the following definition of the term 'scope' in coronial law, as given by the coroner in the case, former Chief Coroner, HH Sir Peter Thornton QC:

> 'The word "scope" has no special meaning of its own. By "scope" all that is generally meant is a list of the topics upon which the coroner, in the coroner's discretion, will call relevant evidence so as to be able to answer the four key statutory questions: Who died? How, when and where did they come by their death?'

The scope of an inquest, although prescribed in principle by statute, can often be a controversial and deeply significant issue between interested persons. In this section, we analyse the statutory provisions of the CJA 2009 relating to scope; consider the distinction between the scope of a *Jamieson* inquest and the scope of a *Middleton* inquest; discuss the wide ambit of discretion traditionally afforded to a coroner when deciding on issues of scope; and provide some brief practical guidance about how scope is actually determined during the investigation and inquest process.

[1] [2018] EWCA Civ 2081.
[2] At [57].

Statutory provisions

3.3 The scope of an inquest is governed by ss 5 and 10 of CJA 2009.

3.4 Section 5 (Matters to be ascertained) is listed in the contents of the Act under the heading, 'Purpose of the investigation'; it is the only section under that heading. It provides as follows:

'5 Matters to be ascertained
(1) The purpose of an investigation under this Part into a person's death is to ascertain—
  (a) who the deceased was;
  (b) how, when and where the deceased came by his or her death;
  (c) the particulars (if any) required by the 1953 Act to be registered concerning the death.
(2) Where necessary in order to avoid a breach of any Convention rights (within the meaning of the Human Rights Act 1998 (c. 42)), the purpose mentioned in subsection (1)(b) is to be read as including the purpose of ascertaining in what circumstances the deceased came by his or her death.
(3) Neither the senior coroner conducting an investigation under this Part into a person's death nor the jury (if there is one) may express any opinion on any matter other than—
  (a) the questions mentioned in subsection (1)(a) and (b) (read with subsection (2) where applicable);
  (b) the particulars mentioned in subsection (1)(c).

This is subject to paragraph 7 of Schedule 5.'

3.5 Section 10 (Determinations and findings to be made) is listed in the contents of the CJA 2009 under the heading, 'Outcome of investigation'; it is the only section under that heading. It provides as follows:

'10 Determinations and findings to be made
(1) After hearing the evidence at an inquest into a death, the senior coroner (if there is no jury) or the jury (if there is one) must—
  (a) make a determination as to the questions mentioned in section 5(1)(a) and (b) (read with section 5(2) where applicable), and
  (b) if particulars are required by the 1953 Act to be registered concerning the death, make a finding as to those particulars.
(2) A determination under subsection (1)(a) may not be framed in such a way as to appear to determine any question of—
  (a) criminal liability on the part of a named person, or
  (b) civil liability.
(3) In subsection (2) "criminal liability" includes liability in respect of a service offence.'

3.6 This framework provides the basis for the consideration of scope in relation to an inquest. Under s 5 the investigation as a whole is directed in the main to answering just four central questions[1] in relation to a death: *who, when, where* and *how*. The investigation must not lead to the expression of an opinion on any matter other than these questions (plus any particulars that may be required by the Births and Deaths Registration Act 1953). Where the investigative obligation under Art 2 ECHR is engaged, then s 5(2) expands the question *how* to *how and in what circumstances*. The test for the engagement of the duty is a question of ECHR law, however, as covered below at **3.70** *et seq*. In order for s 5(2) to be engaged, there needs to have been an arguable breach of one of the substantive duties to protect life under Art 2 ECHR.

[1] This statutory purpose of determining who the deceased was, how, where and when they came by their death is of 'ancient lineage' in the words of Lord Burnett CJ in *R (Hambleton) v Coroner for the Birmingham Inquests (1974)* [2018] EWCA Civ 2081, para 15.

3.7 Any evidence that an interested party may wish to be called at an inquest that does not go to one of these questions may properly be excluded by a coroner as being strictly irrelevant to the purpose of the investigation. Indeed, in light of s 5(3), a coroner must be wary of expressing an *opinion* during the course of the entire investigation on any matter other than the central questions (or particulars to be registered).

3.8 Similarly, by s 10(2), although after hearing the evidence at an inquest, determinations must be made as to the central questions, such determinations must not appear to establish civil liability or any criminal liability of a named person. Therefore, evidence that might suggest any such liability for the death, but that is not strictly relevant to the central questions of the investigation into the death, may properly be excluded by the coroner.

3.9 Section 5 provides for one important exception to that rule: reports made by a coroner in order to prevent future deaths (PFD reports). CJA 2009, Sch 5, para 7 imposes a duty upon a coroner to make such a report where they are of the view that action ought to be taken to prevent the occurrence or continuation of circumstances creating a risk of death (or to eliminate or reduce the risk of death created by such circumstances). See CHAPTER 5 for further detail of PFD reports.

Jamieson inquests and *Middleton* inquests

3.10 The distinction between so-called *Jamieson* and *Middleton* inquests revolves around the interpretation of the fourth, and typically most controversial, of the four central questions: *how* the deceased came by their death.

3.11 The distinction between a *Jamieson* and a *Middleton* inquest is now set down in statue in s 5(2) and s 10(1)(a) CJA 2009. However, it is instructive to examine the authorities in order to understand the relevant principles and the interplay between the two.

3.12 *R v HM Coroner for North Humberside and Scunthorpe, ex p Jamieson*[1] was a case in which the court was considering the suicide of a prisoner. Mr Jamieson was a serving prisoner and was known to be at risk of attempting suicide. He was accommodated at night in a single cell without company and with no arrangements made for special supervision, contrary to Home Office guidance provided at the time, and hanged himself. The coroner refused to leave a verdict of 'lack of care' (ie neglect) to the inquest jury. The deceased's brother sought judicial review of this decision and, after the decision was approved upon review, appealed that outcome to the Court of Appeal.

[1] [1995] QB 1.

3.13 One of the strands of the appeal was that the verdict ought to have been left to the jury in order to allow them fully to answer the statutory question of how the deceased came by their death. The same four central questions now provided by CJA 2009, s 5(1) were, at that time, set out within s 11(5) of the Coroners Act 1988. It was argued on behalf of the appellant that the

3.13 Scope and Article 2 ECHR

question 'how' a deceased had come by their death had to be interpreted as meaning 'in what broad circumstances'; not merely 'by what means'.

3.14 The importance of the Court of Appeal's judgment in *Jamieson* goes beyond just the issue of scope. It remains the key authority on neglect[1]. However, in relation to the interpretation of the 'how' question, Sir Thomas Bingham MR, after completing a comprehensive survey of the history of the statutory provision and the notable judicial authorities, confirmed at p 24 that:

> 'Both in section 11(5)(b)(ii) of the Act of 1988 and in rule 36(1)(b) of the Rules of 1984, "how" is to be understood as meaning "by what means". It is noteworthy that the task is not to ascertain how the deceased died, which might raise general and far-reaching issues, but "how . . . the deceased came by his death", a more limited question directed to the means by which the deceased came by his death.'

[1] See CHAPTER 6 for further detail of cases involving neglect.

3.15 The appeal was subsequently dismissed. Furthermore, although the court's judgment made it clear that a coroner was still duty-bound to investigate all relevant facts fully, fairly and fearlessly, if the coroner decided that certain facts concerned the wider circumstances of the death rather than simply how the deceased came by their death and thus fell outside the scope of their enquiry, that decision could not be impugned.

3.16 The narrower interpretation of the 'how' question required revision following the coming into force of the Human Rights Act 1998 (HRA 1998), which brought the rights set out in the European Convention of Human Rights and Fundamental Freedoms (ECHR) and their interpretation by the European Court of Human Rights in Strasbourg (ECtHR) within the domestic sphere. That revision was undertaken by the House of Lords in *Middleton*.

3.17 *Middleton*[1] also involved a suicide by a prisoner: Colin Middleton, a prisoner serving a long custodial sentence, hanged himself in his prison cell. His family alleged that the prison service knew that he was a suicide risk and should have placed him on 'suicide watch'. If they had done so, the family argued, his suicide would have been prevented. The coroner refused to leave a neglect conclusion to the jury, who returned a verdict of suicide, but also handed the coroner a note containing factual conclusions indicating that the prison had failed in its duty of care to Mr Middleton. The question arose whether the conclusions reached at the inquest were sufficient to satisfy the requirements of Art 2 ECHR.

[1] [2004] UKHL 10.

3.18 Lord Bingham, giving the judgment of the Judicial Committee held as follows:

- Where engaged, Art 2 ECHR required an investigation whose purpose was to ensure the accountability of state agents for deaths occurring under their responsibility, and to be capable of leading to a determination of whether any force used was justified, or the protection afforded to life was adequate, and to the identification of those involved[1].
- That, as the inquest was the means through which the state discharged its Art 2 duty, in order '[t]o meet the procedural requirement of article 2

Scope **3.21**

- an inquest ought ordinarily to culminate in an expression, however brief, of the jury's conclusion on the disputed factual issues at the heart of the case'[2].
- That whilst '[i]n some other cases, short verdicts in the traditional form will enable the jury to express their conclusion on the central issue canvassed at the inquest . . . it is plain that in other cases a strict *ex p Jamieson*[3] approach will not meet what has been identified above as the Convention requirement'[4].
- That there were therefore some cases in which the existing inquest regime did not meet the requirements of the Convention. The change required was to interpret 'how' someone came by their death not simply as meaning 'by what means' but rather 'by what means and in what circumstances'[5].
- That would not require a change of approach in some cases, where a traditional short form conclusion would be satisfactory, but in some cases a broader approach was required. In the latter class of cases 'it must be for the coroner, in the exercise of his discretion, to decide how best, in the particular case, to elicit the jury's conclusion on the central issue or issues'[6].

[1] At [13], [16]–[20].
[2] [2004] UKHL 10 at [20].
[3] [1995] QB 1.
[4] [2004] UKHL 10 at [31].
[5] [2004] UKHL 10 at [35].
[6] [2004] UKHL 10 at [36].

3.19 In due course the ratio of *Middleton* was set out in primary statute under CJA 2009, s 5(2). As a result, where Art 2 ECHR is engaged, the scope of the coroner's investigation and inquest is likely to be required to be broader than would otherwise be the case, in order to determine 'by what means and in what circumstances' a deceased came by their death.

3.20 There is now dicta at the highest level to suggest that there is little difference in scope between a *Jamieson* and *Middleton* inquest at the evidential stage[1]. Indeed, in *R (Maguire) v HM Senior Coroner for Blackpool & Flyde*[2], Lord Burnett CJ in the Court of Appeal stated that the 'scope of the investigation and thus evidence called at the inquest is unlikely to be affected by the question whether the Art 2 procedural obligation applies'[3].

[1] See the speeches of the House of Lords in *R (Hurst) v London North District Coroner* [2007] 2 AC 189.
[2] [2020] EWCA Civ 738.
[3] At [77].

3.21 That position, however, is difficult to reconcile with the words of s 5(2), which draw a clear distinction between the scope of an Art 2 and non-Art 2 inquest. In practice it is commonplace for coroners to restrict or expand the scope of the evidence to be heard at an inquest dependent on whether they consider Art 2 to be engaged or not. It can have an important and often decisive effect, for instance, on a coroner's decision whether to call independent expert evidence, or whether to investigate systemic failures surrounding a death. In any event there is no dispute that its engagement directly affects the range and nature of the conclusions available at the end of the inquest, as

3.21 *Scope and Article 2 ECHR*

confirmed by the Court of Appeal in *Maguire*[1]. In particular it permits critical or judgmental findings to be made. This is of particular significance in jury cases where there will be no factual judgment reached in open court on the evidence itself.

[1] [2020] EWCA Civ 738 at [77].

The coroner's discretion as to scope

3.22 Within the statutory framework provided by CJA 2009, the determination of the scope of a particular investigation or inquest will be highly fact-sensitive. The discretion afforded to a coroner to decide on the scope of an inquest is wide and the higher courts have expressed an unwillingness to interfere with such decisions other than on public law grounds, particularly where there is no dispute that s 5(2) CJA 2009 is not engaged.

3.23 Thus, in *McDonnell v HM Assistant Coroner for West London*[1], Beatson LJ referred to the long line of authority dealing with such inquests as fact-finding exercises where 'decisions by a coroner as to the scope of enquiry and as to which witnesses to call are a matter of judgment which may only be challenged on the ground that they are *Wednesbury* unreasonable, ie irrational'[2].

[1] [2016] EWHC 3078 (Admin).
[2] [2016] EWHC 3078 (Admin) at [28].

3.24 In the words of Hickinbottom LJ, approving this aspect of *McDonnell* at para 41 of the judgment in *R (Worthington) v HM Senior Coroner for Cumbria*[1] 'the scope of enquiry is a matter of judgment for the coroner, to which, quite lawfully, coroners might respond differently subject to challenge on only the usual public law grounds'[2].

[1] [2018] EWHC 3386 (Admin).
[2] [2018] EWHC 3386 (Admin) at [41].

3.25 In *R (Hambleton) v Coroner for the Birmingham Inquests (1974)*[1], a decision relating to the reopened inquests into the deaths of the 21 people killed in the Birmingham bombings, the Court of Appeal confirmed that the same, broad discretion as to scope also applies to *Middleton* inquests in which s 5(2) CJA 2009 is engaged. Indeed, the court reaffirmed the prerogative of a coroner, insofar as defining the scope of an investigation or inquest in general is concerned:

> 'A decision on scope represents a coroner's view about what is necessary, desirable and proportionate by way of investigation to enable the statutory functions to be discharged. These are not hard-edged questions. The decision on scope, just as a decision on which witnesses to call, and the breadth of evidence adduced, is for the coroner. A court exercising supervisory jurisdiction can interfere with such a decision only if it is infected with a public law failing. It has long been the case that a court exercising supervisory jurisdiction will be slow to disturb a decision of this sort [. . .] and will do so only on what is described in omnibus terms as *Wednesbury* grounds. That envisages the supervisory jurisdiction of the High Court being exercised when the decision of the coroner can be demonstrated to disable him from performing his statutory function, when the decision is one which no

reasonable coroner could have come to on the basis of the information available, involves a material error of law or on a number of other well-established public law failings[2].'

[1] [2018] EWCA Civ 2081.
[2] See para 48, Lord Burnett CJ.

3.26 Nevertheless, despite the restrictions provided by the wording of CJA 2009 and the broad ambit of a coroner's discretion on scope, it is still a coroner's duty to ensure that an inquest seeks out and records as many of the facts concerning the death as the public interest requires (as per Lord Lane CJ in *R v HM Coroner for South London, ex p Thompson*[1]).

[1] (1982) 236 SJ 625.

3.27 Thus, the question of how the deceased came by their death is clearly wider than merely finding the medical cause of death. The modern 'Form 2' Record of an Inquest, for instance, requires separate boxes to be filled in at the end of an inquest for the medical cause of death (Box 2), the answers to the CJA 2009, s 5 questions (Box 3) and the conclusion (Box 4).

3.28 As such, a coroner will be required to 'enquire into acts and omissions which are directly responsible for the death' (*R v HM Coroner for East Sussex Western District, ex p Homberg*[1], quoted with approval by Hickinbottom LJ in *R (Worthington) v HM Senior Coroner for Cumbria*[2]). Therefore, the scope of the investigation and inquest 'is almost always going to be wider than the verdict eventually reached' (as per Baroness Hale in *R (Hurst) v London Northern District Coroner*[3], paraphrasing with approval the judgment of Simon Brown LJ in *R v HM Coroner for Inner London West District ex p Dallaglio*[4]).

[1] (1994) 158 JP 357.
[2] [2018] EWHC 3386 (Admin).
[3] [2007] UKHL 13.
[4] [1994] 4 All ER 139.

The determination of scope in practice

3.29 Whether a coroner's investigation and inquest engages Art 2 ECHR or not is likely, in practice, to lead to important differences in scope. In an Art 2 *Middleton* inquest there will generally be grounds for calling evidence from a wider pool of witnesses in order properly to investigate the broader circumstances of the death. At the least, the focus of the evidence that any witnesses of fact may give is likely to be broader in a *Middleton* inquest than in a *Jamieson* inquest; a fact that interested persons may seek to exploit or dampen, depending on the facts of the case.

3.30 Further, whilst coroners have wide discretion as to scope, they must bear in mind the Chief Coroner's Guidance, where relevant. The Chief Coroner's Guidance No 37 on COVID-19 Deaths and Possible Exposure in the Workplace was published during the pandemic[1]. Its original iteration discouraged coroners from investigating issues relating to the provision of personal protective equipment (PPE) at a high level, stating that 'coroners are reminded that an inquest is not the right forum for addressing concerns about high-level

3.30 *Scope and Article 2 ECHR*

government or public policy . . . an inquest would not be a satisfactory means of deciding whether adequate general policies and arrangements were in place for provision of PPE to healthcare workers in the country or a part of it'[2]. However, following concerns raised from various quarters, that language was altered in an amended version of the guidance, which now states 'there have been a number of indications in the judgments of the higher courts that a coroner's inquest is not usually the right forum for addressing concerns about high level government or public policy, which may be causally remote from the particular death . . . However, it is repeated that the scope of the enquiry is a matter for the judgment of coroners, not for hard and fast rules'. The Chief Coroner's Guidance No 27 as amended goes on to provide practical guidance to coroners on the use of their evidence gathering powers in such cases. For further detail on the Chief Coroner's Guidance published during the COVID-19 pandemic see CHAPTER **20**.

[1] Amended 1 July 2020.
[2] At para 13.

3.31 Finally, it is important to remember the role of reg 28 of the 2013 Coroners' Investigation Regulations and reports to prevent future deaths (PFD). These do not have to be causally related to the death. The PFD framework therefore makes it possible for interested persons to submit that certain issues ought to be investigated, or that certain evidence ought to be heard at an inquest, that might not strictly go to the central questions provided by s 5(1) and (2). For example, in relation to a road traffic death, evidence of the speed limit or signage on a particular stretch of road; or in relation to a death in custody, the personnel records of particular prison guards or the risk assessments conducted before and after the death took place. Coroners take different approaches to reg 28 in practice. It is commonplace for PFD evidence to be considered at the close of the inquest after conclusions are reached. In other cases the issue may be considered at the full evidential stage.

3.32 In any case in which the scope of the inquest is likely to be controversial, interested persons ought therefore to ensure that a pre-inquest review (PIR) is held and that they have considered their position fully in advance so that properly reasoned submissions can be made to the coroner at that stage. There may be particular witnesses or pieces of evidence that interested persons wish to ensure are either called at the inquest or ruled to be outside of the inquest's scope. Depending on the facts of the case, these could include medical records, closed-circuit television footage, expert evidence, serious untoward incident reports, local and/or national guidelines, and so on.

3.33 Submissions on the scope of the inquest can then be made at the PIR with reference to the principles set out above, but also with concrete examples of the types of evidence that, it is argued, ought to be called. This is likely to be the most persuasive way of addressing the coroner on the subjects of scope and the engagement of ECHR, Art 2.

3.34 As above, whilst the distinction between a *Jamieson* and *Middleton* inquest at the evidential stage has been called into question, there is no doubt that it directly affects the forms of conclusion that can be returned at the

The European Convention on Human Rights **3.39**

conclusion of an inquest. Conclusions in Art 2 and *Jamieson* inquests are covered in CHAPTER **6** at **6.15**.

THE EUROPEAN CONVENTION ON HUMAN RIGHTS

3.35 This section will provide a short introduction to the ECHR. Readers are referred to the specialist texts on the ECHR and the HRA 1998 for more detailed exposition.

3.36 The ECHR is an international treaty. It was adopted in November 1950 and entered into force in September 1953. It binds the 'High Contracting Parties', the members of the Council of Europe. Under Art 34 ECHR, individual challenges, alleging breaches of the Convention, may be brought to the European Court of Human Rights (ECtHR) against contracting states by individuals, groups, NGOs and other contracting states (although the latter is rare) who claim to be a victim[1]. The UK ratified the ECHR in 1951 and first accepted the jurisdiction of the ECtHR in 1965.

[1] See the ECtHR's Practical Guide on Admissibility Criteria, Updated 31 August 2019. https://www.echr.coe.int/Documents/Admissibility_guide_ENG.pdf.

3.37 As an international treaty, the ECHR binds the UK in international law. Judgments of the ECtHR also bind the UK in international law (in accordance with Art 46 ECHR). Under Art 1 of the Convention, each state party is required to 'secure to everyone within their jurisdiction the rights and freedoms defined in Section 1 of this Convention'. Article 13 provides that individuals have a right to an effective remedy for Convention breaches, in order to ensure that they have a remedy at national level. Article 13 was not incorporated into domestic law in Sch 1 to the HRA 1998 on the basis that the HRA 1998 was considered to ensure Art 13 compliance already.

3.38 Despite the wording of Art 1, a contracting state may be liable for breaches of Convention rights which arise from acts of its authorities outside its territory. In *Al-Skeini v United Kingdom*[1] the Grand Chamber of the ECtHR set out that such jurisdiction will be established:

(a) where diplomatic and consular officials acting within the remit of international law exert authority and control over others;
(b) where the state exercises authority and control over another territory (this is the principle by which jurisdiction is assumed for the ECHR rights of a state's own forces abroad – see *Smith v Ministry of Defence*)[2]; and/or
(c) whenever the state through its agents exercises control and authority over an individual, and thus jurisdiction.

[1] (2011) 53 EHRR 18 at [133]–[137].
[2] [2013] UKSC 41, [2014] AC 52.

The structure of the substantive ECHR rights

3.39 Articles 2, 3 (torture or inhuman or degrading treatment), and 4 (slavery, servitude and forced or compulsory labour) of the EHCR are unqualified, and

3.39 *Scope and Article 2 ECHR*

cannot be derogated from, whereas others are subject to qualifications or limitations. In the case of several qualified rights, state interference is permitted where the interference is prescribed by law, is in pursuit of a legitimate aim and is necessary in a democratic society[1]. The unqualified rights impose positive, as well as negative, obligations upon state parties, and the structure of the positive duties is similar across the three articles. One of the forms of positive duty which has emerged from the ECtHR's case law in relation to Arts 2, 3, and 4, is the investigative duty. This chapter will explore in detail the investigative obligation in relation to Art 2, which in England and Wales is generally fulfilled by an inquest in the absence of a public inquiry or criminal proceedings. But Arts 3 and 4 impose similar obligations[2].

[1] Eg ECHR, Arts 8–11, Protocol No 1, Article 1.
[2] See eg *Aydin v Turkey* (1997) 25 EHRR 251, in respect of Art 3, and *Rantsev v Cyprus* (2010) 51 EHRR 1, in respect of Art 4.

THE HUMAN RIGHTS ACT 1998

3.40 The HRA 1998 was intended to give 'further effect' in domestic law to the rights and freedoms guaranteed under the ECHR[1]. The HRA 1998 did not incorporate the Convention wholesale into English law. Only those Articles and Protocols set out in s 1 of and Sch 1 to the HRA 1998 can be relied upon in English courts. Those Articles have effect for the purposes of the Act under s 1(2) subject to any designated derogation or reservation. Under s 6 of the HRA 1998 it is unlawful for any public authority to act in a manner which is incompatible with a Convention right[2]. Convention rights therefore take precedence over rules of common law. Under s 3, primary and subordinate legislation must be read and given effect in a manner which is compatible with Convention rights 'so far as it is possible to do so'. If it is impossible to resolve a conflict between a Convention right and a provision of primary legislation by construction, the legislation remains valid, operative and enforceable, but under s 4 the higher courts may make a 'declaration of incompatibility'. This legislative mechanism allows for a balance to be struck between the protection of ECHR rights and the principle of parliamentary sovereignty. However, the Convention rights take precedence over secondary legislation, unless primary legislation prevents the relevant incompatibility – see s 3(2).

[1] *Rights Brought Home, White Paper*, Cm 3782, 1997, p 1.
[2] HRA 1998, s 6.

3.41 Under s 7 of the HRA 1998 individuals may bring court or tribunal proceedings against a public authority in respect of acts made unlawful by s 6. An individual may only bring such proceedings provided they are (or would be) a victim for the purposes of Art 34 of the ECHR if proceedings were brought in Strasbourg in respect of that act. Under s 8 of the HRA 1998, in relation to any act of a public authority which a court finds is unlawful, the court 'may grant such relief or remedy, or make such order, within its powers as it considers just and appropriate'. This relief may include an award of damages in respect of an unlawful act.

The relevance of the HRA 1998 to inquests

3.42 Two aspects of the HRA 1998 are of particular significance in an inquest context. The first is the guiding principle that it is 'unlawful for a public authority to act in manner which is incompatible with a Convention right', unless required to do so by the terms of primary legislation which cannot possibly be interpreted in any other way – see s 6(2). An act, for the purposes of s 6, includes a failure to act. In accordance with s 6(3)(a) the acts of all courts and tribunals in England and Wales, including coroners' courts, are bound by the HRA 1998.

3.43 The fact that the HRA 1998 binds only the acts of public authorities also has potential significance when it comes to the determination whether an Art 2 inquest is required or not. In such cases it will be necessary to determine whether a body responsible for the care of a deceased is a public authority under s 6 or not. The definition of a public authority under the HRA 1998 applies to 'any person of whose functions are of a public nature'[1] and not just to bodies that are governmental by constitution. The determining factor in this definition is whether the nature of the relevant function performed by the body was public[2]. Relevant factors include whether the body is exercising statutory authority, the degree of control of its activities by a state authority, the proximity of relationship between the private body and the delegating public authority, and the degree to which the body is 'enmeshed' in the activities of the public authority[3].

[1] HRA 1998, s 6(3)(b).
[2] *Parochial Church Council of Aston Cantlow v Wallbank* [2003] UKHL 37.
[3] *Poplar Housing and Regeneration Community Association v Donoghue* [2002] QB 48.

3.44 In *YL v Birmingham*[1] the House of Lords held, by a 3–2 majority, that a private care home, housing an 84-year-old dementia sufferer whose care was largely funded by the local authority under the National Assistance Act 1948, was nonetheless not a public authority for the purposes of s 6 HRA 1998. In *R (A) v Partnerships in Care*[2] a private provider of state funded mental healthcare was held to be performing public functions under s 6 of the HRA 1998.

[1] [2008] 1 AC 95.
[2] [2002] 1 WLR 2610.

3.45 The second aspect of the HRA 1998 that is particularly relevant to inquests is the obligation on domestic courts and tribunals under s 2 to 'take into account' any decision of the Strasbourg institutions which they consider relevant when determining a question which has arisen in connection with a Convention right. There is conflicting dicta at the highest level as to the content of the obligation imposed by s 2(1). In *R (Ullah) v Special Adjudicator*[1], Lord Bingham stated:

> 'It is of course open to member states to provide for rights more generous than those guaranteed by the Convention, but such provision should not be the product of interpretation of the Convention by national courts, since the meaning of the Convention should be uniform throughout the states party to it. The duty of national

3.45 Scope and Article 2 ECHR

courts is to keep pace with the Strasbourg jurisprudence as it evolves over time: no more, but certainly no less.'

[1] [2004] UKHL 26.

3.46 Lord Bingham's commentary has been referred to establishing the 'mirror principle'. In *R (Al-Skeini) v Secretary of State for Defence (The Redress Trust intervening)*[1], Lord Brown of Eaton-under-Heywood went further, remarking of Lord Bingham's comments in Ullah 'I would respectfully suggest that last sentence could as well have ended: "no less, but certainly no more"'[2].

[1] [2007] UKHL 26, [2008] 1 AC 153.
[2] At [106].

3.47 However, more recently in *D v Commissioner of the Police (Liberty and Others Intervening)*[1], Lords Mance and Kerr suggested that this is too conservative an approach. Lord Mance said[2]:

'There are however cases where the English courts can and should, as a matter of domestic law, go with confidence beyond existing Strasbourg authority . . . If the existence or otherwise of a Convention right is unclear, then it may be appropriate for domestic courts to make up their minds whether the Convention rights should or should not be understood to embrace it.'

[1] [2018] UKSC 11, [2019] AC 196.
[2] At [153].

3.48 Lord Kerr[1] emphasised that in cases following *Ullah* 'a departure from the mirror principle can be detected'. Rabone v Pennine Care Trust (INQUEST intervening)[2] provides an example of the Supreme Court extending the protection of Art 2 ECHR beyond that established by ECtHR authority at the time. Lord Kerr endorsed Lord Wilson's suggestion in *Moohan v Lord Advocate (Advocate General for Scotland Intervening)*[3] that:

'. . . where there is no directly relevant decision of the ECtHR with which it would be possible (even if appropriate) to keep pace, we can and must do more. We must determine for ourselves the existence or otherwise of an alleged Convention right ...'

[1] At [77].
[2] [2012] 2 AC 72.
[3] [2015] AC 901.

3.49 The question whether ECtHR authority should be followed according to a 'mirror principle' or whether it is open for English courts to expand the protection provided by the ECHR beyond Strasbourg authority is a matter of relevance in coroners' courts. It is commonplace for coroners to find themselves facing arguments from interested persons as to whether the investigative duty under Art 2 ECHR applies on a given set of facts: if it does, this widens the scope of the proceedings and the conclusions available to the court at the conclusion of proceedings. Therefore, the more broadly the English courts expand any ECHR protection, the more likely it is that a coroner will need to perform this additional investigative duty.

3.50 The HRA 1998 does not usually have retrospective effect. Generally only state acts or omissions following its coming into force on 2 October 2000 are justiciable under it[1]. However, the ECtHR has held that the investigative Art 2 duty is freestanding from the relevant death itself[2]. The principles governing the circumstances in which an Art 2-compliant investigation will be required into a death that occurred prior to 2 October 2000 were recently reviewed by the Supreme Court in *Re Finucane's Application for Judicial Review*[3].

[1] *Re McKerr* [2004] UKHL 12.
[2] *Janowiec v Russia* (2013) 58 EHRR 30, *Šilih v Slovenia* (2009) 49 EHRR 996.
[3] [2019] UKSC 7.

THE ECHR AND INQUESTS

Scope of Art 2 inquests

3.51 Section 5 of the CJA 2009 sets out the key questions a coroner must answer as part of the inquest (see 3.4 above). The words 'how and in what circumstances' in s 5(2) now provide the statutory gateway through which the investigative duty under Art 2 ECHR is imposed on coroners' courts. In England and Wales, save where a criminal prosecution intervenes or a public inquiry is established pursuant to the Inquiries Act 2005, a coroner's investigation and inquest is the means by which the state discharges its investigative Art 2 duty[1]. Indeed, in cases where there has been a prosecution arising from the death, an inquest may still be necessary as a criminal trial may not satisfy the requirements of the investigative duty. It probably will not investigate systemic failings, state failures to prevent a killing by a civilian, or involve the family of the deceased to a sufficient extent[2].

[1] *Middleton v HM Coroner for West Somerset* [2004] 1 AC 182 at [21].
[2] Thus in *R (Skelton) v Senior Coroner for West Sussex* [2020] EWHC 2813 (Admin) the Administrative Court ordered an Art 2 ECHR compliant inquest into the death of Susan Nicholson, where the coroner had conducted only a short inquest to record a conclusion of unlawful killing and the cause of death following the conviction of her killer for murder. The Administrative Court held an Art 2 inquest was required in order to investigate alleged police failings in the investigation of a previous victim of the murderer, and failures to protect Susan Nicholson prior to her death.

3.52 Whether Art 2 is engaged or not is often a strongly contested issue between properly interested persons at the pre-inquest review stage. It is not uncommon for it to be revisited in submissions at the close of the evidence prior to the conclusion stage, since Art 2 can become engaged (and will therefore need to be taken into consideration) at any stage of the proceedings.

3.53 Whilst s 5(2) states in simple terms the effect of the engagement of Art 2, the conditions necessary for the duty to apply – and its requirements – are not prescribed by the CJA 2009 and remain matters of ECHR law as interpreted by the ECtHR and domestic courts. As a result, it is necessary to consider Art 2 ECHR in some detail in this chapter.

3.54 Because the investigative duty is engaged where there has been an arguable breach of one of the substantive duties, the chapter will consider those first. The test for the engagement of the duty also means that it is not just inquest authorities, but authorities arising from civil claims for breach of Art 2, and applications to the ECtHR in respect of alleged substantive breaches more widely, that must be examined here.

3.55 *Scope and Article 2 ECHR*

ARTICLE 2 ECHR – THE RIGHT TO LIFE

3.55 Article 2 ECHR provides as follows:

> '1. Everyone's right to life shall be protected by law. No one shall be deprived of his life intentionally save in the execution of a sentence of a court following his conviction of a crime for which this penalty is provided by law.
>
> 2. Deprivation of life shall not be regarded as inflicted in contravention of this Article when it results from the use of force which is no more than absolutely necessary:
> (a) in defence of any person from unlawful violence;
> (b) in order to effect lawful arrest;
> (c) in action lawfully taken for the purpose of quelling a riot or insurrection.'

3.56 Article 2 ranks as one of the most fundamental provisions of the Convention and enshrines one of the basic values of the democratic societies making up the Council of Europe. It places a negative duty on the state not to intentionally take life, but also, by the first sentence of s 2(1), creates a positive duty to take appropriate steps to safeguard the lives of those within its jurisdiction[1]. The ECtHR produces a helpful guide on Art 2 which is regularly updated[2].

[1] *Osman v United Kingdom* (1998) 29 EHRR 245 at [115].
[2] See https://www.echr.coe.int/Documents/Guide_Art_2_ENG.pdf.

3.57 Article 2 does not confer a right to life that extends to foetuses in utero. In *Vo v France*[1] the Grand Chamber of the ECtHR held that, given the wide variance in the domestic law of contracting states as to the point of commencement of life, the determination of the point at which life begins is a matter which falls within states' margin of appreciation[2].

[1] (2005) 40 EHRR 12.
[2] For the consideration of the definition of human life in domestic law; see CHAPTER 6 regarding stillbirths.

3.58 Article 2 protects citizens from risks to life; individuals whose lives have been put at serious risk as a result of an Art 2 violation may be victims for the purposes of Art 34 of the Convention (and therefore s 7 HRA 1998) – *Pankov v Bulgaria*[1]. The investigative duty may therefore also be triggered by a situation where there was a risk to, as opposed to loss of, life. Such investigations would of course have to be undertaken outside the coronial jurisdiction. In *R (L (A Patient) v Secretary of State for Justice (Equality and Human Rights Commission Intervening)*[2] the House of Lords considered the circumstances in which it is necessary to hold an Art 2 compliant inquiry into the attempted suicide of a young person in custody.

[1] 12773/03, 7 October 2010.
[2] [2008] UKHL 68, [2009] 1 AC 588.

3.59 In the Supreme Court in *Rabone* Lord Dyson held[1] that the duties arising from Art 2 can be broken down as follows:

(1) A **negative duty** not to take life save in the exceptional circumstances set out in Art 2(2).
(2) **Positive substantive duties** to protect life 'in certain circumstances' as follows:

(a) The **general substantive duty** to protect life (also referred to as the systems, or framework, duty), which requires the state to put in place a legislative and administrative framework which protects the right to life. That includes the need for criminal and civil laws and an effective law enforcement and judicial system, including a system that investigates death. It also includes obligations in the public health sphere, requiring states to make regulations compelling hospitals, whether public or private, to adopt appropriate measures for the protection of patients' lives[2].

(b) The **operational duty** to take preventative measures to protect individuals in specific circumstances (eg those in state detention) from a 'real and immediate' risk to life where the state knows, or ought to know, of that risk[3].

(3) A procedural positive duty to investigate deaths which may arguably amount to a breach of any of the substantive obligations (ie the negative duty, the systemic duty, or the operative duty). This is referred to as the **investigative or procedural duty**.

[1] [2012] 2 AC 72 at [12].
[2] *Tarariyeva v Russia* (2009) 48 EHRR 26 at [73].
[3] *Osman v UK* (1998) 29 EHRR 245.

3.60 This framework will be adopted in this chapter. However, readers should note that the boundaries between the different substantive positive obligations are not always clearly drawn, particularly in the Strasbourg jurisprudence. For present purposes, the terms systemic, operational, and investigative will be used.

The negative duty

3.61 The negative duty on the state and employees or agents of the state to refrain from taking life is subject to the exceptions set out in Art 2(2) ECHR:

'2. Deprivation of life shall not be regarded as inflicted in contravention of this article when it results from the use of force which is no more than absolutely necessary:
(a) in defence of any person from unlawful violence;
(b) in order to effect a lawful arrest or to prevent the escape of a person lawfully detained;
(c) in action lawfully taken for the purpose of quelling a riot or insurrection.'

3.62 A police officer, for example, will not therefore act in breach of Art 2 if they kill someone using force which was 'no more than absolutely necessary' in defence of themselves or of another.

3.63 It is not unusual for inquests to investigate deaths caused directly by the use of lethal force deployed by employees or agents of the state. Such inquests will always have to be Art 2 compliant. Where no criminal prosecution takes place, such violent deaths are likely to be investigated, and the Art 2 investigative duty satisfied, at inquest. Readers are referred to the chapter on conclusions for the law on the potentially relevant conclusions of unlawful killing, neglect, and the requirements of the investigative duty vis-a-vis conclusions.

3.64 However, because the court would have to conduct a thorough inquiry and to consider a conclusion of unlawful killing (which in itself entails a decision as to whether an English homicide offence has been committed) in any event, the role of the negative duty in regulating the content of the proceedings is limited. As a result, the relevance of the substantive law relating to the negative duty under Art 2 to the inquest process is generally restricted to the *compatibility* of English criminal law with the Convention.

3.65 The exceptions in Art 2(2) are not exclusively concerned with intentional killing. They describe situations in which it is permitted to use force which may result in unintended death[1]. Because of the fundamental nature of the right to life, the circumstances in which deprivation of life may be justified as absolutely necessary under Art 2(2) must be strictly construed[2]. In *McCann v United Kingdom*[3], which concerned the killing of three members of the Provisional IRA by British security forces in Gibraltar, the Grand Chamber of the ECtHR held that the lethal use of force by state agents must be subject to careful scrutiny, particularly where it is used deliberately. This should take into account the considerations not only of the direct perpetrators but all the surrounding circumstances including matters such as the planning and control of the operation[4]. The force used by a state agent must be strictly proportionate to the achievement of the relevant aim under Art 2(2). 'Absolutely necessary' under Art 2(2) therefore carries a higher threshold test of necessity than that of being 'necessary in a democratic society' imposed under the second paragraphs of the qualified rights established in Arts 8–11[5].

[1] *McCann v United Kingdom* (App No 18984/91) (1996) 21 EHRR 97, 27 September 1995 at [148].
[2] *Andonicou and Constantinou v Cyprus* (1998) 25 EHRR 20 at [171], [181], [186], [192], [193].
[3] (App No 18984/91) (1996) 21 EHRR 97, 27 September 1995.
[4] (1996) 21 EHRR 97 at [150].
[5] (1996) 21 EHRR 97 at [149].

3.66 In *McCann* it was further held that the Art 2(2) justifications may be made out where they are based on 'an honest belief which is perceived, for good reasons, to be valid at the time but which subsequently turns out to be mistaken'[1]. To impose a stricter duty would place an unrealistic burden on the state and its agents in the execution of their duties.

[1] (1996) 21 EHRR 97 at [200].

3.67 The notion of 'an honest belief' was relevant in *Da Silva v United Kingdom*[1], where the ECtHR considered the case of Jean Charles de Menezes, who was shot dead by police officers following the 2005 London bombings but was subsequently proved to have no connection with the attacks. The family brought ECtHR proceedings arguing that the UK had failed to ensure accountability for Mr De Menezes' death because there was no prosecution arising from the death. Amongst other things, the court considered the honest belief element of the self-defence test in English criminal law. It concluded that this test, which concentrates on the subjective honest belief of the defendant and only considers the reasonableness of such a belief in cases where that is necessary, is compatible with Art 2(2). The ECtHR rejected the submission by the applicants that an objective standard of reasonableness should apply to the *McCann*, honest belief test[2]. Rather, in assessing whether a belief was honestly held, the court 'will have to consider whether the belief was subjectively reasonable, having regard to the circumstances that pertained at the relevant time', as is consistent with English criminal law[3].

[1] (App No 5878/08) (2016) 63 EHRR 12, 30 March 2016.
[2] (2016) 63 EHRR 12 at [245]–[246].
[3] (2016) 63 EHRR 12 at [248].

3.68 In *R (Duggan) v North London Assistant Deputy Coroner*[1] the Court of Appeal applied the decision in *Da Silva*, and held that when self-defence is raised at an inquest, Art 2 does not **require** the jury to be directed that in deciding whether a belief is honestly and genuinely held, the objective reasonableness of that belief is a relevant consideration. Such a direction should not be given unless really necessary in a case where such reasonableness is in issue. Similarly, the court established that there is no requirement for the coroner or jury to reach a conclusion as to whether such a death was lawful according to the different self defence test under civil law in *Ashley v Chief Constable of Sussex Police*[2] (in which consideration of the reasonableness of belief *is mandatory*). Inquests are not concerned with civil liability and there is no necessary obligation under the investigative Art 2 duty to investigate a breach of the civil law[3].

[1] [2017] EWCA Civ 142.
[2] [2008] 1 AC 962.
[3] [2017] EWCA Civ 142 at [94].

3.69 In respect of Art 2(2)(b), the Grand Chamber of the ECtHR emphasised in *Nachova v Bulgaria*[1], that as a legitimate aim, effecting lawful arrest can only justify putting human life at risk in circumstances of absolute necessity. That test is not satisfied if it is 'known that the person arrested poses no threat to life or limb and is not suspected of having committed a violent offence' even if refraining from lethal force leads to the opportunity to arrest being lost[2].

[1] (App Nos 43577/98 and 43579/98) (2006) 42 EHRR 43, 6 July 2005.
[2] [2017] EWCA Civ 142 at [95].

THE POSITIVE SUBSTANTIVE DUTIES

The systemic duty

3.70 The positive obligation to take all appropriate steps to safeguard life for the purposes of Art 2 'entails above all a primary duty on the on the state to put in place a legislative and administrative framework designed to provide effective deterrence against threats to the right to life'[1]. Article 2 therefore requires the establishment and maintenance of 'a framework of laws, precautions, procedures and means of enforcement which will, to the greatest extent reasonably practicable, protect life[2].

[1] *Öneryildiz v Turkey* (2005) 41 EHRR 20 at [89].
[2] *R (Gentle) v Prime Minister* [2008] AC 1356 at [5]–[7], per Lord Bingham.

3.71 In *Middleton*, Lord Bingham emphasised that 'it would not promote the object of the Convention' if English law were to distinguish, in respect of the engagement of the investigative duty, between cases where state agents used lethal force and those 'in which a defective system operated by the state may

3.71 *Scope and Article 2 ECHR*

have failed to afford adequate protection to human life'[1]. However, that tells us little about the kind of systemic state failing which will result in a breach of the systemic duty. Areas where the courts have established that failings breach the systemic duty include:

(a) Dangerous activities and natural hazards.
(b) Certain mental health patients.
(c) Prisoners and certain detainees.
(d) Military operations.
(e) Some instances of general clinical care.

[1] [2004] UKHL 10 at [19].

(a) Dangerous activities and natural hazards

3.72 In *Öneryildiz*[1], the Grand Chamber of the ECHR considered the general duty in the context of the accidental death of a family who lived in slum housing close to a municipal waste site. A methane explosion on the site engulfed the housing causing the deaths of nine members of the applicant's family. The Grand Chamber held that the general duty applies in the context of any activity, whether public or not, in which the right to life may be at stake. It applies a fortiori in the case of industrial activities, which are by their nature dangerous. In the case of dangerous activities, special emphasis must be placed by the state on establishing regulations geared to the protection of lives from relevant potential risks[2]. The Grand Chamber also placed emphasis on the public's right to information regarding relevant risks to life[3].

[1] (2005) 41 EHRR 20.
[2] (2005) 41 EHRR 20 at [90].
[3] (2005) 41 EHRR 20 at [90].

3.73 As to the choice of particular practical measures, the ECtHR has consistently held that where the state is required to take positive measures, it is generally up to that state to decide how they do so. There are different avenues to ensure Convention rights, and even if the state has failed to apply one particular measure provided by domestic law, it may still fulfil its positive duty by other means[1].

[1] *Kolyadenko v Russia* (2013) 56 EHRR 2 at [160].

3.74 Whenever a state undertakes or organises dangerous activities, or authorises them, it must ensure through a system of rules and through sufficient control that the risk is reduced to a reasonable minimum[1]. If nevertheless damage arises, it will only amount to a breach of the State's positive obligations if it was due to insufficient regulation or insufficient control, but not if the damage was caused through the negligent conduct of an individual or a concatenation of unfortunate events[2].

[1] *Mucibabic' v Serbia* (App No 31963/08), 22 January 2013 at [126].
[2] *Stoyanovi v Bulgaria* (App No 42980/04), 9 November 2010 at [61].

3.75 In *Budayeva v Russia*[1] the town in which Budayeva lived was prone to mudslides. The authorities had been advised to repair the mudslide defences and to establish observation posts to alert civilians in the event of a mudslide. However, those measures were not implemented. A mudslide took place at night with no advance warning by the authorities. The ECtHR held that the margin of appreciation afforded to the state in the choice of means as to how it fulfilled its positive obligation with regard to natural disasters was wider than in respect of manmade dangerous activities. Similarly, the principle that an impossible or disproportionate burden must not be imposed on the authorities without consideration being given to the operational choices which they must make in terms of priorities and resources in difficult social and technical spheres must be afforded even greater weight in such cases[2].

[1] (App No 15339/02) (2014) 14 EHRR 2.
[2] (2014) 14 EHRR 2 at [128]–[137].

3.76 In assessing whether there has been a breach of the general duty, the court must consider the circumstances of the case, and amongst other things the domestic legality of the state's acts or omissions, the domestic decision-making process (including appropriate investigations and studies), and the complexity of the issue. In emergency relief cases involving the mitigation of the risk to life from natural hazards, there is likely to be a breach where those factors point to a hazard that was identifiable, especially where it concerned a recurring calamity affecting a distinct area developed for human habitation or use. The scope of the positive obligations in a given case depend on the origin of the threat and the extent to which one or the other risk is susceptible to mitigation[1].

[1] (2014) 14 EHRR 2 at [136]–[137].

3.77 Applying these principles, the ECtHR found a breach of the general duty in *Budayeva*. The authorities had left mudslide defences in a state of disrepair after a previous slide. The slides were natural events. The government had given no reasons why appropriate steps had not been taken to restore those defences or to set up observation posts. In those circumstances, the authorities ought to have acknowledged the increased risk of accidents in the event of a mudslide and to show all possible diligence in informing civilians and making arrangements for emergency evacuation. There was a failure to maintain a defence and warning infrastructure[1].

[1] (2014) 14 EHRR 2 at [147]–[151].

3.78 The state's duty to safeguard the right to life also involves the taking of reasonable measures to ensure the safety of individuals in public places[1]. It further extends to regulation and systems in workplaces in some circumstances, and has been strictly applied. In *Brincat v Malta*[2], the Maltese authorities' failure to provide adequate protection to ship workers exposed to asbestos, such as face masks, breached the framework and operational duties. In *Binisan v Romania*[3], the applicant suffered 70 per cent burns following negligent coordination of railway goods inspections. Despite the existence of regulations, the company being fined and the prosecution of the railway manager, the ECtHR held that the state did not 'display due diligence' in protecting Binisan's right to life and that the domestic legal system failed to provide an adequate response.

[1] *Banel v Lithuania* (App No 14326/11), 18 June 2013.
[2] (App No 60908/11), 24 October 2014.
[3] (App No 39438/05), 13 October 2014.

3.79 *Scope and Article 2 ECHR*

(b) Certain mental health patients

3.79 In *R (Takoushis) v Inner London Coroner and Another*[1], a schizophrenic patient was taken to an accident and emergency department by a member of the public having been found apparently about to jump from a bridge. The hospital operated an emergency mental health triage system under which he should have been seen by a doctor within 10 minutes. A doctor did not arrive for some 40 minutes by which time the patient had left. After leaving the hospital the patient took his own life by jumping from the bridge. The coroner found that there was no systemic failure at the hospital. The Court of Appeal in quashing the verdict held that there was no evidential basis on which he could have made such a finding, and that the possibility of a systemic failing should have been fully investigated in order to comply with the investigative Art 2 duty in any event[2]. See CHAPTER 15 for further detail of inquests touching on the deaths of individuals with mental health difficulties.

[1] [2005] EWCA Civ 1440, [2006] 1 WLR 461.
[2] [2005] EWCA Civ 1440, [2006] 1 WLR 461 at [52].

(c) Prisoners and detainees

3.80 Article 2 imposes a duty on prison authorities to put in place 'systemic precautions' against suicide in prison – *R (L (A Patient) v Secretary of State for Justice (Equality and Human Rights Commission Intervening)*[1]. Every time a suicide 'occurs in a prison the effectiveness of the system is called into question'[2]. In *R (Lewis) v Mid and North Shropshire Coroner*[3], a case investigating the suicide of a prisoner, Sedley LJ in the Court of Appeal emphasised that where death occurs in state custody, the purposes of an Art 2 investigation include ensuring that any shortcomings in the operation of the system are ascertained. In Lewis, failings relating to the training of officers in suicide prevention and first aid and the provision of equipment were held to be required to be recognised in order to satisfy the investigative duty, although it would have been sufficient to do so through the provision of a rule 43 report (the precursor to a report to prevent future deaths under reg 28 of the Coroners (Investigation) Regulations 2013)[4]. See CHAPTER 14 for further detail of inquests touching on the deaths of people in custody and state detention.

[1] [2008] UKHL 68, [2009] 1 AC 588 at [39].
[2] *R (Sacker) v West Yorkshire Coroner* [2004] UKHL 11, [2004] 1 WLR 796 at [11] per Lord Hope.
[3] [2009] EWCA Civ 1403, [2010] 1 WLR 1836.
[4] See CHAPTER 14 regarding prisoners and inquests, and CHAPTER 7 regarding reports to prevent future deaths.

(d) Military operations

3.81 In *Smith and Another v Ministry of Defence*[1], the families of soldiers killed on active duty in Iraq brought systemic and operational claims under the HRA 1998 and claims in negligence relating to failures in the provision of protective equipment (armoured land rovers). Lord Hope stated that although an unrealistic or disproportionate burden should not be imposed on the state in planning and conducting military operations, the court 'must give effect to [the Art 2] obligations where it would be reasonable to expect the individual

The positive substantive duties **3.83**

to be afforded the protection of the Article'. It 'will be easy to find that the allegations are beyond the reach of Article 2' if decisions about training, procurement or operations 'were at a high level of command and closely linked to the exercise of political judgment and issues of policy'[2]. The same would apply the closer the decisions were to actual conflict on the ground. However, there was a middle ground where claims could be properly brought. No 'hard and fast' rules can be laid down, and each case must be assessed on its own facts[3]. See CHAPTER 19 regarding deaths involving the military.

[1] [2013] UKSC 41, [2014] AC 42.
[2] [2013] UKSC 41 at [72].
[3] [2013] UKSC 41 at [76].

3.82 By contrast, civilians who had not undertaken the obligations and risk associated with life in the military should be afforded greater protection by the Convention[1]. The court provided little guidance on the distinction between systemic and operational claims, but did hold that the former 'could extend to issues about training and the procurement of equipment' before forces are deployed on operations. The Court of Appeal in *R (Long) v Secretary of State for Defence*[2], applied *Smith*, and held that a control system failure in relation to an order to provide soldiers with iridium phones fell into Lord Hope's middle ground, and therefore arguably constituted a breach of Art 2 (although the appeal was nevertheless dismissed as the investigative positive duty had already been discharged on the facts)[3].

[1] [2013] UKSC 41 at [71].
[2] [2015] EWCA Civ 770, [2015] 1 WLR 5006.
[3] See CHAPTER 19 for inquests involving the military.

(e) Systemic disfunction in general clinical care

3.83 Article 2 has limited effect in cases where a death has arisen as a result of clinical care (which is not mental health care) provided to the deceased: it has long been clear that 'casual acts of negligence by members of [clinical] staff'[1], 'error[s] of judgment', and 'negligent coordination among health professionals'[2] will not give rise to a breach of Art 2. Further clarity was offered by the decisions of the Grand Chamber of the ECtHR in *Lopes de Sousa Fernandes v Portugal*[3] and the High Court in *R (Parkinson) v Kent Senior Coroner*[4]. A breach of the substantive framework limb of Art 2 in this context will now only arise in two 'exceptional circumstances', namely:

'i. Where an individual's life is knowingly put in danger by denial of access to life-saving emergency treatment . . . [this] does not extend to circumstances where a patient is considered to have received deficient, incorrect or delayed treatment;
ii. Where a systemic or structural dysfunction in hospital services results in a patient being deprived of access to life-saving emergency treatment and:
   a. The authorities knew about or ought to have known about that risk; and
   b. [They] failed to undertake the necessary measures to prevent that risk from materialising, thus putting the patients' lives, including the life of the particular patient concerned, in danger[5].'

[1] *Savage v South Essex Partnership NHS Foundation Trust (MIND Intervening)* [2009] AC 681 at [45], per Lord Rodger.
[2] *Powell v UK* (App No 45305/99) [2000] ECHR 703, 30 EHRR CD 362 (4 May 2000) at [364].

3.83 *Scope and Article 2 ECHR*

[3] (2018) 66 EHRR 28.
[4] [2018] 4 WLR 106.
[5] (2018) 66 EHRR 28 at [195] (line breaks added for clarity).

3.84 It is clear that courts should be careful to distinguish between a genuine objective systemic issue and what may be a tragic series of individual errors[1]. In *R (Humberstone) v Legal Services Commission (Lord Chancellor intervening)*[2] the Court of Appeal held that evidence that an ambulance service was under-provisioned and/or had inappropriate operational systems was enough to engage the investigative duty on the basis of an arguable systemic breach. Smith LJ emphasised that 'it will be necessary for care to be taken to ensure that allegations of individual negligence are not dressed up as systemic failures but, provided that this possibility is always borne in mind, the appropriate conclusion should not be elusive'[3].

[1] (2018) 66 EHRR 28 at [195].
[2] [2010] EWCA Civ 1479, [2011] 1 WLR 1460.
[3] [2010] EWCA Civ 1479, [2011] 1 WLR 1460 at [71].

3.85 Allegations of gross negligence manslaughter against health professionals have been treated differently by English courts.

3.86 A case involving an allegation of gross negligence manslaughter against a servant or servants of the state falls in the middle of the spectrum that extends from allegations of deliberate killing by a servant of the state to allegations of plain negligence by such servants[1].

[1] *R (Khan) v Secretary of State for Health* [2004] 1 WLR 971 at [67], citing *Amin* [2004] 1 AC 653, see also see *R (Takoushis) v Inner London North Coroner and Another* [2006] 1 WLR 461 at [96].

3.87 In *Khan* the Court of Appeal held that a serious allegation of gross negligence manslaughter in a general clinical case meant that Art 2 was engaged and that a police investigation which did not result in a prosecution was insufficient for the investigative duty to be discharged. It should be noted that *Khan* and *Takoushis* pre-date the decision of the Grand Chamber decision in *Lopes de Sousa*, where the ECtHR held that the existence of *recourse* to criminal law is required by the general duty where the fault of medical professionals goes beyond mere fault or negligence[1], but did not go so far as to suggest that such a death would entail a breach in itself. See CHAPTER 13 for further details of inquests considering medical/clinical decisions.

[1] (2018) 66 EHRR 28 at [215] and [223]–[224].

The operational duty

3.88 The positive operational duty to protect life under Art 2 ECHR was first recognised by the ECtHR in *Osman v United Kingdom*[1]. In *Osman* a teacher became obsessed with a pupil and embarked upon a campaign of harassing behaviour that culminated in a shooting incident in which the student was injured and his father was killed. The family's civil claim was dismissed by the Court of Appeal which held that there was no operational duty on the police in civil negligence to protect victims from the violent acts of third parties. The family applied to the ECtHR, which held that in addition to the systemic duty, in 'certain well-defined circumstances' Art 2 places states under an obligation to take preventative operational measures to protect individuals. Although the ECtHR dismissed the application in *Osman* on its facts as not giving rise to a substantive Art 2 breach, it confirmed the existence and scope of the duty. Given the complexities and difficulties of policing modern societies, that duty should not be interpreted in a way that imposes an impossible or disproportionate burden on the authorities[2]: this remains a key part of the legal test. Although the range of factual circumstances in which the operational duty has been applied by the ECtHR and domestic courts has expanded significantly since *Osman*, the essential legal structure of the duty remains as stated by the court in 1998. It must be established that:

(a) the authorities knew or ought to have known;
    (i) of a real and immediate risk to the life of an identified individual or individuals;
    (ii) from the criminal acts of a third party (or a different relevant risk to life in other cases in which the duty applies as set out below); and
(b) the authorities failed to take measures within the scope of their powers which, judged reasonably, might have been expected to avoid that risk[3].

[1] (1998) ECHR 101, (1998) 29 EHRR 245.
[2] *Osman v United Kingdom* (1998) ECHR 101, (1998) 29 EHRR 245 at [116].
[3] *Osman v United Kingdom* (1998) ECHR 101, (1998) 29 EHRR 245 at [116].

3.89 The operational duty applies to real and immediate risks to life from the criminal acts of third parties generally. Note that no higher standard of protection is required simply by virtue of the fact that an individual is a prosecution witness in a criminal case[1].

[1] *Van Colle v Chief Constable of Hertfordshire Police* [2009] 1 AC 226.

3.90 In order to establish a 'real' risk, a 'substantial or significant and not a remote or fanciful one' is sufficient[1]. In *Rabone* a 5 per cent risk of suicide rising to 20 per cent was held to be 'low to moderate (but nevertheless, significant)' at first instance and therefore 'real'. Immediate means 'present and continuing'[2]. The Supreme Court held that the risk posed by the deceased had been sufficient to reach that threshold. Further, the risk must be to life rather than harm, even serious harm[3].

[1] [2009] AC 681 at [38].
[2] [2009] AC 681 at [39].
[3] *R (Skelton) v Senior Coroner for West Sussex and Others* [2020] EWHC 2813 (Admin) at [53.iii] citing *G4S and Care and Justices Services Ltd v Kent County Council* [2019] EWHC 1648 (QB) at [74]-[75] and *R (Kent county Council) v HM Coroner for the County of Kent* [2012] EWHC 2768 (Admin) at [44]-[47].

3.91 The threshold for a breach of the operational duty is high[1]. In *Savage* Lord Rodger stated that it would be harder to establish than mere negligence, although in *Rabone*, Lord Dyson stated that Lord Rodger's observation should be seen in the context of it being sufficient to show in negligence that a risk was reasonably foreseeable[2]. It is not because the assessment of the reasonableness

3.91 *Scope and Article 2 ECHR*

of the actions of the state has a different quality to that involved in establishing negligence[3].

[1] *Savage v South Essex Partnership NHS Foundation Trust (MIND Intervening)* [2009] AC 681 at [41], [66].
[2] [2009] AC 681 at [37].
[3] *R (Skelton) v Senior Coroner for West Sussex and Others* [2020] EWHC 2813 (Admin) at [53(v)].

3.92 Since *Osman* the applicability of the operational duty has been significantly expanded by the domestic courts and ECtHR to cover the following cases. This list does not purport to be exhaustive. Readers may find the ECtHR's Guide to Art 2 a further helpful resource in identifying the scope of the factual circumstances to which the duty applies:

(a) Prisoners whose lives are at risk from the acts of fellow prisoners[1].
(b) Prisoners at risk of suicide or self-harm[2].
(c) The untimely provision of adequate non-mental health clinical care inside prison and the arrangement of clinical care outside prison for prisoners[3]. However, there is no breach of the duty where a prisoner dies of natural causes in detention in circumstances where there were no arguable clinical failures. There is accordingly no obligation to hold an Art 2 compliant inquest in such a case[4]. There is also no arguable breach where a prisoner receives negligent clinical care from services outside of detention – the state's duty in such cases extends to the arrangement of such services only[5].
(d) Detained mental health patients who are at risk of suicide[6].
(e) Voluntary mental health inpatients. The Grand Chamber of the ECtHR confirmed in *Fernandes Oliveira v Portugal*[7] that there is a 'general operational duty with respect to voluntary psychiatric patients'[8]. A 'general' operational duty in respect of such patients may appear to widen the application of the duty beyond the Supreme Court's decision in *Rabone v Pennine Care Trust (INQUEST and others intervening)*[9], where it was held by the Supreme Court to apply to a voluntary psychiatric inpatient on leave when there has been a sufficient assumption of control over the individual by the state. However, in *Oliveira* the Grand Chamber emphasised that 'the specific measures required will depend on the particular circumstances of the case, and those specific circumstances will often differ depending on whether the patient is voluntarily or involuntarily hospitalised'[10]. In the case of detained patients, 'the court, of its own assessment, may apply a stricter standard of scrutiny'[11].
(f) Military conscripts at risk of suicide[12].
(g) Military conscripts undertaking dangerous training exercises such as parachuting[13].
(h) Military operations within the ECHR's jurisdiction which fall into the 'middle ground' discussed by Lord Hope in *Smith and Another v Ministry of Defence*[14].
(i) The transfer of vulnerable and frail elderly residents between care homes (although the ECtHR dismissed the application in this case as not amounting to a breach of the duty on its facts)[15].
(j) Hospitals, orphanages or care homes where particularly vulnerable persons are under the care of the state in some circumstances, in

The positive substantive duties **3.92**

particular where a death arises from a person being kept in appalling conditions, or where there is a shortage of staff or medication, including where the state is aware of those allegations[16]. However, the Court of Appeal in *Maguire* set out that where there is no connection between the cause of death and the reasons why the Art 2 duty to protect has arisen, there will be no breach[17]: in *Maguire* a vulnerable woman detained in a care home under the deprivation of liberty safeguards under the Mental Capacity Act 2005 (DoLS) by reason of her being unable to care for herself died as a result of a medical condition unrelated to the reasons why she was detained. Her death was held to be due to medical negligence only. There was therefore no arguable breach and no requirement for an Art 2 inquest to be held.

(k) Risks to the lives of citizens from industrial activities carried out by the state, which by their nature are deemed to be dangerous – see the judgment of the Grand Chamber of the ECtHR in *Öneryildiz v Turkey*[18] referred to above, where a breach of the operational as well as the general duty was found.

(l) Risks to life from environmental disasters over which the state has no control, although in such situations the duty to take operational measures is limited to the arrangement of preventative operational measures designed to maximise the state's capacity to deal with such phenomena[19].

(m) A failure to provide adequate protection to ship workers exposed to asbestos, including face masks, breached both the systemic and operational duties[20].

[1] *Edwards v United Kingdom* (2002) 35 EHRR 19.
[2] *Keenan v United Kingdom* (2002) 35 EHRR 487.
[3] *Daniel v St George's Healthcare NHS Trust* [2016] EWHC 23 (QB), [2016] 4 WLR 32 at [22]–[29]; *Tarariyeva v Russia* (2006) 48 EHRR 609, *Kats v Ukraine* (2010) 51 EHRR 44.
[4] *R (Tyrell) v HM Senior Coroner for County Durham and Darlington* [2016] EWHC 1892 (Admin).
[5] *Maguire* at [51].
[6] *Savage v South Essex Partnership NHS Foundation Trust (MIND and others intervening)* [2008] UKHL 74, [2009] 1 AC 681.
[7] (2019) 69 EHRR 8.
[8] (2019) 69 EHRR 8 at [124].
[9] [2012] UKSC 2, [2012] 2 AC 72.
[10] (2019) 69 EHRR 8 at [124].
[11] (2019) 69 EHRR 8 at [124].
[12] *Kiliç v Turkey* (App No 40145/98), 7 June 2005, unreported.
[13] *Stoyanovi v Bulgaria* (App No 42980/04), 9 November 2010 at [61].
[14] [2014] AC 42 at [76].
[15] *Watts v United Kingdom* (2010) 51 EHRR SE 66.
[16] *R (Maguire) v HM Senior Coroner for Blackpool & Flyde* [2020] EWCA Civ 738. See *Nencheva v Bulgaria* (App No 48606/06), 18 June 2013, ECtHR and *Câmpeanu v Romania* (App No 47848/08), 17 July 2014, ECtHR, Grand Chamber.
[17] [2020] EWCA Civ 738 at [96].
[18] (2005) 41 EHRR 20.
[19] *M Özel and Others v Turkey* (App No 14350/05), 2 May 2016, *Budayeva v Russia* (App No 15339/02) (2014) 14 EHRR 2.
[20] *Brincat v Malta* (App No 60908/11), 24 October 2014. Again, this engaged both the systemic and operational duties.

3.93 *Scope and Article 2 ECHR*

Features of the operational duty

3.93 In *R (Maguire) v HM Senior Coroner for Blackpool & Flyde*[1], the Court of Appeal established that the 'fact that an operational duty to protect life exists does not lead to the conclusion that for all purposes the death of a person owed that duty is to be judged by Article 2 standards'[2]. The 'unifying feature of the application' of the operational duty is state responsibility[3].

[1] [2020] EWCA Civ 738.
[2] [2020] EWCA Civ 738 at [74].
[3] [2020] EWCA Civ 738 at [72].

3.94 As can be seen from the above categories and examples, the ECHR places a particular emphasis on the protection of mentally ill persons at risk from self-harm, who it considers to be a particularly vulnerable category[1].

[1] See in particular *Fernandes Oliveira v Portugal* (2019) 69 EHRR 8 at [113].

3.95 Submissions at inquests can often focus on the dangers of assessing the conduct of state employees or agents with hindsight, but in *Van Colle v Chief Constable of Hertfordshire Police*[1], Lord Bingham emphasised that the test for whether the operational duty applies includes not just what the authorities knew, but what they ought to have known:

> 'Thus stupidity, lack of imagination and inertia do not afford an excuse to a national authority which reasonably ought, in the light of what it knew or was told, to make further inquiries or investigations: it is then to be treated as knowing what such further inquiries or investigations would have elicited[2].'

[1] [2009] 1 AC 226.
[2] [2009] 1 AC 226 at [32].

3.96 In *Rabone* Lord Dyson observed that the jurisprudence of the operational duty is young and that the ECtHR has tended to expand its remit[1]. In *Rabone*, the key factor militating towards the recognition of the duty was the control assumed by the state over the patient. Lord Dyson observed that 'in circumstances of sufficient vulnerability, the ECtHR has been prepared to find a breach of the operational duty even where there has been no assumption of control by the state'[2]. He gave the example of the protection of children from abuse in *Z v UK*[3] in the context of Art 3 ECHR.

[1] [2012] 2 AC 72 at [25].
[2] [2012] 2 AC 72 at [23].
[3] (2001) 34 EHRR 97.

3.97 However, in *Maguire* the Court of Appeal held that the vulnerability of a care home resident subject to DoLS was not **in itself** sufficient to engage the duty, where there was no correlation between the purpose for which the duty to protect was imposed and the nature of the subsequent alleged failure to protect life. A further example of the limits of the investigative obligation is *R (Kent County Council), HM Coroner for Kent*[1]1, where the High Court held that a local authority was not under an operational duty to protect the life of a 14-year-old boy assessed as being in need within the meaning of s 17 of the Children Act 1989, who was known to be vulnerable and at risk of harm. A risk of harm is insufficient to engage the duty, and despite the existence of the s 17 duty, it would not be proportionate to require a local authority to exercise sufficient control over such children so as an operational duty was engaged in every case. In *R (Lee) v HM Assistant Coroner for Sunderland and Others*[2], the High Court held that the coroner had not adequately considered the relevant evidence and law on the question of whether an extension of the law beyond *Rabone* was required in a case involving the suicide of a young person at high risk and under community mental health care. The court made no finding as to whether the operational duty should have been expanded, but emphasised the relevance of the 'threefold factors of assumed responsibility, vulnerability, and risk' to the assessment[3]. The matter was remitted back to the assistant coroner for a further fact-finding process to take place.

[1] [2012] EWHC 2768 (Admin).
[2] [2019] EWHC 3227 (Admin).
[3] [2019] EWHC 3227 (Admin) at [30], [38].

The investigative duty

3.98 The essential purpose of an Art 2 investigation is to secure the effective implementation of the domestic laws which protect the right to life, and in those cases involving state agents or bodies, to ensure their accountability for deaths occurring under their responsibility[1].

[1] *Jordan v United Kingdom* (2003) 37 EHRR 2, 4 May 2001 at [105].

3.99 Although from the Strasbourg Court's perspective the investigative duty may be satisfied in many different procedural ways, in England and Wales, save where a criminal prosecution intervenes or a public inquiry is ordered into a major accident, a CJA 2009 investigation and inquest is essentially the means by which it is discharged by the state[1]. An Art 2 inquest must, therefore, comply with the requirements of that duty[2]. There must be 'a full investigation of any death involving or possibly involving a violation of the state's substantive obligation to protect human life arising under Art 2 (essentially whenever state agents or bodies may bear responsibility for the death)'[3]. Although the active lethal use of force by state agents is a matter of great seriousness and will always engage the investigative duty, a systemic **failure** to protect human life may call for an investigation which may be no less important and perhaps even more complex[4].

[1] *Middleton v HM Coroner for West Somerset* [2004] 2 AC 182 at [21].
[2] [2004] 2 AC 182 at [21].
[3] *R (on the application of Hurst) v Northern District of London Coroner* [2007] UKHL 13, [2007] 2 WLR 726 at [28].
[4] *R (on the application of Amin) v Secretary of State for Home Dept* [2003] UKHL 51, [2004] 1 AC 653 at [21].

3.100 The compatibility of the inquest system with the investigative duty was considered by the House of Lords in a series of cases in the 2000s following the enactment of the HRA 1998[1]. As a result of those cases and the reforms of the CJA 2009, the role of inquests in fulfilling the procedural duty is well established: there can be no question that the system itself is compatible with the duty and capable of its discharge in full in cases which do not require a public inquiry or a criminal investigation or prosecution. However, it remains possible that decisions by individual coroners, for instance as to whether an issue is in scope, or whether certain evidence should be called, will breach the duty, potentially paving the way for judicial review proceedings.

[1] *Middleton v HM Coroner for West Somerset* [2004] 2 AC 182 at [21], *Sacker v HM Coroner for West Yorkshire* [2004] UKHL 11, *R (on the application of Hurst) v Northern District of London Coroner* [2007] UKHL 13, [2007] 2 WLR 726.

3.101 What follows here is only to intended to set out some of the basic principles which may be most relevant in the inquest forum. It should be remembered that, as observed by Brooke LJ in *R (Khan) v Secretary of State for Health*[1] 'what is required by way of an investigation cannot be reduced to a catechism of rules; a flexible approach is needed, responsive to the dictates of the facts, case by case'. The conclusions reached at an inquest play a key role in discharging the procedural duty. Those are dealt with in detail at CHAPTER 6.

[1] [2003] EWCA Civ 1129, [2004] 1 WLR 971 at [67].

Engagement of the investigative duty

3.102 The threshold for the engagement of the investigative Art 2 duty is low. The death need only have resulted from an 'arguable' – *Middleton* – or 'possible' – *Hurst*[1] – breach of one of the substantive duties. '*Arguable*' is anything more than '*fanciful*': it is a low threshold[2], and one that is reached when there is an issue which requires investigation, not just where the evidence before the court demonstrates something is wrong[3]. In considering whether an arguable breach has taken place, it is important to remember, as set out in CHAPTER 6 at **6.186** that it is not necessary to show 'but for' causation in order to establish an Art 2 breach.

[1] [2007] UKHL 13, [2007] 2 WLR 726 at [28].
[2] *AP v HM Coroner for Worcestershire* [2011] EWHC 1453 (Admin) at [59].
[3] *Moss v HM Coroner for the North and South Districts of Durham and Darlington* [2008] EWHC 2940 (Admin).

3.103 The investigative duty is engaged by implication in all cases where individuals have been killed as a result of the use of force by state agents[1]. All violent deaths in prison, 'whether self-inflicted or otherwise', engage the investigative duty[2]. However, natural causes deaths in custody where no arguable breach of one of the substantive duties has occurred will not give rise to the duty[3]. It is submitted that the same principles should apply to detained mental health patients.

[1] *Jordan v United Kingdom* (2003) 37 EHRR 2 at [105].
[2] *R (Tyrell) v HM Senior Coroner for County Durham and Darlington* [2016] EWHC 1892 (Admin) at [16].
[3] [2016] EWHC 1892 (Admin) at [26].

Criteria for compliance with the investigative duty

3.104 The ECtHR set out the content of the requirements of an Art 2 compliant investigation in *Jordan*[1]. This was endorsed by the House of Lords in *Amin* as the 'minimum' framework criteria that ought to be followed in the England and Wales[2]:

(1) The authorities **must act of their own motion**, once the matter has come to their attention. They cannot leave it to the initiative of the next of kin or family to lodge a complaint or initiate an investigation.
(2) The investigation **must be effective, or adequate,**[3] which requires:
   (a) **Independence on the part of those conducting the investigation.** This means not just hierarchical or institutional independence but also practical independence[4]. In *Amin* the internal prison service investigation into the killing was held to be insufficiently independent, despite the investigator not being employed in the prison in question, as he 'did not enjoy institutional or hierarchical independence'[5]. In *Wright*, the fact that there was no independent expert review of the adequacy of the medical treatment of a prisoner was held to be one reason for a failure of the inquest to comply with the investigative duty[6]. The requirement for an investigation to be independent has limits, however. In *Antoniou v Central and North West London NHS Trust*[7] the Divisional Court held that there is no requirement that pre-inquest investigations in the form of serious untoward incident reports regarding detained psychiatric patients who commit suicide should be independent of the NHS trust involved in the care of the deceased (as is the case with the post-death investigations carried out by the Prison and Probation Ombudsman in prison custody cases).

   (b) **The investigation must be capable of leading to the identification and punishment of those responsible for the death.** An Art 2 investigation 'ensures that those who were at fault will be made accountable for their actions'[8]. This is an obligation of means not result[9]. An Art 2 investigation must be 'based on thorough, objective and impartial analysis of all relevant elements'[10]. The investigation should be broad enough to permit the investigating authorities to take into consideration not only the actions of the employees involved, but also the surrounding circumstances including such matters as the planning, management and control of the operations in question[11].

The restrictions on identifying responsible individuals in inquest conclusions and on conclusions which impart civil or criminal liability at inquests have not been held to raise issues under the investigative duty. The fact-finding nature of the inquest system, provided it investigates with expanded *Middleton* scope, has consistently been held to be capable of discharging the Art 2 duty[12].

Significantly, the process is capable of identifying and leading to the punishment of those responsible: under r 25(4) of the Coroners' (Inquest) Rules 2013 a coroner must adjourn an inquest and notify the Director of Public Prosecutions, if during the course of the inquest, it appears to them that the death of the deceased is likely to have been due to a homicide offence and that a person may be charged in relation to the offence. Schedule 1 of the CJA 2009 contains detailed provisions regarding the suspension of investigations in cases where criminal proceedings

3.104 *Scope and Article 2 ECHR*

are anticipated or started, and where a public inquiry is likely to intervene.

This requirement requires reasonable steps to be taken to secure relevant evidence, including witness evidence, forensic evidence and where appropriate pathology, in order to provide a complete and accurate record of injury and cause of death[13]. Any deficiencies in evidence gathering which undermine the investigation's ability to identify those responsible will risk falling foul of this standard[14].

(3) **The investigation must be brought promptly and with reasonable expedition.** This means acting with 'exemplary diligence and promptness'[15]. Whilst there may be practical difficulties in establishing an investigation and collecting evidence, a prompt investigation is crucial because the passage of time will inevitably erode the amount and quality of the evidence available[16]. It is particularly important in cases of deaths in contentious situations (such as prison deaths) for an investigation to begin promptly (and to be initiated by the state authorities' own motion)[17].

(4) **There must be a sufficient element of public scrutiny of the investigation 'to secure accountability in practice as well as theory.**

The degree of public scrutiny required may well vary from case to case'[18]. In a prison suicide case, the requirement of public scrutiny 'has a vital part to play in the correction of mistakes and the search for improvements. There must be a rigorous examination in public of the operation at every level of the systems and procedures which are designed to prevent self-harm and to save lives'[19].

The requirement for a sufficient degree of public scrutiny to secure accountability does not mean that Art 2 goes 'so far as to require all proceedings following an inquiry into a violent death to be public'[20]. In any event however, inquest proceedings in England and Wales are invariably held in public[21]. On a practical level regarding the limitations on hearing secret evidence in coroners' courts, see the judgment of the Divisional Court in *R (Litvinenko) v Secretary of State for the Home Department*[22], where it was held that the state's duty to investigate an arguable beach of Art 2 had been fulfilled by a criminal investigation, but that the Home Secretary's decision not to set up a statutory inquiry (which is capable of hearing certain relevant evidence in private) was unreasonable on traditional public law grounds.

(5) **In all cases 'the next of kin of the victim must be involved in the procedure to the extent necessary to safeguard' their 'legitimate interests'.**

Whilst the response required of the state by Art 2 varies with the seriousness of the subject matter, in order for an inquiry to be effective, the family of the deceased must be able to play an effective part[23]. In *Amin* the fact that the Commission for Racial Equality (now the Equality and Human Rights Commission) had declined to hold its inquiry in public or to allow the family to participate was a significant factor in the failure to discharge the investigative obligation[24].

This requires more than merely informing the next of kin of the progress of the investigation; it requires their active involvement in it[25]. From this requirement flows the duty to provide representation where it is likely to be necessary to enable the next of kin to play an effective part in proceedings[26]. That function is now served by the exceptional funding regime under the Legal Aid Sentencing and Punishment of Offenders Act 2012[27].

[1] (2003) 37 EHRR 2 at [105]–[109].
[2] *R (on the application of Amin) v Secretary of State for Home Dept* [2003] UKHL 51, [2004] 1 AC 653 at [32], per Lord Bingham.
[3] *Ramsahai v The Netherlands* (2008) 46 EHRR 43.
[4] (2003) 37 EHRR 2 at [106].
[5] [2003] UKHL 51, [2004] 1 AC 653 at [75]–[78].
[6] [2001] EWHC 520 (Admin) at [60].
[7] [2015] 1 WLR 4459.
[8] *Sacker v HM Coroner for West Yorkshire* [2004] UKHL 11 at [11].
[9] *Jordan v United Kingdom* (2003) 37 EHRR 2 at [107], see also *Ramsahai v The Netherlands* (2008) 48 EHRR 43 at [324].
[10] *Nachova v Bulgaria* (2006) 42 EHRR 43 at 113.
[11] *R (Ali Zaki Mousa) v Secretary of State for Defence (No 2)* [2013] EWHC 1412 at [148]–[149].
[12] *R (Smith) v Oxfordshire Deputy Assistant Coroner (Equality and Human Rights Commission Intervening)* [2010] UKSC 29, [2011] 1 AC 1 [88] and *R (Takoushis) v Inner London North Coroner and Another* [2006] 1 WLR 461 at [105]–[107], and pre-*Middleton* see the view of the ECtHR in Jordan at [128].
[13] *Jordan v United Kingdom* (2003) 37 EHRR 2 at [107].
[14] *Ramsahai v The Netherlands* (2008) 46 EHRR 43 at [324].
[15] *Öneryildiz v Turkey* (2005) 41 EHRR 20 at [94].
[16] *R (JL) v Secretary of State for the Home Department* [2009] 1 AC 588.
[17] *Trubnikov v Russia* (App No 49790/99), 5 July 2005 at [91].
[18] *Jordan v United Kingdom* (2003) 37 EHRR 2 at [109].
[19] *Sacker v HM Coroner for West Yorkshire* [2004] UKHL 11 at [11].
[20] *Ramsahai v The Netherlands* (2008) 46 EHRR 43 at [353].
[21] See CHAPTER 5 for further detail.
[22] [2014] EWHC 194 (Admin), [2014] HRLR 6.
[23] *R (Humberstone) v Legal Services Commission* [2011] 1 WLR 1460 at [75].
[24] *R (on the application of Amin) v Secretary of State for Home Dept* [2003] UKHL 51, [2004] 1 AC 653 at [34].
[25] See for instance *Anusca v Moldova* (App No 24034/07), 18 May 2010 at [44].
[26] *R (Humberstone) v Legal Services Commission* [2011] 1 WLR 1460 at [77].
[27] See CHAPTER 9 on costs.

3.105 The formulation set out in *Jordan* was approved by the Grand Chamber of the ECtHR in *Ramasahai v Netherlands*[1]. In *Amin* the deceased, while serving a custodial sentence in a young offender institution, was murdered by his cellmate who had a history of violent and racist behaviour. The Director General of the Prison Service immediately wrote to the deceased's family accepting responsibility for the death. A number of investigations into the death were commenced. An inquest was opened but adjourned when the cellmate was charged with murder and not resumed after he was convicted. An internal prison service investigation recommended changes to the regime but that no individual member of staff could be disciplined. A police investigation concluded with a decision that no prosecution should be brought against the Prison Service. The Commission for Racial Equality conducted an investigation into racial discrimination in the Prison Service, with the circumstances of the deceased's death as one of the terms of reference, but declined, save to a minimal extent, to hold the inquiry's hearings in public or to permit the family to participate. The Secretary of State refused the family's request for a public inquiry into the death on the grounds that such an inquiry would add nothing of substance and would not be in the public interest. The family challenged the

3.105 *Scope and Article 2 ECHR*

Secretary of State's decision in judicial review proceedings. The House of Lords held that, having regard to the absence of an inquest and since none of the investigations which were undertaken satisfied the minimum threshold as set out in *Jordan v UK*, the state's procedural duty under Art 2 had not been discharged. Lord Bingham stated that:

> 'The purposes of such an investigation are clear: to ensure so far as possible that the full facts are brought to light; that culpable and discreditable conduct is exposed and brought to public notice; that suspicion of deliberate wrongdoing is allayed; that dangerous practices and procedures are rectified; and that those who have lost their relative may at least have the satisfaction of knowing that lessons learned from his death may save the lives of others[2].'

[1] (2008) 46 EHRR 43.
[2] (2003) 37 EHRR 2 at [31].

3.106 In *Khan* Brooke LJ stated that 'the procedural obligation introduced by Art 2 has three interlocking aims: to minimise the risk of future like deaths; to give the beginnings of justice to the bereaved; and to assuage the anxieties of the public'[1]. The practical requirements under the investigative duty stem from those purposes.

[1] *R (Khan) v Secretary of State for Health* [2004] 1 WLR 971 at [67].

3.107 The form of investigation required in order to satisfy the purposes of the investigative duty will vary in different circumstances[1]. The Convention is not prescriptive about the manner in which an Art 2 investigation should take place, 'but the more serious the events that call for inquiry, the more intensive should be the process of public scrutiny'[2].

[1] (2003) 37 EHRR 2 [105].
[2] [2004] 1 WLR 971 [62].

Chapter 4

PRELIMINARY ISSUES AND THE PRE-INQUEST REVIEW (PIR)

THE PRE-INQUEST REVIEW

4.1 A pre-inquest review (PIR) is a preliminary hearing which has similarities with plea and trial preparation hearings held in criminal jurisdiction or case management conferences held in civil jurisdiction. The PIR 'should be held in more complex investigations where there is a need for issues to be aired prior to the inquest and which cannot easily be dealt with by email'[1].

[1] Chief Coroner's Guidance No 22, Pre-Inquest Review Hearings (18 January 2016), para 2.

4.2 Although it is not uncommon for complex investigations to require more than one PIR this should be the exception rather that the norm, and most investigations should require no more than one preliminary hearing[1]. It follows that the PIR should be organised and planned in an efficient way with the intention of setting a clear action plan and timetable towards the final hearing. The Chief Coroner's Guidance No 22 makes plain that: 'PIRs should not, however, be used in the guise of regular 'mention' hearings for which there should be no justifiable need'.

[1] Chief Coroner's Guidance No 22, Pre-Inquest Review Hearings, para 4.

4.3 PIR hearings should be held in public[1] but may be subject to reporting restrictions in the usual way. PIR hearings can be held in private in circumstances where the coroner considers it to be in the interests of justice or national security[2].

[1] Coroners (Inquest) Rules 2013, SI 2013/1616, r 11(3).
[2] Coroners (Inquest) Rules 2013, r 11(5).

4.4 In *R (D) v Secretary of State for the Home Department*[1] it was held that a pre-inquest hearing must be held in public unless there are Convention-compatible reasons to hear the evidence of a particular witness or other parts of the hearing in private. Hence, PIRs should only be held in private where there are substantiated and cogent grounds for doing so (eg where holding the hearing in public would give rise to a risk of crime or threat to national security).

[1] [2006] 3 All ER 946 at [13][(i)] and [21]–[35].

4.5 In *R (Coker) v HM Coroner for South London*[1] it was said that:

69

4.5 *Preliminary Issues and the Pre-inquest Review (PIR)*

'it is difficult to see why a pre-inquest hearing should be in private and not in public . . . Article 2 does support the proposition that pre-inquest hearings should be held in public unless there are cogent reasons in any particular case for holding them in private (see paragraph 9(e) of the Master of the Roll's judgment in *D* above).'

[1] [2006] EWHC 614 (Admin) at [18]–[19].

4.6 The coroner has the power to hold a PIR by video conferencing or telephone conferencing if appropriate[1], a measure that has become more common following the coronavirus pandemic. It will not, however, subvert the coroner's duty to hold the PIR in public. See CHAPTER 20 for further detail on the coronial approach to COVID-19.

[1] Chief Coroner's Guidance No 22, Pre-Inquest Review Hearings, para 15.

4.7 The purpose of the PIR is to ensure that the case is managed effectively, efficiently and openly. It will provide the coroner and interested persons with the opportunity to make submissions regarding key topics well in advance of the final hearing dates. It should avoid the unsatisfactory scenario whereby an inquest is adjourned after the parties and witnesses have attended expecting a final hearing because some important issue has not been addressed to everybody's satisfaction.

4.8 The Chief Coroner's Guidance No 22 emphasised the recommendations made by the Chief Coroner in *Brown v HM Coroner for the County of Norfolk*[1] that the PIR should have a three-stage approach: (i) the agenda, (ii) the hearing, and (iii) rulings.

[1] [2014] EWHC 187 (Admin).

4.9 The coroner should send the agenda for the PIR to all potentially interested parties in good time and, where possible, 14 days before the PIR hearing. The Chief Coroner's Guidance No 22 suggests that the coroner should consider whether the following topics apply:

- identity of interested persons;
- scope of the inquest;
- whether Art 2 is engaged;
- whether a jury is required;
- matters for further investigation;
- provisional list of witnesses;
- disclosure;
- jury bundle;
- date of the next PIR hearing;
- date and length of the inquest;
- venue for hearings;
- anonymity of witnesses;
- special measures for witnesses (including video links and screens);
- exclusion of public for part of the inquest (national security);
- public interest immunity;
- apparent bias;
- need for an interpreter;
- CCTV evidence;
- view of the scene;
- other matters.

Interested person status **4.13**

4.10 The coroner should ensure that the interested parties have received sufficient disclosure in advance of the PIR so that they are in a position to make submissions on an informed basis. The coroner may find it necessary to provide additional help to unrepresented parties[1]. After the PIR has been concluded, the coroner should circulate a written document amongst the interested parties containing a minute of the agreed directions and rulings[2]. Rulings should be given at the hearing or in writing within seven working days of the hearing[3] and should set out the reasoning behind any decisions made in relation to contested issues[4].

[1] Chief Coroner's Guidance No 22, Pre-Inquest Review Hearings, paras 10 and 11.
[2] Chief Coroner's Guidance No 22, Pre-Inquest Review Hearings, para 21.
[3] Chief Coroner's Guidance No 22, Pre-Inquest Review Hearings, para 20.
[4] Chief Coroner's Guidance No 22, Pre-Inquest Review Hearings, para 21.

Properly interested persons

4.11 An inquest is not an adversarial process and there are therefore no parties to accuse or defend as there would be within criminal or civil proceedings. The coroner must nonetheless ensure that parties, whether individuals or organisations, who might have a particular interest in the inquest are notified about the investigation and are permitted to play a role. Interested persons benefit from a range of rights, including the right take part in the inquest hearing and to examine witnesses.

4.12 As interested persons have rights that need to be protected at each stage of the investigation process, it is important that they are identified by the coroner at the earliest practicable stage. Although a final decision regarding interested parties is often deferred until the pre-inquest review, and indeed is referred to explicitly on the model agenda, the consideration of interested persons at that stage should be a safeguard to ensure that everybody who should be given status has been identified. It should not be seen as the first opportunity to consider the issue.

INTERESTED PERSON STATUS

4.13 The categories of individuals who could be granted the status of interested parties are defined within s 47 the CJA 2009. An individual cannot be granted the status of interested party unless the coroner is satisfied that they fall within one of these categories:

(a) A spouse, civil partner, partner, parent, child, brother, sister, grandparent, grandchild, child of a brother or sister, stepfather, stepmother, half-brother or half-sister.
(b) A personal representative of the deceased.
(c) A medical examiner exercising functions in relation to the death of the deceased.
(d) A beneficiary under a policy of insurance issued on the life of the deceased.
(e) The insurer who issued such a policy of insurance.

4.13 *Preliminary Issues and the Pre-inquest Review (PIR)*

(f) A person who may by any act or omission have caused or contributed to the death of the deceased, or whose employee or agent may have done so.
(g) A representative of a trade union of which the deceased was a member at the time of death in a case where the death may have been caused by:
 (i) an injury received in the course of employment, or
 (ii) a disease prescribed under the Social Security Contributions and Benefits Act 1992;
(h) A person appointed by, or representative of, an enforcing authority.
(i) A chief constable, where it appears that a person has or have committed:
 (i) a homicide offence involving the death of the deceased, or
 (ii) a related offence (other than a service offence);
(j) A Provost Marshal in similar circumstances to (i) above but involving service offences.
(k) The Independent Office for Police Conduct, where the death of the deceased is or has been the subject of an investigation managed or carried out by the IOPC in accordance with the Police Reform Act 2002.
(l) A person appointed by a government department to attend an inquest into the death or to assist in, or provide evidence for the purposes of, an investigation into the death.
(m) Any other person who the coroner thinks has a sufficient interest.

4.14 Section 47(7) of the CJA 2009 defines 'partner of the deceased person' as a person of the same sex or different sex to the deceased with whom the deceased was living as partners in an enduring relationship at the time of their death. It is significant that the Act does not set a threshold for the duration of any cohabitation. It follows that provided the coroner is satisfied that the deceased was in an enduring relationship with the individual then they might be granted interested party status even if the period of cohabitation was relatively short. The failure to establish a period of cohabitation, or indeed an enduring relationship, will not be an absolute bar to an individual being granted interested party status. In *R (Platts) v HM Coroner for South Yorkshire (East District)*[1], it was held that the former girlfriend of the deceased (as opposed to girlfriend at the time of death, in which case she would have qualified under the listed categories) was a properly interested person, because her 'interest was reasonable and substantial . . . [and also] her wish to participate in the inquest was genuine and directed to a proper motive – namely questioning whether the system had let down the deceased . . . '.

[1] [2008] EWHC 2502 (Admin) at [44].

4.15 Complicated family dynamics can create a particular difficulty for coroners and for those representing families. It is not uncommon for individuals who share a collective status as interested parties by reference to their personal connections with the deceased to have different views about the circumstances that are central to the investigation. Sadly, it is also not uncommon for those individuals to have fragile or even openly hostile relationships with other family members. The practitioner who acts for members of a family must exercise care before asserting that they speak on behalf of the whole family. A coroner should be careful to ensure that all individuals who might be regarded as properly interested parties are aware of their rights or are happy for other family members to take a more dominant role. A coroner's failure to ensure that interested persons are notified of their rights may render the subsequent conclusion void, but each case will be fact sensitive[1].

[1] *R (Dowler) v North London Coroner* [2009] EWHC 3300 (Admin); *Chambers v Preston & West Lancashire Coroner* [2015] EWHC 31 (Admin).

4.16 The coroner retains a general discretion pursuant to s 47(2)(m) of the CJA 2009 to allow any person with a 'sufficient interest' to be granted the status of interested person. 'Sufficient interest' was defined *R v Coroner for Southern District of Greater London ex p Driscoll*[1], where it was stated that:

'[A] properly interested person must establish more than idle curiosity. The mere fact of being a witness will rarely be enough. What must be shown is that the person has a genuine desire to participate more than by the mere giving of relevant evidence in the determination of how, when and where the deceased came by his death.[2]'

[1] (1993) JP 45 DC.
[2] (1993) JP 45 DC at 40.

4.17 There must usually, therefore, be an interest in the specific death, as opposed to the interest of a mere witness or a person or body with a more general interest. It was also made clear, however, that the notion of an interested person should not be unduly restricted:

'The word "interested" should not be given a narrow or technical meaning. It is not confined to a proprietary right or a financial interest in the estate of the deceased. It can cover a variety of concerns about, or resulting from, the circumstances in which the death occurred. The word "interested" is not used in the rule to describe or identify the persons in the categories in Rule 2(a) to (g) [now s 47(2)(a) to (l)] but it may be said that they can each have an interest in the sense contemplated.[1]'

[1] (1993) JP 45 DC at 34.

4.18 It is submitted that an individual or organisation whose conduct is criticised in relation to the death, and may either form the basis of a report to prevent future deaths or engage the investigative duty under Art 2 of the European Convention on Human Rights (ECHR), but in circumstances where the evidence is insufficient to establish the causative requirement in s 47(2)(f) (a person who by act of omission may have contributed to the death), should be considered to meet the test for sufficient interest.

4.19 The individual seeking interested person status must identify interest in the inquest that accords with the investigative scope of the inquest and have some tangible basis in the evidence. A friend's belief that the deceased's death was caused by third party, even if firmly held, does not confer interested person status on that friend, especially where that belief is outside of the scope of the inquiry[1].

[1] See *Allman v West Sussex Assistant Deputy Coroner* [2012] EWHC 534 (Admin).

4.20 An individual may decline to exercise their rights as an interested party. If they do so, a coroner is entitled to continue on the basis that they are not an interested person[1].

[1] *Jervis on Coroners*, 14th edn, at 8–23.

4.21 *Preliminary Issues and the Pre-inquest Review (PIR)*

4.21 The coroner's discretion to name interested persons is not limited to individuals who may have an interest in the proceedings. It is common for public bodies, private companies and other organisations to be found to have a sufficient interest to be granted status. If the actions of an individual employed by such a body are implicated in the death, then most commonly their interests will be represented by the employer as the interested person and its legal team. However, it is not uncommon for such individuals to be made interested persons and to require representation in their own right, particularly where there is or may be a conflict between the position of the organisation and the individual. Advocates representing organisations should be alive to such potential conflicts.

4.22 The police may choose to exercise their right to attend an inquest pursuant to s 47 of the CJA 2009 in order to gather evidence to charge an individual for the purposes of a criminal prosecution. Under the old r 20(2)(g) of the Coroners Rules 1984, it was held that it was not an abuse of the inquest process for the police to do this[1].

[1] *R v Derby and South Derbyshire Coroner ex p Hart* [2000] 164 JP 429.

4.23 The police will not be granted the automatic status of interested person in every case. Under s 47 of the CJA 2009 that role is granted where 'it appears that a person has or may have committed – a homicide offence involving the death of the deceased, or a related offence (other than a service offence)'. For these purposes a homicide death means: murder, manslaughter, corporate manslaughter, infanticide, causing death by dangerous driving, causing death by inconsiderate or careless driving, causing death by driving whilst unlicensed, disqualified or uninsured, causing death by careless driving under the influence of drink or drugs, encouraging or assisting suicide and causing or allowing the death of a child or vulnerable adult. A related offence means an offence involving the death of the deceased (other than a homicide offence) or an offence involving another death committed in circumstances connected with the death of the deceased.

The rights of interested persons

4.24 Once granted interested person status, that person shares common rights in relation to the proceedings and should not be treated differently. A coroner cannot, for example, exclude some of the interested persons or their representatives in order to receive information or submissions in private[1]. Likewise, a coroner should exercise care in their dealings with the interested persons in order to avoid giving the suggestion of bias. Ideally, the coroner should approach each interested person in the same neutral way.

[1] *R (Home Secretary) v Inner West London Assistant Deputy Coroner* [2010] EWHC 3098 (Admin).

4.25 Pursuant to reg 13 of the Coroners (Investigations) Regulations 2013[1], interested persons are entitled to be notified of and represented at the post mortem if they provide the coroner with advance notification of their desire to be present. Interested persons may also fall into one of the following categories and should be given notification of the date, time and place of the post-mortem examination:

(a) The next of kin or the personal representative of the deceased.
(b) The deceased's regular medical practitioner, if they have notified the coroner of their desire to be represented at the post-mortem examination.
(c) If the deceased died in hospital, then the hospital where the deceased died.
(d) If the deceased's death was caused by a notifiable accident or disease the enforcing authority or appropriate inspector or representative of that authority.
(e) A government department which has notified the coroner of its desire to be represented at the examination.
(f) A chief officer of police who has notified the coroner of their desire to be represented at the examination.

[1] SI 2013/1629.

4.26 Interested persons are also entitled to be notified about aspects of the post mortem or toxicological analysis, including the right to receive, on application, a copy of the post-mortem report as soon as reasonably practicable following request[1]. Interested persons are also entitled to be notified of any delay in the release of the body and the reason for that delay, pursuant to the Coroners (Investigations) Regulations 2013, reg 20[2].

[1] Coroners (Investigations) Regulations 2013, SI 2013/1629, reg 23; and Coroners (Inquest) Rules 2013, SI 2013/1616, r 13(2)(a).
[2] SI 2013/1629.

4.27 Interested persons benefit from the rights to receive disclosure of those documents held by the coroner specified in r 13 of the Coroners (Inquests) Rules 2013[1]. These categories are widely defined and include:

(a) Any post-mortem examination report.
(b) Any other report that has been provided to the coroner during the course of the investigation.
(c) The recording of any inquest held in public.
(d) Any other document which the coroner considers relevant to the inquest.

[1] SI 2013/1616.

4.28 Where a coroner has identified interested persons, the coroner should ensure that they are kept informed of any decisions regarding the case management of the inquest and given opportunity to make submissions orally or in writing. In cases where properly interested persons are lay members of the public and unrepresented, it may be preferable for that exercise to take place at a pre-inquest review hearing rather than being dealt with on paper. It is axiomatic that interested persons should be notified of the dates of any pre-inquest reviews.

4.29 Interested persons have the right to be notified of:

4.29 *Preliminary Issues and the Pre-inquest Review (PIR)*

(i) the date, time and place of the inquest hearing within one week of setting the date of the inquest hearing, and of any alteration within a week[1];
(ii) any decision to adjourn an inquest, its date, the reasons for it, and the date, time and place at which the inquest will be resumed[2];
(iii) the resumption of a suspended investigation and the reason for the resumption;[3]
(iv) any transfer of an inquest[4].

They are also entitled to receive, upon request, a written explanation of why an investigation was discontinued under CJA 2009, s 4(4)[5].

[1] Coroners (Inquests) Rules 2013, rr 9–10.
[2] Coroners (Inquests) Rules 2013, r 25.
[3] Coroners (Investigations) Regulations, reg 10.
[4] Coroners (Investigations) Regulations, reg 18.
[5] Coroners (Investigations) Regulations, reg 17.

4.30 A coroner must allow an interested person or their representative the opportunity to ask relevant questions of witnesses[1]. The coroner must allow an interested person to see written evidence and to object to it being admitted at a hearing[2].

[1] Coroners (Inquests) Rules 2013, r 19(1).
[2] Coroners (Inquests) Rules 2013, r 23.

4.31 A decision or omission which is liable to disadvantage an interested person's right to participate in the investigation may be unlawful. The coroner is obliged to behave fairly towards interested persons so that, for example, a delay, which undermines an interested person's ability to participate in the investigatory process, may be unlawful[1].

[1] *R (McLeish) v HM Coroner for the Northern District of Greater London* [2010] EWHC 3624 (Admin); *R v Secretary of State for the Environment ex p Hammersmith and Fulham LBC* [1991] 1 AC 521; *R (Bentley) v HM Coroner for Avon* [2002] 166 JP 297.

SCOPE AND ART 2

4.32 These issues have been considered in detail in the previous chapter.

WITNESS EVIDENCE

Coroner's discretion

4.33 It is the coroner alone who has the power to call a witness[1]. This is a very broad discretion. The discretion was formerly enshrined in statute[2] but is now based upon common law[3]. It is a matter for the coroner based upon what they consider to be relevant, which will be dictated by the scope of the inquest. The coroner must, however, call sufficient evidence to undertake a proper inquiry[4]. In *R (on the application of Hair) v HM Coroner for Staffordshire (South)*[5] the failure to call two witnesses was said to 'totally undermine the integrity of the inquest'[6]. In *R (Mack) v HM Coroner for Birmingham*[7] the Court of Appeal quashed an inquest because the coroner's reason for not expanding the list of witnesses to others who could have given relevant evidence was that it was his

Witness evidence **4.35**

normal practice to accept those nominated by the hospital[8]. There had a been a failure to call any doctor who had charge of Mr Mack's care during the admission in question. The Court of Appeal held that no 'truly rational ground' had been shown for failing to call one of the witnesses, in particular[9].

[1] For examples of failed challenges to the refusal to hear evidence from witnesses proposed by an interested persons, see *R (on the application of Al-Fayed) v Assistant Deputy Coroner of Inner West London* [2008] EWHC 71 (Admin), *R (Maguire) v The Assistant Coroner for West Yorkshire (Eastern Area)* [2018] EWCA Civ 6 and *R (Carwyn Jones) v HM Senior Coroner for North Wales (East & Central) & Ors* [2019] EWHC 1494 (Admin) at [16] and [21].

[2] The Coroners Act 1988, s 11(2), which was repealed and not replaced in the CJA 2009. The discretion is discussed in the Chief Coroner's Law Sheet No 5, paras 9–14. The guidance erroneously suggests that in *Mack v HM Coroner for Birmingham* [2011] EWCA Civ 712 Lord Toulson considered the case law and the 1988 Act in confirming the discretion, but, in fact, he only considered the Act.

[3] It seems to be assumed rather than based upon any direct authority, see *R (Carwyn Jones) v HM Senior Coroner for North Wales (East & Central) & Ors* [2019] EWHC 1494 (Admin) at [16]. In practice this has always been the position. See also *R (Mack) v HM Coroner for Birmingham* [2011] EWCA Civ 712 which referred to the 1988 Act and that it was common ground that the coroner had a 'wide discretion' at [9]. See also *R (Maguire) v The Assistant Coroner for West Yorkshire (Eastern Area)* [2018] EWCA Civ 6 at [3] where Lord Burnett of Maldon CJ said: 'the change [the repeal of s 11(2) of the 1988 Act] has not affected the basis upon which a coroner's decision to decline to call or seek evidence may be challenged'.

[4] See *R v HM Coroner for Lincoln ex p Hay* (1999) 163 JP 666 where a fresh inquest was ordered because the coroner failed to call two material witnesses in an inquest into a death in prison.

[5] [2010] EWHC 2580 (Admin).
[6] [2010] EWHC 2580 (Admin) at [42].
[7] [2011] EWCA Civ 712.
[8] [2011] EWCA Civ 712 at [21].
[9] [2011] EWCA Civ 712 also at [21].

4.34 A coroner is not obliged to produce a list of witnesses before the inquest but it is regarded as good practice[1]. Indeed, the Chief Coroner's Guidance No 22 suggests that a provisional list of witnesses be one of the matters on the agenda[2]. Interested parties are entitled to make submissions as to the witnesses to be called either in writing or at the pre-inquest hearing, or indeed at the inquest itself. The interested parties cannot call witnesses or insist that the coroner does. Interested parties are however entitled to examine a witness[3].

[1] *R v HM Coroner for Lincoln ex p Hay* (1999) 163 JP 666 calling upon the Coroners' Society to publish guidance on the practice.
[2] At para 7.
[3] Coroners (Inquests) Rules 2013, SI 2013/1616, r 19(1).

Power to compel

4.35 Under Sch 5, para 1 to the CJA 2009, the coroner has the power to require a witness to give evidence and to compel the production of evidence by service of a notice[1]. Paragraph 2 restricts the evidence that is compellable to that which would be required in civil proceedings, and states explicitly that public interest immunity is preserved[2]. Offences are set out in the CJA 2009 for failure to observe any such notice by the coroner[3]. The coroner also retains the power to commit for contempt[4]. Certain individuals (sovereigns and heads of state, judges, members of parliament, and diplomatic or consular officials) although competent, are not compellable. In contrast with the position in some

4.35 *Preliminary Issues and the Pre-inquest Review (PIR)*

criminal proceedings, the spouse or civil partner of a person who might be charged with an offence arising out of or connected with the death remains compellable as a witness at the inquest[5]. Similarly, although a person may refuse to answer incriminating questions when sworn and put in the witness box, a witness may not refuse to attend the inquest on grounds of self-incrimination[6].

[1] The coroner also has powers of search and seizure (CJA 2009, Sch 5, para 3) under certain conditions.
[2] Likewise, the coroner cannot compel any evidence that is incompatible with EU law (CJA 2009, Sch 5, para 2(2)).
[3] See the CJA 2009, Sch 6, Pt 2.
[4] *R v HM Coroner for West Yorkshire ex p Smith (No 2)* [1985] QB 1096 and *Peacock v London Weekend Television* (1986) 150 JP 71. See also the Chief Coroner's Guide to the Coroners and Justice Act 2009, para 132.
[5] *Wakley v Cooke* (1847) 4 Ex 511.
[6] *Wakley v Cooke* (1847) 4 Ex 511; *Boyle v Wiseman* (1855) 10 Ex 647.

Protective measures

4.36 The coroner also has power to make anonymity orders with regard to certain witnesses. In *R v Bedfordshire Coroner ex p Local Sunday Newspapers Ltd*[1] it was held this could be done where there is an established fear for the safety of a witness or their family. It is also permissible if it is in the public interest, for example for the protection of the identity of a covert police officer[2]. Any restriction on open justice must be limited to that which is necessary to serve the 'ends of justice'[3]. In the words of the Chief Coroner 'any restriction may be imposed only when it is lawful, necessary and proportionate . . . [and] must be limited to the minimum required to protect the interests in issue'[4]. Although the witness' identity may be kept confidential from the public it must be known by the coroner[5].

[1] (2000) 164 JP 283.
[2] *R v Bedfordshire Coroner ex p Local Sunday Newspapers Ltd* (2000) 164 JP 283 following the unreported case of *Re Jordan's Application* 11 December 1995 and 29 June 1996.
[3] *Attorney-General v Leveller Magazine Ltd and Others* [1979] AC 440 per Lord Diplock at 450D.
[4] Chief Coroner's Guidance No 25, Coroners and the Media (30 September 2016), para 67.
[5] *Re Jordan's Application* in the Court of Appeal, 29 June 1996.

4.37 These matters, like other matters concerning the giving of evidence, should ideally be considered at the pre-inquest hearing or an application made with supportive evidence before the date of the inquest[1]. The interested persons should be permitted to make representations, as should the media, where appropriate[2].

[1] Chief Coroner's Guidance No 22, Pre-Inquest Review Hearings, para 8 as potential agenda items and Coroners and the Media Chief Coroner's Guidance No 25, Coroners and the Media, para 90, to allow any challenge by the media before the final hearing.
[2] Chief Coroner's Guidance No 25, Coroners and the Media, para 91.

4.38 The coroner has the statutory power to direct that witnesses give evidence from behind a screen[1]. As with anonymity orders, this derogation from the principles of open justice should be exercised with care and in circumstances where adherence to principles of natural justice might be said to damage the public interest or make the administration of justice impracticable[2]. When exercising their discretion to permit evidence to be given from behind a screen, a coroner must consider all of the circumstances of the case but is directed to consider in particular whether it would be in the interests of justice or national security to permit evidence to be given from behind a screen, and whether permitting the witness to give evidence from behind a screen might impede the effective questioning of the witness[3].

[1] Coroners (Inquests) Rules 2013, SI 2013/1616, r 18.
[2] To borrow the language of the House of Lords in *Attorney General v Leveller Magazine* [1979] AC 440 at p 450 in considering the court's inherent jurisdiction to limit open justice.
[3] Coroners (Inquests) Rules 2013, r 18(3)(b) and r 18(3)(c).

4.39 The Coroners (Inquests) Rules 2013 (the 2013 Rules) also allow a coroner to permit evidence to be given by video link[1]. This may be a useful consideration in the case of children and other vulnerable witnesses or those witnesses who are physically unable to attend court. The coroner may only direct that evidence be given through a video link if they believe it would improve the quality of the evidence or allow the inquest to proceed more expediently[2]. Factors to be taken into consideration are whether it would be in the interests of justice or national security[3]. The coroner must consider all the circumstances of the case including the wishes of witnesses and interested persons. An order can be made upon an application by the witness, an interested party or at the coroner's own initiative[4].

[1] Coroners (Inquests) Rules 2013, r 17. See also Chief Coroner Guidance No 34, COVID-19 (26 March 2020) which encouraged hearings to take place remotely 'by whatever means' (at para 10).
[2] Coroners (Inquests) Rules 2013, r 18(1) and r 18(2).
[3] Coroners (Inquests) Rules 2013, r 18(3).
[4] Coroners (Inquests) Rules 2013, r 18(4).

4.40 In *R (on the application of Hicks) v Inner North London Senior Coroners*[1] an application was made to challenge a coroner's decision to give anonymity orders to police officers and, because the protection of screens was not available, to exclude the family and the press from the courtroom when their evidence was given[2]. The application was refused because, between the decision and the hearing of the application, arrangements had been made for the relevant part of the inquest to take place in another court with the family present. The court said that orders for protective measures were only to be made when necessary and to the extent necessary[3]. 'It is highly undesirable to exclude family members from the hearing room, and should not be done unless it is absolutely necessary'[4].

[1] [2016] EWHC 1726 (Admin).
[2] Although they were able to hear the evidence by audio link.
[3] [2016] EWHC 1726 (Admin) per Irwin J (as he then was) at [37].
[4] [2016] EWHC 1726 (Admin) per Irwin J at [41].

4.41 In *R (on the application of Dyer) v Assistant Coroner for West Yorkshire (Western)*[1] the coroner allowed police officers, who had already been granted anonymity orders, to give evidence from behind a screen in a case involving a death after a short period in custody. The court held that discretion under the rules was not unfettered and was restricted to improving the quality of the evidence. Open justice was a fundamental principle of the common law. Any incursion into that principle ought to be no more than necessary. Screens

4.41 *Preliminary Issues and the Pre-inquest Review (PIR)*

should only be ordered where, and to the extent, they were necessary[2]. The decision to permit the screens was quashed. *Hicks* was distinguished on the facts because the source of the threats was not the family[3].

[1] [2019] EWHC 2897 (Admin).
[2] [2019] EWHC 2897 (Admin) at [15] and [16], see also the Coroners (Inquests) Rules 2013, r 11.
[3] [2019] EWHC 2897 (Admin) at [64]. The family were not seen as the direct threat in *Hicks* either.

Rule 23 and the use of documentary evidence at the inquest

4.42 As part of the preliminary stages of an inquest, the coroner should consider whether they are going to evidence matters by calling oral evidence from witnesses or by admitting written documents, usually witness statements prepared during the course of the investigation. Whether an issue is proven through live evidence or through documentary evidence is a matter for the coroner's discretion subject to the agreement of the interested parties.

4.43 A coroner may direct that evidence is given by reading a witness statement if: (i) the maker of the statement cannot give evidence at the inquest hearing at all or within a reasonable time; (ii) there is a good and sufficient enough reason to believe that the witness will not attend the inquest; (iii) there is a good and sufficient reason that they should not attend the inquest hearing; or (iv) the evidence is likely to be undisputed[1].

[1] Coroners (Inquests) Rules 2013, r 23.

4.44 Before exercising a decision under r 23 of the Coroners (Inquests) Rules 2013, the coroner should permit the interested parties to see a copy of the evidence if they so wish and make submissions. Under the Coroner's Rules 1984 the objection to the admission of written evidence by an interested person could be overridden by the coroner. The CJA 2009 and 2013 Rules do not provide for such a power. The Chief Coroner's Guide to the CJA 2009 encouraged coroners to admit written evidence wherever possible rather than call oral evidence as a means of saving money and court time and avoiding the inconvenience of bringing witnesses to court unnecessarily[1]. The question whether a coroner can lawfully override an objection to reading a statement under r 23 and the 2009 regime has yet to be determined by a senior court

[1] Chief Coroner's Guide to the Coroners and Justice Act 2009, paras 139–142.

4.45 If the document in question was created by the deceased person and contains material that is relevant to the inquest, then the coroner does not have any discretion and must admit the document[1]. Although the document is admissible the coroner does have the power to redact parts of the document that are not relevant. This situation commonly arises when the coroner has to consider an apparent suicide note left by the deceased. The coroner may wish to redact parts of that note to protect the privacy of the deceased or the persons referred to within the note and limit the evidence to those parts of the note that clearly refer to an intention by the deceased person to end their life. The coroner should however exercise care not to summarise or paraphrase documentary evidence or rely on other people's summaries of documentary evidence as the coroner did in *Mueller v Manchester West Area Coroner*[2]. It would be sensible in most cases for the coroner to discuss these issues with the interested parties in advance of the inquest taking place and where possible provide them with unredacted copies of the document before reading it into evidence.

[1] Coroners (Inquests) Rules 2013, r 23(3).
[2] [2017] EWHC 3000 (Admin).

4.46 Rule 23 provides a comprehensive code relating to all documentary evidence and not just witness statements[1]. Where documents have been created by individuals other than the deceased, the court should consider calling the maker of the document, or if that is not possible an individual who can provide evidence about its contents or creation[2].

[1] In *Assistant Deputy Coroner for Inner West London v Paul and Ritz Hotel* [2007] EWCA Civ 1259 the claimants accepted that the contents of documents could be proved by calling a witness – 'not necessarily the maker of the document or indeed the person who took the statements but any witness giving, if necessary, double or more than double hearsay evidence' at [11] per Waller LJ.
[2] The procedure is set out in the Chief Coroner's Guidance No 29, Documentary Inquests (20 November 2018).

4.47 If all of the interested parties are in agreement there can be a 'documentary inquest' in which all the evidence is read[1].

[1] *Assistant Deputy Coroner for Inner West London v Paul and Ritz Hotel* [2007] EWCA Civ 1259.

DISCLOSURE

Introduction

4.48 The process of disclosure is a two-stage process:

- the first stage of disclosure is to the coroner alone, for the purpose of deciding the scope of the inquest and the witnesses to be called; and
- the second stage is when the coroner decides whether there can and should be onward disclosure to interested persons[1].

[1] Law Sheet No 3, The Worcestershire Case: Disclosure to the Coroner, Not to the Public, 31 January 2014.

4.49 This distinction has always been significant. Coroners have often received documentation which is disclosed no further. Therefore, unless certain documents (often reports)[1] are provided on a voluntary basis for interested persons they may be received by the coroner on a confidential basis. Any further disclosure will be a matter for the coroner under the CJA 2009, the 2013 Rules[2] and relevant case law[3]. There is no right of disclosure under the 2013 Rules where the coroner never comes under an obligation to conduct an investigation, even if they have carried out preliminary inquiries, although the interested persons may have other rights to access the information[4].

[1] For example, reports from the police or the HM Prison Service.
[2] SI 2013/1616.
[3] See Law Sheet No 3, paras 12 and 13.
[4] For example, freedom of information, access to medical records, data protection or pre-action disclosure applications.

4.50 Preliminary Issues and the Pre-inquest Review (PIR)

4.50 The entire process was overhauled by the CJA 2009 and the 2013 Rules[1]. The Chief Coroner's Guide to the CJA 2009 provides some limited guidance[2]. It states that guidance will be issued on disclosure but that has yet to be published[3]. As long as coroners act fairly and allow interested persons to fully participate, they have the discretion to determine the evidence they consider relevant to the investigation[4].

[1] The background to these reforms was in part the Shipman Inquiry and Death Certification and Investigation in England, Wales and Northern Ireland (2003) (Cm 5831). The reforms were also meant to ensure that a coroner was better equipped to conduct an Art 2 compliant investigation (see R *(on the application of Revenue and Customs Commissioners) v HM Coroner for Liverpool* [2014] EWHC 1586 (Admin) at [30]).
[2] Chief Coroner's Guide to the CJA 2009, paras 117–133.
[3] See para 125. There is some further limited guidance in Chief Coroner's Guidance No 30, Judge-led inquests (29 January 2019) and Law Sheet No 3, 31 January 2014.
[4] R v *North Humberside Coroner, ex p Jamieson* [1995] QB 1, and R *(Wilson) v HM Senior Coroner for Birmingham and Solihull* [2015] EWHC 2561 (Admin) at [26]–[27] and R *(Bentley) v HM Coroner in the District of Avon* [2001] EWHC 170 (Admin) at [63].

Disclosure of material to the coroner

4.51 The powers of the coroner to obtain information from third parties are significantly increased under the CJA 2009. Prior to the CJA 2009, the coroner relied principally on the volunteering of information by potential witnesses, the duty of the police to supply all relevant material to the coroner, and the coroner's power to obtain a witness summons from the High Court and county court[1]. Despite the powers under CJA 2009, the Chief Coroner has indicated that:

> 'Coroners should not be too hasty to exercise these powers. They should only be used where necessary and where other methods have failed. Much can be achieved by agreement with, for example, local hospitals, on regular procedures for the production of witness statements, medical notes, and reports.[2]'

[1] An example of the latter method of obtaining information is *Worcester CC v Worcestershire Coroner* [2013] EWHC 1711 (QB). This power is no longer available as a result of the statutory powers under the CJA 2009, see below.
[2] The Chief Coroner's Guide to the Coroners and Justice Act 2009, para 133.

4.52 The relevant powers are found in Sch 5 to the Act. In conducting an investigation, the coroner may require a person by notice, within such period as the coroner things reasonable, to[1]:

- provide evidence in the form of a written statement about any matter specified in the notice;
- produce any documents[2] in their custody or control[3] relating to a matter relevant to the investigation; and
- produce for inspection, examination or testing any other thing in their custody or under their control relating to a matter relevant to the investigation.

[1] CJA 2009, s 32, Sch 5, para 1(2).
[2] 'Document' is not defined by the CJA 2009, but includes information stored in electronic form (s 48(1) of the Act). See also the definition in the Coroners (Inquests) Rules 2013: 'any medium in which information of any description is recorded or stored' (r 2(1)).
[3] A document or item is under a person's custody or control if it is in their possession or they have a right to possession of it (Sch 5, para 1(6)).

4.53 This power relates to the whole period of the investigation, whether before or during any inquest.

4.54 Similarly, in relation to the inquest itself, a coroner may also require a person by notice to attend at a time and place stated in the notice and to[1]:
- give evidence at an inquest;
- produce any documents in their custody or control relating to a matter relevant to an inquest; and
- produce for inspection, examination or testing any other thing in their custody or under their control relating to a matter relevant to an inquest.

[1] CJA 2009, s 32, Sch 5, para 1(1).

4.55 There is therefore no requirement that the production take place at the inquest itself.

4.56 The coroner's powers to obtain information under the CJA 2009 are not limited to the coroner area for which the coroner issuing the notice is appointed, and they therefore extend throughout England and Wales[1]. The coroner's powers also bind the Crown or an agency of the Crown and may therefore be used against government departments such as HMRC: see *R (Commissioners for HMRC) v HM Coroner for the City of Liverpool and the Estate of Roderick Carmichael (deceased) and APIL*[2], in which it was held that a notice under the CJA 2009 requiring disclosure of the deceased's employment history was binding on HMRC.

[1] CJA 2009, Sch 5, para 1(7).
[2] [2014] EWHC 1586 (Admin). It was stated explicitly that the CJA 2009 was intended to strengthen the powers of coroners. Regulation (EU) No 996/2010 on the investigation and prevention of accidents and incidents in civil aviation, which, when read with the Civil Aviation (Investigation of Air Accidents and Incidents) Regulations 1996 (now revoked by SI 2018/321), stipulated that disclosure could only be ordered by the High Court.

4.57 A person may not be required to provide evidence or produce any document or item if they could not be required to do so in civil proceedings (eg on grounds of privilege) or if this would be incompatible with an EU obligation[1]. It is stated explicitly that the law relating to public interest immunity in civil proceedings applies equally to a coroner's investigation or inquest[2]. It is also stated explicitly in the 2013 Rules that no witness is obliged to answer any question leading to self-incrimination[3].

[1] CJA 2009, Sch 5, para 2(2).
[2] Coroners (Inquests) Rules 2013, r 22.
[3] CJA 2009, Sch 5, para 2(1). A recent example of the latter is *R (on the application of Secretary of State for Transport) v HM Senior Coroner for Norfolk* [2016] EWHC 2279 (Admin) in which disclosure by the Air Accident Investigation Branch of cockpit voice and flight data would have been in breach of Art 14 of Regulation (EU) No 996/2010 on the investigation and prevention of accidents and incidents in civil aviation.

Public interest immunity

4.58 The availability of public interest immunity as a shield against disclosure to the coroner was considered in *Worcester CC v Worcestershire Coroner*[1]. In

4.58 *Preliminary Issues and the Pre-inquest Review (PIR)*

that case, the coroner sought access to management reviews and information reports which the Local Safeguarding Children Board had obtained in the course of undertaking a serious case review. It was held that, in circumstances where disclosure was to the coroner and not to the public, the public interest in the pursuit of a full and appropriately detailed inquest into the death outweighed the claim for immunity based on the public interest in encouraging candour from those contributing to such reviews and reports[2].

[1] [2013] EWHC 1711 (QB).
[2] [2013] EWHC 1711 (QB) at [101].

4.59 Law Sheet No 3 was issued in connection with the Worcestershire Case, noting the significance of the distinction between the first stage of disclosure (to the coroner only) and the second (onward disclosure to interested persons), and indicating that:

> 'The benefit of the decision . . . is the extent to which they may justifiably ask for material which they reasonably believe may assist them in their investigation. The decision reflects the trend in the courts towards greater disclosure, at least, as in this case, for the eyes of the coroner.[1]'

[1] Law Sheet No 3, The Worcestershire Case: Disclosure to the Coroner, Not to the Public, 31 January 2014, paras 12, 18.

4.60 A detailed analysis of the extent and scope of public interest immunity is beyond the remit of this work. However, it is worth noting that public interest immunity should not be asserted merely because disclosure is inconvenient, embarrassing or awkward. It must be shown by the person asserting the immunity that there is a real risk that disclosure will cause 'substantial harm' to the public interest[1].

[1] *R v Chief Constable of the West Midlands ex p Wiley* [1995] 1 AC 274 at 281F–G, per Lord Templeman and *R (Mohammed) v Foreign Secretary (No 2)* [2009] 1 WLR 2653 at 34F.

Notices and summonses

4.61 There is no requirement for the coroner to compensate persons for their time in complying with a notice issued under Sch 5 of the CJA 2009. However, an expert can reasonably refuse to prepare and produce an expert report from scratch (as opposed to the production of an existing report) without a proper fee for the work[1].

[1] See, eg, *Brown v Bennett* [2002] 2 All ER 273, [2002] 1 WLR 713, [2002] 02 LS Gaz R 27, in which Neuberger J (as he then was) accepted the general principle that, save in exceptional circumstances, 'it cannot be right for a litigant to get round his obligation to pay an expert witness by use of a witness summons. It would not be fair for an expert witness not to be paid for preparing for trial and giving evidence, while having the burden of preparing for trial and giving evidence while the litigant has the benefit of the evidence without having to pay for it'.

4.62 A notice issued under Sch 5 of the CJA 2009 must explain the possible consequences of not complying with the notice, as set out in paras 6 and 7 of Sch 6[1], namely that the coroner can impose a fine not exceeding £1,000 for a failure to comply with such a notice without reasonable excuse and that is an offence to:

- do anything intended to have the effect either of distorting or altering anything produced for the purposes of an investigation, or of preventing anything from being so produced or provided; and
- intentionally suppress, conceal, alter or destroy a document which that person knows or believes to be one which the coroner (if aware of its existence) would wish to have.

[1] CJA 2009, Sch 5, para 1(3).

4.63 The notice must also indicate what action the recipient should take if they wish to claim that they are unable to comply or that it is not reasonable to require compliance with the notice[1]. This claim is to be determined by the coroner who may revoke or vary the notice[2]. In considering whether to vary or revoke the notice on the ground that it would be unreasonable to require compliance, the coroner must consider the public interest in the information being obtained for the purposes of the inquest or investigation, having regard to the likely importance of the information[3].

[1] CJA 2009, Sch 5, para 1(3), (4).
[2] CJA 2009, Sch 5, para 1(4).
[3] CJA 2009, Sch 5, para 1(5).

4.64 The effect of the statutory provisions in Sch 5 of the CJA 2009 on the coroner's pre-existing powers to summon witnesses, require evidence to be given, and punish for contempt of court is not made explicit. The Chief Coroner's view is that they do not alter these powers[1]. However, the coroner no longer has the power to seek a witness summons from the High Court in aid of inquest proceedings, since that power depended on the fact that coroners previously had no other power to issue a witness summons in relation to their proceedings.

[1] The Chief Coroner's Guide to the Coroners and Justice Act 2009, para 132.

4.65 The general powers of the coroner under Sch 5 of the CJA 2009 may be overridden by specific legislation governing disclosure of information in a specific context. In *R (on the application of the Secretary of State for Transport) v HM Senior Coroner for Norfolk*[1] the Divisional Court held that the CJA 2009 did not override specific legislation (the Civil Aviation (Investigation of Air Accidents and Incidents) Regulations 1996[2]) under which the only court with the power to order disclosure of cockpit voice and flight data recorder was the High Court.

[1] [2016] EWHC 2279 (Admin).
[2] SI 1996/2798 (revoked by the Civil Aviation (Investigation of Air Accidents and Incidents) Regulations 2018, SI 2018/321).

Disclosure by the coroner to interested persons

4.66 The second stage of disclosure requires the coroner to determine whether there should be onward disclosure to interested persons. Normally, a coroner will disclose copies of relevant documents to the interested persons. Historically, advance disclosure of materials had been very problematic for families with the courts frequently leaving matters to the discretion of the coroner[1]. The courts became more disposed to earlier and better disclosure at inquests with the advent of the impact of the ECHR on litigation after the passing of the Human Rights Act 1998 (HRA 1998) and the Civil Procedure Rules. Disclosure of documents by the coroner is now governed by Part 3 of the 2013 Rules (rr 12–15).

[1] See, for example, *R (Hay) v HM Coroner for Lincolnshire* (19 February 1999, unreported) and *R v Hammersmith ex p Peach* [1980] 1 QB 211.

4.67 For the purposes of the 2013 Rules, 'document' means any medium in which information of any description is recorded or stored and 'copy' means anything onto which information has been copied either directly or indirectly[1].

[1] Coroners (Inquests) Rules 2013, r 2.

4.68 The coroner is under a duty, where an interested person asks for disclosure of a document held by the coroner, to provide that document or a copy, or make it available for inspection, as soon as is reasonably practicable[1]. This applies to:

- any post-mortem examination report;
- any other report provided to the coroner during the investigation;
- the recording, where available, of any inquest hearing held in public (but not any part of the hearing from which the public was excluded on the grounds of national security or in the interests of justice);
- any other document which the coroner considers relevant to the inquest.

[1] Coroners (Inquests) Rules 2013, r 13(1).

4.69 This duty applies before, during and after the course of an investigation, pre-inquest review or inquest[1].

[1] Coroners (Inquests) Rules 2013, r 12.

4.70 In considering whether a document is relevant to the inquest or not, it must be borne in mind that the inquest process is inquisitorial. It was stated in *Inner West London Assistant Deputy Coroner v Chanel Four Television Corporation*[1], by Eady J that:

> 'I need to focus upon the distinctive nature of a coroner's inquests, which differs in fundamental respects from that of civil litigation . . . [I]t is possible in the context of civil litigation to define . . . relevance . . . by reference to the statements of case, where the issues are defined. There is nothing closely comparable in relation to a coroner's inquest, which is inquisitorial in nature . . . An unduly selective or narrow approach to evidence may hinder the task of allaying suspicions and/or making any recommendations for the future.[2]'

[1] [2007] EWHC 2513 (QB).
[2] [2007] EWHC 2513 (QB) at [6].

4.71 Disclosure may be by electronic means of a redacted version of a document[1], or by making a document available for inspection at a particular time and place[2]. The Chief Coroner states that disclosure should be by electronic means wherever possible[3].

[1] Obviously, heavily redacted documents may be of little use and the coroner's exercise of these powers will be subject to the usual public law remedies. Excessive redaction is covered in *R (on the application of Smith) v Oxfordshire Assistant Deputy Coroner* [2008] EWHC 694 (Admin).

[2] Coroners (Inquests) Rules 2013, r 14.
[3] The Chief Coroner's Guide to the Coroners and Justice Act 2009, para 119.

4.72 The coroner may not charge a fee for any document or copy disclosed to an interested person before or during an inquest[1]. There may be a charge for disclosure after the investigation is finished[2].

[1] Coroners (Inquests) Rules 2013, r 16.
[2] Coroners (Inquests) Rules 2013, r 16; Coroners Allowances, Fees and Expenses Regulations 2013, SI 2013/1615, reg 12.

4.73 There is a presumption that disclosure should be as full as possible[1]. The coroner must make disclosure as soon as reasonably practicable. In *R (McLeish) v HMC Northern District of Greater London*[2], in which the deceased's mother sought judicial review of the coroner's delay in disclosing the post-mortem report until months after it was received by the coroner's office, despite her requests for further information, it was said that:

> 'It seems to me that the position with unascertained deaths has to be that, if the interested person in the claimant's position is making the sort of requests that she is, then there must be a duty to keep her fully informed rather than leave her in the dark for months.[3]'

[1] *R (on the application of Smith) v Oxfordshire Assistant Deputy Coroner* [2008] EWHC 694 (Admin) at [37] (relying upon *R (Bentley) v HM Coroner for Avon* (2001) 74 BMCRI). *Smith* was reversed in part in the Supreme Court, but not on this point, see [2010] UKSC 29.
[2] [2010] EWHC 3624 (Admin).
[3] [2010] EWHC 3624 (Admin) at [65].

4.74 It was accepted that there is no general duty on a coroner to disclose a post mortem or any other report before the inquest in the absence of any application for disclosure (although, as in that case, the application may be informal). There is no duty on the coroner to tell interested persons what documents they hold.

4.75 The requirement to disclose documents as soon as reasonably practicable does allow coroners some leeway if an interested person is likely to make a number of requests for documents in succession. A coroner may be entitled to wait, but not unreasonably, for a point where a bundle of documents could be disclosed together[1]. Late disclosure should, however, be avoided. The interested persons should be able to address the issues[2].

[1] The Chief Coroner's Guide to the Coroners and Justice Act 2009, para 123.
[2] *Brown v Norfolk Coroner* [2014] EWHC 187 (Admin) at [41] and [45], dealing specifically with a pre-inquest review, but the principle applies broadly, see and *R (Bentley) v HM Coroner in the District of Avon* [2001] EWHC 170 at [67].

4.76 The coroner may refuse to provide a document or copy where[1]:

- there is a statutory or legal prohibition on disclosure;
- the consent of any author or copyright owner cannot reasonably be obtained;
- the request is unreasonable;
- the document relates to contemplated or commenced criminal proceedings; or
- the coroner considers the document irrelevant to the investigation.

[1] Coroners (Inquests) Rules 2013, r 15.

4.77 *Preliminary Issues and the Pre-inquest Review (PIR)*

4.77 In *R (Lagos) v HM Coroner for the City of London*[1], the status of police reports in the inquest process was discussed and it was stated that:

> 'The police report is a document prepared specifically for the Coroner, which summarises the police investigation, the identity and evidence of any witnesses, and the provisional conclusions of the investigating officer. It is intended to assist the Coroner in understanding the issues and deciding which witnesses are to be called. Police reports are not adduced in evidence at inquests because they are not primary evidence.[2]'

[1] [2013] EWHC 423 (Admin).
[2] [2013] EWHC 423 (Admin) at [5].

4.78 The Chief Coroner advises that, following *Lagos*, police reports fall under the category of documents in relation to which there is a statutory or legal prohibition on disclosure[1]. It is not clear why this should be so, however. *Lagos* is not a decision under the new rules. The issue regarding the report in that case was whether it should have been disclosed in the judicial review proceedings – rather than in the inquest – and the comments above were not concerned with disclosure to and by coroners in the course of inquests. The better view, surely, is that any such report is not primary evidence[2] and is therefore unlikely to be 'disclosable'.

[1] The Chief Coroner's Guide to the Coroners and Justice Act 2009, para 121.
[2] This is the analysis by the Chief Coroner in Law Sheet No 3, para 12.

4.79 In relation to documents where the author's or copyright owner's consent cannot be obtained, it was made plain in *R v Hammersmith ex p Peach*[1] and *R v Southwark Coroner ex p Hicks*[2] that an interested person had no power to require the disclosure of witness statements given in confidence.

[1] [1980] 1 QB 211.
[2] [1987] 1 WLR 1624.

4.80 A request for a post-mortem report in circumstances where the police are undertaking a homicide investigation, even from the deceased's doctor, is likely to be met with a refusal until the criminal proceedings have progressed sufficiently.

4.81 The Chief Coroner states that a document that is not relevant to an investigation is one which the coroner does not intend to rely on at inquest[1]. Although relevance is essentially a matter for the coroner, it can be argued by the interested persons that documents are relevant because they are referred to in a different statement, contradict a later statement or are otherwise relevant[2].

[1] The Chief Coroner's Guide to the Coroners and Justice Act 2009, para 122.
[2] See *R (Cohen) v Inner London Coroner* (1994) 158 JP 644.

4.82 Interested persons have no rights under the Coroners (Inquests) Rules 2013 to disclosure from other sources, or other interested persons, only the coroner. There is no disclosure procedure like there is in civil litigation. Decisions about whether documents are relevant and or which documents may be put to a jury are for the coroner. There may, of course, be rights to such documents outside the inquest process[1].

[1] For example; freedom of information, access to medical records, data protection or pre-action disclosure applications.

Medical records

4.83 The deceased's medical records will often be relevant and necessary to the inquest process. An NHS trust or health authority may not refuse to produce the deceased's medical records purely on grounds of confidentiality, or doctor-patient privilege. Whilst those arguments might be said to apply to the records of other patients, it is possible to foresee circumstances where issues arising within the inquest might mean that arguments about confidentiality will be outweighed, especially if records are capable of being anonymised.

4.84 The representative of the deceased (or any person who might have a claim arising from their death) are entitled to be provided with copies of the deceased's medical records pursuant to s 3 of the Access to Health Records Act 1990. The holder of those records, usually an NHS trust or health authority is expected to provide records within 40 days of the request subject to the individual having made a formal request and have paid the statutory fees.

4.85 In *Stobart v Nottinghamshire Health Authority*[1] the court implicitly recognised that the fact that an inquest was not yet complete was not grounds for refusing a request under s 3 of the Access to Health Records 1990 and that it was reasonable for a potential claimant to make an application for pre-action disclosure against a potential defendant to obtain medical records prior to an inquest.

[1] [1992] 3 Med LR 284.

REQUIREMENT FOR A JURY

4.86 Originally, all inquests were held with a jury. Juries were seen as allaying public anxiety over deaths and ensuring a democratic inquiry. The policy behind jury inquests was that there should be public confidence in the inquest[1]. Obviously, the impartiality of a jury is attractive in controversial cases – as a jury cannot be perceived as an organ of the state. From a practical point of view, juries have often been seen to be more ready to criticise state authorities.

[1] *R (Paul) v Deputy Coroner of the Queen's Household and the Assistant Deputy Coroner for Surrey* [2007] EWHC 408 (Admin) at [46].

4.87 Now, however, an inquest must be held without a jury[1] unless the requirements in s 7(2) of the CJA 2009 are met, or the coroner so orders (s 7(3)). The vast majority of inquests are now disposed of by a coroner sitting alone, indeed the explanatory notes to the CJA 2009 says that is the general rule[2].

[1] CJA 2009, s 7(1).
[2] Para 83.

4.88 The jury, where one is called, consists of a minimum of seven and a maximum of eleven people who may come from within or without the coroner's area[1]. Only persons qualified to serve as a juror in the Crown Court, county courts and High Court may serve at an inquest[2]. The number of people

4.88 *Preliminary Issues and the Pre-inquest Review (PIR)*

who are automatically disqualified was substantially reduced in 2004[3] in line with the requirements of other courts.

[1] CJA 2009, s 8.
[2] CJA 2009, s 8(4) – see s 1 of the Juries Act 1974, as amended (registered to vote and a resident for five years and not otherwise disqualified). Disqualified persons are listed in Sch 1 and include the judiciary, clergy mentally disordered persons, persons on bail some ex-prisoners.
[3] Coroners (Amendment) Rules 2004, SI 2004/921, r 1, reflecting the Criminal Justice Act 2003.

4.89 Bias is a ground for disqualification, albeit any detailed analysis is beyond the scope of this work. This applies to apparent bias so the career or employment of a juror may be relevant. A coroner will normally resolve these issues by asking the potential jurors a series of questions before the inquest begins. If there is a risk of bias, a juror should stand down. This should be the case even if it emerges during the inquest. The Chief Coroner has given guidance dealing with apparent bias with regard to coroners themselves, which gives guidance of the law, where similar principles apply[1].

[1] See Chief Coroner's Guidance No 15, Apparent Bias (25 September 2014), paras 12–19.

4.90 A jury is necessary if the coroner has reason to suspect that:

(a) the deceased died while in custody or otherwise in state detention and that either (i) the death was a violent or unnatural one, or (ii) the cause of death is unknown[1]; or that
(b) the death resulted from the act or omission of (i) a police officer, or (ii) a member of a service police force, in the purported execution of their duty[2]; or that
(c) the death was caused by a notifiable accident, poisoning or disease[3].

[1] CJA 2009, s 7(2)(a).
[2] CJA 2009, s 7(2)(b).
[3] CJA 2009, s 7(2)(c).

4.91 The provisions of s 7 are compulsory. When the conditions for summoning a jury are met, a jury inquest 'must' be held. There is no discretion not to summon a jury[1]. 'Reason to suspect' is similar to the wording under the 1988 Act[2] but would appear to be more objective. Indeed, it has been held that it is an objective test[3]. By using 'reason to suspect', s 7(2) imposes a low threshold for holding an inquest with a jury[4]. 'Reason to suspect' does not mean prima facie proof. Any information giving reason to suspect will suffice[5]. 'Suspicion' is the state of conjecture in which obtaining a prima facie proof is the end[6] and could take into account matters which could not be put into evidence[7]. In order to overturn a coroner's decision it must be shown that at the decision was perverse or that the coroner misdirected themselves in law on some material matter[8].

[1] *Handley v HM Coroner for Birmingham* [2011] EWHC 3337 (Admin) at [8], considering s 8 of the Coroners Act 1988.
[2] Coroners Act 1988, s 8(3), The phrase was 'if it appears to the coroner that he has reason to suspect' as opposed to 'if the coroner has reason to suspect'.
[3] *R (Fullick) v HM Senior Coroner for Inner North London* [2015] EWHC 3522 (Admin) at [34].
[4] It is the same language as that used in s 1 of the CJA 2009 concerning the duty to conduct an investigation, so authorities on that provision may be relevant.
[5] *R v Inner North London Coroner ex p Linnane* [1989] 1 WLR 395 at 398.
[6] *R (Ferreira) v HM Senior Coroner for Inner South London* [2017] EWCA Civ 31 at [27].

[7] *R (Fullick) v HM Senior Coroner for Inner North London* [2015] EWHC 3522 (Admin) at [36].
[8] *R (Ferreira v HM Senior Coroner for Inner South London* [2017] EWCA Civ 31 at [28].

4.92 It is no longer necessary to summon a jury, as it was under the 1988 Act, where the death occurred in circumstances, the continuance or possible recurrence of which was, prejudicial to the health and safety of the public, or a section of a public.

Deaths in state detention

4.93 The CJA 2009 defines a person as being in state detention if they are compulsorily detained by a public authority within the meaning of s 6 of the HRA 1998[1]. After the Chief Coroner's recommendation, the definition was amended in 2017 to exclude a person deprived of liberty under s 4A(3) or (5) or 4B of the Mental Capacity Act 2005 (subject to a court order, care home patients, or patients deprived of liberty for life sustaining treatment)[2]. With a death occurring on or after 3 April 2017 any person subject to a deprivation of liberty formally authorised under the MCA 2005 is no longer 'in state detention' for the purposes of the CJA 2009[3]. The reason for the Chief Coroner's recommendation was the huge increase in applications for deprivation of liberty orders under the MCA 2005 between 2013 and 2015, following *P v Cheshire West and Chester Council*[4], in which the Supreme Court held that where the living arrangements made for a mentally incapacitated person involved continuous supervision and control and no freedom to leave the place where they lived those arrangements amounted to a deprivation of liberty. This had the effect of requiring a coroner's investigation and inquest after the death of any person under such restrictions, thereby placing huge pressure on resources[5].

[1] Section 48(2).
[2] Policing and Crime Act 2017, Pt 9, Ch 1, s 178(4).
[3] See the Chief Coroner's Guidance No 16A, Deprivation of Liberty Safeguards (27 March 2017), para 50.
[4] [2014] UKSC 19.
[5] Under s 1(2)(c) of the CJA 2009 a coroner must conduct an investigation if the deceased died while in custody or otherwise in state detention. See further the commentary of the Court of Appeal in *R (Maguire) v HM Senior Coroner for Blackpool & Flyde* [2020] EWCA Civ 738 at [52]–[62].

4.94 The HRA 1998 and the ECHR have a well-developed jurisprudence on what constitutes compulsory detention by the state. The explanatory notes to the CJA 2009 give examples 'such as while the deceased was detained in prison, in police custody or in an immigration detention centre, or held under mental health legislation, irrespective of whether the detention was lawful or unlawful'[1]. State detention does not cover those detained in custody abroad[2].

[1] [2020] EWCA Civ 738 at [61].
[2] *Shafi v HM Senior Coroner for East London* [2015] EWHC 2106 (Admin), see paras 61 and 62.

4.95 Not all deaths within prisons and similar institutions now require a jury. This is a narrowing from the previous position under the Coroners Act 1988, under which a jury was required even where there was no reason to suspect a

4.95 *Preliminary Issues and the Pre-inquest Review (PIR)*

violent or unnatural death or a death of unknown cause. Where there is reason to suspect that the death in state detention was violent or unnatural or of unknown cause, a jury is required. Conversely, this broadens the position from that under the 1988 Act, which required a jury to be summoned in relation to a death in 'prison' (although this was widely defined). A jury will now, therefore, be required where the deceased was detained under the Mental Health Act 1983.

4.96 The question whether the deceased died while in state detention may be a difficult one. For example, those detained under s 2 (for assessment) or s 3 (for treatment) of the Mental Health Act 1983 may be given home leave under s 17 of the same Act. A similar question arises in relation to persons on leave from orders under s 37 (a 'hospital order' of a criminal court) or s 41 (an order of the Crown Court placing restrictions on leave or discharge from hospital)[1].

[1] It is suggested by Christopher Dorries OBE, the author of *Coroner's Courts: A Guide to Law and Practice* (3rd edn, 2014), that in all these situations, a person is best viewed as continuing under state detention while on leave.

4.97 A prisoner who has been removed to hospital for treatment but is still under guard will be considered to be 'in custody'. In *R v Inner North London Coroner ex p Linnane*[1] a prisoner left in hospital without guard was held to be 'in prison' for the purposes of the 1988 Act: his legal status remained that of a prisoner in the custody of the police.

[1] [1989] 1 WLR 395.

4.98 In *Rabone v Pennine Care NHS Trust*[1], it was held that the position of a voluntary patient will in some circumstances equate with that of a detained patient for the purposes of engaging Art 2 ECHR, which may affect the jury requirement in cases of 'state detention'[2].

[1] [2012] UKSC 2.
[2] See also *R (Lee) v HM Assistant Coroner for the city of Sunderland* [2019] EWHC 3227 (Admin) where it was considered, without deciding, that *Rabone* might apply to mentally ill patients at risk of suicide, where the patient was not in hospital but under a programme of care.

4.99 However, in *R (Ferreira) v HM Senior Coroner for Inner South London*[1] it was held that intensive care in a hospital does not constitute 'compulsory detention'. Urgent medical treatment for physical illness was not a deprivation of a person's liberty. This was so even though the deceased had Down's Syndrome and was intubated and sedated. It had been argued that she had been under the 'continuous control and supervision' of the hospital, which, it was accepted, was a public authority. The Court of Appeal said that any deprivation of liberty resulting from life-saving treatment fell within the category of interference described as 'commonly occurring restrictions on movement'. This case did not involve the living arrangements for persons of unsound mind. The root cause of any loss of liberty was her physical condition, not any restrictions placed upon her by the hospital[2]. The treatment was given in good faith and was materially the same treatment as would be given to a person of sound mind with the same physical illness. There were no policy reasons why the death of a person in intensive care of itself should result in an inquest with a jury[3].

[1] [2017] EWCA Civ 31.
[2] [2017] EWCA Civ 31 at [10].
[3] [2017] EWCA Civ 31 at [93].

Death by act or omission of a police officer

4.100 In *R (Fullick) v HM Senior Coroner for Inner North London*[1] the deceased died while apparently sleeping during a police interview when she was not in custody, having attended voluntarily as a witness. Although the coroner decided that she had no reason to suspect that the death arose from any act or omission of a police officer, the decision was quashed because the question 'could or should the police have done more' needed to be answered. The deceased had been accepted by the police to have been a vulnerable person[2].

[1] [2015] EWHC 3522 (Admin).
[2] [2015] EWHC 3522 (Admin) at [39].

Deaths caused by a notifiable accident, poisoning or disease

4.101 A notifiable accident is one where notice is required to be given under any Act to (a) a government department, or (b) to any inspector or other officer of a government department, or (c) to an inspector appointed under s 19 of the Health and Safety at Work etc. Act 1974[1].

[1] CJA 2009, s 7(2)(c), (4).

4.102 The category of deaths caused by a notifiable accident, poisoning or industrial disease largely relates to those reportable by employers or a person in control of premises to the Health and Safety Executive (or sometimes the local authority or other enforcement authority) under the Reporting of Injuries, Diseases and Dangerous Occurrences Regulations 2013 (RIDDOR 2013)[1]. Under reg 6(1) a report must be made if a person dies of a work-related accident which, by reg 2(2), is defined as an accident attributable to the manner of conducting an undertaking, the plant or substances used for the purposes of an undertaking, or the condition of the premises used for the purposes of an undertaking. 'Accident' includes an act of non-consensual physical violence at work but not suicide (reg 2). A 'work-related accident' need not involve a deceased who was at work[2]. A pedestrian falling down a manhole cover left open by workmen in the street, for example, would require a jury inquest.

[1] SI 2013/1471.
[2] RIDDOR 2013, reg 14(1), (2).

4.103 Regulation 14 excludes a range of deaths from the obligation to report. Medical accidents arising directly from the conduct of an operation, examination, or other medical treatment carried out by a supervised doctor or dentist are excluded, although many other deaths in the healthcare sector

4.103 *Preliminary Issues and the Pre-inquest Review (PIR)*

remain reportable[1]. Incidents arising out of or in connection with the movement of a vehicle on a road are excluded with certain exceptions[2].

[1] RIDDOR 2013, reg 14(1), (2).
[2] RIDDOR 2013, reg 14(3).

4.104 In relation to deaths on the railway, deaths of railway staff arising out of their work are reportable. As above, however, possible suicides are not 'notifiable accidents'. The Chief Coroner issued guidance in 2013 dealing with suicides and accidents in railway cases[1], in which it was stated that if on the basis of the evidence available at the outset of an investigation or during one a coroner suspects suicide rather than an accident, the death is not reportable and the inquest can be held without a jury. The guidance referred to guidance on the application of RIDDOR 2013, published by the Office of Rail Regulation which stated that there will be suspicion of suicide where there is, eg a suicide note, a clear statement of suicidal intent, behaviour demonstrating suicidal intent, previous attempts of suicide, prolonged depression or instability.

[1] See *R (Aineto) v HM Coroner for Brighton and Hove* [2003] EWHC 1896 (Admin) where a man was killed by the wheels of a refuse truck although he was not at work and had been out with friends.

4.105 A coroner will also not be required to summon a jury where the circumstances point in the direction of an accident and the accident is not work-related (for example a road traffic accident caused by a driver at work). The guidance states that where the coroner is unable to form a preliminary view as to whether the death is a suicide, accident or a work-related accident, they may wish to err on the side of summoning a jury[1].

[1] Chief Coroner's Guidance No 11, Juries in Railway Cases: Suicides and Accidents, (5 December 2013).

4.106 Regulation 11 requires the reporting of deaths involving the supply or distribution (except by retail) of flammable gas. This does not extend to disposable gas containers.

4.107 Notifiable diseases are covered by the Public Health (Control of Disease) Act 1984 and the Health Protection (Notification) Regulations 2010[1]. They include COVID-19, anthrax, rabies, tuberculosis, rubella, smallpox and many others. However, s 30(1) of the Coronavirus Act 2020 now states that COVID-19 is not a notifiable disease for the purposes of s 7(2)(c) of the CJA 2009. By s 30(2) the provision applies regardless of whether the death predates the coming into force of the 2020 Act.

[1] SI 2010/659, see Sch 1 for the list of notifiable diseases.

Validity of proceedings where a jury is not summoned

4.108 Where it becomes apparent during an inquest hearing that a jury must be summoned, and the jury is only then summoned, anything done by the coroner before the jury is summoned is still effective[1]. It was stated, however, in *R (Aineto) v HM Coroner for Brighton and Hove*[2] that 'there need to be cogent reasons to deny a fresh inquest with a jury when the court decides that the first inquest should have been conducted with a jury'.

[1] Coroners (Inquests) Rules 2013, SI 2013/1616, r 32.
[2] [2003] EWHC 1896 (Admin) at [12].

Discretion to summon a jury

4.109 The coroner should determine the scope of an inquest before deciding whether to summon a jury[1]. Where a jury is not required, the coroner retains a discretion to hold the inquest with a jury if the coroner thinks that 'there is sufficient reason for doing so'[2]. As above, the issue whether a jury should be summoned is a matter for consideration at the PIR[3]. In his first instance ruling into whether a jury should be summonsed under s 7(3) at the inquest into the death of Private Sean Benton[4], HH Peter Rook QC held that there is a presumption under s 7(1) that a coroner will sit alone without a jury which requires to be displaced if the discretion is to be exercised in a case that does not fall within s 7(2)[5].

[1] R (Fullick) v HM Senior Coroner for Inner North London [2015] EWHC 3522 (Admin) at [43].
[2] Coroners and Justice Act 2009, s 7(3).
[3] R (Fullick) v HM Senior Coroner for Inner North London [2015] EWHC 3522 (Admin) at [46].
[4] 28 June 2017, available at: https://www.judiciary.uk/wp-content/uploads/2017/07/inquest-into-the-death-of-private-sean-benton.pdf.
[5] At [4], [50].

4.110 In *R (Collins) v HM Coroner for Inner South London*[1] it was stated that the coroner's discretion must be exercised judicially and that it was a proper exercise of the discretion to take into account that the coroner sitting alone could give a reasoned decision, whereas a jury could not. The relevant events had occurred long before and it was particularly important that any conclusion should be fully reasoned. It was also held to be relevant in weighing against calling a jury that at the end of the inquest the coroner would have to consider a mass of heavy and difficult documentation, which is the sort of exercise best carried out by a professional judge. In his ruling in the Private Sean Benton Inquest[2], HH Peter Rook QC held that this remains a relevant factor to take into account when the discretion is exercised under the CJA 2009[3]. Given the importance recently attached by the High Court to a coroner's reasons when sitting without a jury in satisfying the investigative obligation under Art 2 ECHR in *R (Carole Smith) v HM Assistant Coroner for North West Wales*[4], this may be an important factor in the exercise of the discretion.

[1] [2004] EWHC 2421 (Admin).
[2] 28 June 2017, available at: https://www.judiciary.uk/wp-content/uploads/2017/07/inquest-into-the-death-of-private-sean-benton.pdf.
[3] At [39]–[41].
[4] [2020] EWHC 781 (Admin).

4.111 But the fact that the coroner may or may not take action to prevent further fatalities is not relevant to the decision to summon a jury or not[1]. In the

4.111 *Preliminary Issues and the Pre-inquest Review (PIR)*

Sean Benton Inquest HH Rook QC held that it is neutral factor in the exercise of the discretion: '[t]here is no Convention right to a jury'[2].

[1] *R v West Yorkshire Coroner ex p National Union of Mineworkers (Yorkshire Area)* [1986] CLY 448.
[2] At [10].

4.112 In *R (Paul) v Deputy Coroner of the Queen's Household and the Assistant Deputy Coroner for Surrey*[1] it was stated that factors which might influence the exercise of the discretion include the views of the family and whether the facts of the case bear any resemblance to the situations in which a jury is required. Taking into account the policy considerations lying behind those situations, an important consideration is where there is a possibility that state agents have some responsibility for a death. It was further confirmed that a relevant consideration may be the ability of a coroner sitting alone to provide a reasoned decision.

[1] [2007] EWHC 408 (Admin).

4.113 In *R (Fullick) v HM Senior Coroner for Inner North London*[1], despite finding that the mandatory provisions under s 7(2) had been met, the Divisional Court considered whether a jury should have been convened under s 7(3) of the CJA 2009. The court found that the coroner had acted unreasonably in refusing a jury after the family's request. Having considered *R (Paul) v Deputy Coroner of the Queen's Household and the Assistant Deputy Coroner for Surrey*[2], the court said appropriate matters for consideration were:

- the wishes of the family;
- submissions made on behalf of any other interested person;
- whether the facts of the case bear any resemblance to the types of situation covered by the mandatory provisions;
- the circumstances of the death (in this case in a police station); and
- any uncertainties in the medical evidence[3].

[1] [2015] EWHC 3522 (Admin).
[2] [2007] EWHC 408 (Admin).
[3] See para 42.

Experts

4.114 Medical evidence is given by a pathologist in almost every inquest, either orally or in writing. It is, however, becoming more common for parties to make submissions regarding other forms of expert evidence, particularly in cases involving technical or medical issues. Such evidence will often go to the cause of death or the conduct of persons who may have prevented the death, had they acted appropriately. A coroner who is medically qualified should resist the temptation to give their own expert evidence and should call a medical expert where the circumstances of the case require it[1].

[1] *R v Inner North London Coroner ex p Linnane (No 2)* (1990) 155 JP 343.

Coroner's discretion

4.115 As with witnesses of fact, the coroner has a broad discretion with regard to calling expert witnesses[1]. The coroner's discretion to call expert evidence is not limited purely by factual or technical relevance. In some cases, it may be wise to call an expert witness whom an interested party wishes the coroner to call to give evidence even though it may be strictly unnecessary to do so, if only to allay rumours and suspicion[2].

[1] See the Chief Coroner's Law Sheet No 5, The Discretion of the Coroner, paras 15–18.
[2] *R (LePage) v HM Assistant Deputy Coroner for Inner South London* [2012] EWHC 1485 (Admin) at [60], and referred to in Coroner's Law Sheet No 5, The Discretion of the Coroner. In *LePage* the Divisional Court relied upon dicta from Lord Bingham in *R (Amin) v Secretary of State for the Home Department* [2004] 1 AC 653 at [31].

4.116 The desire or need from the interested persons for expert evidence should be apparent from an early stage, although this is not always the case. If it is apparent, the matter should be raised at any pre-inquest hearing. It is not, however, set out as a standard agenda item in the Chief Coroner's Guidance No 22[1]. It is common for interested persons to have already instructed an expert or experts to advise them on questions of breach of duty and causation. It is open to them, and indeed any party who has already obtained expert evidence to put that before the coroner with a request that the coroner calls that expert or instructs their own expert to advise. In *R (Takoushis) v Inner North London Coroner*[2] it was suggested that an interested person who wished the coroner to call expert evidence should put the substance of the evidence before the coroner so that the coroner may be able to decide whether or not it is appropriate. The coroner's discretion to call expert evidence is subject only to the supervision of the High Court on the ground that its exercise was either *Wednesbury* unreasonable, or in an applicable case, was in breach of the investigative duty under Art 2 ECHR. Nevertheless, the discretion should be exercised with care. As with any witness evidence, a coroner's failure to call expert evidence may result in an inadequate inquiry and the consequence that the inquest is quashed. In *N (a child) v Liverpool City Coroner*[3] it was held that where the coroner refused to call an expert (instructed by the family), whose report was critical of the standard of care received by the deceased, the inquest was ineffective[4]. There is no general principle and each case will be decided upon its own facts[5]. In *R (Warren) v Northamptonshire Assistant Deputy Coroner*[6] the court held that a similar decision by the coroner was not 'obviously wrong'[7]. The fact that the evidence may be similar to that which would be used in civil cases is not of itself, however, a reason to refuse its admission[8].

[1] See Guidance No 22, Pre-Inquest Review Hearings, paras 7 and 8.
[2] [2005] EWCA Civ 1440 at [61], referred to in Coroner's Law Sheet No 5, The Discretion of the Coroner.
[3] [2001] EWHC 922 (Admin).
[4] See also *R (Stanley) v Inner North London Coroner* [2003] EWHC 1180 (Admin) and *N (a child) v HM Coroner for Liverpool* [2001] EWHC 922 (Admin).
[5] *R (Goodson) v Bedfordshire and Luton Coroner* [2004] EWHC 2931 (Admin), where the coroner's decision not to call expert evidence was upheld. At para 71, Richards J said this: 'Everything must depend on the particular circumstances, including the expertise of the coroner himself and the precise nature of the issues and evidence before him'.
[6] [2008] EWHC 966 (Admin).
[7] [2008] EWHC 966 (Admin) at [40].

4.116 *Preliminary Issues and the Pre-inquest Review (PIR)*

⁸   R *(Warren) v Northamptonshire Assistant Deputy Coroner* [2008] EWHC 966 (Admin) at [39] and *N (a child) v HM Coroner for Liverpool* [2001] EWHC 922 (Admin) at [52]. See *R (Mulholland) v HM Coroner for St Pancras* [2003] EWHC 2612 for a decision refusing a new inquest on the basis that the expert evidence fell short of supporting '*Jamieson*' neglect.

4.117 The broad discretion as to whether to call an expert witness to give evidence at an inquest is not turned into a duty by the engagement of Art 2 ECHR[1]. What is required by Art 2 varies according the requirements of the investigative duty in the circumstances of an individual case. In *Goodson* Richards J stated that 'In the context of the sufficiency of an investigation under Art 2, it seems to me that that the court, rather than simply asking whether the coroner's judgment was reasonably open to him in the *Wednesbury* sense, must form its own judgment, in particular by way of independent expert evidence. In forming such a judgment, however, the court must take account of its own lack of medical expertise and must pay an appropriate degree of deference to the judgement of the coroner, who is more experienced in these matters and was closer to the actual evidence in the case'[2].

[1]   *R (LePage) v HM Assistant Deputy Coroner for Inner South London* [2012] EWHC 1485 (Admin).
[2]   *R (Goodson) v Bedfordshire and Luton Coroner* [2004] EWHC 2931 (Admin) at [73].

4.118 The desire or need from the interested persons for expert evidence is frequently apparent from an early stage, although this is not always the case. If it is apparent, the matter should be raised at any pre-inquest hearing. It is not, however, set out as a standard agenda item in the Chief Coroner's guidance. It is common for interested parties in cases where subsequent civil proceedings are contemplated to have already instructed an expert or experts to advise them on questions of breach of duty and causation. It is open to them, and indeed any party who has already obtained expert evidence to put that before the coroner with a request that the coroner calls that expert or instructs their own expert to advise. In *R (Takoushis) v Inner North London Coroner*[1] it was suggested that an interested person who wished the coroner to call expert evidence should put the substance of the evidence before the coroner so that the coroner may be able to decide whether or not it is appropriate.

[1]   [2005] EWCA Civ 1440.

4.119 All witnesses are called by the coroner to give evidence. Interested persons may thus wish to exercise caution in providing a coroner with copies of expert reports obtained in anticipation of litigation, as it could lead to the advance and unilateral disclosure of evidence, that would otherwise be privileged to the detriment of subsequent civil proceedings. Further, a coroner who calls an expert witness instructed initially on a privileged basis by an interested person can request disclosure of the expert's original instructions and the questions put to them as a condition of their being called. Indeed, it is likely that if a coroner does decide to exercise their discretion to call an expert instructed by an interested person, other interested persons will request that the coroner obtains those instructions. Interested persons who intend to rely on experts in consequential civil proceedings may prefer to provide the coroner with summaries of expert evidence, or to rely upon them in putting questions to witnesses, rather than disclosing in full copies of reports themselves.

Requirement for a jury **4.124**

4.120 In *Re Ketcher and Miller*[1] the Northern Ireland Court of Appeal held that litigation privilege did not attach to an expert report obtained by a bereaved family solely for the purposes of an inquest and not for the purpose of civil litigation. The coroner had therefore been entitled to require the family to disclose its report. However, the Northern Ireland Court of Appeal then set out reasons why the public interest would not have favoured disclosure to the coroner in that case. The public interest is a factor coroners must also consider in England and Wales under Sch 5, paras 1 and 5 of the CJA 2009 where an interested person claims that it is not reasonable for them to comply with a disclosure notice.

[1] [2020] NICA 31.

4.121 Where an independent expert is called, there is no obligation on the coroner or jury to accept their evidence. In *R (Carole Smith) v HM Assistant Coroner for North West Wales*[1] the High Court rejected an argument that a coroner's refusal to accept the conclusion of an independent psychiatrist as to causation of death was irrational, where the coroner had carefully questioned the independent expert and where treating clinicians had given evidence to the contrary.

[1] [2020] EWHC 781 (Admin).

4.122 Despite the breadth of their discretion, coroners have been successfully reviewed for their failure to call expert evidence. In *N (a child) v HM Coroner for Liverpool*[1] a coroner was criticised for failing to call expert evidence regarding the standard of care to be expected of a police doctor and issues of causation. On the facts of that case, the Divisional Court considered that the failure to call expert evidence prevented the coroner from holding a full inquiry into the deceased's death in custody. It is notable that this case was approached on the basis of an inquiry within the meaning of *ex p Jamieson* and despite being a death in custody did not raise any issues pursuant to Art 2.

[1] [2001] EWHC 922 (Admin).

4.123 In *R (Duffy) v HM Deputy Coroner for Worcestershire*[1] it was held that the coroner wrongly refused to allow an adjournment sought by the deceased's family at the close of the scheduled evidence to allow them to instruct a further expert. Further, the coroner had in fact called expert evidence but the Divisional Court was critical that the expert was not adequately experienced (in the intensive care of children). In *Thompson v Her Majesty's Assistant Coroner for County Durham and Darlington*[2] the Divisional Court held that a fresh inquest should be held where the pathologist who gave evidence did not have the requisite experience or knowledge but had said that if he had he might have altered his opinion (on the matter of death by epilepsy).

[1] [2013] EWHC 1654 (Admin).
[2] [2015] EWHC 1781 (Admin) at [13]–[14].

4.124 A coroner's decision in a prison suicide inquest not to call a GP and psychiatrist in addition to a nurse to give expert evidence was also found to be unlawful in *R (Warren) v Northamptonshire Assistant Deputy Coroner*[1]. In this case it was also specifically found that the failure to call expert evidence would lead to non-compliance of Art 2 ECHR[2]. This was also held to be the case in *R (Stanley) v HM Coroner for Inner North London*[3] and *R (Wright) v*

4.124 *Preliminary Issues and the Pre-inquest Review (PIR)*

Secretary of State for the Home Department[4]. These cases further emphasised the requirement under Art 2 that any expert evidence called is independent, for example from the medical institution that is under scrutiny.

[1] [2008] EWHC 966 (Admin).
[2] But there is no general rule that psychiatric evidence must be called in every case of a suicide in prison – see *Chambers v HM Coroner for Preston and West Lancashire* [2015] EWHC 31 (Admin) at [31]. That would 'fetter the discretion of the coroner'.
[3] [2003] EWHC 1180 (Admin) at [48] and [49], again relying on *R (Amin) v Secretary of State for the Home Department* [2004] 1 AC 653. In *Stanley* the coroner had refused to call evidence from an expert instructed by the family, the police and his own independent expert.
[4] [2001] EWHC 520 (Admin) at [60], [62].

Experts' duties and fees

4.125 The expert's duties within the context of the inquest are the same as within the criminal or civil courts[1]. The expert owes their duty to the court and not to the party who instructed them. The expert should assist the court by providing objective, unbiased opinions on matters within their expertise, and should not assume the role of an advocate. Experts should consider all material facts, including those which might detract from their opinions. The expert should make it clear where an issue falls outside of their expertise or where they are unable to reach a definitive opinion. Their report should set out the details of their qualifications, identify literature that they have relied upon, make clear which stated facts are within their own knowledge and which are not, identify where others have carried out tests, measurements or experiments on their behalf and whether that was done under their supervision, summarise their conclusions, give reasons for that conclusion and, if relevant, summarise where there would be a range of opinion on any given matter[2].

[1] See CPR Pt 35 and the subsequent Practice Direction for a succinct summary.
[2] See the Practice Direction to CPR Pt 35, sections 2 and 3.

4.126 The fees to be paid by expert witnesses are governed by the Coroners Allowances, Fees and Expenses Regulations 2013[1], rr 9 and 10, which allow a coroner to pay an expert witness for both preparatory work carried out which directly relates to the giving of evidence at an inquest and also for attending and giving evidence at an inquest. The fee to be paid is a fee the coroner considers reasonable, having regard to the nature and complexity of the preparatory work done or evidence provided.

[1] SI 2013/1615.

Chapter 5
THE INQUEST HEARING

CORONER'S INTRODUCTION

5.1 Unlike in a civil trial, there are no parties and there is no 'case' to be presented. Further, r 27 of the Coroners (Inquests) Rules 2013[1] expressly prohibits any person from addressing the coroner or jury as to the facts of the case. Therefore, there is no right to make opening submissions to the coroner. In practice, after formally resuming the inquest, the coroner will begin by reminding the interested persons of their remit, that it is not their function to determine matters of civil or criminal liability, and will then deal with 'housekeeping' matters such as the order in which the witnesses will be called, the issues to which their evidence may go, and the order in which the person's representative may ask questions of the witnesses.

[1] SI 2013/1616.

ORDER OF EVIDENCE

5.2 The coroner will determine the order in which witnesses are called. Conventionally evidence relating to identification and cause of death will be presented first and evidence will often, but not exclusively, follow a chronological sequence thereafter. It is common and sensible for expert witnesses to be called last, as they will prefer to give evidence after all of the factual evidence has been heard and explored (ideally they will be present for any factual evidence in order that they can comment on what it means from their professional perspective). Likewise, it is common for an investigating officer, if the police have been involved, or for the individual who undertook any investigation into the death to give evidence at the conclusion of the inquest so that they can review their conclusions in light of the evidence that has been given. If evidence is being heard about a potential prevention of future deaths report, that evidence is usually given at the very end of the inquest.

5.3 The coroner will also determine the order in which the interested parties examine the witnesses once the coroner has concluded asking their questions. If the witness being questioned has a representative in court, or is part of an organisation who has a representative in court, that representative will ask questions last[1].

[1] Coroners (Inquests) Rules 2013, r 21(c).

5.4 The Inquest Hearing

CALLING AND QUESTIONING WITNESSES

5.4 As inquest proceedings are inquisitorial rather than adversarial in nature, the right to call witnesses is the coroner's and coroner's alone[1]. The coroner's choice of witnesses may be challenged on the grounds of *Wednesbury* unreasonableness via the process of judicial review[2].

[1] Coroners and Justice Act 2009, Sch 5, s 1(1) (CJA 2009).
[2] See CHAPTER 8.

5.5 Evidence at an inquest may be given orally or, in the circumstances set out in r 23 of the Coroners (Inquests) Rules 2013, in writing. These provisions are covered in more detail in CHAPTER 4 at **4.42** *et seq*.

5.6 All evidence shall be given on oath or affirmation[1] save that in the case of a child under the age of 14, or a child who is considered by the coroner to be unable to understand the nature of the oath or affirmation. Such children's evidence may be given unsworn on a promise to tell the truth[2].

[1] Coroners (Inquests) Rules 2013, r 20(1).
[2] Coroners (Inquests) Rules 2013, r 20(2).

5.7 In *Mueller v Her Majesty's Area Coroner for Manchester West*[1], the High Court gave guidance at [31] for coroners reading witness statements or other documents into the inquest record:

> '[I]t is equally important to explain to all concerned, in advance, exactly what that will mean. The coroner should indicate which statements and documents are likely to be read or summarised at the public hearing, and which parts (if any) of the statements or documents are not to be read [. . .] In cases involving suicide it is particularly important to indicate to all concerned whether any note has been found, what it says and whether any other evidence is connected to the note that may shed light on the contents of the note. The family should be alerted to the contents of any statement or document that may cause them concern. Equally where a coroner does not intend to include part of a statement or document, and the family wish it to be included, then subject to relevance, the coroner should have regard to their wishes.'

[1] [2017] EWHC 3000 (Admin).

5.8 The coroner has a positive duty to disallow irrelevant questions[1]. Whether questions are relevant or irrelevant depends on the scope of the inquest, which should have been determined in advance of witnesses being called and questioned, but in some cases can be a more dynamic issue and subject to review. Questioning at an inquest may have a more limited scope than questioning in a criminal or civil trial, where advocates are often permitted greater leeway to raise issues that are purely adversarial or directed towards credibility. That approach has been directly questioned within the context of the coroners' court; indeed, as Griffiths J said in *R v Hammersmith Coroner ex p Peach*[2]:

> 'It is quite true that the coroner must allow interested parties to examine a witness called by the coroner. But that must be for the purposes of assisting in establishing the matters which the inquest is directed to determine. It is not intended by rule [19] to widen the coroner's inquest into adversarial fields of conflict.'

[1] Coroners (Inquests) Rules 2013, r 19(2).
[2] [1980] QB 211.

Calling and questioning witnesses **5.12**

5.9 The modern coroners' court is quite different to the type of environment epitomised in High Court's response to the inquest following the death of Blair Peach in 1979, and coroners are more concerned to ensure they conduct 'full inquiries with ample opportunity for participation'[1]. Nonetheless, relevance will remain a touchstone for most inquests and advocates should plan and direct their questioning carefully so that it remains relevant. If the advocate finds that they are in conflict with the coroner regarding the purpose and relevance of the questions being asked it may be sensible to make submissions and seek further directions regarding the scope of the inquest and the issues that are to be addressed.

[1] *R (on the application of Lin) v Secretary of State for Transport* [2006] EWHC 2575 (Admin) per Moses LJ.

5.10 The coroner may permit questioning regarding the deceased's criminal convictions if they are relevant to the inquest but should not permit those convictions to be admitted into evidence if they are not relevant[1]. Coroners and advocates should bear in mind that questioning may reveal private information about living individuals, including children or vulnerable people, and should be careful that questions are relevant to the purposes of the inquest. In cases of suspected suicide it is usually not necessary to engage in a lengthy and detailed examination of the deceased person's private life and the facts or circumstances that may or may not have triggered them to take their own lives. Their failed business, breakdown of their marriage or personal indiscretions do not, in most cases, help the court answer the central question about intent and are likely to cause unnecessary distress to their families.

[1] *R v Inner South London Coroner ex p Fields* (1998) 162 JP 411 and *R (on the application of Stanley) v Inner North London Coroner* [2003] EWHC 1180 (Admin) are cases in which the deceased's criminal convictions were said to be relevant in one case and irrelevant in the other.

5.11 Where issues are relevant to the inquest, advocates should not hold back when questioning witnesses. They are entitled to test the evidence and put to a witness that their account is wrong[1].

[1] *Re Adam Bithell* (1986) 150 JP 273.

5.12 Whilst the coroner is the person to call those witnesses they think are reasonably required to hold a 'full, frank and fearless' investigation into the death[1], any interested person who wishes to is entitled to ask questions of those witnesses.

[1] The phrase derives from the judgment in *R v HM Coroner for North Humberside, ex p Jamieson* [1995] QB 1, a case relating to a death in custody, Sir Thomas Bingham MR, giving the judgment of the court, said at p 26: 'It is the duty of the coroner as the public official responsible for the conduct of inquests, whether he is sitting with a jury or without, to ensure that the relevant facts are fully, fairly and fearlessly investigated. He is bound to recognise the acute public concern rightly aroused where deaths occur in custody. He must ensure that the relevant facts are exposed to public scrutiny, particularly if there is evidence of foul play, abuse or inhumanity. He fails in his duty if his investigation is superficial, slipshod or perfunctory. But the responsibility is his. He must set the bounds of the inquiry. He must rule on the procedure to be followed.' It has been followed in many subsequent cases. See, eg, the Court of Appeal in *R (on the application of Middleton) v HM Coroner for West Somersetshire* [2002] EWCA Civ 390.

5.13 *The Inquest Hearing*

ADMISSIBILITY OF EVIDENCE AT INQUESTS

5.13 The inquisitorial nature of proceedings in the coroners' court mean that the procedures relating to the admissibility of evidence are unique within the legal systems operating within the United Kingdom. The strict rules of evidence do not apply. There are no exclusionary rules concerning hearsay, opinion evidence or evidence about bad character[1]. The only touchstone that applies to the hearing is that of relevance. A coroner is obliged to disallow any question put to a witness which the coroner considers to be irrelevant. Perhaps the only exclusionary rule relates to privilege, providing a shield against disclosure of information to the coroner and by the coroner to interested persons, and also against revealing privileged information in answer to questions in the witness box.

[1] *R v Divine, ex p Walton* [1930] 2 KB 29; *R v Manchester Coroner, ex p Tal* [1985] 1 QB 67; *R v HM Coroner for Lincoln, ex p Hay* [1999] 163 JP 666.

HEARSAY

5.14 The Chief Coroner's Law Sheet No 4 confirms that all forms of hearsay, even anonymous hearsay witness statements may be admitted in evidence in the coroners' court provided that it is relevant to the investigation[1]. The coroner is obliged to consider what weight should be attached to hearsay evidence. In making this assessment, the coroner or jury must consider all the circumstances and act fairly. The coroner should consider the reliability of the evidence and attach what weight is appropriate in all the circumstances. The coroner is trusted to give a hearsay statement such weight as is appropriate[2]. That may involve attaching no weight to the hearsay evidence, provided that there is good reason to do so[3].

[1] Chief Coroner's Law Sheet No 4, Hearsay Evidence, 15 September 2014.
[2] Chief Coroner's Law Sheet No 4, Hearsay Evidence, para 6, quoting Baroness Hale in *Polanski v Conde Nast Publications Ltd* [2005] UKHL 10.
[3] Chief Coroner's Law Sheet No 4, Hearsay Evidence, para 7.

5.15 The guidance explains that often no point will arise about hearsay evidence and it can be quietly admitted. Where a piece of hearsay evidence is significant or controversial, however, it requires special scrutiny. In such circumstances, the coroner should take care with the evidence and give directions to the jury if there is one[1].

[1] Chief Coroner's Law Sheet No 4, Hearsay Evidence, para 11.

5.16 The guidance gives the following examples of controversial hearsay evidence: a document whose provenance is unknown but whose content is of considerable weight in the circumstances of the case, and evidence which is tinged with false motives so that giving it much weight would be dangerous (para 12).

5.17 In assessing the reliability and worth of such evidence, the guidance explains that coroners may derive assistance in doing so from the statutory provisions applying to civil proceedings. The guidance suggests that the following factors, taken from s 4 of the Civil Evidence Act 1995 may provide assistance in assessing the weight of hearsay evidence:

- whether it would have been reasonable and practicable to produce the maker of the original statement as a witness;
- whether the original statement was made contemporaneously with the occurrence or existence of the matters stated;
- whether the evidence is 'multiple hearsay' (ie information that has been relayed through more than one person before it was recorded);
- whether any person involved had any motive to conceal or misrepresent matters;
- whether the original statement was an edited account, or was made in collaboration with another for a particular purpose; and
- whether the circumstances in which the hearsay is adduced suggest an attempt to prevent proper evaluation of its weight.

5.18 For an example of a liberal application of the discretion to admit hearsay evidence, see the pre-inquest ruling of Lord Justice Scott Baker, sitting as Assistant Deputy Coroner of Inner West London, in the inquests into the deaths of Diana, Princess of Wales and Dodi Al Fayed[1]. Lord Justice Scott Baker considered the admissibility of various classes of documents, the contents of which were disputed and the authors unavailable or unwilling to attend to give oral evidence, comprising:

'(1) Statements made in the French proceedings.
(2) Statements taken in the course of Operation Paget.
(3) Interviews to the media recovered by the Metropolitan Police Service or in proceedings against Channel 4.
(4) Books written by witnesses.'

[1] 7 November 2007.

5.19 In ruling all classes of documents admissible, Lord Justice Scott Baker said:

'In my view the documents in question are properly admissible as hearsay evidence. Accordingly, I am satisfied that the documents in question are admissible at common law. There is no statutory fetter or restriction on the circumstances in which I should admit them, although as I have said, I propose to follow similar procedures to those set out in Rule 37 before admitting them.[1]'

[1] Para 25 of the ruling, 7 November 2007.

5.20 As to the weight that such evidence should be given, he said as follows:

'Allowing the evidence to go before the jury is one thing but of course the weight to be attached to it is quite another. Where the witness does not give evidence in person the jury will of course have to be warned about the weight they should attach to it if it is disputed or conflicts with other evidence. The jury will therefore be given appropriate warnings.[1]'

[1] Para 26 of the ruling, 7 November 2007.

DUTY TO ACT FAIRLY

5.21 The coroner's duty to act fairly has been repeatedly emphasised by the courts[1] and that duty has been re-emphasised by the Chief Coroner[2]. The fact

5.21 The Inquest Hearing

that strict rules of evidence do not apply does not obviate the need to act fairly and reasonably[3].

[1] For example, in *R v Inner South London Coroner, ex p Douglas-Williams* [1999] 1 All ER 344 Lord Woolf MR stated that the coroner's discretion whether to call evidence or leave conclusions must be exercised 'reasonably and fairly'.
[2] Chief Coroner's Law Sheet No 4, Hearsay Evidence, para 17.
[3] *Re McKerr's Application (No 2)* [1993] NI 249.

5.22 The Chief Coroner has therefore emphasised that when approaching hearsay evidence, for instance, the coroner should, where appropriate:

- identify the evidence;
- identify any controversy with the evidence;
- hear submissions on the evidence, if necessary, with the point flagged up at a pre-inquest review;
- consider whether any additional witness is necessary; and
- throughout the process, act fairly to all concerned.

The coroner should not rely on important and controversial hearsay evidence as a short-cut where the witness is available[1].

[1] Indeed, in *R (Bentley) v Avon Coroner* [2001] EWHC 170 (Admin), the court criticised the decision to read statements that were pertinent to key issues in the inquiry.

5.23 Where a coroner sits without a jury, the guidance encourages coroners to refer in their findings to the basic principles above and how they apply.

5.24 Where a jury has been called, the guidance provides an example of a direction to the jury as to how to approach a piece of controversial hearsay evidence that example concludes with the following words:

'. . . This evidence therefore requires careful scrutiny by you, being fair and sensible about it. In the end you must decide what weight, what value, you can give to this piece of evidence. You may give it considerable weight, or some modest weight, or little weight, or no weight at all. That is for you to decide.'¹

[1] Chief Coroner's Law Sheet No 4, Hearsay Evidence, para 22.

PRIVILEGE AGAINST SELF-INCRIMINATION

5.25 No witness is obliged to answer any question/s tending to incriminate them and may refuse to answer questions that are so phrased[1]. Where it appears to the coroner that a witness has been asked a question where the answer may lead to the witness incriminating themselves, the coroner owes a statutory duty to warn the witness that they may refuse to answer the question[2].

[1] Coroners (Inquests) Rules 2013, r 22(1).
[2] Coroners (Inquests) Rules 2013, r 22(2).

5.26 The rule against self-incrimination does not permit a witness to refuse to enter the witness box and swear an oath/make an affirmation[1]. The right to privilege against self-incrimination only comes into existence once the potentially incriminating question has been put to the witness. The coroner may not prevent an advocate from asking a question that may lead to the witness potentially incriminating themselves[2], provided that the question is relevant to the scope of the inquest.

[1] *Wakley v Crooke* (1847) 4 Ex 511; *Boyle v Wiseman* (1855) 10 Ex 647.
[2] *R v Lincoln Coroner ex p Hay* [2000] Lloyd's Rep, Med 264 DC.

5.27 The privilege against self-incrimination only applies in respect of criminal liability on the part of the person being questioned and a witness may not decline to answer the question on the basis that their answer might expose them to civil liability or that their answers might incriminate someone else[1].

[1] *Jervis on Coroners*, 14th edn, Sweet and Maxwell, at 12–94.

5.28 Once the witness has indicated that they will decline to answer a question due to the belief that their answer might incriminate them, it is for the coroner to determine whether that belief is reasonable and whether the witness is entitled to rely upon the privilege. The court should be cautious to ensure that the right is exercised properly and not used as 'an instrument to befool the court and defeat the aims of justice'[1]. If there is likely to be a need to hear detailed submissions regarding the right to the privilege it may be necessary or sensible to send the jury out but in most cases it will probably be very obvious what potential offences the privilege is being exercised in relation to and whether it is being used appropriately.

[1] *Re O'Callaghan* (1899) VLR 957.

5.29 Witnesses may also refuse to breach legal-professional privilege[1], although once waived the privilege is lost and cannot be claimed thereafter.

[1] *R v Derby Justices ex p B* [1996] 1 AC 487.

CLOSING SUBMISSIONS

5.30 Interested persons, whether acting in person or through a solicitor or barrister, are not entitled to address the coroner (or the jury) as to the facts[1]. 'Facts' is generally taken to encompass the 'evidence' in the case (as factual findings can only derive from the evidence given). This prohibition has been held to be consistent with Art 2 of the European Convention on Human Rights (ECHR)[2].

[1] Coroners (Inquests) Rules 2013, r 27 (formerly r 40 of the Coroners Rules 1984).
[2] *R (Hair) v Staffordshire (South) Coroner* [2010] EWHC 2580 (Admin).

5.31 However the interested parties are entitled to make submissions regarding the law and the failure to hear submissions may lead to the subsequent conclusion being set aside[1]. An interested party cannot make submissions regarding the law in a vacuum and must inevitably refer to the evidence and the facts in order to frame their submissions regarding the appropriate conclusions. Referring to the evidence in this context is not inappropriate[2]. Framing submissions on the facts around the legal framework is a useful tool for the inquest advocate and may provide an opportunity to remind the coroner of the salient features of the evidence, and the parties' interpretation of it and the weight that may be attached to it. The advocate should still exercise care, though, as any attempt to engage in a detailed submission

5.31 The Inquest Hearing

regarding the weight to be attached to the evidence of particular witnesses is likely to be met with resistance from the coroner or the other interested parties.

[1] *R v Southwark Coroner ex p Hicks* [1987] 1 WLR 1624.
[2] *R (Syed) v Bradford Council* (4 December 2001, unreported), Collins J.

5.32 In the case of inquests heard with juries, the opportunity to make submissions will be limited as the jury will be sent out whilst the parties make their submissions on the law and potential conclusions[1].

[1] *R v East Berkshire Coroner ex p Buckley* (1992) 157 JP 425.

5.33 In the absence of closing submissions, the coroner's summing up of the evidence takes on increased importance. In *R (Anderson) v Inner North London Coroner*[1], Collins J (at [22]) stated that 'the absence of opening or closing speeches at inquests meant that the need for clarity when summing up became all the more important' and 'the jury must know clearly what they must find as facts in order to justify any verdict'.

[1] [2004] EWHC 2729 (Admin).

THE JURY AT THE INQUEST HEARING

5.34 The circumstances that would lead a coroner to determine that an inquest should be heard with a jury are addressed elsewhere see CHAPTER 4. The question of whether a jury is required will have been determined in almost all cases before the date of the inquest hearing. If it becomes apparent to the coroner and the interested parties at the start of the inquest and before the evidence has been heard that a jury is required then the practicalities involved in summoning a jury will mean that it is almost certain that the inquest will be adjourned to a later date. Whilst the coroner has the power to compel individuals who are in or in the near vicinity of the court to be summoned without notice for jury service if a jury is incomplete[1] that rule does not provide the coroner with the power to create an entire jury from the ranks of people in and around the area of the court[2].

[1] Coroners (Inquests) Rules 2013, r 30.
[2] *R v Solomon* [1958] 1 QB 203.

5.35 The jury at an inquest must be composed of between seven and eleven jurors[1]. An individual is qualified for jury service at an inquest if they are[2]:

(i) aged over 18 but under 76;
(ii) registered as a parliamentary or local government elector;
(iii) resident in the UK, Channel Islands, or Isle of Man for five years since the age of 13;
(iv) not disqualified;

[1] CJA 2009, s 8(1).
[2] CJA 2009, s 8(4) in accordance with the Juries Act 1974.

5.36 The basis for disqualification under the Juries Act 1974 relates to either mental disorder, through detention under the Mental Health Act 1983 or incapacity under the Mental Capacity Act 2005, or involvement in the criminal justice system, either through conviction of specified offences or being on bail

The jury at the inquest hearing **5.41**

facing criminal charges. Membership of the legal profession no longer provides a basis for disqualification.

5.37 If an individual qualifies to be summoned as a potential juror at an inquest the coroner may still refuse to swear an individual juror. *Jervis on Coroners*[1] gives the following examples of cases where the coroner might refuse to swear a juror based upon a proper objection[2]:

(a)   the juror lacks capacity due to an insufficient understanding of English;
(b)   the juror is clearly not impartial, for example because they are employed by a interested person or related to the deceased.

[1] Sweet & Maxwell, 14th edn.
[2] Paras 11–14.

5.38 It is common for coroners to pose questions to potential jurors before administering the oath or affirmation in order to elicit whether they might have conscious or unconscious bias in relation to any of the key issues in the case. Jurors should be asked whether they knew the deceased or any of the witnesses who are due to give evidence, or whether they have connections, either direct or familial, with any of the organisations who are involved as interested parties.

5.39 Once the jury is sworn it is open to the coroner to discharge one or more members of the jury if it is thought that there are sufficient irregularities to warrant doing so[1]. Provided that the number of jurors remains at seven or more the inquest could continue with the remaining jurors[2]. If the number of jurors falls below seven it will be necessary for the coroner to discharge the whole jury and start the inquest again with a fresh jury. It would be unlawful for the coroner to swear a fresh juror once the inquest has commenced and the existing jury have heard some of the evidence[3]. If the coroner considers that the irregularities are sufficiently widespread the coroner has the power to discharge the whole jury and re-list the inquest[4].

[1] Chief Coroner's Guidance No 27, Jury Irregularities (8 February 2018), para 14.3.
[2] CJA 2009, s 8(1).
[3] *R v Yorkshire Coroner* (1863) 9 LT 424.
[4] Chief Coroner's Guidance No 27, Jury Irregularities, para 14.4.

5.40 Examples of the type of jury irregularity that might occur during an inquest are given within the Chief Coroner's Guidance No 27, Jury Irregularities at para 6:

'Irregularities can take many forms: some may clearly appear to be contempt by a juror, for example, searching for material about the inquest on the internet; others may appear to be an attempt by a third party to intimidate or suborn a juror; on other occasions it may not be clear whether it may be a contempt or an attempt at intimidation. The coroner may be made aware of friction between individual jurors.'

5.41 The coroner should take steps to avoid these types of irregularity by giving clear warnings to the jury in writing by way of a written notice[1] and orally in court. Those warnings should be repeated, usually in a shorter form, at the end of each day[2]. The warnings are set out in the Chief Coroner's Guidance No 10[3]:

5.41 The Inquest Hearing

'1. Members of the Jury, you will decide the questions that arise in this inquest on the evidence which you see and hear in court, and on nothing else.
2. Do not discuss the evidence except amongst yourselves when you are all together in private. Do not discuss the inquest with family or friends when you go home, tempting though that may be, because it will be you and not they who hear the evidence in court, and you not they who will come to conclusions in due course.
3. Do not communicate with anyone about the inquest in any way at any time; that includes by phone or text, chat lines, twitter or blogs.
4. During the case, if you happen to travel to court with a fellow juror, or you happen to bump into one another away from court, please do not discuss the evidence you have heard. Any discussions you have about this inquest should be in the privacy of the jury room.
5. Do not be tempted to do your own research; just listen to the evidence. Do not go to the scene or make your own inquiries. Do not look anything up on the internet or on social networking sites such as Facebook. None of that is evidence. Why is this rule so important? Because our whole system of justice relies on open justice. All of those involved in this inquest and the public are entitled to know and hear all the evidence on which you have reached your conclusions. If you want to introduce into the jury room the fruits of your own investigations, be they on the internet, Facebook, or Twitter then they would not have been tested in open court for all to see and hear. We all know how wonderful the internet is and how useful search engines such as Google can be. We also all know unreliable they can sometimes be. Seemingly authoritative pages on the internet can turn out to be completely false. The simple rule is: do not make your own investigations. Of course this does not mean you cannot use the Internet for your personal affairs. It simply means do not use it to investigate this inquest.
6. These are important directions, given by me the coroner, and you must follow them. If you disobey them, any of them, it may amount to contempt of court or even a criminal offence, both of which can be punished by a fine or imprisonment.
7. That is why I must warn you about these things. And if any of it does happen it may bring the inquest grinding to a halt. That might mean having to start all over again with another jury, which would not be good.
8. Do not let anybody talk to you about the inquest. If anyone tries to, tell the coroner's officer, who will tell me.
9. If you have any serious concerns about anything which takes place outside the jury room, or even inside it, do not hesitate to tell the coroner's officer straightaway, so that I get to know about it.
10. [If an inquest is likely to attract publicity: It is possible that there will be some publicity about this inquest and reporting of it in the press. The press are entitled to publish reports of legal proceedings that are held in public. There are rules governing these reports. It is possible you may see, or hear some of those reports. However good the press reports are, they are unlikely to report all of the evidence that is in court. Publicity or press reporting is not evidence. Each of you has taken an oath or affirmation to consider the issues and your conclusion in the inquest on the evidence, and it is on the evidence that you hear in court that you will make your decisions. To ensure fairness to all can I ask each of you makes sure that your focus is on what is said in court in your presence and that you ignore any publicity or press reporting the inquest may attract.]
11. At the end of the evidence I will give you directions on the law and provide you with a summary of the evidence that has been given in court. Please keep an open mind. The evidence will be presented to you over the coming

hours/days/weeks. Do not jump to conclusions. The time to come to any conclusions is once you have heard all of the evidence and the directions I will give to you and you are in the privacy of your jury room.'

[1] The written notice is contained within a document entitled 'Your legal responsibilities as a juror' which should be available to all coroners.
[2] Chief Coroner's Guidance No 27, Jury Irregularities, para 3.
[3] Chief Coroner's Guidance No 10, Warnings to Juries (revised 26 February 2019).

5.42 If the coroner becomes aware of jury irregularities during the course of the inquest they should follow a defined procedure[1]:

(1) Consider isolating the juror(s). This would be appropriate if it appears that the juror has improperly obtained information. There should then be consideration of whether that information has been shared with other members of the jury or whether it could be if they remained together.
(2) Consult with the advocates (if there are any) or the parties if there are no advocates. The coroner should invite submissions. This process should take place in open court unless there is a good reason not to do so.
(3) Consider appropriate provisional measures.
(4) Seek to establish the basic facts of jury irregularity. This may involve questioning the jurors involved. Unless there is a good reason to do otherwise this should be in open court. The coroner's inquiries should be directed towards ascertaining whether the juror(s) can remain faithful to their oath or affirmation. The coroner should not inquire into the deliberations of the jury and should only ascertain what occurred. The coroner may ask the juror(s) a direct question as to whether they feel able to continue and remain faithful to their oath or affirmation.
(5) Further consult with the advocates (if there are any).
(6) Decide what to do in relation to the conduct of the inquest. The coroner may take time to reflect on the appropriate course of action. 'The coroner may consider the stage the inquest has reached and in cases of potential bias whether a fair minded and informed observer would conclude that there was a real possibility that the juror or jury would be biased'.
(7) Consider ancillary matters.

[1] Chief Coroner's Guidance No 27, Jury Irregularities, para 8.

5.43 The coroner should invite the jury to retire whilst considering legal submissions, especially where those submissions relate to issues that the parties are not permitted to address the jury on, such as the available conclusions[1].

[1] *R v East Sussex Coroner ex p Homberg* (1994) 158 JP 357.

5.44 Although there is no obvious statutory basis for it within the coroner's court, it is common for juries to be permitted to put questions to witnesses in order to clarify their evidence. This should occur after the coroner and interested parties have concluded their questions and should be done by way of written questions that will, if appropriate, be put by the coroner. The interested parties should be provided with the opportunity to examine the witness again in light of the answers that they give to the juror(s) question(s).

JURY QUESTIONNAIRES

5.45 In order to assist the jury in their deliberations, the coroner, sometimes with the assistance of the parties' representatives, may draft a questionnaire, or a series of questions, for them to consider. This practice is encouraged. In the case of *R (on the application of Lewis) v Senior Coroner for North West Kent*[1] (Davis LJ, Edis J, Judge Lucraft QC), the judgment of the court emphasised that where the jury were instructed by the coroner to answer a series of questions, they should be reduced to writing and presented to the jury.

1   [2020] EWHC 471 (Admin).

5.46 In *R (on the application of Hamilton-Jackson) v Assistant Coroner for Mid Kent and Medway*[1], a mother applied for judicial review of the questionnaire completed by the jury at the inquest into the death of her son, who had died in prison after hanging himself. The mother's application was granted on the basis, inter alia, that the meaning of various policies had been incorrectly treated as a question of fact for the jury to decide. The Chief Coroner commented that the Assistant Coroner:

> ' . . . should have done more to help the jury in the first instance with an objective view of the meaning of the policies [. . .] rather than leaving to them what he called the polarity of the dichotomy'[2]. Coroners 'should do their best in directing a jury to avoid using language which is not in everyday use, language which may not be clearly understood. Words such as "polarising the dichotomy" and "descriptor" are not helpful'[3].

Conclusions in jury inquests are dealt with at **6.34**.

1   [2016] EWHC 1796 (Admin).
2   [2016] EWHC 1796 (Admin) at [64].
3   [2016] EWHC 1796 (Admin) at [65].

Chapter 6

CONCLUSIONS AND RECORDS OF INQUESTS

6.1 Section 10 of the Coroners and Justice Act 2009 (CJA 2009) is entitled 'Determinations and findings to be made'. Section 10(1) requires that:

'(1) After hearing the evidence at an inquest into a death, the senior coroner (if there is no jury) or the jury (if there is one) must:
 (a) make a determination as to the questions mentioned in section 5(1)(a) and (b) (read with section 5(2) where applicable), and
 (b) if particulars are required by the 1953 Act to be registered concerning the death, make a finding as to those particulars.'

6.2 At the end of the inquest, the coroner or jury is therefore required to formally 'determine' the key four questions cited previously ie who the deceased was, and how, when and where they came about their death. In cases where Art 2 of the European Convention on Human Rights (ECHR) is engaged, in accordance with s 5(2), the question 'how' includes reaching a conclusion as to 'the circumstances in which' they came by their death.

6.3 Rule 34 of the Coroners (Inquest) Rules 2013[1] specifies that the determinations and any findings required by s 10 must be set out in the Record of Inquest (Form 2). This form replaced the previous 'inquisition' under the Coroners Rules 1984. The format of determinations – narrative and short-form, was retained, but the Record of Inquest replaced the word 'verdict' with 'conclusion'. The term 'conclusion' is also used in the Chief Coroner's Guidance No 17[2] and in practice in coroner's courts and will be adopted here.

[1] SI 2013/1616.
[2] Chief Coroner's Guidance No 17, Conclusions: Short-form and narrative (revised 14 January 2016).

6.4 Short-form conclusions are prescribed – and as the name suggests, short – terms to describe the manner of a person's death. Narrative conclusions are longer, descriptive accounts.

6.5 Whilst in some cases a short-form conclusion will suffice as a determination at the end of an inquest, in others, particularly where the investigative duty under Art 2 ECHR is engaged, there may be complexities that are better reflected in a narrative conclusion.

6.6 Conclusions and Records of Inquests

6.6 The Chief Coroner's Guidance No 17 on conclusions sought to simplify the process and introduce some uniformity of practice amongst coroners in this regard, particularly in relation to the fact-finding process and the format of narrative conclusions. The status of the guidance is discussed at CHAPTER 1 at 1.17. Despite its status as guidance only, it is generally treated by coroners as authoritative. Advocates should not lose sight, however, of the fact that the process and determinations at the end of an inquest are required by law to 'seek out and record as many of the facts concerning the death as the public interest requires'[1], and in applicable cases, to satisfy the requirements of the investigative duty under Art 2 see CHAPTER 3.

[1] *R v South London Coroner, ex p Thompson* (1982) 126 SJ 625, per Lord Lane CJ.

A – THE RECORD OF INQUEST

6.7 The Record of Inquest is the name given to the formal document setting out the determination and findings of the coroner (and if relevant the jury). It provides the details to the registrar necessary to register a death and to permit the production of a death certificate.

6.8 Form 2: Record of An Inquest[1] sets out the information required, and the format as to how this information should be presented:

'Form 2
Record of an inquest

The following is the record of the inquest (including the statutory determination and, where requires, findings)—

(1) Name of the deceased)if known):
(2) Medical cause of death:
(3) How, when and where, and for investigations where section 5(2) of the Coroners and Justice Act 2009 applies, in what circumstances the deceased came by his or her death: (see note (ii)):
(4) Conclusion of the coroner/jury as to the death: (see notes (i) and (ii)):
(5) Further particulars required by the Births and Deaths Registration Act 1953 to be registered concerning the death:

1	2	3	4	5
Date and place of death	Name and surname of deceased	Sex	Maiden surname of woman who has married	Date and place of birth

Signature of coroner (and jurors):

NOTES:

(i) One of the following short-form conclusions may be adopted:—
    (I) accident or misadventure
    (II) alcohol/drug related
    (III) industrial disease
    (IV) lawful/unlawful killing
    (V) natural causes
    (VI) open
    (VII) road traffic collision
    (VIII) stillbirth
    (IX) suicide
(ii) As an alternative, or in addition to one of the short-form conclusions listed under NOTE (i), the coroner or where applicable the jury, may make a brief narrative conclusion.

(iii) The standard of proof required for the short form conclusions of "unlawful killing" and "suicide" is the criminal standard of proof. For all other short-form conclusions and a narrative statement the standard of proof is the civil standard of proof[2].'

[1] Required by Coroners (Inquest) Rules 2013, SI 2013/1616, r 34.
[2] As below at **6.53** this note has now been overruled by the Supreme Court's decision in *R (Maughan) v HM Senior Coroner for Oxfordshire* [2020] UKSC 46 which confirmed that the standard of proof for all short form conclusions is the balance of probabilities.

Box 1: name of the deceased

6.9 This should be the name by which the person was known, rather than for example their name at birth.

Box 2: medical cause of death

6.10 The medical cause of death is the formal cause of death. Whilst in some inquests the medical cause of death will be immediately apparent from the report of a pathologist and uncontested, in others coroners may hear detailed oral evidence before reaching a judgment on the issue.

6.11 Box 2 of the Record of Inquest mirrors Medical Certificates of Cause of Death[1] in that there is scope to list not only the immediate cause of death, but also any underlying contributory conditions. The guidance provided to doctors completing Medical Certificates of Cause of Death therefore similarly applies to Box 2. That guidance gives examples of how to identify not only the immediate cause of death, but also morbid or underlying conditions giving rise to that immediate cause:

Examples of cause of death section from MCCDs (including example of COVID-19 as underlying cause of death):

Cause of death *the disease or condition thought to be the underlying cause should appear in the lowest completed line of part I*		
I	(a) *Disease or condition leading directly to death*	Interstitial pneumonitis
	(b) *other disease or condition, if any, leading to* I(a)	COVID-19
	(c) *other disease or condition, if any, leading to* I(b)	primary adenocarcinoma of ascending colon
II	*Other significant conditions*	diabetes mellitus
	Contributing to death *but not related to the disease or condition causing it*	

Cause of death *the disease or condition thought to be the underlying cause should appear in the lowest completed line of part I*		
I	(a) *Disease or condition leading directly to death*	Intraperitoneal haemorrhage
	(b) *other disease or condition, if any, leading to* I(a)	Ruptured metastatic deposit in liver

6.11 *Conclusions and Records of Inquests*

Cause of death *the disease or condition thought to be the underlying cause should appear in the lowest completed line of part I*		
	(c) *other disease or condition, if any, leading to* I(b)	primary adenocarcinoma of ascending colon
II	*Other significant conditions*	diabetes mellitus
	Contributing to death *but not related to the disease or condition causing it*	Non-insulin dependent diabetes

The colon cancer on line I(c) led directly to the liver metastases on line I(b), which ruptured, casing the fatal haemorrhage on I(a). Adenocarcinoma of the colon is the underlying cause of death.

[1] Guidance for Doctors Completing Medical Certificates of Cause of Death in England and Wales, F66 Guidance.

6.12 Where it is impossible to say which of two competing conditions caused the death, Form 66 instructs doctors to include them on the same line of the form with a note indicating they were 'joint causes of death'. For example:

- I*a. Hepatic failure;*
- I*b. Liver cirrhosis;*
- I*c. Chronic hepatitis C infection and alcoholism (joint causes of death).*

The same should apply to Box 2 on a Record of Inquest.

Box 3: how, when and where the deceased came about their death

6.13 The questions when and where the deceased died are not usually contentious. If it is unclear exactly when or where a death occurred, however, it may be acceptable to give ranges, if the evidence supports it. If even this is not possible, the coroner can instead record the time and place the deceased's body was discovered.

6.14 The third aspect of Box 3, the question **how** the deceased came about their death, is usually the key focus of an inquest. As discussed in CHAPTER 3, in a non-Art 2 case, in accordance with the decision of the Court of Appeal in *R v HM Coroner for North Humberside and Scunthorpe ex p Jamieson*[1], how is to be interpreted as 'by what means', and there is no requirement to ascertain the wider circumstances of the death.

[1] [1995] QB 1.

Box 3 and Art 2: in what circumstances did the deceased come about their death?

6.15 Article 2 inquests are explained in fuller detail in CHAPTER 3.

6.16 In inquests where the Art 2 duty of the ECHR is engaged, the question of how the deceased came about their death includes ascertaining 'in what circumstances' they came by their death, as initially determined in *R (Middleton) v West Somerset Coroner*[1] and now required by s 5(2) CJA 2009. This is so that the inquest can form an effective means by which the state can

A – The Record of Inquest 6.21

meet its procedural investigative duty under Art 2 of the ECHR[2]. The core differences between a *Middleton* inquest and a non-Art 2 *Jamieson* inquest are considered in detail at **3.10**.

[1] [2004] AC 182.
[2] See CHAPTER 3.

6.17 What difference does this additional question make in practice for the purposes of a conclusion? It was acknowledged by the House of Lords in *Middleton* that in an Art 2 case, 'an inquest ought ordinarily to culminate in an expression, however brief, of the jury's conclusion on the disputed factual issues at the heart of the case'[1].

[1] [2004] AC 182 at [20].

6.18 This ought to be reflected in the court's approach to answers in both Boxes 3 and 4. Indeed many coroners approach the content of Boxes 3 and 4 together, as appears to have been envisaged by the court in *Middleton*[1]. It is however important to bear in mind that when *Middleton* was decided there was no separation of Box 3 and Box 4 in the Record of Inquest form. *Middleton* did not envisage separating the question 'how' someone came about their death from a narrative *conclusion* as to that death. That was clearly altered by the 2013 form. The Chief Coroner's Guidance now states that coroners and juries are 'required' to undergo a three-stage process:

(1) make findings of fact (referred to above as 'reasons'[2];
(2) answer the question when where and how the deceased came by their death and record that in Box 3; and
(3) reach a conclusion and record that in Box 4[3].

[1] *R (Middleton) v HM Coroner for West Somerset* [2004] 2 AC 182.
[2] See **6.30** below.
[3] Chief Coroner's Guidance No 17, Conclusions, para 18.

6.19 The guidance envisages that in a non-Art 2 case Box 3 will normally be one brief sentence describing the mechanism of death'. Examples given include:

- 'by hanging from an exposed beam using a ligature made from a bedsheet'; and
- 'from trauma consistent with an unwitnessed fall downstairs'.

6.20 Note these are short sentences giving a very brief overview. They focus on questions of legal causation (see **6.188**): coroners need not investigate every issue raised by interested person, nor the 'underlying responsibility for every circumstance which may be said to have contributed to the death'[1].

[1] *R v East Sussex Coroner ex p Homberg* [1994] 158 JP 357 DC.

6.21 In cases where a narrative conclusion is reached, the guidance envisages that Box 3 will either read 'see Box 4' or be a short record of the mechanism of the death with 'the wider narrative conclusion in Box 4'[1].

[1] Chief Coroner's Guidance No 17, Conclusions, para 34.

6.22 Conclusions and Records of Inquests

Box 4: conclusion as to the death

6.22 The conclusion is often one of the most contentious aspects of the Record of Inquest. It must 'flow' from the content of Boxes 1, 2 and 3[1] and as noted above at para **6.18** these two aspects of the Record of Inquest are often approached together. The conclusion is recorded in either short-form (ie one of the 'short-form conclusions' listed on Form 2) (see **6.8**), as a brief narrative conclusion, or both. The requirement to seek out and record as many of the facts as the public interest requires may mean in certain circumstances that a short-form conclusion will be insufficient, in which case a narrative conclusion will be required in Box 4. On narrative and short form conclusions, see **6.49** and **6.160** below. A narrative conclusion can be reached alone or in conjunction with a short-form.

[1] Chief Coroner's Guidance No 17, Conclusions, para 18.

6.23 Whilst many families hope, or even expect, to see details and perhaps an analysis of how their loved one came to die on the court record, the courts have been clear that this is not the purpose of the conclusion. Indeed, it has been expressly confirmed that the coroner does not have to reach a conclusion on every issue raised, but only those that are the '*core issues which the inquest raised*'[1]. The court does not have to resolve every difference in the evidence, but only those that go to the core issues in the case, even in an Art 2 case[2].

[1] R (Cash) v HM Coroner for Northamptonshire [2007] EWHC 1354 (Admin) at [49].
[2] R (Allen) v Inner London North Coroner [2009] EWCA Civ 623.

6.24 The conclusion must not determine any question of criminal liability on the part of a named person, or civil liability[1]. These principles apply to Art 2 and non-Art 2 inquests alike.

[1] Coroners and Justice Act 2009, s 10(2) (CJA 2009); *Middleton*, [2004] 2 AC 182 at [37].

Box 5: further particulars

6.25 Box 5 of Form 2 provides for information required when registering a death, namely the deceased's:

(a) Date and place of death.
(b) Name and surname.
(c) Sex.
(d) Maiden surname if the person has married and changed their surname.
(e) Date and place of birth.
(f) Occupation and usual address.

6.26 These are self-explanatory. Coroners will also routinely include details of any spouse or partner of the deceased. If representing the family at an inquest, it helps to obtain all this information from them at the start of the inquest so that details can be provided to the coroner in court, or sometimes their officer outside court, at an opportune moment.

Attestation

6.27 The space for the signatures of the coroner and, if relevant, jurors, is sometimes called the attestation. The Record should be completed at the conclusion of the inquest and signed by the coroner, and where there is a jury, those members of the jury who agree with the content of the Record.

Caption

6.28 In addition to the aspects of the Record required by the Coroners Rules, it is common for the Record to set out some other basic information about the inquest itself, including:

(a)   where the inquest has been held;
(b)   which coroner heard the inquest;
(c)   the date on which the investigation commenced;
(d)   the dates the inquest was held (including any adjournments); and
(e)   whether a jury heard the inquest.

This is usually included at the start of the Record of Inquest.

B – CONCLUSIONS: PRACTICALITIES

Making submissions

6.29 At the conclusion of the evidence the coroner will invite the interested parties to address them as to the correct approach to the task of completing the Record of Inquest. Further detail regarding this is set out in CHAPTER 4.

Reasons

6.30 The aim of the Record of Inquest is to sum up the key elements of the deceased's death as succinctly as possible, whilst satisfying the statutory requirements under the CJA 2009, the death registration regime, and where necessary, the procedural obligation under Art 2 ECHR. However, that leaves a question as to how wider factual findings and judgments on the issues and evidence are to be made at an inquest. The Chief Coroner's Guidance No 17 sets out that these should be made at stage 1 of the three-stage process – the 'reasons'.

6.31 In non-jury cases, the reasons should be given in open court. Often a coroner will deliver a summary of the facts, a consideration of the issues, and/or set out her reasons for reaching certain conclusions in what is commonly referred to as her 'reasons'. If lengthy, reasons may be provided in writing to persons taking part in the inquest. Once delivered in public, the reasons form a part of the public record.

6.32 The use and importance of the reasons stage of the three-stage process in the Chief Coroner's Guidance No 17 was approved by the High Court in *R (Carole Smith) v HM Assistant Coroner for North West Wales*[1]. There, the

6.32 Conclusions and Records of Inquests

High Court took the view that it was unnecessary for the Record of Inquest to reflect the negative findings of the coroner in respect of the local health board's failings because they were already stated in the reasons: 'the argument that more of what appeared in the reasons should have been repeated in the Record has the appearance of an argument of form over substance and we would reject it on that ground alone'[2]. This is an indication of the significant role the reasons can play at the conclusion of an inquest.

[1] [2020] EWHC 781 (Admin).
[2] *R (Carole Smith) v HM Assistant Coroner for North West Wales* [2020] EWHC 781 (Admin) at [77].

6.33 In jury cases, the wider factual reasons cannot be stated in open court. This can make the process of reaching conclusions in jury cases more complex. Narratives in jury cases are dealt with below at **6.36**.

Conclusions in jury inquests

6.34 When the coroner sits with a jury they will sum the case up to the jury in order that they can carry out the three-stage process. Prior to the coroner summing up to the jury and as noted above, the parties will have the opportunity to address the coroner, in the absence of the jury, as to which conclusions should be left to the jury. No one other than the coroner may address the jury[1].

[1] Coroner's (Inquest) Rules 2013, r 27.

6.35 Rule 33 requires the coroner to 'direct the jury as to the law and provide them with a summary of the evidence'[1]. The coroner must remind the jury of the remit (and limitations) of the inquest, in particular that[2]:

- they are limited to reaching conclusions on who the deceased was, when, where and how they died (and where Art 2 is engaged, in what circumstances they came by their death);
- they must not express an opinion on any other matter;
- the conclusion must not be framed in such a way as to appear to determine any questions of criminal liability on the part of a named person, nor civil liability.

[1] Coroner's (Inquest) Rules 2013, r 33.
[2] CJA 2009, ss 5(3) and 10(2).

6.36 Written directions on law may be given to the jury by the coroner and are likely to be helpful. Interested parties should be permitted to address the coroner on a draft version prior to the summing up[1]. Following any such submissions, the coroner should give a short ruling as to which conclusions should and should not be left to the jury. Where the jury are required to write, for example in Box 3, or in a narrative conclusion, they should be provided with assistance in how best to approach that task[2].

[1] Chief Coroner's Guidance No 17, Conclusions, para 24.
[2] Chief Coroner's Guidance No 17, Conclusions, paras 39 and 40.

6.37 It is generally improper for any part of the Record of Inquest to be pre-typed in advance of any jury deliberations. It is however improbable that

B – Conclusions: practicalities 6.42

an inquisition would be quashed if the jury were presented with a Record of Inquest where uncontroversial details had been pre-recorded in advance[1].

[1] *R v East Berkshire Coroner ex p Buckley* (1992) 157 JP.

6.38 When the jury retire the jury bailiff will be responsible for keeping them together and alone for their deliberations. The bailiff is usually a coroner's officer. Jury deliberations must be in private, with all jurors together[1]. Attempts to interfere with the confidentiality of a jury's deliberations on a case may amount to an offence under s 8 of the Contempt of Court Act 1981. Juries must be given adequate time to deliberate and reach a conclusion. They must not be required to sit for a whole days without adequate breaks[2], or be put under pressure to reach a conclusion by a certain time[3].

[1] *R v Fitzgerald ex p O'Brien and Bourchier* (1883) 17 IRLT 34.
[2] *R v Southwark Coroner ex p Hicks* [1987] 1 WLR 1624.
[3] *Clayton v South Yorkshire Coroner* [2005] EWHC 1196 (Admin).

6.39 Section 9 of the Coroner's and Justice Act 2009 regulates majority conclusions in jury inquests. A 'determination or finding' that a jury is required to make by s 10 must be unanimous unless:

(a) only one or two of the jury do not agree on it; and
(b) the jury has deliberated for a period of time that the senior coroner thinks reasonable in view of the nature and complexity of the case.

6.40 As the maximum number of inquest jurors is eleven, this will often mean the minimum majority required to reach a conclusion at inquest is nine, unless jurors have already been discharged. If a jury still cannot reach a conclusion following an appropriate period of time after a majority direction the direction in *R v Watson*[1] may be given, although again a jury should not be put under pressure to reach a majority conclusion[2]. Following a *Watson* direction if the jury state they are unable to reach a conclusion, s 9(3) of CJA 2009 provides the coroner with the power to discharge the jury and to summons another in its place.

[1] [1988] QB 690.
[2] *Clayton v South Yorkshire Coroner* [2005] EWHC 1196 (Admin).

6.41 See CHAPTER 5 for more detail of the role of juries in inquests, including how they are appointed.

Conclusions in cases where there have been related criminal proceedings

6.42 In inquests where there have been previous, related criminal proceedings, any determination of the resumed inquest must be consistent with the outcome of the proceedings in the criminal court[1]. Where there has been a substantive hearing in the criminal courts it may not be necessary to resume the inquest, in which case the coroner will simply inform the registrar of this. However, in some cases, for example where arguable failings by state bodies contributed to a person committing a homicide offence, an inquest may be required to investigate issues that could not be determined in a criminal trial. See CHAPTER

6.42 *Conclusions and Records of Inquests*

21 for further detail on the interplay between inquests and criminal proceedings.

[1] CJA 2009, Sch 1, para 9(11).

Admissions by an interested person

6.43 There are instances when an interested person will make admissions prior to or during an inquest that there were failings in the care or treatment extended to the deceased. To what extent should any such admissions be reflected in the coroner's or jury's conclusions?

6.44 In the case of *R (Tainton) v HM Senior Coroner for Preston and W Lancashire*[1], admissions had been made by an NHS trust that there had been shortcomings in the care provided to the deceased in that they had delayed in diagnosing him with cancer. On judicial review the Divisional Court agreed that the coroner, having left only the short-forms of natural causes and open conclusion, should have directed the jury to include within the Record of Inquest a brief narrative of the admitted shortcomings:

> 'Putting the point another way, in an inquest such as this, where the possibility of a violation of the deceased's right to life cannot be wholly excluded, sections 5(1)(b) and 5(2) of the 2009 Act should require the inclusion in the Record of Inquest of any admitted failings forming part of the circumstances in which the deceased came by his death, which are given in evidence before the coroner, even if, on the balance of probabilities, the jury cannot properly find them causative of the death.'[2]

[1] [2016] EWHC 1396 (Admin).
[2] *R (Tainton) v HM Senior Coroner for Preston and W Lancashire* [2016] EWHC 1396 (Admin) at [74].

6.45 In this case the relevant NHS trust had admitted that they had delayed in diagnosing the deceased with cancer, but there was no way of knowing whether this delay had contributed to his death (see **6.175** below for consideration of *Tainton* in respect of causation in coronial law). Without recording the failings in Box 3, the Record of Inquest would simply have stated that the deceased died of 'natural causes', which the Divisional Court deemed 'inadequate to describe properly the circumstances in which the deceased met his death. In our judgment, the admitted failings of the Trust's staff [. . .] should have formed part of the inquest findings precisely because they were admitted, and formed part of the evidence heard by the jury'[1]. Without the additional information, the Record of Inquest when looked at as a whole would not have fully answered the question of 'in what circumstances' the deceased came about his death, and therefore would have been incomplete[2].

[1] [2016] EWHC 1396 (Admin) at [80], [81].
[2] [2016] EWHC 1396 (Admin) at [73].

6.46 This principle was further considered by the High Court in *R (Carole Smith) v HM Assistant Coroner for North West Wales*[1], where it was determined that the test set out in *Tainton* could be met by including reference to any admitted failings in the coroner's reasons (not just in the Record of Inquest)[2]. Ostensibly this is at odds with the explicit direction of the court in *Tainton*. However, it is notable that whilst a jury sat in *Tainton*, this was not the case in *Smith*; there, a coroner, sitting alone, heard the inquest. In a jury inquest, no findings of fact can be delivered other than those recorded on the Record of Inquest itself. There is no mechanism for the jury to deliver 'reasons' in the way that a coroner, sitting alone, can. Indeed, the court noted in *Smith* that 'both the reasons and the Record were delivered in public. Both, therefore, were part of the public record'. It is submitted that this explains the apparent discrepancy between the two decisions.

[1] [2020] EWHC 781 (Admin).
[2] *R (Carole Smith) v HM Assistant Coroner for North West Wales* [2020] EWHC 781 (Admin) at [77].

6.47 How the procedural Art 2 obligation is satisfied is a matter of domestic law[1]. Art 2 does not require a particular format of finding. However, in a jury case, matters required to be found in open court in order to satisfy the procedural obligation will require to be on either the face of the Record of Inquest, or possibly in a report to prevent future deaths[2].

[1] *R (Lewis) v Mid and North Shropshire Coroner* [2009] EWCA Civ 1403, [2010] 1 WLR 1836 at [24].
[2] See CHAPTER 7.

6.48 This interpretation as to why these cases take different approaches is bolstered by the decision in *Worthington* where the question of whether there is a material difference between (i) a coroner's findings of fact, and (ii) the '"determination" of the matters to be ascertained under section 5(1)' was considered: the Administrative court 'doubted' that there is any real distinction between the two[1]. Whilst this is not an Art 2 case, the principle may well still be of relevance.

[1] *R (Worthington) v Senior Coroner for Cumbria* [2018] EWHC 3386 (Admin) at [34].

C – SHORT-FORM CONCLUSIONS

Overview

6.49 As has been set out at **6.22** above, there are two alternatives for conclusions which are permitted by the Record of Inquest form and the case law: (i) a short-form conclusion, and (ii) a narrative conclusion[1]. It is also permissible to combine the two types of conclusion[2].

[1] Chief Coroner's Guidance No 17, Conclusions, para 19.
[2] Note (ii) to Form 2, Record of Inquest.

6.50 Wherever possible coroners should conclude with a short-form conclusion, as this 'has the advantage of being simple, accessible for bereaved families and public alike, and also clear for statistical purposes'[1].

[1] Chief Coroner's Guidance No 17, Conclusions, para 26.

6.51 It is a matter for the coroner to decide whether a short-form or narrative conclusion is more appropriate, or if there is a jury, which type of conclusion should be left to the jury (see **6.34**). However, in more complex cases, the coroner should hear submissions from interested parties as to whether there should be a short-form or narrative conclusion, and the particular short-form conclusion (see **6.29** above).

6.52 Conclusions and Records of Inquests

6.52 The notes to the Record of Inquest lists nine short-form conclusions that may be adopted:

(I) accident or misadventure;
(II) alcohol/drug related;
(III) industrial disease;
(IV) lawful/unlawful killing;
(V) natural causes;
(VI) open;
(VII) road traffic collision;
(VIII) stillbirth;
(IX) suicide.

6.53 The coroner is not obliged to record a short-form conclusion in the terms suggested in the notes to Form 2. This is apparent from note (i) to Form 2, which states that one of the short-form conclusions *may* be adopted, and note (ii) which makes clear that in addition to or in the alternative to a short-form conclusion, the coroner or jury may reach a narrative conclusion[1]. It was made clear by the majority in the Supreme Court in *R (Maughan) v HM Senior Coroner for Oxfordshire Senior Coroner*[2] that the notes appended to Form 2 do not have the substantive status of rules, but simply set out, for the convenience of coroners, an understanding of the common law. However, as the Chief Coroner's Guidance states, 'as before (old Form 22) the list is not exclusive but straying from the list will usually be unwise'. In practice, if none of the list of short-form conclusions are suitable, a narrative conclusion will usually be more appropriate.

[1] See also *R v Inner South London Coroner, ex p Kendall* [1988] 1 WLR 1186.
[2] [2020] UKSC 46.

6.54 Neglect is not a conclusion in itself but is best described as a finding. Nonetheless it must be recorded as part of the conclusion (in Box 4)[1] and so is considered alongside the short-form conclusions below.

[1] Coroner's Guidance No 17, Conclusions, para 74.

I. Accident or misadventure

6.55 In practice, there is little, if any, distinction between accidental death and misadventure. In terms of definition, in *McDonnell v HM Assistant Coroner for West London*[1] the Divisional Court stated that death by misadventure is a death in which some deliberate but lawful human act has unexpectedly resulted in death, whereas 'accident' connotes something over which there is no human control[2]. In that case, the deceased suffered from chronic pain and died of an overdose of codeine that he had been prescribed. The court held that the coroner had been entitled to conclude that taking codeine was a deliberate human act which contributed to the deceased's death, and her conclusion of death by misadventure was not therefore open to challenge.

[1] [2016] EWHC 3078 (Admin), 154 BMLR 188.
[2] Approving *Jervis on Coroners* (13th edn), at 13–37.

6.56 Despite historic judicial discouragement of the term 'misadventure'[1], the Chief Coroner's Guidance[2] confirms that misadventure may be used as a conclusion – it remains on the list – and 'may be the right conclusion when a death arises from some deliberate human act which unexpectedly and unintentionally goes wrong'.

[1] *R v Portsmouth Coroner's Court, ex p Anderson* [1987] 1 WLR 1640; *R v Inner South London Coroner, ex p Kendall* [1988] 1 WLR 1186.
[2] Chief Coroner's Guidance No 17, Conclusions, para 67.

6.57 As is also made clear by the Chief Coroner's Guidance No 17, authorities have approved the use of additional words in accident conclusions, such as 'the deceased was drowned when his sailing dinghy capsized in heavy seas', or 'accidental death resulting from the inhalation of Tippex thinners'[1]. After all, the coroner's obligation is to record 'how' the deceased came by their death. These additional words in Box 3 in combination with a short-form conclusion of 'accident' should not be confused for narrative conclusions.

[1] Chief Coroner's Guidance No 17, Conclusions, paras 65–66.

6.58 In the context of medical treatment which unexpectedly causes death, a conclusion of accident may well be the right conclusion. In *R v Birmingham and Solihull Coroner ex p Benton*[1], the High Court held that where an underlying medical condition causes death, then even in the context of inadequate medical treatment, a conclusion of natural causes will be appropriate. However:

> 'On the other hand, where a person is suffering from a condition which does not in any way threaten his life and such person undergoes treatment which for whatever reason causes death. Then assuming that there is no question of unlawful killing the verdict should be death by accident/misadventure. Just as the recording of death by natural causes does not absolve the doctors of fault so the recording of death by accident/misadventure does not imply fault.'

[1] (1997) 162 JP 807, [1997] 8 Med LR 362.

II. Alcohol/drug related

6.59 The wording 'alcohol/drug related' in the 2013 list replaced the previous wording in the notes to the old Form 22, which was 'dependent/non-dependent abuse of drugs'. The new wording is clearly much wider in its scope, and by omitting the word 'abuse' carries less stigma to the memory of the deceased. This may reflect social policy, which is to treat drug addiction and chronic alcoholism as an illness or disease rather than as a choice. The current wording would appear to be wide enough to encompass the whole spectrum of alcohol/drug related deaths, from deaths due to chronic drug abuse/dependence and alcoholism though to accidental death due to excess drinking on a night out or a 'one-off' drug overdose. In principle, there seems no reason why this conclusion could not also include deaths related to the use of prescription or over the counter medicines, as well as 'recreational' drugs.

6.60 In *R v Inner South London Coroner, ex p Kendall*[1], the deceased died after inhaling Tippex thinning fluid containing the solvent trichloroethane at the age of 14. At the inquest the coroner recorded a verdict of death by acute abuse of a drug. The Court of Appeal held that trichloroethane could not be classed as a 'drug' and that solvent abuse deaths were not therefore to be

6.60 *Conclusions and Records of Inquests*

designated as 'acute abuse of a drug'. There should instead be a conclusion of accident in combination with words such as 'abuse of volatile substances' or 'solvent abuse'. Simon Brown J observed that it was established policy within the coroner's jurisdiction to avoid any unnecessary stigma to the memory of the deceased and that the 'very word "drugs" evokes clear overtones of addiction and criminality'. The verdict had been both unnecessarily wounding to the memory of the deceased and failed in its purpose of warning the public of the danger of solvent abuse. It must be questionable whether *ex p Kendall* would now be decided the same way under the new wording, perhaps reflecting the change in attitude towards drug taking together with the vastly greater variety and availability of drugs.

[1]   [1988] 1 WLR 1186.

III. Industrial disease

6.61 There is no clear definition of 'industrial diseases' for the purposes of this conclusion. The conclusion is not restricted to the list of industrial diseases set out in the Social Security (Industrial Injuries) Prescribed Disease Regulations 1985[1]. The definition is probably wide enough to include any disease contracted in the workplace due to exposure to a harmful substance or activity. The Chief Coroner's Guidance No 37 on COVID-19 deaths and possible exposure in the workplace[2] focusses on the opening of investigations and not potential conclusions in such cases. But it is submitted that industrial disease may be an appropriate conclusion if it can be established on evidence that the disease was contracted at work.

[1]   SI 1985/967; see *R v HM Coroner for South Glamorgan* (1987) 151 JP 799.
[2]   Published 26 March 2020.

IV. Lawful killing/unlawful killing

6.62 Historically coronial proceedings were used as a means for finding criminal liability. It was the duty of a coroner's jury to state in their verdict the name of the person considered to have committed the offence or of being an accessory to the fact. The inquisition would then act as an indictment and the accused would be committed for criminal trial. However, since s 56(1) of the Criminal Justice Act 1977 was passed, inquest verdicts have been forbidden from making any finding that any person is guilty of murder, manslaughter or infanticide[1]. Inquests are now also forbidden by s 10(2)(a) CJA 2009 from making a determination that appears to determine any question of criminal liability, hence the use of the term unlawful killing, as opposed to a specific criminal offence. Thus Lady Arden observed in the Supreme Court in *Maughan* that retaining the criminal standard of proof 'has lost some of its historical purpose'[2].

[1]   *R (Maughan) v HM Senior Coroner for Oxfordshire Senior Coroner* [2020] UKSC 46 at [88]–[89].
[2]   *Maughan* at [89].

6.63 Despite the historical divergence of criminal and inquest proceedings, unlawful killing, which following *Maughan* must established to the civil

C – Short-form conclusions **6.67**

standard of proof, remains a short-form conclusion listed in Form 2. Thus, in order for an unlawful killing determination to be made, the coroner or jury must be satisfied that the elements of a relevant English homicide offence are made out on balance. Somewhat counter-intuitively, therefore, whilst inquests are required to avoid naming both the perpetrator and the offence, they need to consider whether the person was in fact killed by a homicide offence.

In response to the Supreme Court's decision in *Maughan* the Chief Coroner published Law Sheet No 6, which states:

> 'At any inquest where unlawful killing may be in issue, it will now be particularly important for the coroner to explain the distinction between criminal proceedings and inquests. The explanation should set out the nature of the inquest process as a fact-finding inquiry with the objective of answering the four statutory questions (who the deceased was; and when, where and how the deceased came by his or her death). Where a coroner or coroner's jury comes to a conclusion of unlawful killing, that finding has no bearing on criminal proceedings, which are subject to a materially higher standard of proof (as well as entirely different procedural rules).'[1]

[1] See para 3.

6.64 Cases in which an unlawful killing conclusion is in issue are often amongst the most intensely fought of all inquests. This section will therefore set out in brief the relevant constituent elements of the law of intentional homicide. It is recommended, however, that practitioners consult the relevant specialist criminal law texts where unlawful killing is directly in issue.

6.65 Not all criminal homicide offences can result in an unlawful killing conclusion. The Chief Coroner's Law Sheet No 1 on Unlawful Killing[1] states that conclusions of unlawful killing are restricted to the offences of:

(a) murder;
(b) manslaughter;
(c) infanticide.

[1] Chief Coroner, Law Sheet No 1, Unlawful Killing (revised 18 January 2016).

6.66 It is clear that unlawful killing does not cover the homicide driving offences causing death by careless or dangerous driving[1]. Causing death by driving will only amount to unlawful killing if amounts to either murder (where a vehicle is used to kill intentionally), or more commonly manslaughter (by gross negligence or unlawful act). Law Sheet No 1 provides helpful examples of circumstances in which causing a death by driving may amount to unlawful killing. It further avers that by analogy with driving offences unlawful killing does not extend to Health and Safety Act 1974 offences that result in death[2].

[1] *R (Wilkinson) v HM Coroner for Greater Manchester South District* [2012] EWHC 2755 (Admin).
[2] Chief Coroner, Law Sheet No 1, Unlawful Killing, para 38.

6.67 For the procedural links between the criminal and coronial jurisdictions, including when a criminal homicide investigation will lead to the suspension of a coronial investigation, see CHAPTER 2. Practitioners should bear in mind that if at any time during the course of an inquest it appears to the coroner that the death of the deceased is likely to have been due to a homicide offence and that

6.67 *Conclusions and Records of Inquests*

a person may be charged in relation to the offence, the coroner must adjourn the inquest and notify the Director of Public Prosecution in accordance with r 25 of the Coroners (Inquests) Rules 2013[1] (the 2013 Rules).

[1] SI 2013/1616.

Lawful killing

6.68 Form 2 provides for the possibility of a 'lawful killing' conclusion. Lawful killing is the intentional killing of another where a valid justificatory criminal defence is made out, such as self-defence or defence of another. There is a dearth of authority on lawful killing and it is not covered in the Chief Coroner's Law Sheets or Guidance. It relates to the previous short conclusion of 'justifiable homicide'. It appears to be restricted to cases where but for the defence the death would amount to either murder or voluntary manslaughter. If there is no legal or evidential basis for concluding that a death was deliberately caused but legally justified, then a lawful killing conclusion will be inappropriate[1]. Criminal defences are covered below at **6.106**.

[1] Chief Coroner, Law Sheet No 1, Unlawful Killing, para 2.

Unlawful killing

MURDER

6.69 Murder is a common law offence. It is the killing of a person by another with the intent either to kill the person or to do them grievous bodily harm. The intent is defined by the old wordage 'with malice aforethought'[1].

[1] *R v Durham Coroner ex p Attorney General*, The Times, 29 June 1978, DC.

Physical elements

6.70 The offence can only involve the killing of a human being. Prior to its birth, a child is not a legal person[1]. The death of a fetus in utero cannot therefore constitute murder, although it may constitute child destruction. If a fetus is injured whilst in utero and goes on to die having been born alive, that could constitute murder or manslaughter, depending on the intent[2].

[1] Coke's Institutes, 3 Co Inst 47.
[2] *Criminal Injuries Compensation Authority v First Tier Tribunal (Social Entitlement Tribunal)* [2015] QB 459.

Mental elements

6.71 Murder is crime of specific intent based on an intention to kill or cause serious bodily harm. In the rare cases where the primary desire of the defendant was not to harm the person it is sufficient that death or serious bodily harm was a virtual certainty (barring some unforeseen intervention) and that the accused appreciated that was the case[1].

[1] *A-G's Ref (No 3 of 1994)* [1998] AC 245.

6.72 Mercy killing remains unlawful in England and Wales. Thus the Court of Appeal upheld the murder conviction of a mother who had deliberately killed

C – Short-form conclusions 6.77

her son by injecting him with heroin in his hospital bed[1]. Voluntary euthanasia cannot provide a defence of necessity to murder and such a defence is not required by the ECHR[2]. For the distinction between the lawful withdrawal of treatment that maintains life, and the unlawful termination of a patient's life see *Airedale NHS Trust v Bland*[3].

[1] *R v Nedrick* [1986] 3 All ER 1.
[2] *R v Inglis* [201] EWCA Crim 2637.
[3] [1993] AC 789.

Partial defences

6.73 There are three specific statutory partial defences to murder each of which has the effect of reducing the offence of murder to one of manslaughter. These forms of voluntary manslaughter will, of course, still result in an unlawful killing conclusion at inquest and a detailed exposition is beyond the scope of this book. The defences are:

(1) Loss of control under the CJA 2009.
(2) Diminished responsibility under s 2 of the Homicide Act 1957.
(3) Killing in pursuance of a suicide pact under s 4 of the Homicide Act 1957.

6.74 The defence of loss of control repealed the defence of provocation under s 3 of the Homicide Act 1957 and abolished the common law offence of provocation from October 2010.

6.75 Murder or manslaughter committed outside the United Kingdom may be tried in England in accordance with s 9 of the Offences Against the Person Act 1861.

MANSLAUGHTER

6.76 A distinction is to be drawn between voluntary and involuntary manslaughter[1]. Voluntary manslaughter consists of cases covered by the partial defences to murder set out above. Involuntary manslaughter covers the forms of manslaughter which are indictable criminal offences in their own right where there is no intention to kill. There are two forms of involuntary manslaughter:

(a) unlawful act or constructive manslaughter; and
(b) gross negligence manslaughter

[1] *R (Nicklinson) v Ministry of Justice* [2013] EWCA Civ 961, [2014] 2 All ER 32.

Unlawful act manslaughter

6.77 Unlawful act manslaughter is made out where a person commits a criminal offence which is not a homicide offence, which then causes another's death. The majority of cases of unlawful act manslaughter will be offences against the person such as an assault, which result in death. But other offences, such as criminal damage and arson[1], and burglary[2] will suffice.

[1] *R v Goodfellow* (1986) 83 Cr App R 23; *R v F (J)* [2015] EWCA Crim 167.

6.77 *Conclusions and Records of Inquests*

² R v Watson [1989] 2 All ER 865.

Mental element

6.78 It must be established that the accused had the requisite *mens rea* for the free-standing unlawful act, so subjective recklessness would be required, eg for an assault[1].

[1] R v Spratt [1990] 1 WLR 1073.

Physical element

6.79 As well as establishing the physical element of the unlawful act, there is an additional objective requirement in respect of the act in order for unlawful act manslaughter to be made out:

' . . . the unlawful act must be such as all sober and reasonable people would inevitably recognise must subject the other person to, at least, the risk of some harm resulting therefrom, albeit not serious harm.'

6.80 Because this element is objective, it is not necessary to establish that the accused themselves foresaw harm to another from their unlawful conduct[1]. The relevant harm resulting from the act must be physical, thus emotional disturbance to a petrol attendant who had a weak heart and who went on to die following a robbery was not sufficient to satisfy the test[2].

[1] DPP v Newbury [1977] AC 500.
[2] R v Dawson (1985) 81 Cr App R 150.

GROSS NEGLIGENCE MANSLAUGHTER

6.81 Gross negligence manslaughter occurs when a person breaches a duty of care imposed by civil law, causing death in circumstances so reprehensible as to amount to criminal gross negligence. In the landmark case of *R v Adomako*[1] an anaesthetist failed to notice a disconnection at an endotracheal tube during an eye operation, resulting in oxygen deprivation, cardiac arrest and death. He was convicted at trial of manslaughter by gross negligence. The House of Lords resolved that gross negligence in relation to a civil breach of duty, and not recklessness, constitutes the proper test for the offence. Lord Mackay of Clashfern held at [187]:

' . . . the ordinary principles of the law of negligence apply to ascertain whether or not the defendant has been in breach of a duty of care towards the victim who has died. If such breach of duty is established the next question is whether that breach of duty caused the death of the victim. If so, the jury must go on to consider whether that breach of duty should be characterised as gross negligence and therefore as a crime. This will depend on the seriousness of the breach of duty committed by the defendant in all the circumstances in which the defendant was placed when it occurred. The jury will have to consider whether the extent to which the defendant's conduct departed from the proper standard of care incumbent upon him, involving as it must have done a risk of death to the patient, was such that it should be judged criminal.'

[1] [1995] 1 AC 171.

6.82 The common law rules of the law of negligence thus govern whether a relevant duty of care exists, and the standard of that duty. Although much of the case law regarding gross negligence manslaughter concerns clinical negligence, there are obviously examples of inquest juries finding unlawful killing by gross negligence manslaughter in other contexts, for instance against the police in the second Hillsborough Inquests. The question is simply whether a relevant duty exists in civil law. Again, readers are referred to the relevant practitioner texts of the law of negligence in that regard. However, it is only if the additional element of criminal grossness is established that a breach of such a duty may constitute gross negligence manslaughter.

6.83 The elements of gross negligence manslaughter must be proved in relation to one identifiable person. They may not be stablished through the cumulative actions of several people – *R (Secretary of State for Justice) v HM Deputy Coroner for the Eastern District of West Yorkshire*[1].

[1] [2012] EWHC 1634 (Admin).

Grossness

6.84 The classical formulation of the test for grossness is per Lord Hewart CJ in *R v Bateman*[1] where he held it was required that:

> 'the negligence of the accused went beyond a mere matter of compensation between subjects and showed such disregard for the life and safety of others as to amount to a crime against the state and conduct deserving punishment.'

[1] (1925) 19 Cr App R 8.

6.85 Post-*Adomako* cases have clarified the nature of the value judgment inherent in deciding whether a breach of duty is properly characterised as 'gross' and therefore criminal.

6.86 In *R v Misra*[1], which concerned breach of duty arising out of the omission to treat post-operative infection Lord Judge CJ approved [at 150] the following direction to the jury by Langley J:

> 'Over the years, the courts have used a number of expressions to describe this vital element of the crime, but the key is that it must be gross in the perhaps slightly old-fashioned sense now of the use of that word. So in this case, when you are considering the conduct of each doctor, I think you will find it most helpful to concentrate on whether or not the prosecution has made you sure that the conduct of whichever one you are considering, in all the circumstances you have heard about and as you find them to be, fell so far below the standard to be expected of a reasonably competent and careful senior house officer that it was something, in your assessment, truly exceptionally bad, and which showed such an indifference to an obviously serious risk to the life of Sean Phillips and such a departure from the standard to be expected as to amount, in your judgment, to a criminal act or omission, and so to be the very serious crime of manslaughter.'

[1] [2004] EWCA Crim 2375, [2005] 1 Cr App R 21.

6.87 In *R (Oliver) v DPP*[1] Davis LJ summarised the position, referring to the 'truly exceptionally bad' criterion in *R v Misra*[2]:

6.87 Conclusions and Records of Inquests

'Mistakes, even very serious mistakes, and errors of judgment, even very serious errors of judgment, will not of themselves suffice . . . The bar is thus set high: perhaps unsurprisingly so, given that such cases ordinarily involve no criminal intent.'

[1] [2016] 1771 (Admin).
[2] [2004] EWCA Crim 2375, [2005] 1 Cr App R 21, as follows at [11].

6.88 The question of grossness is one for the jury. In the clinical case of *R v Sellu*[1] the deceased underwent elective total knee replacement surgery but later died of a perforated bowel following failures in treatment on the part of a colorectal surgeon. The surgeon was convicted of gross negligence manslaughter. His grounds of appeal included the prosecution's use of expert clinical evidence on the question of grossness. The Court of Appeal held amongst other things, that the law had developed to the position where an expert was permitted to give his opinion on the 'ultimate issue' of grossness. Sir Brian Leveson P stated that it was necessary that:

'The jury are assisted sufficiently to understand how to approach their task of identifying the line that separates even serious or very serious mistakes or lapses, from conduct which . . . "was truly exceptionally bad" and was such a departure from that standard that it consequently amounted to being criminal.'

[1] [2016] EWCA Crim 1716, [2017] 4 WLR 64.

6.89 However, in such a case the judge remains required to make clear to the jury that they are not bound by the expert's opinion and the question of grossness is ultimately one for them. The judge's directions to the jury had been deficient in that respect and the conviction was quashed.

Causation

6.90 The negligence must be a substantial, but not necessarily the sole or the major cause of death; see *R v Misra*[1]. The conduct in question need not be the sole cause of death so long as it is proved to be a material cause. 'Further, in this regard it is also well-established that the prosecution is not required to demonstrate scientific or mathematical certainty. The facts have to be looked at as a whole. That a medical expert is not able to rule out a possibility other than the breach of duty as the cause of death is not of itself necessarily a bar to a jury being sure of guilt' (*R v Sellu*[2], citing *Dawson*)[3].

[1] At [70].
[2] At [12].
[3] (1985) 81 CAR 150 at p 154.

6.91 If the jury are not sure that the victim would have survived in any event, either however well they had been treated or because they might not have received appropriate treatment anyway, then causation will not be made out. Equally, if there is a time beyond which the jury is not sure the victim would have survived, then any grossly negligent conduct beyond that point cannot result in a finding of guilt (*R v Misra*[1]).

[1] At [70].

Mental element

6.92 Proving gross negligence does not require proof of any particular state of mind on the part of the accused. The test is in its essence objective and subjective recklessness as to the results of conduct is not required (*A-G's Ref (No 2 of 1999)*[1]). '[A]ctual foresight of perception of the risk is not a prerequisite of the crime of gross negligence'; see *R v Mark*[2]. However, an objectively foreseeable risk of death is required: 'the circumstances must be such that a reasonably prudent person would have foreseen a serious and obvious risk not merely of injury, even serious injury, but of death' (*R v Singh*[3], approved in *R v Misra*).

[1] [2000] QB 796.
[2] [2004] EWCA Crim 2490.
[3] [1999] Crim LR 582.

CORPORATE MANSLAUGHTER

6.93 Historically, because of the 'identification principle', whereby a company is fixed with criminal liability through its 'directing mind', corporate manslaughter, although theoretically possible, had been very rarely established. It was for this reason that Parliament passed the Corporate Manslaughter and Corporate Homicide Act 2007 (CMCHA 2007). The act established a new offence of corporate manslaughter and abolished the common law offence of gross negligence. Section 20 CMCHA 2007 abolished common law manslaughter by gross negligence insofar as it concerns corporations or other organisations.

The offence

6.94 Section 1(1) sets out as follows:

'1 The offence
(1) An organisation to which this section applies is guilty of an offence if the way in which its activities are managed or organised—
(a) causes a person's death, and
(b) amounts to a gross breach of a relevant duty of care owed by the organisation to the deceased.'

6.95 Section 1(2) specifies that offence can be committed only by corporations, police forces, partnerships, trade unions or employers' associations that are employers, or governmental department or other bodies listed in Sch 1 to the Act. The offence cannot be committed by an individual and an individual cannot be guilty of aiding, abetting, counselling or procuring the commission of an offence under the act (s 18 CMCHA 2007).

6.96 Section 1(3) sets out an important qualification to the offence as follows:

'(3) An organisation is guilty of an offence under this section only if the way in which its activities are managed or organised by its senior management is a substantial element in the breach referred to in subsection (1).'

6.97 *Conclusions and Records of Inquests*

Duty of care

6.97 Section 2 CMCHA 2007 defines a 'relevant duty of care' for the purposes of s 1. By contrast with the common law offence of gross negligence manslaughter, the CMCHA 2007 excludes many specific situations in which a duty of care may or may not exist in civil law, from the operation of the criminal act. It is a detailed provision which requires careful attention in order to assess whether the offence may be committed in a given context. Section 2(1)–2(6) set out as follows:

'2 Meaning of "relevant duty of care"
- (1) A *"relevant duty of care"*, in relation to an organisation, means any of the following duties owed by it under the law of negligence—
  - (a) a duty owed to its employees or to other persons working for the organisation or performing services for it;
  - (b) a duty owed as occupier of premises;
  - (c) a duty owed in connection with—
    - (i) the supply by the organisation of goods or services (whether for consideration or not),
    - (ii) the carrying on by the organisation of any construction or maintenance operations,
    - (iii) the carrying on by the organisation of any other activity on a commercial basis, or
    - (iv) the use or keeping by the organisation of any plant, vehicle or other thing;
  - (d) a duty owed to a person who, by reason of being a person within subsection (2), is someone for whose safety the organisation is responsible.
- (2) A person is within this subsection if—
  - (a) he is detained at a custodial institution or in a custody area at a court, a police station or customs premises;
  - (aa) he is detained in service custody premises;
  - (b) he is detained at a removal centre, a short-term holding facility or in pre-departure accommodation;
  - (c) he is being transported in a vehicle, or being held in any premises, in pursuance of prison escort arrangements or immigration escort arrangements;
  - (d) he is living in secure accommodation in which he has been placed;
  - (e) he is a detained patient.
- (3) Subsection (1) is subject to sections 3 to 7.
- (4) A reference in subsection (1) to a duty owed under the law of negligence includes a reference to a duty that would be owed under the law of negligence but for any statutory provision under which liability is imposed in place of liability under that law.
- (5) For the purposes of this Act, whether a particular organisation owes a duty of care to a particular individual is a question of law. The judge must make any findings of fact necessary to decide that question.
- (6) For the purposes of this Act there is to be disregarded—
  - (a) any rule of the common law that has the effect of preventing a duty of care from being owed by one person to another by reason of the fact that they are jointly engaged in unlawful conduct;
  - (b) any such rule that has the effect of preventing a duty of care from being owed to a person by reason of his acceptance of a risk of harm.'

6.98 Sections 3–7 of CMCHA 2007, in accordance with s 2(3) above, limit the scope of the application of the duties of care set out in s 2 in specific circumstances regarding:

- public policy decisions, public functions and statutory inspections – s 3;
- military activities – s 4;
- policing and law enforcement – s 5;
- the responses emergency services to emergencies – s 6;
- child protection and probation functions – s 7.

6.99 The specific limitations require detailed analysis by practitioners in order to assess whether a relevant duty of care exists for the purposes of CMCHA 2007 in a given scenario. Set out below are the exclusions in relation to certain categories of case that are commonly considered at inquests:

(1) Military activities are excluded in respect of:
  (a) operations, including peacekeeping operations and operations for dealing with terrorism, civil unrest or serious public disorder, in the course of which members of the armed forces come under attack or face the threat of attack or violent resistance (s 4(1)(a) and s 4(2)), and activities carried on in preparation for, or directly in support of, such operations;
  (b) training of a hazardous nature, or training carried out in a hazardous way, which it is considered needs to be carried out, or carried out in that way, in order to improve or maintain the effectiveness of the armed forces with respect to such operations (s 4(1)(c));
  (c) any activities carried out by members of the special forces (s 4(3)).

(2) Policing and law enforcement activities are excluded by s 5 in respect of:
  (a) operations which are operations:
   (i) for dealing with terrorism, civil unrest or serious disorder;
   (ii) that involve the carrying on of policing or law–enforcement activities;
   (iii) where officers or employees of the public authority in question come under attack, or face the threat of attack or violent resistance (s 5(1)(a) and s 5(2));
  (b) activities carried on in preparation for, or directly in support of, such operations (s 5(1)(b));
  (c) training of a hazardous nature, or training carried out in a hazardous way, which it is considered needs to be carried out, or carried out in that way, in order to improve or maintain the effectiveness of officers or employees of the public authority with respect to such operations (s 5(1)(c));
  (d) any duty of care which is not a duty of care that falls within s 2(1)(a), (b), or (c).

It can thus be seen that the vast majority of operational functions of the police are excluded from the operation of the Act.

(3) The activities of an emergency service are excluded broadly in respect of 'any duty of care owed . . . in respect of the way in which it responds

to emergency circumstances' (s 6(1)). However, for the purposes of emergency medical services this broad exclusion does not include:
(a) the way in which medical treatment is carried out (s 6(3)(a)); or
(b) the way in which decisions as to the carrying out of medical treatment are made, other than decision as to the order in which persons are to be given such treatment – s 6(3)(b) and s 6(4).

Thus corporate negligence in relation to the carrying out of clinical emergency services may amount to the offence under CMCHA 2007.

Gross breach

6.100 Whether a breach was gross must be determined in accordance with s 8 CMCHA 2007 which sets out a series of factors that the jury must consider:

'8 Factors for jury
(1) This section applies where—
   (a) it is established that an organisation owed a relevant duty of care to a person, and
   (b) it falls to the jury to decide whether there was a gross breach of that duty.
(2) The jury must consider whether the evidence shows that the organisation failed to comply with any health and safety legislation that relates to the alleged breach, and if so—
   (a) how serious that failure was;
   (b) how much of a risk of death it posed.
(3) The jury may also—
   (a) consider the extent to which the evidence shows that there were attitudes, policies, systems or accepted practices within the organisation that were likely to have encouraged any such failure as is mentioned in subsection (2), or to have produced tolerance of it;
   (b) have regard to any health and safety guidance that relates to the alleged breach.'

6.101 However, s 8 does not the prevent the jury from having regard to any other matters they consider relevant; see s 8(4).

6.102 The relationship between the requirement to consider whether there was a failure to comply with health and safety legislation, the burden of proof on the prosecution, and the reverse burden of proof in relation to certain matters under the Health and Safety at Work Act 1974 was considered by the Court of Appeal in *R v Cotswold Geotechnical Holdings Ltd*[1].

[1] [2011] EWCA Crim 1337.

INFANTICIDE

6.103 As observed in the Chief Coroner's Law Sheet No 1, the offence of infanticide under s 1 of the Infanticide Act 1938 is rarely prosecuted. In criminal proceedings it may be charged as a sole offence or as an alternative to murder or manslaughter. The elements of the offence of infanticide are as follows:

(i) a woman by wilful act or omission causes the death of her child under the age of 12 months;
(ii) at the time of the act or omission the balance of her mind was disturbed by reason of her not having fully recovered from the effect of giving birth or by reason of the effect of lactation consequent on the birth;
(iii) the circumstances are such that but for the above the offence would have amounted to murder or manslaughter.

6.104 As regards element (ii), the failure to fully recover from the effect of giving birth or the effect of lactation consequent on the birth do not have to be the sole cause of the balance of mind being disturbed[1].

[1] *R v Tunstill* [2018] EWCA Crim 1696.

6.105 As regards the mental element of the crime, point (iii) above does not require the prosecution to prove that there was an intention to cause death or grievous bodily harm. The *mens rea* for the offence is simply 'by any wilful act or omission' – thus the remit of the offence is widened and 'a distressed young mother . . . is not forced to confront what may be the stark truth that, for whatever reason, however disturbed she may have been at the time, she killed her child intending to kill of cause really serious harm'[1].

[1] *R v Gore* [2007] EWCA Crim 2789, per Hallet LJ at [35].

Defences

6.106 A non-exhaustive list of the most common general defences in criminal law which apply to homicide offences are as follows:

(i) **Mistake:**
This involves a denial of the *mens rea* of the particular crime charged. A mistake can provide a defence to a crime of negligence but such a mistake must be a reasonable one, in keeping with the nature of breach of duty; see *DPP v Morgan*[1].

(ii) **Automatism:**
The defence of automatism applies only where there is a total loss of voluntary control. The question is whether there was 'a complete destruction of voluntary control'; see *R v Coley*[2].

(iii) **Intoxification:**
Where such intoxification is voluntary then it may only amount to a defence to a crime of specific intent, such as murder; see *DPP v Majewski*[3].

(iv) **Insanity**
The defence of insanity is still governed by the nineteenth century M'Naghten's rules from *M'Naghtens' Case* (1843) As observed in Law Sheet No 1, the defence of insanity has the operates to deprive the accused of the requisite *mens rea* necessary to commit the offence. The test is: is the coroner (or the jury) sure that the person was not legally insane at the time of the killing?

(v) **Duress:**
The defence of duress is not available to the crime of murder; see *R v Howe*[4]. Duress by threats generally requires a threat of death or grievous bodily harm and the further requirement that 'a person of

6.106 *Conclusions and Records of Inquests*

reasonable firmness sharing the characteristics of the defendant would not have given way to the threats; see *R v Hassan*[5], *R v Howe*[6].

(vi) **Self-defence, defence of another, defence of property, and the prevention of crime**
Self-defence, along with defence of property and defence of another are common law defences. The defence of using such force as is reasonable in the circumstances in the prevention of crime is found in s 3 of the Criminal Law Act 1967. In the case of each of these defences a person may use 'such force as is reasonable in the circumstances'. The meaning of 'reasonable force' in the case of each defence is now governed by s 76 of the Criminal Justice and Immigration Act 2008 (CJIA 2008).

[1] [1976] AC 182, *R v Lamb* [1967] 2 QB 981.
[2] [2013] EWCA Crim 223.
[3] [1977] AC 443.
[4] [1987] AC 417.
[5] [2005] UKHL 22.
[6] [1987] AC 417.

6.107 There are two questions to be answered by the jury in determining whether these defences are made out:

(i) WERE THE FACTS AS THE ACCUSED BELIEVED THEM TO BE SUCH THAT THE USE OF FORCE WAS NECESSARY FOR THE PURPOSES OF THE DEFENCE?

6.108 This is a subjective question[1]. The previous common law rule that the accused's belief had to be a reasonable one (thus including objective factors) remains the test for self-defence in civil law. The difference between the two tests was approved by the Divisional Court in *R (Duggan) v HM Assistant Deputy Coroner for the Northern District of Greater London*[2]. This approach is compatible with the EHCR[3]. Good reasons for a belief, and the reasonableness of the accused's belief, are nonetheless relevant evidentially to whether the belief was genuinely held.

[1] *R v Williams* [1987] 3 All ER 411.
[2] [2017] EWCA Civ 42, [2017] 1 WLR 2199.
[3] *Da Silva v UK* (2016) 63 EHRR 12, see CHAPTER 3 on Art 2 ECHR.

(ii) WAS THE DEGREE OF FORCE USED REASONABLE IN THE CIRCUMSTANCES?

6.109 This is ostensibly an objective test. But it has been applied, first by the common law[1], and now by statute under the CJIA 2008 to necessitate the consideration of subjective factors. Thus s 76(3) CJIA 2008 states that the question whether the degree of force used by D was reasonable in the circumstances is to be decided *by reference to the circumstances as D believed them to be,* and sub-ss (4)–(8) set out detailed considerations for the jury in applying the test.

[1] *Palmer v The Queen* [1971] AC 814.

Parties and causation

6.110 The criminal law governing parties and causation is vast, and it would not be practicable to set it out here. The law relating to 'joint enterprise' as

C – Short-form conclusions 6.114

accessories (secondary parties) to an offence was fundamentally restated in *R v Jogee*[1]. Again practitioners are referred to the relevant specialist criminal law texts in this regard.

[1] [2016] UKSC 8, [2017] AC 387.

Standard of proof

6.111 Following *Maughan*, all elements of the relevant intentional homicide offence must be proved on the balance of probabilities in order for a conclusion of unlawful killing to be reached. The justification for the change in the standard of proof for unlawful killing was set out by Lady Arden in *Maughan* at [93], where she stated:

> '. . . It is said that it would not promote public confidence in the legal system if a conclusion of unlawful killing is reached in an inquest on the civil standard, and a prosecution is mounted as a result which then fails. But that can happen in any event, even if the existing criminal standard is maintained, and it is at least as likely that public confidence in the legal system will be diminished if the evidence at the inquest cannot lead to clear findings on a balance of probabilities. It would appear to the public as if the system has conspired to prevent the truth from being available to them. It seems to me that the public are likely to understand that there is difference between a finding at an inquest and one at a criminal trial where the accused has well-established rights to participate actively in the process.'

Directions to the jury

6.112 If unlawful killing is left to the jury with any other conclusion, the jury must consider unlawful killing first[1]. An unlawful killing conclusion is of course subject to the Galbraith Plus test set out at **6.198** in this chapter.

[1] *R v Wolverhampton Coroner ex parte McCurbin* [1990] 1 WLR 719.

6.113 In accordance with s 10(2) CJA 2009 an inquest conclusion may not name a person found to be responsible for an unlawful killing. However, Law Sheet No 1 states that 'that person must still be capable of being identified (in the mind of the decision maker), whether by name, description or otherwise, as the person who caused the death'.

6.114 In respect of directions to the jury, Law Sheet No 1 states:

> 'In the summing up the coroner should direct the jury clearly as to what needs to be proved, ie all the ingredients of the criminal offence. Since a conclusion of unlawful killing involves a decision that a criminal offence has caused death, a jury must know clearly from the summing up what they have to find as facts (Box 3) in order to justify the conclusion (Box 4): see Anderson above. In any event every summing up must be tailored to the facts of the case and not just a recital of the necessary ingredients of the conclusion in question: see *R (Brown) v HM Coroner for Neath and Port Talbot* [2006] EWHC 2019 (Admin) at [22].'

The Chief Coroner's Law Sheet No 6 gives guidance to coroners in unlawful killing cases in the light of the Supreme Court's decision in *Maughan*. It states that in the cases where unlawful killing does arise 'the Chief Coroner would expect coroners to take a well-reasoned and fact-specific approach when faced with submissions and/or decisions as to the conclusions that are open to consideration'[1]. It reiterates that coroners and juries will need to direct themselves as to the elements that need to be established in respect of the relevant homicide offence and then to apply the civil standard to the facts as they related to each element[2]. Further:

> 'Where a coroner is sitting with a jury, if unlawful killing is a conclusion properly open on the facts, the coroner will need to give a reasoned judgment explaining why, and direct the jury accordingly. A reasoned decision will equally be expected of the coroner if unlawful killing is not, in the coroner's judgment, a conclusion properly open to the jury on the facts of the case.[3]'

[1] At para 8.
[2] See para 9.
[3] At para 15.

6.115 In *Brown* the Administrative Court quashed an unlawful killing verdict in a case where a boy had called another in to swim in a small pool, when the latter boy could not swim, and he subsequently downed. The evidence of an expert was that it was not foreseeable that the boy could have drowned in the pool, and he would not have done so if he had not thrashed so violently for so long in the water. The High Court held as follows:

(i) Although the decision to interfere with the ruling of a coroner could not be taken lightly, the evidence in the case, taken at its highest, could not be sufficient to allow a jury to return a verdict of unlawful killing. The court reiterated the importance of the application of the Galbraith plus test in unlawful killing cases.

(ii) '[I]t behoves a coroner to sum up the law relating to unlawful killing, ie, manslaughter, with the very greatest care. The direction must be tailored to the facts of the case. To give what can be described as a general direction can be positively misleading.[1]'

[1] [2006] EWHC 2019 (Admin) at [22].

6.116 *Brown* was an extreme case, in the sense that the coroner's directions to the jury were plainly defective. However, it demonstrates well that, in part because of the different roles of coroners and interested persons to an inquest, as opposed to the Crown and defence in criminal proceedings, the possibility of an unlawful killing conclusion may arise in factual circumstances at an inquest where, for instance, the CPS would have been likely to make the decision that a prosecution would not be in the public interest following any criminal investigation. It seems inevitable that following *Maughan*, there will be a rise in unlawful killing conclusions, and that coroners will be more willing to leave the conclusion to juries to consider. It seems further inevitable, that there will be challenges to unlawful killing conclusions by way of judicial review. It is submitted that coroners directing juries in unlawful killing cases post-*Maughan* would do well to have in mind the dicta of Bennett J in the Administrative Court in *Brown*.

V. Natural causes

6.117 The short form conclusion of natural causes includes deaths due to natural illnesses or disease processes that run their full course with no other intervening factors. There is an exception for natural disease processes that

C – Short-form conclusions 6.120

meet the definition of an 'industrial disease' conclusion, where that short-form conclusion should be used in the alternative. Natural causes as a conclusion therefore encompasses many of the major causes of death, such as heart disease, stroke, cancer and dementia. The Chief Coroner's Guidance on COVID-19 deaths in the workplace makes clear that COVID-19 is a naturally occurring disease. Although the guidance concerns the question whether a death is natural for the purposes of opening an investigation, it must follow that a conclusion of natural causes will be appropriate in a COVID-19 death unless other circumstances require additional conclusions to be made[1].

[1] Chief Coroner's Guidance No 37, COVID-19 deaths and possible exposure in the workplace.

6.118 Coronial law draws a distinction between the interpretation of the word 'unnatural' for the purposes of establishing coronial jurisdiction under s 1 CJA 2009, and the definition of 'natural' causes for the purposes of that short form conclusion. Therefore, a death may be properly investigated as being 'unnatural' due to there being reason to suspect that there was a wholly unexpected death resulting from 'culpable human failure'[1], (see CHAPTER 2) but following investigation, the inquest may nevertheless return a conclusion of natural causes. A conclusion of natural causes will be appropriate:

> '. . . where a person is suffering from a potentially fatal condition and medical intervention does no more than fail to prevent death. In such circumstances the underlying cause of death is the condition that proved fatal and in such a case, the correct verdict would be death from natural causes. This would be the case even if the medical treatment that had been given was viewed generally by the medical profession as the wrong treatment. All the more so is this the case where such a person is not treated at all, even if the failure to give treatment was negligent . . . [2]'

[1] *R v Poplar Coroner* [1993] QB 610, see also *R (Touche) v Inner London North Coroner* [2001] 1 QB 1206.
[2] *R v Birmingham and Solihull Coroner ex p Benton* (1997) 1962 JP 807, 8 Med LR 362.

VI. Open conclusion

6.119 An open conclusion is one in which there is insufficient evidence to reach any of the other short-form conclusions. Form 22 of the Coroners Rules 1984 defined an open verdict as arising 'when the evidence did not fully or further disclose the means whereby the cause of death arose', although this definition has not been repeated in the 2013 Rules[1]. The Chief Coroner's Guidance[2] instead explains that 'an open conclusion is the only conclusion when the evidence fails to satisfy the coroner or the jury (to the appropriate standard of proof) that another short-form conclusion (or some necessary element of it) has been proved'. An open conclusion does not have its own standard of proof.

[1] SI 2013/1616.
[2] Chief Coroner's Guidance No 17, Conclusions, para 69.

6.120 Open conclusions are to be discouraged, save where strictly necessary. In *Re Tabarn* the Court of Appeal stated that 'an open verdict should only be used as a last resort, notably when the coroner is simply unable to reach any conclusion on the balance of probabilities'[1]. The court confirmed that the fact that there may be uncertainty as to other parts of the inquisition, such as the precise cause, time or place of death, does not authorise recording an open verdict if there is sufficient evidence to record how the deceased came by his death.

[1] Re Tabarn [1998] EWHC 8 (Admin), [2000] Inquest LR 52.

6.121 An open conclusion should not be used because members of the jury disagree amongst themselves on the other short form conclusion(s). Thus, an open conclusion is not equivalent to a hung jury in a criminal trial, but should only represent circumstances where it is their agreed decision that there is insufficient evidence to reach any of the short-form conclusions.

6.122 In *R (Barber) v City of London Coroner*[1] Lord Widgery, CJ stated:

> 'I would impress upon coroners that if they find themselves compelled to return an open verdict, that is not in any sense a reflection on them. It does not suggest that they are not doing their job properly or are insufficiently perceptive. There are many, many cases where there is real doubt as to the cause of death and where an open verdict is right, and where anything else is unjust to the family of the deceased.'

[1] [1975] 1 WLR 1310.

6.123 This is reflected in the current Chief Coroner's Guidance[1] where it is suggested that the coroner should tell the jury that if they do come to an open conclusion, they should not consider that they will be criticised for it or that they have failed in their duty in any way. They should however avoid using that conclusion simply on the basis that they disagree between themselves as to the other short-form conclusions.

[1] Chief Coroner's Guidance No 17, Conclusions, para 70.

6.124 That being said, even if an open conclusion is properly reached, it can still feel unsatisfactory for the relatives of the deceased, and in some cases it will be preferable for a narrative conclusion to be given setting out what findings that can be made and what cannot, or to add extra words to the conclusion by way of explanation[1].

[1] Chief Coroner's Guidance No 17, Conclusions, para 73.

6.125 Where the conclusion is an open one, the Chief Coroner's Guidance states that Box 3 still needs to be completed[1]. An open conclusion once entered and recorded my not be revisited at a later date without the intervention of the High Court[2].

[1] Chief Coroner's Guidance No 17, Conclusions, para 71.
[2] Chief Coroner's Guidance No 17, Conclusions, para 72.

VII. Road traffic collision

6.126 'Road traffic collision' as a short form conclusion was introduced for the first time in the 2013 list of short-form conclusions by virtue of Coroners (Inquest) Rules 2013[1]. Previously, most road traffic accidents would have resulted in a conclusion of accident or misadventure.

[1] SI 2013/1616.

6.127 There are no authorities or guidance relating to this conclusion. In the vast majority of cases it can be anticipated that the conclusion will present few difficulties – it will usually be obvious that the death was due to a road traffic collision, unless there is evidence that justifies a conclusion of unlawful killing or suicide. Of course, it would be open to the coroner or jury to return a road traffic collision conclusion in conjunction with other conclusions. It is suggested that there are two elements needed to reach a conclusion of 'road traffic collision': first, that the death resulted from a collision involving at least one vehicle, and second that the collision took place on a road. It remains to be seen whether coroners will apply definitions in the Road Traffic Act 1988[1] and the body of case law relating to road traffic offences in the interpretation of this conclusion. Road traffic collision deaths are considered in fuller terms in CHAPTER 17.

[1] Road Traffic Act 1988, s 192(1): 'road' means any highway and any other road to which the public has access and includes bridges over which a road passes. See also CPR 45.9(4) for a definition of 'road traffic accident'.

VIII. Stillbirth

6.128 A 'stillborn child' is defined by s 41 of the Births and Deaths Registration Act 1953 (as amended by the Still-birth (Definition) Act 1992, as meaning:

> 'A child which has issued forth from its mother after the *twenty-fourth week* of pregnancy and which did not at any time after being completely expelled from its mother breathe or show any other signs of life, and the expression "*still–birth*" shall be construed accordingly.'

6.129 As the law currently stands, the coroner has no jurisdiction under s 1 of the CJA 2009 to investigate or conduct an inquest into the 'death' of a stillborn child (or a foetus that has died in utero), because in each case there has been no life independent of the mother and thus no death. Neither the stillborn child nor the foetus can be regarded as a 'deceased person' as a matter of law[1].

[1] *Attorney General's Reference (No 3 of 1994)* [1998] AC 245: the destruction of a foetus is not homicide. See also *In Re MB (Medical Treatment)* [1997] 2 FLR 426: the common law affords no independent rights to a foetus.

6.130 However, the Court of Appeal in *R (T) v West Yorkshire Senior Coroner*[1] concluded that a coroner **can investigate** a death of a baby where there is doubt as to whether a baby was born alive or stillborn, without first being satisfied on the balance of probabilities that the child was born alive, provided there were reasonable grounds to suspect one of the matters set out in s 1(2) CJA 2009. The facts of that case were that the mother brought the body of her dead baby daughter, born some time earlier, to hospital in a shoebox, and it was not clear from the subsequent post-mortem examination whether the baby had been born alive or stillborn. The Court of Appeal considered that there was a public interest in establishing whether a child was or was not stillborn, and if it was born alive, how it came to its death, and held that the coroner was correct that the CJA 2009 enabled him to investigate these matters.

[1] [2018] 2 WLR 211.

6.131 If the conclusion at any such inquest is that there was a stillbirth, this should be recorded in Box 4 of the Record of Inquest, but the rest of the form should not be completed.

6.132 On 26 March 2019 the government launched a consultation on proposals to give coroners the power to investigate all full-term stillbirths, with the objective of helping to provide parents with vital information from an independent inquest on what went wrong and why, while ensuring any mistakes are identified to prevent future deaths. The proposals are:

- Coroners will have powers to investigate all full-term stillbirths occurring from 27 weeks pregnancy.
- The coroner will consider whether any lessons can be learned which could prevent future stillbirths.
- Coroners will not have to gain consent or permission from any third party in exercising this power.
- Coronial investigations will not replace current investigations undertaken by the hospital or NHS agencies.

6.133 At the time of writing Parliament had not chosen to implement these proposals.

IX. Suicide

6.134 Suicide is the intentional taking by the deceased of their own life. It has been defined as 'voluntarily doing an act for the purpose of destroying one's own life while one is conscious of what one is doing, and in order to arrive at a verdict of suicide there must be evidence that the deceased intended the consequences of the act'[1].

[1] *R v Cardiff City Coroner ex p Thomas* [1970] 1 WLR 1475, per James J at 1478H.

6.135 In *R (Maughan) v HM Senior Coroner for Oxfordshire* the Supreme Court confirmed the decisions of the High Court and Court of Appeal that the standard of proof for suicide is the balance of probabilities and not beyond reasonable doubt. Two elements must be established: (i) the deceased took their own life, and (ii) they intended to do so. The Chief Coroner's Guidance states that the coroner must make express reference in each case of possible suicide to these two elements[1].

[1] Chief Coroner's Guidance No 17, Conclusions, para 62.

6.136 Suicide should never be presumed but must be affirmatively proved to justify the finding[1]. In *R (Barber) v City of London Coroner*[2] a caretaker fell from the roof of a block of flats after he had been out with his wife for a few drinks, but without evidence that he was drunk. There was no evidence of suicidal intent. Lord Widgery, CJ, said:

> '... One of the most important rules that coroners should bear in mind in cases of this class, namely that suicide must never be presumed. If a person dies a violent death, the possibility of suicide may be there for all to see, but it must not be presumed merely because it seems, on the face of it, to be a likely explanation.

Suicide must be proved by evidence, and if it is not proved by evidence, it is the duty of the coroner not to find suicide, but to find an open verdict.'

[1] *Southall v Cheshire County News Co Ltd* (1912) 5 BWCC 251, *In re Davis, decd* [1968] 1 QB 72, *R (Maughan) v HM Senior Coroner for Oxfordshire Senior Coroner* [2020] UKSC 46 per Lady Arden at [62].
[2] [1975] 1 WLR 1310.

6.137 It follows that there must be sufficient evidence that the deceased intended to take their own life. This has been emphasised in a number of authorities, for example *Jenkins v HM Coroner for Bridgend and Glamorgan Valleys*[1]. On the evening before his death, the deceased, a young man aged 23, had been drinking very heavily, but appeared in good mood and was intending to go to the England against Wales rugby match the following day. He died when he was struck by a train, the train driver's evidence being that he appeared asleep. The Divisional Court held that the verdict of suicide could not be sustained. Pitchford LJ emphasised that there needs to be a structured approach to the two essential strands of evidence (i) that which went to the circumstances of the deceased's death, and (ii) that which went to the state of his mind during the critical period of two to three hours before his death.

[1] [2012] EWHC 3175 (Admin). Care must be taken in relation to this and other authorities decided before *R (Maughan)* above. To the extent that the court referred to the criminal standard of proof, it is no longer good law.

6.138 The Chief Coroner's Guidance states[1]:

'The conclusion of suicide should not be avoided by coroners simply out of sympathy for family relatives or for any other reason. Parliament has decided that suicide should remain as a short-form conclusion. The word "suicide" is expressly used in the Rules . . . It is therefore the coroner's judicial duty, when suicide is proved on the evidence, to record the conclusion of suicide according to the law and findings which justify it. It would be wrong, for example, to record an "open" conclusion when the evidence is clear.'

[1] Chief Coroner's Guidance No 17, Conclusions, para 61.

6.139 Family members may need to be advised sensitively on the obligation to record a suicide conclusion if supported by the evidence. Short-form suicide conclusions are important for statistical and preventative purposes, particularly in cases involving deaths in custody or deaths of patients sectioned under the Mental Health Act 1983. In *Maughan* the coroner had decided that the jury could not safely reach a short form conclusion of suicide because they could not be sure to the criminal standard of proof that James Maughan had intended to kill himself. The coroner instead asked the jury to reach a narrative conclusion, setting out whether they believed, applying the lower civil standard of proof, James Maughan had intended to kill himself by hanging. The jury confirmed to the civil standard that he had intended to take his own life. James Maughan's brother brought judicial review proceedings against the coroner claiming that the conclusion was unlawful because the coroner was wrong to have directed the jury to apply the civil standard of proof.

6.140 In the Supreme Court the majority dismissed the appeal and emphasised that the strong links between inquests and the criminal process are now matters of historical fact only. Lady Arden observed that instead, 'inquests are concerned today not with criminal justice . . . They take a new and different

6.140 *Conclusions and Records of Inquests*

purpose in a case such as this'[1] ie to 'identify lessons to be learnt for the future'[2] and prevent future deaths. Lady Arden commented on the changing attitudes towards suicide as one reason to justify lowering the standard of proof required, implicitly rejecting the submission that there is a 'close affinity between suicide and a criminal offence'[3] and instead noting that there is no longer such a stigma associated with intentional self-inflicted death. This reflects society's changing attitudes towards mental health in general, and marks the fact that the balance is now in favour of reporting suicides whenever they occur in order to ensure statistics are as accurate (and therefore as helpful) as possible.

[1] *R (Maughan) v HM Senior Coroner for Oxfordshire Senior Coroner* [2020] UKSC 46 at [81].
[2] *R (Maughan) v HM Senior Coroner for Oxfordshire Senior Coroner* [2020] UKSC 46 at [8].
[3] *R (Maughan) v HM Senior Coroner for Oxfordshire Senior Coroner* [2020] UKSC 46 at [67].

6.141 According to the Chief Coroner's Guidance No 17, there is usually no longer any need to add the words 'whilst the balance of his mind was disturbed'[1]. However, these words can still be added if there is evidence on which to base such a conclusion, although in practice this is now rare. Words in these or similar terms can be helpful to families in alleviating the impact of the suicide conclusion.

[1] Chief Coroner's Guidance No 17, Conclusions, para 63.

D – NEGLECT

6.142 Neglect is not a free-standing conclusion in itself, but it best described as a finding. It should not be considered as a primary cause of death[1]. Neglect can rarely, if ever, be an appropriate conclusion on its own[2]. A finding of 'contributed to by neglect' may be attached to short-form conclusions, such as natural causes, accident/misadventure, suicide and industrial disease, or form part of a narrative conclusion. The Chief Coroner's Guidance No 17 indicates that neglect, formerly lack of care, may be recorded as part of the conclusion in Box 4[3].

[1] Chief Coroner's Guidance No 17, Conclusions, para 74.
[2] *R v HM Coroner for North Humberside and Scunthorpe ex p Jamieson* [1995] QB 1 at 24D.
[3] Chief Coroner's Guidance No 17, Conclusions, para 75.

Definition of neglect

6.143 Neglect is not the same as negligence but is narrower in meaning: it is not to be equated with negligence or even gross negligence[1]. 'Neglect' should be treated as a 'term of art'[2].

[1] Chief Coroner's Guidance No 17, Conclusions, para 76. See also *R (Longfield Care Homes) v HM Coroner for Blackburn* [2004] EWHC 2467 (Admin) at [27]: the direction to jury focused upon the lack of a risk assessment, which 'more accurately fell to be considered as negligence in civil law, rather than neglect in the law relating to inquests'.
[2] *R (on the application of Middleton) v West Somerset Coroner* [2004] UKHL 10, [2004] 2 AC 182 at [37].

6.144 The starting point for any consideration of 'neglect' is the landmark decision of Sir Thomas Bingham in *R v HM Coroner for North Humberside and Scunthorpe ex p Jamieson*[1]. It defined neglect in the following terms:

> 'Neglect in this context means a gross failure to provide adequate nourishment or liquid, or provide or procure basic medical attention or shelter or warmth for someone in a dependent position (because of youth, age, illness or incarceration) who cannot provide it for himself. Failure to provide medical attention for a dependent person whose physical condition is such as to show that he obviously needs it may amount to neglect. So it may be if it is the dependant person's mental condition which obviously calls for medical attention . . . In both cases the crucial consideration will be what the dependant person's condition, whether physical or mental, appeared to be.'

[1] [1995] QB 1.

6.145 The deceased, a prisoner serving a long sentence for murder, hanged himself in his cell. In addition to the classic definition of neglect set out above, Bingham MR set out the following important conclusions:

- Much of the difficulty in relation to verdicts of lack of care had been due to 'the almost inevitable confusion' between lack of care in the context of an inquest and the lack of care which is the foundation for a successful claim in common law negligence. Lack of care in the context of an inquest should be deleted from the lexicon and replaced by 'neglect'.
- 'Self-neglect' is a gross failure to take adequate nourishment or liquid, to obtain basic medical attention, or to obtain adequate shelter or housing. Neglect is the obverse of self-neglect.
- Neglect can rarely, if ever, be an appropriate verdict on its own, but it may be factually accurate to say that it contributed to the death. It is preferable for the verdict to be stated as (for example) 'the deceased died from natural causes to which neglect contributed', rather than that the deceased died from natural causes 'aggravated by neglect', as 'neglect probably did not make the fatal condition worse but sacrificed the opportunity to halt it'.
- Where the deceased took his own life, it is possible for there to be a finding that neglect contributed to the suicide, but this finding would not be justified simply on the ground that the deceased was given an opportunity to take his own life, even if was careless to afford the deceased that opportunity. Such a finding would only be appropriate in a case where gross neglect was directly connected with the deceased's suicide (for example, if a prison warder observed a prisoner in his cell preparing to hang a noose around his neck but passed on without any attempt to intervene).
- Neither neglect nor self-neglect should ever form any part of any verdict unless a clear and direct causal connection is established between the neglect/self-neglect and the cause of death.

6.146 In *R (Scott) v HM Coroner for Inner West London*[1] Keane LJ said that the passages in *Jamieson* are 'not to be treated as if they were statutory enactments. They are part of the process of judicial interpretation of the law, which is a developing process. None the less, they represent a valuable distillation of the case law on the subject'.

[1] [2001] EWHC 105 (Admin), 62 BMLR 222 at [23].

6.147 It follows from the classic definition of neglect in *Jamieson* set out above, that neglect has three principal components:

(1) The deceased must have been in a dependent position, because of youth, age, illness or incarceration.
(2) There must have been a failure to have provided basic care or attention to the deceased whose physical or mental condition obviously needed it.
(3) The failure must be 'gross'.

6.148 As the Chief Coroner stated in Guidance No 17, the definition in *Jamieson*:

> 'Has been expanded more by illustration than by changes in the law, testing the words "gross failure" and "basic" against particular facts. In broad terms there must be a sufficient level of fault to justify a finding of neglect. That does not mean that, for example in a medical context, there has to have been no action, simply that that action (or lack of it) on an objective basis must be more than a failure to provide medical attention. It must be a gross failure. The difference will be highly fact-specific.'

Failure v 'gross' failure

6.149 The difference between a failure and a gross failure was considered in *R (Nicholls) v Coroner for City of Liverpool*[1], a case concerning the alleged failure of a police forensic medical examiner properly to recognise the fact that the deceased had swallowed drugs, believed to be heroin. The court plainly thought that his failure could amount to neglect. Sullivan J, with whom Rose LJ agreed, stated (at para 52):

> 'Notwithstanding [Counsel's] submission that neglect and negligence are two different "animals", there is, in reality, no precise dividing line between "a gross failure to provide ... basic medical attention" and a "failure to provide ... medical attention". The difference is bound to be one of degree, highly dependent on the facts of the particular case.'

[1] [2001] EWHC 922 (Admin) at [52].

6.150 An obvious example of seemingly gross failings is *R (Lewis) v Senior Coroner for North West Kent*[1] where a detained psychiatric patient died of malnutrition. She had suffered pronounced weight loss in the months before she died, accompanied by obvious manifestations of physical decline and malnutrition. Medical records were not maintained and the written policy on hydration and nutrition was not adhered to. Despite this background, described by Davis LJ as 'disconcerting', the senior coroner refused to leave neglect to the jury. Given the circumstances revealed in the evidence, the Divisional Court could not see how neglect was not properly available to the jury (applying *Galbraith* principles – see below at **6.198**) or how it could not be safe for the jury to make such a finding.

[1] [2020] EWHC 471 (Admin).

Neglect as a series of acts or omissions

6.151 Neglect is not confined to the acts and omissions of one person but may constitute a series of acts and omissions which combine to form 'the total picture which amounts to neglect'[1] or a continuous series of shortcomings[2]. In *R (Clegg) v HM Coroner for Wiltshire*, a young woman took an overdose of aspirin at home, was taken to hospital and died 12 hours later. An independent review concluded that her treatment was 'grossly inadequate'. Phillips LJ held that the failure to provide appropriate medical attention to a dependent patient in hospital is capable of constituting 'neglect' and stated:

> 'In this case the deceased was dependent upon the hospital staff for a period of nearly 12 hours before she died. If the findings of the Review and of the Panel are correct . . . the care which she received during that period suffered from a continuous sequence of shortcomings. Those findings suggest that it is at least possible that, but for those shortcomings, her life would have been saved. In these circumstances my conclusion is that, applying the approach in Jamieson, it is possible that if a new inquest were to be held the verdict would be that Lucy killed herself but that neglect contributed to her death.[3]'

[1] *Scott v HM Coroner for Inner West London* [2001] EWHC 105 (Admin).
[2] *R (Clegg) v HM Coroner for Wiltshire* (1996) 161 JP 521.
[3] *R (Clegg) v HM Coroner for Wiltshire* (1996) 161 JP 521 at para 25.

6.152 In medical cases, it is now clearly established that neglect is not limited to a complete failure to provide basic medical care or attention but can include errors in clinical judgment that lead to the wrong diagnosis and treatment[1].

[1] See eg *R v Surrey Coroner ex p Wright* [1997] QB 786, *R v Birmingham and Solihull Coroner ex p Benton* (1997) 162 JP 807.

6.153 *Scott v HM Coroner for Inner West London*[1] was one such case. The deceased, who had been diagnosed as suffering from paranoid schizophrenia and suicidal tendencies, hanged himself with his shoelaces in his cell at Wandsworth Prison. He had undergone a very brief medical examination, following which his shoelaces were returned to him and he was put in his cell on his own with no observations. The Divisional Court held that there was evidence of a gross failure to provide medical attention upon which a jury could properly make a finding of neglect. The fact that this seems to have flowed from the views formed by the medical practitioners at the prison did not rule out neglect, Keene LJ stating that 'omissions on the part of medical practitioners are capable of forming part of the total picture which amounts to neglect'.

[1] [2001] EWHC 105 (Admin) at [28]–[29].

6.154 The decision of Keene LJ in *Scott* was cited with approval in *R (on the application of Davies) v Birmingham Deputy Coroner*,[1] a case involving the death of a prisoner by dehydration in which there were shortcomings in the medical care he received. Brookes LJ made it clear that gross failures are not limited to those cases where an individual has failed to take any action at all but can apply to purported clinical decisions or diagnosis. The nurse's failure to seek assistance was at least capable of constituting neglect even though she exercised a clinical judgment as to whether assistance was necessary.

[1] [2003] EWCA Civ 1739.

6.155 *Conclusions and Records of Inquests*

6.155 However, as the Chief Coroner's Guidance makes clear[1], in a medical context it is not the role of an inquest to criticise every twist and turn of a patient's treatment. As stated in *Nicholls*[2], neglect is not concerned with the correctness of complex and sophisticated medical procedures but rather the consequences of, for example, failing to make simple ('basic') checks. In that case, the steps that 'would have been taken by any doctor were neither complex, nor sophisticated. They amounted to doing no more than checking the patient's respiratory rate and then arranging for it to be checked after about another hour'[3].

[1] Chief Coroner's Guidance No 17, Conclusions, para 80.
[2] *R (Nicholls) v Coroner for City of Liverpool* [2001] EWHC 922 (Admin).
[3] [2001] EWHC 922 (Admin) at [54].

6.156 In *R (Touche) v Inner London North Coroner*[1], the court considered that the failure to provide basic and routine blood pressure monitoring after the deceased had given birth to twins, a failure that was described as 'astonishing' by the family's expert witness, and 'wholly unacceptable' by the coroner, gave reasonable grounds to suspect that Mrs Touche's death was contributed by neglect.

[1] [2001] 1 QB 1206.

6.157 It was suggested in *R v Surrey Coroner, ex p Wright*[1] that neglect means 'continuous or at least non-transient neglect'. The applicant's son was admitted to hospital for minor surgery under anaesthetic but died from cerebral anoxia because his airway was not maintained. Tucker J held that a conclusion of neglect was not open to the coroner, and that the negligent lack of care alleged to have led to the death was better decided in a civil action. This is a surprising decision and was doubted by Phillips LJ in *Re Clegg*. It is suggested that it is arguable that that the failure to provide oxygen to an unconscious patient constituted a gross failure to provide basic medical attention.

[1] [1997] QB 786.

Neglect in cases involving self-harm and accidents

6.158 Cases in which neglect may be found to have contributed to death by self-harm or accident will only arise where neglect was gross and a clear or direct causal connection is established[1]. In *Jamieson*[2] the Court of Appeal held that neglect could not be found to have contributed to the suicide of a prisoner merely on the ground that the deceased had been given an opportunity to kill himself. Sir Thomas Bingham MR (as he then was) giving the judgment of the court, stated as follows with regard to the question of neglect in self-harm and medical cases:

> 'Failure to provide medical attention for a dependent person whose physical condition is such as to show that he obviously needs it may amount to neglect. So it may be if it is the dependent person's mental condition which obviously calls for medical attention (as it would, for example, if a mental nurse observed that a patient had a propensity to swallow razor blades and failed to report this propensity to a doctor, in a case where the patient had no intention to cause himself injury but did

thereafter swallow razor blades with fatal results). In both cases the crucial consideration will be what the dependent person's condition, whether physical or mental, appeared to be.' [p 25, para (8)]

1   *R (Longfield Care Homes) v HM Coroner for Blackburn* [2004] EWHC 2467 (Admin) at [26], referred to at para 85 of the Chief Coroner's Guidance No 17, Conclusions.
2   *R v HM Coroner for North Humberside and Scunthorpe, ex p Jamieson* [1995] QB 1.

6.159 In the recent case of *R (Carole Smith) v HM Assistant Coroner for North West Wales*[1]. Griffiths J concluded that 'a finding of neglect is exceptional, particularly in suicide cases, and requires proof, not only that it was causative of death, but that it is in the nature of "gross failure" or "gross neglect"'. The reference to 'gross neglect' is not helpful in this context as the term 'neglect' necessarily involves a 'gross failure'. It is submitted that the case is not authority for the proposition that coroners or juries should only return conclusions of neglect if they are satisfied that the failures are exceptionally gross.

1   [2020] EWHC 781 (Admin).

E – NARRATIVE CONCLUSIONS

What is a narrative conclusion?

6.160 As noted above the coroner (or jury as directed by the coroner) may record a brief narrative conclusion in Box 4 as an alternative (or in addition) to a short-form conclusion. We return to the overarching principle that 'the function of an inquest is to seek out and record **as many of the facts concerning the death as the public interest requires**'[1] (emphasis added). Narrative conclusions therefore play an important role, particularly in jury cases, where there will be no factual reasons provided, and a short form conclusion alone may be insufficient to satisfy that inquisitorial function.

1   *R v South London Coroner, ex p Thompson* (1982) 126 SJ 625, per Lord Lane CJ.

6.161 Prior to the publication of the Chief Coroner's Guidance No 17 on conclusions in 2015, it was not unusual for coroners to reach lengthy narrative conclusions, making significant factual findings. That practice was disparaged in Guidance No 17, which formalised the three-stage fact-finding process, and stated:

6.162 There has been a tendency for narrative conclusions from coroners to become lengthy and far-reaching, both as statements and in questionnaires to juries (see below). That is not what the authorities envisage. Long narratives should not be given. They achieve neither clarity nor accessibility in that form. They make it difficult to assess for statistical purposes.

6.163 A narrative conclusion should be a brief, neutral, factual statement dealing with the issues that were central to the inquest. The requirement for brevity has been repeatedly emphasised by the courts and more recently by the Chief Coroner in his guidance where he observes that 'a few sentences or one or two short paragraphs at the most will be sufficient'[1].

1   Chief Coroner's Guidance No 17, Conclusions, para 35.

6.164 *Conclusions and Records of Inquests*

The content of a narrative conclusion

Article 2 inquests

6.164 In *Middleton* the House of Lords held that in order to satisfy the investigative duty under Art 2 ECHR the jury at the close of the inquest had to be able to express its conclusion on the 'central issue[s] canvassed at the inquest'[1]. In *Middleton* those included whether the deceased prisoner should have been recognised as a suicide risk and whether appropriate precautions should have been taken to protect his life. The traditional short form conclusion of suicide alone had been inadequate to do that[2].

[1] R *(on the application of Middleton) v West Somerset Coroner* [2004] UKHL 10, [2004] 2 AC 182 at [33].
[2] 2004] UKHL 10, [2004] 2 AC 182 at [45]–[49].

6.165 As set out in CHAPTER 3, in order for the Art 2 duty to be satisfied, an investigation must be effective, which includes ensuring accountability for the death and reaching a determination as to whether adequate steps were taken to protect life. The procedure as a whole, including the conclusions, must satisfy the criteria in *Jordan v UK*[1], as set out in CHAPTER 3 at 3.98. In *Middleton* the House of Lords suggested that the following conclusion would have been adequate to satisfy the Art 2 duty in the circumstances of the case:

> 'The deceased took his own life, in part because the risk of his doing so was not recognised and appropriate precautions were not taken to prevent him doing so.'

[1] *Jordan v United Kingdom* (2003) 37 EHRR 2.

6.166 This was described by the court as embodying 'a factual conclusion of a judgmental nature'[1]. In *Lewis*, the Court of Appeal held that a 'failure to report on a systemic failure' would be a breach of the Art 2 duty[2]. The Chief Coroner's Guidance No 17 confirms that permissible judgmental words in narrative Art 2 conclusions include: inadequate, insufficient, inappropriate, lacking, unsuitable, unsatisfactory and failure[3]. 'Words donating causation such as "because" and "contributed to" are permissible'[4].

[1] [2004] UKHL 10, [2004] 2 AC 182 at [45].
[2] *R (Lewis) v Mid and North Shropshire Coroner* [2009] EWCA Civ 1403, [2010] 1 WLR 1836 at [38]. Although in that case the duty was satisfied by the making of a rule 43 report (now a report to prevent future deaths under the 2013 Rules).
[3] Guidance No 17, Conclusions, para 52.
[4] Guidance No 17, Conclusions, para 52.

6.167 The decision of the High Court in *R (Carole Smith) v HM Assistant Coroner for North West Wales*[1], an Art 2 suicide case, reiterated the warning in *Jamieson* that an inquest conclusion 'must be factual, **expressing no judgment or opinion** and it is not the jury's function to prepare detailed factual statements'[2]. It is submitted that insofar as the High Court appeared to suggest that in Art 2 cases juries cannot return judgmental conclusions, it fell into error.

[1] [2020] EWHC 781 (Admin).
[2] [2020] EWHC 781 (Admin) at [78]–[79] (emphasis added).

6.168 The practice of providing juries with questionnaires in order to complete narrative conclusions is disparaged in the Chief Coroner's Guidance.

E – Narrative conclusions **6.171**

However, this approach has been adopted in long, complex inquests, such as those into the deaths arising from the Hillsborough disaster[1], and the death of Mark Duggan[2].

[1] At the time of publication the Hillsborough Inquests website had been taken down temporarily due to legal proceedings.
[2] See the Report to Prevent Future Death in the Inquest into the Death of Mark Duggan, 29 May 2014, https://www.judiciary.uk/wp-content/uploads/2014/06/Duggan-2014-0182.pdf.

6.169 A complicating factor in Art 2 conclusions can be the interaction of inquest procedure (in particular whether or not the coroner sits with a jury and makes a report to prevent future deaths), with the looser test for causation under the ECHR. This will be dealt with below at **6.186**.

Non-Article 2 inquests

6.170 Can a jury or coroner in a non-Art 2 inquest return a conclusion that expresses a judgment or opinion? In *Jamieson* the Court of Appeal held that this was prohibited, although its judgment was based in large part on the wording of r 36(1)(b) of the 1984 Rules, which expressly prohibited the coroner and jury from expressing 'any opinion on any other matters' other than the four statutory questions. There is no such express prohibition in the CJA 2009 or the 2013 Rules. The Chief Coroner's Guidance No 17 suggests that judgmental language should not be used in non-Art 2 inquests: 'in a non-Article 2 case judgment words such as 'missed opportunities' or 'inadequate failures' should probably be avoided'[1]. This question has yet to be definitively determined by a senior court. Indeed, the wording of the guidance (that judgment language should 'probably' be avoided) leaves open the possibility that in exceptional cases, it may be appropriate for the coroner or jury to depart from the norm. If the use of the 'judgmental' word failure in an Art 2 case does not offend against the s 10(2) prohibition on imparting civil or criminal liability, then by logical extension it cannot in a non-Art 2 case. However, the only non-Art 2 case of which the authors are aware in which it has been suggested that a jury should be able to return a judgmental conclusion is *R (Bodycote HIP Ltd) v HM Coroner for the County of Hertfordshire*[2]. That case concerned the death of two men in an industrial accident. Blake J held that the coroner had erred in law in failing to direct the jury on the question of corporate gross negligence manslaughter at common law. He further held as follows:

> 'Narrative verdicts may have a particular relevance in cases where the jury record particular breaches of duties, or particular failures to foresee risks, which should be recorded so that the industry can be alerted and all others concerned with the tragedy in this case can learn lessons for the future.[3]'

[1] Chief Coroner's Guidance No 17, Conclusions, para 34.
[2] [2008] EWHC 164 (Admin).
[3] [2008] EWHC 164 (Admin) at [24].

6.171 In any event, where acts or omissions are recorded in purely factual, non-judgmental terms, that is not to say that the conclusion should be anodyne[1]. For example, where a delay in the arrival of an ambulance contributed to the death of a patient, the court may return a conclusion along these lines:

6.171 *Conclusions and Records of Inquests*

'An ambulance was called at 13.00 but did not arrive until 15.00. Had the ambulance attended on an urgent basis, as requested by the GP, it is likely that the deceased would have survived.'

[1] See the Chief Coroner's Guidance No 17, Conclusions, para 34.

F – STANDARD OF PROOF

6.172 Following the decision of the Supreme Court in *R (Maughan) v HM Senior Coroner for Oxfordshire* the standard of proof required for all short-form conclusions is now the civil standard of proof ie the balance of probabilities[1]. This means the coroner or jury must take the view that a certain conclusion is more likely than not to have been the cause of death before they can make a finding as such. In that case, the majority of the judges hearing the case in the Supreme Court held that to the extent that Note (iii), Form 2 (as set out in the Schedule to the 2013 Rules), states that the standard of proof for suicide and unlawful killing conclusions is beyond reasonable doubt, the form is expressing the draftsman's (incorrect) understanding of the common law position and does not constitute a legal rule imposed by Parliament. Whilst it remains in the Schedule to the 2013 Rules, therefore, Note (iii) to Form 2 should now be ignored by practitioners.

[1] [2020] UKSC 46.

6.173 There is no separate standard of proof for open conclusions: essentially, this is the only available conclusion when the evidence does not meet the standard of proof for any other conclusion.

G – CAUSATION

6.174 Box 2 of the Record of Inquest requires a coroner to set out the medical cause of death (see **6.10** above). In considering the cause of death, in addition to considering the specific 'medical' cause for the purposes of Box 2, a coroner or jury will often be required to consider whether certain action, or inaction, was a causative factor. This is part of the analysis which forms the answers to Boxes 3 and 4.

6.175 The test for causation of death in coronial law is set out in *R (Tainton) v HM Senior Coroner for Preston & West Lancashire*[1]:

'It is common ground that the threshold for causation of death is not the same thing as the standard of proof required to prove causation of death. In cases such as this, the latter is proof on the balance of probabilities. It is agreed that the threshold that must be reached for causation of death to be established, is that the event or conduct said to have caused the death must have 'more than minimally, negligibly or trivially contributed to the death' (see eg *R (Dawson) v HM Coroner for East Riding and Kingston upon Hull Coroners District* [2001] EWHC Admin 352; [2001] Inquest LR 233, per Jackson J at paras 65–67). Putting these two concepts together, **the question is whether, on the balance of probabilities, the conduct in question more than minimally, negligibly or trivially contributed to death.**' [emphasis added]

[1] [2016] EWHC 1396 (Admin).

6.176 This will, in some instances, include investigation into the action or inaction of a third party eg where the deceased suffered from a natural illness but received treatment from medical professionals, and the medics may have had the opportunity to prevent the death.

6.177 One such case was *R (Chidlow) v Senior Coroner for Blackpool and Flyde*[1], in which Mr Justice Pepperall undertook a comprehensive review of the law relating to causation; this was a case in which the deceased had become ill, and there had been a delay, caused by the ambulance service, in him obtaining the necessary medical assistance. The coroner had originally refused to put the question of causation to the jury (ie whether the delay had contributed to the death), on the basis that the underlying medical cause of death was actually unclear.

[1] [2019] EWHC 581 (Admin).

6.178 This case management decision was challenged by way of a judicial review. On appeal, the Divisional Court addressed to what extent statistical evidence can assist a coroner or jury when considering the question of causation, particularly in the context of medical treatment or intervention. The following key principles can be taken from the case:

(1) Causation cannot be determined on the basis of survivability statistics alone.
(2) There is a distinction between saying what caused someone's death, and being able to determine whether, regardless of the cause of death, they could have survived with earlier or different medical treatment.

6.179 Pepperall J determined that causation evidence in any particular inquest may include general statistical evidence not specific to the deceased eg survival rates in a particular age group or other generic population data. However, the statistics alone cannot prove causation. For instance, just because it is the case that 60 per cent of black females aged between 40 and 50 would survive a particular operation if performed in a timely manner, it does not mean that this deceased would have done. That statistic in itself is not enough for a jury to safely conclude that the deceased would have been one of the survivors if there had not been a delay. The court must go further and hear evidence in which the statistics are applied and considered in the context of the deceased's own unique situation: given her particular circumstances, is it likely that she would have been one of the majority?

6.180 A coroner or jury is entitled to consider the impact of delayed or poor medical treatment (and whether it had a causative role in the deceased's death) even in circumstances where the actual underlying cause of death is unknown. In *Chidlow* itself, the reason for the deceased's illness was unclear, but the coroner heard evidence that if he had been treated more quickly, he would likely have survived. Clearly it would have been useful to know the medical cause of death, but it was not crucial to being able to take a view on the impact of the delay in medical attention. It was appropriate, in those circumstances, for the jury to consider the question of whether the delays in treatment were a causative factor in his death.

6.181 *Conclusions and Records of Inquests*

Causation and neglect

6.181 Unless the alleged neglect is causative of the death, there can be no finding of neglect. The test set out in *Jamieson* is that there must be a 'clear and direct causal connection is established between the neglect/self-neglect and the cause of death'[1].

[1] *Jamieson* (above) at 991G.

6.182 The requirement for a 'clear and direct causal connection' is not to be read in an over literal manner[1] and the coroner or jury is entitled to take a common-sense approach, making appropriate inferences[2]. Neglect does not need to be the sole or predominant cause of death.

[1] *Nicholls v HM Coroner for Liverpool* [2002] AC 89 at [56].
[2] *R (on the application of Khan) v HM Coroner for West Hertfordshire* [2002] EWHC 302 Admin at [43].

6.183 In *R (on the application of Khan) v HM Coroner for West Hertfordshire*[1] Richards J concluded and that it was sufficient to establish on the balance of probabilities that the conduct made a material contribution to death. But it was still necessary to establish causation on the balance of probabilities; it was therefore not enough for a finding of neglect on the facts of that case that there was a 'possibility' that the deceased's life would have been saved through the administration of an antidote (after a package of drugs he was carrying in his mouth burst). It had to be shown that an antidote would have made a difference in terms of saving or prolonging life.

[1] [2002] EWHC 302 (Admin).

6.184 In *R v HM Coroner for Coventry ex p Chief Constable of Staffordshire Police*[1] Tomlinson J said:

> 'The causal connection which is relevant in the context of consideration by an inquest jury of the addition of a neglect rider is, in my judgment, not the same as the causal connection for which one may look in the context of other, perhaps more familiar, enquiries. The touchstone in the present context is, I believe, the opportunity of rendering care, in the narrow sense of the work, which would have prevented the death... That does not mean that a conscientious person would necessarily have done that which would have successfully prevented death. The question is whether he had opportunity of doing something effective.'

[1] [2000] 164 JP 665 at [41]: The condition of a prisoner in police custody deteriorated so fast for it to be impossible to provide care that would have saved him.

6.185 If there is no opportunity of rendering care which would have prevented the death, then there will be no finding of neglect[1].

[1] *R v Inner South London Coroner, ex p Douglas-Williams* [1999] 1 All ER 344.

Article 2 and causation

6.186 There is an additional test regarding causation when it comes to Art 2 inquests. The test for causation of 'damage' under the ECHR is not akin to a common law test. In the Art 3 case *O'Keefe v Ireland*[1], the Grand Chamber of the ECtHR summed up the Convention approach to causation and breach in the following terms:

'... it was not necessary to show that "but for" the state's omission, the ill treatment would not have happened. A failure to take reasonably available measures which could have had a real prospect of altering the outcome or mitigating the harm was sufficient to engage the responsibility of the state.[2]'

[1] [2014] 59 EHRR 15.
[2] [2014] 59 EHRR 15 at [149]–[150].

6.187 The same principle applies in respect of Art 2. In *Sarjantson*[1], in the Court of Appeal, Lord Dyson held that it is not necessary to demonstrate that, had the authorities acted in a manner compliant with their *Osman* duty to protect individuals from a real and immediate risk to life under Art 2, the steps taken would in fact have prevented a loss of life: '[t]he fact that a response would have made no difference is not relevant to liability'.

[1] [2014] QB 411.

Causation, conclusions and Art 2 in jury inquests

6.188 A series of authorities has grappled with the requirements in respect of conclusions in Art 2 cases. This issue has been particularly significant in jury inquests, where the first of the three fact-finding stages advocated in Guidance 17, the 'reasons' (see **6.30** above), must take place in private and the findings are not made public.

6.189 In *R (Lewis) v Mid and North Shropshire Coroner*[1] the Court of Appeal determined that in Art 2 cases a coroner has the option, but not a duty, to direct a jury to consider any 'fact or circumstance which could have caused or contributed to the death but cannot be shown probably to have done so'[2]. The court emphasised that whilst the coroner/jury was required to make findings in relation to failures of training and systems in suicide prevention in prison in order to satisfy Art 2, 'the question whether it should also form part of the jury's verdict is then a question of domestic law'. Essentially, the content of what should be considered was prescribed by Convention law, but the way in which it was presented in public was a matter for Member States. The Court of Appeal decided that in the circumstances the making of a Report to Prevent Future Deaths on the issues was sufficient to satisfy Art 2.

[1] [2009] EWCA Civ 1403.
[2] [2009] EWCA Civ 1403 at [34].

6.190 The Divisional Court developed (or amended) this principle in *R (Tainton) v Senior Coroner for Preston and West Lancashire*[1]. The court firstly confirmed that it is right that a coroner has discretion as to whether to put certain causation questions to a jury (see below at **6.198** in respect of Galbraith Plus[2] and **6.203** in respect of *Tainton*). However it also determined that in an Art 2 inquest such as this, juries **should** be directed to record in Box 3 on the Record of Inquest 'any **admitted** failings forming part of the circumstances in which the deceased came by his death ... even if, on the balance of probabilities, the jury cannot properly find them causative of the death'[3]. These should be considered 'as forming part of the narrative'[4].

[1] [2016] EWHC 1396 (Admin).
[2] *R v Galbraith* [1981] 1 WLR 1039; see Chief Coroner's Law Sheet No 2, 'Galbraith Plus'.
[3] [2016] EWHC 1396 (Admin) at [74]–[75] (emphasis added).

[4] [2016] EWHC 1396 (Admin) at [78].

6.191 The court emphasised that any such entry on the Record of Inquest should be supplemented by an explanation that 'it could not be concluded that these shortcomings significantly shortened [the deceased's] life'[1]. See **6.175** above for further consideration of *Tainton* in respect of how to approach admitted failings by interested persons.

[1] [2016] EWHC 1396 (Admin) at [73].

6.192 It has been suggested that the decision in *Tainton* is at odds with that taken in *Lewis*.

6.193 In unpublished guidance circulated to coroners following *Tainton*, the Chief Coroner drew attention to the fact that in *Lewis* the coroner provided a rule 43 report (the equivalent now is a report to prevent future deaths), which formed a mechanism by which the state's Art 2 obligations were discharged. In *Tainton*, a report to prevent future deaths could not be made because the NHS trust had addressed the relevant risks prior to the inquest hearing[1]. The Divisional Court in *Tainton* cited this as one of the reasons why the additional information should have been reflected on the Record of Inquest: the coroner could not discharge the Art 2 obligations any other way[2].

[1] [2016] EWHC 1396 (Admin) at [55].
[2] [2016] EWHC 1396 (Admin) at [75] and [79].

6.194 The Chief Coroner suggests that:

'A coroner sitting with a jury in an Article 2 case such as this (ie involving admitted failings by a state body) should consider asking himself/herself the following questions:
a. Is there evidence that the admitted failings probably made any contribution to the death? If so, would it be safe (on a Galbraith plus basis) for a jury so to find?
b. If not, is there evidence that the admitted failings possibly made any contribution to the death? The coroner has a discretion, not a duty (see *Lewis* and *LePage*), whether to leave this question to the jury. The discretion must be exercised reasonably and fairly.
c. If questions 1 and 2 are not left to the jury, should the admitted failings be entered briefly in Box 3 of the Record of Inquest in order to complete the account of the circumstances in which the deceased came by his death? Would the account be incomplete without them? If so, the jury should be directed to do so and to add an explanation that the failings did not make any contribution to the death.'[1]

[1] Chief Coroner's Note: The Decision in *Tainton* (18 June 2016).

6.195 It is submitted that it is clearer, and therefore preferable, to have a proscribed procedure for considering how, and where, to discharge Art 2 obligations, and therefore the *Tainton* approach (and the considerations set out by the Chief Coroner in the accompanying note) is perhaps more helpful than that in *Lewis*.

6.196 A further case on this issue is *R (Carole Smith) v HM Assistant Coroner for North West Wales*[1]. Crucially, *Smith* was not a jury case, and so the coroner gave his findings in his reasons in public in court. As set out above in respect of admitted failings by interested parties (see **6.43**), in *Smith* the High Court took the view that it was unnecessary for the formal narrative conclusion to reflect the local health board's admitted failings, which were potentially causative of death, because they were already stated in the reasons: 'the argument that more of what appeared in the reasons should have been repeated in the Record has the appearance of an argument of form over substance and we would reject it on that ground alone'[2]. The emphasis on substance over form accords with the established principle of Convention law that the investigative Art 2 obligation is one of means, not results (see CHAPTER 3). How the duty is satisfied is a matter of domestic law, as above. It is submitted that as the law presently stands, Art 2 will be satisfied provided that Convention breaches are found and recognised **in public** at the close of the coronial proceedings.

[1] [2020] EWHC 781 (Admin)
[2] *R (Carole Smith) v HM Assistant Coroner for North West Wales* [2020] EWHC 781 (Admin) at [77].

6.197 These cases show that advocates should be sensitive to how these Art 2 requirements interact with the complexities of inquest procedure in a given case.

Galbraith Plus – leaving decisions to the jury

6.198 When considering which conclusions or findings to leave to a jury, a coroner is required to consider the 'Galbraith Plus' test[1]. There are two stages:

(1)   The coroner must ask whether there is evidence upon which the jury, properly directed, could properly reach a particular finding[2].
(2)   The coroner must consider whether it would be safe for the jury to reach the conclusion or finding on the evidence.

[1] Chief Coroner's Law Sheet No 2, 'Galbraith Plus'.
[2] This is the test applied by Crown Court judges in determining whether to leave a particular criminal charge to the jury: *R v Galbraith* (1981) 73 Cr App R 124, CA.

6.199 The first limb is that which is used in criminal proceedings. Essentially, if there is insufficient evidence to support a conclusion, the question should not be left for the jury to decide.

6.200 The second limb of the Galbraith Plus test has been described as a 'wider and more subjective filter'[1] than just applying the test used in the Crown Court. In the judgment in which he established the Galbraith Plus principle, Haddon-Cave J (as he was then) reflected that 'in my view, this extra layer of protection makes sense in the context of a coronial inquiry where the process is inquisitorial rather than adversarial, the rights of interested parties to engage in the proceedings are necessarily curtailed and coronial verdicts are at large'[2].

[1] Haddon-Cave J, in *R (Secretary of State for Justice) v HM Deputy Coroner for the Eastern District of West Yorkshire* [2012] EWHC 1634 (Admin) at [23].
[2] Haddon-Cave J, in *R (Secretary of State for Justice) v HM Deputy Coroner for the Eastern District of West Yorkshire* [2012] EWHC 1634 (Admin) at [23].

6.201 Conclusions and Records of Inquests

6.201 In reality, there is often little to be added by applying the second limb of the Galbraith Plus test. The key difference is that question of the safety of a verdict as opposed to sufficiency of the evidence.

6.202 The Chief Coroner's Law Sheet No 2 tells us that 'safe' should be given 'its ordinary English meaning, the coroner exercising their own discretion judicially on a case by case basis'[1]. The Law Sheet notes that in other cases, the principle has been described as 'a filter to avoid injustice'[2] and a means by which a coroner can decide not to leave a conclusion from a jury 'when the interests of justice require it'[3]. Essentially, the second limb is an additional mechanism to ensure the proceedings remain fair.

[1] Law Sheet No 2, para 9.
[2] Lord Woolf MR, *R v HM Coroner for Exeter and East Devon ex p Palmer* (10 December 1997, unreported).
[3] *R (Longfield Care Homes Ltd) v HM Coroner for Blackburn* [2004] EWHC 2467 (Admin) at [21].

6.203 One example of when the court has considered it inappropriate to leave a matter to a jury is the case of *Tainton:* the Divisional Court agreed with the coroner that it was not safe to leave the jury to consider the question of whether a delay in diagnosis of the deceased's cancer caused or accelerated his death because 'there were too many unknowns in the factual history'[1]. The court even agreed it was unsafe to ask the jury to consider whether the delay 'possibly' accelerated the death in the circumstances of that case.

[1] [2016] EWHC 1396 (Admin) at [68].

Chapter 7

REPORTS TO PREVENT FUTURE DEATHS

7.1 A coroner has a duty, where appropriate, to provide a report on a particular death with a view to preventing future deaths[1]. These are known as reports to prevent future deaths or 'PFD reports'. As the Chief Coroner's Guidance on PFD reports notes: 'these reports are important . . . a bereaved family wants to be able to say: "his death was tragic and terrible, but at least it shouldn't happen to somebody else"'[2]. However, it should be borne in mind that these reports have in the past been described as 'ancillary to the inquest procedure and not its mainspring'[3].

[1] This duty arises from the CJA 2009, Sch 5, para 7 and the Coroners (Investigations) Regulations 2013, SI 2013/1629, regs 28 and 29.
[2] Chief Coroner's Guidance No 5, Reports to Prevent Future Deaths (revised 4 November 2020), para 2.
[3] *Re Kelly (deceased)* (1996) 161 JP 417.

7.2 The Chief Coroner's Guidance No 5 is helpful in setting out the scope of PFD reports. It observes that:

> 'Broadly speaking reports should be intended to improve public health, welfare and safety. They should not be unduly general in their content; sweeping generalisations should be avoided. They should be clear, brief, focused, meaningful and, where possible, designed to have practical effect.[1]'

[1] Chief Coroner's Guidance No 5, Reports to Prevent Future Deaths, para 5.

WHEN ARE PFD REPORTS REQUIRED?

7.3 PFD reports are only appropriate in certain circumstances. But where the following criteria are met, the coroner has a duty, and not a discretion, to make a report:

(1) The coroner has been investigating the circumstances of a person's death;
(2) 'Anything revealed by the investigation' into the death has given rise to a concern 'that circumstances creating a risk of other deaths will occur, or will continue to exist, in the future[1]'. This has been considered a relatively low threshold[2];
(3) The coroner has considered all the documents, evidence and information that in the opinion of the coroner is relevant to the investigation[3]; and

7.3 Reports to Prevent Future Deaths

(4) The coroner believes that action should be taken to reduce the risk to life or to prevent the concerning circumstances from arising again in the future.

[1] CJA 2009, Sch 5, para 7(1)(b).
[2] Coroners Inquests into the London Bombings of 7 July 2005, 6 May 2011, p 15.
[3] Coroners (Investigations) Regulations 2013, reg 28(3).

7.4 Note that point (3) is a pre-requisite: the coroner may **not** write a PFD report if they have not yet considered all the relevant documents, evidence and information.

SUBMISSIONS/EVIDENCE REGARDING PFD REPORTS

7.5 It is up to the coroner whether they accept submissions from interested persons at the inquest with regard to whether a PFD report is required.

7.6 The coroner also has discretion as to whether to hear evidence which is relevant to any potential PFD report but which is not strictly relevant to the outcome of the inquest itself. One example of this might be when, in a case involving a death in a hospital, a medical director not involved with the deceased's care gives evidence on any changes the hospital/NHS trust has made as a result of the death.

7.7 Bear in mind though that coroners are encouraged not to allow an inquest to become unduly lengthened by evidence or submissions relating to a PFD report as opposed to the death itself[1].

[1] Chief Coroner's Guidance No 5, Reports to Prevent Future Deaths, para 15.

PFD REPORTS IN CASES INVOLVING JURIES

7.8 As noted in the Chief Coroner's Guidance No 5 'a jury is not permitted to make riders or recommendations'[1]. The jury should therefore be expressly directed not to express an opinion on anything other than the four questions they are tasked with answering ie who, how, when and where.

[1] Chief Coroner's Guidance No 5, Reports to Prevent Future Deaths, para 39.

7.9 However there have been situations where juries have been permitted to consider 'facts which are relevant to the coroner's reporting power under paragraph 7 of Schedule 5 [ie the power to create a PFD report], particularly where those facts are disputed or uncertain'[1]. Note that this is distinct from inviting an **opinion** from the jury – they remain arbiters of fact.

[1] Chief Coroner's Guidance No 5, Reports to Prevent Future Deaths, para 40.

TIMING

(a) When should the PFD report be produced?

7.10 It is not necessary for the inquest to have concluded for a PFD report to be written, though they are most commonly completed at the end of an inquest because of the requirement to have considered all relevant documents, evidence and information.

7.11 One example of a PFD report having been completed before the conclusion of the inquest is the PFD report produced in March 2018 in respect of the Grenfell Tower tragedy: the inquests had been opened but then suspended pending the public Grenfell Inquiry, and despite the fact that the inquests had not yet been held the coroner produced a report setting out concerns which had arisen during her investigation[1].

[1] https://www.judiciary.uk/wp-content/uploads/2018/09/Grenfell-Tower-2018-0262.pdf.

(b) When should the PFD report be sent?

7.12 The report should be sent out either within 10 working days of the end of the inquest, or within 10 working days of the time prior to the inquest when the matter is revealed and considered within the scope of the coroner's investigation[1].

[1] Chief Coroner's Guidance No 5, Reports to Prevent Future Deaths, para 36.

CONTENT OF A PFD REPORT

7.13 The Chief Coroner's Guidance on PFD reports provides a template report for coroners to use when creating a PFD report. The PFD report must state:

- the details of the investigation (and if applicable the inquest);
- the circumstances of the death;
- the coroner's concerns;
- that in the coroner's opinion action should be taken to prevent future deaths.

7.14 The PFD report should not contain a confidentiality clause. It should also be complete in itself and there ought not be any need to send any extraneous documents such as the Record of Inquest[1].

[1] Chief Coroner's Guidance No 5, Reports to Prevent Future Deaths, para 21.

(a) What can form the basis for the coroner's concerns?

7.15 Note that the coroner's concerns do not need to arise from something causative of the death: they can arise from 'anything' arising from the coroner's investigation into that death[1]. This means the subject of a PFD report can sometimes be something that is peripheral to the death being investigated in that particular inquest.

[1] CJA 2009, Sch 5, para 7(1)(b).

7.16 The matter giving cause for concern also does not have to have arisen out of evidence at the actual inquest: it may have arisen during the investigation which led to the inquest. This is particularly pertinent when the coroner considers that certain issues need to be urgently addressed.

7.17 Reports to Prevent Future Deaths

7.17 Again, the PFD report produced in March 2018 in respect of Grenfell Tower was one example of this (see **7.11** above): some of the coroner's concerns were to do with ongoing provision of healthcare services to survivors, and so there was a material benefit in that report being produced earlier than the conclusion of the inquests (which will not be for some years after the event).

(b) How should the concerns be expressed?

7.18 The coroner should express clearly, simply and 'in neutral and non-contentious terms' the factual basis for each of the concerns raised in the PFD report[1]. This should be centred around the evidence obtained during the investigation and/or inquest and should be as to the point as possible.

[1] *R v Shrewsbury Coroner's Court, ex p British Parachute Association* (1988) 152 JP 123.

7.19 Coroners are expressly guided by the Chief Coroner to 'ensure that a bereaved family's expectations are not raised unrealistically' by the PFD report[1]. This is particularly important when considered in the context of the fact that a coroner cannot actually compel the recipient of the report to take action (see below at **7.25**).

[1] Chief Coroner's Guidance No 5, Reports to Prevent Future Deaths, para 25.

7.20 In respect of the requirement to state that the coroner believes that action should be taken, the template report provided in the Chief Coroner's Guidance suggests the following wording: 'In my opinion action should be taken to prevent future deaths and I believe you have the power to take such action'[1].

[1] Chief Coroner's Guidance No 5, Reports to Prevent Future Deaths, Annex A.

(c) What should the coroner avoid in a PFD report?

7.21 The PFD report should be neutral. The Chief Coroner's Guidance sets out things to avoid when drafting reports:

> 'Reports should not apportion blame, be defamatory, prejudice law enforcement action or the administration of justice, affect national security, put anyone's safety at risk, or breach data protection for example by naming children or breaching medical confidentiality.'[1]

[1] Chief Coroner's Guidance No 5, Reports to Prevent Future Deaths, para 26.

7.22 The PFD report should not make specific recommendations as to what the action to be taken to prevent future deaths should be (though at times this will be perfectly obvious). This was considered by Hallett LJ in the 7/7 London Bombings Inquests. She noted that:

> 'It is neither necessary, nor appropriate, for a coroner making a report under rule 43 [now reg 28] to identify the necessary remedial action. As it apparent from the final words of rule 43(1), the coroner's function is to identify points of concern, not to prescribe solutions.'[1]

[1] Coroners Inquests into the London Bombings of 7 July 2005, 6 May 2011, p 15.

7.23 A coroner is however permitted to make general recommendations as to an area or practice that the recipient of the PFD report should review. In the 7/7 Bombings Inquests for instance Hallett LJ made nine recommendations in such terms; one example is 'I recommend that the London Resilience Team reviews the provision of inter-agency major incident training for frontline staff, particularly with reference to the London Underground system'[1]. The recommendation is about a particular part of the work carried out by the London Resilience Team, as opposed to a specific solution to the problem.

[1] Rule 43 (now reg 28); letter arising from the Coroners Inquests into the London Bombings of 7 July 2005, 6 May 2011.

WHAT HAPPENS TO THE REPORT?

7.24 The coroner must send the PFD report to 'a person who the coroner believes may have power' to take the action required to eliminate or reduce the risk of death[1]. The term 'person' can include organisations, though when sent to an organisation a coroner is expected to seek to identify a specific person within the organisation who is senior enough to be able to take the action sought.

[1] CJA 2009, Sch 5, para 7(1)(c).

7.25 Whilst that person is expected to (and generally does) answer the report, there is no coronial power compelling them to implement any recommended changes nor to force them to respond. If they do wish to respond this should be done within 56 days[1].

[1] Section 7, Template Form.

7.26 A copy of the report, plus a copy of any response, must be sent to the Chief Coroner[1].

[1] CJA 2009, Sch 5, para 7(3).

LETTER INSTEAD OF REPORT

7.27 If the duty to make a report does not arise but the coroner still wishes to raise a matter of concern with a particular body, the coroner may choose to write a letter to that organisation.

7.28 This situation might arise in circumstances where there is not a risk of future deaths but there is still something that the coroner wishes to draw to the organisation's attention.

RELATIONSHIP BETWEEN PFD REPORTS AND ART 2

7.29 In an Art 2 inquest the PFD report can be one of the ways in which the state fulfils its obligations under Art 2 (see **3.80** regarding the case of *Lewis*)[1].

[1] *R (Lewis) v Mid and North Shropshire Coroner* [2009] EWCA Civ 1403, [2010] 1 WLR 1836.

7.30 *Reports to Prevent Future Deaths*

CHALLENGING A PFD REPORT

7.30 The correct approach, should a recipient wish to challenge a PFD report, was considered in *R (Dr Siddiqi and Dr Paeprer-Rohricht) v Assistant Coroner for East London*[1]. The claimants were partners in a GP practice which had received a PFD report from the coroner following the death of one of their patients. They made an application for judicial review to challenge the coroner's decision to send the report. They considered the factual basis upon which the report had been issued was incorrect and invited the coroner to withdraw the report.

[1] *R (Dr Siddiqi and Dr Paeprer-Rohricht) v Assistant Coroner for East London* CO/2892/2017 (28 September 2017), Admin Court.

7.31 The court confirmed that a coroner has no power to withdraw a PFD report once it has been made. The correct approach, if a party wishes to challenge a PFD report, is to send a response to the coroner in writing ie follow the procedure set out at para 7(2) of Sch 5, CJA 2009.

Chapter 8

CHALLENGING CORONIAL DECISIONS: JUDICIAL REVIEW AND STATUTORY REVIEW

INTRODUCTION

8.1 There is no power to **appeal** the conclusion of an inquest or the decision of a coroner. An intended appeal provision in s 40 to the Coroners and Justice Act 2009 (CJA 2009) was repealed prior to its coming into force. However, there are two procedural routes through which coronial decisions may be **challenged**: (i) statutory review under s 13 of the Coroner's Act 1988; and (ii) judicial review in the High Court. This chapter will set out a guide to both routes of challenge.

STATUTORY REVIEW: THE STATUTORY POWER TO ORDER A (NEW) INQUEST OR INVESTIGATION

8.2 The first way in which it is possible to challenge coronial decisions is by way of a statutory review. This power to apply to 'review' the decision of the coroner is set out in statute, hence the name. Under s 13 of the Coroners Act 1988[1] (CA 1988) the High Court has the power to:

(i) quash 'any inquisition on, or the determination or finding' (all referred to together in this chapter as 'findings') reached at an inquest and/or order a second, new investigation or inquest to be held; and

(ii) direct that an investigation or inquest be commenced where a coroner has 'refuse[d] or neglect[ed]' to do so previously.

[1] As amended by s 2(5) of the Coroners and Justice Act 2009 (Consequential Provisions) Order 2013, SI 2013/1874. Note that this power was originally provided for in s 6 of the Coroners Act 1887, and as a result some of the relevant case law derives from prior to 1988.

8.3 They may also direct that any new investigation or inquest should be held by a different coroner to the original. There are of course caveats to these powers, as set out below. Overall, however, this is a powerful statutory mechanism which provides a check on the powers held, and conclusions reached, by coroners.

8.4 Challenging Coronial Decisions: Judicial Review and Statutory Review

Practical matters

Who can make an application under s 13?

8.4 Unlike applications for judicial review, there is no requirement for judicial permission to make an application pursuant to s 13 of the CA 1988[1].

[1] Re Rapier [1988] QB 26, DC.

8.5 An application under s 13 can be made by any person with sufficient interest. If new evidence has arisen which means it is likely that a different finding will be made, it is often the coroner themselves who makes the application[1].

[1] See for instance Re HM Senior Coroner for the Eastern Area of Greater London [2017] EWHC 3201 (Admin); Re HM Senior Coroner for Birmingham and Solihull [2018] EWHC 3443 (Admin); Re HM Senior Coroner for North West Wales [2017] EWHC 2557 (Admin).

The Attorney General must authorise any application under s 13 CA 1988

8.6 Any application under s 13 CA 1988 must have the authorisation (or 'fiat') of, or be made by, the Attorney General (AG)[1].

[1] Section 13(1) CA 1988.

8.7 To seek the AG's authorisation, the prospective applicant must draft a 'Memorial' document. There is no specific format for this document, but it must contain:

(a) The detail of the application being made.
(b) The reasons for that application.
(c) A statutory declaration.

The Memorial should also be accompanied by supporting documentation if at all possible.

8.8 The AG then gives the coroner in question the opportunity to respond to the Memorial prior to deciding whether to authorise the application. The test that is applied by the AG is not formally proscribed; however, it is widely accepted that the test is broadly similar to the test applied on applications for permission to seek judicial review, ie is there an arguable case for the statutory review[1]?

[1] Jervis on Coroners (Sweet & Maxwell, 14th edn), at 19–21.

Making the application

8.9 The application is then made, either by the AG or by the person who drafted the Memorial, by way of a Pt 8 claim and is governed by the Civil Procedure Rules (see in particular CPR 8 and CPR PD8A).

A coroner must have jurisdiction over the death for s 13 CA 1988 to bite

8.10 Section 13 allows the court to review a particular coroner's decision or findings. If the specific area coroner subject to the review never had jurisdiction

Statutory review **8.15**

over the death in question, then the court has no statutory power to order a coroner to conduct an investigation[1].

[1] *Connah v Plymouth Hospitals NHS Trust* [2010] EWHC 1727 (Admin); see s 1 CJA 2009 for the circumstances in which a coroner's jurisdiction arises, and CHAPTER 2 above.

Power to order an investigation where the coroner has refused or neglected to do so (s 13(1)(a) CA 1988)

8.11 A coroner may decline to hold an investigation for various reasons, such as that they do not have jurisdiction, or because they do not consider one is required pursuant to their duties under s 1 of the CJA 2009. These are considered in more detail in CHAPTER 2, but in key terms, s 1 states:

'(1) A senior coroner who is made aware that the body of a deceased person is within that coroner's area must as soon as practicable conduct an investigation into the person's death if subsection (2) applies.
(2) This subsection applies if the coroner has reason to suspect that—
(a) the deceased died a violent or unnatural death,
(b) the cause of death is unknown, or
(c) the deceased died while in custody or otherwise in state detention.'

8.12 Upon receiving an application to exercise this power, the court will assess whether the coroner has properly applied the tests for conducting an investigation, or if relevant, whether the coroner has correctly declined jurisdiction.

Jurisdiction (s 1(4) CJA 2009)

8.13 The matter of jurisdiction under s 1(4) tends to be a practical question. This is considered in detail in CHAPTER 2.

Section 1(2) CJA 2009 – duty to investigate because of the nature of the death

8.14 The duty to investigate because of the nature of the death arises under s 1(2) CJA 2009. These are generally factual questions; instances where the duty arises are considered in detail in CHAPTER 2.

8.15 In *Connah*[1], the court also considered whether the Cornwall Coroner should have made a report to the Secretary of State under the terms of s 15 Coroners Act 1988 (CA 1988) (the equivalent of which is now s 1(4) CJA 2009). Section 15 stated a report should have been made, if the coroner had reason to believe that the death had occurred in such circumstances that an inquest ought to be held; however, the deceased's doctor had reported to the then Cornwall Coroner that there was no requirement for an inquest and as such the deceased's body had been released for cremation. There was no basis for the current Cornwall Coroner to make any such report.

[1] [2010] EWHC 1727 (Admin).

8.16 Challenging Coronial Decisions: Judicial Review and Statutory Review

Power to quash the findings made at an inquest and order a new investigation (s 13(1)(b) CA 1988)

8.16 In order to exercise the s 13(1)(b) power, the determinations or findings must already have been produced, and the investigation and inquest must actually have been completed. In *Flower v Devon, Plymouth, Torbay, and South Devon Coroner*[1], the court held that s 6 of the CJA 2009 made it clear that the inquest is part of the investigation. In that case the coroner had held an investigation and commenced an inquest but had decided not to resume it after the conclusion of related criminal proceedings. Without completion of the inquest, therefore, the investigation could not be complete. An investigation could not be considered to have been 'held' for the purposes of s 13(1)(b) CA 1988.

[1] [2016] 1 WLR 2221.

8.17 Secondly the High Court must be satisfied that:

'whether by reason of fraud, rejection of evidence, irregularity of proceedings, insufficiency of inquiry, the discovery of new facts or evidence or otherwise [. . .] it is necessary or desirable in the interests of justice that [. . .] another investigation should be held.'[1]

[1] Section 13(1)(b) CA 1988.

8.18 In practice, these broadly amount to: (i) situations where new evidence has arisen; (ii) situations where there has been a fraud of some kind; (iii) situations where there has been a material irregularity or error in the way the investigation or inquest proceeded.

What makes it necessary or desirable in the interests of justice to conduct another investigation or inquest?

8.19 Necessity and desirability are:

' . . . the critical words. The court is not to attend to mere formalities, nor to criticise minutely the summing up, or the nature of the evidence or of the procedure. But if the inquest has been so conducted, or the circumstances attending it are such that there is a real risk that justice has not been done, a real impairment of security which the right procedure provides that justice is done and is seen to be done, the court ought not to allow the inquisition to stand.'[1]

[1] *R v Divine ex parte Walton* [1930] 2 KB 29.

8.20 More recently in considering the same question, Burnett J (as he then was) observed (when considering whether to quash the original inquests into the deaths arising from the Hillsborough disaster – 'the *Hillsborough* application') that 'the interests of justice, as they arise in the coronial process, are undefined, but dealing with it broadly [. . .] the decision is not based on problems with process, unless the process adopted in the original inquest has caused justice to be diverted or for the inquiry to be insufficient'[1].

[1] *Attorney General v South Yorkshire (West) Coroner* [2012] EWHC 3783 (Admin) at [10].

8.21 Often, the way in which the test is met is by showing the court that a different outcome is 'likely' if a fresh inquest is held[1]. For obvious reasons, this is one of the most compelling justifications for reopening an inquest: the original findings as to how someone came by their death may been wrongly made. Equally, if a new investigation will inevitably lead to the same conclusions as the original one, this is a factor against quashing the findings and listing a new inquest. However:

> '[I]t is not a precondition to an order for a further inquest that this court should anticipate that a different verdict to the one already reached will be returned. If a different verdict is likely, then the interests of justice will make it necessary for a fresh inquest to be ordered, but even when significant fresh evidence may serve to confirm the correctness of the earlier verdict, it may sometimes nevertheless be desirable for the full extent of the evidence which tends to confirm the correctness of the verdict to be publicly revealed.[2]'

[1] *Attorney General v South Yorkshire (West) Coroner* [2012] EWHC 3783 (Admin) at [10].
[2] *Attorney General v South Yorkshire (West) Coroner* [2012] EWHC 3783 (Admin) at [10].

8.22 The passage of time makes the success of an application less likely[1], but does not rule it out[2].

[1] *R v HM Coroner for East Sussex Western District ex parte Homburg* [1994] 1 WLUK 555, (1994) 158 JP 357.
[2] *Frost v HM Coroner for West Yorkshire (Eastern District)* [2019] EWHC 1100 (Admin), in which the application was successful despite 57 years having passed since the death; and *Re HM Senior Coroner for Birmingham and Solihull* [2018] EWHC 3443 (Admin), a successful application despite over 40 years having passed.

8.23 Ultimately, what constitutes necessity and desirability in the interests of justice will vary depending on the nature of the inadequacy within the original inquest, or the new circumstances which have arisen. Each of the three categories identified from s 13(1)(b) CA 1988 above are therefore examined in turn.

New evidence

8.24 The first of these, where new evidence has arisen, is perhaps the most straightforward. As Burnett J observed in the *Hillsborough* application:

> 'It seems to us elementary that the emergence of fresh evidence which may reasonably lead to the conclusion that the substantial truth about how an individual met his death was not revealed at the first inquest will normally make it both desirable and necessary in the interests of justice for a fresh inquest to be ordered.[1]'

[1] [2012] EWHC 3783 (Admin) at [10].

8.25 New evidence is any evidence that[1]:

(a) was not available at the time of the original inquest;
(b) would have been admissible at the time;
(c) is relevant and credible in respect of a significant issue; and
(d) might have made a material difference to the findings.

[1] *R v HM Coroner for Derbyshire (Scarsdale) ex parte Fletcher* [1992] 1 WLUK 273, cited with approval in *Attorney General v HM Coroner for South Yorkshire (West)* [2012] EWHC 3783 (Admin).

8.26 Again, the question of whether 'fresh evidence' meets the test is highly fact-specific. Examples include:

8.26 *Challenging Coronial Decisions: Judicial Review and Statutory Review*

- a case where significant new evidence was uncovered after the inquest which led to another individual being convicted of the murders of two deceased men[1];
- an instance in which significant advances in DNA profiling gave an indication as to the probable identity of a previously unidentified man[2];
- a case where, over 40 years after the original inquest, fresh evidence regarding the mechanism and cause of death contradicted the opinion of the pathologist upon whose evidence the original verdict (as it was then) had been made[3]; and
- cases where new and contradicting medical evidence which was previously unavailable has come to light[4].

[1] *Re HM Senior Coroner for the Eastern Area of Greater London* [2017] EWHC 3201 (Admin).
[2] *Re HM Senior Coroner for North West Wales* [2017] EWHC 2557 (Admin).
[3] *Re HM Senior Coroner for Birmingham and Solihull* [2018] EWHC 3443 (Admin). Note that also in this case the fact that the original verdict had been an 'open verdict' ie the 'verdict of last resort' was a supporting reason why reopening the matter was desirable.
[4] For instance, *HM Coroner for the Southern District of Manchester v Stockport NHS Foundation Trust* [2015] EWHC 2675 (Admin).

8.27 Note that in all these cases the coroners themselves made the application for the original findings to be quashed upon receipt of new evidence, rather than this task being left to the families of the deceased.

8.28 In some instances, the evidence may be more speculative than in others. In one instance, the suspect for the deceased's murder had died prior to any arrest or charge and so had never been tried for the offence, but the police had referred the matter to the CPS for a charging decision prior to his death, and had made a public statement after he died that they considered him to be responsible. Despite the fact that the court had not seen the police file, this was considered sufficient 'fresh evidence [. . .] which might reasonably lead to the conclusion that the substantial truth about how [the deceased] died had not been revealed at the first inquest'[1].

[1] *Frost v HM Coroner for West Yorkshire (Eastern District)* [2019] EWHC 1100 (Admin) at [41].

8.29 The outcomes of other investigations, both public and private, can at times provide the fresh evidence required to quash findings and order another inquest. For instance, following the first inquests into the deaths of those who died in the Hillsborough disaster, the fresh evidence was brought to light as part of the publicly funded Hillsborough Independent Panel investigation into the tragedy. This evidence included the results of alcohol testing on the deceased, new evidence around rescue attempts and safety concerns, and evidence of the extent to which professionals' statements for the inquest had been amended (with the intention of concealing criticism of the police and rescue operation), was justification for quashing the inquest and ordering a new one[1].

[1] *Attorney General v HM Coroner for South Yorkshire (West)* [2012] EWHC 3783 (Admin). Note that in addition to the importance of the fresh evidence presented, the High Court also found one of the coroner's procedural decisions 'seriously flawed'.

8.30 There is inconsistent case law on whether new expert opinion evidence constitutes 'new evidence'. See for instance *Chambers v HM Coroner for*

Preston and West Lancashire[1], in which the claimant's independent psychiatrist's expert report containing an opinion of the deceased's treatment was not considered 'new evidence' for these purposes.

[1] [2015] EWHC 31 (Admin).

8.31 However, the production of a new expert report which showed that the determination as to cause of death was wrong did mean it was overall 'necessary or desirable' to hold a new investigation in *Hopkins v HM Coroner for Swansea, Neath and Port Talbot*[1].

[1] [2018] EWHC 1604 (Admin). The author questions whether the court considered the report as formal 'fresh evidence' or whether it determined that it was otherwise 'necessary and desirable' for it to be admitted due to its value in the proceedings.

Fraud

8.32 Fraud should be given its common sense, natural meaning. For obvious reasons, when it transpires that evidence has been given to the coroner's court fraudulently, this provides a basis to quash the inquest and rehear the genuine evidence. There is no direct coronial authority on the test that the court should apply when considering whether a determination has been tainted by fraud so it is likely that the court will adopt the formulation in *Royal Bank of Scotland plc v Highland Financial Partners LP*[1] as endorsed by the Supreme Court in *Takhar v Gracefield Developments Ltd*[2]:

- There must have been 'conscious and deliberate dishonesty' in relation to the relevant evidence given, which itself is relevant to the judgment now sought to be impugned.
- The relevant dishonest evidence or action must be 'material', ie the fresh evidence adduced after the relevant judgment would have 'entirely changed the way in which the first court approached and came to its decision'. The dishonesty must be causative of the judgment.
- The materiality of the new evidence 'is to be assessed by reference to its impact on the evidence supporting the original decision', not its likely impact if the claim were to be retried on correct and honest evidence now[3].

[1] [2013] EWCA Civ 328.
[2] [2019] UKSC 13.
[3] At [106], *RBS v Highland*.

Material irregularities or errors

8.33 There are a multiplicity of things that fall into the other 'headings' provided in s 13(1)(b) CA 1988: 'rejection of evidence, irregularity of proceedings, insufficiency of inquiry'. These are largely fact- and case-specific. Examples include:

– the coroner's decision in the original Hillsborough Inquests not to consider events on the day of the deaths past 3.15pm, which resulted in material evidence not being heard or considered[1].
– undue pressure inadvertently being placed upon a jury to reach a decision[2].
– inadequate investigations which do not provide adequate information as to the nature of the death[3].

8.33 Challenging Coronial Decisions: Judicial Review and Statutory Review

– a coroner, in investigating the death of a British tourist in Dubai, who simply admitted written evidence from witnesses in Dubai under r 23 Coroners (Inquests) Rules 2013[4] without setting out the 'good and sufficient reason' why he believed the witnesses in question did not need to attend in person to give evidence, and seemingly without having made enquiries as to whether they could attend remotely. This constituted a significant failure in due process[5].

[1] *Attorney General v HM Coroner for South Yorkshire (West)* [2012] EWHC 3783 (Admin) at [13]–[21].
[2] *Clayton v HM Coroner for South Yorkshire (East District)* [2005] EWHC 1196 (Admin).
[3] *Thompson v Durham & Darlington Assistant Coroner* [2015] EWHC 1781 (Admin).
[4] SI 2013/1616.
[5] *Shafi v HM Senior Coroner for East London* [2015] EWHC 2106 (Admin).

8.34 The High Court has been known to draw a clear distinction between an 'irregularity' and a 'material irregularity'. For example, the failure to notify a family member of the inquest hearing date after she had registered interest with the coroner was an irregularity but not a material one in *Chambers v HM Coroner for Preston and West Lancashire*[1], since other family members had been present and had been represented by counsel.

[1] [2015] EWHC 31 (Admin).

8.35 In some cases, there are multiple less-material irregularities which, when combined, mean it is 'necessary or desirable' to quash the findings and hold a new inquest. In *Sylvia Rushbrooke v HM Coroner for West London*[1], the deceased was subject to a deprivation of liberty safeguards standard authorisation[2], and had sustained numerous fractures prior to her death which were unexplained and which had resulted in her admission to hospital, where she contracted pneumonia. The coroner knew that a safeguarding investigation was currently underway into the deceased's death, but declined to even consider adjourning the inquest pending the outcome. In addition, the coroner had declined to hear other relevant evidence relating to the potential medical cause of death. This combination, alongside other smaller procedural irregularities such as a failure to give the family adequate notice of various matters, meant that the inquest was quashed and a new one was ordered.

[1] [2020] EWHC 1612 (Admin).
[2] See CHAPTER 15 for details of inquests involving questions of mental capacity.

JUDICIAL REVIEW

Practical matters

Who can make an application for judicial review of coronial decisions?

8.36 The test for standing ie whether someone will be permitted to make an application for judicial review is whether a person has 'sufficient interest' in the matter to which the application relates[1].

[1] Section 31(3) Senior Courts Act 1981 (SCA 1981).

8.37 The modern public law test for sufficient interest is 'interest-based rather than right-based'[1], further:

Judicial review **8.39**

'A personal interest need not be shown if the individual is acting in the public interest and can genuinely say that the issue directly affects the section of the public that he seeks to represent.[2]'

[1] *R (Bancoult) v Secretary of State for Foreign and Commonwealth Affairs* [2007] EWCA Civ 498, [2008] QB 365 at [61] per Sedley LJ.
[2] *AXA General Insurance v The Lord Advocate* [2011] WKSC 46, [2012] 1 AC 868 at [63] per Lord Hope.

8.38 In an inquest context this means that the cohort of persons who have standing to challenge a coronial decision is not restricted to those who are determined to be 'properly interested persons' under s 47 of the CJA 2009[1]. The question of sufficient interest is related to the decision that the applicant seeks to challenge. Family members of the deceased and persons whose conduct may be called into question during coronial proceedings plainly will have standing. The wider cohort of persons who have been determined to have sufficient interest to challenge coronial decisions include:

(a) A person punished by a coroner for contempt of court[2].
(b) A person who may be charged with a homicide offence in relation to a person's death, in relation to a decision to release a body for disposal or removal out of the country[3].
(c) Newspapers and the press in relation to decisions to hold an inquest in private or to grant witness anonymity[4].
(d) The Medical Defence Union where the conduct of a member clinician is criticised[5].
(e) The campaigning BME womens' rights organisation, Southall Black Sisters, was held to have sufficient interest in judicial review proceedings to challenge the decision of a coroner not to grant it properly interested person status, despite the High Court finding in the same application that it was not arguable that the coroner had erred in law in failing to grant them that status[6].
(f) A charitable organisation responsible for managing the burials of a large proportion of the Orthodox Jewish population in the relevant area, in relation to a coroner's policy refusing to prioritise burials on the basis of religion[7].

[1] See **4.13**.
[2] *R v West Yorkshire Coroner, ex parte Smith (No 2)* [1985] QB 1096 (DC).
[3] *R v Bristol Coroner, ex parte Kerr* [1974] QB 652 (DC).
[4] *R v Bedfordshire Coroner ex parte Local Sunday Newspapers Ltd* (1999) 164 JP 283l, *R v Felixstowe Justices ex parte Leigh* [1987] QB 582.
[5] In *Re Medical Defence Union v Bascombe Sinclair* [1990] 1 Med LR 359.
[6] *R (Southall Black Sisters) v West Yorkshire Coroner* [2002] EWHC 1914 (Admin).
[7] *R (Adath Yisroel Burial Society v HM Senior Coroner for Inner North London* [2018] EWHC 969 (Admin), [2019] QB 251.

Procedure – s 31 SCA 1981, CPR Pt 54

8.39 The procedure and rules applicable to judicial review are set out in s 31 of the Senior Courts Act 1981 (SCA 1981), and Pts 8 and 54 of the Civil Procedure Rules 1998. What follows is only a brief outline of significant aspects of judicial review procedure for coronial purposes. Readers are referred to the specialist texts on judicial review and procedure for more detailed analysis.

8.40 *Challenging Coronial Decisions: Judicial Review and Statutory Review*

PRE ACTION PROTOCOL

8.40 The Pre-Action Protocol for Judicial Review sets out a code of good practice and the steps that parties should generally follow before making an application for judicial review, including a letter of claim and an opportunity for the defendant coroner to provide a letter of response[1]. As with other civil proceedings, failure to follow the Protocol may result in judicial sanction or be reflected in costs. The protocol states that it 'will not be appropriate in very urgent cases'. The majority of coronial decisions, it is submitted, will not require urgent review. Though there may be fact specific exceptions in relation to procedural decisions regarding, eg witnesses and anonymity.

[1] https://www.justice.gov.uk/courts/procedure-rules/civil/protocol/prot_jrv.

LIMITATION AND CLAIM FORM

8.41 The claim form for judicial review is the N461 form. CPR 54.5 specifies, amongst other things, as follows:

'(1) The claim form must be filed—
  (a) promptly; and
  (b) in any event not later than 3 months after the grounds to make the claim first arose.

(2) The time limits in this rule may not be extended by agreement between the parties

[. . .]'

8.42 Claimants should be aware that a claim filed within three months will not necessarily meet the test for promptness[1]. The time limit runs from the date when the grounds for review arose. In an inquest context that means claimants should concentrate on the date of the decision they are seeking to challenge. The time limit will run from the date of a decision not to order a post mortem, for example, and not from the date of any subsequent inquest into that death[2].

[1] See eg *R (Sustainable Development Capital LLP) v Secretary of State for Business, Energy and Strategy* [2017] EWHC 771 (Admin).
[2] *Re Jacobs Application for Judicial Review* (1999) 53 BMLR 21, CA.

8.43 The court may grant an extension of time for filing the claim form under CPR 3.1(2)(a). However, the courts recognise that public law clams by their nature should be brought quickly and require strict adherence to time limits[1]. Previous authority to the effect that delay in the grant of grant of public funding would justify an extension[2], should now be doubted. In *R (Kigen) v Secretary of State for the Home Department*[3] the Court of Appeal held that a lack of legal aid, or waiting for a grant of legal aid, is not normally a reason to extend the three-month issue period for judicial review.

[1] *R v Institute of Chartered Accountants in England and Wales, ex parte, Andreou* (1996) 8 Admin LR 557.
[2] *R v Stratford upon Avon DC ex parte Jackson* [1985] 1 WLR 1319.
[3] [2016] 1 WLR 723.

8.44 The requirements for the contents of the claim form are set out in CPR 8.2 and 54.6 and Practice Direction 54A, and include a request for permission to proceed with a claim for judicial review, any remedy which is being claimed, a statement of the facts relied upon and a detailed statement of the claimant's grounds.

PERMISSION

8.45 The court's permission to proceed is required in a claim for judicial review[1]. The test for permission is whether the court is satisfied that there is an arguable case for a ground of judicial review that merits a full oral hearing with all relevant parties and evidence[2]. The court will generally, in the first instance, consider the question of permission without a hearing[3]. If permission is refused, the claimant has a right to request that any decision to refuse or limit the grant of permission be reconsidered at an oral hearing[4]. In appropriate cases the court may order a 'rolled up' hearing where the question of permission and the substantive merits of the claim are considered at a single hearing. If permission is refused, the claimant has seven days to make a paper application for permission to appeal to the Court of Appeal[5].

[1] SCA 1981, s 31; CPR 54.4.
[2] *R v Legal Aid Board ex parte Hughes* (1992) 5 Admin L Rep 623.
[3] Practice Direction 54, para 8.4.
[4] *R (Sahthivel) v Secretary of State for the Home Department* [2018] EWHC 913 (Admin).
[5] CPR 52.8.

Coronial decisions susceptible to judicial review

8.46 Judicial review is a discretionary remedy. As Lord Goff said in *R v Greater Manchester Coroner, ex p Tal*[1], after explaining why the ordinary approach to the principles of judicial review applied to coroners:

> '... we wish to add the caveat that in every case the grant of an application for judicial review is discretionary and that it does not follow that an order of certiorari will be made merely because some error of law has been committed during an inquest.'

[1] [1984] 3 All ER 240 at 249, [1985] QB 67 at 83.

8.47 Nevertheless, the vast majority of coronial decisions are in principle *susceptible* to judicial review (susceptibility being a different question to whether a ground of judicial review is made out in law). Advocates should be mindful to ask for reasons for a decision from a coroner, where they suspect it may be susceptible to challenge. Interlocutory decisions are susceptible to challenge, as are the outcomes and conclusions of inquests and investigations; but so in principle are administrative decisions and policies made by individual local coroners. Permission to proceed to judicial review has therefore been granted with regard to a very wide range of coronial decisions. Those will not be set out in full here. However, a list of key coronial decisions subject to challenge on review includes:

(a) Whether to exhume and x-ray a body[1].
(b) Whether to hold a post mortem or additional post mortem[2].
(c) Whether or not a local policy refusing to prioritise burials according to religion was lawful[3].

8.47 *Challenging Coronial Decisions: Judicial Review and Statutory Review*

(d) Whether or not to open an investigation into a death/assume jurisdiction under s 1 of the CJA 2009[4].
(e) Whether or not to include a particular issue in the scope of the inquest[5].
(f) Whether to call witnesses of fact[6].
(g) Whether or not to grant anonymity or special measures to a witness[7].
(h) Whether the investigative duty under Art 2 of the European Convention on Human Rights (ECHR) is engaged[8].
(i) Whether or not to leave a particular verdict or conclusion to the jury[9].
(j) Whether the content of the Art 2 ECHR investigative duty has been adhered to[10].
(k) Whether a report to prevent future deaths should have been made[11].
(l) Alleged coronial bias[12].
(m) Failure to conduct a sufficient enquiry[13].

[1] *R (Trivedi) v Southwark Coroner* [2016] EWHC 2764 (Admin).
[2] *R v South London Coroner ex parte Ridley* [1985] 1 WLR 1347.
[3] *R (Adath Yisroel Burial Society v HM Senior Coroner for Inner North London* [2018] EWHC 969 (Admin), [2019] QB 251.
[4] *R (T) v HM Senior Coroner for West Yorkshire* [2017] EWCA Civ 318, [2018] 2 WLR 211; *R (Touche) v HM Coroner for Inner London North* [2001] EWCA Civ 383, [2001] QB 1206.
[5] Eg *Hambleton R (Hambleton) v Coroner for the Birmingham Inquests (1974)* [2019] 1 WLR 3417; *R (Sturgess) v HM Senior Coroner for Wiltshire and Swindon* [2020] EWHC 2007 (Admin).
[6] *R (Maguire) v Assistant Coroner for West Yorkshire* [2017] EWHC 2039 (Admin).
[7] *R (T) v HM Senior Coroner for West Yorkshire* [2017] EWCA Civ 318.
[8] *R (Hurst) v HM Coroner for Northern District London* [2007] UKHL 13, [2007] 2 WLR 726, *R (Parkinson) v Kent Senior Coroner* [2018] 4 WLR 106.
[9] *R v HM Coroner for Inner London South District ex parte Douglas-Williams* [1999] 1 All ER 344, *Middleton*, above, *R v HM Coroner for Northamptonshire, ex parte Cash* [2007] EWHC 1354 (Admin).
[10] *R (Amin) v Secretary of State for the Home Department* [2003] UKHL 51, [2004] 1 AC 653, [2003] 3 WLR 1169, [2003] 4 All ER 1264, HL(E).
[11] RPFD should have been made authority!.
[12] *R (on the application of Gabriele Shaw) (Claimant) v (1) HM Coroner for Leicester City & South Leicestershire (2) Assistant Deputy Coroner for Leicester City & South Leicestershire (Defendants) & University Hospitals of Leicester NHS Trust & Ors (Interested Parties)* [2013] EWHC 386 (Admin).
[13] *R v HM Coroner for Portsmouth ex parte Keane* (1989) 153 JP 658, *R v Avon Deputy Coroner, ex parte Lambourne*, 29 July 2002, DC. See further the section on statutory review.

Timing of challenge

8.48 Generally, a challenge by way of judicial review, even to an interlocutory decision, should await the conclusion of the coronial proceedings, when the High Court will be in a better position to review the overall lawfulness of proceedings and what contribution any errors of law made to the overall process[1]. It is only in exceptional circumstances that that the court will intervene in inquests that are still proceeding[2]. One example of such a cases is *Chief Constable of Devon and Cornwall Police v HM Coroner for Plymouth, Torbay and South Devon*[3], where the High Court listed an urgent rolled up oral hearing one week after the claim was issued and quashed the decision of the coroner to submit to the jury a question regarding 'defects in . . . state organisations which contributed to the death', when there was no evidence that the police's procedures or systems for protecting vulnerable suicidal persons were in anyway deficient. Further examples of permission being granted to review interlocutory decisions prior to the full inquest hearing taking place are *R (Sturgess) v HM Senior Coroner for Wiltshire and Swindon*[4], where the coroner's decision not to investigate the involvement of the Russian state in Dawn Sturgess' death from Novichok exposure was quashed, and *R (T) v HM Senior Coroner for West Yorkshire*[5], where the Court of Appeal upheld the decision of a coroner to assume jurisdiction to open an investigation into the death of a baby who could not be said on balance to have been born alive.

[1] Re Officers C, D, H and R NICA 47; R (Khan) v West Hertfordshire Coroner [2002] EWHC 302 (Admin) at [3]; R (Cooper) v HM Coroner for North East Kent [2014] EWHC 586 (Admin).
[2] R v HM Coroner for Wiltshire & Swindon, ex parte Craik [2004] EWHC 2653 (Admin).
[3] [2017] EWHC 3729 (Admin).
[4] [2020] EWHC 2007 (Admin).
[5] [2017] EWCA Civ 318.

8.49 There is a distinction, it is submitted, between a review of an interlocutory decision taken prior to an inquest taking place, and one of a decision taken during the course of an inquest itself. Reviews in the latter group, such as the Devon and Cornwall case[1], will be rarer, especially where a jury has been sworn.

[1] [2017] EWHC 3729 (Admin).

Grounds of review

Common law

8.50 In principle the full range of grounds for judicial review of administrative action are available to claimants seeking to challenge coronial decisions. The most likely relevant grounds of review are summarised shortly here.

ILLEGALITY

8.51 This ground includes the following categories of errors of law:

(i) Misinterpretation of a statute or secondary legislation.
(ii) A lack of legal authority to reach the decision.
(iii) Failure to act in accordance with a legal duty.

8.52 Coroners hold a unique position in the English legal system as judicial decision makers in an inquisitorial jurisdiction. Many decisions made within the framework of the CJA 2009 are discretionary. A discretionary coronial decision may generally only be challenged on the grounds of *Wednesbury* unreasonableness, as set out below. However, representatives should be careful to distinguish between a challenge which is truly to the exercise of a discretion, and one which is to a legal element of a discretionary power. Thus in *R (Touche) v Inner London North Coroner*[1], the Court of Appeal held that a decision by a coroner as to whether there is reason to suspect that a death was violent or unnatural may be challenged on the basis that 'it is *Wednesbury* unreasonable (see *Associated Provincial Picture Houses Ltd v Wednesbury Corpn*[2]) or involves a self-misdirection in law' [emphasis added]. The question in *Touche* was whether a coroner had lawfully refused to exercise

8.52 *Challenging Coronial Decisions: Judicial Review and Statutory Review*

his discretion to open an inquest. But the lawfulness of the decision depended on the correct interpretation of the word 'unnatural' for the purposes of s 8 of the Coroners Act 1988, and so the relevant ground of review was an error or law.

[1] [2001] QB 1206.
[2] [1948] 1 KB 223.

8.53 A further recent example of a common law error of law ground succeeding is in the challenge to the decision of the coroner in the inquest into the death of Dawn Sturgess[1], who died after coming into contact with the nerve agent Novichok in Salisbury in July 2018. The coroner held that the inquest would investigate the two Russian nationals widely understood to be directly responsible for the death, but not whether other members for the Russian state were directly responsible for the death or the source of the Novichok. The Divisional Court held that in giving his reasons for this decision the coroner made two material and distinct errors of law: investigating the Russian state's role would not infringe the prohibitions on reaching a conclusion that imparts either (i) civil or (ii) criminal liability in s 10 CJA 2009.

[1] *R (Sturgess) v HM Senior Coroner for Wiltshire and Swindon* [2020] EWHC 2007 (Admin).

PROCEDURAL UNFAIRNESS

8.54 Procedural unfairness includes the following categories of error of law relevant to coronial decision making:

(i) Fettering of discretion: in *R (Adath Yisroel Burial Society) v HM Senior Coroner for Inner North London*[1] Singh LJ held that the common law power to retain the body of a deceased was akin to a power derived from statute and that the coroner's rigid policy of refusing to prioritise the release of bodies for burial by religion constituted an unlawful fettering of her discretion.
(ii) The prohibition on actual and perceived bias[2].

[1] [2018] EWHC 969 (Admin), [2019] QB 251.
[2] On which in a coronial context see *R (on the application of Gabriele Shaw) (Claimant) v (1) HM Coroner for Leicester City & South Leicestershire (2) Assistant Deputy Coroner for Leicester City & South Leicestershire (Defendants) & University Hospitals of Leicester NHS Trust & Ors (Interested Parties)* [2013] EWHC 386 (Admin).

IRRATIONALITY OR UNREASONABLENESS

8.55 Examples of coronial decisions that may only be challenged on the ground of substantive *Wednesbury* unreasonableness are those as to the scope of the inquest under s 5 CJA 2009, and which witnesses (including experts) to call to give evidence at an inquest. In *R (Hambleton) v Coroner for the Birmingham Inquests (1974)*[1] Burnett LCJ stated:

'48. A decision on scope represents a coroner's view about what is necessary, desirable and proportionate by way of investigation to enable the statutory functions to be discharged. These are not hard-edged questions. The decision on scope, just as a decision on which witnesses to call, and the breadth of evidence adduced, is for the coroner. A court exercising supervisory jurisdiction can interfere with such a decision only if it is infected with a public law failing. It has long been the case that a court exercising supervisory jurisdiction will be slow to disturb a decision of this sort (see Simon Brown LJ in *Dallaglio* at [155] cited in [21] above) and will do so only on what is described in omnibus terms as *Wednesbury* grounds. That envisages the supervisory jurisdiction of the High Court being exercised when the decision of the coroner can be demonstrated to disable him from performing his statutory function, when the decision is one which no reasonable coroner could have come to on the basis of the information available, involves a material error of law or on a number of other well-established public law failings.'

[1] [2019] 1 WLR 3417.

8.56 In *R (Maguire) v Assistant Coroner for West Yorkshire*[1], the Administrative Court held that a coroner had been entitled to refuse to call as witnesses at the inquest into the murder of a school pupil fellow pupils who had been interviewed by the police and had had contact with the murderer in the days leading up to the killing. Holdroyde J emphasised as follows:

'36. In judicial review proceedings, a decision by a coroner as to the scope of an inquest as to which witnesses are to be called may only be challenged on the grounds of Wednesbury unreasonableness, ie irrationality: see *R (Mack) v HM Coroner for Birmingham* [2011] EWCA Civ 712, in which Toulson LJ said (at paragraph 9) that the coroner has –

" . . . a wide discretion – or perhaps more appropriately a wide range of judgment – whom it is expedient to call. The court will only intervene if satisfied that the decision made was one which was not properly open to him on *Wednesbury* principles."'

[1] [2017] EWHC 2039 (Admin), [2017] Inquest LR 248.

8.57 Holdroyde J accepted[1] that the test for unreasonableness 'includes circumstances in which a coroner is said to have taken into account irrelevant matters, or failed to take into account relevant matters . . . The test may be summed up by saying that a party who seeks to challenge a decision by a coroner must show that the coroner acted in a way which was not reasonably open to them, and made a decision which could not reasonably be reached'.

[1] [2017] EWHC 2039 (Admin) at [38].

Article 2 ECHR

8.58 A coroner's court is a public authority for the purposes of s 6 of the Human Rights Act 1998 (HRA 1998). Coroners must therefore act compatibly with Convention rights in accordance with s 6 HRA 1998. They must also read and give effect to primary and secondary legislation, 'so far as it is possible to do so' under s 3. An alleged failure to adhere to either of these duties on the part of a coroner may be challenged by way of judicial review. A coroner's court cannot issue a declaration of compatibility under s 4 HRA 1998. The interpretative obligation imposed by s 3 is wide[1], the most famous example of its use in an inquest context being the addition of the words 'and in what circumstances' to the question 'by what means the deceased came by her death' by Lord Bingham in *Middleton*[2] in order to satisfy the requirements of the investigative duty under Art 2 ECHR. The law in relation to inquests and the positive duties to protect life under Art 2 ECHR is set out at CHAPTER 3. Practitioners should further note that judicial reviews of coronial decisions

8.58 *Challenging Coronial Decisions: Judicial Review and Statutory Review*

on Convention grounds are not limited to those in respect of Art 2. A decision regarding witness anonymity, for example, may engage Arts 3 and 8 ECHR[3], as well as Art 2[4], a decision on burials may engage Art 9[5], and a decision regarding reporting restrictions will engage Art 10[6]. In these cases the relevant ground of review will be a failure to adhere to or to interpret legislation compatibility with Convention rights. Readers are referred to the relevant substantive chapters dealing with these areas of coronial law.

[1] See *Ghaidan v Godin-Mendoza* [2004] UKHL 30, [2004] 2 AC 557.
[2] [2004] 2 AC 182.
[3] The prohibition of torture, inhuman or degrading treatment, and the right to respect for private and family life, home and correspondence.
[4] See CHAPTER 12 on witness anonymity.
[5] The right to freedom of thought, conscience and religion.
[6] The right to freedom of expression.

8.59 The standard and intensity of review applicable by the High Court in cases where a coroner's decision that the Art 2 investigative duty is not engaged is under challenge was considered recently by the Administrative Court in *R (Skelton) v Senior Coroner for West Sussex*[1]. The Court observed that the crucial element of the test for Art 2 engagement is the low, arguable threshold in relation to a breach of one of the substantive Art 2 duties. In practice, because of the nature of the test, which is black and white and objective[2] 'a rationality challenge collapses into a merits review because the answer to the question as posed is the same whether the route to it is through *Wednesbury* or an examination of the merits'[3]. Popplewell LJ continued:

> '92. That is not to say, however, that the conclusion and the reasons given by the Coroner are entirely irrelevant . . . the court in reaching its own conclusion will take account of those reasons . . . The weight to be accorded to them by the court in reaching its own decision will vary according to their nature and cogency, as well as the degree to which they can properly be regarded as informed by specialist knowledge and experience in relation to the particular factual questions in issue.
>
> 93. In conclusion, therefore, the nature of the exercise being conducted by the Coroner means that her options were limited to one, as are ours. In practice, we must ask ourselves whether her conclusion was right or wrong.'

[1] [2020] EWHC 2813 (Admin).
[2] At [22].
[3] At [91].

Remedies

8.60 Section 31(1) of the SCA 1981 sets out the forms of relief available to the High Court on an application for judicial review, including awarding damages, mandatory, prohibiting and quashing orders; and declarations or injunctions. Because a coroner is a judicial officer and can be expected to comply with a direction or suggested course of action by the High Court (thus not normally requiring a mandatory order to be made), in practice the most widely used of these powers in judicial reviews of coronial decisions are quashing orders, and where appropriate, declarations.

8.61 The High Court may quash the inquisition or Record of Inquest in its entirety and order a new inquest. The more prejudicial to the outcome of the inquest proceedings as a whole the relevant error of law, the more likely the court is to make such an order. For example, a failure to hold an inquest with a jury was held to be such a serious procedural irregularity in *R (Aineto) v HM coroner for Brighton and Hove*[1], that the 'there would need to be cogent reasons to deny a fresh inquest' where that was the outcome sought by the family. However, it will not be in the interests of justice to set aside an inquest on the basis of a misdirection if the misdirection would not have affected the outcom – *R v Wolverhampton Coroner, ex p McCurbin*[2].

[1] [2003] EWHC 1896 (Admin).
[2] [1990] 2 All ER 759 at 767, [1990] 1 WLR 719 at 730.

8.62 In other cases, the Administrative Court has quashed *elements* of the outcome or particular conclusions, but avoided the need for a fresh inquest. In the *Longfield Care Homes* case, the court ordered that the inquisition was to be quashed and the conclusion of accidental death was to be substituted by a narrative verdict suggested by the court[1]. In *R (Wilkinson) v HM Coroner for the Greater Manchester South District*[2] the Divisional Court held that driving offences causing death could not equate to unlawful killing. The court quashed the conclusion but, as no party desired a fresh inquest and it was not in the public interest to hold one, substituted a conclusion of accident for unlawful killing[3]. Similarly, despite successful judicial reviews on the basis of Art 2 ECHR, the court refused to quash the inquisition/Record of Inquest and order a fresh inquest in *R (P) v HM Coroner for the District of Avon*[4], because no further benefit would ensue[5], and in *R (Tainton) v HM Senior Coroner for Preston and West Lancashire*[6], because it was unnecessary and 'would serve no useful purpose'[7]. The flexible nature of public law remedies will permit the High Court to correct inaccuracies in a conclusion[8]. or to expunge specific criticism of an individual, where appropriate[9].

[1] *R (Longfield Care Homes Ltd) v HM Coroner for Blackburn* [2004] EWHC 2467 (Admin) at [32].
[2] [2012] EWHC 2755 (Admin).
[3] At [86].
[4] [2009] EWCA Civ 1367.
[5] At [33].
[6] [2016] EWHC 1396 (Admin).
[7] At [83].
[8] *R v Inner North London Coroner ex parte Linnane (No 2)* (1990) 155 JP 343, DC.
[9] *R (Worthington) v HM Coroner for the County of Cumbria* [2018] EWHC 3386 (Admin), although in *Worthington* the claimant's application was dismissed.

8.63 Where the court finds that the act of any public authority is unlawful under the HRA 1996, it may grant such relief and remedy as is within its existing powers and it 'considers to be just and appropriate' – s 8(1) HRA 1996. A declaration may be more appropriate where there has been an infringement of an interested person's Convention rights, but the public interest would not be served by the quashing of the Record of Inquest and the ordering of a fresh inquest. Thus, declarations were made in the cases of *Tainton* and *P* set out above, and in the Court of Appeal in *Middleton*[1].

[1] [2002] EWCA Civ 390. This decision was overturned by the House of Lords on appeal but on substantive legal grounds relating to the original decision not the making of the declaration).

8.64 Challenging Coronial Decisions: Judicial Review and Statutory Review

8.64 Section 141 of the Tribunals, Courts and Enforcement Act 1981 amended s 31 of the SCA 1981 to add s 31(5A) with effect from 6 April 2008. Under s 31(5A), where the High Court 'quashes the decision to which the application relates', it may substitute its own decision for the decision in question (as opposed to remitting it to the coroners court with a direction to reconsider the matter and reach a fresh decision in accordance with the findings of the High Court), but only if the decision was quashed on the ground that there has been an error of law, 'and without the error, there would have been only one decision which the court or tribunal could have reached'. In *R (O'Connor) v Avon Coroner (Visser Intervening)*[1], the Divisional Court applied s 31(5A) and despite concluding that the coroner had erred in law in returning a conclusion of unlawful killing, refused to substitute its own narrative conclusion, as it could not be satisfied that there was only one decision which without the error of law the coroner would have come to[2]. The conclusion was therefore quashed but the matter remitted for further consideration by the coroner.

[1] [2009] EWHC 854 (Admin), [2011] QB 106.
[2] At [32].

Costs

8.65 Where the decision of a coroner is found to be unlawful on review, then costs may follow the event, dependent on the conduct of the coroner in the proceedings. In *R (Davies) v Birmingham Deputy Coroner*[1] the Court of Appeal held that[2]:

> '(1) the established practice of the courts was to make no order for costs against an inferior court or tribunal which did not appear before it except when there was a flagrant instance of improper behaviour or when the inferior court or tribunal unreasonably declined or neglected to sign a consent order disposing of the proceedings;
>
> (2) the established practice of the courts was to treat an inferior court or tribunal which resisted an application actively by way of argument in such a way that it made itself an active party to the litigation, as if it was such a party, so that in the normal course of things costs would follow the event;
>
> (3) if, however, an inferior court or tribunal appeared in the proceedings in order to assist the court neutrally on questions of jurisdiction, procedure, specialist case law and such like, the established practice of the courts was to treat it as a neutral party, so that it would not make an order for costs in its favour or an order for costs against it whatever the outcome of the application;
>
> (4) there are, however, a number of important considerations which might tend to make the courts exercise their discretion in a different way . . . in cases in category (3) above, so that a successful applicant . . . who has to finance his own litigation without external funding, may be fairly compensated out of a source of public funds and not be put to irrecoverable expense in asserting his rights after a coroner, or other inferior tribunal, has gone wrong in law, and [where] there is no other very obvious candidate available to pay his costs.'

[1] [2004] 1 WLR 2739.
[2] At [47].

8.66 As regards orders for costs made against claimants upon dismissal of an application for judicial review, in principle these follow the event as a matter of civil procedure. A claimant who loses at a full judicial review hearing is thus likely to be held liable to pay the coroner's costs of the defending the proceedings. That position was recently confirmed by the Divisional Court in *R (Parkinson) v Kent Senior Coroner*[1], where the unsuccessful claimant was ordered to pay the costs of the coroner and the two interveners. The initial costs of filing an acknowledgement of service and defence to the claim may be claimed by a successful coroner, although PD54A para 8.6 sets out the that where a defendant does not attend a permission hearing, the court will not generally make an order for costs against the claimant.

[1] [2018] 4 WLR 106.

STATUTORY REVIEW OR JUDICIAL REVIEW?

8.67 Following the repeal of the intended appeal provision in the CJA 2009, it is a quirk of inquest procedure that the two routes of challenge set out in this chapter remain available alongside one another. Which route of challenge should properly or sufficiently interested persons adopt?

8.68 The answer to this question depends on the type of decision to which the challenge is sought, and the desired outcome from the review. Funding may also be a relevant consideration.

8.69 The statutory power to quash is an all or nothing remedy. If successful the court's only power is to quash the entirety of the coroner's or jury's findings and remit the matter to be reheard[1]. It does not apply to interlocutory decisions taken by coroners eg whether to obtain an expert report, or whether Art 2 ECHR applies in a particular inquest[2]. Where, therefore, a party seeks to challenge the inclusion of a particular fact in an inquest conclusion, but does not want the strain of going through another full inquest, judicial review will be the preferred route.

[1] *Re Bithell* [1986] 1 WLUK 114.
[2] *Re Bithell* [1986] 1 WLUK 114.

8.70 The court's discretion under the statutory review power is wide, but parties must bring themselves within one of the relevant statutory categories. These relate to broad concerns of justice in relation to the original proceedings – whether there was sufficiency of inquiry, whether material evidence was omitted, etc. By contrast, judicial review may be seen as a more procedural remedy. If the result of an inquest can be quashed on a procedural point on judicial review, then a claimant may avoid having to establish that it is 'necessary and desirable in the interests of justice' that a further hearing take place. The discretion is wide, but necessity may be a high hurdle.

8.71 There is little judicial learning which compares the forms of review. In *R v HM Coroner for Inner London South District ex parte Douglas-Williams*[1], Lord Woolf MR emphasised the discretionary nature of the power to quash the outcome of an inquest on judicial review, and stated that in such cases he could not 'suggest a better test for a court to apply when deciding whether it should

8.71 *Challenging Coronial Decisions: Judicial Review and Statutory Review*

give relief than that it should be "necessary or desirable to do so in the interest of justice"¹ as per the statutory review test.

1   [1999] 1 All ER 344.

8.72 In *Terry v HM Coroner for East Sussex*¹ Simon Brown LJ stated in the Court of Appeal²:

'It seems to me that the selfsame test should apply under section 13(1)(a) as applies on a judicial review challenge. The court cannot conclude that "an inquest . . . ought to be held" unless the coroner has misdirected himself in law or his factual conclusion is irrational. *R (Touche) v Inner London North Coroner* [2001] QB 1206 itself had been brought before the court as a section 13 application as well as a judicial review challenge (see p 162c) yet no one suggested that the court's powers of intervention there were wider under the statute than at common law — indeed, the section 13 application was simply sidelined.'

1   [2001] EWCA Civ 1094.
2   At [21].

8.73 In *Jones v Gwent Coroner*¹ however, Elias LJ held that a statutory review challenge to a coroner's decision that there was insufficient evidence to sustain an unlawful killing conclusion, was in substance an attempt to judicially review the outcome of the proceedings five years out of time. Elias rejected an attempt to conflate the two tests such that an error of law sufficient to found an application for judicial review will always satisfy the s 13 statutory review test².

1   [2015] EWHC 2178 (Admin).
2   At [18].

8.74 Parties should consider carefully the decision in respect of which review is sought, the desired outcome on review, and the wider circumstances of the case before choosing one route of review over another. It should also be remembered that, as in *Touche*, cited above, there is no legal principle that prohibits a challenge being brought under both routes simultaneously.

Chapter 9
FUNDING AND COSTS

FUNDING

Inquest funding

9.1 The coroner does not have funds to pay for interested parties to be legally represented and there is no automatic right to public funding for inquests by way of legal aid. The circumstances where legal aid is available to the deceased's family are discussed later in this chapter.

9.2 Most organisations that commonly attend inquests eg NHS Trusts are able to privately instruct a lawyer (or have lawyers in-house) to deal with inquests; in short, there are far fewer funding issues for organisations when attending inquests. This chapter therefore primarily considers questions of funding for families and their representatives. We consider representation of organisations more widely at CHAPTER 11.

9.3 The absence of reliable or consistent public funding means that those representing families must investigate alternative means of funding legal costs can include:

– privately paying for representation;
– conditional fee agreements;
– before the event insurance cover;
– union membership funding;
– more recently utilising crowd funding websites.

Although some charities will provide or fund representation, their resources are usually stretched, and in many circumstances, they rely on pro bono legal assistance from solicitors and counsel.

9.4 The government's justification for limiting the availability of legal aid to fund representation at inquests is that an inquest is inquisitorial in nature and not adversarial[1]. Although this is true in theory, most practitioners who have participated in inquests will know that in many inquests the evidence is contentious and the outcome can depend on the extent to which that evidence can be effectively challenged. In most cases coroners can often be relied upon to investigate the case themselves but it would be wrong to conclude from this that the coroner is not assisted by advocates who may expertly test evidence, or widen the coroner's perspective on legal or factual matters. Sometimes it is

9.4 *Funding and Costs*

only through advocates' discussions with their clients that additional and important information is provided for the coroner.

[1] Lord Chancellor's Exceptional Funding Guidance (Inquests), para 4.

9.5 Most public bodies and other interested organisations will have legal representation at the inquest and may attend with counsel and solicitors in addition to the legal officers of the company or organisation. An unrepresented party may feel that the odds are stacked against them, may feel intimidated and may struggle to put questions or arguments confidently in the face of able and experienced advocates.

9.6 The effect of this imbalance is that frequently, unrepresented parties feel they are denied access to justice during the proceedings, particularly if the enquiry has not been as broad or thorough as they would have wished.

The role of legal representatives

9.7 Before considering how to fund legal representation it is useful to consider why representation for interested parties is beneficial to the inquest process. When acting for a family, legal representatives act as a conduit between them and the coroner. Their role is to raise any relevant legal arguments regarding scope, evidence, witnesses, conclusions and Prevention of Future Death reports. This is done by first communicating with the family to identify what the issues are, to explain any relevant law and to clarify the purpose of the inquest. It is a two-way process and the ability to communicate on many different levels is essential when representing families. It can be an involved and emotional role for an advocate.

9.8 For most families an inquest will be the first time they will have had any experience of a court process. They will be grieving and often feel that a death has been unnecessary and negligent. Feeling a fundamental part of the process is an important step in their grieving journey. See CHAPTER 10 for further detail on representing families at inquests.

Legal aid

9.9 The benefit of legal aid funding for interested persons is that it does not place a financial burden on the individual and payment of legal fees is not conditional upon achieving a particular outcome. Funding can be awarded in matters where there will be no subsequent civil claim or where costs would be vastly disproportionate to any damages arising from a civil claim. It can also provide a degree of certainty of payment of fees for the legal representatives before and during the inquest in matters where the prospects of success of a subsequent civil claim are limited.

9.10 The type of legal aid that can be granted for inquests is split into two categories: (i) legal help, which allows for solicitor assistance before the inquest; and (ii) full representation at the inquest. Full details on the award of legal aid can be found in the Lord Chancellor's Exceptional Funding Guidance (Inquests)[1].

[1] Lord Chancellor's Exceptional Funding Guidance (Inquests) https://assets.publishing.service.gov.uk.

9.11 To apply for legal aid the proposed solicitor's firm must have a legal aid franchise and the application is all completed online via a portal. The current number of firms that have a legal aid franchise is relatively small and continues to fall. The application process for a legal aid franchise is cumbersome and the payments made by the Legal Aid Agency for legal costs are at much lower than rates paid for civil legal work. In recent years it has become uneconomical for many firms to apply and maintain a legal aid franchise.

9.12 To qualify for legal aid (either legal help or full representation) the inquest must meet the means and merits tests.

Means test

9.13 The client and solicitor must complete a means test form[1] and submit it, along with all the required evidence, to the Legal Aid Agency. This form is cumbersome and more than one family member may be required to complete the application. It requires extensive disclosure of financial information. Just obtaining all the relevant information is a daunting task for most families, especially in circumstances where they have recently suffered a traumatic bereavement. Many clients will not qualify for legal aid under the means test if they have any savings or property interests even if they are in receipt of benefits.

[1] CIVMEANS1 https://www.gov.uk/government/publications/civ-means-1-financial-assessment-form-not-passported.

9.14 The Legal Aid Agency has the power to award a partial certificate and instruct the family to make a financial contribution to legal costs. A solicitor can request that the Legal Aid Agency use their discretion to waive any financial contribution in whole or part, ignoring financial eligibility limits, if in all the circumstances it would not be reasonable to expect the applicant to bear the costs of legal assistance.

9.15 Using current guidance, it is unclear who will be granted a waiver from the means test and a decision on a waiver of the means test would be more beneficial before it is completed. There will be circumstances where it is clear an interested person will not meet the means test for public funding but a waiver will be appropriate. In these circumstances the burden of completing the means test is unnecessary but currently there is no process to omit this step. We understand this process is being reviewed and may be subject to change in due course.

9.16 *Funding and Costs*

Merits test

9.16 Once the means test is completed the solicitor will also need to complete the merits part of the application. This is formed of two parts: the civil legal aid application[1], and the exceptional circumstances form[2].

[1] CIV APP https://www.gov.uk/government/collections/civil-legal-aid-application-forms.
[2] CIV ECF1 https://www.gov.uk/government/publications/legal-aid-exceptional-case-funding-form-and-guidance.

9.17 The guidance confirms there are only two categories of inquests where funding can be granted. This is either (i) where Art 2 is engaged or (ii) where there is a wider public interest. For further information about where Art 2 is engaged, see CHAPTER 3. The coroner will need to formally confirm that Art 2 is engaged for this to apply.

9.18 The test for granting funding extends to cases where it is arguable that there has been a violation of one of the deceased's rights under the European Convention on Human Rights (ECHR) and there is no requirement for it to be established that a violation has occurred before granting funding.

9.19 The wider public interest basis for legal aid is less frequently relied upon to request funding. The test is whether the granting of funding is in the public interest (as opposed to whether there is public interest in the inquest). In circumstances where other regulatory bodies such as the CQC or HSE are involved, or there has been an investigation by an NHS trust resulting in changes of procedures funding is unlikely to be granted.

Legal help

9.20 The initial stage of public funding is legal help. Legal help provides for a solicitor to prepare written questions and submissions to the coroner, and to advise the interested person in the period leading up to the inquest. It can include an allowance for the expenses of a 'Mackenzie Friend' if approved by the coroner. A Mackenzie Friend is a non-lawyer who attends court with the interested person and assists them in making submissions and asking questions. The Mackenzie Friend is not allowed to speak on behalf of the party.

9.21 The solicitor is required to detail the circumstances and work to be completed, and then to apply for a certificate for the requested amount at legal aid rates. Once all the forms are submitted then the Legal Aid Agency will review the submissions and provide a response. If the application is rejected there is an appeals process. If a certificate is issued it will be for a stated maximum amount. This is often not the requested amount. There is also an opportunity to appeal the authorised amount.

9.22 Once the work is completed, it must be evidenced; the request for payment should then be made to the Legal Aid Agency providing this evidence. This process can be very protracted and if urgent decisions are required then it will be imperative that the solicitor has a contact within the Legal Aid Agency to chase up responses and the progress of the application.

9.23 There are many solicitors who would comment that the time taken to complete an application is disproportionate to any amounts granted by the Legal Aid Agency, particularly if the inquest is not going to be long and/or complex.

Legal representation

9.24 As noted above an application can also be made for funding to cover legal representation at the inquest. Again the means and merits tests will need to be completed and approved. Once approved, an application should then be made to cover advocacy costs.

9.25 If granted, the funding will be set out in a certificate. The total sum awarded will be limited to set amounts for a brief fee plus refresher rate. It is also possible to apply for a certificate for solicitor attendance, travel and subsidence costs; the case would need to be exceptional to justify funding for both.

9.26 As above, it is possible to request a means test waiver if the interested person would not qualify for legal aid under the current means testing criteria. Often, unless Art 2 is automatically engaged, detailed submissions will need to be made to demonstrate that the exceptional funding criteria are met before a certificate is issued.

9.27 The guidance is clear that in most circumstances legal representation is not required and will not be publicly funded.

9.28 Charities and legal representatives continue to lobby parliament for a change in the law and provision of legal aid for families to access legal help for the inquest process[1].

[1] https://www.inquest.org.uk/legal-aid-for-inquests.

Conditional fee agreements

9.29 The most common form of funding for families at inquests, particularly medical related deaths, is by way of a conditional fee agreement ('CFA'). These spring from the fact that there may be prospects of succeeding in a linked civil claim arising from the death eg a clinical negligence claim against the NHS Trust that was providing care for the deceased. In such claims, lawyers representing a family will be paid for the work they do by the defendant if successful. Sometimes, lawyers will also be paid for time they spent on the associated inquest (or at least part of it). In other instances, lawyers will recover solely for the time they spend on the civil claim, but consider that this is sufficient to justify their time in both arenas.

9.30 CFAs will often be underpinned by an 'after the event' insurance policy. Before entering into a CFA a solicitor must consider that the prospects of a successful civil claim are reasonable – generally, that the prospects of success are over 50%. This will mean that there will be a number of families seeking inquest representation where solicitors will refuse instructions under a CFA as

9.30 Funding and Costs

prospects are not sufficiently high, or the value of damages would make the matter disproportionate. Of course, the costs will also only be recovered upon successful conclusion of a civil claim and that may mean that there is a long delay between incurring costs and cost recovery.

9.31 When entering into a CFA, solicitors must consider who the client will be for a civil claim and ensure that is the same person that is providing instructions as the interested person, consider who the defendant in the civil claim is and what evidence can be secured via the inquest process. The evidence heard during the inquest can form part of the evidence in a civil case. It is not determinative but can be persuasive and can form part of the overall evidence before a civil judge.

9.32 The provision of an after the event insurance policy should allow for obtaining expert evidence in relation to liability for the civil claim. Once this expert evidence is obtained the reports will retain privilege but can be used by the legal representatives to direct questions to the witnesses. In some instances, it may be indicated to serve the expert report on the coroner and waive privilege. Not all coroners will admit this evidence, some may wish to call the expert and some coroners will instruct their own expert. The disclosure of expert evidence will need to be considered on a case by case basis and with clear instructions from the client.

9.33 Most civil cases do not reach trial and as such the inquest may be the only opportunity to ask questions of the witnesses and allow your client to give their account of the events leading to death. This process lays the foundation for the civil proceedings, and setting out the sequence of events and assisting the coroner to make findings of fact that might later be disputed can be very beneficial for swift settlement of civil claims.

Before the event insurance and union membership

9.34 There are some insurance policies and union memberships that may provide cover for inquest representation. The terms and conditions of any pre-existing cover should be checked before applying for legal aid or entering into a conditional fee agreement with after the event insurance (which is usually less favourable to the client). Failure to fully investigate possible funding routes would not be acting in your client's best interests and may prevent recovery of after the event premiums at conclusion of the matter.

9.35 Some insurers and unions will direct the insured to their preferred panel solicitor, whilst some will have exceptions that can allow the insured a solicitor of choice in particular circumstances; this often includes fatal cases and those with a particular complexity. Regardless of what the insurer's general policy is, bear in mind the recent European Court of Justice ruling in *Orde van Vlaamse Balies v Ministerraad*[1] where the court concluded that the insured has the right to choose which lawyer to instruct if they are doing so at the outset of proceedings. This case did not arise from inquest proceedings, but the principle is comparable. However, there will be terms of appointment which must be adhered to.

[1] C-667/18, judgment 14 May 2020, ECLI:EU:C:2020:372.

Privately funded retainer

9.36 A private retainer for inquest representation can be agreed with a client. This can be agreed where a family does not wish to pursue a civil claim (or there are no prospects of success in a civil claim) or where the matter is unsuitable for any alternative funding arrangements. Solicitors may choose to act on an hourly rate retainer or may prefer to act under a fixed fee agreement. All possible funding arrangements should be discussed with the client to ensure solicitors are acting in their best interest and the client is aware of potential liabilities.

9.37 Inquests are often complex and what may appear to be a relatively straightforward matter may increase in complexity as it progresses. A coroner will progress the matter as the evidence leads without consideration of funding arrangements. Families could potentially be left with a much larger bill than anticipated or find that representation has to stop when funds are exhausted. If there is a successful civil claim after the inquest then the costs of a private retainer can form part of the interpartes costs if the retainer covered the inquest and civil claim. A detailed bill should be prepared and served, and will be subject to assessment. However, the client should be aware that costs recovered interpartes may not be the same as the private retainer and there is likely to be shortfall which the client will remain liable to pay. For more information on the recoverability of inquest costs in civil proceedings please refer to **9.41** *et seq.*

Charitable assistance

9.38 There are several charitable organisations that can assist with inquests. These include INQUEST[1] and Action Against Medical Accidents (AVMA)[2]. Others are listed in the Ministry of Justice publication 'Guide to Coroner Services'[3].

[1] www.inquest.org.uk.
[2] www.avma.org.uk.
[3] https://www.gov.uk/government/publications/guide-to-coroner-services-and-coroner-investigations-a-short-guide.

9.39 INQUEST focuses on assisting families with deaths in state detention.

9.40 AvMA focus on deaths relating to medical treatment and improving patient safety; they are able to provide assistance to families with the inquest process. They are also able to signpost families to specialist solicitors who will offer CFAs.

9.41 *Funding and Costs*

COSTS RECOVERY

9.41 There are two key High Court decisions in this area, namely *Fullick v Commissioner of Police of the Metropolis*[1] and *Roach v Home Office*[2]. These are supplemented by a patchwork of first instance decisions by costs judges that provide some practical examples of the application of the relevant principles.

[1] [2019] EWHC 1941 (QB).
[2] [2009] EWHC 312 (QB).

General principles of costs recovery

9.42 A coroner has no power to make costs orders. Costs can, however, be recovered in subsequent civil proceedings under the civil court's general discretion pursuant to s 51 SCA 1981.

9.43 Inquest costs are recoverable where they are 'of and incidental to' the civil claim[1]. The assessing court will approach the issue in two stages[2]:

– Firstly, were the costs incurred relevant to pursuing a live issue in the civil claim?
– Secondly, were the costs incurred in pursuing the issue proportionate?

[1] Section 51 Senior Courts Act 1981; *Roach v Home Office* [2009] EWHC 312 (QB).
[2] *Roach v Home Office* [2009] EWHC 312(QB) at [58] and [60]; *Fullick v Commissioner of Police of the Metropolis* [2019] EWHC 1941 (QB) at [69].

Relevance

9.44 The first threshold is one of relevance. In *Fullick v Commissioner of Police of the Metropolis*[1] Slade J explained the position as follows:

> 'The costs incurred by claimants in connection with the inquest must be relevant to the issues in the civil claim to be recoverable costs in that claim. That requires identification of outstanding issues which are necessary to the civil claim in respect of which the claimants' case would be advanced by participation in that inquest. The assessment also required the identification of what it was in the participation which assist with the civil claim.'[2]

[1] [2019] EWHC 1941 (QB).
[2] 2019] EWHC 1941 (QB) at 69.

9.45 The exercise of identifying and evaluating the relevance and utility of the inquest, or parts of the inquest process, can prove onerous, time consuming and contentious. The authorities from the Senior Courts Costs Office are also not clear as to whether this exercise should be guided by hindsight or not. In *Lynch v Chief Constable of Warwickshire*[1] Master Rowley considered that 'the well-spring of this test is redolent of hindsight being applied'. He assessed relevance not from the position that the solicitor was in at the time of the inquest but from the assessing court's perspective at the conclusion of the proceedings. The threshold could only be met where it was demonstrable that the costs incurred in the inquest had actually contributed to the civil proceedings[2]. In the more recent case of *Douglas v Ministry of Justice*[3], Master Leonard took a different approach concluding that hindsight should not be deployed[4]. It is submitted that this must be the proper approach. It accords with the general manner of assessment in other recent High Court authorities[5]. Further, the consideration of utility through the lens of hindsight could lead to injustice. Necessary work done on issues that were live in the civil proceedings at the time of incurring the costs might be disallowed if, later down the line and prior to assessment, the work became less or not relevant as a result of a fresh admission or finding at the inquest.

[1] [2014] Inquest LR 247.
[2] [2014] Inquest LR 247 at paras 68–70.
[3] [2018] Inquest LR 71.
[4] [2018] Inquest LR 71 at para 96.
[5] See for example *Fullick v Commissioner of Police of the Metropolis* [2019] EWHC 1941 (QB).

9.46 Relevance becomes much harder to establish where defendants admit liability prior to the inquest. Such admissions can act as a bar to recovery. Claimants may, however, be able to argue successfully that such admissions were equivocal or not binding pursuant to CPR 14.1A, albeit that there is an expectation that claimants will reasonably seek to clarify any areas of uncertainty and explore settlement if instigated by the defendant. It may also be open to claimants to argue that notwithstanding admissions as to liability, live issues still remained, particularly as to the quantification of damages. The facts that emerge at an inquest may be relevant to pain, suffering and loss of amenity[1]. The nature, blameworthiness and egregiousness of any failure may be relevant to quantification of damages under the Human Rights Act 1998 (HRA 1998). In *Douglas v Ministry of Justice*[2] inquest costs were recovered despite the defendant's full and unqualified admission of liability to every claim endorsed on the claim form. The court held that the level of damages and the question of vindication were still in issue at the time of the inquest and it mattered not that the process itself did nothing to contribute materially to the formulation or settlement of the claim[3].

[1] *Ross v Owners of Bowbelle and Another* [1997] 2 Lloyd's Rep 196.
[2] [2018] Inquest LR 71.
[3] *Douglas v Ministry of Justice* [2018] Inquest LR 71 at paras 89–96.

Proportionality

9.47 Proportionality has long been an important principle in inquest costs[1]. Its importance has been amplified in the post-Jackson era. Pursuant to CPR 44.3(2) costs which are disproportionate in amount may be disallowed or reduced even if they were reasonably and necessarily incurred.

[1] *Roach v Home Office* [2009] EWHC 312 (QB) at [60].

9.48 The monetary value of the claim is always relevant to the issue of proportionality but should not be looked at in isolation, particularly in fatal cases where the damages can be quite limited. CPR 44.3(5) and CPR 44.4(3) require the court, when assessing proportionality, to consider, aside from monetary value, the importance of any non-monetary relief such as, it is suggested, a declaration under the HRA 1998, the complexity of the litigation and the importance of the proceedings to the parties, including reputational and public interest. This point was stressed by Slade J in the case of *Fullick v Commissioner of Police of the Metropolis*[1] where the claim was settled for just over £18,000. Notwithstanding the settlement for a *relatively small* sum,

9.48 *Funding and Costs*

the costs incurred had also to be judged from the perspective that the inquest and the claim had caused the police to revise its policies, protocols and training[2].

[1] [2019] EWHC 1941 (QB).
[2] [2019] EWHC 1941 (QB) at [66].

9.49 In assessing proportionality, it can be relevant to be mindful of the fact that inquest proceedings can lead to the expeditious and therefore economical compromise of civil claims[1]. That said, it was held in the case of *Lynch v Chief Constable of Warwickshire*[2] that the inquest proceedings were so long and the costs so substantial that this assumption was turned on its head – instead of it being a cost effective method of gathering evidence, it becomes a disproportionately expensive way of doing so[3].

[1] *Roach v Home Office* [2009] EWHC 312 (QB) at [48]; *Fullick v Commissioner of Police of the Metropolis* [2019] EWHC 1941 (QB) at [67].
[2] [2014] Inquest LR 247.
[3] [2014] Inquest LR 247 at para 66.

9.50 Whilst proportionality of costs, like the test of relevance, needs to be considered on an issue by issue basis, it is nonetheless prudent to stand back and consider whether the total costs of participation at the inquest are proportionate to its utility and relevance to the outstanding issues in the civil claim[1].

[1] *Fullick v Commissioner of Police of the Metropolis* [2019] EWHC 1941 (QB) at [70].

9.51 In *Lynch v Chief Constable of Warwickshire*[1] the inquest costs as a whole were found to be 'globally disproportionate'[2]. The relatively unique facts of the case must however be noted. The inquest in question lasted seven weeks and the claimant enjoyed representation from leading counsel, junior counsel, a partner and a trainee. All the lawyers attended for significant portions of the inquest, with all four attending for ten of the days. The costs of attendance claimed were around £600,000 but the court found that the claimant had sufficient basis to prepare the particulars of claim in the subsequent civil proceedings from the pre-inquest disclosure alone[3]. Indeed, the Costs Master concluded that attendance of junior counsel alone, or a sufficiently experienced solicitor, would have been reasonable and proportionate and awarded costs accordingly[4].

[1] [2014] Inquest LR 247.
[2] *Lynch v Chief Constable of Warwickshire* [2014] Inquest LR 247 at para 64.
[3] *Lynch v Chief Constable of Warwickshire* [2014] Inquest LR 247 at para 80.
[4] *Lynch v Chief Constable of Warwickshire* [2014] Inquest LR 247 at paras 91 and 93.

Examples and authorities in practice

9.52 Determination as to what is recoverable is always highly fact sensitive. The courts have declined to provide overly prescriptive guidance instead advising costs judges to apply the relevant rules and their broad discretion under s 51 SCA 1981[1].

[1] See for example *Roach v Home Office* [2009] EWHC 312 (QB) at [62]; *Fullick v Commissioner of Police of the Metropolis* [2019] EWHC 1941 (QB) at [71].

9.53 To the extent that previous authorities do assist, pre-Jackson cases remain relevant as they deal with the interpretation of extant rules on costs[1]. The existence of a public funding certificate has no bearing on the issue of recoverability[2].

[1] *Fullick v Commissioner of Police of the Metropolis* [2019] EWHC 1941 (QB) at [44].
[2] *Roach v Home Office* [2009] EWHC 312 (QB) at [51].

9.54 The following parts of the inquest process have been held to be recoverable in the circumstances of the cases in question:

– attendance at the pre-inquest review hearing to secure disclosure of documents as well as lay or expert witness evidence[1];
– securing disclosure from parties aside from the tortfeasor[2];
– proofing and preparing witness statements from relevant witnesses[3];
– pre-inquest conferences[4];
– lawyer's preparation for the inquest hearing[5];
– attendance at the inquest to take a note of the evidence and ask questions of witnesses[6];
– attendance even where no questions are asked by the party's representative[7];
– making written submissions with the aim of securing a conclusion that was helpful to the claimant in the civil claim[8];
– attendance to receive conclusions and review the same with the family[9].

[1] *Fullick v Commissioner of Police of the Metropolis* [2019] EWHC 1941 (QB) at [54]–[56].
[2] *Fullick v Commissioner of Police of the Metropolis* [2019] EWHC 1941 (QB) at [60].
[3] *Roach v Home Office* [2009] EWHC 312 (QB) at [59].
[4] *Fullick v Commissioner of Police of the Metropolis* [2019] EWHC 1941 (QB) at [59].
[5] *Fullick v Commissioner of Police of the Metropolis* [2019] EWHC 1941 (QB) at [57].
[6] *Roach v Home Office* [2009] EWHC 312 (QB); *Lynch v Chief Constable of Warwickshire* [2014] Inquest LR 247; *Fullick v Commissioner of Police of the Metropolis* [2019] EWHC 1941 (QB) at [71].
[7] *Lynch v Chief Constable of Warwickshire* [2014] Inquest LR 247 at para 87.
[8] *Douglas v Ministry of Justice* [2018] Inquest LR 71 at para 104, although note the contrary conclusion in *Lynch v Chief Constable of Warwickshire* [2014] Inquest LR 247 at para 81.
[9] *Douglas v Ministry of Justice* [2018] Inquest LR 71 at para 106.

9.55 Various segments of the inquest process have been challenged by defendants. Costs related to inquest housekeeping, apart from that aimed at obtaining disclosure and witness evidence, have been disallowed[1]. Even the obtaining of disclosure and witness evidence may not be recoverable where the issues to which they go are agreed[2]. Attendance to hear statements being read, as well as client care and 'hand-holding', have been held not to be recoverable[3]. Once the evidence at the inquest is concluded, the assessing court's scrutiny will intensify. In *Douglas v Ministry of Justice*[4] attendance for the summing up and waiting for the jury was disallowed, albeit in circumstances where broad pre-action admissions had been made by the defendant[5].

[1] *Lynch v Chief Constable of Warwickshire* [2014] Inquest LR 247 at para 78.
[2] *Fullick v Commissioner of Police of the Metropolis* [2019] EWHC 1941 (QB) at [52].
[3] *Lynch v Chief Constable of Warwickshire* [2014] Inquest LR 247 at paras 99 and 77.
[4] [2018] Inquest LR 71.
[5] [2018] Inquest LR 71 at para 105.

Chapter 10
REPRESENTING FAMILIES AT INQUESTS

10.1 For bereaved families navigating through the inquest process there are no single truths – one family's experience of an inquest can be positive, perhaps even cathartic; another could find it damaging or degrading. The family's experience of the process can be affected positively or negatively by the actions of those who represent them and by the coroner. Thus, the parent of one victim was able to describe the cross-examination of Lord Robens at the inquiry in to the Aberfan disaster as 'balm to my soul', whereas the daughter of a victim of the Hillsborough disaster described the first inquest as 'dehumanising'. The role of the lawyer who represents families at inquests combines a duty to represent the interests of that family but also to guide them through a uniquely difficult and traumatising process. The environment is a challenging one for lawyers whose clients can be very vulnerable and who may have unrealistic expectations about what the inquest into the death of their loved one can deliver. Their solicitor and barrister should be bear in mind that it is their duty to advise and advocate but not take away from the family their autonomy to make choices.

10.2 This chapter is intended to follow the process from the first client meeting through to the conclusion of the inquest hearing. It is an adjunct to other chapters, which deal in more detail with the procedural and legal aspects of those processes. It tries to provide guidance whilst bearing in mind that each family and their experience of grief is different.

IMMEDIATELY AFTER THE DEATH

10.3 The coroner's jurisdiction is triggered by the occurrence of an unnatural or unexplained death. In many cases this will be communicated to the family at the outset by the coroner or coroner's officer. Their early interactions with the coroner and their officers, and sometimes even the lawyers whom they instruct, will occur in the days and weeks following that death. The lawyers representing them, and in particular their solicitor, should be prepared to intrude into their lives during this particularly difficult and emotionally volatile stage. In other cases, the family may not instruct a solicitor until much later in the process. They may go through the initial steps without legal representation.

10.4 *Representing Families at Inquests*

10.4 If the death has been reported to the coroner, the coroner will issue an interim death certificate so the family can start to deal with property and financial affairs.

10.5 If the death is not reported to the coroner, the family have five days following the death to register the death at the local registrar's office. Often a registrar will ask if the family have any concerns and if they do the registrar can refer the death to the coroner.

10.6 Once the coroner has jurisdiction to investigate the family will be appointed a coroner's officer who will liaise with them. There is a huge variation in the level of information and support that families receive from coroner's officers. This is owing not only to the different working practices of each coroner, but also to the fact that each coroner is appointed and funded locally[1], meaning there is a variety of local authority funding provisions.

[1] See CHAPTER 1.

10.7 As a minimum a family should receive A Guide to Coroner Services ('the Guide')[1].

[1] https://assets.publishing.service.gov.uk/government/uploads/system/uploads/attachment_data/file/859076/guide-to-coroner-services-bereaved-people-jan-2020.pdf.

10.8 The Guide details the steps to be taken by the coroner including ordering a post mortem and opening the inquest. The Guide also covers how and where a family might seek legal advice. It states that there is no requirement to appoint a lawyer for the inquest but families may wish to do so, especially if other interested persons have legal representation.

10.9 The Guide also confirms that legal help may be available via legal aid for preparation for the inquest, though legal aid is subject to means and merits tests (see CHAPTER 9).

10.10 Assuming the family wish to seek legal advice, they are directed to the Law Society website. Unfortunately, there is no category for inquests in the search fields on that website. However the useful contacts at the back of the Guide include INQUEST, a charity which supports families through inquests into state-related deaths, who do have a list of specialist firms providing representation and who also seek to put families in touch with advocates who may represent them on a pro bono (no fee) basis.

10.11 Once a family has managed to locate a specialist solicitor, they should be given a full picture of the various stages of the investigation and inquest, and more importantly advised on what the inquest can and cannot provide in way of conclusions and accountability.

THE POST MORTEM AND POST-MORTEM REPORT

10.12 These quotes go some way towards indicating the difference between some family members' approach to the post mortem and the evidence that it generates:

The post mortem and post-mortem report **10.14**

'We were never actually prohibited from seeing [our daughter] but were talked out of doing so at every stage . . . when I went to the undertaker's expecting to see her, the coffin was already sealed . . . I could not sit in a room with a box and so walked out the funeral parlour. I feel very strongly that I should have had the opportunity of time alone with her. [Her mother] . . . has since seen photographs of [our daughter] and from the photographs there really is no reason why we should not have seen her.[1]'

'At no stage was there any mention of the fact that families had the right to be present at the post mortem – either personally or to have their own doctor attend on their behalf. That right should have been communicated to the families when they had to identify their loved one . . . [2]'

'Mortuary photographs were included as part of my witness bundles at the recent inquests. I couldn't understand why they were there. We raised it with the solicitor to the inquests and I was told that they should not have been there. Seeing those photographs affected me deeply.[3]'

[1] The experience of the parent of a victim of the *Marchioness* disaster, Dr Richard Shepherd *Unnatural Causes* (Penguin Books, 2019) p 230.
[2] The words of Barry Devonside, the father of a victim of the Hillsborough disaster quoted by the Right Reverend James Jones KBE in 'The patronizing disposition of unaccountable power': A report to ensure the pain and suffering of the Hillsborough families is not repeated (1 November 2017, HC 511).
[3] The words of Dave Golding, the nephew of a victim of the Hillsborough disaster also quoted by the Right Reverend James Jones KBE.

10.13 Most families will have no experience of a post mortem or the process by which the examination is carried out beyond having seen or read about it in fiction. It is important that this process is discussed with family members and they are given the opportunity of understanding why the process is necessary. They should also be offered reassurance that the examination and handling of the body of their loved one will be conducted with dignity. Details of how a post mortem takes place, and to what extent the family and other parties can be present at the post mortem, are set out in CHAPTER 2.

The post-mortem report

10.14 Having completed their examination the pathologist will prepare a report setting out the nature of the examination carried out and the findings. The report will usually conclude with a proposed cause of death, although that may sometimes be deferred pending further evidence. There is an expectation that the pathologist will provide a copy of that report to the coroner within 14 days. The coroner is thereafter obliged to make copies of that report available to the family upon their request[1]. Because the right to see the post-mortem report arises upon request, coroners usually will not send copies of the report to family members without first being asked. This is sensible: many family members do not wish to read details of a post mortem, and simply being informed of the overall conclusions is enough. It is common for coroners' officers to explain the contents of the report to the next of kin but it is important that lawyers representing families are proactive in obtaining copies of the report themselves, rather than relying on second or third hand accounts of what was found.

[1] Coroners (Investigations) Regulations 2013, SI 2013/1629, reg 23; Coroners (Inquests) Rules 2013, SI 2013/1616, r 13(1), (2)(a).

10.15 Representing Families at Inquests

10.15 Lawyers should take care to discuss the contents of the post-mortem report with the next of kin but should not send it out to them unsolicited. There continues to be occasional incidents where a careless lawyer simply forwards on a copy of the post-mortem report to the family members without (a) asking them whether they want to see it, or (b) warning them that it is about to arrive. It is important not to underestimate the impact of receiving a post-mortem report through the post. Lawyers should be sensitive about how the report is passed on or its contents are communicated to the family, even in circumstances where they are apparently keen to review the report themselves.

10.16 It is unusual for a post-mortem report to contain photographs of the deceased, and even more unusual for those photographs to be passed on to the family of the deceased. When discussing the evidence of the pathologist with the family, it is important to remind them that the evidence will not include photographs of their loved one, if that is the case, as many believe that it is routine for pathologists to take photographs during their examinations. If there are photographs or moving images of the deceased or the scene of their death or injury within the evidence, it is important to discuss this with the family in advance of the inquest and elicit their views on whether they want to see that material or not. It is a matter of personal choice for any family member as to whether they want to see images of their loved one and it is important for the lawyer not to be paternalistic. As with the post-mortem report, the contents of those images should be carefully explained and discussed before they are witnessed for the first time and the family should be reminded that there will be a prohibition on publishing those images to others without the coroner's permission.

Oral evidence

10.17 It is common, although not inevitable, for pathologists to give evidence at the inquest. This can sometimes involve very detailed descriptions of how they conducted the post mortem, or aspects of their findings. Families should be reminded well in advance of the inquest that it is their choice whether they are present in court for this part of the hearing. They should not be discouraged from hearing that evidence if they want to but nor should they be left with the misapprehension that the coroner will draw some unconscious and adverse inference against them if they do not. It is common for some or all of the deceased's family members to leave court rather than hear the post-mortem examination described in evidence and no coroner will be surprised by their decision to wait outside whilst the pathologist's evidence is heard. Family members who prefer to remain in court during the pathologist's evidence should also be reminded that they are entitled to leave court if, having begun to hear the evidence, they change their mind.

10.18 Where bodily materials have been retained following the post mortem, the coroner must notify the next of kin or personal representative of the deceased person of: (i) the nature of the materials retained; (ii) the periods for which it will be retained; and (iii) the options for dealing with that material once the period has come to an end. Those options are: (i) for the material to be buried, cremated or lawfully disposed of; (ii) for it to be returned to the next of kin; or (iii) for it to be retained for the purposes of research[1].

[1] Coroners (Investigations) Regulations 2013, reg 14(5) and (6).

FIRST CONTACT WITH A SOLICITOR

10.19 For the vast majority of clients, an inquest will be their first involvement in legal proceedings and usually it is a new and alien experience. Not only are they recently bereaved, most probably in difficult circumstances, but they are thrust into a world of legal terminology and formality that is completely unfamiliar to them.

10.20 Where possible it is best to arrange a meeting with the family so they can identify the issues they have surrounding the death and the solicitor can advise them on the purpose of the inquest and likely process they will have to go through. In many instances funding will place restrictions on meetings in person and telephone calls will be the only option for the initial contact.

10.21 At an early stage it is important to manage expectations about the timescales, the process and conclusions. Where possible a detailed letter should be provided explaining the terminology and process; the family may not recall details of what is said at the meeting, particularly if it takes place soon after the death, so this letter will become a useful reference point.

10.22 Families will have different expectations about what the function of an inquest is and what sort of outcome it can deliver in their case. If the proper parameters of the process are not explained to them, or worse still they are misled by a bombastic or inexperienced lawyer, then they might be excused for having a profound sense of cognitive dissonance when the inquest does not meet with their expectations. This issue was remarked upon by Kay J in *R v HM Coroner for Birmingham and Solihull, Ex p Julie Benton*[1]:

> 'It is of critical importance to recognize the true purpose of an inquest. Sadly, the public's perceptions of such purpose does not always match the reality, and those caught up in the process expect more . . . than it can, or is permitted to, deliver thereby adding to their distress.'

[1] [1997] 8 Med LR 362.

10.23 It is important to remind family members that in a conventional inquest the coroner will try to find the answers to four important questions: who the deceased was, where they died, when they died and how they died. Although at times it will appear like a trial the inquest hearing will not be an adversarial trial and in many cases the coroner will avoid transgressing into areas that they may think are better placed within a civil trial. The family must also be reminded that there is a statutory prohibition on the coroner or jury returning any conclusion that appear to determine any issues of civil or criminal liability against a named person pursuant to s 10 of the CJA 2009.

10.24 Each inquest will be an individual set of circumstances that have to be applied to the rigid framework of the CJA 2009 and the particular practices of each individual coroner. The family must be reassured they are at the heart of the process and should have the opportunity to feel they have fully participated at each stage.

10.25 There will be very little certainty that can be given to families at an early stage with the exception that you will assist them through the process and explain what is happening as they progress. The one mantra to apply is that it is impossible to predict just about everything during the inquest process. There will be numerous twists and turns to the evidence and timeline.

10.26 Building a relationship with the family at this time is essential to the smooth running of the entire matter. They will need confidence in their representatives' ability and understanding of the process, and will benefit from empathy for the fact they are bereaved. It is a useful for all solicitors dealing with families at inquests to have a basic understanding of the grieving process and the likely paths families might take as they deal with grief.

10.27 Funding and money may be an issue for many families and many will be unclear as to the way in which conditional fee agreements, insurance cover and legal aid certificates all work. Repeated reassurances may be required to deal with these issues as the inquest progresses. In complex or long running matters costs can escalate and families must feel comfortable with the funding arrangements. It is often a worry that funding will run out before the inquest and they will be left with no assistance at the hearing. Where possible, depending on the funding arrangements, this information and risks must be provided to families at the earliest opportunity. See CHAPTER 9 for further detail on funding.

CLIENT CARE THROUGHOUT THE PROCESS

10.28 One of the most important factors for families is a continued updating of any progress on the case and full discussions about next steps. Often there are additional proceedings running alongside the inquest, such as a clinical negligence claim, and consideration has to be taken as to when and how these processes are blended. Some families look to the inquest as the end point and want quantum dealt with by the time of the inquest, whilst others can only focus on the inquest and will be unable to deal with consideration of quantum at the same time. It is important to consider this and discuss it with your clients so you can manage expectations and ensure that they understand the processes and how they merge.

10.29 This can be particularly important where funding is by Conditional Fee Agreement; issues with cost recoverability and liability are intertwined, as are incurring costs for quantum evidence when liability has yet to be established.

10.30 As a minimum, clients should be contacted on a monthly basis to provide an update and diary reminders are a useful tool to do this.

10.31 Some solicitors also make diary reminders for particular key dates in very sensitive matters such as the deceased's birthday or anniversary of the

Disclosure 10.38

death to ensure that this is either acknowledged if communication is required or those dates are avoided if possible.

10.32 This type of consideration and preparation will build a strong relationship of trust with the client and when things are difficult, which they always are at some point, there will be a firm foundation that can withstand the inevitable bumps that an inquest process will have.

10.33 Where counsel is instructed it is useful to arrange a meeting as early as possible. Any pre-inquest review hearing taking place in person can be combined with a family meeting to discuss the issues, take instructions and ascertain what the family is hoping to achieve.

CLIENT CARE AT PRE-INQUEST REVIEW HEARINGS

10.34 In complex inquests the coroner should list a pre-inquest review hearing (PIR). If one is not listed written representations can be made seeking for one to be listed in order to iron out any potential complications that could risk the inquest not being completed in the allocated time-slot. A part-heard inquest can be difficult for families: it can give the impression that their loved one's case did not receive proper consideration or planning, and many find it difficult to wait, sometimes for long periods of time, for the next stage of evidence to be heard or to receive the conclusion.

10.35 The pre-inquest review (or reviews, in some cases) is often referred to as a housekeeping hearing, at which the coroner goes through a list of points that require judicial direction or decision-making. It is generally not as difficult for the families to attend a PIR as the actual inquest as it does not involve hearing evidence about the deceased. It will clearly however bring emotions to the forefront.

10.36 The hearing is an opportunity for the family to see the coroner conducting a hearing, see inside the court room and see the other legal teams and how they are conducting the process. This will allow the family to feel more prepared for the final hearing.

10.37 Any submissions, written or oral, should be made on the family's instructions. Any written submissions should be seen by the family for approval in advance of being sent to the coroner. If written submissions are not prepared, then instructions need to be taken in advance of the hearing as to the points to be raised. The family will need to be consulted during the hearing and should feel able to ask their legal representatives questions. It is good practice for them to write things down as they occur to them and for the advocate to briefly 'turn their back' and speak with them to ensure all points are covered before the hearing ends.

DISCLOSURE

10.38 As an 'interested person' the family will have access to all the disclosure available.

10.39 It is vital to get any relevant or additional disclosure at the earliest opportunity; this can be requested by letter to the coroner or at a PIR. The coroner has wide ranging powers to order disclosure of documents if they consider it appropriate. In addition, solicitors or the family can make disclosure requests of other holders of information. If relevant, copies of that information can then be sent to the coroner.

10.40 It should not be underestimated how frustrated families can feel if they are denied disclosure in an open and transparent manner. The perception of collusion and cover-up runs through many inquests where the death and evidence may lead to civil or criminal consequences. This adds to the distress of the family and will need to be anticipated and managed.

10.41 As with the content of the post-mortem report, the family should be asked if they actually want to see all the disclosure. Some things, particularly medical evidence and photographs, can be very distressing and solicitors will need to consider how this information is shared.

10.42 As with the post-mortem report it is good practice to telephone clients to inform them that potentially distressing material is being emailed or posted. This can allow the family time to prepare to read difficult information. In some cases it may even be prudent to send the information at a particular time of day to ensure that it does not arrive at the most difficult moments.

WITNESS STATEMENTS

Statements from members of the family

10.43 Often a coroner's officer will have requested a witness statement from the family before solicitors are instructed. Generally (and unless family members are required as specific witnesses of fact), a single witness statement from one family member will suffice to represent them as a unit. If the coroner has indeed already obtained a statement from the family, solicitors will need to carefully review it and see if an additional statement is required to provide a more detailed account of events.

10.44 Depending on the circumstances, a well-prepared and full witness statement will allow the family's evidence to be read under r 23 and avoid the distress of giving evidence during the inquest. In most inquests, other interested persons (particularly if they are organisations) do not ask family members any questions about the deceased.

10.45 Bear in mind the key principle that statements should be factual and provide a first-hand account of matters relevant to the death. In cases where there is the potential to bring a secondary victim claim it can be particularly useful to take this evidence from the client early and ensure that it forms part of the court record.

10.46 The exception to this is that where a family member provides a witness statement for the inquest, it should also say something about the deceased person and their life more widely. The inquest process can feel dehumanising for family members and whilst it is impossible to prevent the inquest from seeming formal or intimidating it often helps family members if they feel that they are allowed to say something about their loved one other than the way in which they died. Witness statements should begin by telling something of the deceased's life story and what they meant to the person giving evidence. Some personal photographs of the deceased person could be exhibited to the family member's statement, if they wish to share them. This may help remind the coroner that the individual at the heart of the inquest was more than the sum of their death.

10.47 If a civil claim is likely to progress after the inquest, the process of taking a witness statement can be split into two parts, one for the inquest and secondly to consider losses that might be recoverable. The latter is not relevant to the inquest so ought not to feature in the statement served in those proceedings.

Statements from other witnesses

10.48 There will also be statements prepared by other witnesses. The family may dispute some of what is said and consideration needs to be given as to when and how the family should respond to any perceived inaccuracies. Where possible the family statement should be served after receipt of all the other witness statements so they can address any issues in that statement. Where a witness statement responds to issues within the statements served by other interested parties it is important that the response remains factual in nature. The witness statement should not appear overly aggressive or adversarial.

INQUEST HEARING

10.49 This is clearly a very emotional time for families and the environment can feel volatile if not managed carefully. It is not uncommon for family members to want to bring photographs of the deceased into court. Whether photographs can be displayed in the courtroom will be at the discretion of the coroner. If the family would like to provide the coroner or the jury with a photograph of the deceased then that issue should be raised in advance of the final hearing as attempts to ambush the coroner or the jury are likely to prompt a negative reaction from the coroner. At the very least, the family members might choose to exhibit photographs of the deceased to their witness statement.

10.50 If the family has attended PIR hearings they will be familiar with the court layout and the coroner. If they have not it is useful to take them into court before the hearing starts so they can see the layout.

10.51 At most courts the family will be allowed a private room to sit with legal representatives and discuss the matter so instructions can be taken before the hearing, during any breaks and for a short period at the end of the day.

10.52 In general, the legal representatives will sit in the front row of court and family members behind their legal representatives. There is some inconsistency

10.52 *Representing Families at Inquests*

before certain coroners but guidance will be given by the coroner's officer as to who should sit where.

10.53 Some hearings have a lot of family members, witnesses and press in attendance; others have very few people present. Each hearing will be unique. See CHAPTER 12 at **12.22** *et seq* for consideration of managing the media when representing a family at an inquest.

10.54 Obviously, there can be some bad feeling between the parties if the family feels that there have been failings by individuals leading to the death. Families must be advised that they are in a court and cannot voice opinions or disrupt proceedings. It is worth reminding them of the fact that their advocate is there to speak on their behalf, and also that they have a pen and paper and can pass the advocates notes if they need to communicate anything urgently. The coroner has wide-ranging powers to exclude people from the court, hold them in contempt of court and has been known to seek police assistance to have people removed.

10.55 If a solicitor feels that there could be issues with the family attending, they should warn the family that proceedings cannot be disrupted and they must behave in an appropriate manner. If problems are anticipated it should be drawn to the coroner's officer's attention so that perhaps other witnesses can be moved out of the direct vision of some family members, or arrangements can be made to keep the parties separate where possible.

10.56 The client relationship will be of fundamental importance during the days of the hearing and the solicitor should be alive to any anticipated problems during the course of the evidence, during conclusions and immediately afterwards.

10.57 If the inquest is likely to be prolonged then several team members may cover the hearing days. Consideration must be given to the emotional strain the family are likely to be feeling over long periods of travelling and sitting in court. If there are likely to be logistical problems these should be raised with the coroner at the earliest opportunity in order that they can be accommodated.

GIVING EVIDENCE AT THE INQUEST

10.58 Families need to be advised that if they give a witness statement, they may be called to give oral evidence at an inquest; they can be called by the coroner, or any other interested persons may wish to raise questions (though as noted above this is less common).

10.59 Families should be reassured and prepared to give evidence without witness coaching. It is their evidence given under oath and they must say what they believe to be true. If they do not understand some of the terminology they can be assisted with an understanding of the evidence before the court. If they are likely to be called, it is imperative that they have received all the documentation so they are well prepared.

10.60 If written statements are prepared, generally these will be admitted under r 23, in which case the coroner will not actively seek to call the family member. Therefore, it is often left for family members to decide if they want to give evidence; a good understanding of how they are feeling and what they want to say will be vital in order to properly advise them. Again, the advocate should be guided by the wishes of the family.

10.61 For most families the inquest is their only opportunity to have their say in open court and they must be fully advised as to what the coroner will allow, and the potential effect of what they say on any civil or criminal claim and any press interests. Again, a good understanding of the family will assist practitioners in advising them on this.

10.62 If the inquest relates to a medical death then much of the evidence is given by clinicians; this can be technical and difficult to dispute without expert evidence. However, if there are factual disputes as to what was said and done then allowing a family member to give evidence after clinical witnesses have been heard can allow them to respond to any issues that have arisen.

EXPERT EVIDENCE

10.63 If there have been issues that the family consider have caused or contributed to the death the coroner can be invited to instruct an expert. An expert should be independent and the family may find reassurance in their opinion, whether it confirms their concerns or rejects them.

10.64 The family should be advised of the various options, including obtaining their own expert evidence and serving it on the coroner. This allows the family some degree of control over the choice of expert and what is disclosed. However, all experts have a primary duty to the court. Unless and until disclosed, any evidence obtained by the family will attract legal privilege until privilege is waived.

10.65 Submissions can be made to the coroner to invite them to instruct an independent expert. These submissions can be made writing or at a PIR. It is entirely dependent upon the coroner whether they choose to instruct an expert. There are wide variations in a coroners' use of expert evidence in the 96 different areas. In an effort to save costs the coroner may state that the family are free to obtain their own evidence and serve it on the coroner. This will of course waive privilege in the report, but will also not mean the coroner will introduce it into evidence, call the expert to give evidence or later instruct their own expert who may have a difference of opinion.

10.66 It is likely if the family's expert is used, any additional costs of attending the inquest will be borne by the family. This must be considered when advising them on the merits and risks of instructing their own expert evidence. It is a balance between control of the expert used and evidence disclosed, against the risks of incurring costs which may be difficult to recover. See CHAPTER 23 for reference to the use of experts in inquests when there are linked civil or negligence proceedings.

MEDICAL CAUSE OF DEATH

10.67 The pathologist is usually independent of the interested persons although occasionally they may be employed by the same trust in healthcare cases. If that is the case it is helpful to inform the family so that they are aware of any links between the individuals involved in the inquest.

10.68 As noted above at **2.75** the pathologist will have completed a post mortem and provided an opinion on the cause of death. The medical cause of death can be an important declaration by which the family feel that any failings have been recognised. It can also be significant to subsequent civil or criminal proceedings. However, since it is often merely a word or sentence, it will not always fulfil this function, and the family will look to the conclusion for that acknowledgement instead. See **10.71** below.

10.69 Often there can be concerns raised by families that incidents such as falls resulting in fractures do not form part of the chain to death where conditions such as pneumonia are the terminal event. Very often the fall, fracture or surgery etc can directly contribute to development of pneumonia and as such should form part of the causal chain. It is important to get this detail correct if possible as it can affect damages such as recovery of bereavement awards and loss of dependency damages. See CHAPTER 6 in respect of the Record of Inquest for detail on how the medical cause of death should be recorded.

10.70 If there are any valid concerns from the family that the medical cause of death is incorrect then the pathologist should be called as a witness. Questions can be put to them that may result in a change of opinion.

CONCLUSIONS

10.71 In some inquests the conclusion is of vital importance to the family; for others a particular conclusion will always be inevitable, but it is the opportunity to explore the evidence that is the most important part of the inquest.

10.72 It is good practice to explain to the family all the potential conclusions open to the coroner and if relevant, to explain why conclusions, particularly short form ones such as 'accidental death' or 'natural causes', do not necessarily mean that nobody was at fault or a civil claim will not be successful.

10.73 For many families the conclusion develops an importance that outweighs the value of the words that will be used. In most cases families should be reminded that the conclusion is unlikely to address the concerns that they have regarding the death of their loved one or express them in terms that are sufficient, particularly since conclusions are often far shorter than families expect them to be. Families should be warned about the possibility that the coroners conclusion will even appear to exonerate the individuals or organisation whom they blame for the death of their loved one.

10.74 It is not uncommon for families to focus on conclusions such as 'unlawful killing' or the rider of 'neglect' without appreciating that these conclusions apply to a very limited number of cases where negligence has contributed to the deceased's death. It is not surprising that a family who have lost a loved one due to the apparent negligence of another person or organisation would expect the coroner to recognise this in their conclusion. They should be reminded throughout that the inquest process is not adversarial and that coroners (generally) are not permitted to apportion blame. Failing to obtain a critical conclusion at the culmination of the inquest hearing does not mean that the coroner has rejected the notion that the death might have been caused or contributed to by negligence.

10.75 If the family are likely to pursue a civil claim following the inquest then it is often helpful to explain to them that the purpose of the inquest will be to find the answers to their questions, insofar as they can be answered, and gather and test evidence for the purpose of the subsequent civil claim, in which concepts of blame and negligence will have greater primacy.

10.76 Matters may be different in cases where Art 2 of the European Convention on Human Rights is engaged. In those cases, the family should be advised that identifying fault does fall within the scope of the coroner or juries' decision-making process. They should nonetheless be reminded that not every act of negligent or poor care will result in an adverse finding (see CHAPTER 6 at 6.142 for further detail).

10.77 In some cases, the family may hope that the inquest will galvanise the Crown Prosecution Service (CPS) into re-opening criminal proceedings. In that context it is important to bear in mind that whilst a conclusion of 'unlawful killing' makes the prospect of subsequent criminal proceedings much more likely it does not make them inevitable. This conclusion will prompt the CPS to consider, or re-consider, a decision to prosecute but does not place an obligation on the CPS to actually prosecute. There are numerous examples of cases where the CPS has declined to prosecute an individual or an organisation despite a coroner or inquest jury delivering a conclusion of unlawful killing.

PREVENTION OF FUTURE DEATHS

10.78 One of the most important aspects of an inquest for some families is the wish to see change and help save lives in the future. It is important to discuss this with families and where possible prepare submissions on whether the coroner should make a report to prevent future deaths in respect of the points that are causing the family concern.

10.79 Helping effect change can help families come to terms with their loss, although there is a common and perhaps not entirely unreasonable belief that some organisations direct their resources towards redrafting safety protocols or mission statements without effecting real or fundamental change in their practices. In most cases the family will have seen a copy of any report to prevent future deaths and should be provided with the opportunity to discuss it with their team in a candid way. There is sometimes a temptation to regard the report as an afterthought, without realising that preventing future tragedies

10.79 *Representing Families at Inquests*

is a common motivation amongst bereaved families. If a witness attends court to speak about the steps that have been taken and the measures that have been put in place, they should be asked to confirm the progress that has been made and whether there have been further events or near misses.

AFTER THE INQUEST

> 'After the [fresh] inquests I was at an all-time low. It made me look at things I thought I had dealt with . . . if people thought that families would be coming home celebrating that was not the case.'[1]

[1] Jenni Hicks, mother of Sarah and Victoria Hicks, quoted by the Right Reverend James Jones KBE in 'The patronizing disposition of unaccountable power': A report to ensure the pain and suffering of the Hillsborough families is not repeated (1 November 2017, HC 511).

10.80 The inquest is an emotional journey for a family and can often take a year or longer to conclude. Families should be prepared for feeling very different after the inquest. Sometimes if the journey has felt like a fight then the end of that may leave them feeling very depressed and without purpose. Equally, there is often just grieving left and families can find this very difficult. The more difficult the inquest has been, the more adversarial, the greater the level of failings and press interest, the more likely it will be that the conclusion of the inquest has a greater emotional impact.

10.81 It is not uncommon for families who have previously appeared to be coping well to dramatically change after the inquest. There is often a temptation for advocates to move straight from the inquest process into the civil claim, sometimes seeking to hold a case conference in the family room after the conclusion has been handed down. For most families the conclusion of the inquest is not the time to be going through the details of a potential civil claim and the best advice is to go home and contact their solicitor again in a week or two's time. As with all aspects of representing families at inquests, though, the approach for one family will not be the same for every family. No family member should be told that they cannot speak about the civil process at the conclusion of the inquest if that is what they want.

Chapter 11

REPRESENTING ORGANISATIONS AT INQUESTS

11.1 Public and private bodies involved in coronial proceedings can face a kaleidoscopic range of risks and concerns. The inquest may be the preliminary stage of potential civil or criminal proceedings. Reputational damage, via media coverage or otherwise, may be a consequence of the evidence that emerges in the investigation, the approach taken by the organisation at the inquest, the conclusions, or a reg 28 report[1] to prevent future deaths. Officers of the relevant organisations may also be in fear of personal repercussions, impacting their continued employment and/or regulatory or criminal investigation. Many of these areas of risk and concern may be in tension with one another and practitioners often need to balance the countervailing goals they are seeking to achieve.

[1] Coroners (Investigations) Regulations 2013, SI 2013/1629.

FIRST INVOLVEMENT

11.2 The point at which practitioners representing organisations first become aware of a coronial investigation (or likely investigation) can vary. They may be involved shortly after the death itself occurs, if the circumstances raise particular or obvious concerns. The first approach may instead follow criticisms being made in an internal or external investigation. In the alternative, practitioners may first be instructed shortly before a pre-inquest review hearing or when the coroner first invites the organisation to participate as an interested person.

11.3 Whatever the stage, practitioners will often be met by a requirement to gather documentation for disclosure to the coroner or by the need to review material already collated in an earlier investigation. It is important, at such a preliminary stage, to identify the key issues and obtain instructions. This may sound obvious but inquests develop in a way that can be alien to some. There are no pleadings. The issues emerge as the investigation progresses. Clients may have little understanding of the process. Without a grasp of where things are likely to lead, a practitioner cannot properly advise an organisation as to the best way forward. Getting instructions can be a challenge. It may sometimes not be clear who is in the best position, or has the authority, to provide them. In large organisations, several layers of management may need to be consulted before clear instructions are obtained. Practitioners need to try

11.3 *Representing Organisations at Inquests*

and ensure that they are in contact with the relevant decision makers as soon as reasonably practicable in the process. An early conference usually assists.

11.4 The position taken by an organisation at an inquest can sometimes be rather nuanced. Organisations need to understand that in some circumstances fighting every point may not be in their best interests. There can sometimes be a tension between opposing certain criticisms and ensuring the coroner sees that relevant lessons have been learned (and thereby avoid a reg 28 report to prevent future deaths).

Conflicts of interest

11.5 A timely understanding of the organisation's position can also assist lawyers to advise as to conflicts of interest. Conflicts arise, or may arise, when the position at the inquest of an officer of the organisation is, or will be, materially at odds with those of their employer. In such circumstances, a lawyer cannot advance two incompatible positions and the relevant officer should be informed of the same and allowed an opportunity to obtain separate representation. The mere fact that an individual is criticised, or may be criticised, by the body does not raise a conflict if the officer accepts the error/criticism. The need to recognise conflicts of interest, and to advise on the same, is an ongoing duty. Practitioners need to grapple with such issues as soon as practicable, otherwise the inquest could be delayed when separate lawyers need to be brought in and up to speed late in the day. It follows that where the organisation explicitly criticises one of its employees regarding their conduct in relation to some important issue, it should at an early stage ask the employee whether they accept that criticism. If that criticism is not accepted, the employee should be separately represented at the inquest. The same conflict applies in circumstances where an employee who is due to give evidence at the inquest criticises the organisation's conduct on material issues. If the organisation does not accept that criticism it should ensure that the employee is represented by a different legal team, if representation is required.

Previous reports and investigations

11.6 Following a death, an organisation may undertake its own investigation. Further or alternatively, there may an investigation by an outside body, such as an ombudsman or regulatory authority. These investigations seek to reach conclusions as to the factual circumstances of the death for the purposes of learning and preventing deaths in the future. The investigators interview relevant witnesses and collect evidence. Such investigations can be important sources of evidence. The first-hand accounts of witnesses are likely to be prima facie admissible. The status of a report and its conclusions may, however, be another issue. Those representing organisations therefore need to ensure they have instructions as to the contents of the relevant investigation reports and must consider whether they wish to challenge the admissibility of the report and/or its conclusions. Such reports are prepared for a different purpose than the inquest. They may be based on extraneous evidence or evidential standards. Admission of their conclusions may therefore be unfair and the basis of challenge[1].

[1] See *R v Her Majesty's Coroner forInner North London, ex parte Stanley* [2003] EWHC 1180 (Admin) per Silber J; the Northern Ireland case of *Siberry's Application (No 2)* [2008] NIQB 147 per McCloskey J; and *Lagos v HM Coroner for the City of London* [2013] EWHC 423 (Admin).

Media

11.7 Organisations need to be advised as early as possible as to the risks of adverse media coverage. A risk assessment and media plan may be required. For further on this, see CHAPTER 12.

PRE-INQUEST REVIEW HEARING

11.8 The pre-inquest review hearing (PIR) is a key part of the coronial process and the capability of a practitioner to meet the goals of an organisation may be determined at that hearing. Those representing public and private bodies must be ready to argue issues such as scope of the inquest, engagement of Art 2, the need for a jury, witness lists and disclosure. A failure by an organisation to prepare for a PIR hearing properly can be costly down the line both in terms of money and reputation. Issues of scope are addressed in detail in other chapters and are not repeated here. Those representing organisations should always be cautious to ensure that the arguments raised on behalf of the deceased person's family fall properly within the scope of the coroner's jurisdiction, are causatively relevant and are not simply directed towards arguing civil or criminal liability.

PREPARING FOR THE INQUEST

11.9 It is helpful for practitioners to meet key witnesses before the inquest so that those witnesses understand the purpose of the hearing and the relevance of their evidence within it. Lawyers should be mindful that witnesses may be anxious about giving evidence and the repercussions that may follow. Practitioners can provide reassurance if appropriate but in relevant cases organisations should ensure that their officers are properly supported, whether by a colleague, by management or more formal therapeutic input.

11.10 Subject to instructions, organisations should also consider whether any matters of fact or law should be admitted in open correspondence prior to the inquest. Providing such clarity, and therefore reducing the ostensible areas of contention, can be a way for an organisation to assist a family in advance of a difficult inquest hearing. Such admissions, if binding under the civil procedure rules, can also have costs benefits in any future civil claim[1]. By narrowing the issues between the parties at an early stage, costs of attendance at the inquest may not be recoverable in subsequent civil proceedings. See further as regards this at CHAPTER 9. Making admissions does, however, carry risks. The evidence at the inquest may not support the position taken. Further,

11.10 Representing Organisations at Inquests

admitted failings may be included in the Record of Inquest or the court's reasons even if they are not probably or possibly causative of the death[2]. The organisation should bear in mind that having made admissions prior to the inquest its approach to the evidence at the inquest must be consistent with those admissions. If the organisation, by the way it presents its evidence at the inquest, seeks to resile from those admissions, it may undermine its position in relation to costs, especially in circumstances where those representing the family might argue that the admission made was not binding on the organisation[3].

[1] Pursuant to CPR 14.1A, an admission is binding if made after receipt of a letter of claim or when such admission is explicitly stated to be made under CPR Pt 14.
[2] See *R (Tainton) v HM Senior Coroner and West Lancashire* [2016] EWHC 1396 (Admin) where the practice of the putting admitted failings in the record was approved; in *R (Carole Smith) v HM Assistant Coroner for North West Wales* [2020] EWHC 781 (Admin) the court considered that a coroner sitting alone may better mention such admitted failures when giving reasons.
[3] Pre-action admissions are not absolutely binding and can be resiled from, especially if the admission is made outside of the relevant pre-action protocol.

11.11 An organisation will also need to consider what evidence it produces to assist the coroner on their duty under reg 28 of The Coroners (Investigation) Regulations 2013[1]. A body will need to identify who is best placed to inform the coroner of any internal reviews undertaken, their outcome and the steps taken to rectify any concerns identified. An internal or external investigation may be the starting point for this evidence, but coroners will expect to see an action plan following on from the same. The court will, however, be realistic. Not all steps can be quickly implemented. As a minimum a coroner will expect to see that a plan is in place and will be executed at some reasonable point in the future.

[1] SI 2013/1629.

THE INQUEST HEARING

11.12 The inquest hearing can be emotionally charged. Those representing organisations, whilst at all times ensuring they fully and fearlessly represent their client, need to be mindful that their approach, style and tone in court can add to the distress of the family or others involved in the process. An unsympathetic or overly aggressive approach can alienate the tribunal, especially if the inquest is heard before a jury. Tactless or unguarded comments by lawyers, officers of the organisation, and/or witnesses can attract adverse comment in the media and cause reputational damage. Those who represent the organisation at the inquest must be reminded, if they don't already know, about the need to behave appropriately, professionally and sympathetically, during the inquest.

11.13 Some consideration needs to be given as to the stance taken as to family witness evidence. Often this can be read, or the evidence elicited without any challenge, thereby avoiding any distress for the family. Unlike in adversarial proceedings, an interested party is not taken to admit evidence just because they do not challenge it in open court. It is reasonable and common for those representing organisations to advise the court that they do not accept a witness's evidence but out of a desire not to cause distress to the family member they will not cross examine that witness. In some cases the proposed evidence is highly relevant and contentious, and it may be professionally inappropriate for those representing an organisation to allow it to pass without challenge. If questions are being put to a witness, especially a family member, they should be asked in an appropriate manner. In the alternative, the material may be better elicited from and challenged during the testimony of other witnesses. In such circumstances, the interested persons and the coroner might agree to exclude contentious parts from family statements so as to avoid the need for additional distressing questions.

11.14 Many or sometimes all of the factual witnesses at an inquest may come from the organisation involved. Accordingly, the practitioner will be asking questions of the witness last in sequence and should ensure that any helpful areas not covered are elicited and any wrong impressions arising from the witness' evidence are corrected. Even before this, a lawyer representing an organisation must, when others are examining the witness, be in a position to protect the interests of their client and of the witness by objecting to inappropriate questions, such as those that go outside the scope of the inquest or those that are unfair or invite speculation or conjecture.

AFTER THE INQUEST

11.15 The client will need to be taken through the court's findings, its conclusion and the position as to reg 28 reports. A media statement may be required. Further, the organisation will need to know the risks and next steps going forwards. Advice as to any potential criminal, civil or regulatory liability will be required. The organisation may also, in due course, require assistance with its response to any report to prevent future deaths.

Chapter 12

PRESS AND PUBLICITY AT INQUESTS

12.1 In accordance with the principle of open justice, the vast majority of inquests and pre-inquest hearings will be held in public[1] and members of the press have the right to attend and report, and often to have access to relevant documentation. The coroner must generally ensure that the court is accessible to the public both in principle and in practice[2]. Details of witnesses and other individuals named in proceedings will also usually be made public. There are exceptions to the principle of open justice and these are explored further below.

[1] Coroners (Inquests) Rules 2013, r 11; see also The Chief Coroner's Guidance No 25, Coroners and the Media (30 September 2016), para 13 (and para 12 which expressly refers to the press).
[2] Chief Coroner's Guidance No 25, Coroners and the Media, para 11.

12.2 Media attention can arise whether the interested parties involved in the inquest want it or not. It is important that practitioners advise their clients, whether the family or an organisation, from the outset as to what the publicity ramifications might be and take instructions as to the appropriate response. A client's position may change as matters unfold, so it is sensible to keep this issue under constant review.

12.3 The key documents and legislation that practitioners should be aware of that relate to inquests and the media are:

- The Coroners (Inquests) Rules 2013[1];
- Chief Coroner's Guidance No 25, Coroners and the Media;
- The Contempt of Court Act 1981.

Further, the Independent Press Standards Organisation (IPSO) provides a helpful guide titled 'Press reporting on a death – information for the public'[2] which practitioners may wish to provide to their clients alongside their advice gleaned from experience.

[1] SI 2013/1616.
[2] https://www.ipso.co.uk/media/1535/reporting-on-deaths-public-18.pdf.

APPLICATIONS BY THE MEDIA FOR DISCLOSURE OF DOCUMENTS

12.4 The press can make an application for disclosure of any document referred to in an inquest. Under the Coroners (Investigations) Regulations 2013[1] the coroner may provide any document or a copy of any document to any person who, in the opinion of the coroner, is a proper person to have

12.4 Press and Publicity at Inquests

possession of it. The Chief Coroner's Guidance No 25, 'Coroners and the Media', states that members of the media should normally be considered proper persons for these purposes[2].

[1] SI 2013/1629.
[2] Chief Coroner's Guidance No 25, Coroners and the Media, paras 27 and 29.

12.5 Any such request for access to documents 'must specify precisely the document sought and explain why it is required. Where any of this is unclear, the coroner may ask for clarification'[1].

[1] Chief Coroner's Guidance No 25, Coroners and the Media, para 38.

12.6 In considering a request for access to documents, the coroner must conduct a 'fact-specific proportionality exercise'[1] and should bear in mind:

(a) The *'open justice principle'*. A request from the press supports public scrutiny of the judicial system and so there is a presumption that the document will be disclosed[2].
(b) The media is not entitled to see documents not referred to in court[3].
(c) Generally members of the media are not entitled to have access to any documents before the inquest, 'save where disclosure is necessary to enable the media itself to make representations (when entitled to be heard), for example in relation to a proposed restriction on reporting'[4].
(d) If appropriate, 'the competing rights of (1) the media under Art 10 of the European Convention on Human Rights (freedom of expression) with the rights of (2) a particular person (including Interested Persons, witnesses and any individual who could be affected by the disclosure) under Art 8 (right to respect for private and family life) where disclosure could give rise to a risk of harm or otherwise interfere with those rights'[5].

[1] Chief Coroner's Guidance No 25, Coroners and the Media, para 51.
[2] Chief Coroner's Guidance No 25, Coroners and the Media, paras 41–42.
[3] Chief Coroner's Guidance No 25, Coroners and the Media, para 43.
[4] Chief Coroner's Guidance No 25, Coroners and the Media, para 44.
[5] Chief Coroner's Guidance No 25, Coroners and the Media, para 51.

12.7 The coroner should normally accede to a media request unless there is a 'some strong contrary argument' or 'countervailing reasons' not to[1], but redaction is permitted. Reasons for refusal include national security, prejudice to ongoing/future criminal proceedings, to protect rights under Art 8 of the European Convention on Human Rights (ECHR), the protection of sensitive personal information or that disclosure would put a great burden on the court[2].

[1] *R (Guardian News and Media Ltd) v City of Westminster Magistrates' Court* [2012] EWCA Civ 420, [2013] QB 618.
[2] Chief Coroner's Guidance No 25, Coroners and the Media, para 48.

12.8 When granting or refusing any such application, the corner should give brief reasons for the decision. If they refuse the application, these reasons should refer to[1]:

(1) the application;
(2) the nature of the material requested;
(3) whether the application has 'journalistic purpose';

(4) the principle of open justice;
(5) Art 10 freedom of expression;
(6) the presumption in favour of disclosure;
(7) the 'countervailing reasons';
(8) the refusal of the application;
(9) the reasons for refusal.

If access to the document is granted, this may take place by way of inspection or copying; 'a journalist may take a photograph of a document as a copy'[2].

[1] Chief Coroner's Guidance No 25, Coroners and the Media, para 53.
[2] Chief Coroner's Guidance No 25, Coroners and the Media, para 56.

ATTENDANCE AT INQUESTS

12.9 As noted above, in general terms both the press and the general public are entitled to attend all inquest hearings[1]. There are exceptions to this rule, but they are limited broadly to pre-inquest hearings and inquests where there are issues of national security[2]. In any case, the media should be entitled to make representations as to whether they should be permitted to attend[3].

[1] Chief Coroner's Guidance No 25, Coroners and the Media, para 10.
[2] Coroners (Inquests) Rules 2013, r 11(2)–(5).
[3] Chief Coroner's Guidance No 25, Coroners and the Media.

REPORTING RESTRICTIONS

12.10 The coroner may put reporting restrictions in place but these may only be imposed when it is lawful, necessary and proportionate[1]. Again, the coroner should always keep in mind the principle of open justice as a starting point. In any case, as with any application concerning them, the coroner should give the media a chance to make representations so they should make any such decision at a pre-inquest review hearing if at all possible[2].

[1] Chief Coroner's Guidance No 25, Coroners and the Media, para 67.
[2] Chief Coroner's Guidance No 25, Coroners and the Media, para 68.

12.11 As an alternative to reporting restrictions, a coroner can always ensure that personal and sensitive information not required to enable a sufficient enquiry is not referred to in public. If it is not referred to in open court, the press is unlikely to obtain disclosure of it.

12.12 Under the Contempt of Court Act 1981, s 4(2), a coroner may order that publication of a media report be postponed for such period as they think necessary to avoid a substantial risk of prejudice to the administration of justice[1]. Equally, as noted in the Chief Coroner's Guidance, 'in practice, coroners may wish, in appropriate instances and for good reason, to invite the press not to report something'[2].

[1] Contempt of Court Act 1981, s 4(2).
[2] Chief Coroner's Guidance No 25, Coroners and the Media, para 71.

12.13 *Press and Publicity at Inquests*

LIVE COMMUNICATIONS/PUBLICATIONS DURING A HEARING

12.13 Members of the press are permitted to make 'live text-based communications' during a hearing, though any phones or laptops must be used silently. This same right is not afforded to members of the public. They must apply to the coroner for permission[1].

[1] Chief Coroner's Guidance No 25, Coroners and the Media, paras 34–35.

ANONYMITY

12.14 A coroner does have the power to permit witnesses to remain anonymous, or to give evidence from behind a screen. The law on applications for anonymity is comprehensively set out at paras 55–64 of *R (on the application of T) v HM Senior Coroner for the County of West Yorkshire (Western Area)*[1], where Lord Thomas LCJ stated:

(a) Open justice is the starting point for any such application;
(b) 'One very important aspect of the principle of open justice is the naming of those before the court'[2];
(c) There must be cogent evidence for restricting these basic principles; and
(d) The balancing act in any such application is highly fact-specific, taking into account the benefits of open justice versus the risk of harm any disclosure of the person's identity might cause to either 'the maintenance of an effective judicial process or to the legitimate interests of others'[3].

[1] [2017] EWCA Civ 318.
[2] [2017] EWCA Civ 318 at [58].
[3] [2017] EWCA Civ 318 at [63].

12.15 By way of example, in *R (on the application of T) v HM Senior Coroner for the County of West Yorkshire (Western Area)*[1], the mother of a baby contended that her child had been stillborn and had concealed the body at home for several days before reporting the death. The mother sought anonymity, alleging that if her identity were made public that she would suffer: (i) a real and immediate risk of inhuman and degrading treatment under Art 3 ECHR (from family and acquaintances, if they were to find out what she had done); (ii) a real and immediate threat to her life within the meaning of Art 2 ECHR (for the same reasons); and (iii) her rights under Art 8 ECHR ie the right to a private and family life. The application was refused, an approach that was endorsed by the Court of Appeal. It was noted that the mother had already been named in some internet reports, meaning the anonymity order would not provide complete protection in any event. The Court of Appeal also considered the suggestion she would be at risk was highly speculative. Finally, the coroner had offered alternative measures to afford her some privacy, including screens, and exclusion of questions which might indicate where she now lived.

[1] [2017] EWCA Civ 318.

12.16 Any application for a witness to remain anonymous, or to give evidence from behind a screen, should be heard in public[1].

[1] Coroners (Inquests) Rules 2013, r 18.

CHILDREN IN CORONIAL PROCEEDINGS

(a) Child witnesses

12.17 Special considerations concerning reporting a child's identity may apply. Under s 39, Children and Young Person's Act 1933, a coroner has a discretionary power to restrict reporting of a child witness's name[1]. Such an order may only be made for 'necessary and proportionate reasons' and yet again the coroner is required to take into account the principle of open justice[2].

[1] Children and Young Person's Act 1933, s 39.
[2] Chief Coroner's Guidance No 25, Coroners and the Media, para 75.

12.18 The Chief Coroner's guidance confirms that 'where a section 39 direction, which is discretionary, is given, it prohibits the reporting of the name, address or school or any particulars calculated to lead to the identification of the child witness, including publication of a picture'[1]. Any order made under s 39 would expire on the child's majority[2].

[1] Chief Coroner's Guidance No 25, Coroners and the Media, para 74.
[2] *JC and RT v Central Criminal Court and others* [2014] EWHC 1041 (QB).

(b) Deceased children

12.19 The identity of a deceased child may be protected where the Family Court or High Court has imposed an order restricting reporting and the order remains in force[1].

[1] Chief Coroner's Guidance No 25, Coroners and the Media, para 78.

12.20 It is worth noting that in practice, where a coroner asks the media to refrain from publishing a child's identity, such a request is usually acceded to.

CHALLENGES TO A CORONER'S DECISION REGARDING MEDIA ACCESS

12.21 There is no right of appeal when a coroner makes a decision regarding media access. The only avenue available is to challenge the coroner by way of a judicial review (see CHAPTER 8).

FAMILIES AND THE MEDIA

12.22 Practitioners will often have been instructed because the family of the deceased believes the cause of their loved one's death to be linked to the act or omission of another person, company or organisation. Tensions can run high and family members who wish to speak out must be careful not to make allegations or provide information to the press that could prejudice the coroner's investigation. Further, they should be prepared that the press coverage may not be sympathetic.

12.23 Many families will be extremely concerned about what they may consider to be an intrusion on their privacy and grief. They may have suffered

12.23 *Press and Publicity at Inquests*

negative experiences around the time of death such as 'doorstepping', publication of personal photographs obtained from social media, or misreporting of facts. It is important to explain to the family that the press have a job to do and that steps can be taken to minimise any intrusion.

12.24 It is wise to check at first instruction whether the family have previously made any statements to / spoken to the press or published anything on social media. They may want to ensure that their social media settings are private as soon as possible. Those assisting families may also want to conduct an internet sweep of what has already been reported or is already in the public domain. The death may well have been reported contemporaneously in the local press. The family should also be aware that if friends or colleagues have paid tribute to the deceased on social media, then the press may choose to reproduce information and photographs from public sites.

12.25 Whether press coverage is welcomed or not, the family may want to consider taking certain steps to help to minimise intrusion and maintain some control over events. First, providing a contact at the firm for all press queries can provide a buffer for the family. Second, in advance of the inquest, the family may wish to release a photograph of the deceased to the press, along with a short quote about what the deceased meant to the family, perhaps revealing something of the deceased's personality. This can satisfy the needs of the press for their story whilst protecting the family from making any inadvertent prejudicial comments, as well as providing a higher chance of a photograph that the family are happy with being the one that is published. If the family is happy to do so, notifying the press that they will stop for a brief photo opportunity on the way into court can alleviate concerns that they will be pursued for a photograph. It is also sensible to notify the press in advance that a statement will be given at the conclusion of the inquest, once the conclusion has been recorded. This can be given by a member of the family or their representative. Again, this step can help to give the press what they need for their story and obviate the requirement for further attempted questioning of the family.

12.26 If the coroner makes a report to prevent future deaths, the family may choose to campaign for change around the issue or issues raised[1]. We have seen changes to the law suggested and made as a result of this sort of activity and campaigning can sometimes provide the family with the sense that something good has come out of their loved one's death via changes made for the future.

[1] These are published on the judiciary website by the Chief Coroner along with any responses that have been received – see Chief Coroner's Guidance No 5, Reports to Prevent Future Deaths (revised 4 November 2020).

12.27 Press reporting of inquests can draw attention to areas of concern and can lead to pressure for reform. By highlighting the facts that have led to a tragedy, there is always the hope that another may be prevented.

12.28 Practitioners should manage expectations and prepare the family for what they may consider to be negative outcomes. The press will not always be sympathetic. Journalists are able to choose what information they are going to report and so will not always report everything that has been said or necessarily the elements of the inquest that are of most concern to the family.

Where a family has been hoping for a particular verdict or a prevention of future deaths report, they may not get it. Further, the inquest or the outcome of the inquest may not get reported. Where the inquest takes place over a number of days / weeks, the press may not have the resources to cover the whole proceedings and reporting may be patchy. Similarly, key parts of the inquest or its entirety may be overshadowed or excluded completely from the media as a result of other news cycles.

12.29 An inquest can be an exhausting and emotional process for a family even in normal circumstances. If the inquest has been high-profile, the family may need additional emotional support and should be prepared for when the coverage stops.

12.30 Where there are genuine concerns about a story or the way a journalist has behaved, these can be raised with the Independent Press Standards Organisation (IPSO), who are the independent regulator of most of the UK's newspapers and magazines.

See CHAPTER 10 for further detail about representing families at inquests.

ORGANISATIONS AND THE MEDIA

12.31 Press reporting can pose risks to the reputation of organisations, as well as their officers. In particularly sensitive or concerning cases, the damage can be sufficient to jeopardise the professional standing and livelihoods of individuals linked to the death as well as the management of an organisation. Accordingly, it is essential to prepare a press strategy.

12.32 Legal representatives, from the outset of their involvement, should undertake, or invite the organisation to undertake, a publicity risk assessment. This will be guided by the extent and tone of coverage to date and the anticipated reporting during the course of investigation. Areas of likely coronial and press interest and criticism, as well as the departments, teams or individuals that may be the subject of reporting, need to be identified. On the basis of that assessment, a publicity action plan should be, if necessary, put in place. The relevant steps might include:

- a press statement at the preliminary stage of the proceedings;
- in cases where particularly intense coverage is expected, arranging a media point of contact at the organisation or their representative's firm is helpful;
- adducing evidence in the proceedings that may avoid or mitigate unfair press comment;
- providing support to members of the organisation that may come to be the subject of reporting. This can include colleague/union assistance, managerial oversight, counselling and/or psychological input. In some cases, this can extend to individuals being encouraged to take steps to protect their privacy, such as amending their social media settings and profile;

12.32 *Press and Publicity at Inquests*

- identifying the publicity risks with relevant managers of the organisation in order to guide expectations and see what steps are necessary to demonstrate changes to internal processes and lesson learning.

The publicity risk assessment is a dynamic tool that needs to be, along with the relevant action plan, updated as the investigation proceeds.

12.33 Press releases, whether given at a preliminary stage or at the conclusion of the inquest, require careful consideration. Legal oversight will usually be required. Statements to the press must be tailored to the circumstances of the case, the result (if you have one) and the position taken by the organisation at the inquest. Guidance cannot be prescriptive. Organisations would usually be well advised to be mindful of a range of considerations including the sensitivities of the family, protecting the reputation of the organisation and its officers, correcting any unfair media impressions, making relevant admissions of fault and/or avoiding any admissions of liability, not prejudicing the investigation (if indeed it is ongoing), and ensuring that any lessons learnt and internal improvements are publicly identified.

See CHAPTER 11 for further detail about representing organisations at inquests.

Chapter 13
CLINICAL INQUESTS

13.1 This chapter looks at the extent to which an inquest can be a forum for investigating the role that medical treatment played in the circumstances surrounding a death. That can encompass a broad range of clinical scenarios ranging from omissions in the form of failures to diagnose and treat, to circumstances where surgery or other medical treatment becomes the direct cause of death. We will identify the issues that are common to clinical inquests without reviewing each and every circumstance in which medical treatment, or the absence of it, can bring about death. We will not look at the issue of mental health in any detail, for example, as this is addressed elsewhere in CHAPTER 15.

REPRESENTING FAMILIES AT CLINICAL INQUESTS

13.2 Families who have suffered traumatic deaths often struggle to accept that the coronial system is not looking to blame individuals. Even if the family understands the limitations of the statutory remit of the coroner's court, they are still likely to be frustrated. They may feel strongly that clinicians have failed their loved ones, with devastating results. The reporting requirements for clinicians are set out in CHAPTER 4. However, there remain occasions when the hospitals and/or clinicians fail to report the death, and the family do so. Even if the NHS trust recognises failings through an investigation or the position it takes at the inquest, individual clinician witnesses may not do so when giving evidence. Expectation management at the outset and frequent reminders about the limitations of what can be achieved through the process are key. Nevertheless, where the inquest is being used to also investigate a civil claim, representatives should be mindful that the vast majority of clinical negligence claims settle prior to trial and therefore the inquest is likely to be the only opportunity for the family to hear what the clinicians have to say about what happened.

CLINICAL NEGLIGENCE

13.3 It is not the role of the coroner in the ordinary course of events to determine whether the care provided to the deceased person was negligent. This was made clear by Lord Justice McCowan in *R v HM Coroner for Birmingham ex p Cotton*[1]:

> 'The real question in this case, in my judgment, is whether there was negligence on the part of the hospital and/or the doctors that treated the deceased. Whether they

13.3 Clinical Inquests

were negligent and, if so, whether there was a clear and direct causal connection between that negligence and the deceased's death, would in my judgment, be much better determined by a judge trying a pleaded case sitting alone and calmly and dispassionately weighing up the evidence on each side assisted by factual submissions from counsel. But, in any event, a coroner's jury is prohibited from determining a verdict which determines or appears to determine any question of civil liability. The purpose of an inquest is to discover the cause of death, not to get a negligence claim on its feet.'

[1] (1996) 160 JP 123.

13.4 That is not to say that inquests are not a used as a forum for establishing a potential claim for damages or laying the foundations of a defence. In *Roach v Home Office*[1], *Lynch v Chief Constable of Warwickshire*[2] and *Powell and Others v The Chief Constable of West Midlands Police*[3] it was recognised that the inquest could be a useful mechanism for gathering evidence and examining witnesses and that: 'The benefit of a positive verdict to the claimants is entirely in the possible crumbling of the defendants' resolve to defend the claim. The verdict might have had this effect in bringing the defendants to the settlement table as the claimants suggest'[4].

[1] [2009] EWHC 312 (QB).
[2] [2014] 11 WLUK 332.
[3] [2018] EWHC B12 (Costs).
[4] *Lynch v Chief Constable of Warwickshire Police* [2014] 11 WLUK 332.

13.5 Despite the comments in *ex parte Cotton*, the presence of alleged clinical negligence surrounding the death can be important in a number of respects: it can provide the coroner with jurisdiction to hold an inquest into a death that would otherwise be certified as natural; it can affect the conclusion that the coroner or the jury delivers; it could be the basis of an investigation into an alleged breach of Art 2 of the European Convention on Human Rights (ECHR); it could provide the basis of a report to prevent future deaths[1].

[1] For more on reports to prevent future deaths see CHAPTER 7.

JURISDICTION

13.6 As is discussed in more detail elsewhere, the coroner derives their power to investigate death from s 1 of the Coroners and Justice Act 2009 (CJA 2009). Section 1(2) of the CJA 2009 provides that this duty arises only in circumstances where:

'. . . the coroner has reason to suspect that—
(a) the deceased died a violent or unnatural death,
(b) the cause of death is unknown, or
(c) the deceased died while in custody or otherwise in state detention.'

13.7 Pursuant to s 4(1) of the CJA 2009, a senior coroner who is responsible for conducting an investigation into a death *must* discontinue that investigation if a post-mortem examination reveals the cause of death and it is the coroner's belief that it is not necessary to continue the investigation. It is reasonable to conclude from this that where the cause of death is known and is natural, then assuming that the death did not occur in custody of state detention then the investigation must be discontinued.

13.8 Whilst it is obvious that a death caused by alleged negligence during the course of surgery or some other medical treatment will lead to an unnatural death, it is less clear as to whether the negligent failure to treat a natural disease process could bring about an unnatural death. A number of cases address the question of whether a death by natural causes might be regarded as unnatural if caused by clinical negligence in the form of an omission to treat a natural disease process[1].

[1] This issue would not arise in the case of clinical staff treating an individual who sustained traumatic injuries. In those circumstances the death would be regarded as unnatural whether by virtue of the alleged clinical failings or the trauma that brought about the need for that medical treatment in the first place.

13.9 In *R v Poplar Coroner, Ex p Thomas*[1] a coroner declined to hold an inquest into the death of the 17-year-old girl who died following a severe asthma attack despite evidence suggesting that she would not have died if an ambulance not been delayed. In finding that this decision was unlawful, Dillon LJ said[2]:

'Whether Miss Thomas's death was natural or unnatural must therefore depend on what was the cause of death. At this point, I remind myself of the observations of Lord Salmon in *Alphacell Ltd v Woodward* [1972] AC 824, 847, where he said: "I consider . . . that what or who has caused a certain event to occur is essentially a practical question of fact which can best be answered by ordinary common sense rather than by abstract metaphysical theory" . . . [having considered the potential reasons why the ambulance was delayed] I do not suggest that any of these scenarios actually fits the facts of Miss Thomas's case. I do not know what the cause of the delay was. But in each of these scenarios common sense indicates that what caused the patient's death was, on Lord Salmon's test in *Alphacell v Woodward* [1972] AC 824, 847, the asthmatic attack, not the congestion of traffic, the bursting of the water main, the malfunction of the computer or the inefficiency of the ambulance service. But the asthmatic attack is a natural cause of death, and the death is not, in my judgment, turned into an unnatural death by any of the facts suggested in any of the alternative scenarios . . . The coroner was saying that, even when all of the other evidence is taken into account, the cause of death was still the asthmatic attack and the death was not an unnatural death . . .'

[1] [1993] QB 610.
[2] At p 628.

13.10 Farquharson LJ agreed with Dillon LJ; Simon Brown LJ however went on to say:

'I agree . . . that the question whether or not a death is natural or unnatural depends ultimately on the view one takes as to the cause of death. But I do not find the question of causation in this context susceptible of quite the same sort of robust approach that the House of Lords advocated in a very different context in cases such as *McGhee v National Coal Board* [1973] 1 WLR 1. The question arising there was: can the court properly infer, in the absence of a provable direct link, that one particular state of affairs caused or contributed to another. In those cases the possibility of there being more than one cause was immaterial . . . The question posed in the present context is surely therefore different: given that all the important facts are known to the coroner, what view should he take of causes that may well be secondary but are not self-evidently irrelevant? As in litigation why should he not sometimes find a death to be the result of two causes, either one of which could serve to make it unnatural? . . . It seems to me necessary to recognise that cases may

13.10 Clinical Inquests

well arise in which human fault can and properly should be found to turn what would otherwise be a natural death into an unnatural one, and one into which therefore an inquest should be held.'

13.11 In *R v HM Coroner for East Sussex Western District Ex p Homberg*[1], Simon Brown LJ observed (at p 370) that:

'Although I myself would have been disposed to include within the proper scope of such a verdict [neglect] the death of someone seriously ill or injured who would have been saved by medical care but for wholly unreasonable delay in the arrival of the emergency services, such a view is obviously inconsistent with the majority decision of the Court of Appeal in [*ex p Thomas*]. That is not to say, however, that a lack of care verdict, whether freestanding or in terms of aggravating some other cause of death, would offend *Ex p Thomas*. On the contrary, Dillon LJ's judgment clearly recognises the legitimate continuance of such verdicts whenever properly founded on the facts. I would therefore accept Mr Fitzgerald's submission that *Ex p Thomas* must be confined to the section 8(1)(a) context in which it arose: essentially it decides no more than that a broad common sense view must be taken when deciding the bald question whether a death is unnatural so as to determine whether to hold an inquest. Whereas, however, for that purpose one shuts one's mind to all but the dominant cause of death, once an inquest is held, the duty to inquire into 'how the deceased came by his death' requires one then to take a broader view and investigate not merely the dominant but also (in Jervis's language) any 'acts or omissions which are directly responsible for the death.'

[1] (1994) 158 JP 357.

13.12 *R v HM Coroner for Inner North London Ex p Touche*[1] concerned the death of a woman from a cerebral haemorrhage following the birth of twins. It was thought that her death was related to eclampsia, a condition that could have been identified and treated if her blood pressure had been monitored. The coroner declined to hold an inquest on the basis that the death was caused by a natural process. The hearing before the Divisional Court and Court of Appeal was concerned amongst other things as to whether there was a conflict between the judgment of Dillon LJ and Simon Brown LJ in *Ex p Thomas*. Having determined that an inquest should be held given the possibility that the coroner might add a rider of 'neglect' to a conclusion that the death was due to natural causes Simon Brown LJ added[2]:

'But undoubtedly there will be cases which fall outside the category of "neglect" and yet appear to call for an inquest on the basis already indicated, namely, cases involving a wholly unexpected death from natural causes which would not have occurred but for some culpable human failure . . . It is the combination of their unexpectedness and the culpable human failing that allowed them to happen which to my mind makes such deaths unnatural. Deaths by natural causes though undoubtedly they are, they should plainly never have happened and in that sense are unnatural'.

[1] [2001] QB 1206.
[2] [2001] QB 1206 at 1219.

13.13 Robert Walker LJ said[1]:

'The expression "unnatural death" in section 8(1)(a) of the Coroners Act 1988 does not have a single clearly defined meaning (As Lord Sumner said in a different context in *Weld-Blundell v Stephens* [1920] AC 956, 983, Everything that happens, happens in the order of nature and is therefore "natural".) Often "unnatural" means little more than abnormal and unexpected, and that rather muted shade of meaning would appear to be consistent with the legislative purposes of the Coroners Act 1988.

In particular, I doubt whether the naturalness or unnaturalness of a death should be determined exclusively in terms of causation, especially if that is seen as requiring a search for a single "dominant cause of death" . . . The better way forward is to look for a combination of circumstances rather than a single dominant cause.'

[1]   [2001] QB 1206 at 1222.

13.14 It follows that the omission to treat a natural disease process can give rise to the obligation to investigate a death that would otherwise be regarded as occurring by natural causes if that death was abnormal or unexpected. This might be taken to indicate that negligence during the lead up to an expected death by natural causes may not be sufficient to trigger the obligation to investigate. This is probably too simplistic an approach to take and even in those circumstances a death could be regarded as unnatural if it were caused or contributed to by failures in medical care, especially if those failures were sufficient to amount to 'neglect'.

SCOPE AND ART 2 OF THE ECHR

13.15 The question of scope is dealt with in more detail in CHAPTER 3.

13.16 Section 5 of the CJA 2009 provides that a coroner or jury may not express any opinion on any matter other than to answer the four statutory questions of who, when, where, and how (and if applicable in what circumstances) a person came by their death.

13.17 Section 10(2) of the CJA 2009 prohibits any determination of these issues being framed in such a way as to appear to determine any question of criminal liability or civil liability on the part of a named person. It follows from this that the coroner does not have the power to determine that an individual died as the consequence of clinical negligence, indeed a conclusion expressed in those terms would be unlawful. It does not however follow that acts or omissions that could amount to clinical negligence fall outside of the scope of the coroner's inquiry. Despite the prohibition under s 10(2) of the CJA 2009, a coroner is required to 'enquire into acts and omissions which are directly responsible for the death'[1]. The scope of the investigation and inquest 'is almost always going to be wider than the verdict eventually reached'[2]. That is not to say however that clinical negligence will not have a bearing upon the conclusion expressed by the coroner: positive acts, such as administering drugs, or undertaking surgery, would plainly fall within the scope of an inquest that sought to determine 'how' a deceased person came by their death and could result in conclusions of accident/misadventure or even unlawful killing[3]. Clinical omissions could in extreme cases amount to unlawful killing and certainly might lead the coroner to consider adding neglect to any conclusion. Similarly, conclusions regarding the contribution that medical care or the lack of it made to a death might feature within a narrative conclusion provided that the language adopted was reasonable[4].

[1]   *R v HM Coroner for East Sussex Western District, ex parte Homberg* (1994) 158 JP 357.

13.17 Clinical Inquests

[2] Per Baroness Hale in *R (Hurst) v London Northern District Coroner* [2007] UKHL 13.
[3] *R v Birmingham and Solihull Coroner ex p Benton* (1997) 1962 JP.
[4] See CHAPTER 6.

13.18 If s 5(2) of the CJA 2009 is engaged, the scope of the inquest will be broader and the coroner's conclusions directed more towards failings in the care provided to the deceased. The Art 2 duty is not generally imposed by the occurrence of clinical negligence in the context of state provided healthcare[1]. The position with regard to the interaction between clinical negligence and the coroner's obligations arising under Art 2 of the ECHR were summarised by Lord Burnett of Maldon CJ in *R (Maguire) v HM Senior Coroner for Blackpool and Fylde*[2] (himself making reference to the European Court of Human Rights case of *Lopes de Sousa*[3]) as follows[4]:

- In a medical negligence case the state's positive obligation under Art 2 ECHR is regulatory ie they must ensure appropriate measures to 'ensure implementation, including supervision and enforcement'.
- However, in very exceptional circumstances the state's substantive duty under Art 2 ECHR may also arise in medical negligence cases if the following criteria are met:
  - There must be much more than negligence alone – the patient's life must have been knowingly put in danger by denial of access to life-saving emergency treatment. This does *not* include situations where a patient has received deficient, incorrect or delayed treatment.
  - There must be a dysfunction in hospital services which is objectively and genuinely identifiable as systemic or structural in nature (ie not just something going badly wrong).
  - There must be a link between the dysfunction and the harm sustained.
  - The dysfunction must have resulted from the failure of the state to meet its obligation to provide a regulatory framework.

[1] *Iroko v HM Senior Coroner for Inner London South and others* [2020] EWHC 1753 (Admin); *R (Maquire) v HM Senior Coroner for Blackpool and Fylde* [2020] EWCA Civ 738; *R (Parkinson) v HM Senior Coroner for Inner London South* [2018] EWHC 1501 (Admin) following *Lopes de Sousa Fernandes v Portugal* (App No 56080/13) (2018) 66 EHRR 28, ECtHR.
[2] [2020] EWCA Civ 738.
[3] *Lopes de Sousa Fernandes v Portugal* (App No 56080/13) (2018) 66 EHRR 28, ECtHR.
[4] (2018) 66 EHRR 28 at [22]–[26].

13.19 The coroner should therefore draw distinction between 'ordinary' cases of clinical negligence, to which the procedural obligation under Art 2 of the ECHR does not apply and cases of systemic failure, to which it does apply[1]. The coroner should also take care to ensure that what are in truth allegations of individual fault are not 'dressed up' as systemic failures[2].

[1] Per Singh LJ in *R (Parkinson) v HM Senior Coroner for Inner London South* [2018] EWHC 1501 (Admin) at [90].
[2] Per Hickinbottom LJ in *Iroko v HM Senior Coroner for Inner London South and others* [2020] EWHC 1753 (Admin) at para 29, quoting Smith LJ in *R (Humberstone) v Legal Services Commission* [2010] EWCA Civ 1479 at [71].

CLINICAL NEGLIGENCE AND THE OPERATIONAL DUTY

13.20 Although most ordinary incidents of clinical negligence will not lead to an allegation of a breach of Art 2 of the ECHR, distinction must be drawn between ordinary patients receiving healthcare and the special category of individuals to whom the state owes an operational duty to protect life pursuant to Art 2. In *Rabone v Pennine Care NHS Foundation Trust*[1], the Supreme Court concluded that a voluntary patient receiving psychiatric treatment was owed an operational duty in relation to real and immediate risks to her life arising from the risk of suicide. It was however the risk of suicide and the extent to which she was vulnerable to being detained by the state that created with nexus in that case, as Baroness Hale observed[2]:

> 'In the light of all this, there can be little doubt that the operational duty under Article 2 is engaged in the case of a patient such as Miss Rabone. She was admitted to hospital precisely because of the risk that she would take her own life. The purpose of the admission was to prevent that happening and to bring about an improvement in her mental health such that she no longer posed a risk to herself . . . Although she was an informal patient, the hospital could at any time have prevented her leaving . . .
>
> The analogy with a patient detained under the Mental Health Act 1983 is much closer than the analogy with a patient admitted for treatment of a physical illness or injury. A patient receiving treatment in hospital for a physical illness or injury is in a quite different position. She has made an informed and autonomous choice to be in hospital and to receive the treatment in question. There is no power to detain her should she decide to leave. Any risk to her life stems from her physical condition. Any failure to prevent her death is likely to stem from what in the *Savage* case [2009] AC 681 Lord Rodger of Earlsferry called 'casual acts' of medical negligence rather than a deliberate decision. If there is a deliberate decision to take a risk, she should have given her informed consent to it. By contrast, if in fact she is known to be at risk of harm from the criminal acts of a third party (a risk which ironically it appears may well have arisen at this very hospital) the operational duty under Article 2 would indeed be engaged in her case too.'

[1] [2012] 2 AC 72.
[2] [2012] 2 AC 72 at [105] and [106].

13.21 It follows that in circumstances where an operational duty is owed to a psychiatric patient, whether voluntary or detained, acts of clinical negligence leading to the death of that patient by suicide or inadvertent or deliberate self-harm are capable of amounting to a breach of Art 2.

13.22 There is authority in support of the proposition that the state can owe an operational duty in relation to general healthcare provided to prisoners and thus Art 2 can be breached by acts of clinical negligence. In *Anguelova v Bulgaria*[1] the ECtHR held that the police breached an individual's Art 2 rights by delaying the provision of medical assistance to a prisoner who sustained a fractured skull prior to his arrest and thus 'contributed in a decisive manner to the fatal outcome'. In *Tais v France*[2] the ECtHR found that the failures of police officers to provide or arrange medical care to a prisoner who sustained accidental injuries in his cell amounted to a violation of the Art 2 obligation to protect life. In *Kats v Ukraine*[3] the death of a prisoner who was HIV positive and suffering from various chronic illnesses was found to be caused by inadequate medical treatment given to her by prison authorities and medical

13.22 Clinical Inquests

staff, in violation of Art 2. In *Tarariyeva v Russia*[4] the ECtHR found that a prisoner with gastro-duodenitis was not given competent or adequate medical care in violation of Art 2. The court cited the proposition from *Keenan v United Kingdom*[5] that 'persons in custody are in a vulnerable position and that the authorities are under a duty to protect them'[6].

[1] (2004) EHRR 31.
[2] (App No 39922/03), 1 June 2006, ECtHR.
[3] (2010) EHRR 44.
[4] (2009) 48 EHRR 26.
[5] (2001) 33 EHRR 38.
[6] (2009) 48 EHRR 26 at [73]–[74].

13.23 In *R (Hall) v University College Hospital and the Secretary of State for Justice*[1] the Divisional Court accepted that the operational duty under Art 2 was engaged in a claim based upon the alleged lack of care by prison medical staff and errors of clinical judgment on the part of an NHS trust in discharging a chronically sick and disabled prisoner from hospital to prison, although in that case the court did not identify a violation of that prisoner's Art 2 rights.

[1] [2013] EWHC 198 (Admin).

13.24 In *Dolly Daniel and Owen Daniel v St George's Healthcare NHS Trust and London Ambulance Service*[1] Lang J accepted that in the case of a prisoner: 'since it is the state which is subject to the operational duty, it can apply not only to the detaining authority but also to other public authorities who from time to time may have responsibility for the detainee, such as a hospital or ambulance staff'[2]. It follows that if proven to be causatively relevant, failures that might otherwise be described as clinical negligence on the part of NHS staff providing care to prisoners, inside or outside of prison can give rise to a violation of the operational duty under Art 2.

[1] [2016] EWHC 23 (QB).
[2] [2016] EWHC 23 (QB) at [29].

13.25 Given the analogous position between prisoners and those detained under the Mental Health Act 1983, there is no obvious reason why acts of clinical negligence relating to the provision of general health care to detained psychiatric patients. The position is likely to be different for voluntary psychiatric patients to whom a narrower operational duty is owed, relating specifically to the risk of suicide and analogous forms of self-harm[1].

[1] *Rabone v Pennine Care NHS Foundation Trust* [2012] 2 AC 72.

DISCLOSURE AND MEDICAL RECORDS

13.26 This is addressed at length within CHAPTER 4. Within the context of healthcare inquests, the main source of documentary evidence is likely to be the deceased person's medical records. These may be sought by the coroner, who has the power to order the production of any documents in the custody or control of an individual or organisation which relate to a matter that is relevant to an inquest[1]. In most if not all cases this will not be necessary and there will be an expectation that relevant documents, such as medical records, will be provided to the coroner without the need to serve a specific notice

Serious untoward incident reports and the duty of candour 13.31

requiring that. The Chief Coroner's Guide to the Coroners and Justice Act 2009 notes that:

> 'Coroners should not be too hasty to exercise these powers. They should only be used where necessary and where other methods have failed. Much can be achieved by agreement with, for example, local hospitals, on regular procedures for the production of witness statements, medical notes and reports.[2]'

[1] CJA 2009, Sch 5, s 1(1)(b) and s 1(2)(b).
[2] Paragraph 133.

13.27 The coroner is obliged to provide copies of documents held by the coroner to interested parties where those documents are relevant to the inquest[1]. Thus, if medical records are disclosed to the coroner, they are likely to be disclosed to all of the interested parties. When disclosing medical records to the coroner it would be sensible to ensure that only those records that are relevant to the inquest are disclosed and preferably in an organised, easily navigated and paginated bundle, which can be of use to the parties and witnesses at any inquest hearing.

[1] Coroners (Inquests) Rules 2013, SI 2013/1616, r 13(1).

13.28 Unlike the civil courts, the coroner has no power to order that a party give disclosure of documents directly to another interested party. Control over the documentary evidence and decisions about their relevance are within the coroner's discretion, although that must be exercised reasonably and fairly.

13.29 The family or representatives of the deceased have a free-standing right to obtain copies of the deceased's medical records pursuant to s 3 of the Access to Health Records Act 1990. The NHS trust or health authority holding those records will be expected to provide them within 40 days of any formal request and upon payment of a statutory fee. The fact that an inquest is ongoing and not yet complete is not a valid basis for refusing to comply with a request pursuant to s 3 of the Access to Health Records Act 1990[1].

[1] *Stobart v Nottinghamshire Health Authority* [1992] 3 Med LR 284.

13.30 The relevant documents will not necessarily be limited to clinical notes, they will also include any serious untoward incident report prepared by the NHS trust and any other documentation created in response to the death, subject to its relevance.

SERIOUS UNTOWARD INCIDENT REPORTS AND THE DUTY OF CANDOUR

13.31 Pursuant to reg 20 of the Health and Social Care Act 2008 (Regulated Activities) Regulations 2014[1], healthcare providers registered with the CQC owe the following statutory duty:

(a) To act in an open and transparent way with relevant persons in relation to care and treatment provided to service users in carrying out a regulated activity[2].
(b) In the event of a notifiable safety incident[3] occurring involving the death of a patient, to notify a person acting on behalf of the deceased person that the incident has occurred[4].

13.31 *Clinical Inquests*

(c) The notification must provide an account, which to the best of the registered person's knowledge is true, of all the facts the registered person knows about the incident as at the date of notification[5].
(d) This notification must be followed by a written notification setting out the same information, details of any enquiries to be undertaken and the results of those enquiries and an apology[6].

[1] SI 2014/2936.
[2] Regulation 20(1).
[3] A notifiable safety incident means 'any unintended or unexpected incident that occurred in respect of a service user during the provision of a regulated activity that, in the reasonable opinion of a health care professional, could result in, or appears to have resulted in: the death of the service user, where the death relates directly to the incident rather than to the natural course of the service user's illness or underlying condition, or severe harm, moderate harm or prolonged psychological harm to the service user' (reg 20(8)).
[4] Regulation 20(2).
[5] Regulation 20(3).
[6] Regulation 20(4).

13.32 The practical effect of this is that those who believe that they have caused death through their clinical negligence, or through the clinical negligence of their employees, owe a statutory duty to notify the family of the deceased of that fact. The obligation to investigate is wider, though, and pursuant to reg 20(8), a registered healthcare provider will be obliged to undertake an investigation into any unintended or unexpected death and provide a written account of that investigation. That investigation must be open and transparent. Following the Health and Social Care Act 2008, NHS England set up a Serious Incident Framework, which was revised following implementation of the Health and Social Care Act 2012. In cases where it is suspected or suggested that a death occurred due to clinical acts or omissions the NHS trust responsible for the deceased patient's care should undertake a Serious Untoward Incident Investigation (SUII). The findings of that investigation should be recorded in a report and provided to the family of the deceased. The report is also likely to be considered to be a relevant document for the purposes of the inquest, both in its findings and in its recommendations to prevent future deaths. There is no obligation that the investigation be undertaken by an independent body and the report is commonly prepared by employees of the NHS trust. Following the duty of candour that investigation should however be undertaken in an open and transparent way.

EXPERT EVIDENCE

13.33 An individual or organisation investigating a potential claim for damages arising from alleged clinical negligence is likely to obtain independent expert evidence. Whilst it is often tempting for a family or those representing a healthcare provider to reinforce their arguments about the standard of care provided to the deceased person by disclosing their expert evidence to the coroner, this practice carries the inevitable consequence that copies of those reports will be disclosed to the other interested parties[1]. As disclosure of expert evidence in clinical negligence proceedings is usually undertaken on a mutual basis after the commencement of the claim there is a clear tactical disadvantage in many cases in providing early unilateral disclosure of expert evidence that would otherwise be privileged. That tactical disadvantage would be increased

Expert evidence **13.37**

if the expert witness to be used in litigation were to be called at the inquest and be subject to cross-examination by the other interested parties. Although a strong performance by the expert might add force to the interested party's arguments in the subsequent litigation, it would also provide the other parties with the opportunity to test that evidence and adapt their case in response to it. If the expert performed badly under cross-examination, it could severely undermine the party's position in subsequent litigation. In most cases it is better for the interested parties to avoid bringing their litigation experts into the inquest forum and instead use their evidence behind the scenes.

[1] The Court of Appeal (Northern Ireland) concluded in *Re Ketcher's Application for Judicial Review* [2020] 6 WLUK 195 that litigation privilege did not apply to expert reports provided to the coroner by interested parties, in this case the families of the deceased, and that as a consequence the coroner was entitled to order that those reports should be disclosed to all of the interested parties.

13.34 The coroner has the discretion to instruct medical experts and should call an expert if the scope of the enquiry requires it[1]. In *R (Goodson) v Bedfordshire and Luton Coroner*[2] Richards J observed that in relation to the lawfulness of the decision not to call expert evidence[3]: 'Everything must depend on the particular circumstances, including the expertise of the coroner himself and the precise nature of the issues and evidence before him'.

[1] *R v Inner North London Coroner Ex p Linnane (No 2)* (1990) 155 JP 343.
[2] [2004] EWHC 2931 (Admin).
[3] [2004] EWHC 2931 (Admin) at [71].

13.35 Although the engagement of the ECHR in the inquest process does not automatically obligate a coroner to call expert evidence[1] it is difficult to see how a coroner could fairly determine questions relating to the quality of healthcare provided in an Art 2 case without calling independent expert evidence. Various cases before the Divisional Court demonstrate that a coroner who proceeds to hear an Art 2 inquest involving alleged clinical negligence in the absence of independent expert evidence does so at considerable risk[2].

[1] *Re (LePage) v HM Assistant Deputy Coroner for Inner South London* [2012] EWHC 1485 (Admin).
[2] *R (Warren) v Northamptonshire Assistant Deputy Coroner* [2008] EWHC 966 (Admin), *R (Stanley) v HM Coroner for Inner North London* [2003] EWHC 1180 (Admin), *R (Wright) v Secretary of State for the Home Department* [2001] EWHC 520 (Admin).

13.36 The same argument could be advanced in any case where the scope of the inquest involves an enquiry into technical medical issues. In *N (a child) v HM Coroner for Liverpool*[1] a coroner was criticised by the Divisional Court for not calling expert evidence regarding the standard of care to be expected of a police doctor and issues relating to causation. In the view of the Divisional Court, this prevented the coroner from holding a full enquiry into the deceased's death in custody. It is notable that this case was not one conducted pursuant to Art 2 of the ECHR.

[1] [2001] EWHC 922 (Admin).

13.37 Nevertheless, inquests touching upon deaths in clinical care are common, and frequently coroners will hear complex medical evidence from treating clinicians without relying upon the assistance of an independent expert. As a representative how can you challenge such evidence? Consider

13.37 Clinical Inquests

what resources you can deploy. If you are able to obtain an expert's report critical of the care prior to inquest, you could rely on it for the purposes of cross examination of witnesses only, without disclosing it to the coroner and waiving privilege. Where you have no report, check whether there are relevant guidelines or protocols accessible online. Consider:

- NICE guidelines.
- Local guidance.
- Standard clinical texts eg GP's handbook, The British National Formulary, the Handbook of Emergency Medicine.
- Websites such as patient.co.uk.

These documents may assist you as clinical lay person questioning professional clinician witnesses.

IMPACT OF CLINICAL NEGLIGENCE ON CONCLUSIONS

13.38 In the absence of the broader investigatory obligation pursuant to s 5 of the CJA 2009, many incidents of casual clinical negligence, whether by deliberate act or omission will have only a limited impact upon the conclusion that the coroner or jury return. In *R v Birmingham and Solihull Coroner ex p Benton*[1] the Divisional Court addressed the effect that clinical negligence might have upon a short-form conclusion, per Kay J:

> 'The first [scenario] is where a person is suffering from a potentially fatal condition and medical intervention does no more than fail to prevent death. In such circumstances the underlying cause of death is the condition that proved fatal and in such a case, the correct verdict would be death from natural causes. This would be the case even if the medical treatment that had been given was viewed generally by the medical profession as the wrong treatment. All the more so is this the case where such a person is not treated at all, even if the failure to give the treatment was negligent . . .
>
> On the other hand, where a person is suffering from a condition which does not in any way threaten his life and such person undergoes treatment which for whatever reason causes death, then assuming that there is no question of unlawful killing the verdict should be death by accident/misadventure. Just as the recording of death by natural causes does not absolve the doctors of fault so the recording of death by accident/misadventure does not imply fault.'

[1] (1997) 1962 JP 807.

13.39 It follows that in the absence of a basis for stating that the alleged clinical negligence would also amount to neglect[1] clinical negligence would lead to a short-form conclusion of accident/misadventure in the case of death arising from a deliberate clinical action or natural causes (if the precipitating cause of death was natural) in most cases of omission. If representing a family at an inquest involving issues of healthcare it is therefore sensible to warn them as soon as possible that the conclusion of the inquest may not describe the concerns that they have, and will be prohibited from appearing to determine any questions of civil liability and in particular will not contain words such as 'negligent'[2].

[1] See CHAPTER 6.
[2] CJA 2009, s 10(2).

13.40 The coroner has a broader discretion when delivering a narrative conclusion. Although they will still be prohibited from appearing to determine any questions of civil liability the conclusion could nonetheless cover the medical care provided to the deceased. The Chief Coroner's Guidance No 17 says that[1]:

> 'In a non-Article 2 case a narrative conclusion should be a brief, neutral, factual statement; it should not express any judgment or opinion. By contrast a conclusion in an Article 2 case may be judgmental . . . the difference in some cases may be slight and not much more than a matter of words. For example, in a non-Article 2 case judgmental words such as "missed opportunities" or "inadequate failures" should probably be avoided. Bur rather than, for example, saying that "There was a missed opportunity when the registrar failed to seek advice from the consultant", the coroner could say just as effectively: The evidence leads me to find that the registrar did not seek advice from the consultant who was nearby and available at the time and the registrar knew that. The registrar acted on his own.'

[1] Chief Coroner's Guidance No 17, Conclusions: Short-form and narrative (revised 14 January 2016), para 34.

Chapter 14

DEATHS IN CUSTODY

14.1 Inquests concerning deaths in prisons, young offender institutions, police custody and psychiatric hospitals touch upon the nexus between the state's role as a custodian and the lives of some of the most vulnerable in society. There is therefore a high public interest in scrutinising the circumstances of such deaths, which is reflected in the requirements of coronial law. In light of the encompassing role the state plays when detaining an individual, the obligations on the custodial body are high and subject to rigorous investigation.

14.2 Further, these types of inquest are almost inevitably emotive. Families may have had limited contact with the deceased prior to the fatal events. They may also have limited trust in the relevant institution, as it will often have been only officers of that institution that came into contact with the deceased in the crucial final minutes, hours or days.

14.3 Deaths in custody can be separated into three types of fatal incident:
(a) suicide/self-inflicted deaths;
(b) use of excessive force/restraint;
(c) failures in medical care.

Each of these categories of inquest are considered in turn below.

14.4 In light of the holistic needs of detainees that custodial bodies are required to meet, inquests in this area are often multi-party affairs. As well as the family and institution (for example the Ministry of Justice/Prison service; Home Office in immigration deaths; police constabulary), the providers of medical care are often an interested person, as well as private organisations that might provide ancillary clinical services or detainee conveyance. Where a conflict of interest arises, or a relevant officer/professional fears the repercussions of the investigation's findings, individuals involved in the care provided to the detainee may also need to be separately represented.

14.5 In accordance with s 1(2) of the CJA 2009, a coronial investigation must be opened into every death in custody or otherwise in state detention. Inquests touching upon deaths in state detention usually engage Art 2 of the European Convention on Human Rights[1]. An exception applies to custody deaths in which are established to be from natural causes and which do not therefore give rise to arguable state responsibility[2]. Article 2 extends to investigations relating to those detained for mental health treatment and also extends to voluntary patients, who are not formally sectioned under the Mental Health

14.5 Deaths in Custody

Act 1984, if the custodial authority would have been in a position to detain the patient if they chose to leave[3]. Custody does not include custody overseas[4]. A person is considered to be in custody if they are serving a custodial sentence at the time of death, even if they are not physically in custody when the death occurs[5].

[1] The definition of 'state detention' is considered in CHAPTER 15; the engagement of Art 2 is considered fully in CHAPTER 3.
[2] *R (Tyrell) v HM Senior Coroner for County Durham and Darlington* [2016] EWHC 1892 (Admin).
[3] *Rabone v Pennine Care NHS Trust* [2012] UKSC 2; *Letts v Lord Chancellor* [2015] EWHC 402 (Admin).
[4] *Shafi v HM Senior Coroner for East London* [2015] EWHC 2106 (Admin).
[5] *R v HM Coroner for Inner London North District ex parte Linnane* [1989] 1 WLR 395.

14.6 A jury is also required by statute where the death in custody is a violent or unnatural one, or the cause of death is unknown[1]. Legal aid funding is in principle available to families by reason of the engagement of the investigative duty under Art 2 of the European Convention on Human Rights (ECHR)[2].

[1] Section 7(2)(a) CJA 2009.
[2] See CHAPTER 9 for further as regards legal aid funding.

14.7 The short form conclusions most often in the court's mind in death in custody inquests include suicide, accidental death and unlawful killing. A rider of neglect may also be relevant[1].

[1] See CHAPTER 6 as to the law on different short form conclusions and as to neglect riders.

SUICIDE AND SELF-INFLICTED DEATHS

14.8 Over a quarter of all deaths in prison are self-inflicted and such fatalities will be the subject of coronial investigation[1]. Inquests into self-inflicted deaths in custody are sadly commonplace, and have played an important role in developing coronial law. In *R (Sacker) v West Yorkshire Coroner*[2], Lord Hope said[3]:

> 'It is hard to fault the attention that has been given to this problem by senior management in the Prison Service and by the Prison Inspectorate. There is a high level of awareness, and much effort has been devoted to improving the system for the prevention of suicides. But every time one occurs in a prison the effectiveness of the system is called into question. So all the facts surrounding every suicide must be thoroughly, impartially and carefully investigated. The purpose of the investigation is to open up the circumstances of the death to public scrutiny. This ensures that those who were at fault will be made accountable for their actions. But it also has a vital part to play in the correction of mistakes and the search for improvements. There must be a rigorous examination in public of the operation at every level of the systems and procedures which are designed to prevent self-harm and to save lives.'

[1] *Safety in Custody Statistics, England and Wales – Deaths in Prison Custody to March 2020* (Ministry of Justice, 30 April 2020).
[2] [2004] UKHL 11.
[3] At [11].

14.9 A number of common themes and issues arise in this type of investigation. The starting point will often be whether a care plan and risk assessment were in place for the deceased[1]. If so, consideration will need to be given to

Suicide and self-inflicted deaths **14.14**

whether the plan/assessment was devised with appropriate rigour. This will need to be considered in light of the relevant national and local guidance. Common issues include: was sufficient background information obtained? Was there engagement with the detainee, friends and family? Were other records, in particular clinical records, considered and were other professionals and bodies contacted to ensure the requisite multi-disciplinary approach? Were the conclusions of the assessment appropriate, clearly set out and communicated? Was the level of risk and observation requirements properly categorised? Were relevant triggers or suicide signatures identified? Was the plan formulated in the timescales required[2]?

[1] In the prison setting this would usually be contained in the Assessment, Care in Custody and Teamwork (ACCT) document, which is intended to be a central source of information when dealing with prisoners that are at risk of suicide or self-harm. In prisoner deaths touching upon events outside of prison, the Person Escort Record (PER) forms will be high relevant. For young offenders the ASSET assessment will be the key framework. For mental health patients it is the Care Programme Approach documentation.

[2] The ACCT process in particular has a number of steps that must be undertaken in the first hour (discussion with the prisoner and formulation of an Immediate Action Plan) and first 24 hours (a first case multidisciplinary case review) once the framework is opened. Prison Service Instruction 64/2011 is the policy which sets out the requirement of the ACCT process.

14.10 The mere formulation of a plan is, of course, only a starting point. Plans must be put into action. Observations need to be undertaken as prescribed. Usually the local and national guidelines require observations to be more than a visual check. They have a therapeutic purpose and should be an opportunity for interaction and reassurance.

14.11 Internal communication of the risk assessment is also important. Handovers can be a point of vulnerability in institutional systems and care should be taken by practitioners to check that systems were in place to allow officers coming onto the shift to undertake their protective work adequately. A prisoner arriving at a prison, most commonly from court, should be accompanied by a Prisoner Escort Record, which should record any concerns of custodial staff at court and where applicable a police station regarding a risk of self-harm or harm to others. Staff numbers and training may also be relevant.

14.12 Risk assessments are not snapshots. The care plan for a detainee should be a live document and subject to updates as and when required. Further the plan and its enforcement should be supervised properly.

14.13 Property management and environmental issues can become the focus of some inquests. In hanging cases, the source and point of any ligature are relevant. Were sufficient property restrictions, checks and searches in place? Should any ligature points have been addressed? Contraband policies are also relevant to drug-induced fatalities.

14.14 The emergency response of officers to acute events can also come into issue. Whilst the window of opportunity to assist can be narrow, early detection of an event, attendance and the rendering of first aid/resuscitation can save lives. Attention should be given to the training of staff, procedures and protocols, the availability of resuscitation equipment and the competence of the responders on the day.

14.15 *Deaths in Custody*

14.15 Where the alleged deficiencies relate to the absence of timely observations or a delayed response to an acute event, establishing that a particular failure caused or contributed to the death can be difficult. It can be the case that earlier observations would not have provided the institution with sufficient opportunity to prevent the death. That said, the therapeutic nature of observations may lead a jury to conclude that observations would have changed the outcome even if they had not come across the detainee taking or preparing to take their own life. As regards the response to acute events, windows of rendering life-saving care are narrow. The court may need the assistance of an expert intensivist to reach safe conclusions. Advocates should be careful to consider how the evidence and factual circumstances of a particular death fit into the complex framework of potential domestic and ECHR law inquest conclusions.

See CHAPTER 15 for further detail of inquests involving suicides.

EXCESSIVE FORCE

14.16 Deaths arising from the use of force or restraint by custodial officers are, for obvious reasons, highly emotive. Families will be deeply concerned that their loved ones have died from the positive acts of state officials, whilst the officers themselves may be at risk of loss of their employment and/or criminal prosecution.

14.17 The precise circumstances of the particular engagement will be highly relevant and should be judged alongside the training provided to the officers and guidelines (local and national) on the use of force and restraint. The police and regulatory bodies, such as the Prisons and Probation Ombudsman or the Independent Office for Police Complaints, may be involved in the proceedings or at least will want to keep a close eye on the investigation.

MEDICAL CARE

14.18 Where the death results from failures of clinical judgement, treatment and advice, the proceedings will mirror those for non-detainees in comparable clinical settings. The nuances for cases involving those in detention often arise from systemic or communication problems. Unfortunately, there can be delays in identifying that vulnerable individuals require medical care at all. Appointments may be delayed through administrative failures or missed through lack of secure conveyance. In modern custodial institutions clinical care is invariably contracted out to a separate healthcare provider (whether an NHS trust or a private provider). There may be breakdowns in communication between the custodial institution, the medical care provider associated with the institution and the NHS services in the community. Accordingly, deaths arising from such systemic or communication failures often involve multiple parties beyond the family of the deceased. The operational duty to protect life under Art 2 ECHR applies to the untimely provision of adequate non-mental health clinical care inside prison and the arrangement of clinical care outside prison for prisoners[1].

[1] *Daniel v St George's Healthcare NHS Trust* [2016] EWHC 23 (QB), [2016] 4 WLR 32 at [22]–[29]; *Tarariyeva v Russia* (2006) 48 EHRR 609, *Kats v Ukraine* (2010) 51 EHRR 44.

DISCLOSURE

14.19 The extent of relevant disclosure will be fact sensitive. The following types or categories of document may be relevant depending on the circumstances:

- post-mortem report – a forensic pathology report will often be required;
- the deceased's medical records;
- risk assessments and care plans[1];
- observation records;
- search, property and detention logs;
- any footage, either from CCTV or body worn;
- 999 recordings or ambulance records – emergency responders may be the first independent eyes to attend the scene;
- staff training records;
- local policies and procedures;
- national policies and procedures;
- incident investigations, whether by the institution or regulatory/inspecting bodies;
- material arising from investigations, such as witness statement or interviews.
- PPO or IOPC reports and material.

[1] In the prison setting this would usually be contained in the Assessment, Care in Custody and Teamwork (ACCT) document, which is intended to be a central source of information when dealing with prisoners that are at risk of suicide or self-harm. In prisoner deaths touching upon events outside of prison, the Person Escort Record (PER) forms will be high relevant. For young offenders the ASSET assessment will be the key framework. For mental health patients it is the Care Programme Approach documentation.

PARALLEL STATE INVESTIGATIONS

14.20 Where an individual dies in prison custody, including deaths by apparent natural causes, an investigation must be carried out by the Prison and Probation Ombudsman. The Independent Office for Police Conduct similarly investigates every death following contact with the police. These organisations reach conclusions regarding the factual circumstances of the death for the purposes of learning and preventing deaths in the future. The investigators interview relevant witnesses and collect evidence. The investigations and reports of the IOPC and PPO are often important sources of evidence later at inquest. The status of a report and its conclusions may be contested, and an issue is likely to arise as to its admissibility at the inquest. However, the evidence on which the reports are based, often including interviews with witnesses, is likely to be prima facie admissible and can be of important evidential value.

14.21 *Deaths in Custody*

EXPERT EVIDENCE

14.21 In most cases the medical cause of death will be clearly identified by the pathologist. Expert evidence, most likely from an intensivist, may be necessary to consider whether earlier or better emergency intervention by staff might have saved the deceased's life. Similarly, expert medical evidence may be required to consider issues of causation in medical deaths. In a mental health setting, a report from a forensic psychiatrist can assist where the overall care and treatment plan may have been deficient. Coroner's have a wide discretion as to whether instruct and call expert witnesses which is dealt with at CHAPTER 4.

14.22 Coroners will often be tempted to try and rely on treating clinicians to comment on causation. In contentious cases, their lack of independence may be problematic. It may even raise issues as to the compliance with the investigative duty under Art 2 ECHR. Further, where their evidence might touch on complex or nuanced issues, it may be overly burdensome to require a treating clinician to undertake the necessary review of evidence and literature required to form a sufficiently authoritative opinion.

CLIENT CARE

14.23 Whether representing the family or an institution, deaths in custody can be a harrowing experience for those involved. The process needs to be clearly explained by practitioners. The expectations of family members – who may consider that foul play, criminal conduct or negligence is involved – need to be managed. If representing an institution, practitioners need also to be mindful of the welfare of officers that have been involved in traumatic incidents, which can result in psychological distress and fear as to personal repercussions.

Chapter 15
MENTAL HEALTH AND MENTAL CAPACITY

INTRODUCTION

15.1 This section is intended to assist practitioners with the legal and practical issues that are likely to arise during coronial proceedings where the deceased was suffering from a mental illness and/or lacked capacity. Mental capacity and mental health law are areas of legal practice in their own right. A detailed exposition of either area is beyond the scope of this book and chapter, and readers are referred to the specialist texts in the fields[1]. However, inquests touching upon the deaths of persons suffering from mental illness and/or lacking capacity are sadly common place. Further, the care received by mental health patients and those lacking capacity, and their legal status under the Mental Health Act 1983 (MHA 1983) and Mental Capacity Act 2005 (MCA 2005), are of relevance to inquest practitioners in that they can affect: (i) coronial law questions of jurisdiction; (ii) the scope of the inquiry and the engagement of Art 2 of the European Convention on Human Rights (ECHR); (iii) whether the inquest should be heard by a jury; and (iv) the determinations and conclusions reached at inquest.

[1] See for instance *Court of Protection Practice* (Lexis Nexis, 2020).

15.2 Representatives at inquests may appear on behalf of mental health trusts, local authorities, private care homes, individual doctors, registered mental health nurses, or carers. They may represent the families of vulnerable persons who were receiving mental health care and/or lacked capacity at the time of their death. Such families may be considering bringing fatal accident, clinical negligence and/or Human Rights Act 1998 (HRA 1998) civil claims after the conclusion of the inquest. This chapter will therefore provide brief outlines of the principles and practice of modern mental health care and capacity law as they are relevant to the inquest practitioner. See also the chapter regarding healthcare and inquests at **13.3** for further detail in that respect.

MENTAL HEALTH

Representing clients at mental health inquests

15.3 In 2019 there were 4,620 suicide conclusions in coroners' courts in England and Wales. As discussed below, a conclusion of suicide requires a

15.3 Mental Health and Mental Capacity

finding of intent to take one's own life in English law. It follows that the number of deaths resulting directly from intentional self-harm where there was no intent to die, or indirectly from other mental health conditions, will be higher. Suicide and self-harm are a sad feature of coronial practice. Cases involving self-inflicted deaths, especially where the deceased was in the care and custody of the state, have established some of the key principles of coronial law.

15.4 In the landmark majority decision in *R (Maughan) v HM Senior Coroner for Oxfordshire*[1] the Supreme Court emphasised the important role played by inquests in suicide prevention in England and Wales. Lady Arden stated 'inquests are concerned today not with criminal justice . . . They take a new and different purpose in a case such as this'[2] ie to 'identify lessons to be learnt for the future'[3] and prevent future deaths. Lady Arden commented on the changing attitudes towards suicide as one reason to justify lowering the standard of proof for suicide to the balance of probabilities, implicitly rejecting the submission that there is a 'close affinity between suicide and a criminal offence'[4] and instead noting that there is no longer such a stigma associated with intentional self-inflicted death. This reflects society's changing attitudes towards mental health in general, and marks the fact that the balance is now in favour of reporting suicides whenever they occur in order to ensure statistics are as accurate (and therefore as helpful) as possible.

[1] [2020] UKSC 46.
[2] [2020] UKSC 46 at [81].
[3] [2020] UKSC 46 at [8].
[4] [2020] UKSC 46 at [67].

15.5 Mental health inquests by their nature relive traumatic events, and they can take their toll on the wellbeing of coroners and practitioners. But for the family of the deceased, and those involved in the deceased's care prior to their death, the process may be traumatising in itself[1]. It is important that representatives are sensitive to clients' needs and wellbeing at all times. However, they should also be careful to manage expectations regarding the process and what it can achieve, to set out the purpose of the proceedings and the prohibition on imparting blame and civil or criminal liability, the relevance of scope and the matters that will not be investigated, and what the likely outcomes may be. It is, of course, not always possible to get the answers clients want at inquests, but it is the role of the representative (insofar as the law permits them to do so) to ask the questions they want answered, to assist them in putting forward their account of events (where relevant), and to ensure as positive an outcome as possible for them in challenging circumstances.

[1] See eg the 2020 Royal College of Psychiatrists and University of Oxford resource for practising psychiatrists on when patients commit suicide, which can be found at: https://www.psych.ox.ac.uk/news/new-resource-for-psychiatrists-patient-suicide.

Inquest law and mental healthcare

Jurisdiction

STATE DETENTION

15.6 An investigation must be opened under s 1 of the CJA 2009 into the death of every patient who dies whilst detained under s 2 or 3 of the MHA 1983[1]. As set out in CHAPTER 2 at **2.86**, once an investigation is opened, an inquest must take place in every case unless the power to discontinue is used following post mortem under s 4 of the CJA 2009. This is unlikely to be applied in the case of a death in mental health detention. Whilst a post mortem may well reveal the medical cause of death prior to inquest, given the need for public scrutiny of deaths in state detention and care, the coroner is likely to think that the investigation remains necessary.

[1] Because s 1(2) CJA 2009 applies wherever the coroner has reason to suspect that the deceased died whilst in custody or state detention.

VIOLENT DEATHS

15.7 An investigation must also be opened under s 1 CJA 2009 into all self-inflicted deaths, whether intentional or not, and whether they occur whilst the deceased is receiving mental health care or not, because such deaths are 'violent deaths' within the meaning of s 1(2) CJA 2009.

15.8 Whether an investigation must be opened into the death of a voluntary inpatient (a mental health inpatient who is not detained under s 2 or 3 MHA 1983) in a mental hospital which occurred for physical health reasons, such as a naturally occurring disease process or due to active medical treatment, will be determined in accordance with the normal principles of coronial jurisdiction set out in CHAPTER 2 at **2.22**.

Scope, determinations and Art 2 ECHR

15.9 The law relating to inquests and Art 2 ECHR is set out in CHAPTER 3. The positive operational duty to protect life applies to all patients detained under the MHA 1983 at risk of suicide[1]. According to the judgment of the Grand Chamber of the ECtHR in *Fernandes Oliveira v Portugal*, it also applies to all voluntary mental health *inpatients* at risk of suicide[2]. As discussed at **3.92**, a 'general' operational duty in respect of such patients, as referred to in *Oliveira*, may appear to widen the application of the duty beyond the Supreme Court's decision in *Rabone*[3], where it was held by the Supreme Court to apply only when there has been a sufficient assumption and control by of the individual by the state. However, in *Oliveira* the Grand Chamber emphasised that 'the specific measures required will depend on the particular circumstances of the case, and those specific circumstances will often differ depending on whether the patient is voluntarily or involuntarily hospitalised'[4]. In the case of detained patients, 'the court, of its own assessment, may apply a stricter standard of scrutiny'[5].

[1] *Savage v South Essex Partnership NHS Foundation Trust (MIND and others intervening)* [2009] AC 681.

15.9 *Mental Health and Mental Capacity*

² *Fernandes Oliveira v Portugal* (2019) 69 EHRR 8.
³ *Rabone v Pennine Care Trust (INQUEST and others intervening)* [2012] UKSC 2, [2012] 2 AC 72.
⁴ (2019) 69 EHRR 8 at [124].
⁵ (2019) 69 EHRR 8 at [124].

15.10 A question arises as to whether the operational duty to protect life will ever arise in a community mental health care context. In the Supreme Court in *Rabone* Lord Dyson observed that the jurisprudence of the operational duty is young and that the ECtHR has tended to expand its remit[1]. In *Rabone*[2] the key factor militating towards the recognition of the duty was the control assumed by the state over the deceased. Lord Dyson observed that 'in circumstances of sufficient vulnerability, the ECtHR has been prepared to find a breach of the operational duty even where there has been no assumption of control by the state'[3]. Lord Dyson gave the example of *Z v UK*[4] in the context of Art 3 ECHR.

¹ (2019) 69 EHRR 8 at [25].
² *Rabone v Pennine Care Trust (INQUEST and others intervening)* [2012] UKSC 2, [2012] 2 AC 72.
³ 2012] UKSC 2, [2012] 2 AC 72 at [23].
⁴ (2001) 34 EHRR 97.

15.11 However, in *R (Maguire) v HM Senior Coroner for Blackpool & Flyde & Others*[1] the Court of Appeal held that the vulnerability of a care home resident subject to the Deprivation of Liberty Safeguards (DoLS) under the MCA 2005 was not *in itself* sufficient to engage the duty, where there was no correlation between the purpose for which the duty to protect was imposed and the nature of the subsequent alleged failure to protect life (the deceased died as a result of complications unconnected to the reasons why she was deprived of her liberty).

¹ [2020] EWCA Civ 738.

15.12 In *R (Lee) v HM Assistant Coroner for Sunderland and Others*[1], the High Court held that the coroner had not adequately considered the relevant evidence and law on the question of whether an extension of the law beyond *Rabone* was required in a case involving the suicide of a young person at risk in community mental health care. The court made no finding as to whether the operational duty should have been expanded, but emphasised the relevance of the 'threefold factors of assumed responsibility, vulnerability, and risk' to the assessment[2].

¹ [2019] EWHC 3227 (Admin).
² [2019] EWHC 3227 (Admin) at [30], [38].

15.13 The patient in *Lee* was young (unhelpfully her age is not set out in the judgment), had a diagnosis of emotionally unstable personality disorder, was subject to crisis community care as the time of her death, had been detained previously under the MHA, and was considered at the time of her death to be a 'moderate risk of self-harm which did not justify her readmission to hospital'. She may be considered to have been in the upper range of community mental healthcare patients in terms of the state's assumption of responsibility to her. It is unhelpful that the High Court did not resolve for itself the question whether the Art 2 duty applied in her case. Community mental health suicides of that type are not uncommon, and it would assist coroners, practitioners, and families to have clarity in whether Art 2 applies in such cases. The ECtHR places particular importance on the protection of the mentally ill. In cases where the deceased was particularly vulnerable, and there had been a significant level of assumption of responsibility by crisis services, advocates should consider carefully arguments for and against the engagement of the Art 2 operational duty.

15.14 Practitioners should also bear in mind the Art 2 systemic duty in mental health care cases. In *Lee*, HHJ Mark Raeside QC applied the restrictive criteria for a systemic breach established in *Lopes de Sousa Fernandes v Portugal*[1] to this question[2]. It is respectfully submitted that he did so in error. Mental health patients are considered to be a particular category of persons deserving of the protection of the Convention by the ECtHR, they are particularly vulnerable and dependent on state services, and it is submitted that restrictive principles regarding alleged systemic breaches in general clinical care should not apply.

[1] (2018) 66 EHRR 28.
[2] See CHAPTER 3 for details of these criteria.

15.15 It has not been categorically determined by any authority that every self-inflicted death in mental health detention or inpatient care should trigger the investigative duty as amounting to a suspected or arguable breach of the operational duty. This is the case for prisoners[1], however, and it is submitted that the same principles should apply to mental health inpatients, who are in any event likely to be patients for their own protection, by contrast with sentenced prisoners, who are detained for the purposes of punishment.

[1] *R (Tyrell) v HM Senior Coroner for County Durham and Darlington* [2016] EWHC 1892 (Admin) at [16].

Suicide conclusions

15.16 In *Maughan*[1] the Supreme Court confirmed that the standard of proof for a suicide conclusion is the balance of probabilities. The elements of suicide conclusions are dealt with in full in the conclusions CHAPTER 6 at **6.134**.

[1] [2020] UKSC 46.

Neglect conclusions

15.17 Neglect in cases involving self-harm is dealt with in full in the conclusions CHAPTER 6 at **6.142**.

Juries

15.18 The requirements for a jury under s 7 CJA 2009 are dealt with in full in CHAPTER 4. A jury will be required in the case of all self-inflicted deaths in mental health detention under the MHA 1983 in accordance with s 7(2).

MENTAL HEALTHCARE

Mental health trusts and service providers

15.19 Mental healthcare in England is provided by services administered by specialist mental health trusts, who are separate entities to the NHS trusts that

15.19 *Mental Health and Mental Capacity*

provide physical clinical care. Specialist mental health care is usually accessed via referral from a patient's primary care GP, via accident and emergency services at hospital, or via 'psychiatric liaison' or assessment services provided by mental health trusts but operating at general hospitals. Primary GP services may provide general practice mental healthcare, including prescribing medication. Some GP surgeries also offer community mental health nurse and therapy services. Mental health services for young persons up to the age of 18 are provided by Child and Adolescent Mental Health Services (CAMHS) within trusts (although the age at which a young person transfers from CAMHS to other services varies between local trusts) .

15.20 Sentenced and remanded prisoners and police detainees may receive mental health care or assessment whilst in custody. Such services are likely to be contracted in by the police, private custodial services, or the Ministry of Justice in the case of prisons. They may be provided by NHS mental health trusts or by private providers. In each of these cases, however, the provision of the service will amount to the provision of a public function and the service provider will therefore be considered a public authority for the purposes of s 6 HRA 1998 (see s 73 Care Act 2014 for the definition of a 'public authority' in relation to private care homes that receive state funding). The investigative duty under Art 2 ECHR will therefore apply where the other conditions for its engagement are satisfied. In *R (A) v Partnerships in Care*[1] a private provider of state funded mental healthcare was held to be performing public functions under s 6 of the HRA 1998.

[1] [2002] 1 WLR 2610.

Inpatient and tertiary mental health services

15.21 Terminology in mental healthcare can be bewildering. Generally speaking, inpatient mental health care is provided in hospitals to 'voluntary' or 'informal' inpatients (so called in the vernacular because they are not detained) and those detained under the MHA 1983. Such hospitals form part of secondary mental health services along with the community-based services outlined below. There are further specialist units within inpatient care. A Psychiatric Intensive Care Unit (PICU) is a secure unit for acutely disturbed detained patients. Low forensic and medium forensic services provide care on wards for those with the most complex needs and who require to be managed closely in order to maintain their and others' safety. Rampton, Broadmoor, and Ashworth are the only three high security hospitals in England and Wales. 'Tertiary services' is a term generally used to refer to specialised services such as secure forensic services, prison mental health care and inpatient CAMHS. Forensic service patients may be detained under s 2 or s 3 MHA 1983 or by virtue of a hospital order imposed by a criminal court under Pt III of the MHA 1983.

The Mental Health Act 1983

15.22 The MHA 1983 sets out a legal framework for the treatment and assessment, including detention and other restrictions on liberty, of persons

Mental healthcare **15.24**

with mental disorders. Mental health law, particularly regarding the lawful use and review of the powers under the Act, is an area of legal practice in itself. Coroners of course have no functions under the MHA 1983, and do not apply or follow the terms of the act. But the MHA 1983 may be of important factual relevance to coronial practice. Those treating patients under the Act are bound by the MHA 1983 and the Guidance in Mental Health Act Code of Practice (2015) (MHA Code of Practice). The MHA 1983 and MHA Code of Practice provide a framework which may assist coroners in determining whether alleged failures in treatment or risk management contributed to the death of a patient. Identifying such failures in detained patients at risk of self-harm or suicide is a requirement of Art 2 ECHR.

15.23 Section 1 of the MHA 1983 sets out that it applies to the reception, care and treatment of mentally disordered patients, the management of their property and related matters. 'Mental disorder means any disorder or disability of the mind'[1]. Part II of the Act governs compulsory admission to hospital and guardianship. As is well known, patients may be admitted to hospital and detained there by the state under s 2 (for assessment) and s 3 (for treatment) of the MHA 1983 (hence the vernacular reference to a patient being 'sectioned'), provided that the requirements under the Act are made out. Section 2 requires, amongst other things, that two registered medical practitioners are of the view that the patient 'ought to be detained in the interests of his own health and safety or with a view to the protection of others'. Section 3 requires that that two registered medical practitioners are of the view that the patient's detention for treatment 'is necessary for the health and safety of the patient or for the protection of others'. Part III governs patients concerned in criminal proceedings or under criminal sentence. The overarching importance in respect of these patients for the purposes of inquest proceedings is that detained patients are acutely vulnerable persons, who are detained for treatment, and generally in order to protect themselves or others. There is a clear purpose to their detention that is relevant to the issues likely to be canvassed at an inquest.

[1] See s 1(2) MHA 1983.

15.24 The MHA Code of Practice provides statutory guidance to mental health clinicians, staff, and approved mental health professionals on how the functions and powers under the MHA 1983 should be used. The MHA Code of Practice is a lengthy and detailed document and will not be discussed here save to mention some key principles. The MHA Code of Practice sets out that five guiding principles should be considered by those performing functions under the Act. These provide important context for assessing a patient's treatment under the MHA 1983[1]:

'Least restrictive option and maximising independence for patients

Where it is possible to treat a patient safely and lawfully without detaining them under the Act, the patient should not be detained. Wherever possible a patient's independence should be encouraged and supported with a focus on promoting recovery wherever possible.

Empowering and involvement

Patients should be fully involved in decisions about care, support and treatment. The views of families, carers and others, if appropriate, should be fully considered when taking decisions. Where decisions are taken which are contradictory to views expressed, professionals should explain the reasons for this.

Respect and dignity

Patients, their families and carers should be treated with respect and dignity and listened to by professionals.

Purpose and effectiveness

Decisions about care and treatment should be appropriate to the patient, with clear therapeutic aims, promote recovery and should be performed to current national guidelines and/or current, available best practice guidelines.

Efficiency and equity

Providers, commissioners and other relevant organisations should work together to ensure that the quality of commissioning and provision of mental healthcare services are of high quality and are given equal priority to physical health and social care services. All relevant services should work together to facilitate timely, safe and supportive discharge from detention.'

[1] See p 21 and Chapter 1.

15.25 Important roles under the MHA 1983 and MHA Code of Practice for inquest purposes include that of the 'responsible clinician' (RC), who is the approved clinical with overall responsibility for the patient's case. The RC, who is normally a psychiatrist, plays a crucial role in directing a patient's care. The RC will be an important witness at a detained inpatient inquest. The 'nearest relative' of the patient is defined by s 26 MHA 1983. Chapter 5 of the MHA Code of Practice sets out the requirements on clinicians and staff under the Act to communicate effectively with the patient and the nearest relative regarding their care and to involve them in specific decisions regarding their care. This may be important if family members wish to challenge the extent to which they were provided with information or involved in decisions regarding the care of the deceased.

Community mental health services

15.26 Secondary mental health services are provided in the community. There is no consistent national framework setting out different roles for services and the different teams who may provide secondary mental healthcare services. The format of services varies from trust to trust. However, the following services are most commonplace:

- Community mental health teams, through which, for instance a patient may attend a clinic at specified intervals to be assessed by a psychiatrist or registered mental health nurse (RMN) or to receive psychological or other therapy.
- Assertive outreach and early intervention teams, who may play a specific role with patients, for instance suffering from the early stages of a psychotic illness or who require specific risk management.
- Crisis or home treatment teams, who typically provide a level of treatment and risk management and assessment that is more intense and direct than that provided by community mental health care teams, and offer an important bridge between community and inpatient care.

Crisis teams visit patients in their homes and tailor the frequency and intensity of treatment to the risks and needs of the patient.

The Care Programme Approach

15.27 The Care Programme Approach (CPA) is a system of individualised care planning and case management in the community for those suffering from severe mental illness, or who are at risk of suicide, self-harm, or harming other people, as well as other categories of vulnerable persons. Its use has been established in England and Wales since 1991.

15.28 Every mental health trust that provides secondary mental health services is likely to utilise the CPA and will have an established written policy setting out its requirements. There is no national unified NHS policy governing the CPA and representatives should request and rely upon local policies.

15.29 The CPA is intended to be a holistic package of care which assesses, treats, and manages the risks of those requiring community mental healthcare. All those subject to CPA should have:

- a care plan;
- a crisis plan; and
- an identified care coordinator.

15.30 The role of the care coordinator is to coordinate and monitor the care of the person subject to the CPA, including ensuring that their care plan is complete and up to date. The role of the care coordinator may be fulfilled by a social worker, an RMN or an occupational therapist. The care coordinator should be in regular contact with the person subject to the CPA. The coordination role is crucial in mental health care, where a single patient may receive care from different service providers such as GPs, social workers, crisis mental healthcare teams, and inpatient mental health services. The management and sharing of information between such services, facilitated by the role of the care coordinator, may be crucial. The care coordinator also plays a key role in managing the movement of patients between services, for instance meeting and assessing a patient whilst in hospital in order to assist them in preparing to return to the community and secondary mental health services.

15.31 In an inquest context the following are key elements of the CPA which should be dealt with in a local policy, and may have an important impact on the facts to be determined at inquest and an assessment of the care provided to the deceased. They are likely to provide a framework against which the quality of the care provided to the deceased can be assessed:

- Care planning including:
    - ongoing risk assessment;
    - risk management plan;
    - crisis plan;
    - treatment plan; and
    - the role of the family as carers for the patient.

15.32 The NHS website refers those looking for information on the CPA to this factsheet prepared by the charity Rethink Mental Illness[1].

[1] https://damdev.rethink.org/advice-and-information/living-with-mental-illness/treatment-and-support/care-programme-approach-cpa/.

Experts and elements of mental healthcare

15.33 The focus of a mental healthcare inquest is likely to be on:

(a) whether sufficient steps were taken to assess and manage the risk of the deceased to themselves, and
(b) whether any failures or inadequacies in the care contributed to the death.

15.34 Risk management and assessment, along with care planning, diagnosis, the use of prescription medication and psychological therapy are core functions of modern mental healthcare. The assessment of the efficacy and standard of these functions should be a matter of expert opinion. Most lawyers and coroners are not mental health experts or clinicians. Even if clinically qualified, their professional role in inquests is legal and they are lay persons for the purposes of clinical practice and opinion. Although coroners have a wide discretion as to whether to instruct and call expert witnesses, it is submitted that where the inquest will be required to reach a conclusion on the *standard* (not used as a term of art) of the care provided to the deceased, a coroner should carefully consider instructing an independent expert to give opinion evidence. In an Art 2 case, the independence required and the need to identify any relevant state failings, adds weight to that argument.

15.35 Even in a *Jamieson* inquest, if neglect is a possible conclusion on the evidence, then recording as many facts 'as the public interest requires', as per Lord Lane in *R v South London Coroner, ex parte Thompson*[1], may also require independent expert evidence to be called. Otherwise, the coroner may not be in a position to identify gross basic failures in mental health care. Whilst in some cases such failures may amount, as per Lord Bingham's suggestion in *Jamieson*[2], to a failure to make basic observations, in others a complex series of errors, including in relation to medication and diagnosis, may contribute to an overall picture of neglect.

[1] (1982) 126 SJ 625.
[2] *R v HM Coroner for North Humberside and Scunthorpe ex parte Jamieson* [1995] QB 1 at 28, para 8, per Lord Bingham MR: 'Failure to provide medical attention for a dependent person whose physical condition is such as to show that he obviously needs it may amount to neglect. So it may be if it is the dependent person's mental condition which obviously calls for medical attention (as it would, for example, if a mental nurse observed that a patient had a propensity to swallow razor blades and failed to report this propensity to a doctor, in a case where the patient had no intention to cause himself injury but did thereafter swallow razor blades with fatal results). In both cases the crucial consideration will be what the dependent person's condition, whether physical or mental, appeared to be', p 25, para (8).

15.36 Where a patient dies whilst in mental healthcare, the relevant mental health trust will undertake an investigation which will result in a report, usually referred to as a serious untoward incident report, or a root cause analysis report. These are important sources of information and, potentially, of evidence. Family representatives should request that the coroner obtains disclosure not just of the report, but of all supporting documents, including any witness statements taken or records of interviews with witnesses, and where relevant any internal correspondence regarding the content of the report. It is common, and entirely legitimate, for a coroner to call the author of the report to give evidence regarding steps the trust has taken to mitigate the risk of future deaths arising in similar circumstances, for the purposes of assessing whether or not to make report to prevent future deaths.

15.37 Coroners may also be tempted to use the report to assist them in reaching judgmental conclusions. They may even seek to call the author of the report to give evidence with the intention of asking them to comment on the standard of the care provided. However, this is likely to raise issues of independence (in particular in Art 2 cases). In *Siberry's Application (No 2)*[1], McCloskey J held that, despite the wide discretion afforded to coroners in calling witnesses, a coroner's decision to call evidence from the author of a Northern Ireland Prisoner Ombudsman's report which had found failings in clinical care, was *Wednesbury* unreasonable, because the author did not have the requisite independent clinical expertise to give expert evidence at the inquest (despite having himself relied upon the evidence of two experts in writing the report).

[1] [2008] NIQB 147.

15.38 Practitioners should be careful to identify the correct expert in a mental health case. Modern mental healthcare is administered by multidisciplinary teams (MDTs). Inpatient MDTs are likely to include a psychiatrist, registered mental nurses, a psychologist and where appropriate social workers. As above, where a patient is treated or assessed under the MHA 1983, they will have a 'responsible clinician' who has overall charge and responsibility for their care. This will invariably be a consultant psychiatrist, and a consultant psychiatrist may be in the best position to give the most authoritative overall view of the care provided to the deceased. But where the real issue relates, eg to mental health nursing and assessment (for instance in relation to nursing risk assessment and observations), then a mental health nursing expert should be called.

Witnesses and disclosure

15.39 The following are potentially important witnesses in a mental health inquest. If their identity is not apparent from the notes then advocates should request that they are identified and asked to provide a statement by the NHS trust:

- The responsible clinician, as discussed above.
- The care coordinator, as discussed above.
- Most trusts will operate a 'named nurse' system, where a specific nurse is given particular responsibilities in relation to a specific patient and ensures continuity in their care.
- The nearest relative in a detained case and/or the patient's carer/s. Family members may not recognise themselves as 'carers' as such, but

15.39 *Mental Health and Mental Capacity*

carers in mental healthcare (provided the patient consents to information being shared with them) have an important role and clinicians have important obligations (including legal obligations) towards them.

15.40 Because of the need for observations to be carried out in inpatient care, and because of the narrative nature of the notes, mental health clinical notes can be voluminous. Practitioners should ensure that disclosure has been received or requested of these key documents:

- The patient's updated care plan.
- The patient's risk management and crisis plans if not included in the above.
- Observation records.
- Narrative daily clinical notes.
- Handover records.
- Any DATIX or other serious incident reports.
- Relevant trust polices which are likely to include a risk assessment and management policy; a CPA policy, and an observations policy.

MENTAL CAPACITY

15.41 Much of the law around mental capacity derives from the Mental Capacity Act 2005 (MCA 2005). In inquests, the other key documentation is the Chief Coroner's Guidance Nos 16 and 16A[1]. When lawyers talk about mental capacity, this is a reference to a person's capacity to make certain specified decisions for themselves eg capacity to make a decision as to where they should live or the medical care they should receive.

[1] Chief Coroner's Guidance No 16, Deprivation of Liberty Safeguards (DoLS) 5 December 2014 (revised 14 January 2016); Chief Coroner's Guidance No 16A, Deprivation of Liberty Safeguards (DoLS) 3 April 2017 onwards (27 March 2017).

15.42 If someone lacks capacity, decisions must be taken on their behalf by others, be it friends, family or the state. Because of the obvious vulnerabilities of someone lacking capacity, the courts generally apply a greater degree of scrutiny to anything that happens to them; this principle extends to their deaths. It is particularly the case if the state has a duty of care towards the individual in some way, and/or they have been formally 'deprived of their liberty'. In an inquest context, it can mean that an inquest takes place when it otherwise might not, or that Art 2 ECHR is engaged when it otherwise might not be. For inquest practitioners, usually the most important aspect of capacity law is whether someone was 'deprived of their liberty'.

Basic principles of mental capacity

What is the test for lacking capacity?

15.43 The test for whether someone has capacity is set out at s 2(1) MCA 2005:

'... a person lacks capacity in relation to a matter if at the material time he is unable to make a decision for himself in relation to the matter because of an impairment of, or a disturbance in the functioning of, the mind or brain.'[1]

[1] Note that the definition of 'making a decision' is set out at s 2(2) MCA 2005, but broadly it follows common sense.

15.44 The MCA 2005 confirms that it does not matter if that impairment or disturbance is temporary or permanent, and a lack of capacity cannot be established merely be reference to 'a person's age or appearance' or 'a condition of his, or an aspect of his behaviour, which might lead others to make unjustified assumptions about his capacity'[1]. There is a presumption of capacity: it must be shown on the balance of probabilities that someone lacks capacity in order for a finding to be made as such[2].

[1] Section 1(2) and s 1(3) MCA 2005.
[2] Section 1(2) and s 2(4) MCA 2005.

15.45 The test is decision-specific: for instance, someone may have capacity to decide where they want to live, but lack capacity to decide how to spend their money. If it is determined that P lacks capacity to make a particular decision, the person who is charged with making the decision for them must do so on the basis of P's best interests, considering the factors set out at s 4 MCA 2005.

15.46 When there is uncertainty or disagreement as to whether someone lacks capacity, what might be in their best interests, or whether they should be deprived of their liberty in some way, the issue should be dealt with by the Court of Protection.

What does it mean if someone is deprived of their liberty?

15.47 Deprivations of liberty under the MCA 2005 have the same meaning as those referenced in ECHR, Art 5(1) set out in the HRA 1998, namely:

'... the right to liberty and security of person. No one shall be deprived of his liberty save in the following cases and in accordance with a procedure prescribed by law:

...

(e) the lawful detention of persons for the prevention of the spreading of infectious diseases, **of persons of unsound mind**, alcoholics or drug addicts, or vagrants.' (emphasis added)

As is clear from the above, the right not to be deprived of one's liberty is a qualified right and there are certain circumstances in which it is legal.

15.48 In 2014 the Supreme Court set out the 'acid test' for whether someone is deprived of their liberty. It consists of two questions[1]:

(a) Is the person subject to continuous supervision and control?
(b) Is the person free to leave?

This is an objective test[2].

[1] *P v Cheshire West & Chester Council; P & Q v Surrey County Council* [2014] UKSC 19.
[2] [2014] UKSC 19 at [76].

When is it legal to deprive someone of their liberty? What is a DoLS?

15.49 Someone can be deprived of their liberty in any setting or location if this is authorised by the Court of Protection. There is also a streamlined statutory scheme set up for cases involving individuals who are in hospitals or in care/nursing homes. These are referenced in the Chief Coroner's Guidance No 16A:

> 'Under the MCA 2005 a person who lacks capacity and is in a hospital or care home for the purpose of being given care or treatment may be subjected to restrictions and/or detention which amount to deprivation of liberty. Steps amounting to deprivation of liberty may be permitted by authorisation under the statutory scheme. Deprivation of liberty without such authority may otherwise be unlawful. The statutory scheme, set out in Schedule A1 to the MCA 2005, provides safeguards known as Deprivation of Liberty Safeguards (DoLS).[1]'

[1] Chief Coroner's Guidance No 16A, Deprivation of Liberty Safeguards (DoLS), para 3.

DoLS authorisations by the relevant local authority

15.50 The Chief Coroner's Guidance No 16A provides a very helpful summary, for the purposes of an inquest practitioner, of when it is lawful to deprive someone of their liberty and how that is achieved at paras 18–33. For a basic overview, this text can do no better than to refer readers to that summary. In very short terms, however, a deprivation of liberty can be authorised by either a local authority or by the Court of Protection. The way in which a local authority achieves this is through what is known as standard or urgent 'DoL' authorisations. These can be applied to individuals who are deprived of their liberty in a hospital or care home[1]. Standard authorisations are the most common way in which people lacking capacity are deprived of their liberty.

[1] See paras 18–31 of the Guidance, which itself is based on Sch A1, MCA 2005.

Orders issued by the Court of Protection

15.51 The Court of Protection may also authorise a deprivation of liberty either in a care, medical or domestic setting by way of a court order; the Court of Protection will also hear any challenges to a DoL authorisation granted by the local authority under s 21A MCA 2005[1].

[1] Chief Coroner's Guidance No 16A, Deprivation of Liberty Safeguards (DoLS), paras 32–33.

15.52 There is no basis upon which an authorisation or court order to deprive someone of their liberty can be challenged before or by a coroner[1]. Equally, the Court of Protection is only able to make decisions about a living person: as soon as that person dies, its jurisdiction ceases.

[1] Chief Coroner's Guidance No 16A, Deprivation of Liberty Safeguards (DoLS), para 34.

Mental capacity 15.57

Jurisdiction and 'state detention' for the purposes of an inquest

What does the CJA 2009 mean by 'state detention'?

15.53 A coronial investigation is mandatory when the coroner has reason to suspect that the death occurred 'in state detention'[1]. It is therefore important to establish whether being deprived of one's liberty in the above circumstances constitutes being 'in state detention'.

1   CJA 2009, s 1(2)(c).

15.54 'State detention' is defined by the CJA 2009 as follows: 'a person is in state detention if he or she is compulsorily detained by a public authority within the meaning of s 6 of the Human Rights Act 1998'[1], referring to 'acts of public authorities'[2].

1   CJA 2009, s 48(2).
2   Human Rights Act 1998, s 6.

15.55 Clearly hospitals and publicly run care homes are public authorities for these purposes. There has been some debate as to whether certain privately run hospitals or care homes constitute 'public authorities' for these purposes. However, if the private hospital or care home carries out 'functions of a public nature', it will fall within the meaning of 'public authority' in s 6(3)(b) of the HRA 1998. Whether a care provider will be a public authority for the purposes of the HRA 1998 is regulated by s 73 of the Care Act 2014 (HRA 1998: provision of regulated care or support etc a public function), which sets out that:

'(1)   This section applies where—
   (a)   in England, a registered care provider provides care and support to an adult or support to a carer, in the course of providing—
      (i)   personal care in a place where the adult receiving the personal care is living when the personal care is provided, or
      (ii) residential accommodation together with nursing or personal care;
      . . .
(2)   The provider is to be taken for the purposes of section 6(3)(b) of the Human Rights Act 1998 (acts of public authorities) to be exercising a function of a public nature in providing the care or support, if the requirements of subsection (3) are met.'

15.56 The requirements under s 74(3) confirm that a local authority or health and social care trust must either arrange the care and support or pay (directly or indirectly) for that care and support pursuant to certain sections of the Care Act 2014 (see the table produced at s 74 for full details of the relevant sections). In short, any placement arranged with the involvement of a local authority constitutes a 'public authority' for these purposes.

Deaths after 3 April 2017

15.57 Section 48(2A) CJA 2009 (implemented on 3 April 2017) provides an important caveat to this. It states that 'a person is not in state detention at any time when he or she is deprived of liberty under s 4A(3) or (5) or 4B of the Mental Capacity Act 2005'. This exception means that there is no mandatory

261

15.57 *Mental Health and Mental Capacity*

requirement to commence an investigation on the basis that the person was 'in state detention' if their deprivation of liberty falls under s 48(2A) CJA 2009.

15.58 This legislative change is an indication as to how a deprivation of liberty for capacity reasons is treated differently from deprivations of liberty for other reasons such as being held in custody; see CHAPTER 14 for further detail on deaths which occur in custody.

15.59 Bear in mind that there is no requirement for someone in a care home or hospital to have been legally deprived of their liberty by way of a court order or DoL authorisation for it to constitute a deprivation of their liberty for the purposes of Art 5 ECHR, and to constitute being 'in state detention' for the purposes of s 48(2) CJA 2009. Whether someone is deprived of their liberty is a question of fact. In *R (on the application of Ferreira) and HM Senior Coroner for Inner London South, King's College Hospital NHS Foundation Trust, the Intensive Care Society and the Faculty of Intensive Care Medicine and Secretary of State for Health and Secretary of State for Justice*[1] the court confirmed that the deceased, who had died in a hospital whilst sedated in an intensive care unit, had been deprived of their liberty in state detention despite the fact that no DoL authorisation nor court order had been made approving that deprivation[2]. Indeed, if a person is deprived of their liberty but the legal procedures have not been followed, either correctly or at all, then this does constitute an instance where the person is 'in state detention' but the exception under s 48(2A) CJA 2009 does not apply. Therefore the death must be investigated under s 1(2)(c) CJA 2009.

[1] [2017] EWCA Civ 31.
[2] *R (on the application of Ferreira) and HM Senior Coroner for Inner London South, King's College Hospital NHS Foundation Trust, the Intensive Care Society and the Faculty of Intensive Care Medicine and Secretary of State for Health and Secretary of State for Justice* [2017] EWCA Civ 31; Chief Coroner's Guidance No 16A, Deprivation of Liberty Safeguards (DoLS), paras 35–36.

Deaths prior to 3 April 2017

15.60 Note that s 48(2A) CJA 2009 was added by way of s 178 Policing and Crime Act 2017 and took effect from 3 April 2017. Any deaths prior to this point are still subject to the previous legislation and practitioners should consider Chief Coroner's Guidance No 16 rather than 16A. In short terms, the exception provided under s 48(2A) does not apply, and the death of someone subject to a DoL authorisation should be considered as having taken place 'in state detention' (subject to the above discussion regarding the definition of 'a public authority'). It should therefore be subject to a coronial investigation.

15.61 As above for deaths after 3 April 2017, deaths in a hospital or care home prior to 3 April 2017 where someone was deprived of their liberty, but where the legal processes were not followed, also constitute a deprivation of liberty 'in state detention' and should also be investigated by a coroner under s 1(2) CJA 2009.

Mental capacity 15.69

When is a jury required?

15.62 The requirement for a jury under s 7 CJA 2009 is dealt with in full in CHAPTER 4.

15.63 As above, for deaths after 3 April 2017 a jury will not be required in a DoLS detention case by virtue of the amendment to the CJA 2009. For deaths prior to 3 April 2017 the definition of state detention will be as set out above but for s 7 to be engaged the coroner must also have reason to suspect that the death was violent or natural or that the cause of death was unknown.

When is Art 2 ECHR engaged in cases involving the death of someone deprived of their liberty?

15.64 The fact that there is state involvement, and at times, responsibility, for those who are deprived of their liberty is also relevant to the question of whether a *'Jamieson'* or a *'Middleton'* inquest is carried out ie whether Art 2 ECHR is engaged.

15.65 The relevance of Art 2 ECHR to inquests is covered in detail in CHAPTER 3 at 3.51 *et seq*. However, in brief, where the procedural investigative Art 2 ECHR duty is engaged, an inquest must consider not just how, but 'how and in what circumstances' someone came by their death[1]. That has important consequences, in particular for the nature and format of the conclusions reached at an inquest.

[1] CJA 2009, ss 5 and 10.

15.66 The procedural Art 2 duty is engaged where there has been an arguable breach by the state of one of its substantive duties to protect life[1].

[1] Again, further detail of this can be found in CHAPTER 3 at 3.55 *et seq*.

15.67 What relevance does Art 2 ECHR have for cases involving someone who was deprived of their liberty?

15.68 This was considered in *R (Maguire) v HM Senior Coroner for Blackpool & Flyde & Others*[1] by the Court of Appeal. The deceased had lived in a care home funded by her local authority and was subject to a standard DoL authorisation under Sch A1 MCA 2005. She died as a result of alleged medical negligence unconnected to her deprivation of liberty. The issue was whether there had been an arguable breach of either: (i) the operational duty to protect certain individuals from a real and immediate risk to their life; or (ii) the general duty to put in place a regulatory framework sufficient to protect life. The coroner had originally decided that Art 2 ECHR was not engaged, but the deceased's family appealed this decision.

[1] [2020] EWCA Civ 738.

Maguire and the Art 2 ECHR operational duty

15.69 In *Maguire* the Court of Appeal held that the 'fact that an operational duty to protect life exists does not lead to the conclusion that for all purposes

15.69 *Mental Health and Mental Capacity*

the death of a person owed that duty is to be judged by Article 2 standards'[1]. The 'unifying feature of the application' of the operational duty is state responsibility[2].

[1] [2020] EWCA Civ 738 at [74].
[2] [2020] EWCA Civ 738 at [72].

15.70 The Court of Appeal held that the vulnerability of a care home resident subject to DoLS was not in itself sufficient to engage the duty in circumstances where there was no correlation between the purpose for which the duty to protect was imposed and the nature of the subsequent alleged failure to protect life. In short, 'the Article 2 operational duty is owed to vulnerable people under the care of the state for some purposes', but where there is no connection between the cause of death and the reasons why the Art 2 duty to protect has arisen, there will generally be no breach, and Art 2 ECHR is not engaged for the purposes of the inquest[1]. In future then the coroner should consider the scope of any operational duty owed on a case by case basis, and judge the circumstances of the death by reference to it. If, for instance, someone subject to a DoLS died of a condition or event connected with the reason behind their deprivation of their liberty, it is submitted that different principles should apply, and a breach may well be found.

[1] [2020] EWCA Civ 738 at [96].

Maguire and the general Art 2 ECHR duty to put in place a regulatory framework sufficient to protect life

15.71 Having held that the relevant failures related to 'ordinary medical treatment', the court made short work of dismissing the appellants' argument that there had been a breach of the general Art 2 ECHR duty. The principles in relation to the general duty to put in place an adequate regulatory framework to protect life, as authoritatively set out by the Grand Chamber of the ECtHR in *Lopes de Sousa*[1], did not apply. There was no arguable systemic dysfunction.

[1] *Lopes de Sousa Fernandez v Portugal* (2018) 66 EHRR 28; see paras 194–196.

How does the judgment in Maguire square with other existing decisions?

15.72 The court used *Dumpe*[1] and *Lopes de Sousa* as cornerstones for this decision. This is somewhat surprising given neither case concerned detained people. In *Lopes de Sousa*, the Grand Chamber clearly set out that different considerations would apply to people deprived of their liberty and/or those considered particularly vulnerable[2]. The Court of Appeal in *Maguire* held that that caveat 'does not affect the outcome in a case of this sort'[3] but did not explain why that is the case. The ECtHR has always considered those in state detention to be a particularly vulnerable group warranting the protection of Art 2. The lack of focus by the Court of Appeal on the detention issue is surprising.

[1] *Dumpe v Latvia* (App No 71506/13).
[2] (2018) 66 EHRR 28 at [163].
[3] [2020] EWCA Civ 738 at [99].

15.73 Further, the court did not cite the High Court authority of *Daniel v St George's Healthcare NHS Trust*[1]. In *Daniel*, the court deemed that Art 2 was engaged in circumstances where Mr Daniel died in prison from a heart attack and there were real concerns around the medical care provided to him. The operational duty applied to the medical treatment within prison of detainees who were at a real and immediate risk to life. This is arguably more analogous to the facts of Jackie's death than *Tyrell v HM Senior Coroner for County Durham and Darlington*[2], the prisoner case the Court of Appeal did cite, in which Mr Tyrell died in prison of natural causes and in which, for that reason, Art 2 was not engaged. In *Daniel* Lang J surveyed the ECtHR case law and stated that 'medical practitioners, both inside, and outside a prison setting, are also subject to the Article 2 duty, as well as prison officers and police officers'[3].

[1] [2016] EWHC 23 (QB).
[2] [2016] EWHC 1892 (Admin).
[3] [2016] EWHC 1892 (Admin) at [28].

15.74 It may be that the court in *Maguire* was concerned that the blanket imposition of an operational duty to protect life in respect of those subject to DoLs would be unworkable, given the recent rise in numbers. However, the result of the decision is that Art 2 will be engaged in respect of the medical treatment of certain state detainees and not of others. An analytical framework was imposed on the operational duty which is not explicitly stated in previous judgments of the domestic courts or the ECtHR. Practitioners dealing with DoLS cases must now look carefully at the reasons for the imposition of the deprivation and whether there is a link between that and any harm suffered.

Suicide conclusions

15.75 Practitioners should bear in mind that issues of capacity may be relevant to the question whether a deceased acted with the requisite intent for a suicide conclusion. Suicide conclusions are dealt with in full in the conclusions in CHAPTER 6 at **6.134**.

Working with families of people lacking capacity

15.76 Inquests into the deaths of individuals who lacked capacity can be emotive. The close families of individuals who lack capacity may well have had a degree of control over intimate decisions in their relative's life, or even a part to play in representing that person's best interests in formal and informal capacities, thus holding some responsibility for them and their wellbeing. They may therefore feel a sense of guilt at the person's death which is otherwise unjustified.

15.77 Equally, the families of those who lack capacity are routinely involved with a variety of medical and social care professionals, and sometimes lawyers and courts, as a result of their loved one's vulnerability and need for additional care and support. They should have been consulted as part of any standard DoL authorisation and should certainly have been offered the opportunity to play a role in any court proceedings that have taken place. As a result, they may wish to play a particularly active role in seeking answers on behalf of their loved one.

Chapter 16

WORKPLACE DEATHS

INTRODUCTION TO WORKPLACE DEATHS

16.1 Inquests into workplace deaths present a unique set of challenges for practitioners. The interaction between the police, relevant regulators and the coroner can add a layer of complexity and often delay that means that inquests can end up taking place many months or even several years after the death. Practitioners need to be mindful of the often-impending risk of criminal proceedings, which can raise the stakes further in already difficult circumstances.

16.2 The Chief Coroner has issued specific guidance on COVID-19 and possible exposure in the workplace[1]. This is covered in CHAPTER 20 on Inquests and COVID-19.

[1] Chief Coroner's Guidance No 37, COVID-19 deaths and possible exposure in the workplace (amended 1 July 2020).

16.3 Regulation 3(1)(a) of the Notification of Deaths Regulations 2019 specifies that a death must be reported to the coroner if the certifying medical practitioner 'suspects that the person's death was due to . . . (ix) an injury or disease attributable to any employment held during a person's lifetime'. There was an average of 137 worker deaths each year between 2015/16 to 2019/20[1]. Statistics suggests that some occupations have greater risk of death. Most deaths occur in construction, agriculture, forestry and fishing, and manufacturing (see Figure 1 below[2]) with agriculture, forestry and fishing and the waste and recycling industries having by far the worst fatal injury rate per 100,000 workers[3]. Men are much more likely to die at work than women, accounting for 97 per cent of all worker fatalities in 2019/20, which likely reflects the predominantly male workforces that occupy the more dangerous industries[4].

16.3 Workplace Deaths

Figure 1

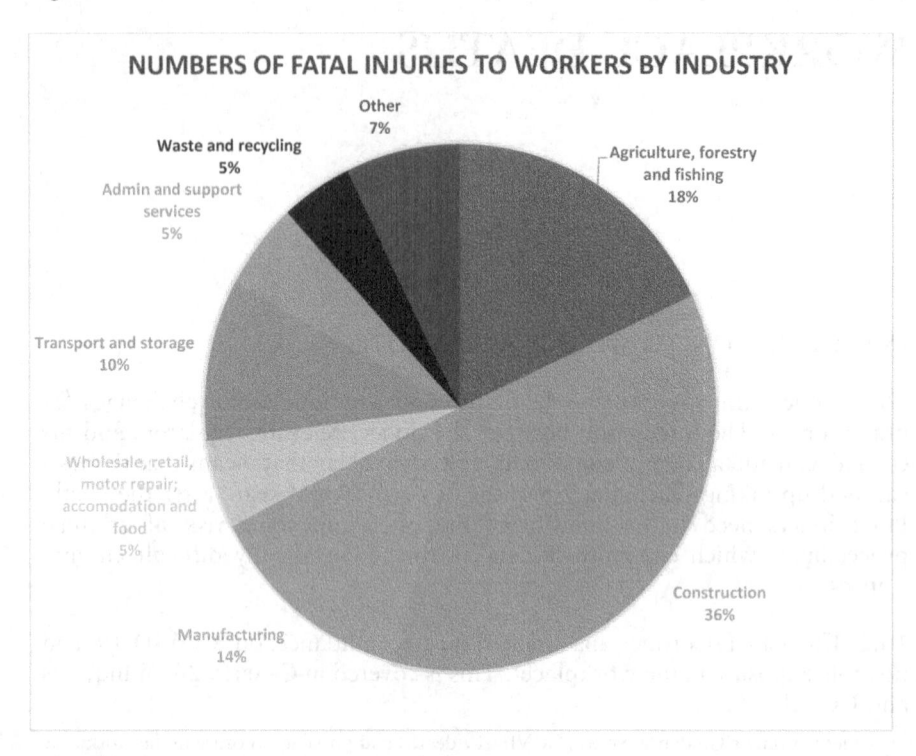

NUMBERS OF FATAL INJURIES TO WORKERS BY INDUSTRY

- Other 7%
- Waste and recycling 5%
- Admin and support services 5%
- Transport and storage 10%
- Wholesale, retail, motor repair; accomodation and food 5%
- Manufacturing 14%
- Construction 36%
- Agriculture, forestry and fishing 18%

[1] HSE Workplace fatal injuries in Great Britain, 2020, 1 July 2020. The figures are based on reportable deaths under RIDDOR 2013. These exclude fatal accidents of workers travelling on public highways, workers travelling by air or sea and deaths due to occupational disease (including COVID-19). Please note the figures are provisional and will be finalised in July 2021 to take into account of any necessary adjustments.
[2] HSE Workplace fatal injuries in Great Britain, 2020, 1 July 2020, p 5.
[3] HSE Workplace fatal injuries in Great Britain, 2020, 1 July 2020, pp 5, 6.
[4] HSE Workplace fatal injuries in Great Britain, 2020, 1 July 2020, p 8.

16.4 Certain activities are much more likely to result in worker death than others. The most common causes are falls from height and being struck by a moving vehicle or object (see Figure 2[1]).

Figure 2

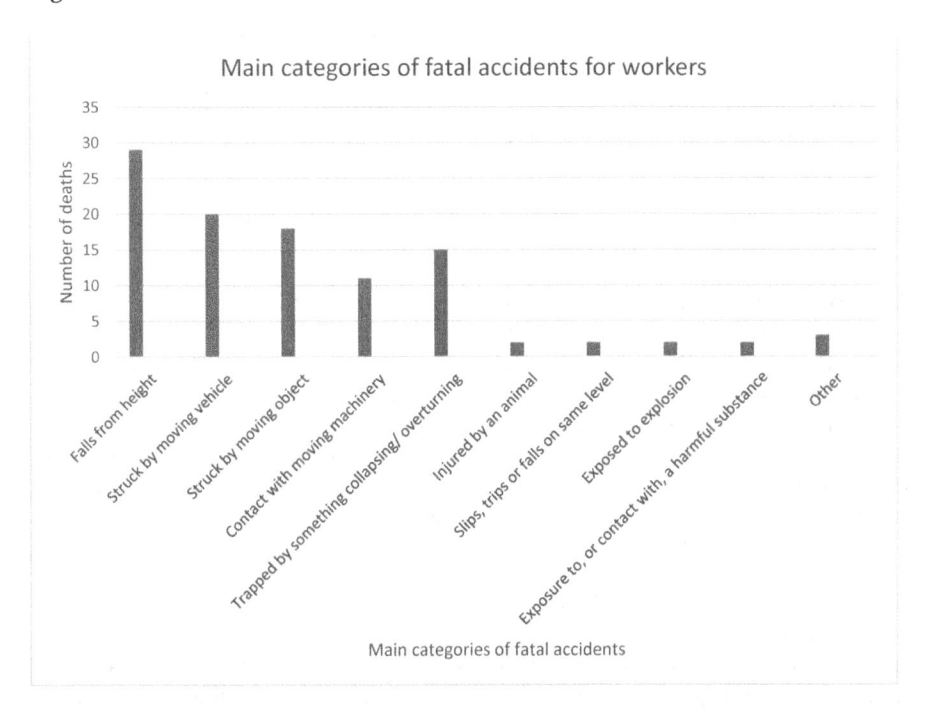

```
Main categories of fatal accidents for workers
```

Chart showing number of deaths by category:
- Falls from height: ~29
- Struck by moving vehicle: ~20
- Struck by moving object: ~18
- Contact with moving machinery: ~11
- Trapped by something collapsing/overturning: ~15
- Injured by an animal: ~2
- Slips, trips or falls on same level: ~2
- Exposed to explosion: ~2
- Exposure to, or contact with, a harmful substance: ~2
- Other: ~3

Main categories of fatal accidents

[1] HSE Workplace fatal injuries in Great Britain, 2020, 1 July 2020, p 7.

INTERPLAY WITH REGULATORY PROCEEDINGS

16.5 The vast majority of workplace deaths are investigated by the relevant regulator, and in some cases the police, in order to explore whether criminal offences have been committed. Given this, the involvement of enforcement authorities must be considered from the outset.

16.6 The Work-related Deaths Protocol[1] outlines how the police, Crown Prosecution Service, Health and Safety Executive (HSE), local authorities and other regulators will work together when investigating work-related deaths. In most cases the police initially have primacy over an investigation, and will consider whether any homicide offences have been committed. Where homicide offences have been ruled out, primacy of the investigation passes to the HSE or the local authority[2] to consider whether any health and safety offences have been committed. The transfer of primacy often happens early on, once the police are satisfied there is no evidence of homicide offences. It is possible for the police to reassume primary, should new evidence come to light or following a conclusion of 'unlawful killing' at the inquest.

[1] Work-related Deaths: A protocol for liaison, Version 4, https://www.hse.gov.uk/pubns/wrdp1.pdf.
[2] Enforcement responsibility is allocated to HSE or local authority according to the main activity carried out at a premises (see the Health and Safety (Enforcing Authority) Regulations 1998). Local authorities are the main enforcing authority in retail, wholesale distribution, warehousing, hotel and catering premises, offices, and the consumer/leisure industries.

16.7 *Workplace Deaths*

Homicide offences

16.7 Generally, whilst the police investigate whether any homicide offences have been committed, the inquest will be suspended[1]. In a workplace death, the relevant homicide offences are likely to be corporate manslaughter[2] in respect of organisations and/or gross negligence manslaughter as regards individuals.

[1] CJA 2009, Sch 1, para 1(2) states that the coroner must suspend an inquest if a prosecuting authority requests the inquest be suspended on the grounds that a person may be charged with a homicide offence involving the death of the deceased or a related offence.
[2] Corporate Manslaughter and Corporate Homicide Act 2007, s 1.

16.8 Where a prosecution for a homicide offence is brought, the coroner will only resume an inquest where there is sufficient reason to do so. Generally, this means that there will not be an inquest where there has been a prosecution for a manslaughter offence following a workplace death. Exceptions would be where the coroner considers there are issues surrounding the death that still need to be explored. This may be the case, for example, where the criminal trial has been limited in scope or has not heard from the defendant (such as would be the case following a successful submission of no case to answer).

16.9 If the coroner considers that the state's procedural obligation to investigate arguable breaches of Art 2 has not been fulfilled by the criminal proceedings, then the coroner must resume the inquest following the prosecution. See CHAPTER 21 for further detail of the links between criminal and inquest proceedings, and CHAPTER 2 for circumstances in which an inquest can be suspended.

Other offences

16.10 Where homicide offences have been discounted, the investigation will be handed from the police to the HSE or local authority to investigate whether any offences under the Health and Safety at Work etc. Act 1974 (HSWA 1974) have been committed.

16.11 The HSWA 1974 is a wide-ranging piece of legislation and creates a number of different duty holders. Employers have duties not just to their own employees but also to others affected by their undertaking. Directors and managers may be investigated, and prosecuted, in relation to their part in the commission of offences by their employer. Employees have duties to take reasonable care for their own and others' health and safety whilst at work. This means that the HSE or local authority may be investigating a number of different organisations and individuals in relation to the circumstances surrounding one fatal incident.

16.12 An investigation into potential offences under the HSWA 1974, has a different focus to the coroner's investigation. Under the HSWA 1974, an offence can be committed without it being causative of harm, so the HSE or local authority may be investigating matters that had no causal link with the death.

Memorandum of understanding between the Chief Coroner and HSE

16.13 There is a Memorandum of Understanding (MOU) between the Chief Coroner of England and Wales and the HSE which sets out how coroners and the HSE work together following a workplace death and the different roles that each has. The latest MOU is dated 21 May 2019[1] and states that it is to be reviewed every five years or more frequently should the need arise. The purpose of the MOU is to facilitate cooperation between the HSE and coroners and to avoid misunderstandings and disputes about each's remit and responsibility.

[1] Memorandum of Understanding between The Chief Coroner or England and Wales and The Health and Safety Executive, 21 May 2019.

16.14 Whilst the MOU does not strictly apply between coroners and local authorities, coroners are likely to take a similar approach as they would where the HSE is leading the investigation.

Timeline of proceedings

16.15 The MOU states that where the HSE has primacy of an investigation it will provide an initial report to the coroner within four months of the start of its investigation, summarising its investigation to date and providing an estimate for the time required to produce a final report. Following this, quarterly written reports will be provided to the coroner until the completion of its investigation and the submission of a final factual report with supporting evidence to the coroner.

16.16 The MOU provides that coroners should normally suspend the inquest whilst the criminal investigation is ongoing (this is using the coroner's power to suspend an inquest where appropriate to do so, Sch 1, para 5 of the CJA 2009) but once the HSE's investigation is complete it will be a matter for the HSE to decide whether to prosecute at that stage or await the conclusion of the inquest.

16.17 The HSE has a wide discretion as to whether to prosecute pre or post inquest but its usual practice is to await the conclusion of the inquest before prosecuting.

16.18 There are two main reasons for this:

(1) additional evidence may come to light as a result of the inquest; and
(2) where there is a conclusion of 'unlawful killing', the police/CPS will consider whether to bring proceedings for a homicide offence. A previous prosecution for a health and safety offence may be a bar to a prosecution for another serious criminal offence such as manslaughter[1].

[1] Work-related deaths: Guidance on the timing of criminal proceedings in a work-related death case (England and Wales), www.hse.gov.uk/pubns/wrdp3.pdf.

16.19 Whilst commencement of criminal proceedings pre-inquest is not usual, it is common for the HSE to indicate its position to the coroner and those under investigation before the inquest. Where the HSE's decision is to take 'no

16.19 Workplace Deaths

further action' (abbreviated to 'NFA') this is stated to be a provisional decision and subject to any further evidence coming out of the inquest. On occasions, the HSE will indicate pre-inquest that it intends to prosecute following the inquest. Alternatively the HSE may simply reserve its decision until post-inquest.

16.20 Clearly the HSE's position is likely to influence interested persons' approaches to the inquest, for example in relation to arguments put forward as to scope and witnesses.

16.21 Although the HSE say that the rationale for normally waiting for conclusion of the inquest before prosecuting is not designed to afford it (nor any potential defendants) the opportunity to test the evidence before any enforcement proceedings, this is clearly a consequence of this order of proceedings.

16.22 Should the conclusion of the inquest be one of 'unlawful killing' then the police will reassume primacy of the investigation.

PREPARING FOR AN INQUEST

16.23 Following a death in the workplace, organisations and their legal representatives should complete an investigation into the incident. This is necessary to understand if any changes are needed to prevent further accidents or improve current processes, to respond to any criminal investigation or civil proceedings and also to prepare for the inquest. Understanding the company's position early on, the risk of a prosecution and any areas of concern will help to inform the approach to the inquest.

16.24 The investigation should include taking statements from eye witnesses, managers and other relevant witnesses and collating relevant documents and material. What material is relevant will depend on the circumstances, but the following are normally required:

- CCTV and photographs of the incident and scene;
- any risk assessments, method statements, standard operating procedures, work instructions, manuals and permits to work relevant to the work being carried out;
- time sheets, visitor books or sign-in sheets for the site and relevant workers;
- the organisation's health and safety policy and arrangements;
- details of recruitment processes;
- induction records;
- training records and course syllabi where available;
- human resources records for the deceased and others involved including any disciplinary records;
- organograms showing the structure of the organisation; and
- records for any relevant equipment including declarations of conformity, operating manuals, maintenance records and statutory inspection records.

16.25 It may be necessary to obtain an opinion from an independent expert to understand the cause of the incident and any failings by an organisation or others. An organisation may wish to challenge evidence in relation to the cause and is often in a better position to do so having obtained its own expert evidence. Expert evidence can also assist in understanding whether an organisation may have committed an offence which will inform an organisation's approach to the inquest.

16.26 Legal privilege is a complex topic and outside the scope of this book. Internal investigation reports and other documents not protected by legal privilege may need to be disclosed to the police, regulators, the coroner and potential claimants in civil proceedings, if requested.

16.27 In certain circumstances, internal investigations can be protected by legal privilege, which means an organisation can examine itself and reach potentially harmful conclusions which it will not have to share with others. Organisations should seek early legal advice about the scope of legal privilege and not assume it automatically applies to an internal investigation.

16.28 Having completed an investigation and gathered evidence, organisations will be better equipped to respond to requests from regulators and the coroner.

16.29 Following the death of a family member at work, relatives will want to understand more about the circumstances of the death and in some cases explore whether they will be able to bring a claim for compensation. Where there is a regulatory or criminal investigation into the incident, family members and their representatives should be updated on the status and progress of the investigation by the police liaison officer or inspector leading the investigation. They may also be asked to provide a statement about their family member and anything else that may be relevant to the circumstances of the death.

INTERESTED PERSONS

16.30 Full detail as to who may be an interested person is set out in CHAPTER 4. Examples of common interested persons in workplace death inquests are set out below.

Family members

16.31 The deceased's family will have a right to be in attendance and ask questions about their relative's death.

The deceased's employer

16.32 Whatever their involvement in the death, it will often be in the deceased's employer's interests to seek interested person status in order to

16.32 *Workplace Deaths*

protect their position and also to be in a position to assist the coroner during the inquest.

16.33 The coroner is likely to require disclosure from the employer and witness statements from other employees. Early engagement and assistance to the coroner will help to set the tone for the inquest and demonstrate that the employer is a responsible organisation. Attendance at the inquest by a director or senior management will also help to show that the organisation is taking the process seriously at the highest level.

Other organisations

16.34 Often in workplace deaths, there will be more than one organisation involved in the circumstances of the death and subject to investigation by HSE.

16.35 For example, in construction related deaths, there may be a principal contractor as well as various different sub-contractors, a client organisation and an architect who may all be involved in some way and who may wish to seek interested person status.

16.36 Where there has been an accident involving a piece of equipment, the manufacturer of any of the equipment, the company that installed the equipment and/or the company that tested the equipment may be involved depending on the circumstances of the death and the evidence as to the cause of the accident.

Trade union representative

16.37 In cases where death may have been caused by an injury received in the course of employment, a representative of a trade union of which the deceased was a member at the time of death will have standing as an interested person[1].

[1] CJA 2009, s 47(2)(g).

Individuals

16.38 It may be advisable for individuals who were involved in the circumstances of the death to seek interested person status separate from that of their employer. This will be vital where individuals themselves are under investigation for potential offences so that their position can be protected through the right to address the coroner and ask questions of witnesses. Representatives of organisations should consider at an early stage and throughout the course of the investigation and inquest whether there is a need for separate legal representation of individuals so they can be advised of their right to avoid answering questions that may tend to incriminate them[1].

[1] Coroners (Inquests) Rules 2013, r 22.

Enforcing authority

16.39 The MOU states that 'HSE will usually be an interested person in an inquest concerning a work related death' and representatives of enforcing authorities have automatic standing as an interested person[1]. Often the HSE will attend to assist the coroner and to take note of the evidence, rather than actively seeking to ask questions of witnesses.

[1] CJA 2009, s 47(2)(h).

16.40 The HSE is not normally legally represented at inquests, but may be represented at more complex or high profile inquests or where issues have arisen between the HSE and coroner as to each's role.

DISCLOSURE

16.41 As mentioned at **16.15–16.22**, the HSE will provide a final factual report on its investigation to the coroner. Whilst this report is not primary evidence, there will be evidence accompanying the report, such as witness statements, risk assessments, safe systems of work, training records and disciplinary records which may be relevant to the coroner's investigation.

16.42 The MOU recognises the two-stage process from the *Worcestershire* case[1]; that disclosure will be made to the coroner who will then decide whether to provide onward disclosure to interested persons. The HSE may raise objections to onward disclosure, however it will be the coroner's decision as to whether there should be onward disclosure to interested persons. The MOU also confirms that if the coroner has material that HSE has not seen then normally the coroner will share this.

[1] *Worcestershire County Council and Anor v HM Coroner for the County of Worcestershire* [2013] EWHC 1711 (QB).

16.43 In addition to evidence collated by the HSE, it is possible that the coroner may seek additional evidence from interested persons, and organisations should be willing to assist if asked. However, the coroner will not normally want to repeat investigatory work already undertaken by the HSE or others.

JURY INQUEST

16.44 Inquests relating to deaths arising out of accidents in the workplace will generally be heard by a jury. Section 7(2)(c) of the CJA 2009 provides that inquests must be heard with a jury if the coroner has reason to suspect 'that the death was caused by a notifiable accident, poisoning or disease'. 'Notifiable accident' includes those required to be reported under the Reporting of Injuries, Diseases and Dangerous Occurrences Regulations 2013 (RIDDOR 2013) regime[1]. Regulation 6(1) of RIDDOR 2013 requires that where any person dies as a result a work-related accident it must be reported to the relevant enforcing authority. Also, where an employee suffers a reportable

16.44 *Workplace Deaths*

injury which is the cause of his death within one year of the day of the accident, it must be reported.

[1] SI 2013/1471.

WITNESSES

16.45 The witnesses in an inquest following a workplace death will usually include colleagues who were working with the deceased at the time of the death and/or who witnessed it.

16.46 As mentioned at **16.31–16.40**, individuals who are suspects in an ongoing criminal investigation or liable to come under criticism, are likely to need independent legal representation, due to the risk of a conflict of interest between employer and employee. It is normally advisable for legal representatives of individuals to seek interested person status for their client in order to have standing to make representations to the coroner, including in respect of r 22 of the Coroners (Inquests) Rules 2013, and so that they are able to ask questions of witnesses.

16.47 It is not uncommon for the coroner to ask for a manager, director or in-house health and safety advisor to give evidence about the risk assessments and safe systems of work relevant to the work being carried out at the time of the incident. In other types of inquests, organisations may be asked to arrange to collect employees' witness statements. This is less common in workplace death inquests where the coroner will already have witness statements taken by the police or HSE.

16.48 The coroner will normally ask the HSE inspector dealing with the investigation to give evidence about their investigation and the circumstances of the incident. This is often given towards the start of the inquest, to set the scene for the jury as to the evidence the HSE has gathered and the status of the investigation, before the coroner calls other witnesses to give more detailed evidence.

16.49 As part of the HSE investigation, a HSE Specialist Inspector may have written a report setting out findings and their conclusions on issues relevant to their expertise. This may include evidence as to any testing that the HSE has carried out, for example, on a vehicle or piece of equipment involved in the incident. Where the coroner deems this relevant to their investigation then the coroner may want this evidence to form part of the inquest evidence. The position in the MOU is that whilst the decision as to who to call is for the coroner, it is recognised that specialist inspectors are in high demand and 'proper consideration' should be given to reading their reports rather than requiring them to give evidence in person. The MOU seeks to confine the role of the Specialist Inspector in an inquest and make clear that they can only answer questions on matters within their report and on matters which assist the coroner to answer the statutory questions.

16.50 In some cases, particularly where there is a fundamental dispute as to the cause of the incident, interested persons may wish to suggest that the coroner hears evidence from an expert they have instructed. The coroner has discretion whether to hear this evidence. It is also possible that the coroner may decide to instruct their own expert, for example if they feel that relevant issues are not covered by the HSE Specialist Inspector.

INQUEST CONCLUSIONS

16.51 Common short form conclusions following workplace deaths are 'accident' and 'misadventure'. Whilst it has not been the focus of this chapter, 'industrial disease' may be applicable where death has been due to exposure to a hazardous substance while at work.

16.52 Should a conclusion of 'unlawful killing' be returned, then the matter will be referred back to the police/CPS to consider whether to bring criminal proceedings. Unlawful killing does not mean an offence under the HSWA 1974, but rather a homicide offence, which could include corporate manslaughter or gross negligence manslaughter.

16.53 Where the cause of death is complicated or where death results from a chain of events, the coroner or jury may determine that a narrative conclusion is most appropriate. See CHAPTER 6 for full analysis of the various conclusions available to coroners.

REPORT TO PREVENT FUTURE DEATHS

16.54 Reports to prevent future deaths are a regular feature of inquests following workplace deaths. Common concerns for coroners include perceived deficiencies in risk assessments and safe systems of work, concerns about the adequacy or maintenance of equipment and gaps in training. It is not unusual for reports to prevent future deaths to be directed at the HSE or other government departments if there are concerns about HSE guidance or about broader industry practice.

16.55 In advance of issuing the report, coroners may be willing to provide an indication of areas of potential concern and those representing organisations should prepare submissions in response to these concerns to try to avoid a report directed towards their organisation. If there is anything that the coroner has misunderstood then this should be clarified and any evidence to allay the coroner's concerns should be provided. This may include details of any review of the relevant risk assessment, changes to the safe system of work or equipment and refresher training provided to staff.

16.56 The coroner may specifically ask for a witness to deal with prevention of future death matters or an organisation may propose a witness. The witness should be well prepared to answer the coroner's questions in relation to the incident and any changes to the workplace that have been made subsequently.

16.57 When dealing with report to prevent future death issues, it is of key importance for organisations and their legal advisors to have a clear view on

16.57 *Workplace Deaths*

the organisation's own position and to consider any implications for any related criminal investigation or potential civil claims for damages.

16.58 A failure to address issues raised by the coroner in a report to prevent future deaths, may constitute an ongoing breach of health and safety legislation, which may be an aggravating feature in a future prosecution as well as an ongoing risk to employees or others. However, changes made to a workplace post-accident, may be perceived by the HSE as reasonably practicable steps that could have been taken before the accident. This may be unfair where a gap in systems that led to the death could not have been foreseen beforehand or where an organisation now goes above and beyond standard industry practice in response to a fatal incident. Clearly these considerations should not stop organisations making improvements, but thought should be given to how these changes are presented and explained.

16.59 Reports to prevent future deaths are considered in fuller terms in CHAPTER 7.

Chapter 17

ROAD TRAFFIC COLLISION DEATHS

17.1 We live on a small island and our roads are perilously busy[1]. In 2018, there were 1,782 reported road deaths. That number has remained broadly the same since 2010, hovering at around 1,800, despite attempts by police, local authorities, the Department for Transport and vehicle manufacturers to reduce it.

[1] According to one survey, the busiest in Europe and the tenth busiest in the world; source: Inrix.

17.2 Road traffic deaths are the leading cause of death for children and young adults aged 5–29, with males more likely to be killed than females[1]. About three quarters (73 per cent) of all road traffic deaths occur among young males under the age of 25 who are almost three times as likely to be killed as young females. The World Health Organisation cites the main risk factors in causing accidents as: speed; driving under the influence of alcohol and other psychoactive substances; non-use of helmets; seat-belts and child restraints; distracted driving (for example through mobile-telephone-use); unsafe road infrastructure; unsafe vehicles; and inadequate post-crash care.

[1] World Health Organisation data, 'Road traffic injuries', 7 February 2020.

DO ALL ROAD TRAFFIC COLLISION DEATHS REQUIRE AN INQUEST?

17.3 The CJA 2009, s 1 duty to investigate will typically be triggered by a road traffic collision death. The combination of the s 1(1) and s 1(2)(a) provisions requires an investigation to be conducted as soon as practicable once: (i) a senior coroner is made aware that the body of a deceased person is within that coroner's area, and (ii) the coroner has reason to suspect that the deceased died a violent or unnatural death.

17.4 Road traffic collision deaths are by definition 'violent or unnatural' and therefore, once reported to the local senior coroner, an investigation must ensue. The reporting of the death (thus making the senior coroner aware that the body of a deceased person is within that coroner's area) is typically a formality, with the death being reported by police and/or emergency medical services. Additionally, all deaths of children and young people under the age of 18, even if due to natural causes, must be reported to the coroner, for safeguarding purposes.

17.5 Road Traffic Collision Deaths

17.5 Under CJA 2009, s 6, the coroner's investigation into such a death must include the holding of an inquest. Notably, the CJA 2009, s 4 duty to discontinue an inquest where the cause of death has been revealed by post-mortem examination expressly does not apply to violent or unnatural deaths (CJA 2009, s 4(2)(a)). Therefore, assuming that the coroner's investigation is not suspended and then discontinued following criminal proceedings, road traffic collision deaths will always be investigated at an inquest. Circumstances in which an investigation and/or inquest is held in broader terms are set out at CHAPTER 2.

IDENTIFICATION OF INTERESTED PERSONS

17.6 Section 47(2) of CJA 2009 lists those who come within the definition of the term 'interested person'. An 'interested person' is someone who has the right to actively participate in the inquest proceedings, whether by virtue of their relationship to the deceased, involvement in the circumstances of the death or at the discretion of the coroner. Any party who might, reasonably, be thought to be 'involved' in the death, or who might by criticised by the coroner or jury in their findings, will ordinarily be an 'interested person' in an inquest. The list includes any person whom the senior coroner thinks has a sufficient interest in the deceased person, the investigation or the inquest. Thus, the senior coroner has a broad discretion about who is entitled to take an active role in the proceedings.

17.7 Whilst in each case the identification of interested persons will ultimately be a matter for the coroner and will be inevitably fact-specific, in the case of a road traffic collision death it can be envisaged that the following groups may be identified as interested persons (the list of potential interested parties is extensive but non-exhaustive):

- Family of the deceased.
- Drivers of the vehicles involved in the collision (or those most centrally involved, in the case of a multi-vehicle collision).
- Companies or organisations responsible for providing transport (for example bus companies, or coach companies).
- Local highway authority and/or local authority (where, for example, the road layout, road maintenance, and/or signage is criticised).
- Owners or controllers of land adjoining the highway in circumstances where their acts or omissions have potentially led to a danger on the highway, including for example the Rivers Agency, where danger has arisen due to flood waters.
- Individuals or organisations undertaking work on or near to the highway.
- Emergency services (where the response time, or aftercare, may be the subject of criticism).
- Vehicle manufacturers (where for example there is a suspicion that the design or build of the vehicle contributed to the death, for instance by seat belts not working properly, or air bags not deploying).

PRE-INQUEST REVIEW AND CONDUCT OF THE INQUEST

17.8 Where the case is complex, one or more pre-inquest review hearings (PIRs) may be held. At a PIR, amongst other matters, the coroner may give directions as to the identity of the interested persons; the future conduct of the inquest, including which witnesses are to be called and whether any witness statements or other documentary evidence will be read; the scope of the inquest; and whether a jury is required. See CHAPTER 4 for further detail of these matters.

17.9 In the case of a road traffic collision death, the coroner will need to consider evidence of how the accident or collision came about, where such evidence is relevant to the question how the deceased came about their death.

17.10 In the vast majority of road traffic collision death inquests, such evidence will be highly relevant to that question. Therefore, the coroner ought to give consideration to the issue of whether or not a police investigation report should be admitted as evidence and/or whether an independent road traffic accident investigator should be instructed by the coroner to produce a report for use at the inquest. The latter course may be appropriate (and/or may be urged upon the coroner by the family of the deceased at a PIR) where, for example, there is reason to believe that a police vehicle was involved in the accident or collision itself.

17.11 The scope of the inquest is restricted by CJA 2009, s 5(1) to ascertaining who the deceased person was; how, when and where they came by their death; and any particulars required to be registered concerning the death. The question of 'how' the person came by their death can in certain cases be treated more broadly, to be read as including the purpose of ascertaining *in what circumstances* the deceased came by their death, as provided for by CJA 2009, s 5(2). This provision applies to so-called 'Article 2' or '*Middleton*' inquests[1], where the state's duties under Art 2 of the Convention for the Protection of Human Rights and Fundamental Freedoms (ECHR) are engaged.

[1] See *R (Middleton) v HM Coroner for Western Somerset* [2004] 2 AC 18 and, more generally in CHAPTER 3 at 3.10 *et seq*.

17.12 Most road traffic inquests are unlikely to engage the rights and duties of the ECHR and thus their scope will be restricted to the four questions as per CJA 2009, s 5(1). However, as noted above, there will be road traffic collision deaths in which state agents are interested parties or the deceased is formally detained by the state at the time of the collision; the most obvious example being where a prison van, police car or other emergency state vehicle is itself involved in a fatal accident or collision. In such circumstances, the coroner can be expected to invite submissions from the interested persons about the scope of the inquest (including the applicability or otherwise of CJA 2009, s 5(2)) in advance of the PIR, and then make a formal ruling on the issue at the PIR itself. Scope is dealt with at CHAPTER 3 of this book in further detail.

17.13 Under CJA 2009, s 7(2), an inquest must be held with a jury if a senior coroner has reason to suspect that 'the death resulted from an act or omission of (i) a police officer, or (ii) a member of a service police force'. Thus, if one of

17.13 Road Traffic Collision Deaths

the vehicles involved in the accident causing the death was a police car, a jury will be required, in addition to the likely widening of the inquest's scope. The death of a prisoner or individual detained pursuant to the Mental Health Act 1983, whilst being transported on a road by a vehicle would amount to an unnatural death in custody or state detention within the meaning of CJA 2009, s 7(2)(a) as would the death in a road traffic collision of a prisoner or detained person who had escaped or otherwise left the place of their detention, assuming that they continued to meet the definition of detained persons. In all of those circumstances, a jury would be mandatory. Again, the coroner can be expected to invite submissions from the interested persons about this issue prior to the PIR, and then make a formal ruling on the matter at the PIR itself.

CRIMINAL PROCEEDINGS

17.14 Road traffic collision deaths are typically followed by police investigations in order to ascertain whether there are reasonable grounds for charging any of the surviving drivers with a criminal offence. Naturally, not all police investigations result in criminal proceedings.

17.15 In principle, a coroner's investigation into the death can proceed alongside the police investigation. However, Sch 1 to the CJA 2009 sets out when a coroner can or must suspend investigations (and when they can or must resume them). There are three specific situations where there is a duty to suspend and one general power:

(i) Paragraph 1 of Sch 1 provides that a coroner must suspend an investigation if asked to do so by a prosecuting authority because someone may be charged with a homicide or related offence involving the death of the deceased (as defined in para 1(6) of Sch 1). The suspension must be for at least 28 days but the coroner has the power to extend the period of the suspension (more than once if needed) if asked to do so by the person or authority who requested the original suspension.

(ii) Paragraph 2 of Sch 1 provides that a coroner must suspend an investigation if they become aware that a person has appeared in the magistrates' courts or the Crown Court charged with a homicide offence involving the death, or if they are informed of the same in relation to a related offence by a prosecuting authority and asked to suspend their investigation accordingly. The coroner need not suspend their investigation if the prosecuting authority informs them that they have no objection with it continuing (including while the prosecution in question is continuing itself: Sch 1, para 8). The coroner also has the power not to suspend the investigation if they think that there is an exceptional reason for continuing.

(iii) Paragraphs 3 and 4 of Sch 1 set out the circumstances in which a coroner's investigation must be suspended where a public inquiry is created under the Inquiries Act 2005. The terms of reference of that inquiry must include the purposes set out in s 5(1) of the CJA 2009 in relation to the death in question; namely, who the deceased was and how, when and where the deceased came by their death.

Criminal proceedings **17.20**

(iv)   Paragraph 5 of Sch 1 provides a general power to a coroner to suspend an investigation where appropriate. The example given in the Chief Coroner's Guidance is where, for example, another investigation is being conducted into the death by the Independent Police Complaints Commission, the Health and Safety Executive or an Accident Investigation Branch, or if an investigation is being conducted in another jurisdiction, for example, if the death occurred abroad[1].

[1]   Chief Coroner's Guidance No 33, Suspension, Adjournment and Resumption of Investigations and Inquests (7 October 2019), para 14.

17.16 The suspension of an investigation (and/or the adjournment of an inquest) should be dealt with publicly, in court and a review date ought to be set even if this leads to further review dates or the review date being brought forward[1].

[1]   Chief Coroner's Guidance No 33, Suspension, Adjournment and Resumption of Investigations and Inquests, para 7.

17.17 The term 'homicide offence' is defined in Sch 1 to include any offence under s 1 of the Road Traffic Act 1988 (RTA 1988) (causing death by dangerous driving); s 2B of RTA 1988 (causing death by careless, or inconsiderate, driving); s 3ZB of RTA 1988 (causing death by driving whilst unlicensed or uninsured); s 3ZC of RTA 1988 (causing death by driving whilst disqualified) and s 3A of RTA 1988 (causing death by careless driving when under the influence of drink or drugs).

17.18 A 'related offence' is either (a) an offence that involves the death of the deceased but is not a 'homicide offence' (or the service equivalent), or (b) an offence (be it a homicide offence or otherwise) involving the death of a person other than the deceased committed in circumstances connected with the death of the deceased.

17.19 It follows from the Sch 1 provisions therefore that the requirement for a coroner to suspend an investigation will not apply to fatal accidents or collisions where another driver has been charged only with careless or dangerous driving, as opposed to death by careless driving or death by dangerous driving.

17.20 In these cases, where it cannot be shown that the driving caused the death, the criteria for a 'homicide offence' or a 'related offence' will not be satisfied. As such, the coroner is perfectly entitled to continue with their investigation and even hold an inquest. Indeed, such an inquest ought ordinarily to take precedence over, and be held in advance of, any summary criminal trial that the other driver or drivers may face in the magistrates' courts[1]. For details of circumstances in which inquests can be suspended whilst criminal proceedings are ongoing, see CHAPTER 2; for further detail about the interplay between inquests and criminal proceedings more generally, see CHAPTER 21.

[1]   See *Smith v DPP* [2000] RTR 36, [2000] 164 JP 96 and *Re Beresford* (1952) 36 Cr App R 1, (1952) 116 JP Jo 194. These authorities suggest that any criminal trial of a summary-only offence ought ordinarily to be adjourned until after the inquest has taken place, although

17.20 Road Traffic Collision Deaths

ultimately this is a matter within the ambit of the magistrates' court's discretion. Query how such reasoning would apply now in relation to an indictable offence such as dangerous driving (s 2 of RTA 1988).

CONCLUSIONS: SHORT-FORM AND NARRATIVE

17.21 'Road traffic collision' is a short-form conclusion that was introduced in the Coroners (Inquests) Rules 2013, Sch 1, para 1 and approved in the Chief Coroner's Guidance No 17 on conclusions.

17.22 Coroners are encouraged, 'wherever possible' to 'conclude with a short-form conclusion'[1]. Other short-form conclusions that may be appropriate where the death is caused by a road traffic collision are 'accident or misadventure' or 'alcohol/drug related'. The Chief Coroner's Guidance highlights the appropriate use of additional words in accident cases such as 'the deceased was killed when his car was run down by an express train on a level crossing'. The phrase 'accidental death' may also be used. Alternatively, a narrative conclusion, defined as 'a brief, neutral, factual statement', may be deployed. See also **6.126** on 'road traffic collisions' as a short-form conclusion.

[1] Chief Coroner's Guidance No 17, Conclusions: Short-form and narrative (revised January 2016), para 26.

17.23 If the road traffic death results in an Art 2 or *Middleton* inquest, then the coroner must record 'in what circumstances' the deceased came by their death (CJA 2009, s 5(2)). The Chief Coroner's Guidance confirms that the conclusion in an Art 2 case may still be in short-form or narrative form (or a combination of the two)[1].

[1] Chief Coroner's Guidance No 17, Conclusions, para 45.

17.24 In practice, there are limited circumstances where a road traffic death is likely to engage ECHR, Art 2, but a death occurring when a prisoner is being transported to prison would seem to meet the definition of a 'death in custody'. In such circumstances, it is submitted that an appropriate determination of the case could be a short-form conclusion of 'road traffic collision' with a narrative addressing the wider circumstances of the death appended, as described (albeit in the context of a prison death) in *R (P) v HM Coroner for Avon*[1] and referred to with approval by the Chief Coroner in Guidance No 17 at paras 45 and 55.

[1] [2009] EWCA Civ 1367.

17.25 The crucial point is that the inquest process in such a case must enable the coroner or the jury to express their conclusions on the central factual issue or issues raised by the evidence without infringing either CJA 2009, s 5(3) (expressing an opinion on matters set out in s 5(1) or (2)) or s 10(2) (appearing to determine any question of civil or criminal liability)[1].

[1] Chief Coroner's Guidance No 17, Conclusions, paras 46 and 51 and see more generally CHAPTER 3.

PREVENTION OF FUTURE DEATHS

17.26 Under CJA 2009, Sch 5, para 7, a coroner has the power to make a Report to Prevent Future Deaths ('PFD reports'). These are considered in detail at CHAPTER 7.

17.27 In the case of a road traffic collision death which has been caused by the negligent driving of a motorist, it is therefore unlikely that the duty to prepare a PFD report would arise. However, where there are external factors contributing to the death, such as road layout, medication causing drowsiness, poor signage, or an inappropriate speed limit, the duty may be engaged and the coroner will be obliged to issue one or more PFD reports to the relevant agencies who may be able to take appropriate remedial action.

Chapter 18

PRODUCT-RELATED DEATHS

18.1 Inquests which consider the involvement of a product in how the deceased came by their death are often complex proceedings, frequently raising novel issues for all involved. Each case will turn on its own facts. Such inquests often attract national and sometimes international attention given the public interest element relating to the safety profile of what are often mass-produced items. They tend to be characterised as lengthy proceedings which involve a more developed disclosure process and the need for multiple factual witnesses and areas of specialist expert evidence. Because of all this they normally require significant resources, and it is generally helpful for interested persons to be represented.

WHICH 'PRODUCTS'?

18.2 The term 'product' is a broad church, spanning items which can be wholly distinct in their nature and purpose. For example, pharmaceutical drugs, electricity, fridge freezers, toys and food are all products, but each is produced by very different industries for very specific markets. Each has distinctly different regulatory regimes. The definition of a product is also a fluid concept. The age of the internet has seen this definition stretch to incorporate things which might not necessarily spring to mind such as software, mobile phone apps etc. Artificial intelligence permeates many product markets and looks set to push the boundaries of this definition further. Gone are the days when most of our products were manufactured in domestic factories to be sold in local high street shops. Rather, most products are manufactured in countries across the world and supplied on an international level often via a complex supply chain involving multiple parties, any of whom may be an interested person, depending upon the perceived fault in the product.

INTERESTED PERSONS

18.3 CHAPTER 2 considers who might be an interested person at an inquest in general terms. The paragraphs below set out common interested persons in inquests arising from product-related deaths.

18.4 The family of the deceased should be invited to become interested persons.

18.5 Product-related Deaths

18.5 It should be remembered that interested person status cannot be forced upon anyone. Further, the coroner's jurisdiction ends at the boundaries of England and Wales in terms of witness summonses. This can sometimes prove to be a problem in product-related inquests where the company is based abroad and there is no UK subsidiary or equivalent. The coroner is still able to write to an international witness with a request however, even if there is no subsequent enforcement power to compel attendance. An invitation for interested person status can also be sent to a foreign company. If this is not an option, or proves fruitless, the UK importer or retailer/supplier of the product might be approached to see whether they could assist the coroner in any way.

18.6 If the producer takes an active part in the proceedings, it is often worthwhile for them to consider engaging a specialist product liability, health and safety, regulatory and group action practice legal team and media relations consultants. Producers may need to be looking beyond the inquest to the potential ramifications with their regulator and the possibility of a future civil claim or even group litigation. Whilst the coroner will have no interest in such matters, practitioners attending inquests involving deaths where a product might be at fault should familiarise themselves with the regime established under the Consumer Protection Act 1987 (CPA 1987) and the Council Directive 85/374/EEC on the approximation of the laws, regulations and administrative provisions of the Member States concerning liability for defective products (Directive 85/374/EEC). The CPA 1987 and Directive 85/374/EEC are relatively short documents, in the context of consumer regulation. An action in negligence might also be brought under the general rules of tort and civil litigation.

18.7 The regime under the CPA 1987 and Directive 85/374/EEC is 'no-fault' in terms of a civil claim, in that negligence by the producer of the product need not be proved[1]. The regime makes 'producers' liable for the 'damage' caused by any 'defect' in the product.

[1] See the wording of the CPA 1987, s 2 'shall be liable' and the second paragraph of the text in the recitals to the Directive 'liability without fault on the part of the producer is the sole means of adequately solving the problem'.

18.8 A producer is the manufacturer of a finished product or any raw material or component part, and any party with a trademark or other distinguishing feature on the product[1]. Further, any person who imports the product into the UK in the course of his business will also be responsible as a producer. If the producer cannot be identified suppliers in line of the product will be treated as the producer unless they can provide the identity of the producer or of the person who supplied them with the product.

[1] See the CPA 1987, s 2 and Directive 85/374/EEC, Art 3.

18.9 The injured person must prove the damage, the defect and the causal relationship between defect and damage[1].

[1] See Directive 85/374/EEC, Art 4.

18.10 Damage is damage to property, death or personal injury[1].

[1] CPA 1987, s 5 and Directive 85/374/EEC, Art 9.

18.11 There is extensive case law now on what constitutes 'defect' but under the CPA 1987 a product is defective when it does not provide the safety which 'persons generally are entitled to expect', taking all relevant circumstances into account, including the reasonable use of the product and when it was put into circulation[1]. A defect might be an individual manufacturing defect, such as a brittle component or a design defect which is common to all products of that class.

[1] CPA 1987, s 3 and Directive 85/374/EEC, Art 6.

18.12 Although unlikely to be an issue at an inquest, it is a defence for the producer under the regime that the state of scientific and technical knowledge at the time when they put the product into circulation was not such as to enable the existence of the defect to be discovered[1]. This is often referred to as the 'development risks defence'.

[1] CPA 1987 s 4(e) and Directive 85/374/EEC, Art 7(e).

18.13 It is important to note that there is a 10-year longstop after the product was put into circulation when the right of action under the CPA 1987 and Directive 85/374/EEC is 'extinguished'. There is no provision for any extension of this period[1]. Other than that, the normal personal injury limitation periods apply, albeit under a different section of the Limitation Act 1980[2].

[1] Limitation Act 1980, s 11A and Directive 85/374/EEC, Art 10.
[2] Limitation Act 1980, s 11A.

FURTHER INFORMATION

18.14 At an early stage in the inquest proceedings, it is always advisable to carry out research to see whether there are any reports of other individuals being harmed or killed by the same product in question. There is no central database of product-related injuries or deaths and interplay between different coroners who have dealt with similar cases can be patchy. It is worth checking the government's website to see whether prevention of future death reports (see CHAPTER 7) have been issued in cases involving the same product or similar product types, or even the same company in question. Media reports of other seemingly relevant inquests involving the same product can be followed up with a written request to that coroner for a copy of the case file. The Chief Coroner's Guidance No 25 on Coroners and the Media states:

'Disclosure to others
27. The coroner _may_ provide any document or a copy of any document, including a recording, "to any person who in the opinion of the coroner is a proper person to have possession of it": regulation 27(2)).
28. In relation to a request by anyone other than an Interested Person for a recording or any other document, the discretion of the coroner on this issue (derived from the word "may") must be exercised judicially. The coroner should take into account:
    - the person requesting the document
    - the reason for the request
    - the public interest
    - the sensitivities of particular passages of evidence
    - the need for editing or redaction (if any, bearing in mind this was a public hearing), and

18.14 Product-related Deaths

- other relevant factors
29. Although coroner's have a discretion on this point, members of the media (who can show identification where necessary) should normally be expected to be considered proper persons for these purposes.
30. A copy of a recording should also be accompanied by a notice warning against improper use. A charge of £5.00 may be made for a copy of a recording or other document.
31. Coroners are not obliged to product transcripts of hearings.'

DISCLOSURE AND REGULATORY ISSUES

18.15 The reputational and commercial stakes for the producer of a product which may have caused or contributed to an individual's death can be significant. In any product-related inquest, it is crucial to understand the specific regulatory system in place at the relevant time. If it turns out that a product was in breach of the relevant safety regulations, that could be highly relevant when addressing the 'how' question. Practitioners should also consider any causal role that the regulator itself may have in the case and whether it might be of assistance to the coroner to argue that they should be invited to become an interested party or provide witness evidence. The most common regulators of products in the UK are Trading Standards for consumer products and the Medicines and Healthcare Regulatory Agency for pharmaceuticals and medical devices. The involvement of the regulator in the proceedings is normally the only point that a product-related inquest might satisfy the criteria to be made an Art 2 inquest.

18.16 There may be scope to argue that the regulatory system itself is inadequate. This might more persuasively be advanced in respect of whether the coroner should issue a report under Sch 5 para 7 to the CJA 2009 in that respect. To phrase the point in terms of causal relevance to the death would normally fall outside the scope of most inquests.

18.17 Disclosure tends to be a more significant task in inquests of this sort and something that might require numerous pre-inquest hearings to achieve before expert evidence and the witness list can be finalised. Some products are inherently more complicated to understand than others.

18.18 If any relevant issues have happened historically relating to the product in question, practitioners will want to know about them. The coroner may be more persuaded to grant a specific disclosure direction if the request can be phrased in terms of relevant classes of documents. Producers might raise counter-arguments that requests for information constitute a fishing expedition. Whilst some producers take an open approach to disclosure, others take a much narrower approach to what has been asked of them. This can make it difficult for families to prepare for an inquest, especially where the main hearing is imminent. It is open to the interested persons to consider asking the coroner to exercise their powers in terms of issuing a notice under Sch 5, para 1(2).

18.19 On a practical level, the legal team will need to be appropriately structured shortly after first instruction so that it will be ready to consider complex and most likely voluminous disclosure within a tight timeframe well in advance of the inquest itself. Counsel is likely to become overwhelmed if the outcome of the disclosure review is only provided to them just prior to the inquest itself, or even worse, not at all. The disclosure process often throws up issues including but not limited to (a) whether further disclosure is required, (b) the choice of factual witnesses, and (c) the choice of expert witnesses. The coroner may have read all, most, some or none of the disclosure. Access to online disclosure software can be of great assistance in terms of getting through a large review. Failure to properly grapple with disclosure at an early stage has often been seen to result in inquests being adjourned mid-hearing and going part-heard which is less than satisfactory. The worst scenario is where the inquest concludes and fresh evidence comes to light afterwards. Disclosure is further addressed in CHAPTER 4.

FACTUAL AND EXPERT EVIDENCE

18.20 A coroner has discretion as to which witnesses they call to give evidence. The coroner is not required to call every witness who might have relevant evidence, but sufficient witnesses to undertake a proper inquiry[1]. This can be a difficult line to draw in product-related deaths.

[1] *R (Ahmed) v South and East Cumbria Coroner* [2009] EWHC 1653 (Admin) at [35] and *Mack v HM Coroner for Birmingham* [2011] EWCA Civ 712, per Toulson LJ at [8].

18.21 It is not normally until full disclosure has been given that the court and interested persons can properly consider which witnesses from the producer need to be called in order to ensure a proper investigation. It is not uncommon for producers to start by putting forward what is known as an 'overview' witness, normally a relatively senior member of the company (but who does not sit on the management board) who tends to hold a regulatory position. Whilst that can be helpful to a certain degree, an overview witness is likely to give retrospective summary evidence and is rarely in a position to give any first hand evidence of the direct events which might have led to the death in question (such as the mechanic who works for a giant motor car producer who failed to fit a set of brakes properly). The interested persons should make attempts to contact factual witnesses who may hold crucial evidence. Again, the sooner these issues can be bottomed out in the proceedings the better.

18.22 The complex subject matter of most product-related inquests usually gives rise to the need for specialist expert evidence. Ultimately it is at the coroner's sole discretion as to whether expert evidence should be adduced. The Court of Appeal has observed in *Mack*[1] that this discretion is wide.

[1] *Mack v HM Coroner for Birmingham* [2011] EWCA Civ 712, per Toulson LJ at [9].

18.23 Coroners have limited budgets and some types of expert evidence can be expensive. It can also be challenging for an under-resourced court to identify the right expert for the job. It is advisable to try to be in a position to assist the court in terms of the expert search from the earliest point possible. Coroners are quite rightly wary about their courts being used to fund the investigation of a future civil claim. However, sometimes their duties can

18.23 *Product-related Deaths*

only be discharged if they do acquire expert evidence. Each case will turn on its own facts.

18.24 In certain circumstances, the interested persons may already be in possession of their own expert evidence. Where this is the case, practitioners should be clear, as far as possible, as to what the coroner's thoughts are about the potential admission of such evidence before disclosing it, remembering that legal privilege is waived once it has been disclosed. Expert evidence is considered in fuller terms in CHAPTER 4.

MEDIA

18.25 Finally, practitioners should ensure that the interested party they represent has received appropriate media advice well in advance of any product-related inquest as the presence of journalists covering the inquest is significantly more likely in a case of this sort. Producers may have a media plan in place. Inquests and the media are considered in fuller terms in CHAPTER 12.

Chapter 19
MILITARY INQUESTS

19.1 Inquests into deaths in the military raise a number of difficult issues. Firstly, they can present significant investigatory and evidential challenges, involving sensitive material which may not be suitable for public disclosure and, in some cases, deaths which have occurred in overseas combat zones. The essential legal principles remain the same as in other inquests. In this section, we will cover some of the practical challenges which may arise in military inquests in particular and offer some suggested solutions.

19.2 Additionally, however, it is important to bear in mind that military personnel are often particularly close colleagues and friends as a result of living and working together in extreme conditions. There may be divided senses of loyalty both to a deceased friend, but also to the military itself. These individuals may well be required as witnesses at an inquest, adding a further layer of complexity. All of this brings an obvious need for sensitivity.

19.3 This section covers[1]:

- organisation of military inquests;
- legal and practical assistance available for families;
- disclosure, including restrictions on sensitive material and the use of redactions;
- internal military investigations;
- deaths in combat;
- combat and Crown immunity.

[1] This chapter does not cover deaths of civilians overseas as part of UK combat operations, which give rise to a number of very difficult issues and can, in certain circumstances, trigger investigative obligations whether they occur in British custody facilities abroad or as part of military activity – see eg *R (Ali Zaki Mousa No 2) v Secretary of State for Defence* [2013] EWHC 1412 (Admin), which led to the establishment of an extensive investigation process concerning civilian deaths in Iraq. Nor do we cover so-called legacy inquests arising out of deaths in the Northern Ireland Troubles, which continue to be the subject of protracted litigation. Each of those subjects raises a number of difficult issues which fall beyond the scope of this book.

ORGANISATION OF MILITARY INQUESTS

19.4 The starting point for military deaths within England and Wales is the same as for any other death ie if it had a violent or unnatural cause, or if the cause is unknown, the local coroner will be under a duty to hold an inquest.

19.5 Military Inquests

19.5 Where such a death occurs abroad, but the body is repatriated to the UK (as now happens in almost all cases), the coroner to whose district the body is returned is obliged to hold an inquest if the circumstances were such that they would have been so obliged if the death had occurred in England and Wales[1].

[1] *R v HM Coroner for West Yorkshire ex parte Helen Smith* [1983] QB 335.

19.6 Prior to the CJA 2009, where there was a single death overseas, the inquest was held where the body was to be buried, but where there were multiple deaths, inquests were to be held where the body entered the UK. That led to a large number of inquests being held in Oxfordshire, being the location of RAF Brize Norton which was used for the repatriation of personnel killed in operations in Afghanistan and Iraq.

19.7 In 2013, the Chief Coroner created a specially trained cadre of coroners to conduct investigations and inquests into the deaths of service personnel 'on active service', which was said to include 'training and preparation for active service'. The purpose was said to be:

> 'to provide a specialist, well-trained, experienced group of coroners to conduct where necessary investigations and inquests into service deaths. It is also hoped that under this scheme a sensible and flexible approach can be adopted in all service death cases. This would clearly be to the benefit of bereaved families, the military and the wider public.'[1]

[1] Chief Coroner's Guidance No 7, A Cadre of Coroners for Service Deaths (26 July 2013), para 10.

19.8 Under these arrangements, any coroner who has a service death reported to their office should inform the Chief Coroner within 24 hours. If the next of kin wish the inquest to be held in their local area, that will normally occur, but with the Chief Coroner nominating one of the specially trained cadre to take on the investigation and inquest unless a local coroner has particular experience in such matters. Where there has been more than one death arising out of the same incident overseas, the normal arrangement will be for the inquest to be held in Oxfordshire[1].

[1] Chief Coroner's Guidance No 7, Service Deaths, para 12.

19.9 It is also relevant to note that treatment for serious traumatic injuries occurring to military personnel, which often present very differently to injuries which occur in civilian life, is generally provided in a specialist unit in Birmingham. Patients tend to be transferred to that unit if possible, including from overseas. In practical terms, this means that many service deaths which occur following unsuccessful treatment for traumatic injury will occur in the Birmingham and Solihull area. In such cases, the inquests will normally take place there before a highly trained and experienced local coroner.

19.10 As with other potentially complex and challenging inquests, the Chief Coroner has the power to ask the Lord Chief Justice to nominate a judge to hear a particular inquest. That occurred with the Deepcut inquests.

LEGAL AND PRACTICAL ASSISTANCE FOR FAMILIES

19.11 Families will often have strong associations with the military, potentially if they have lived on military bases with the deceased or through having multiple family members in the forces. In practical terms, pursuant to the Armed Forces Covenant, the MoD undertakes to enable those families who live in service accommodation to remain there for up to two years following a bereavement, and to transfer any resettlement entitlement which the deceased would have had to their spouse or civil partner in order to assist them with moving on.

19.12 Ordinarily, whenever a member of service personnel is killed, injured, or reported missing, their service will arrange some pastoral support for family members through a Visiting Officer. While the Visiting Officer will be part of that armed service, they will not be involved in such matters as instructing lawyers to act for the Ministry of Defence, so the risk of conflicts of interest arising is minimised.

19.13 More delicate personal issues tend to arise around senior personnel from the regiment, ship etc in which the deceased served. They are likely to be heavily involved in the inquest, but may also know the family personally and be some of the best placed to provide support. Provided it is understood that they might find themselves giving evidence at the inquest which the family would not wish to hear, it will normally be appropriate for them to offer such support as the family wish to receive. They may wish to nominate someone from their regiment who knew the deceased and the family well, but who was not closely involved in the circumstances of the death and who is not so senior in the chain of command as to be closely involved in advising on the position which the MoD should take, to be in regular contact with the family.

19.14 Under the Armed Forces Covenant, the MoD has committed to provide funding for up to three members of the deceased's family to attend the inquest, with funding for further family members available on application. It has produced a video about the inquest process which is intended to assist the family.

REPRESENTATION AND ATTENDANCE AT INQUESTS

19.15 In some inquests, the MoD may choose not to have legal representation and will instead send a case officer. The intention is to reduce the impression that the inquest is adversarial. At inquests which are higher profile or where civil claims may arise out of the incidents concerned, however, it remains common practice for a barrister to be instructed.

19.16 During the inquest hearing itself, large numbers of military personnel may attend, either to give evidence or simply because they are friends of the deceased and the family. A large military presence in court can feel intimidating for some family members. It is advisable to consider how many personnel really need to be physically present in court at any one time, and also to consider how many need to be wearing military uniforms. One suggestion, if representing the MoD, is to advise that personnel should only wear their uniforms when actually giving their evidence and should otherwise simply wear smart civilian clothes.

19.17 The Royal British Legion offers an Independent Inquest Advice Service, providing free, independent advice, including legal advice, to family members following deaths in the military. They are able to refer family members to specialist lawyers where appropriate.

19.18 In some cases, there will be potential civil claims for damages arising out of the deaths which are the subject of an inquest. Where this arises, families may be able to obtain assistance and representation from a specialist firm which deals with such civil claims. In other cases, where there is no civil claim arising, the Royal British Legion may be able to assist with finding pro bono legal representation for family members.

DISCLOSURE

19.19 The Defence Inquests Unit was established as part of the MoD in 2008. Its role is to co-ordinate disclosure and to assist coroners in understanding the issues which arise in military inquests. Since it was established, it has conducted training for coroners, including demonstrations of military equipment and visits to military training environments.

19.20 In many cases, a Board of Inquiry, Service Inquiry or similar will be held by the military (see more below on these internal inquiries.) From a disclosure point of view, the evidence gathered for these internal investigations will often produce relevant material for the coroner to consider. The report of the internal investigation may itself be relevant. In some cases, the coroner may wish to delay the inquest so that the internal investigation can be completed first.

19.21 The Defence Inquests Unit states that it aims for completion of inquests where there is no Service Inquiry within nine months of the death, and for completion where there is a Service Inquiry within 18 months. The Chief Coroner's aim is for inquests to be completed within 12 months of a death unless there is a good reason to depart from this[1]. Awaiting the outcome of a Service Inquiry may well be one such good reason.

[1] See CJA 2009, s 16.

19.22 The armed forces have extensive policies, procedures and standing orders governing how particular exercises are to be undertaken, what equipment is to be used, how material such as ammunition is to be stored and transported etc. Advocates for parties other than the MoD should seek disclosure of such documents in preparation for the inquest. As a matter of practice, individual regiments or squadrons may produce brief summaries of the key relevant rules and procedures, potentially in pocket sized format, for distribution ahead of a given exercise. It may be helpful to ask individual military witnesses what documents they were actually given in preparation for the exercise or operation in question.

Disclosure 19.28

19.23 In some cases, the potentially relevant material may include classified documents about military plans, equipment capabilities etc, and could conceivably include classified material obtained from allied nations. The MoD is likely to have concerns about disclosing such material. It is important to consider such material in two stages. The first question for the MoD to ask itself is whether or not it is relevant to the inquest, regardless of its classification. Coroners will only expect to see relevant material. The second, separate, question, is what reasons there may be for withholding or redacting disclosure – first to the coroner, then to the parties, then to the public at large.

19.24 It will often be appropriate, when dealing with sensitive material, for the MoD to disclose material at an early stage to the coroner only, under the *Worcestershire* principles[1], making clear that it does not consent to any further disclosure of that material. Such an approach can be helpful in delimiting the scope of the inquest at an early stage and may avoid unnecessary disputes about what material should and should not be disclosed publicly.

[1] See the Chief Coroner's Law Sheet No 3 for details of this case and the disclosure principles it set up.

19.25 Even disclosing classified material to the coroner may be problematic, as they and their staff may not have security clearance at a sufficient level to allow them to consider all of the material identified as potentially relevant. In such cases, the MoD may apply redactions on a public interest immunity basis, effectively declassifying the material by redacting sensitive contents.

19.26 In practical terms, Board of Inquiry reports will often be handled in this fashion. Information which is sensitive for security reasons (such as foreign intelligence or equipment specifications) will be redacted from these reports before they are sent to the coroner. Information which is sensitive for other reasons, such as references to individuals, may be redacted in versions of the report which are sent out to family members or published on government websites, but it will not be redacted for the coroner.

19.27 Disputes may arise, often between family representatives and the MoD, about the disclosure of material. Cases where unredacted material is disclosed to the coroner, but where redactions are permitted before onward disclosure under the *Worcestershire* principles, are relatively unproblematic. In such cases, the coroner will know what has been redacted and why and will be able to make a judgment about relevance. For instance, the detailed specifications of a given weapon system may be sensitive on security grounds. The fact that it is capable of causing lethal damage at a certain range is likely to be obvious. In most inquest scenarios, the latter fact will plainly be relevant and the former will then be ruled to be unnecessary detail for the inquest, and therefore capable of redaction or gist.

19.28 The most problematic disputes are likely to arise where material has been withheld from the coroner on security grounds, so that they do not know what lies beneath a set of redactions complained of by family representatives. In such cases, if the MoD wishes to withhold the material in the face of objections, it will need to make a formal application for public interest immunity (PII). This is only likely to arise rarely, and in the most difficult of

19.28 *Military Inquests*

cases. When a similar scenario arose in the Perepilichnyy Inquest, the Secretary of State issued a PII certificate over certain material and applied to the High Court for it to be withheld from the coroner[1]. Following that successful application, a new coroner with adequate security clearance which allowed him to view the material was appointed (HHJ Hilliard QC). He affirmed the High Court's finding on the PII application and went on to hold an inquest based only on openly disclosed material. Had it not been possible to do so fairly, he would have had to consider asking the Secretary of State to hold a public inquiry, under the Inquiries Act 2005, so that closed material could be reviewed.

[1] *Secretary of State for the Home Department v HM Senior Coroner for Surrey & Ors* [2016] EWHC 3001 (Admin).

19.29 In most military inquests, though, the fact that such inquests are held before a small number of specially trained and experienced coroners is likely to mean that disputes about the disclosure or publication of sensitive military material are capable of being dealt with in a fair and sensible fashion.

INTERNAL MILITARY INVESTIGATIONS

19.30 Where any service death occurs, consideration will be given to holding a Board of Inquiry. If it is felt, after an initial review, that the facts are clear and no lessons are likely to be learned from the manner of the death, no Board of Inquiry will be held. This may happen if a death occurs as part of an operation abroad, as opposed to as part of a training exercise.

19.31 Any Board of Inquiry investigation will seek to establish facts and will make recommendations of any lessons which need to be learned and any procedures which require amendment. Members of the deceased's family will not be invited to participate. The proceedings will take place in private, potentially in a military facility outside the UK. That investigation does not purport to be independent of the MoD[1].

[1] Ministry of Defence JSP 832, Guide to Service Inquiries, paras 2.4, 2.53, Annex C.

19.32 In cases where the Defence Safety Authority conducts an investigation, the practice is to appoint a lead investigator from one of the services which was not involved in the death – so for instance, an investigation into an Army death may be led by a Naval or an RAF officer[1]. While this still gives a greater degree of impartiality than a regular Service Inquiry, it is not designed to replicate the independence of the coroner.

[1] See for instance DSA/SI/02/17/TAJI, a DSA-convened Service Inquiry into the death of a soldier at Camp Taji, Iraq. The identities of the individuals investigating are redacted but it is clear that there was RAF involvement in the investigation of an Army death. The Convening Authority is DG DSA, a military officer of 3-star rank with direct access to the Secretary of State and operational independence guaranteed under the DSA Charter, most recently issued on 2 April 2020.

19.33 Reports of Boards of Inquiry, Service Investigations (which are similar) or the Defence Safety Authority (which tends to review a small number of higher profile incidents, or those which involve technical failures) are likely to be disclosable to the coroner. Statements made, and other material provided, for those investigations is also likely to be disclosable, regardless of what assurances of confidentiality may have been given when the statements were taken. They do not benefit from any statutory immunity. There is an important exception for material collected by or for the Air Accidents Investigation Branch, which does benefit from statutory immunity and is therefore likely to be exempt from disclosure[1].

[1] See *R (Secretary of State for Transport) v HM Senior Coroner for Norfolk, British Airline Pilots Association intervening* [2016] EWHC 2279 (Admin), a non-military case.

19.34 Many coroners adopt a practice of calling the author of such reports, if available, as one of the final witnesses at an inquest. Where such evidence is to be considered, it is important to recall that the report will usually be opinion evidence, prepared by someone who is not and does not purport to be independent of the MoD, who will not normally have sat through the oral evidence actually given at the inquest (which may differ in some respects from that given by the same individuals to his investigation), and who will have authority to make recommendations for future practice, but not to implement those recommendations.

19.35 In some cases, investigations may have been conducted by the Royal Military Police or, in the case of service deaths in the UK, by the local civilian police force. Material produced by those investigations will be disclosable to the coroner in the usual way.

DEATHS IN COMBAT

19.36 The requirements of Art 2 are capable of applying to deaths overseas. In *Smith (No 1)*[1], the Supreme Court considered the position of a soldier who had died of heat stroke whilst on a British Army base in Iraq. It found that he did fall within UK jurisdiction and that an Art 2-compliant inquest was required. On the facts of that case, there was said to be reason to think that the death could have occurred because of the default of the Army. The deceased had reported feeling sick from heat, but was ordered to carry on working outside.

[1] *R (on the application of Smith) v Secretary of State for Defence* [2010] UKSC 29.

19.37 The court also concluded that Art 2 duties would not apply to soldiers off the base. However, this was overturned in *Smith (No 2)*[1], which applied *Al-Skeini v UK*[2] and found that Art 2 requirements did in fact apply in circumstances where soldiers were said to have died as a result of defective equipment or of so-called friendly fire. The Supreme Court said that the doctrine of combat immunity continues to apply, but that it should be construed narrowly[3].

[1] [2013] UKSC 41.
[2] (2011) 53 EHRR 18.
[3] *Smith & ors v Ministry of Defence* [2013] UKSC 41, Lord Hope at [90].

19.38 In practical terms, coroners can be expected to adopt a relatively generous approach to the parameters of inquests involving controversial deaths of service personnel overseas. It will often be at least arguable that any particular death would have been avoided but for a particular plan or but for

19.38 Military Inquests

a particular alleged deficiency of equipment. However, the Court of Appeal has said that 'the right of a soldier under Art 2 [. . .] to have his life protected by law does not include a right to be safeguarded from human error, including negligent error, in the conduct of military operations which results in the risk of death on active service being greater than it would otherwise have been'[1].

[1] *R (Long) v Secretary of State for Defence* [2014] EWHC 2391 (QB).

19.39 Since 2014, there has been a significant reduction in inquests into the deaths of service personnel in combat zones. That reduction has come from a reduction in overseas operations rather than from any change in the law. The scope for argument about the limits of Art 2 in any future inquests arising from combat-related deaths overseas remains broad.

COMBAT AND CROWN IMMUNITY

19.40 Combat immunity normally applies as a shield to civil claims arising from deaths in combat. For its scope and limitations, see *Smith (No 2)* and the litigation which followed around Snatch Landrovers and Challenger tanks[1].

[1] *Smith & ors v Ministry of Defence* [2013] UKSC 41.

19.41 Following many ordinary inquests which raise health and safety concerns, such as defective equipment or inappropriate training practices, enforcement proceedings may be taken by the Health and Safety Executive or a similar body. The Ministry of Defence enjoys Crown immunity in respect of such proceedings, and therefore cannot be prosecuted in the manner in which a corporation might be for serious health and safety failings. However, the HSE is able to issue a Crown censure in appropriate circumstances, which has no criminal consequences but which is taken seriously by the MoD. The HSE does not investigate any accidents occurring outside the UK.

PRACTICAL EXAMPLES

Brecon Beacons SAS training

19.42 In very hot conditions in July 2013, three men died whilst taking part on an SAS selection march in the Brecon Beacons[1]. The inquest took place in 2015 in Solihull before HM Senior Coroner Louise Hunt, one of the specially trained cadre of coroners to deal with military inquests. Details of SAS membership, selection and training are obviously sensitive.

[1] Releasable Extracts of the Service Inquiry into the deaths of 3 soldiers in the Brecon Beacons Wales, in July 2013 – available through the Defence Safety Authority.

19.43 The names of participants other than the deceased were not released. Numerical codes were used to identify them. Details of the routes used were released. Public evidence was given by a number of military personnel, identified by ciphers and in some cases giving evidence in public but from behind a screen, and by an independent expert in the effects of heat on military personnel.

19.44 An application was made by media organisations for the release of written statements which had been used in the inquest. The coroner refused that application on the basis that to release the statements to the media could prejudice any future criminal proceedings (courts martial did in fact follow the inquest). She stated that she was only relying on evidence which was given in open court. The use of ciphers was also challenged by the media: the coroner ruled that revealing the identity of the witnesses could compromise their own safety, the safety of others, and national security. She commented that, in the circumstances, the use of measures to protect the identities of witnesses had the overall effect of improving the quality of the evidence given. The legal basis for such measures in coroners' inquests remains controversial and could well be the subject of a challenge to the High Court in a suitable future case.

19.45 The coroner gave a detailed narrative conclusion, made findings of neglect, and issued a report to prevent future deaths. Following the inquest, the HSE investigated, but was unable to prosecute because of Crown immunity. It instead issued a Crown censure against the MoD.

19.46 In July 2016, a soldier died in the army's annual fitness test in South Wales. His death was found to have been contributed to by heat stress. The inquest into his death was held before the same coroner. She issued a further report to prevent future deaths, and commented that the failure to learn from previous mistakes was very concerning[1].

[1] Coroner's comments following inquest into the death of Cpl Joshua Hoole, 19 July 2016, as reported by BBC News https://www.bbc.co.uk/news/uk-wales-50179071.

Jason Smith (Iraq)

19.47 Jason Smith's death was the subject of *Smith No 1*[1], in which his mother brought proceedings seeking an Art 2-compliant inquest. Following the Supreme Court's judgment, the inquest was held in Oxfordshire in 2013. He was a reservist who was deployed to Iraq in 2003. He was given little time to acclimatise to the very challenging climate, which saw temperatures exceeding 50C. The evening before his death, he was sent to help guard a power station, which involved spending prolonged periods in a very hot armoured personnel carrier. He suffered a cardiac arrest. After his death, his body temperature was 41.4C.

[1] *R (Smith) v Secretary of State for Defence* [2010] UKSC 29.

19.48 At the inquest, the army's policies around heat illnesses were examined. The inquest also considered the suitability of the equipment provided and of the briefings which were given to the soldiers.

Deepcut

19.49 Following a high-profile public campaign, extensive police investigations, judicial review proceedings, and a report by Nicholas Blake QC in 2006, in 2016–2019 fresh inquests were held into the deaths of Privates Cheryl James, Sean Benton and Geoff Gray[1]. The three were young cadets at Deepcut Barracks, who were each found dead with gunshot wounds to the head whilst

19.49 *Military Inquests*

alone on guard duty. Given the public importance of the cases, senior judges were appointed to act as coroner in these cases – HHJ Brian Barker QC in the first inquest and latterly HHJ Peter Rook QC.

[1] The Deepcut Review, Nicholas Blake QC, 29 March 2006, HC 795, https://assets.publishin g.service.gov.uk/givernment/uploads/system/uploads/attachment_data/file/228930/0795.pdf; *Geoffrey Gray, Diane Gray v HM Coroner for Surrey* [2017] EWHC 3648 (Admin); *Desmond James, Doreen James v HM Coroner for Surrey* [2014] EWHC 2585 (Admin); High Court judgment granting a fresh inquest in the case of Sean Benton not reported.

19.50 While suggestions of third party involvement were rejected in each case and suicide conclusions were returned, the inquests considered issues around safeguarding of the young cadets, bullying, a culture of sexual misconduct, and a lack of awareness around mental health issues in general and the risks of suicide specifically.

Chapter 20
INQUESTS AND COVID-19

20.1 Tens of thousands of people died as a result of COVID-19 in 2020. This had a significant impact on coroners' work, not only because there were a large number of deaths which potentially needed to be investigated, but because 'lockdown' restrictions affected the way in which coroners' courts could operate. The Chief Coroner published several guidance documents:

- Guidance No 34, Chief Coroner's Guidance for coroners on COVID-19;
- Guidance No 35, Hearings during the pandemic;
- Guidance No 36, Summary of the Coronavirus Act 2020, provisions relevant to coroners;
- Guidance No 37, COVID-19 deaths and possible exposure in the workplace;
- Guidance No 38, Remote participation;
- Guidance No 39, Recovery from the COVID-19 pandemic.

20.2 The Chief Coroner also released some COVID-19 notes. This book does not consider in detail the guidance or notes which set out the procedural amendments to the ways in which hearings were carried out, because these changed regularly over the course of the year and will continue to change in line with wider government guidance regarding social distancing (Guidance Nos 35, 38 and 39). Practitioners attending any hearings should check the latest Chief Coroner's Guidance as to how hearings are presently being conducted.

20.3 It is important to bear in mind that guidance from the Chief Coroner is intended to 'assist coroners with the law and their legal duties, and to provide a commentary and advice on policy and practice'. The guidance emphasises that it should not be taken as an indication of the Chief Coroner's views on the way in which coroners should exercise their duties. But it also claims to be 'an expression of the law as it currently stands,' and in practice, guidance notes are generally followed by sitting coroners.

THE CORONAVIRUS ACT 2020

20.4 Section 30 of the Coronavirus Act 2020 specifies that COVID-19 is not a notifiable disease for the purposes of s 7(2) of the Coroners and Justice Act 2009 (CJA 2009). Despite the fact that COVID-19 *is a notifiable disease* for

20.4 Inquests and COVID-19

the purposes of the Health Protection (Notification) Regulations 2010, there is therefore no requirement for a coroner to sit with a jury at a COVID-19 inquest.

GUIDANCE NO 34 – CHIEF CORONER'S GUIDANCE FOR CORONERS ON COVID-19

20.5 This guidance[1] contains several aspects of specific practical guidance for attempting to conduct coronial business whilst subject to lockdown conditions and restrictions. As noted above this aspect of the guidance is not addressed in this text.

[1] Published 26 March 2020.

(a) COVID-19 as a natural cause of death

20.6 Most substantially, Guidance No 34 advises in respect of treating COVID-19 as a 'natural' cause of death, relying on reg 24 of the Notification of Deaths Regulations 2019[1], which states:

> 'A death is typically considered to be unnatural if it has not resulted entirely from a naturally occurring disease process running its natural course, where nothing else is implicated.'

[1] SI 2019/1112.

20.7 The guidance therefore makes clear at para 18 that whilst every case is different, in general terms:

(a) COVID-19 is an acceptable direct or underlying cause of death for the purposes of completing the Medical Certificate of Cause of Death.
(b) COVID-19 as the cause of death is not in and of itself a reason to refer a death to a coroner under CJA 2009.
(c) Furthermore there is no requirement to refer it simply on the basis that COVID-19 is a notifiable disease under the Health Protection (Notification) Regulations 2010[1].

[1] SI 2010/659.

20.8 Paragraph 19 states that:

> 'Covid-19 is a naturally occurring disease and therefore is capable of being a natural cause of death. There may of course be additional factors around the death which mean a report of death to the coroner is necessary – for example where the cause is not clear, or where there are other relevant factors. This is set out in the Notification of Death Regulations 2019[1]. There may also be cases where an otherwise natural causes death could be considered unnatural.'

[1] SI 2019/1112.

20.9 The Chief Coroner, in conjunction with the National Medical Examiner, emphasises that the aim should be for any death that doesn't require a referral to simply be dealt with by way of a Medical Certificate of Cause of Death (MCCD) (para 20).

20.10 Of course, there will be instances where COVID-19 deaths are referred to a coroner despite this guidance. The question of whether a death is referred to a coroner is a separate issue to whether a coroner has a duty to open an investigation into a death under s 1 of the CJA 2009: just because a death is reported, it doesn't mean the coroner is bound to commence an investigation. Instead, that duty is engaged where a coroner has 'reason to suspect' that the death was violent or unnatural, its cause is unknown, or the deceased died whilst in state detention.

20.11 The Chief Coroner provides guidance to coroners to whom a death is referred when there is no Medical Certificate of Cause of Death (MCCD), namely (para 23):

- To open a dialogue with the doctor who reported the death or who was involved in the person's care, and if relevant to provide advice as to circumstances in which it is in fact appropriate to sign a MCCD.
- If there is no MCCD, to consider whether a post-mortem can be arranged. If this produces a natural cause of death, the coroner can decline jurisdiction and enable the death to be registered using a Form 100B. it is noted that this approach can also be used 'where the pathologist confirms a natural cause of death even if the exact cause is not ascertained'.
- If a post-mortem examination is not an option due to infection risk or 'because of capacity problems in the system', coroners are invited to take 'a pragmatic approach'. If the coroner thinks an investigation may well not be necessary, but cannot arrange a post-mortem within a reasonable time frame, they are advised to open an investigation and proceed to inquest. As part of this the coroner should assemble 'all the relevant medical and other evidence'. The coroner may then, if possible, hold a 'rule 23 inquest' ie a short inquest based on the documents alone, 'which considers the evidence and arrives at a conclusion (possibly of natural causes) with a medical cause of death either providing COVID-19 as the cause, or if there is still uncertainty, an unknown cause'.
- Alternatively, if circumstances require a more detailed explanation or if it is impossible to hold an inquest, for whatever practical reason, the coroner is directed to open an investigation, assemble the relevant evidence, release the body for burial or cremation, and list the inquest for a future date.

20.12 The Chief Coroner does note that the pandemic may create exceptional circumstances and introduce previously unrealised pressures on the system. He therefore invites coroners to remember 'their usual statutory duties' and to conduct 'proper investigations', whilst using their discretion, being pragmatic and flexible.

(b) COVID-19 and post mortems

20.13 In respect of post mortems, the Chief Coroner observes that there may well be difficulties for pathologists in conducting a post mortem during the pandemic as they might otherwise expect to. Coroners 'may need to consider

20.13 Inquests and COVID-19

partial or external examinations by pathologists, as well as non-invasive examinations, or no examination at all. Cases of particular complexity and sensitivity may need to be prioritised' (para 29).

(c) COVID-19 and deaths occurring in prison or otherwise in state detention

20.14 The Chief Coroner considers inquests arising from deaths in prisons or other state detention during the pandemic. He notes that 'there is no necessary requirement to have an inquest with a jury when the death is from natural causes' and that 'all coroners will make decisions carefully on the facts and merits of each case. it is obviously important that deaths in custody or otherwise in state detention are scrutinised carefully'. He notes that 'there may be deaths which occur which are not by natural causes and these should be given as much attention and resource as is available by investigators in the circumstances . . . The Chief Coroner considers it important that sufficiency of inquiry should be maintained as much as possible in prison deaths' (paras 38–42).

GUIDANCE NO 36 – SUMMARY OF THE CORONAVIRUS ACT 2020, PROVISIONS RELEVANT TO CORONERS

20.15 As the name suggests, this guidance[1] offers a summary of ways in which the Coronavirus Act 2020 may impact coroners.

[1] Published 30 March 2020.

(a) COVID-19 and Medical Certificates of Cause of Death (MCCD)

20.16 The rules surrounding which medical professionals can complete the MCCD have changed. As the Chief Coroner notes, 'signing and attendance are effectively decoupled, but with safeguards. Any practitioner can sign an MCCD, even if the deceased was not attended during their last illness and not seen after death, provided that they are able to state the cause of death to the best of their knowledge and belief'.

20.17 This affects the options open to the registrar when it comes to registering the death:

> 'First, if a medical practitioner (who does not have to be the same medical practitioner who signed the MCCD) attended the deceased within 28 days before death (a new, longer timescale) or after death, then the registrar can register the death in the normal way. Second, if there was no attendance either within 28 days before death or after death, then the registrar would need to refer that to the coroner. [. . .]
>
> The General Register Office position is that attendance before death can be visual (ie in person) or by video (eg Skype), but cannot be audio (ie telephone) only. Attendance after death must be in person. Clearly, some form of attendance would be ideal since it will reduce natural cause referrals to the coroner.'

20.18 In conjunction with this, reg 3(1)(e) and (f) of the Notification of Deaths Regulations 2019 (referrals to the coroner in certain circumstances arising from a lack of attending medical practitioner) are disapplied. Instead, 'the duty on a medical practitioner to notify the coroner only applies during the emergency period where it is reasonably believed that there is no other medical practitioner who may sign the MCCD (or that such a medical practitioner is not available within a reasonable time of the person's death to do so)'. This is taken from Sch 13, Pt 1, para 7(1) Coronavirus Act 2020.

(b) Documentation required for cremations during the coronavirus pandemic

20.19 The Chief Coroner makes reference to amendments to the certification requirements for cremation; the requirement for a confirmatory certificate, Cremation Form 5, is suspended, and instead there is only a requirement for one medical certificate ie Cremation Form 4 (s 19 of the Coronavirus Act 2020).

(c) Jury inquests and COVID-19 deaths

20.20 Finally, the Chief Coroner states that s 30 of the Coronavirus Act 2020 removes the requirement to hold a jury inquest if the coroner has reason to suspect that death was caused by COVID-19, even though it is listed as a notifiable death under the Health Protection (Notification) Regulations 2010[1] (which would normally mean a jury should sit at any such inquest).

[1] SI 2010/659.

20.21 The provisions of the Coronavirus Act 2020 are not retrospective. Provisions regarding death registration came into force on 26 March 2020, and provisions regarding MCCDs will remain effective 'during the life of the Act'.

GUIDANCE NO 37 – COVID-19 DEATHS AND POSSIBLE EXPOSURE IN THE WORKPLACE

20.22 Guidance No 37 was first published on 28 April 2020 with an amended version published on 1 July 2020.

(a) What does the Guidance say, and when should a COVID-19-related death be referred to the coroner?

20.23 This guidance, similarly to Guidance No 34, reminds us that COVID-19 can constitute a 'natural' cause of death. As previously established, COVID-19 as a cause of death does not in itself, therefore, require a referral to a coroner. However in this Guidance the Chief Coroner places COVID-19 in the context of the work environment. The Guidance states that there 'may be' exceptions to the general rule that it doesn't need to be referred, 'such as where the virus may have been contracted in the workplace setting' (para 7).

20.23 *Inquests and COVID-19*

Indeed, the Notification of Deaths Regulations 2019[1] **require** that a death is reported to a coroner where it is suspected that it was due to a disease 'attributable' to the deceased person's employment. Obvious candidates for referrals therefore include NHS and care workers and public transport staff who have died as a result of COVID-19 and who may have contracted it in the workplace.

[1] SI 2019/1112.

20.24 The guidance reiterates that where 'there is no reason to suspect that any culpable human failure contributed to the particular death, there will usually be no requirement for an investigation to be opened' (para 9).

20.25 As per *R (Touche) v Inner London Coroner*[1], a death 'may be "unnatural" where it has resulted from the effects of a naturally occurring condition or disease process but where some human error contributed to death' (para 11). This definition provides an important safeguard to ensure coroners investigate certain deaths from otherwise 'natural causes' when it is in the public interest to do so. COVID-19 deaths may therefore require investigation where it is suspected that 'failures of precautions in a particular workplace caused' the contraction of the illness.

[1] [2001] QB 1206.

(b) Can/should coroners consider any COVID-19 deaths involving PPE issues or matters of public policy?

20.26 During the COVID-19 epidemic the provision of PPE to workers has become a matter of national concern. The guidance as originally published discouraged coroners from investigating issues regarding the provision of PPE at a policy level, stating:

> 'Coroners are reminded that an inquest is not the right forum for addressing concerns about high-level government or public policy [. . .] an inquest would not be a satisfactory means of deciding whether adequate general policies and arrangements were in place for provision of PPE [personal protective equipment] to healthcare workers in the country or a part of it.' (para 13)

20.27 Following interventions by, amongst others, the charity INQUEST, the amended guidance now uses more tempered language in this respect. It emphasises that an inquest is an investigation into a particular death and that whilst it must be full, fair and fearless, it should also be focused on the circumstances of the particular death (para 15). It goes on to cite, in a more neutral fashion, the authorities (which particularly concern Art 2 of the European Convention on Human Rights (ECHR)) which it says provide 'indications in the judgments of the higher courts that a coroner's inquest is not usually the right forum for addressing concerns about high-level government or public policy, which may be causally remote from the particular death'. Before, however, emphasising that 'the scope of the enquiry is a matter for the judgment of coroners, not for hard and fast rules' (para 16).

20.28 The guidance goes on to provide practical guidance for coroners on how to obtain evidence or material relevant to matters of policy or resourcing.

It states that coroners may wish to suspend an investigation until it is clear how such enquiries can be pursued, it advises that 'coroners pursuing enquiries with hospitals and clinicians should be sensitive to the additional demands upon them during this period', whilst also emphasising that 'it may be in the best interests of a bereaved family to proceed in a prompt and timely way to inquest' (para 18).

20.29 The amended guidance does not, therefore, seek to prohibit coroners from investigating concerns regarding PPE at a high level, but emphasises the relevant authorities. Indeed, neither the original or amended guidance has stated that coroners cannot consider PPE issues at all. Local policies, such as within a particular employer or organisation, or the way in which a policy has been implemented in practice, are still potentially very much within the coroner's scope.

20.30 In one sense the original guidance could be read as an indication that the Chief Coroner's view was that some issues are better left to be investigated at a public inquiry, as opposed to at an inquest into a given individual's death. However at the time of writing (November 2020), despite much public speculation, the government has not given any indication that they are commencing a public inquiry into any aspect of COVID-19.

20.31 Furthermore, the guidance does not and cannot alter the primary duties of coroners to investigate appropriate deaths under the CJA 2009 and Art 2 ECHR. As Lord Lane stated in *R v South London Coroner, ex Parte Thompson*[1], a coroner should 'seek out and record as many of the facts concerning the death as the public interest requires'.

[1] (1982) 126 SJ 625.

20.32 Investigating civilian deaths that are suspected to have been caused by a failure to provide a safe workplace is a well-established coronial function, whether at common law or because of Art 2 ECHR. In the absence of the establishment of a public inquiry, coroners are likely to face arguments that the deaths of keyworkers should be fully and fearlessly investigated. Any refusal to investigate, or decision to suspend an investigation under para 5 in such cases may well be challenged by way of judicial review.

Chapter 21

INQUESTS AND CRIMINAL PROCEEDINGS

21.1 Many deaths engage both the coroner's jurisdiction and criminal jurisdiction. The senior coroner's duty under s 1(2) of the Coroners and Justice Act 2009 (CJA 2009) is to investigate a violent or unnatural death, deaths in custody, and cases where the cause of death is unknown. Those broad terms encompass all alleged criminal homicides. Specific provisions therefore govern which investigation and process takes precedence, and the relationship between the two jurisdictions. This chapter will consider the law governing the relationship between the coronial and criminal jurisdictions. As well as the rules on precedence of process, it will cover cases where an inquest prompts a criminal investigation or criminal prosecution, and practical questions regarding the distribution and disclosure of material between jurisdictions.

INITIAL JURISDICTION

21.2 Coronial jurisdiction is considered in detail in CHAPTER 2. However, once a coroner is made aware that the body of a deceased person that they have reason to believe falls within the scope of s 1 CJA 2009 is in their jurisdiction, it is the coroner alone who assumes jurisdiction over the body[1], and an 2009 Act investigation must be opened. Further, the coroner alone has the authority to carry out a post-mortem on the deceased[2]; although if the coroner is informed by a chief officer of police that a homicide offence is suspected, they must consult the chief officer about who should carry out the post-mortem examination[3]. These are matters of coronial jurisdiction. However, in practice, in deaths which are also homicide investigations from the beginning, these processes will be carried out by coroners and officers in cooperation with the police, who will have commenced their criminal investigation prior to a decision being taken as to the suspension of an investigation[4].

[1] *R v Bristol Coroner Ex p Kerr* [1974] QB 652 and CJA 2009 s 15.
[2] Human Tissue Act 2004, s 11, CJA 2009, s 14.
[3] Coroners (Investigations) Regulations 2013, reg 12.
[4] For further detail on the procedure governing post-mortems and jurisdiction over the body in a homicide investigation see *Jervis on Coroners* (14th edn), Chapter 14.

RULES FOR PRECEDENCE

21.3 Precedence between the criminal and coronial jurisdictions is primarily established by CJA 2009, Sch 1. In addition to CJA 2009, Sch 1, practitioners should refer to the Chief Coroner's Guidance No 33, issued 7 October 2019, which covers suspension, adjournment and resumption of investigations and inquests.

21.4 The aim of the system is to avoid overlapping investigations into a death, to establish clear rules for which investigation occurs first, to avoid confusion that might arise in parallel investigations and to avoid unnecessary duplication of investigation and the waste of resources. In the most common of the three circumstances, priority is given to the criminal investigation and any consequential criminal case. However, there remains a discretion that allows a coroner's investigation to continue. The coroner, in addition to the duties to suspend an investigation under paras 1–4 has power to suspend an investigation if it appears 'it would be appropriate to do so' under CJA 2009, Sch 1, para 5.

CORONER'S DUTY TO SUSPEND; CASES WHERE A PERSON MAY BE CHARGED

21.5 CJA 2009, Sch 1, para 1 places a duty on a coroner to suspend an investigation into a death where a 'prosecuting authority' requests the suspension on the ground that a person 'may be charged' with a 'homicide offence' or 'an offence . . . alleged to be a related offence'. Under CJA 2009, s 48, 'prosecuting authority' is effectively defined as the Director of Public Prosecutions. The section makes provision to extend the definition to others by order made by the Lord Chancellor; up to October 2020, however no extension had been made. The DPP's powers may be exercised by a Crown Prosecutor (Prosecution of Offences Act 1985, s 1(7)). Schedule 1, para 1 also covers the armed services equivalents of a 'prosecuting authority' and 'homicide offences', with the definitions of service offences and service police force under CJA 2009, s 48.

21.6 The full definition of both 'homicide' and 'related' offence is in CJA 2009, Sch 1, para 1(6). 'Homicide offence' has a broad definition which includes the most serious homicide offences, as well as the road traffic offences where a death is involved, encouraging or assisting suicide, and causing or allowing the death of a child or vulnerable adult . 'Related offence' takes the definition wider still. A related offence is one that:

(a) involves the death of the deceased, but is not a homicide offence or the service equivalent of a homicide offence, or
(b) involves the death of a person other than the deceased (whether or not it is a homicide offence or the service equivalent of a homicide offence) and is committed in circumstances connected with the death of the deceased.

21.7 The effect is that any criminal investigation with any effective connection with a death may trigger the duty to suspend a coroner's investigation.

21.8 Under CJA 2009, Sch 1, para 1(4) and (5), the period of suspension is initially 28 days, or for whatever longer period the coroner specifies. The period may be extended on further request by the prosecutor (Sch 1, para 7).

21.9 The paragraph therefore covers cases where a criminal investigation is under way and moving towards a decision to charge a suspect. The provisions reflect the reality that the prosecutor will normally be better placed than any other authority to know the progress of a police investigation, and that in many cases a month will be sufficient for the likely outcome to be clear.

CORONER'S DUTY TO SUSPEND; CASES WHERE A PERSON HAS BEEN CHARGED

21.10 If a coroner's investigation has not already been suspended under para 1(1), a similar duty to suspend the investigation arises when, under CJA 2009, Sch 1, para 2, the coroner becomes aware of a person charged with a homicide offence involving the deceased:

- either appearing in a magistrates' court charged with the offence;
- or appearing in the Crown Court on indictment.

21.11 The slightly convoluted provision thus covers all the homicide offences, whether triable either way (such as offences under Road Traffic Act 1988, ss 2B and 3ZB), or triable only indictment, and covers the different statutory provisions for sending a case to a Crown Court under Crime and Disorder Act 1998, ss 51 and 52. The provision also covers the rare occurrence of an appearance in the Crown Court resulting from a voluntary bill of indictment.

21.12 Schedule 1, para 2(4) extends the coroner's duty to suspend to 'related offences'. Schedule 1, para 2(3) and (5), make similar provision for armed services charges and offences

21.13 There is no formal requirement on magistrates' courts or the Crown Court to keep their area coroner informed of such cases, although many areas have established practical links.

21.14 There is also, unsurprisingly, a duty to suspend when there is to be a public inquiry under Sch 1, paras 3 and 4.

DISCRETIONARY SUSPENSIONS

21.15 In addition to the *duty* to suspend an investigation under Sch 1, para 5, the coroner has a general discretion to do so under para 5 where 'it appears to the coroner that it would be appropriate do so'. Guidance No 33 suggests that this broad power may be used where a death is under investigation by another authority such as the Health and Safety Executive or the Independent Office for Police Conduct, both of which would bring an expertise to the enquiry into a death. Alternatively, a death overseas may be being investigated where it occurred by a suitable authority.

21.16 Guidance No 33 emphasises that the discretion is 'wide but not unlimited and must be exercised reasonably and fairly'[1]. The principles set out on discretionary decisions in CHAPTER 8 on Judicial Review and Statutory review will be applicable.

[1] Chief Coroner's Guidance No 33, Suspension, Adjournment and Resumption of Investigations and Inquests, para 16.

EFFECT OF SUSPENSION OF INVESTIGATION, GOOD PRACTICE ON SUSPENSION

21.17 If the coroner suspends the investigation, they must adjourn any inquest being held as part of the investigation and may discharge the jury, CJA 2009, Sch 1, para 6. The adjournment will be made under Coroners (Inquest) Rules 2013, r 25(1).

21.18 Any suspension or adjournment should be dealt with publicly, and with review dates set[1]. On suspending an investigation or the adjournment of an inquest the coroner should provide the registrar of deaths with the particulars required to register the death[2].

[1] Chief Coroner's Guidance No 33, Suspension, Adjournment and Resumption of Investigations and Inquests, para 7.
[2] Chief Coroner's Guidance No 33, Suspension, Adjournment and Resumption of Investigations and Inquests, para 19.

EXCEPTIONS TO COMPULSORY SUSPENSION

21.19 CJA 2009, Sch 1, para 2(5) provides that the coroner need not suspend the investigation where the prosecuting authority (or Director of Services Prosecutions) indicates that there is no objection to the investigation continuing. Or 'In any case, if the coroner thinks there is an exceptional reason for not suspending the investigation'.

21.20 A decision not to suspend a coroner's investigation is unusual. It is a power that requires an 'exceptional reason', or the express agreement of the prosecuting authority. Further statutory provisions make it clear that the expectation is that the criminal proceedings will take precedence. CJA 2009, Sch 1, para 8(2) bars the resumption of a coroner's investigation while proceedings are continuing in the court of trial in respect of a homicide offence or related offence (or the similar service offences). Further, if at any time there is a resumed inquest, any determination made at the inquest may not be inconsistent with the verdict of the criminal trial, CJA 2009, Sch 1, para 8(5).

21.21 The Chief Coroner's Guidance No 33, which covers cases where there are criminal proceedings states unequivocally at para 9 that:

'The coroner will await the outcome of the criminal proceedings.'

The guidance adds, at paras 10 and 11, that in cases where the criminal investigation or proceedings have not made progress and are over 12 months old it may be open to a coroner to form the opinion that there is exceptional

COMPULSORY ADJOURNMENT UNDER THE CORONERS RULES

21.22 In addition to the Sch 1 suspension provisions r 25(4) of the Coroners Rules 2013 states:

> '(4) A coroner must adjourn an inquest and notify the Director of Public Prosecutions, if during the course of the inquest, it appears to the coroner that the death of the deceased is likely to have been due to a homicide offence and that a person may be charged in relation to the offence.'

21.23 Coroners will need to give careful consideration to the point during an inquest that r 25(4) is engaged. It should be noted that the duty refers to the adjournment of an inquest hearing alone. In practice the duty is likely to be engaged at the time as the discretionary power to suspend the *investigation* as a whole under Sch 1, para 5 of the CJA 2009 where it appears to the coroner that it is appropriate to do so.

DISCLOSURE

Disclosure of material from criminal process to parties at resumed inquest

21.24 If a coroner decides to continue or to resume an investigation or inquest following a criminal trial, there is likely to be available large quantities of material generated by the criminal process.

21.25 Disclosure of material held by the coroner is made under Coroners (Inquests) Rules[1]. The procedure covers the entire period from investigation to inquest[2]. Disclosure must be made by the coroner at the request of an interested party, and the obligation to disclose extends to all documents which the coroner considers relevant to the inquest[3]. Coronial disclosure is dealt with generally in CHAPTER 4.

[1] SI 2013/1616, Pt 3, rr 12–16.
[2] Rule 12.
[3] Rule 13.

Disclosure and use of material limited by statutory or legal prohibition on disclosure

21.26 There are statutory provisions which affect disclosure and use of made of material from criminal proceedings. Some of the provisions constrain the coroner. Other provisions may affect the duty of disclosure by parties to an inquest (such as a police force) to the coroner. In addition, the duty to comply with any conditions as to how the material may be used or passed on falls on any party in receipt of disclosed material; this may be of particular relevance to such interested parties as relatives of the deceased.

21.27 The statutory constraints include:

21.27 Inquests and Criminal Proceedings

- Any order made under Contempt of Court Act 1981, s 4(2) which gives the criminal court power to order that reporting of some or all aspects be postponed until the conclusion of criminal proceedings. Reporting includes reports appearing on social media. Details of what the prohibition covers will be available from the court office where the order was made.
- The use made of disclosure made to the accused at the criminal trial is limited by Criminal Procedure and Investigations Act 1996, ss 17–18 which restricts any use of the disclosed material to the criminal trial.
- There is potential lifelong protection of the identity of young offenders (those under 18) and of young witnesses and victims under the Youth Justice and Criminal Evidence Act 1999, ss 45 and 45A.
- The Youth Justice and Criminal Evidence Act 1999, s 46 gives the criminal court the power to restrict the reporting of the identity of a limited category of adult witnesses during witnesses lifetime
- The Sexual Offences (Amendment) Act 1992, ss 1–4 gives lifetime anonymity to complainants in sexual cases.

The coroner's discretion on disclosure

21.28 Additionally, depending on the timing of any request for or distribution of the material, the coroner may refuse to provide disclosure of a document or copy of a document if it 'relates to contemplated or commenced criminal proceedings'[1]. Disclosure of such material held by the coroner to the interested parties will, at least to that extent, be discretionary and not by right. In practice it may be made subject to interested parties undertaking not to make any use of the disclosure until a suitable time such as the conclusion of a criminal trial or resumption of an investigation or inquest.

[1] Coroners (Inquests) Rules 2013, r 15(d)).

21.29 In cases where the coroner does have documents relating to contemplated or commenced criminal proceedings, disclosure of the documents to the interested parties at the inquest will subject to the timing of a decision to suspend the investigation or adjourn an inquest, but would almost certainly arise should the coroner decide that despite the criminal proceedings there should be a resumption of an investigation or inquest.

Documents publicly available

21.30 Even without disclosure from the coroner, a great deal of the relevant material deployed at the criminal trial is potentially available to the public generally and particularly to those who can show a recognisable and proper interest in the provision of the material. The Criminal Procedure Rules 2020, rr 5.7–5.9 cover the provision by the court to any person of certain basic information about a criminal case (the charges, the dates, the result, etc.) These rules are supplemented by the Criminal Practice Directions 2015[1], Directions 5B.1–30. The Practice Directions give practical application to the principle of public justice re-iterated by Lord Toulson in *R (Guardian News and Media Ltd) v City of Westminster Magistrates' Court*[2].

[1] [2015] EWCA Crim 1567.
[2] [2012] EWCA Civ 420, [2013] QB 618.

21.31 Application for documents should be made first to the 'party who presented them to the court' (Crim PD 5B.6). Application for Prosecution documents should therefore be made to the Crown Prosecution Service and not to the police. Defence documents may be obtainable from the defendant or their solicitors; evidently a defendant is under no obligation to serve any interest but their own.

21.32 If the approach to the supplier of the document proves unsatisfactory, it is open to a party to apply to the court under Crim PR, r 5.8(7). The Criminal Practice Direction guides the exercise of the court's discretion to grant requests. Members of the family of the deceased will readily have an answer to any question asked as to why they seek the material. However, a criminal court faced by a request for disclosure from a party to an inquest will almost certainly also want a satisfactory answer to the question of why the application is to the criminal court and not to the coroner.

21.33 A request for a transcript of the public parts of criminal proceedings under Crim PR, r 5.5(2) is also to controlled by a similar discretion. Any transcript obtained will be covered by any publication order made under statute. Transcripts are available on payment of the fees for transcription

Material generated by a police criminal investigation

21.34 A coroner is likely to ask the police to assist an inquest following a criminal trial by producing some or all of their material to the coroner's court. Whether a criminal trial has occurred or not, it is common place in cases where the police have opened an investigation, for the officer in the case to provide a report to the coroner summarising the investigation. The normal rules of and law relating to coronial disclosure, as set out in CHAPTER 4 apply to such reports. Individual coroners, however, may adopt different approaches to disclosure of such reports and interested persons may need to specifically request the document. It is also common for coroners in jury cases to call investigating officers to an inquest to provide a summary in oral evidence of the investigation and action taken. If there is disclosure by the coroner to interested parties of the material generated by a criminal investigation, other than reports produced specifically for coroners, the police documents will be in standard formats.

Disclosure in criminal proceedings – 'relevant', 'sensitive' and 'non-sensitive' material'

21.35 For those representing interested persons where criminal material may be relevant to the inquest proceedings, it is helpful to understand the procedures that govern disclosure by the prosecution in criminal process. Disclosure in criminal proceedings is governed by the Criminal Procedure and

21.35 *Inquests and Criminal Proceedings*

Investigations Act 1996 (CPIA 1996), along with the Code of Practice issued under that Act and the Attorney General's Guidelines on Disclosure 2013. It is a continuing process with prosecution duties extending to trial, and beyond, to disclose 'relevant' material; that is 'any prosecution material which might reasonably be considered capable of undermining the prosecution against the accused or of assisting the case for the 'accused'. In criminal proceedings the prosecution assessment of what material falls into this disclosable category is assisted and informed by the statement of nature of the defence case required under CPIA 1996, ss 5, 6 and 6A. 'Sensitive' and 'non-sensitive' material are descriptions of categories of material that must be considered for disclosure in the criminal proceedings. Sensitive material that is not relevant to a defence, in that that neither undermines nor assists is not disclosable. Sensitive material that is capable of undermining the prosecution case or assisting the defence should be disclosed, possibly in redacted form or via admission, or made the subject of an application to the court to withhold the material based on public interest immunity from disclosure. Questions of disclosure should have been resolved during the criminal process.

21.36 In practice, material that has not been assessed as 'relevant' in the criminal proceedings is likely to require a carefully reasoned application for disclosure in any coronial proceedings. Reasons will need to explain why an area that was not relevant to the criminal proceedings would be relevant in an inquest.

Practical guidance on material to look for in criminal disclosure

21.37 The Home Office Manual of Guidance is agreed between the Home Office, CPS and Police Chiefs. It sets out the format of a series of 'MG forms' used to build a prosecution case file. These are the basic building blocks of a criminal investigation and prosecution. Likely to be of interest to parties looking for disclosure are:

- MG 5 – the offence report from the police; it produces the results of the investigation to date and is used to inform the court and defence at the first court appearance of the nature of the case and the available evidence.
- MG 6C – the form listing all non-sensitive unused material. Unused material is all the items gathered during the enquiry that are not used in the prosecution's case. The Schedule should describe this material in sufficient detail to allow the crown prosecutor to decide as to whether to disclose it to the defence. The prosecutor's decision is recorded on the form and served on the defence.
- MG 11 – each witness statement will be on an MG11 form.
- MG 12 – the exhibits Schedule.
- MG 15 – records of interview under caution of suspects.

21.38 The forms that will not generally be available for disclosure are the:
- MG 3 reports to the CPS for advice, a decision log and action plan which will be covered either by legal privilege or alternatively by a public interest immunity from disclosure – the relevant public interest

being in allowing the free flow of information between police and CPS and the inhibiting effect disclosure in a particular case might have on the general process.
- Parts of MG 6 forms such as the MG6 itself which will have 'sensitive information' provided to assist CPS decision making and the MG6D, the Schedule of sensitive material.

Other criminal process material

21.39 In addition, a criminal investigation may also produce:
- A contemporaneous record of earliest stages of enquiries, typically notes detailing the call/s to emergency services and the initial police radio traffic (in some police areas called the CAD (computer aided despatch) report).
- A crime report. Generally, within 24 hours the despatch record will be taken over by a crime report, which will then become a log of the investigation.
- Most murder inquiries and some other large or complex police enquires are run and recorded using the Home Office computer software known as HOLMES (Home Office Large Major Enquiry System). The system categorises such material as Actions (eg 'collect CCTV from . . . '), Statements (from witnesses), Reports, Interviews, Messages, and Electronic transmissions
- A road traffic death should generate from the police investigation a vehicle examiner's report – checking for pre-collision mechanical defects and the state of vehicles when recovered, and a collision investigator report which will describe the scene before and after the collision, attempt to reconstruct what happened and offer an opinion about the cause of the collision.

RESUMPTION OF INVESTIGATION OR INQUEST

Later resumption of the investigation

21.40 Where a coroner's investigation has been suspended under Sch 1, para 1 (ie at the prosecuting authority's request where a suspect may be charged), the coroner has a duty to resume the investigation at the end of the either the initial suspension period or of any extension to that period under Sch 1, para 7.

21.41 However, if criminal proceedings are brought (and so the investigation is suspended either under Sch 1, para 2 or the initial suspension is extended under Sch 1, para 2(7)(d)), the investigation 'may not be resumed unless, but must be resumed if, the senior coroner thinks there is sufficient reason for resuming it'[1]. There is an exception to this rule, which allows an investigation to be resumed where criminal proceedings are continuing, if the prosecuting authority informs the coroner that it has no objection to the investigation being resumed (Sch 1, para 8(3)).

[1] Coroners and Justice Act 2009, Sch 1, para 8(1).

21.42 *Inquests and Criminal Proceedings*

21.42 If the investigation or inquest was suspended in the exercise of the coroner's general discretion (under Sch 1, para 5), the coroner may resume the investigation at any time if they think that there is sufficient reason for doing so (Sch 1, para 10).

Sufficient reason

21.43 There is no statutory guidance on what may constitute 'sufficient reason' for a resumption.

21.44 Some indication of what may provide sufficient reason for resumption is found in the Chief Coroner's Guidance No 33, paras 26–27, 32–38. Suggested reasons for resumption include the wishes of the family, other parties' submissions, inadequacies in the medical evidence and 'the circumstances of the death'.

21.45 The coroner will also need to consider the public interest in a further investigation, and whether an inquest will investigate topics not already explored in public, perhaps with a view to the coroner exercising their duty to write a report to prevent future deaths under reg 28.

21.46 The coroner will need to consider if the Crown Court proceedings involved a thorough consideration of all the facts, and in particular whether the criminal court hearing has sufficiently answered the questions of who the deceased was, and how, when and where they came by their death. If those questions are answered then a coroner may well conclude that there is no sufficient reason for a resumption. The coroner's discretion is not however confined to cases involving 'exceptional circumstances'; the section itself requires only 'sufficient cause' (and see *R v HM Coroner for Inner London West Section, ex p Dallaglio*[1]).

[1] [1994] 4 All ER 139 at p 155.

21.47 In discussion of the breadth of the discretion the Chief Coroner's Guidance No 33 invites parallels with the exercise of the discretion under CJA 2009, s 7(3) to hold an inquest with a jury if the coroner 'thinks there is sufficient reason', and the cases decided under s 7(3).

21.48 Where there has been a thorough consideration of the facts in a substantive hearing in criminal proceedings at the Crown Court (or magistrates' court) it may be unusual to resume a coroner's investigation or the inquest, as the criminal trial will be likely to answer the questions of the identity of the deceased, and how when and where they came by their death. A factual example of a case where a trial has taken place but issues remain so that it is in the public interest to determine these at a further inquest, is where arguable failures in probation supervision, policing or mental health care contributed to a homicide offence being committed. Inquests post-criminal homicide proceedings in these types of cases have become increasingly common in recent years. In such cases Art 2 of the European Convention on Human Rights (ECHR) is also likely to be engaged.

Resumption under Art 2

21.49 Coroners approaching a resumption hearing will need to consider whether the Art 2 ECHR duty to investigate is triggered. The most likely issues will be whether the death was arguably caused or contributed to by the acts or omissions of a public authority, and if the criminal proceedings have fulfilled the state's investigative duty – *R (on the application of Silvera) v HM Senior Coroner for Oxfordshire*[1]. The investigative duty under Art 2 ECHR and the conditions for its engagement are considered in detail at CHAPTER 3.

[1]   [2017] EWHC 2499 (Admin).

21.50 Criminal proceedings in general provide little scope for relatives' direct participation. It may be limited to the provision to the court by a relative of the deceased of a 'Victim Personal Statement' (see Criminal Practice Direction VII, Sentencing F). The relatives are not represented, save in the most general terms, by the prosecution which represents the family's interest only as part of the full public interest. They have no opportunity to cross examine witnesses or to have explored any aspect of evidence that the prosecution considers irrelevant or unnecessary to the charge brought.

21.51 The seminal Art 2 authority in *R (Amin) v Secretary of State for the Home Department*[1] provides an example of a homicide case where a criminal trial for murder did not satisfy the investigative duty. The *Amin/Jordan* criteria are considered in detail in CHAPTER 3 at 3.104. In relation to the provision of relevant material to the deceased's family, which was an aspect of the decision in *Amin*, practice has changed since 2003. Much more material from a criminal trial can now be obtained by members of a victim's family (see under Documents Publicly Available, above).

[1]   [2003] UKHL 51.

Inquest findings must be consistent with the result of the criminal process

21.52 A resumed investigation or inquest cannot be used as a means of collateral attack on the verdict in the criminal trial. Any determination made by the resumed investigation or inquest must be consistent with the result of the criminal proceedings which triggered the suspension[1].

[1]   CJA 2009, Sch 1, paras 8(5) and 9(11).

CRIMINAL PROCEEDINGS INITIATED FOLLOWING INQUEST VERDICT

21.53 In certain cases the outcome of coronial proceedings will lead to a criminal prosecution. Such an outcome is by no means, however, an automatic response to an unlawful killing conclusion. That is because coroners' proceedings are not adversarial; an inquest jury is not considering a specific criminal charge against an individual; any person charged will be individually represented in criminal proceedings; and there are different rules affecting who may call witnesses and how they may be examined, and who may address the jury.

21.53 *Inquests and Criminal Proceedings*

The decision on whether to prosecute will be made by the Crown Prosecution Service

21.54 The decision can be affected by a previous decision not to prosecute. There is a presumption that if a suspect is informed of a decision not to prosecute that they may rely on that decision, and it should not ordinarily be revoked. However, the Code for Crown Prosecutors section 10.2 includes among reasons when a prosecution may be restarted:

> '. . . cases involving a death in which a review following the findings of an inquest concludes that a prosecution should be brought, notwithstanding any earlier decision not to prosecute.'

21.55 Nonetheless, where there has been a decision not to prosecute the CPS encourages reviewing lawyers to attend relevant parts of an inquest, for example to see and hear how witnesses give evidence. This is particularly so for deaths in custody cases (and see also para 6.11 CPS Policy for Prosecution Cases of Bad Driving).

21.56 Any further review of a decision not to prosecute will take account of evidence that has emerged in the course of the inquest, and any of the jury's conclusions that indicate which parts of the evidence they accepted or rejected as well as judgments, where possible as to the effectiveness with which witnesses gave evidence; all of the these factors can assist the prosecutor's assessment. The decision will be subject to the 'The Full Code Test' requirements in the Code for Crown Prosecutors, ie that there is sufficient evidence to provide a realistic prospect of a conviction, and that a prosecution is in the public interest.

Victim's right of review

21.57 The CPS, following *R v Killick*[1], provides for a victim's right to review a decision not to prosecute an offence. 'Victims' include close relatives of a person whose death was directly caused by criminal conduct. Full details of the scheme are available from https://www.cps.gov.uk/legal-guidance/victims-right-review-scheme.

[1] [2011] EWCA Crim 1608.

Criminal trial not bound by inquest verdict

21.58 There is no equivalent in criminal proceedings of CJA 2009, Sch 1, para 8(5), that requires an inquest's findings to be consistent with the verdict of a criminal trial. If there is a criminal trial as a result of an inquest, the criminal jury are not bound by the inquest verdict and may acquit or convict of the offence before them, uninhibited by the inquest's result.

Chapter 22

INQUESTS AND FAMILY PROCEEDINGS

22.1 In tragic cases involving the death of a child and where there are allegations of harm or non-accidental injury inflicted by an adult who has had care of that child, the local authority may make an application for a care or supervision order in relation to siblings or other children[1]. Care orders place a child in the care of the local authority, whilst supervision orders mean they have a duty to 'advise, assist and befriend the supervised child'[2]. Care proceedings involving the death of a child are among the most serious and difficult that the Family Court must deal with. The local authority should investigate fully. At a fact-finding hearing, the Family Court will usually hear extensive evidence, including evidence from the parent(s), other carers, professionals involved with the child or the family such as social workers, health visitors and teachers, and any relevant experts. The parents are eligible for public funding and are often represented by leading counsel as a result of the seriousness of the case. At the conclusion of the hearing, the Family Court judge will make detailed findings of fact[3].

[1] The power to make a care or supervision order arises from Children Act 1989, s 31.
[2] Children Act 1989, ss 33 and 35.
[3] See *Re JS* [2012] EWHC 1379 (Fam) for distillation of principles to be applied by the court in making findings of fact.

22.2 It should be noted that the Family Court does not have the power to investigate the death of a child unless the local authority makes an application in respect of other children whose welfare is in issue: if the deceased child has no siblings for instance, such proceedings cannot arise.

22.3 Whilst there is a clear statutory framework which governs the relationship between coronial investigations and criminal proceedings, there is nothing similar relating to family proceedings. The Chief Coroner has issued Guidance No 13[1], which suggests that findings of fact of the Family Court should be admitted into inquests investigating the same death; there would be good reason to do so. There is a public interest in relying upon the findings of the Family Court and not rehearing evidence, which would be time-consuming, costly and stressful. There is also the risk that the coroner could make different and inconsistent findings.

[1] Chief Coroner's Guidance No 13, Family Court Proceedings – Findings of Fact Admissibility in the Family Court (10 April 2014).

22.4 Inquests and Family Proceedings

22.4 The Chief Coroner stresses that the law has not been conclusively decided on this point, but makes the following observations[1]:

(1) The findings of fact in the Family Court are opinion evidence, specifically the opinion of the judge who has heard and assessed the evidence, and they are relevant evidence. A coroner's inquest is not bound by strict rules of evidence, and there is no restriction to the admissibility of opinion evidence in an inquest.

(2) The findings of the Family Court judge in Children Act proceedings may carry additional weight because the Family Court is 'far from adversarial', and the higher courts have emphasised both the partly inquisitorial nature of care proceedings and the relaxation of the strict rules of evidence. The Chief Coroner therefore suggests that the rule in *Hollington v Hewthorn*[2], that findings of fact are ordinarily inadmissible in other proceedings, has no application in relation to the findings of fact of the Family Court being adduced in the coroner's court.

(3) It is at least arguable that Parliament intended the Children Act 1989, and matters arising from it, to be an exception to the rule in *Hollington v Hewthorn*.

[1] Chief Coroner's Guidance No 13, Family Court Proceedings, paras 5–8.
[2] [1943] KB 587.

22.5 Whilst it is for coroners to make up their own mind having heard submissions from interested persons, the guidance concludes that 'coroners may . . . take the view, after legal submissions, that they are not barred from relying upon findings of fact in the Family Court. There is both good sense and potentially good law for taking that view'[1].

[1] Chief Coroner's Guidance No 13, Family Court Proceedings, para 9.

22.6 Before admitting the findings of fact into evidence, the coroner should consider whether it is fair and just to do so. Such circumstances may arise where:

(1) the coroner has closely scrutinised the judgment of the Family Court in order to be satisfied that the Family Court heard all the relevant evidence about the death;

(2) relevant members of the family of the deceased had the opportunity to challenge the evidence in the Family Court;

(3) other relevant matters not covered by the findings in the Family Court may be raised in further evidence at the inquest;

(4) interested persons have had the opportunity to consider making submissions about the law and findings of the Family Court at a pre-inquest review hearing; and

(5) the coroner is satisfied in all the circumstances that there is 'sufficiency of evidence' for the purposes of the inquest[1].

[1] Chief Coroner's Guidance No 13, Family Court Proceedings, para 10.

22.7 As a practical matter, unless the judgment has already been released for publication by the Family Court, the coroner must obtain the permission and an order for disclosure of the Family Court judge before relying upon the judgment. Redaction may be necessary[1].

[1] Chief Coroner's Guidance No 13, Family Court Proceedings, paras 12–13.

22.8 In *A v HM Coroner for Central and North West London*[1] an infant was found on the floor with severe injuries from which he died. Although the coroner was informed that a 15-day fact-finding hearing had been listed in care proceedings, in a letter which stated that 'you may want to take this into account when considering whether or not to proceed to a final inquest', the coroner nevertheless proceeded with the inquest and determined that the baby's injuries were caused by his 4½-year-old brother. Subsequently Peter Jackson J concluded the in the fact-finding hearing that the infant had been fatally injured by his father and listed no fewer than 22 separate factors which told against the sibling being the perpetrator. The Divisional Court had no hesitation in quashing the inquest findings on the grounds of insufficiency of enquiry and procedural irregularity, as the coroner had taken no steps to notify the local authority of the inquest, or that they may wish to take steps to protect the sibling's interests. Laws LJ stated:

> 'It is worth noting that recent helpful guidance from the Chief Coroner, who sits in this case with me today, advances the view that findings in care proceedings such as those made by Peter Jackson J in this case may be admitted at an inquest. The question for the coroner would be whether it is fair and just to admit such material. That seems to me, with respect, to be right.
>
> *HM Senior Coroner for the County of Cumbria v Ian Smith* [2015] EWHC 2465 (Admin) was a well-publicised case arising from the tragic death of Poppi Worthington at the age of 13 months. Jackson J had conducted a family law fact-finding hearing relating to the cause of injuries sustained before Poppi's death and concluded that the cause of the death itself was unascertained. His judgment was subject to embargo to avoid prejudicing criminal proceedings, and there were orders preventing identification of the mother and siblings. At the inquest, the coroner indicated he had taken account of and adopted the factual findings made by the judgment in the parallel Family Court proceedings, but because of the restriction on using the judgment publicly, he was unable to refer to those findings, and thus there was no evidence put into the public domain concerning the circumstances in which Poppi died. The part of the record which is headed 'How, when and where the deceased came by his or her death' was left blank. Unsurprisingly the Divisional Court held that the inquest was irregular because it failed to perform its central function of determining how, when and where Poppi came by her death, there was no recording of the facts required, and evidence was taken in private. A fresh inquest was ordered, to take place after a further fact finding hearing in the Family Court, with the court suggesting that there would need to be close cooperation between the two courts to ensure that any embargo has been lifted and necessary redactions made to the judgment.'

[1] [2014] EWHC 2676 (Admin).

22.9 Although the Divisional Court declined to express a view as to whether the Chief Coroner's Guidance represented the law, having not heard submissions upon it, Burnett LJ stated that it was 'apparent that all lawful steps should be taken to avoid unnecessary duplication of effort'.

22.10 The Chief Coroner's Guidance sensibly advises good co-operation between the coroner and the local Family Court, as the family judge may require material from the coroner or vice-versa. Either way, judges and coroners are expected to make requests of each other, not orders, and in complex cases it would be helpful if coroner and judge set out a joint timetable

22.10 Inquests and Family Proceedings

providing for the timing of disclosure and the sharing of conclusions and determination[1].

[1] Chief Coroner's Guidance No 13, Family Court Proceedings, para 14.

22.11 The Family Court may admit into evidence in the family proceedings any relevant evidence that has been obtained for the purpose of an inquest. In the case of expert evidence, such evidence must be necessary to assist the court to resolve the proceedings justly, fall within the expertise of the expert, and the expert must understand their duty to the court. Further detail of the rules of evidence in the Family Court is set out in the Family Procedure Rules 2010.

REPORTING RESTRICTIONS IN RESPECT OF CHILDREN INVOLVED IN OR AFFECTED BY AN INQUEST

22.12 Children who are witnesses in an inquest can be the subjects of an order under s 39 Children and Young Person's Act 1933, which restricts the reporting of their name or identifying information.

22.13 It is also important however to bear in mind that any disclosure of a deceased person's identity may lead to the accidental disclosure of the identity of a child, such as a sibling, son or daughter. This could have real and adverse consequences for them. If there appears to be a risk of accidental disclosure in this way, the coroner should invite the relevant local authority, or a children's guardian acting on behalf of the child, to apply to the High Court for an order which restricts the reporting of information which might lead to identification of the child[1]. Any such application will be determined by an application of the principles set out in the criminal case of *Re S (A Child) (Identification: Restrictions on Publication)*[2], as modified and endorsed in *Re LM (Reporting Restrictions: Coroner's Inquest)*[3] and in the Chief Coroner's Guidance No 25.

[1] *Re LM (Reporting Restrictions: Coroner's Inquest)* [2007] EWHC 1902 (Fam).
[2] [2005] 1 AC 593.
[3] [2007] EWHC 1902 (Fam).

22.14 Fuller details of reporting restrictions in inquests are dealt with in CHAPTER 12.

Chapter 23
INQUESTS AND CIVIL PROCEEDINGS

23.1 An inquest, representing the culmination of a coroner's investigation, is a complete legal process. It is free-standing, in terms of its practice and procedure, and unusual in that it is inquisitorial rather than adversarial.

23.2 In many cases, the inquest will be the sole legal proceedings following a death, but sometimes the conclusion of the inquest will be the beginning, rather than the end, of legal proceedings arising from the death, and a civil claim for damages or other remedy will be the next step.

23.3 Whilst a coroner is expressly forbidden from expressing a conclusion which determines any civil or criminal liability for the death[1], the family of the deceased, and/or their lawyers, will often see the inquest as part of a fact gathering process for subsequent civil proceedings. Indeed, the family's lawyers may only be paid for their participation in the inquest in the event of a successful civil case arising out of it. Thus, their focus throughout the inquest may have been on the prospect of a civil claim all along. This may lead to a mismatch between the function of an inquest, and the expectations of the family of the deceased of the inquest process. This was remarked upon by Kay J in *R v HM Coroner for Birmingham and Solihull, Ex p Julie Benton*[2]:

> 'It is of critical importance to recognise the true purpose of an inquest. Sadly, the public's perception of such purpose does not always match the reality, and those caught up in the process expect more . . . than it can, or is permitted to, deliver thereby adding to their distress.'

[1] CJA 2009, s 10(2).
[2] (1997) 162 JP 807, [1997] 8 Med LR 362.

23.4 The reasons for this mismatch may be nuanced, but simple human desire to see someone held to account for the death, often fuelled in part by guilt that 'more could have been done' to have avoided the death, may be powerful drivers[1]. Arguably this mismatch also derives in part from the rules governing inquest procedure which are, as has been observed by the judicial committee of the House of Lords, partly adversarial in content: See *R (Middleton) v West Somerset Coroner*[2]: 'The 1984 Rules prescribe a hybrid procedure, not purely inquisitorial or purely adversarial'.

[1] See the remarks of Kay J in *R v Bimingham Coroner, ex p Benton*: 'The medical report suggests that the parents in some way think that the finding of death by natural causes in some way reflects blame on them. Nothing could be further from the position than that. There is not the slightest reason to think that the parents were in any way open to the slightest criticism'.
[2] [2004] 2 AC 182 at [26].

23.5 *Inquests and Civil Proceedings*

TYPES OF CIVIL PROCEEDINGS THAT MAY FOLLOW AN INQUEST

23.5 The types of civil proceedings that may follow from, and in a sense arise out of, inquest proceedings, are many and varied. Most commonly, an action in negligence may be brought against the party or parties who, as the evidence develops, the family come to see as responsible for the death. This party may be a NHS trust, who through their employees' individual negligence, or system failures, may be seen as the guilty party by the family; or it may be the emergency services, who the family believe failed to respond quickly enough or adequately to an emergency call; or it may be a primary care provider such as a general practitioner. In other types of cases, the party may be an employer, in the case of an industrial accident, or other motorists, in the case of a road traffic death, or a local authority, in the case of a death of a child in care.

23.6 There is an obvious tension between the function of an inquest (expressly not to determine questions of civil liability) and those costs cases in which it has repeatedly been held that the costs of inquest proceedings, the purpose of which was (in part) to obtain information and evidence for a contemplated civil claim for damages by the estate, were recoverable in principle; as to which, see CHAPTER 9. In those cases, the principle followed is that what was determinative of a party's right to recover costs was not the purpose of the proceedings in which the costs were incurred, but the purpose of the party incurring the costs. Thus, if the purpose of the party attending an inquest was to obtain evidence from that process (via cross-examination of witnesses or the production of documentary evidence) which may be helpful in a subsequent civil claim, those costs are, in principle, recoverable in a subsequent civil claim.

IS THE CONCLUSION OF AN INQUEST BINDING OR ADMISSIBLE IN SUBSEQUENT CIVIL PROCEEDINGS?

23.7 It is neither binding nor admissible. This has long been established in the case law. There is nothing in a coroner's conclusion that confers civil liability on any party. That is expressly forbidden in the rules.

23.8 The coroner's conclusion is inadmissible in any subsequent civil proceedings. This has been described both as a 'rule' and a 'doctrine'; see Lord Justice Christopher Clarke in *(1) Julia Mary Rogers (2) Jade Nicola Lucinda Rogers v Scott Hoyle*[1]:

'The rule in *Hollington v Hewthorn*

32. In this case the Court of Appeal held that the conviction of the defendant in the magistrates' court for careless driving was inadmissible in a subsequent action in which the plaintiff and his son (who had since died) claimed damages on the ground of the defendant's negligent driving. The rule extends so as to render factual findings made by judges in civil cases inadmissible in subsequent proceedings (unless the party against whom the finding is sought to be deployed is bound by it by reason of an estoppel per rem judicatam).

33. This doctrine is not new. It is to be found in the Duchess of Kingston's case (1776) 2 Sm L.C., 13th edn, 644, where Sir William Grey, Lord Chief Justice of the Common Pleas, said:

Is conclusion binding or admissible? **23.10**

"What has been said at the bar is certainly true, as a general principle, that a transaction between two parties, in judicial proceedings, ought not to be binding upon a third; for it would be unjust to bind any person who could not be admitted to make a defence, or to examine witnesses, or to appeal from a judgment he might think erroneous; and therefore the depositions of witnesses in another cause in proof of a fact, the verdict of a jury finding the fact, and the judgment of the court upon facts found, although evidence against the parties, and all claiming under them, are not, in general, to be used to the prejudice of strangers. There are some exceptions to this general rule, founded upon particular reasons, but, not being applicable to the present subject, it is unnecessary to state them."

34. The rule also applies to the findings of facts of arbitrators: *Land Securities Plc v Westminster City Council* [1993] 1 WLR 286; of coroners or coroners' juries: *Bird v Keep* [1918] 2 KB 692; of persons conducting a Wreck Inquiry: *Waddle v Wallsend Shipping Co* [1952] 2 Lloyd's Rep 105, where Devlin J suggested that the law should be changed; and The European Gateway where Steyn J repeated the suggestion [1987] QB 206; and to the findings of individuals, of however great distinction, conducting extra statutory inquiries such as Lord Bingham's Report into the Supervision of BCCI: *Three Rivers District Council v Bank of England (No 3)* [2003] 2 AC 1. The judge treated the rule as applicable to judicial findings, being, for this purpose, "an opinion of a court or other tribunal whose responsibility it is to reach conclusions based solely on the evidence before it". If that definition was intended to exclude a tribunal whose remit is to carry out its own investigation it is too narrow.[2]'

[1] [2014] EWCA Civ 257 at [32]–[34].
[2] Cited with approval by Leggatt J in *R (on the application of RJ) (Claimant) v Director of Legal Aid Casework (Defendant) v HM Senior Coroner for Manchester (Interested Party)* [2016] EWHC 645 (Admin): 'it is settled law that findings of a coroner or a coroner's jury are not admissible as evidence against any person in subsequent proceedings: *Bird v Keep* [1918] 2 KB 692; *Rogers v Hoyle* [2015] QB 265, 304, para 34'.

23.9 But under the Civil Evidence Act 1995, s 1(1), a transcript of the evidence given at an inquest is admissible as hearsay evidence in a subsequent civil trial, and may be used in cross examination at that trial[1]. But the transcript is not admissible as proof of the truth of its contents.

[1] Even where the application to do so comes very late in the day; see *(1) James Lavelle (a child) (2) Megan Lavelle (a child) (by their mother & litigation friend Michelle Lavelle) v (1) Ceri Noble (2) Philip Lawless (3) Leslie Gibbs (4) Dennis McCarthy (5) Jean McCarthy* [2011] EWCA Civ 441.

23.10 It is therefore the position that a conclusion or finding at an inquest may be helpful in subsequent civil proceedings but no more. In practice, a coroner's conclusion and/or excerpts from the evidence given at an inquest are commonly pleaded in a statement of claim by the party who believes it to be helpful. But such pleading, it is suggested, has more to do with the perceived persuasive quality of a statement of case to induce an admission or offer of settlement, than with legal coherence.

Chapter 24
INQUESTS AND PUBLIC INQUIRIES

24.1 The topic of public inquiries is broad enough to constitute a book in itself. However, as an inquest practitioner, it is important to understand in outline the role of public inquiries in relation to certain investigations, and the interplay between such inquiries and coroners' investigations.

24.2 This chapter provides a brief outline of what a public inquiry is under the law of England and Wales and the principal similarities and differences between public inquiries and coroners' investigations. It then considers the relationship between inquests and inquiries, insofar as the state's investigation of death is concerned, by considering in what circumstances a public inquiry might prove to be a more appropriate forum for such an investigation than an inquest.

WHAT IS A PUBLIC INQUIRY?

24.3 Broadly speaking, a public inquiry is a means of establishing facts, learning lessons, restoring public confidence and, where appropriate, determining accountability in relation to an accident, disaster or significant failure of public policy[1]. Public inquiries are held where there is substantial public concern about the occurrence of a particular event or events. Although typically initiated by government, public inquiries are usually independent of government and charged with making objective findings of fact and recommendations for the future.

[1] See, for example, Graeme Cowie and Mark Sandford, *Statutory Commissions of Inquiry: The Inquiries Act 2005*, Briefing Paper No SN06410, House of Commons Library, 24 September 2018, p 3.

24.4 The history of public inquiries is bound up with the history of parliamentary scrutiny of the executive. By the early twentieth century it was recognised that, in circumstances involving widespread public concern, there was some merit in passing the responsibility of such scrutiny from parliamentary committees to a non-parliamentary forum less likely to be coloured by party politics. Statutory powers for convening, and calling evidence in, such inquiries were subsequently created by the Tribunal of Inquiry (Evidence) Act 1921; although various non-statutory forms of public inquiry continued to be utilised by governments throughout the twentieth century and into the twenty-first.

24.5 Inquests and Public Inquiries

24.5 The Inquiries Act 2005 (IA 2005) repealed the 1921 Act and created a new statutory framework for public inquiries. Under s 1 of the IA 2005, an inquiry may be established by a minister where it appears to them that:

'(a) particular events have caused, or are capable of causing, public concern, or
(b) there is public concern that particular events may have occurred.'

The discretion afforded to a minister by the IA 2005 is thus a broad one and the Act contains no further definitions or guidance as to the term 'public concern'. Nevertheless, a minister's decision to cause an inquiry to be held, or not to be held, under s 1 can be the subject of judicial review[1]. The minister who establishes the inquiry under the IA 2005 also decides upon the identity of the chairperson and whether the chairperson should sit alone or with a panel[2], specifies the setting-up date of the inquiry and, prior to that date, sets out the inquiry's terms of reference[3].

[1] As per the recommendation of the House of Lords Select Committee, ministers should give reasons to Parliament for any decision not to hold an inquiry under s 1 and particularly upon a request by a coroner for an inquest to be converted into a public inquiry (House of Lords Select Committee on the Inquiries Act 2005, *The Inquiries Act 2005: Post-legislative Scrutiny*, 11 March 2014; see, in particular s 107). Therefore, in practice, one would expect most such decisions to be subjected to parliamentary scrutiny prior to any application for judicial review being considered. Nevertheless, successful applications for judicial review have been made; most notably in *R (Litvinenko) v Secretary of State for the Home Department* [2014] EWHC 194 (Admin).
[2] IA 2005, s 3.
[3] IA 2005, s 5(1).

24.6 The 'terms of reference' of an inquiry are defined under s 5(6) of the IA 2005 as being:

'(a) the matters to which the inquiry relates;
(b) any particular matters as to which the inquiry panel is to determine the facts;
(c) whether the inquiry panel is to make recommendations;
(d) any other matters relating to the scope of the inquiry that the Minister may specify.'

The minister retains a power to amend the inquiry's terms of reference if they consider that is required in the public interest[1]. However, the chairperson (or proposed chairperson) must be consulted, in relation to both the setting of the original terms of reference and to any amendment (they must also be consulted before appointment of a member to the inquiry panel[2].

[1] IA 2005, s 5(3).
[2] IA 2005, s 4(3).

24.7 Often, but not always, the chairperson of a public inquiry chosen by a minister will be a senior member of the judiciary, particularly in large-scale or particularly controversial inquiries. Where the minister in question wishes to appoint a judge (as either chairperson or panel member), s 10 of the IA 2005 provides that either the Lord Chief Justice or the Senior Lord of Appeal in Ordinary[1] must first be consulted. Where the terms of reference of the inquiry touch upon matters of government policy, it is likely to be inappropriate for a serving judge to take up the post; however, retired senior judges are often invited to take up such positions.

[1] Presumably this is now a reference to the President of the Supreme Court, although s 10 does not appear to have been updated in line with the provisions of the Constitutional Reform Act 2005 in this regard.

24.8 Regardless of the terms of reference, s 2 of the IA 2005 maintains the traditional restriction on a public inquiry determining any person's civil or criminal liability. This allows for flexibility in the evidence-gathering and hearing process as neither the common law nor European Convention rights to a fair trial will be engaged; it is also presumed to encourage candour and engagement amongst participants. Parliament nevertheless deemed it necessary to emphasise the expectation that public inquiries under the IA 2005 will not shrink from reaching conclusions about accountability by including the s 2(2) provision: 'But an inquiry panel is not to be inhibited in the discharge of its functions by any likelihood of liability being inferred from facts that it determines or recommendations that it makes'.

24.9 Sections 17–23 of the IA 2005, together with the Inquiry Rules 2006[1], provide significant powers to an inquiry to gather and hear evidence. Under s 17, evidence can be heard under oath and under s 21 the chairperson can require a person to give evidence or produce documents, with criminal sanctions for non-compliance[2].

[1] SI 2006/1838.
[2] As created by s 35.

24.10 There is a presumption of openness and transparency written into the inquiry process by s 18 of the IA 2005. Indeed, the chairperson is under a duty, insofar as they consider reasonable, to allow the public (including reporters) to attend the inquiry proceedings or see and hear a simultaneous transmission of them, and to provide access to the documents provided to the inquiry as well as a record of evidence. However, s 19 also allows for the inquiry to restrict public access to the proceedings and to documents provided, where appropriate, by creating a regime of 'restriction orders' (made by the chairperson) and 'restriction notices' (specified by the relevant minister). Any restrictions so specified must either be restrictions required by law or considered by the chairperson or minister 'to be conducive to the inquiry fulfilling its terms of reference or to be necessary in the public interest'[1]. Section 19(4) provides four matters to which regard must be paid when considering the issue:

'(a) the extent to which any restriction on attendance, disclosure or publication might inhibit the allaying of public concern;
(b) any risk of harm or damage that could be avoided or reduced by any such restriction;
(c) any conditions as to confidentiality subject to which a person acquired information that he is to give, or has given, to the inquiry;
(d) the extent to which not imposing any particular restriction would be likely—
 (i) to cause delay or to impair the efficiency or effectiveness of the inquiry, or
 (ii) otherwise to result in additional cost (whether to public funds or to witnesses or others).'

24.10 *Inquests and Public Inquiries*

The term 'harm or damage' is stated to include, in particular, death or injury, damage to national security, international relations or the economic interests of the country and damage caused by disclosure of commercially sensitive information. Taken together, these sections provide an important means by which an inquiry under the IA 2005 can remain 'public' insofar as possible, whilst also being able to consider inherently non-public and non-publishable evidence. Notably, the discretion given to the chairperson (and/or minister) is broad and subject only to judicial review, thus encouraging a flexibility of approach tailored to the individual, and likely unique, circumstances of each inquiry.

[1] Section 19(3)(b).

24.11 Insofar as making findings is concerned, the IA 2005 is silent as to the standard of proof to be applied. Instead, this is a further matter falling within the ambit of the chairperson's discretion, depending on the particular facts and circumstances of the inquiry and its terms of reference. Thus, in the Baha Mousa Inquiry, the chairman, Sir William Gage, held that the usual starting point for his findings would be the civil standard of proof, regardless of the fact that criminal culpability might be inferred from them[1]. This has echoes of the approach taken by the Bloody Sunday Inquiry panel (an inquiry established under the 1921 Act)[2].

[1] The Baha Mousa Public Inquiry, *Ruling on the Standard of Proof*, 7 May 2010.
[2] Cf The Bloody Sunday Inquiry, *Ruling on the Requisite Standard of Proof for Inquiries of this Nature*, 11 October 2004, sections 17–18: 'In our view, therefore, the cases cited to us do not provide any support for the proposition that as a matter of principle we cannot make any findings implying criminality unless we are satisfied to the criminal standard of proof or of serious misconduct unless we are satisfied to the enhanced civil standard. As we have said earlier, since we are an Inquiry and not a Court (criminal or civil) we cannot give a verdict or pass a judgment on the question whether an individual was guilty of a specific crime or legally recognised serious wrongdoing. For the same reason the terminology and requirements of the criminal or civil law are largely inapplicable. Thus it seems to us that we can and should reach conclusions without being bound by rules designed for court cases, such as who has the burden of proof and the strict rules of evidence'.

24.12 An even more explicitly flexible approach to the standard of proof was adopted in the subsequent Undercover Policing and Grenfell Tower Inquiries. Thus, for example, in the latter, the chairman Sir Martin Moore-Bick held that:

'Since the Inquiry is inquisitorial in nature, there is no burden of proof and no fixed standard by reference to which findings of fact must be made. I have therefore adopted the flexible approach that has been followed in many other inquiries. That allows me to express my conclusions in terms of the likelihood that an event did or did not occur. In some cases I have been left in no doubt that an event occurred; in others, I think it more likely than not that it did; in others, that it is possible, and so on. In my view that is likely to be more helpful and to assist the reader to understand the complex factual circumstances which the Grenfell Tower fire presented.'[1]

[1] The Grenfell Tower Inquiry, *Phase 1 Report*, Volume 1, section 1.17, October 2019.

24.13 Once findings have been made and a report completed, the chairperson must deliver the report to the relevant minister for publication. Under s 25(3) the report must be published in full, save where material is required by law not to be published, or non-publication is considered 'necessary in the public interest'[1] having regard to:

'(a) the extent to which withholding material might inhibit the allaying of public concern;
(b) any risk of harm or damage that could be avoided or reduced by withholding any material;
(c) any conditions as to confidentiality subject to which a person acquired information that he has given to the inquiry.[2]'

[1] Section 25(4).
[2] Section 25(5).

24.14 Rules 13–16 of the 2006 Rules[1] codify the traditional requirement on an inquiry chairperson to send a warning letter in advance to any person who may be, or has been, subject to criticism in the inquiry's report. The inquiry panel must not include any explicit or significant criticism of a person in the report, or any interim report, unless that person has been sent a warning letter and been given a reasonable chance to respond.

[1] SI 2006/1838.

24.15 There is power under s 14 of the IA 2005 for the minister in question to halt an inquiry. However, in such circumstances, they must consult with the chairperson of the inquiry first. If notice is then given to bring the inquiry to an end, s 14(4) requires that the minister sets out the reasons for the decision and lays a copy before Parliament (or the relevant Assembly) for public scrutiny.

24.16 It should be noted that nothing in the IA 2005 does away with the government's power to launch a *non-statutory* public inquiry instead of an inquiry under the Act, where considered appropriate. Furthermore, under s 15 of the IA 2005, although a minister has the power to convert '*an inquiry*' into a 2005 Act public inquiry (assuming the s 1 criteria and other procedural conditions are satisfied), there is no requirement for such a conversion to occur.

24.17 Despite the passing of the IA 2005, non-statutory public inquiries (including Royal Commissions and Committee of Privy Council inquiries) have continued to be established. This appears to be due to the perceived speed and flexibility with which they can be set up and conducted in comparison to statutory inquiries.

24.18 There is no power for a non-statutory inquiry to compel persons to give evidence or to take evidence on oath. However, since non-statutory inquiries need not be conducted in public, they have often been deployed where the subject matter of the inquiry included highly sensitive material that could only be considered in private. Committee of Privy Council inquiries are often thought to be particularly appropriate for such exercises since, by definition, the committee members will have sufficient security clearance to consider all of the relevant material.

24.19 High-profile examples of non-statutory inquiries include the Hutton Inquiry into the death of Dr David Kelly (an *ad hoc* inquiry) and, since the passing of the IA 2005, the Chilcot Inquiry into the Iraq war (a Committee of Privy Council inquiry).

24.20 However, the House of Lords Select Committee on the Inquiries Act 2005 has stated that inquiries arising out of a death but involving significantly wider public concern ought ordinarily to be established under the 2005 Act. Where the death engaged the state's investigative duty under Art 2 of the European Convention this was considered to be *'essential'* by the Committee since only under the Act could such an inquiry compel the attendance of witnesses and the production of evidence. However, in any event, the Committee recommended that:

> 'No inquiry should be set up without the power to compel the attendance of witnesses unless ministers are confident that all potential witnesses will attend [and] Ministers should give reasons for any decision to hold an inquiry otherwise than under the Act.[1]'

[1] House of Lords Select Committee on the Inquiries Act 2005, *The Inquiries Act 2005: Post-legislative Scrutiny*, 11 March 2014, sections 81–82.

SIMILARITIES AND DIFFERENCES

24.21 It follows from the above that there are a number of broad similarities between inquests and public inquiries. Both are inquisitorial processes proscribed from determining issues of liability. Both are concerned with making findings of fact about particular events, but also have a role to play in satisfying public concern that certain events are properly investigated and, where appropriate, lessons are learned. Both inquests and, at least, statutory inquiries, have the power to compel witnesses to give evidence and take evidence on oath.

24.22 However, it will be seen that the scope of a public inquiry will almost inevitably be far broader than an inquest's, constrained as that is by the CJA 2009, s 5 questions. By contrast, the scope of a public inquiry will be as broad as its terms of reference require. In addition, whereas a coroner's inquest findings are strictly limited by CJA 2009, ss 5 and 10, there are no such constraints on a public inquiry. An inquiry will be concerned with the production of a report and, if so instructed, the making of recommendations, rather than distilling its findings down into a short-form, or short narrative, conclusion. In so doing, a public inquiry may call what evidence it sees fit and apply a standard of proof accordingly. The ability to hold closed hearings and consider highly sensitive material, where appropriate, means that even inquiries under the IA 2005 can consider a much wider spectrum of evidence in certain circumstances than would be open to a coroner. An example of this is the Manchester Arena Bombing where the inquest into the deaths of the victims of the attack was converted by the coroner into an inquiry in order that sensitive material could be considered in the appropriate procedural framework.

24.23 A public inquiry under the IA 2005 affords special status to 'core participants' in a similar fashion to the way coroners identify 'interested persons'. However, in sharp contrast to the coronial jurisdiction, a public inquiry will typically ensure that core participants are legally represented, and provision can even be made for the costs of such representation to be borne by the inquiry itself.

24.24 Furthermore, under r 11 of the Inquiry Rules 2006[1], a core participant may make opening and closing statements to the inquiry (not only limited to legal submissions). Rule 17 also requires the chairperson of the inquiry to give to each core participant (and their recognised legal representative) a copy of the inquiry's final report prior to its publication.

[1] SI 2006/1838.

WHY A PUBLIC INQUIRY RATHER THAN AN INQUEST?

24.25 Following a death engaging CJA 2009, s 1, there is nothing to prevent a public inquiry being established in addition to the coroner's investigation; the public inquiry may even supersede the coroner's investigation, such as happened with the Manchester Arena Inquiry.

24.26 However, for the vast majority of such deaths, this will be inappropriate and unnecessary. In what circumstances might a public inquiry therefore represent a necessary or more appropriate investigation into a person's death?

24.27 Broadly speaking, there are two main reasons for a public inquiry to be held in addition to, or instead of, an inquest. First, where the scope of the coroner's investigation, as provided for by CJA 2009, is simply too narrow to deal with all of the matters of public concern arising from the circumstances of the death. Second, where the practical, procedural or evidential differences between inquests and public inquiries entail that only the latter form of investigation would be effective (or that certain interested parties may strongly prefer one form of investigation over the other).

24.28 As will be seen, these two reasons are interrelated. Each will be considered in turn in the remainder of this chapter.

REASONS OF SCOPE

24.29 The most obvious reason for establishing a public inquiry in addition to a coronial investigation into a death is that the circumstances of the death require a broader investigation than a coroner is permitted by CJA 2009 to undertake (see CHAPTER 3 for further detail on the scope of inquests). This may be the case where a particular event has caused multiple deaths. The CJA 2009, s 5 questions will still need to be answered in relation to each death, but there may be sufficient public concern to require a broader investigation into what happened and how such an event can be prevented from happening again. Even where rights under the European Convention are engaged, the coroner's discretion as to the scope of an inquest is still limited by the requirement to focus on the CJA 2009, s 5 questions[1]. Therefore, a public inquiry will typically be the appropriate tool for carrying out the necessary, broader investigations.

[1] See CHAPTER 3 at 3.22–3.28 for further discussion of the coroner's discretion as to the scope of their investigation.

24.30 Nothing in either CJA 2009 or the Inquiries Act 2005 requires that a public inquiry must be established following a particular event. However,

24.30 Inquests and Public Inquiries

under CJA 2009, Sch 1, para 3(1), a coroner's investigation into a death must be suspended where:

'(a) the Lord Chancellor requests the coroner to do so on the ground that the cause of death is likely to be adequately investigated by an inquiry under the Inquiries Act 2005 (c. 12) that is being or is to be held,
(b) a senior judge has been appointed under that Act as chairman of the inquiry, and
(c) the Lord Chief Justice has indicated approval to the Lord Chancellor, for the purposes of this paragraph, of the appointment of that judge.'

Notably, this duty is subject to the caveat that a coroner need not suspend an investigation 'if there appears to be an exceptional reason for not doing so'[1]. No further definition or guidance as to the meaning of this phrase is provided in the Act[2].

[1] CJA 2009, Sch 1, para 3(2).
[2] There is also no discussion of this provision in the Chief Coroner's Guidance No 33, Suspension, Adjournment and Resumption of Investigations and Inquests (7 October 2019).

24.31 Under CJA 2009, Sch 1, para 4, where a coroner's investigation has been suspended pursuant to para 3:

'(2) The terms of reference of the inquiry must be such that it has as its purpose, or among its purposes, the purpose set out in section 5(1) above[1]; and section 5 of the Inquiries Act 2005 has effect accordingly.'

[1] Read with s 5(2) where applicable.

24.32 Insofar as resuming such an investigation is concerned, CJA 2009, Sch 1, para 9 provides that the investigation 'may not be resumed unless, but must be resumed if, the senior coroner thinks that there is sufficient reason for resuming it'. In any event, the investigation cannot be resumed until after 28 days have passed since either the date that the Lord Chancellor has notified the coroner as the date of conclusion of the public inquiry or, where the coroner has received no such notification, the date of publication of the findings of the public inquiry.

24.33 It is important to note that under CJA 2009, Sch 1, para 9(11) the coroner's investigation, once resumed, cannot reach a conclusion which is inconsistent with the outcome of the inquiry which triggered the suspension. This provision in itself may bear on the decision whether to resume an investigation (and hold or resume an inquest) following a 2005 Act inquiry into the same event, particularly given the requirement under para 4 for the inquiry to answer the CJA 2009, s 5 questions itself.

24.34 The wording of CJA 2009, Sch 1 in this regard suggests a desire to prevent, where possible, situations arising in which the findings of different investigations by the state into multiple-death disasters produce inconsistent results.

24.35 The notorious verdicts of accidental deaths reached by coroners in inquests following the Aberfan and Hillsborough disasters serve as potent reminders of the public outrage that such inconsistencies are likely to spark (not to mention the additional pain and distress caused to the families of the deceased). In Aberfan, the verdicts were reached despite the earlier publication of the highly critical conclusions of the Aberfan Disaster Tribunal (a public inquiry created under the Tribunals of Inquiry (Evidence) Act 1921) about the actions of the National Coal Board. In Hillsborough, the verdicts appeared to be in stark contrast to the conclusions of Taylor LJ's 1989 interim report which criticised the role played by South Yorkshire Police in the disaster, triggering a campaign for justice by the bereaved families which ultimately resulted in the quashing of the verdicts and the ordering of fresh inquests, upon the Attorney-General's own application, in 2012[1].

[1] *Attorney General v HM Coroner for South Yorkshire (West)* [2012] EWHC 3783 (Admin), the decision of a three-judge Divisional Court made up of Lord Judge CJ, Burnett J and the Chief Coroner, HHJ Peter Thornton QC.

24.36 In contrast to such cases, the CJA 2009, Sch 1 provisions allowed the Grenfell Tower Inquiry simply to absorb the coroner's duties under CJA 2009, s 5 within its terms of reference. Thus, in the introduction to its Phase 1 Report, the Grenfell Tower Inquiry's chairman, Sir Martin Moore-Bick, stated[1]:

> 'Between 20 June and 22 November 2017 Her Majesty's Senior Coroner for London (Inner West), in whose jurisdiction Grenfell Tower is situated, opened 70 separate inquests into the deaths of those who perished in the fire. She subsequently suspended those inquests pending the outcome of this Inquiry and, if necessary, that of the police investigation. I decided that, in discharging my Terms of Reference, I should carry out, as far as I properly could, an investigation into the deaths caused by the fire corresponding to that which the coroner would be required to undertake in order to discharge her responsibilities. By doing so I hoped to minimise as far as possible the need for her to re-open any of the inquests and thereby to spare the relatives of those who died the need to endure further proceedings in relation to the deaths of their family members.'

[1] The Grenfell Tower Inquiry, *Phase 1 Report*, Volume 1, section 1.9, October 2019. At Volume 4, section 34.2 Sir Martin reasserted this intention, noting that where the circumstances of the deaths required further investigation, this would be undertaken in Phase 2 of the Inquiry 'with a view to making the findings which the coroner requires'.

24.37 It is submitted that this approach is preferable in most multiple-death disaster cases. As such, the operation of CJA 2009, Sch 1, para 9 should make it far rarer for inquests to be resumed after the conclusion of a 2005 Act inquiry into such a disaster.

24.38 However, it is notable that the duty to suspend under CJA 2009, Sch 1, para 3 will only arise in the specific circumstances set out therein. Arguably this creates an uncomfortable grey area where the coroner's duty to suspend does not arise as no minister has taken the steps set out in para 3, and yet the death in question may well become the subject of a public inquiry in due course.

24.39 Concerns of this nature were expressed during the 2020 COVID-19 pandemic in relation to the deaths of 'key workers' whose exposure to the virus may have occurred in the course of their employment by the state and/or been exacerbated by public health policy failings in terms of the provision of personal protective equipment. The Chief Coroner's Guidance No 37 notoriously advised coroners that 'an inquest would not be a satisfactory means of

24.39 *Inquests and Public Inquiries*

deciding whether adequate general policies and arrangements were in place for provision of personal protective equipment (PPE) to healthcare workers in the country or a part of it'[1]. However, without the CJA 2009, Sch 1, para 3 duty triggered by the government establishing a public inquiry, coroners were left with little choice but to try and satisfy their investigative duties as best they could in the circumstances of such cases, or suspend their investigations under CJA 2009, Sch 1, para 5 (the general power to suspend) in the hope that the broader investigation required could be effected in due course.

[1] Chief Coroner's Guidance No 37, COVID-19 deaths and possible exposure in the workplace (published on 28 April 2020, amended 1 July 2020), para 13.

24.40 In addition to multiple-death disaster cases, a public inquiry may prove to be a more appropriate forum for investigating even a single death, in certain circumstances. The death may have caused sufficient public concern to necessitate an investigation going well beyond the scope of an inquest, as in the case of the death of Stephen Lawrence, for instance. In the words of the House of Lords Select Committee on the Inquiries Act 2005:

> 'Where public concern extends significantly beyond a death itself to wider related issues, an inquiry may be preferable to an inquest. If such issues emerge in the course of an inquest, consideration should be given to suspending the inquest and appointing a senior judge as chairman of an inquiry under the Inquiries Act 2005.'[1]

[1] House of Lords Select Committee on the Inquiries Act 2005, *The Inquiries Act 2005: Post-legislative Scrutiny*, 11 March 2014, section 92.

24.41 Public inquiries may also be preferable to a coronial investigation and inquest where the circumstances of the death or deaths involve, for instance, non-fatal injuries to other persons or historical events falling outside of the scope of CJA 2009, s 5. No such statutory limitation applies to public inquires. Thus, for example, the Bloody Sunday Inquiry was able to report as follows[1]:

> 'In addition to those killed, people were also injured by Army gunfire on Bloody Sunday. We took the view at the outset that it would be artificial in the extreme to ignore the injured, since those shooting incidents in the main took place in the same circumstances, at the same times and in the same places as those causing fatal injuries. [. . .] We found it necessary not to confine our investigations only to what happened on the day. Without examining what led up to Bloody Sunday, it would be impossible to reach a properly informed view of what happened, let alone of why it happened. An examination of what preceded Bloody Sunday was particularly important because there had been allegations that members of the United Kingdom and Northern Ireland Governments, as well as the security forces, had so conducted themselves in the period up to Bloody Sunday that they bore a heavy responsibility for what happened on that day.'

[1] The Bloody Sunday Inquiry, *Report of the Bloody Sunday Inquiry*, Volume 1, Chapter 1, sections 1.4–1.5, 15 June 2010.

24.42 Where Art 2 of the European Convention is engaged, the state's investigative duty may require that an independent investigation is held even where no death has occurred (for example, in the case of an attempted suicide by a state prisoner resulting in long-standing injury). In such circumstances, there would be no scope for a coroner's investigation or inquest as there would have been no death. However, the investigative duty could still be discharged by the establishment of a public inquiry (although it might also be discharged by another form of investigation, as long as that investigation was independent, promptly and expeditiously conducted, involved the victim's family and provided for sufficient public scrutiny)¹.

¹ *R (JL) v Secretary of State for the Home Department* [2009] 1 AC 588.

24.43 On a related note, Arts 2 and 3 of the European Convention (not to mention the general public interest) might require investigations, in certain circumstances, into deaths involving state agents outside of the jurisdiction. The UK invasion of Iraq provided the context for testing some of the legal principles involved in such circumstances. Thus, allegations of the ill-treatment and unlawful killing of Iraqi nationals at the hands of UK soldiers in Iraq in 2004 were investigated not via inquests (the CJA 2009, s 1 duty having not arisen) but ultimately by the establishment of the Al-Sweady Inquiry under the Inquiries Act 2005 on 29 November 2009. By contrast, a claim for judicial review of the government's decision not to establish a public inquiry into the legality of the UK's invasion of Iraq itself, brought by the families of deceased UK soldiers, failed in *R (Gentle) v Prime Minister*¹. Although the Appellate Committee of the House of Lords ultimately considered that Art 2 could not be read as requiring a state to undertake such an inquiry, there was also no dispute that, where appropriate, inquests had been held in order to investigate the particular circumstances surrounding the deaths of the deceased soldiers.

¹ [2008] 1 AC 1356.

PRACTICAL, PROCEDURAL AND EVIDENTIAL DIFFERENCES BETWEEN AN INQUEST AND INQUIRY

24.44 Any practitioner advising on the difference between coronial investigations and a public inquiry needs to be aware of the likely difference in timescales between the two. A coronial investigation is intended to be a swift and focused examination of the circumstances of a death. Under CJA 2009, s 16 a senior coroner is formally required to notify the Chief Coroner about any investigation lasting longer than 12 months. By contrast, public inquiries, given their wider scope and employment of national (and often novel) resources, can take years before they report.

24.45 The idea of a public inquiry may often seem initially more attractive than an inquest to a bereaved family member angry and/or suspicious about the circumstances of their relative's death. However, even in the rare circumstances where a public inquiry might be a viable alternative to an inquest, the latter may well serve their purposes as effectively, if not more so.

24.46 In addition to the timescales involved, the coronial process may be thought to have the advantage of being entirely independent from government. Thus, for example, under s 14 of the Inquiries Act 2005, a government minister may bring even a statutory inquiry to an end at any point prior to it fulfilling its terms of reference (subject to laying before Parliament their reasons for so doing). By the same token, inquests are still conducted with juries in certain circumstances. Again, this visible sign of independence can be important to bereaved family members in particular.

24.47 In addition, there is no scope for a coroner to hold closed hearings as part of their inquest proceedings. This is in contrast to public inquiries where, again, even statutory inquiries are given this power despite the general presumption of public access (cf ss 19 and 20 of the IA 2005). One could even envisage circumstances where a bereaved family's demands for a public inquiry were granted by the establishment of a non-statutory inquiry, able to consider evidence in private and unable to compel the attendance of witnesses or take evidence under oath. In such circumstances, the moral might be to be careful what one wishes for.

24.48 Despite the similarities between 'core participant' status at a public inquiry and 'interested person' status at an inquest, there are also some important differences. Under CJA 2009, s 47(2)(a) most close family members of the deceased will automatically be 'interested persons' at an inquest. As such, a coroner *must* allow them to examine any witness called at the inquest if they so request[1]. By contrast, there is no automatic entitlement for core participants to question witnesses called to give oral evidence at a public inquiry. Rather, their recognised legal representative must apply to the chairperson for permission, setting out the issues for questioning along with an explanation for why permission should be granted if no new issues are being raised[2]. Nevertheless, as noted above, under r 11 of the Inquiry Rules 2006, a core participant may make opening and closing statements to the inquiry (not only limited to legal submissions). Rule 17 also requires the chairperson of the inquiry to give to each core participant (and their recognised legal representative) a copy of the inquiry's final report prior to its publication.

[1] Coroners (Inquests) Rules 2013, r 19(1), subject to the coroner's duty to disallow any irrelevant questions under r 19(2).
[2] Inquiry Rules 2006, r 10.

24.49 Furthermore, a core participant in a public inquiry will typically be expected to have a legal representative acting on their behalf and, where this is the case, the inquiry must recognise that representative formally under r 6 of the Inquiry Rules 2006. Under s 40 of the IA 2005, an inquiry chairperson even has the power to award expenses covering the costs of legal representation at the inquiry.

24.50 Insofar as final determinations are concerned, a public inquiry is always likely to produce a broader and, potentially, deeper analysis of the relevant evidence than an inquest. Coroners are now advised to make (and state orally in open court, if sitting alone[1]) key findings of fact upon which their conclusions are based. Nevertheless, the conclusions themselves will generally be concise and summary in nature. The Chief Coroner's Guidance No 17 on conclusions advises that: 'Wherever possible coroners should conclude with a short-form conclusion'[2] and that, even where a narrative conclusion has been adjudged to be more appropriate: 'A few sentences or one or two short paragraphs at the most will be sufficient'[3].

[1] Chief Coroner's Guidance No 17, Conclusions: Short-form and narrative (revised 14 January 2016), para 18.
[2] Chief Coroner's Guidance No 17, Conclusions, para 26.
[3] Chief Coroner's Guidance No 17, Conclusions, para 35.

24.51 Interested persons, and particularly bereaved relatives, are often keen for juries to sit as the tribunal of fact at inquests. Whilst this may provide a further mark of independence to the proceedings, it of course also means that the findings of fact and reasons upon which the conclusion of the inquest is subsequently based, will not normally be recorded or made public. This by-product of the jury system can sometimes be overlooked by interested persons keen for an independent investigation into the death and ought to be borne in mind if the issue of a jury is raised at a pre-inquest review hearing or otherwise.

24.52 The different standards of proof that can be applied in coronial investigations may also be relevant to the question of whether a particular person would prefer a death to be investigated by means of an inquest or a public inquiry. As noted above, public inquiry panels can often apply a flexible standard and will rarely commit themselves to, for instance, only making findings of fact of which they can be sure to the criminal standard.

24.53 By contrast, a coroner cannot reach the short-form conclusion of, for example, unlawful killing other than by applying the criminal standard of proof[1]. As such, a party whom some of the evidence suggests may have perpetrated an unlawful killing may much prefer the matter to be determined at an inquest. At an inquest, such a conclusion could only be reached if the coroner (or jury) were sure beyond reasonable doubt; whereas at a public inquiry, factual findings entailing that the death must have been an unlawful killing could lawfully be reached merely on the balance of probabilities.

[1] Cf, for example, Chief Coroner's Guidance No 17, Conclusions, para 5.

24.54 In some cases, evidence requested by the coroner as part of their investigation into a death may be such that the holder of the material asserts that its disclosure would be damaging to the public interest. Where such material is disclosable to the coroner and the issue is simply onward disclosure to interested parties, that is a matter that can be determined by the coroner in the usual way: by hearing a public interest immunity application and balancing the public interest in the material being disclosed against the public interest in it not being disclosed[1].

[1] As per para 22 of the Chief Coroner's Guidance No 30, Judge-led Inquests (29 January 2019).

24.55 There may however be cases in which the holder of the material in question asserts that its disclosure, even to the coroner, would be damaging to the public interest or proscribed by statute (for example, material related to national security or interception communications obtained by the police or other authorities under the Investigatory Powers Act 2016). In those circumstances, the coroner may appoint counsel with the appropriate level of security clearance to consider the material, advise on whether it is likely to be relevant to the investigation and, where appropriate, agree a suitable gist with the holder of the material[1]. If a disclosable gist cannot be agreed and/or it becomes obvious that the security sensitive material will be central to the investigation, then CJA 2009, Sch 10 provides a procedure whereby the coroner in question can be replaced for the purposes of the inquest by a judge. The judge can then consider the material themselves and make rulings accordingly.

[1] See paras 27–28 of the Chief Coroner's Guidance No 30, Judge-led Inquests.

24.56 In certain cases, a judge appointed under the CJA 2009, Sch 10 procedure may reach the paradoxical conclusion that the material is sufficiently relevant to the investigation and therefore ought to be disclosed to the interested persons as part of the inquest proceedings, and yet its disclosure would be sufficiently damaging to the public interest to mean that it cannot be so disclosed. In such circumstances, since there is no mechanism for an inquest to hold closed hearings in which the evidence is considered, the judge would be left unable to comply with their duty to carry out a proper investigation into the death. The solution is for the inquest, in these particular and unusual circumstances, to be converted into a public inquiry, as happened in the Manchester Arena Inquiry. The powers provided by the IA 2005 to hold closed hearings and make restriction notices where appropriate were used to ensure that the evidence was considered as part of the investigation into the death and that it informed the inquiry's findings and recommendations.

24.57 In such circumstances, pursuant to CJA 2009, Sch 1, paras 3 and 4, the coronial investigation into the death would then formally be suspended, and determination of the CJA 2009, s 5 questions would become part of the terms of reference of the public inquiry. Procedurally, the coroner or judge in such circumstances is required to write to the Lord Chancellor or other appropriate minister in order to request that a public inquiry be held. Generally, such advice is followed; as occurred, for example, in the cases concerning the deaths of Azelle Rodney and Anthony Grainger, both of whom were tragically killed by police gunfire. In the Grainger Inquiry's report, the chairman, HHJ Teague QC, set out the chronology as follows[1]:

> 'After hearing submissions from all properly interested persons, I concluded that an inquest jury would not be able to ascertain the circumstances in which Mr Grainger came by his death without access to the evidence that I had decided must be withheld from disclosure. Further, an inquest that was precluded from investigating those circumstances would not provide the level of scrutiny required by Article 2 of the European Convention on Human Rights. On 20 November 2015, I wrote to the Home Secretary (then the Rt Hon Theresa May MP), setting out my views and inviting the Government to convert the inquest into an inquiry under the Inquiries Act 2005 ('the 2005 Act'). On 17 March 2016, the Home Secretary appointed me Chairman of the present Inquiry into Mr Grainger's death under the provisions of the 2005 Act. In her statement to the House of Commons, the Home Secretary set out the Terms of Reference [. . .], stating that the Government had considered it necessary to convert the inquest into a statutory inquiry "so as to permit all relevant evidence to be heard by the judge".'

[1] The Anthony Grainger Inquiry, *Report into the Death of Anthony Grainger*, 11 July 2019, sections 1.24–1.26.

24.58 Notoriously, the Home Secretary initially refused such an invitation in the case concerning the death of Alexander Litvinenko, a Russian national who was killed in London as part of an operation by the Russian federal security service, the FSB. The Home Secretary's decision was subsequently quashed by a three-judge Divisional Court of the High Court, leading her to reassess and ultimately decide to establish an inquiry under the IA 2005. One of the original reasons given by the Home Secretary for not establishing a public inquiry into the death was that an inquiry in such circumstances would serve no useful purpose because it could only reveal *publicly* what a conventional inquest would reveal anyway. This justification was given short shrift by the High Court, with Richards LJ concluding in the following terms[1]:

> 'The Secretary of State's assertion that an inquiry could reveal publicly only that which the inquest would reveal publicly is at best implausible. Of course, a statutory inquiry would have to consider the HMG material in closed session and would be precluded from disclosing it; but the chairman of the inquiry would almost certainly be able to state publicly some useful conclusion based on the material without disclosing the material itself. It is extremely difficult to envisage a situation in which no conclusion could be stated publicly without infringing the restriction notice. All this applies even more forcefully in relation to an inquiry of the kind sought by the coroner, which would look at all the open evidence as well as the closed material, not only increasing the chances that some useful finding could be made but also making it that much easier to express conclusions without revealing the closed material. The proposition that a statutory inquiry would be incapable of achieving any useful purpose is therefore in my view a bad one.'

[1] *R (Litvinenko) v Secretary of State for the Home Department* [2014] EWHC 194 (Admin) at [67]–[68].

24.59 As such, the conversion of coroners' inquests into 2005 Act inquiries (or the suspension of investigations pursuant to the establishment of such an inquiry), where requested by a coroner or judge in these sorts of circumstances, seems likely only to become more common[1].

[1] For a further example, see the Home Secretary's decision on 22 October 2019 to convert the inquests touching the deaths of those killed in the Manchester Arena bombing on 22 May 2017 into a IA 2005 public inquiry at the request of the coroner Sir John Saunders (following his ruling upholding an application for public interest immunity; Sir John was subsequently appointed chairman of the public inquiry). For reference, see both the Home Secretary's announcement, published 22 October 2019, and Sir John's formal letter of request, dated 27 September 2019.

Appendix

STATUTORY MATERIAL

CORONERS AND JUSTICE ACT 2009

PART 1
CORONERS ETC

CHAPTER 1

INVESTIGATIONS INTO DEATHS
Duty to investigate

A1.1

1 Duty to investigate certain deaths
(1) A senior coroner who is made aware that the body of a deceased person is within that coroner's area must as soon as practicable conduct an investigation into the person's death if subsection (2) applies.
(2) This subsection applies if the coroner has reason to suspect that—
  (a) the deceased died a violent or unnatural death,
  (b) the cause of death is unknown, or
  (c) the deceased died while in custody or otherwise in state detention.
(3) Subsection (1) is subject to sections 2 to 4.
(4) A senior coroner who has reason to believe that—
  (a) a death has occurred in or near the coroner's area,
  (b) the circumstances of the death are such that there should be an investigation into it, and
  (c) the duty to conduct an investigation into the death under subsection (1) does not arise because of the destruction, loss or absence of the body,
may report the matter to the Chief Coroner.
(5) On receiving a report under subsection (4) the Chief Coroner may direct a senior coroner (who does not have to be the one who made the report) to conduct an investigation into the death.
(6) The coroner to whom a direction is given under subsection (5) must conduct an investigation into the death as soon as practicable.
This is subject to section 3.
(7) A senior coroner may make whatever enquiries seem necessary in order to decide—
  (a) whether the duty under subsection (1) arises;
  (b) whether the power under subsection (4) arises.
(8) This Chapter is subject to Schedule 10.

A1.1 *Coroners and Justice Act 2009*

Investigation by other coroner

2 Request for other coroner to conduct investigation

(1) A senior coroner (coroner A) who is under a duty under section 1(1) to conduct an investigation into a person's death may request a senior coroner for another area (coroner B) to conduct the investigation.

(2) If coroner B agrees to conduct the investigation, that coroner (and not coroner A) must conduct the investigation, and must do so as soon as practicable.

(3) Subsection (2) does not apply if a direction concerning the investigation is given under section 3 before coroner B agrees to conduct the investigation.

(4) Subsection (2) is subject to—
- (a) any direction concerning the investigation that is given under section 3 after the agreement, and
- (b) section 4.

(5) A senior coroner must give to the Chief Coroner notice in writing of any request made by him or her under subsection (1), stating whether or not the other coroner agreed to it.

3 Direction for other coroner to conduct investigation

(1) The Chief Coroner may direct a senior coroner (coroner B) to conduct an investigation under this Part into a person's death even though, apart from the direction, a different senior coroner (coroner A) would be under a duty to conduct it.

(2) Where a direction is given under this section, coroner B (and not coroner A) must conduct the investigation, and must do so as soon as practicable.

(3) Subsection (2) is subject to—
- (a) any subsequent direction concerning the investigation that is given under this section, and
- (b) section 4.

(4) The Chief Coroner must give notice in writing of a direction under this section to coroner A.

(5) A reference in this section to conducting an investigation, in the case of an investigation that has already begun, is to be read as a reference to continuing to conduct the investigation.

Discontinuance of investigation

4 Discontinuance where cause of death revealed by post-mortem examination

(1) A senior coroner who is responsible for conducting an investigation under this Part into a person's death must discontinue the investigation if—
- (a) an examination under section 14 reveals the cause of death before the coroner has begun holding an inquest into the death, and
- (b) the coroner thinks that it is not necessary to continue the investigation.

(2) Subsection (1) does not apply if the coroner has reason to suspect that the deceased—
- (a) died a violent or unnatural death, or
- (b) died while in custody or otherwise in state detention.

(3) Where a senior coroner discontinues an investigation into a death under this section—
- (a) the coroner may not hold an inquest into the death;
- (b) no determination or finding under section 10(1) may be made in respect of the death.

This subsection does not prevent a fresh investigation under this Part from being conducted into the death.

(4) A senior coroner who discontinues an investigation into a death under this section must, if requested to do so in writing by an interested person, give to that person as soon as practicable a written explanation as to why the investigation was discontinued.

Purpose of investigation

5 Matters to be ascertained
(1) The purpose of an investigation under this Part into a person's death is to ascertain—
- (a) who the deceased was;
- (b) how, when and where the deceased came by his or her death;
- (c) the particulars (if any) required by the 1953 Act to be registered concerning the death.

(2) Where necessary in order to avoid a breach of any Convention rights (within the meaning of the Human Rights Act 1998 (c 42)), the purpose mentioned in subsection (1)(b) is to be read as including the purpose of ascertaining in what circumstances the deceased came by his or her death.

(3) Neither the senior coroner conducting an investigation under this Part into a person's death nor the jury (if there is one) may express any opinion on any matter other than—
- (a) the questions mentioned in subsection (1)(a) and (b) (read with subsection (2) where applicable);
- (b) the particulars mentioned in subsection (1)(c).

This is subject to paragraph 7 of Schedule 5.

Inquests

6 Duty to hold inquest
A senior coroner who conducts an investigation under this Part into a person's death must (as part of the investigation) hold an inquest into the death.
This is subject to section 4(3)(a).

7 Whether jury required
(1) An inquest into a death must be held without a jury unless subsection (2) or (3) applies.

(2) An inquest into a death must be held with a jury if the senior coroner has reason to suspect—
- (a) that the deceased died while in custody or otherwise in state detention, and that either—
  - (i) the death was a violent or unnatural one, or
  - (ii) the cause of death is unknown,
- (b) that the death resulted from an act or omission of—
  - (i) a police officer, or
  - (ii) a member of a service police force,

  in the purported execution of the officer's or member's duty as such, or
- (c) that the death was caused by a notifiable accident, poisoning or disease.

(3) An inquest into a death may be held with a jury if the senior coroner thinks that there is sufficient reason for doing so.

(4) For the purposes of subsection (2)(c) an accident, poisoning or disease is "notifiable" if notice of it is required under any Act to be given—
- (a) to a government department,

A1.1 Coroners and Justice Act 2009

    (b)   to an inspector or other officer of a government department, or
    (c)   to an inspector appointed under section 19 of the Health and Safety at Work etc Act 1974 (c 37).

NOTES

Modification
Para (2) modified, with temporary effect, by the Coronavirus Act 2020, s 30.

8 Assembling a jury

(1) The jury at an inquest (where there is a jury) is to consist of seven, eight, nine, ten or eleven persons.

(2) For the purpose of summoning a jury, a senior coroner may summon persons (whether within or without the coroner area for which that coroner is appointed) to attend at the time and place stated in the summons.

(3) Once assembled, the members of a jury are to be sworn by or before the coroner to inquire into the death of the deceased and to give a true determination according to the evidence.

(4) Only a person who is qualified to serve as a juror in the Crown Court, the High Court and the county court, under section 1 of the Juries Act 1974 (c 23), is qualified to serve as a juror at an inquest.

(5) The senior coroner may put to a person summoned under this section any questions that appear necessary to establish whether or not the person is qualified to serve as a juror at an inquest.

NOTES

Amendment
Amended by the Crime and Courts Act 2013, s 17(5), Sch 9, Pt 3, para 73.

9 Determinations and findings by jury

(1) Subject to subsection (2), a determination or finding that a jury is required to make under section 10(1) must be unanimous.

(2) A determination or finding need not be unanimous if—
    (a)   only one or two of the jury do not agree on it, and
    (b)   the jury has deliberated for a period of time that the senior coroner thinks reasonable in view of the nature and complexity of the case.

Before accepting a determination or finding not agreed on by all the members of the jury, the coroner must require one of them to announce publicly how many agreed and how many did not.

(3) If the members of the jury, or the number of members required by subsection (2)(a), do not agree on a determination or finding, the coroner may discharge the jury and another one may be summoned in its place.

9A Surrender of electronic communications devices by jurors

(1) A senior coroner holding an inquest with a jury may order the members of the jury to surrender any electronic communications devices for a period.

(2) An order may be made only if the senior coroner considers that—
    (a)   the order is necessary or expedient in the interests of justice, and
    (b)   the terms of the order are a proportionate means of safeguarding those interests.

(3) An order may only specify a period during which the members of the jury are—
    (a)   in the building in which the inquest is being heard,
    (b)   in other accommodation provided at the senior coroner's request,
    (c)   visiting a place in accordance with arrangements made for the purposes of the inquest, or
    (d)   travelling to or from a place mentioned in paragraph (b) or (c).

(4) An order may be made subject to exceptions.

(5) It is a contempt of court for a member of a jury to fail to surrender an electronic communications device in accordance with an order under this section.

(6) Proceedings for a contempt of court under this section may only be instituted on the motion of a senior coroner having jurisdiction to deal with it.

(7) In this section, "electronic communications device" means a device that is designed or adapted for a use which consists of or includes the sending or receiving of signals that are transmitted by means of an electronic communications network (as defined in section 32 of the Communications Act 2003).

NOTES

Amendment
Inserted by the Criminal Justice and Courts Act 2015, s 75, Sch 13, para 1.

9B Surrender of electronic communications devices: powers of search etc

(1) This section applies where an order has been made under section 9A in respect of the members of a jury.

(2) A coroners' officer must, if ordered to do so by a senior coroner, search a member of the jury in order to determine whether the juror has failed to surrender an electronic communications device in accordance with the order.

(3) Subsection (2) does not authorise the officer to require a person to remove clothing other than a coat, jacket, headgear, gloves or footwear.

(4) If the search reveals a device which is required by the order to be surrendered—
   (a) the officer must ask the juror to surrender the device, and
   (b) if the juror refuses to do so, the officer may seize it.

(5) Subject to subsection (6), a coroners' officer may retain an article which was surrendered or seized under subsection (4) until the end of the period specified in the order.

(6) If a coroners' officer reasonably believes that the device may be evidence of, or in relation to, an offence, the officer may retain it until the later of—
   (a) the end of the period specified in the order, and
   (b) the end of such period as will enable the officer to draw it to the attention of a constable.

(7) A coroners' officer may not retain a device under subsection (6)(b) for a period of more than 24 hours from the time when it was surrendered or seized.

(8) The Lord Chancellor may by regulations make provision as to—
   (a) the provision of written information about coroners' officers' powers of retention to persons by whom devices have been surrendered, or from whom devices have been seized, under this section,
   (b) the keeping of records about devices which have been surrendered or seized under this section,
   (c) the period for which unclaimed devices have to be kept, and
   (d) the disposal of unclaimed devices at the end of that period.

(9) In this section—
   "electronic communications device" has the same meaning as in section 9A;
   "unclaimed device" means a device retained under this section which has not been returned and whose return has not been requested by a person entitled to it.

NOTES

Amendment
Inserted by the Criminal Justice and Courts Act 2015, s 75, Sch 13, para 1.

A1.1 Coroners and Justice Act 2009

Outcome of investigation

10 Determinations and findings to be made

(1) After hearing the evidence at an inquest into a death, the senior coroner (if there is no jury) or the jury (if there is one) must—
- (a) make a determination as to the questions mentioned in section 5(1)(a) and (b) (read with section 5(2) where applicable), and
- (b) if particulars are required by the 1953 Act to be registered concerning the death, make a finding as to those particulars.

(2) A determination under subsection (1)(a) may not be framed in such a way as to appear to determine any question of—
- (a) criminal liability on the part of a named person, or
- (b) civil liability.

(3) In subsection (2) "criminal liability" includes liability in respect of a service offence.

Suspension

11 Duty or power to suspend or resume investigations

Schedule 1 makes provision about suspension and resumption of investigations.

Death of service personnel abroad

12 Investigation in Scotland

(1) This section applies to the death outside the United Kingdom of a person within subsection (2) or (3).

(2) A person is within this subsection if at the time of the death the person was subject to service law by virtue of section 367 of the Armed Forces Act 2006 (c 52) and was engaged in—
- (a) active service,
- (b) activities carried on in preparation for, or directly in support of, active service, or
- (c) training carried out in order to improve or maintain the effectiveness of those engaged in active service.

(3) A person is within this subsection if at the time of the death the person was not subject to service law but—
- (a) by virtue of paragraph 7 of Schedule 15 to the Armed Forces Act 2006 was a civilian subject to service discipline, and
- (b) was accompanying persons subject to service law who were engaged in active service.

(4) If—
- (a) the person's body is within Scotland or is expected to be brought to the United Kingdom, and
- (b) the Secretary of State thinks that it may be appropriate for the circumstances of the death to be investigated under the Inquiries into Fatal Accidents and Sudden Deaths etc (Scotland) Act 2016,

the Secretary of State may notify the Lord Advocate accordingly.

(5) If—
- (a) the person's body is within England and Wales, and
- (b) the Chief Coroner thinks that it may be appropriate for the circumstances of the death to be investigated under that Act,

the Chief Coroner may notify the Lord Advocate accordingly.

NOTES

Amendment
Amended by SI 2016/1142, art 7(1), Schedule, Pt 3, para 13(1), (2).

13 Investigation in England and Wales despite body being brought to Scotland

(1) The Chief Coroner may direct a senior coroner to conduct an investigation into a person's death if—

- (a) the deceased is a person within subsection (2) or (3) of section 12,
- (b) the Lord Advocate has been notified under subsection (4) or (5) of that section in relation to the death,
- (c) the body of the deceased has been brought to Scotland,
- (d) no inquiry into the circumstances of the death under the Inquiries into Fatal Accidents and Sudden Deaths etc (Scotland) Act 2016 has been held (or any such inquiry that has been started has not been concluded),
- (e) the Lord Advocate notifies the Chief Coroner that, in the Lord Advocate's view, it may be appropriate for an investigation under this Part into the death to be conducted, and
- (f) the Chief Coroner has reason to suspect that—
  - (i) the deceased died a violent or unnatural death,
  - (ii) the cause of death is unknown, or
  - (iii) the deceased died while in custody or otherwise in state detention.

(2) The coroner to whom a direction is given under subsection (1) must conduct an investigation into the death as soon as practicable.

This is subject to section 3.

NOTES

Amendment
Amended by SI 2016/1142, art 7(1), Schedule, Pt 3, para 13(1), (3).

Ancillary powers of coroners in relation to deaths

14 Post-mortem examinations

(1) A senior coroner may request a suitable practitioner to make a post-mortem examination of a body if—

- (a) the coroner is responsible for conducting an investigation under this Part into the death of the person in question, or
- (b) a post-mortem examination is necessary to enable the coroner to decide whether the death is one into which the coroner has a duty under section 1(1) to conduct an investigation.

(2) A request under subsection (1) may specify the kind of examination to be made.

(3) For the purposes of subsection (1) a person is a suitable practitioner if he or she—

- (a) is a registered medical practitioner, or
- (b) in a case where a particular kind of examination is requested, a practitioner of a description designated by the Chief Coroner as suitable to make examinations of that kind.

(4) Where a person informs the senior coroner that, in the informant's opinion, death was caused wholly or partly by the improper or negligent treatment of a registered medical practitioner or other person, that practitioner or other person—

- (a) must not make, or assist at, an examination under this section of the body, but
- (b) is entitled to be represented at such an examination.

This subsection has no effect as regards a post-mortem examination already made.

A1.1 Coroners and Justice Act 2009

(5) A person who makes a post-mortem examination under this section must as soon as practicable report the result of the examination to the senior coroner in whatever form the coroner requires.

15 Power to remove body
(1) A senior coroner who—
- (a) is responsible for conducting an investigation under this Part into a person's death, or
- (b) needs to request a post-mortem examination under section 14 in order to decide whether the death is one into which the coroner has a duty under section 1(1) to conduct an investigation,

may order the body to be removed to any suitable place.
(2) That place may be within the coroner's area or elsewhere.
(3) The senior coroner may not order the removal of a body under this section to a place provided by a person who has not consented to its being removed there.
This does not apply to a place within the coroner's area that is provided by a district council, a county council, a county borough council, a London borough council or the Common Council.

Miscellaneous

16 Investigations lasting more than a year
(1) A senior coroner who is conducting an investigation under this Part into a person's death that has not been completed or discontinued within a year—
- (a) must notify the Chief Coroner of that fact;
- (b) must notify the Chief Coroner of the date on which the investigation is completed or discontinued.

(2) In subsection (1) "within a year" means within the period of 12 months beginning with the day on which the coroner was made aware that the person's body was within the coroner's area.
(3) The Chief Coroner must keep a register of notifications given under subsection (1).

17 Monitoring of and training for investigations into deaths of service personnel
(1) The Chief Coroner must—
- (a) monitor investigations under this Part into service deaths;
- (b) secure that coroners conducting such investigations are suitably trained to do so.

(2) In this section "service death" means the death of a person who at the time of the death was subject to service law by virtue of section 367 of the Armed Forces Act 2006 (c 52) and was engaged in—
- (a) active service,
- (b) activities carried on in preparation for, or directly in support of, active service, or
- (c) training carried out in order to improve or maintain the effectiveness of those engaged in active service.

CHAPTER 2

Notification, Certification and Registration of Deaths

18 Notification by medical practitioner to senior coroner
(1) The Lord Chancellor may make regulations requiring a registered medical practitioner, in prescribed cases or circumstances, to notify a senior coroner of a death of which the practitioner is aware.
(2) Before making regulations under this section the Lord Chancellor must consult—
- (a) the Secretary of State for Health and Social Care, and
- (b) the Chief Coroner.

NOTES

Amendment
   Amended by SI 2018/378, art 15, Schedule, Pt 1, para 15(a).

19 Medical examiners
(1) Local authorities (in England) and Local Health Boards (in Wales) must appoint persons as medical examiners to discharge the functions conferred on medical examiners by or under this Chapter.
(2) Each local authority or Board must—
- (a) appoint enough medical examiners, and make available enough funds and other resources, to enable those functions to be discharged in its area;
- (b) monitor the performance of medical examiners appointed by the local authority or Board by reference to any standards or levels of performance that those examiners are expected to attain.

(3) A person may be appointed as a medical examiner only if, at the time of the appointment, he or she—
- (a) is a registered medical practitioner and has been throughout the previous 5 years, and
- (b) practises as such or has done within the previous 5 years.

(4) The appropriate Minister may by regulations make—
- (a) provision about the terms of appointment of medical examiners and about termination of appointment;
- (b) provision for the payment to medical examiners of remuneration, expenses, fees, compensation for termination of appointment, pensions, allowances or gratuities;
- (c) provision as to training—
  - (i) to be undertaken as a precondition for appointment as a medical examiner;
  - (ii) to be undertaken by medical examiners;
- (d) provision about the procedure to be followed in connection with the exercise of functions by medical examiners;
- (e) provision conferring functions on medical examiners;
- (f) provision for functions of medical examiners to be exercised, during a period of emergency, by persons not meeting the criteria in subsection (3).

(5) Nothing in this section, or in regulations under this section, gives a local authority or a Local Health Board any role in relation to the way in which medical examiners exercise their professional judgment as medical practitioners.

(6) In this section "the appropriate Minister" means—
- (a) in relation to England, the Secretary of State;
- (b) in relation to Wales, the Welsh Ministers.

(7) For the purposes of this section a "period of emergency" is a period certified as such by the Secretary of State on the basis that there is or has been, or is about to be,

A1.1 *Coroners and Justice Act 2009*

an event or situation involving or causing, or having the potential to cause, a substantial loss of human life throughout, or in any part of, England and Wales.

(8) A certification under subsection (7) must specify—
- (a) the date when the period of emergency begins, and
- (b) the date when it is to end.

(9) Subsection (8)(b) does not prevent the Secretary of State certifying a new period of emergency in respect of the same event or situation.

NOTES

Amendment
Amended by the Health and Social Care Act 2012, s 54(1), (2).

20 Medical certificate of cause of death

(1) The Secretary of State may by regulations make the following provision in relation to a death that is required to be registered under Part 2 of the 1953 Act—
- (a) provision requiring a registered medical practitioner who attended the deceased before his or her death (an "attending practitioner")—
  - (i) to prepare a certificate stating the cause of death to the best of the practitioner's knowledge and belief (an "attending practitioner's certificate"), or
  - (ii) where the practitioner is unable to establish the cause of death, to refer the case to a senior coroner;
- (b) provision requiring a copy of an attending practitioner's certificate to be given to a medical examiner;
- (c) provision allowing an attending practitioner, if invited to do so by the medical examiner or a registrar, to issue a fresh attending practitioner's certificate superseding the existing one;
- (d) provision requiring a senior coroner to refer a case to a medical examiner;
- (e) provision requiring a medical examiner to make whatever enquiries appear to be necessary in order to confirm or establish the cause of death;
- (f) provision requiring a medical examiner to whom a copy of an attending practitioner's certificate has been given—
  - (i) to confirm the cause of death stated on the certificate and to notify a registrar that the cause of death has been confirmed, or
  - (ii) where the examiner is unable to confirm the cause of death, to refer the case to a senior coroner;
- (g) provision for an attending practitioner's certificate, once the cause of death has been confirmed as mentioned in paragraph (f), to be given to a registrar;
- (h) provision requiring a medical examiner to whom a case has been referred by a senior coroner—
  - (i) to issue a certificate stating the cause of death to the best of the examiner's knowledge and belief (a "medical examiner's certificate") and to notify a registrar that the certificate has been issued, or
  - (ii) where the examiner is unable to establish the cause of the death, to refer the case back to the coroner;
- (i) provision for a medical examiner's certificate to be given to a registrar;
- (j) provision allowing a medical examiner, if invited to do so by the registrar, to issue a fresh medical examiner's certificate superseding the existing one;
- (k) provision requiring a medical examiner or someone acting on behalf of a medical examiner—

(i) to discuss the cause of death with the informant or with some other person whom the examiner considers appropriate, and
(ii) to give him or her the opportunity to mention any matter that might cause a senior coroner to think that the death should be investigated under section 1;
(l) provision for confirmation to be given in writing, either by the informant or by a person of a prescribed description, that the requirement referred to in paragraph (k) has been complied with;
(m) provision prescribing forms (including the form of an attending practitioner's certificate and of a medical examiner's certificate) for use by persons exercising functions under the regulations, and requiring the forms to be made available to those persons;
(n) provision requiring the Chief Medical Officer of the Department of Health and Social Care, after consulting—
(i) the Officer with corresponding functions in relation to Wales,
(ii) the Registrar General, and
(iii) the Statistics Board,
to issue guidance as to how certificates and other forms under the regulations are to be completed;
(o) provision for certificates or other forms under the regulations to be signed or otherwise authenticated.

(2) Regulations under subsection (1) imposing a requirement—
(a) may prescribe a period within which the requirement is to be complied with;
(b) may prescribe cases or circumstances in which the requirement does, or does not, apply (and may, in particular, provide for the requirement not to apply during a period of emergency).

(3) The power under subsection (1)(m) to prescribe forms is exercisable only after consultation with—
(a) the Welsh Ministers,
(b) the Registrar General, and
(c) the Statistics Board.

(4) Regulations under subsection (1) may provide for functions that would otherwise be exercisable by a registered medical practitioner who attended the deceased before his or her death to be exercisable, during a period of emergency, by a registered medical practitioner who did not do so.

(5) The appropriate Minister may by regulations provide for a fee to be payable to a local authority or Local Health Board in respect of—
(a) a medical examiner's confirmation of the cause of death stated on an attending practitioner's certificate, or
(b) the issue of a medical examiner's certificate.

(6) Section 7 of the Cremation Act 1902 (c 8) (regulations as to burning) does not require the Secretary of State to make regulations, or to include any provision in regulations, if or to the extent that he or she thinks it unnecessary to do so in consequence of—
(a) provision made by regulations under this Chapter or by Coroners regulations, or
(b) provision contained in, or made by regulations under, Part 2 of the 1953 Act as amended by Part 1 of Schedule 21 to this Act.

(7) In this section—
"the appropriate Minister" has the same meaning as in section 19;
"informant", in relation to a death, means the person who gave particulars concerning the death to the registrar under section 16 or 17 of the 1953 Act;

A1.1 Coroners and Justice Act 2009

"period of emergency" has the same meaning as in section 19;
"the Statistics Board" means the body corporate established by section 1 of the Statistics and Registration Service Act 2007 (c 18).

NOTES

Amendment
Amended by the Health and Social Care Act 2012, s 54(1), (3); SI 2018/378, art 15, Schedule, Pt 1, para 15(b).

Modification
This provision is affected by temporary measures by the Coronavirus Act 2020, s 18(1), Sch 13, Pt 1, para 4(7).

21 National Medical Examiner

(1) The Secretary of State may appoint a person as National Medical Examiner.
(2) The National Medical Examiner is to have—
 (a) the function of issuing guidance to medical examiners with a view to securing that they carry out their functions in an effective and proportionate manner;
 (b) any further functions conferred by regulations made by the Secretary of State.
(3) Before appointing a person as National Medical Examiner or making regulations under subsection (2)(b), the Secretary of State must consult the Welsh Ministers.
(4) A person may be appointed as National Medical Examiner only if, at the time of the appointment, he or she—
 (a) is a registered medical practitioner and has been throughout the previous 5 years, and
 (b) practises as such or has done within the previous 5 years.
(5) The appointment of a person as National Medical Examiner is to be on whatever terms and conditions the Secretary of State thinks appropriate.
(6) The Secretary of State may pay to the National Medical Examiner—
 (a) amounts determined by the Secretary of State by way of remuneration or allowances;
 (b) amounts determined by the Secretary of State towards expenses incurred in performing functions as such.
(7) The National Medical Examiner may amend or revoke any guidance issued under subsection (2)(a).
(8) The National Medical Examiner must consult the Welsh Ministers before issuing, amending or revoking any such guidance.
(9) Medical examiners must have regard to any such guidance in carrying out their functions.

CHAPTER 3

Coroner Areas, Appointments etc

22 Coroner areas
Schedule 2 makes provision about coroner areas.

23 Appointment etc of senior coroners, area coroners and assistant coroners
Schedule 3 makes provision about the appointment etc of senior coroners, area coroners and assistant coroners.

24 Provision of staff and accommodation
(1) The relevant authority for a coroner area—
 (a) must secure the provision of whatever officers and other staff are needed by the coroners for that area to carry out their functions;

(b) must provide, or secure the provision of, accommodation that is appropriate to the needs of those coroners in carrying out their functions;
(c) must maintain, or secure the maintenance of, accommodation provided under paragraph (b).

(2) Subsection (1)(a) applies to a particular coroner area only if, or to the extent that, the necessary officers and other staff for that area are not provided by a local policing body.
(3) Subsection (1)(c) does not apply in relation to accommodation the maintenance of which is the responsibility of a person other than the relevant authority in question.
(4) In deciding how to discharge its duties under subsection (1)(b) and (c), the relevant authority for a coroner area must take into account the views of the senior coroner for that area.
(5) A reference in subsection (1) to the coroners for an area is to the senior coroner, and any area coroners or assistant coroners, for that area.

NOTES

Amendment
Amended the Police Reform and Social Responsibility Act 2011, s 99, Sch 16, Pt 3, para 372.

CHAPTER 4

Investigations Concerning Treasure

25 Coroner for Treasure and Assistant Coroners for Treasure

Schedule 4 makes provision about the appointment etc of the Coroner for Treasure and Assistant Coroners for Treasure.

26 Investigations concerning treasure

(1) The Coroner for Treasure must conduct an investigation concerning an object in respect of which notification is given under section 8(1) of the Treasure Act 1996 (c 24).
(2) The Coroner for Treasure may conduct an investigation concerning an object in respect of which notification has not been given under that section if he or she has reason to suspect that the object is treasure.
(3) The Coroner for Treasure may conduct an investigation concerning an object if he or she has reason to suspect that the object is treasure trove.
(4) Subsections (1) to (3) are subject to section 29.
(5) The purpose of an investigation under this section is to ascertain—
(a) whether or not the object in question is treasure or treasure trove;
(b) if it is treasure or treasure trove, who found it, where it was found and when it was found.
(6) Senior coroners, area coroners and assistant coroners have no functions in relation to objects that are or may be treasure or treasure trove.
This is subject to paragraph 11 of Schedule 4 (which enables an assistant coroner acting as an Assistant Coroner for Treasure to perform functions of the Coroner for Treasure).

27 Inquests concerning treasure

(1) The Coroner for Treasure may, as part of an investigation under section 26, hold an inquest concerning the object in question (a "treasure inquest").
(2) A treasure inquest must be held without a jury, unless the Coroner for Treasure thinks there is sufficient reason for it to be held with a jury.
(3) In relation to a treasure inquest held with a jury, sections 8 and 9 apply with the following modifications—
(a) a reference to a senior coroner is to be read as a reference to the Coroner for Treasure;

A1.1 *Coroners and Justice Act 2009*

    (b)   the reference in section 8(3) to the death of the deceased is to be read as a reference to the matters mentioned in section 26(5).

28 Outcome of investigations concerning treasure

Where the Coroner for Treasure has conducted an investigation under section 26, a determination as to the question mentioned in subsection (5)(a) of that section, and (where applicable) the questions mentioned in subsection (5)(b) of that section, must be made—

    (a)   by the Coroner for Treasure after considering the evidence (where an inquest is not held),

    (b)   by the Coroner for Treasure after hearing the evidence (where an inquest is held without a jury), or

    (c)   by the jury after hearing the evidence (where an inquest is held with a jury).

29 Exception to duty to investigate

(1) Where the Coroner for Treasure is conducting, or proposes to conduct, an investigation under section 26 concerning—

    (a)   an object that would vest in the Crown under the Treasure Act 1996 (c 24) if the object was in fact treasure and there were no prior interests or rights, or

    (b)   an object that would belong to the Crown under the law relating to treasure trove if the object was in fact treasure trove,

the Secretary of State may give notice to the Coroner for Treasure disclaiming, on behalf of the Crown, any title that the Crown may have to the object.

(2) Where the Coroner for Treasure is conducting, or proposes to conduct, an investigation under section 26 concerning—

    (a)   an object that would vest in the franchisee under the Treasure Act 1996 if the object was in fact treasure and there were no prior interests or rights, or

    (b)   an object that would belong to the franchisee under the law relating to treasure trove if the object was in fact treasure trove,

the franchisee may give notice to the Coroner for Treasure disclaiming any title that the franchisee may have to the object.

(3) A notice under subsection (1) or (2) may be given only before the making of a determination under section 28.

(4) Where a notice is given under subsection (1) or (2)—

    (a)   the object is to be treated as not vesting in or belonging to the Crown, or (as the case may be) the franchisee, under the Treasure Act 1996, or the law relating to treasure trove;

    (b)   the Coroner for Treasure may not conduct an investigation concerning the object under section 26 or, if an investigation has already begun, may not continue with it;

    (c)   without prejudice to the interests or rights of others, the object may be delivered to a person in accordance with a code of practice published under section 11 of the Treasure Act 1996.

(5) For the purposes of this section the franchisee, in relation to an object, is the person who—

    (a)   was, immediately before the commencement of section 4 of the Treasure Act 1996, or

    (b)   apart from that Act, as successor in title, would have been,

the franchisee of the Crown in right of treasure trove for the place where the object was found.

30, 31
(*Not reproduced*)

CHAPTER 5

FURTHER PROVISION TO DO WITH INVESTIGATIONS AND DEATHS

32 Powers of coroners
Schedule 5 makes provision about powers of senior coroners and the Coroner for Treasure.

33 Offences
Schedule 6 makes provision about offences relating to jurors, witnesses and evidence.

34 Allowances, fees and expenses
Schedule 7 makes provision about allowances, fees and expenses.

CHAPTER 6

GOVERNANCE ETC

35 Chief Coroner and Deputy Chief Coroners
(1) Schedule 8 makes provision about the appointment etc of the Chief Coroner and Deputy Chief Coroners.
(2) The Lord Chief Justice may nominate a judicial office holder (as defined in section 109(4) of the Constitutional Reform Act 2005 (c 4)) to exercise any of the functions of the Lord Chief Justice under Schedule 8.

36 Reports and advice to the Lord Chancellor from the Chief Coroner
(1) The Chief Coroner must give the Lord Chancellor a report for each calendar year.
(2) The report must cover—
 (a) matters that the Chief Coroner wishes to bring to the attention of the Lord Chancellor;
 (b) matters that the Lord Chancellor has asked the Chief Coroner to cover in the report.
(3) The report must contain an assessment for the year of the consistency of standards between coroners areas.
(4) The report must also contain a summary for the year of—
 (a) the number and length of—
  (i) investigations in respect of which notification was given under subsection (1)(a) or (b) of section 16, and
  (ii) investigations that were not concluded or discontinued by the end of the year and in respect of which notification was given under subsection (1)(a) of that section in a previous year,
 as well as the reasons for the length of those investigations and the measures taken with a view to keeping them from being unnecessarily lengthy;
 (b) . . .
 (c) the matters recorded under paragraph 4 of Schedule 5;
 (d) the matters reported under paragraph 7 of that Schedule and the responses given under sub-paragraph (2) of that paragraph.
(5) A report for a year under this section must be given to the Lord Chancellor by 1 July in the following year.
(6) The Lord Chancellor must publish each report given under this section and must lay a copy of it before each House of Parliament.

A1.1 *Coroners and Justice Act 2009*

(7) If requested to do so by the Lord Chancellor, the Chief Coroner must give advice to the Lord Chancellor about particular matters relating to the operation of the coroner system.

NOTES

Amendment
Amended by the Public Bodies Act 2011, s 33(2).

37 Regulations about training
(1) The Chief Coroner may, with the agreement of the Lord Chancellor, make regulations about the training of—
- (a) senior coroners, area coroners and assistant coroners;
- (b) the Coroner for Treasure and Assistant Coroners for Treasure;
- (c) coroners' officers and other staff assisting persons within paragraph (a) or (b).

(2) The regulations may (in particular) make provision as to—
- (a) the kind of training to be undertaken;
- (b) the amount of training to be undertaken;
- (c) the frequency with which it is to be undertaken.

38 Medical Adviser and Deputy Medical Advisers to the Chief Coroner
Schedule 9 makes provision about the appointment etc of the Medical Adviser to the Chief Coroner and Deputy Medical Advisers to the Chief Coroner.

39 ...
...

NOTES

Amendment
Repealed by SI 2012/2401, art 2(6), Sch 1, paras 33, 34.

40 ...
...

NOTES

Amendment
Repealed by the Public Bodies Act 2011, s 33(1).

41 Investigation by Chief Coroner or Coroner for Treasure or by judge, former judge or former coroner
Schedule 10 makes provision for an investigation into a person's death to be carried out by the Chief Coroner or the Coroner for Treasure or by a judge, former judge or former coroner.

42 Guidance by the Lord Chancellor
(1) The Lord Chancellor may issue guidance about the way in which the coroner system is expected to operate in relation to interested persons within section 47(2)(a).
(2) Guidance issued under this section may include provision—
- (a) about the way in which such persons are able to participate in investigations under this Part into deaths;
- (b) ...
- (c) about the role of coroners' officers and other staff in helping such persons to participate in investigations . . . ..

This subsection is not to be read as limiting the power in subsection (1).
(3) The Lord Chancellor may amend or revoke any guidance issued under this section.

(4) The Lord Chancellor must consult the Chief Coroner before issuing, amending or revoking any guidance under this section.

NOTES

Amendment
Amended by the Public Bodies Act 2011, s 33(2).

CHAPTER 7

Supplementary
Regulations and rules

43 Coroners regulations

(1) The Lord Chancellor may make regulations—
- (a) for regulating the practice and procedure at or in connection with investigations under this Part (other than the practice and procedure at or in connection with inquests);
- (b) for regulating the practice and procedure at or in connection with examinations under section 14;
- (c) for regulating the practice and procedure at or in connection with exhumations under paragraph 6 of Schedule 5.

Regulations under this section are referred to in this Part as "Coroners regulations".

(2) Coroners regulations may be made only if—
- (a) the Lord Chief Justice, or
- (b) a judicial office holder (as defined in section 109(4) of the Constitutional Reform Act 2005 (c 4)) nominated for the purposes of this subsection by the Lord Chief Justice,

agrees to the making of the regulations.

(3) Coroners regulations may make—
- (a) provision for the discharge of an investigation (including provision as to fresh investigations following discharge);
- (b) provision for or in connection with the suspension or resumption of investigations;
- (c) provision for the delegation by a senior coroner, area coroner or assistant coroner of any of his or her functions;
- (d) provision allowing information to be disclosed or requiring information to be given;
- (e) provision giving to the Lord Chancellor or the Chief Coroner power to require information from senior coroners;
- (f) provision requiring a summary of specified information given to the Chief Coroner by virtue of paragraph (e) to be included in reports under section 36;
- (g) provision with respect to the preservation, retention, release or disposal of bodies (including provision with respect to reinterment and with respect to the issue of orders authorising burial);
- (h) provision, in relation to authorisations under paragraph 3 of Schedule 5 or entry and search under such authorisations, equivalent to that made by any provision of sections 15 and 16 of the Police and Criminal Evidence Act 1984 (c 60), subject to any modifications the Lord Chancellor thinks appropriate;
- (i) provision, in relation to the power of seizure conferred by paragraph 3(4)(a) of that Schedule, equivalent to that made by any provision of section 21 of that Act, subject to any modifications the Lord Chancellor thinks appropriate;

A1.1 *Coroners and Justice Act 2009*

      (j)   provision about reports under paragraph 7 of that Schedule.
This subsection is not to be read as limiting the power in subsection (1).
(4) Coroners regulations may apply any provisions of Coroners rules.
(5) Where Coroners regulations apply any provisions of Coroners rules, those provisions—
      (a)   may be applied to any extent;
      (b)   may be applied with or without modifications;
      (c)   may be applied as amended from time to time.

44 Treasure regulations

(1) The Lord Chancellor may make regulations for regulating the practice and procedure at or in connection with investigations under this Part concerning objects that are or may be treasure or treasure trove (other than the practice and procedure at or in connection with inquests concerning such objects).
Regulations under this section are referred to in this Part as "Treasure regulations".
(2) Treasure regulations may be made only if—
      (a)   the Lord Chief Justice, or
      (b)   a judicial office holder (as defined in section 109(4) of the Constitutional Reform Act 2005 (c 4)) nominated for the purposes of this subsection by the Lord Chief Justice,
agrees to the making of the regulations.
(3) Treasure regulations may make—
      (a)   provision for the discharge of an investigation (including provision as to fresh investigations following discharge);
      (b)   provision for or in connection with the suspension or resumption of investigations;
      (c)   provision for the delegation by the Coroner for Treasure (or an Assistant Coroner for Treasure) of any of his or her functions;
      (d)   provision allowing information to be disclosed or requiring information to be given;
      (e)   provision giving to the Lord Chancellor or the Chief Coroner power to require information from the Coroner for Treasure;
      (f)   provision requiring a summary of specified information given to the Chief Coroner by virtue of paragraph (e) to be included in reports under section 36;
      (g)   provision of the kind mentioned in paragraph (h) or (i) of section 43(3).
This subsection is not to be read as limiting the power in subsection (1).
(4) Treasure regulations may apply any provisions of Coroners rules.
(5) Where Treasure regulations apply any provisions of Coroners rules, those provisions—
      (a)   may be applied to any extent;
      (b)   may be applied with or without modifications;
      (c)   may be applied as amended from time to time.

45 Coroners rules

(1) Rules may be made in accordance with Part 1 of Schedule 1 to the Constitutional Reform Act 2005 (c 4)—
      (a)   for regulating the practice and procedure at or in connection with inquests;
      (b)   . . .
      (c)   . . .
Rules under this section are referred to in this Part as "Coroners rules".
(2) Coroners rules may make—

(a) provision about evidence (including provision requiring evidence to be given on oath except in prescribed cases);
(b) provision for the discharge of a jury (including provision as to the summoning of new juries following discharge);
(c) provision for the discharge of an inquest (including provision as to fresh inquests following discharge);
(d) provision for or in connection with the adjournment or resumption of inquests;
(e) provision for a senior coroner to have power to give a direction, in proceedings at an inquest, allowing or requiring a name or other matter not to be disclosed except to persons specified in the direction;
(f) provision for the delegation by—
 (i) a senior coroner, area coroner or assistant coroner, or
 (ii) the Coroner for Treasure (or an Assistant Coroner for Treasure),
of any of his or her functions, except for functions that involve making judicial decisions or exercising any judicial discretion;
(g) provision with respect to the disclosure of information;
(h) provision for persons to be excused from service as jurors at inquests in cases specified in the rules;
(i) provision as to the matters to be taken into account by the Coroner for Treasure in deciding whether to hold an inquest concerning an object that is or may be treasure or treasure trove;
(j) . . ..

(3) Coroners rules may make provision conferring power on a senior coroner or the Coroner for Treasure—
(a) to give a direction excluding specified persons from an inquest, or part of an inquest, if the coroner is of the opinion that the interests of national security so require;
(b) to give a direction excluding specified persons from an inquest during the giving of evidence by a witness under the age of 18, if the coroner is of the opinion that doing so would be likely to improve the quality of the witness's evidence.

In this subsection "specified persons" means persons of a description specified in the direction, or all persons except those of a description specified in the direction.

(4) Subsections (2) and (3) are not to be read as limiting the power in subsection (1).
(5) Coroners rules may apply—
(a) any provisions of Coroners regulations;
(b) any provisions of Treasure regulations;
(c) any rules of court that relate to proceedings other than inquests.

(6) Where any provisions or rules are applied by virtue of subsection (5), they may be applied—
(a) to any extent;
(b) with or without modifications;
(c) as amended from time to time.

(7) Practice directions may be given in accordance with Part 1 of Schedule 2 to the Constitutional Reform Act 2005 (c 4) on any matter that could otherwise be included in Coroners rules.

(8) Coroners rules may, instead of providing for a matter, refer to provision made or to be made by practice directions under subsection (7).

(9) In this section "rules of court" include any provision governing the practice and procedure of a court that is made by or under an enactment.

A1.1 *Coroners and Justice Act 2009*

NOTES

Amendment
Amended by the Public Bodies Act 2011, s 33(2).

Coroner of the Queen's household

46 Abolition of the office of coroner of the Queen's household
The office of coroner of the Queen's household is abolished.

Interpretation

47 "Interested person"
(1) This section applies for the purposes of this Part.
(2) "Interested person", in relation to a deceased person or an investigation or inquest under this Part into a person's death, means—
- (a) a spouse, civil partner, partner, parent, child, brother, sister, grandparent, grandchild, child of a brother or sister, stepfather, stepmother, half-brother or half-sister;
- (b) a personal representative of the deceased;
- (c) a medical examiner exercising functions in relation to the death of the deceased;
- (d) a beneficiary under a policy of insurance issued on the life of the deceased;
- (e) the insurer who issued such a policy of insurance;
- (f) a person who may by any act or omission have caused or contributed to the death of the deceased, or whose employee or agent may have done so;
- (g) in a case where the death may have been caused by—
    - (i) an injury received in the course of an employment, or
    - (ii) a disease prescribed under section 108 of the Social Security Contributions and Benefits Act 1992 (c 4) (benefit in respect of prescribed industrial diseases, etc),

    a representative of a trade union of which the deceased was a member at the time of death;
- (h) a person appointed by, or representative of, an enforcing authority;
- (i) where subsection (3) applies, a chief constable;
- (j) where subsection (4) applies, a Provost Marshal;
- (k) where subsection (5) applies, the Director General of the Independent Office for Police Conduct;
- (l) a person appointed by a Government department to attend an inquest into the death or to assist in, or provide evidence for the purposes of, an investigation into the death under this Part;
- (m) any other person who the senior coroner thinks has a sufficient interest.

(3) This subsection applies where it appears that a person has or may have committed—
- (a) a homicide offence involving the death of the deceased, or
- (b) a related offence (other than a service offence).

(4) This subsection applies where it appears that a person has or may have committed—
- (a) the service equivalent of a homicide offence involving the death of the deceased, or
- (b) a service offence that is a related offence.

(5) This subsection applies where the death of the deceased is or has been the subject of an investigation managed or carried out by the Director General of the Independent Office for Police Conduct in accordance with Part 3 of Schedule 3 to the Police Reform Act 2002 (c 30), including that Part as extended or applied by or under any statutory provision (whenever made).

(6) "Interested person", in relation to an object that is or may be treasure or treasure trove, or an investigation or inquest under Chapter 4 concerning such an object, means—

- (a) the British Museum, if the object was found or is believed to have been found in England;
- (b) the National Museum of Wales, if the object was found or is believed to have been found in Wales;
- (c) the finder of the object or any person otherwise involved in the find;
- (d) the occupier, at the time the object was found, of the land where it was found or is believed to have been found;
- (e) a person who had an interest in that land at that time or who has had such an interest since;
- (f) any other person who the Coroner for Treasure thinks has a sufficient interest.

(7) For the purposes of this section, a person is the partner of a deceased person if the two of them (whether of different sexes or the same sex) were living as partners in an enduring relationship at the time of the deceased person's death.

NOTES

Amendment
Amended by the Policing and Crime Act 2017, s 33(9), Sch 9, Pt 3, para 71.

48 Interpretation: general

(1) In this Part, unless the context otherwise requires—
"the 1953 Act" means the Births and Deaths Registration Act 1953 (c 20);
"the 1988 Act" means the Coroners Act 1988 (c 13);
"active service" means service in—

- (a) an action or operation against an enemy (within the meaning given by section 374 of the Armed Forces Act 2006 (c 52)),
- (b) an operation outside the British Islands for the protection of life or property, or
- (c) the military occupation of a foreign country or territory;

"area", in relation to a senior coroner, area coroner or assistant coroner, means the coroner area for which that coroner is appointed;
"area coroner" means a person appointed under paragraph 2(3) of Schedule 3;
"assistant coroner" means a person appointed under paragraph 2(4) of Schedule 3;
"Assistant Coroner for Treasure" means an assistant coroner, designated under paragraph 7 of Schedule 4, acting in the capacity of Assistant Coroner for Treasure;
"body" includes body parts;
"chief constable" means—

- (a) a chief officer of police (within the meaning given in section 101(1) of the Police Act 1996 (c 16));
- (b) the Chief Constable of the Ministry of Defence Police;
- (c) the Chief Constable of the Civil Nuclear Constabulary;
- (d) the Chief Constable of the British Transport Police;

"the Chief Coroner" means a person appointed under paragraph 1 of Schedule 8;

"the Common Council" means the Common Council of the City of London, and "common councillor" is to be read accordingly;
"coroner area" is to be read in accordance with paragraph 1 of Schedule 2;
"the Coroner for Treasure" means a person appointed under paragraph 1 of Schedule 4;
"Coroners regulations" means regulations under section 43;
"Coroners rules" means rules under section 45;
"the coroner system" means the system of law and administration relating to investigations and inquests under this Part;
"the court of trial" means—
- (a) in relation to an offence (other than a service offence) that is tried summarily, the magistrates' court by which the offence is tried;
- (b) in relation to an offence tried on indictment, the Crown Court;
- (c) in relation to a service offence, a commanding officer, a Court Martial or the Service Civilian Court (depending on the person before whom, or court before which, it is tried);

"Deputy Chief Coroner" means a person appointed under paragraph 2 of Schedule 8;
"document" includes information stored in an electronic form;
"enforcing authority" has the meaning given by section 18(7) of the Health and Safety at Work etc Act 1974 (c 37);
"functions" includes powers and duties;
"homicide offence" has the meaning given in paragraph 1(6) of Schedule 1;
"interested person" is to be read in accordance with section 47;
"land" includes premises within the meaning of the Police and Criminal Evidence Act 1984 (c 60);
"local authority" means—
- (a) in relation to England, a county council, the council of any district comprised in an area for which there is no county council, a London borough council, the Common Council or the Council of the Isles of Scilly;
- (b) in relation to Wales, a county council or a county borough council;

"medical examiner" means a person appointed under section 19;
"person", in relation to an offence of corporate manslaughter, includes an organisation;
"prosecuting authority" means—
- (a) the Director of Public Prosecutions, or
- (b) a person of a description prescribed by an order made by the Lord Chancellor;

"related offence" has the meaning given in paragraph 1(6) of Schedule 1;
"relevant authority", in relation to a coroner area, has the meaning given by paragraph 3 of Schedule 2 (and see paragraph 2 of Schedule 22);
"senior coroner" means a person appointed under paragraph 1 of Schedule 3;
"the service equivalent of a homicide offence" has the meaning given in paragraph 1(6) of Schedule 1;
"service offence" has the meaning given by section 50(2) of the Armed Forces Act 2006 (c 52) (read without regard to any order under section 380 of that Act) and also includes an offence under—
- (a) Part 2 of the Army Act 1955 (3 & 4 Eliz 2 c 18) or paragraph 4(6) of Schedule 5A to that Act,
- (b) Part 2 of the Air Force Act 1955 (3 & 4 Eliz 2 c 19) or paragraph 4(6) of Schedule 5A to that Act, or

(c) Part 1 or section 47K of the Naval Discipline Act 1957 (c 53) or paragraph 4(6) of Schedule 4A to that Act;

"service police force" means—
- (a) the Royal Navy Police,
- (b) the Royal Military Police, or
- (c) the Royal Air Force Police;

"state detention" has the meaning given by subsection (2) (read with subsection (2A));

"statutory provision" means provision contained in, or in an instrument made under, any Act (including this Act);

"treasure" means anything that is treasure for the purposes of the Treasure Act 1996 (c 24) (and accordingly does not include anything found before 24 September 1997);

"Treasure regulations" means regulations under section 44;

"treasure trove" does not include anything found on or after 24 September 1997.

(2) Subject to subsection (2A), a person is in state detention if he or she is compulsorily detained by a public authority within the meaning of section 6 of the Human Rights Act 1998 (c 42).

(2A) But a person is not in state detention at any time when he or she is deprived of liberty under section 4A(3) or (5) or 4B of the Mental Capacity Act 2005.

(3) For the purposes of this Part, the area of the Common Council is to be treated as including the Inner Temple and the Middle Temple.

(4) A reference in this Part to a coroner who is responsible for conducting an investigation under this Part into a person's death is to be read as a reference to the coroner who is under a duty to conduct the investigation, or who would be under such a duty but for the suspension of the investigation under this Part.

(5) A reference in this Part to producing or providing a document, in relation to information stored in an electronic form, is to be read as a reference to producing or providing a copy of the information in a legible form.

NOTES

Amendment
Amended by the Policing and Crime Act 2017, s 178.

Northern Ireland and Scotland amendments

49

(*Section 49 applies to Northern Ireland only and is not reproduced*)

50 . . .

. . .

NOTES

Amendment
Repealed by the Inquiries into Fatal Accidents and Sudden Deaths etc (Scotland) Act 2016, s 39(2), Sch 2, para 14.

. . .

51 . . .

. . .

A1.1 *Coroners and Justice Act 2009*

NOTES

Amendment
Repealed by the Legal Aid, Sentencing and Punishment of Offenders Act 2012, s 39(1), Sch 5, Pt 2.

SCHEDULE 1
DUTY OR POWER TO SUSPEND OR RESUME INVESTIGATIONS

Section 11

PART 1
SUSPENSION OF INVESTIGATIONS

Suspension where certain criminal charges may be brought

1
(1) A senior coroner must suspend an investigation under this Part of this Act into a person's death in the following cases.
(2) The first case is where a prosecuting authority requests the coroner to suspend the investigation on the ground that a person may be charged with—
    (a)   a homicide offence involving the death of the deceased, or
    (b)   an offence (other than a service offence) that is alleged to be a related offence.
(3) The second case is where a Provost Marshal or the Director of Service Prosecutions requests the coroner to suspend the investigation on the ground that a person may be charged with—
    (a)   the service equivalent of a homicide offence involving the death of the deceased, or
    (b)   a service offence that is alleged to be a related offence.
(4) Subject to paragraphs 2 and 3, a suspension of an investigation under this paragraph must be for—
    (a)   a period of 28 days beginning with the day on which the suspension first takes effect, or
    (b)   whatever longer period (beginning with that day) the coroner specifies.
(5) The period referred to in sub-paragraph (4) may be extended or further extended—
    (a)   in the first case, at the request of the authority by which the suspension was originally requested;
    (b)   in the second case, at the request of—
        (i)   the Provost Marshal by whom the suspension was originally requested, or
        (ii)   the Director of Service Prosecutions.
(6) In this Act—
        "homicide offence" means—
            (a)   murder, manslaughter, corporate manslaughter or infanticide;
            (b)   an offence under any of the following provisions of the Road Traffic Act 1988 (c 52)—
                (i)   section 1 (causing death by dangerous driving);
                (ii)   section 2B (causing death by careless, or inconsiderate, driving);
                (iii)   section 3ZB (causing death by driving: unlicensed... or uninsured drivers);
                (iiia)   section 3ZC (causing death by driving: disqualified drivers);

(iv) section 3A (causing death by careless driving when under the influence of drink or drugs);
(c) an offence under section 2(1) of the Suicide Act 1961 (c 60) (encouraging or assisting suicide);
(d) an offence under section 5 of the Domestic Violence, Crime and Victims Act 2004 (c 28) of causing or allowing the death of a child or vulnerable adult;

"related offence" means an offence (including a service offence) that—
(a) involves the death of the deceased, but is not a homicide offence or the service equivalent of a homicide offence, or
(b) involves the death of a person other than the deceased (whether or not it is a homicide offence or the service equivalent of a homicide offence) and is committed in circumstances connected with the death of the deceased;

"the service equivalent of a homicide offence" means an offence under section 42 of the Armed Forces Act 2006 (c 52) (or section 70 of the Army Act 1955 (3 & 4 Eliz 2 c 18), section 70 of the Air Force Act 1955 (3 & 4 Eliz 2 c 19) or section 42 of the Naval Discipline Act 1957 (c 53)) corresponding to a homicide offence.

Suspension where certain criminal proceedings are brought

2
(1) Subject to sub-paragraph (6), a senior coroner must suspend an investigation under this Part of this Act into a person's death in the following cases.
(2) The first case is where the coroner—
(a) becomes aware that a person has appeared or been brought before a magistrates' court charged with a homicide offence involving the death of the deceased, or
(b) becomes aware that a person has been charged on an indictment with such an offence without having appeared or been brought before a magistrates' court charged with it.
(3) The second case is where the coroner becomes aware that a person has been charged with the service equivalent of a homicide offence involving the death of the deceased.
(4) The third case is where a prosecuting authority informs the coroner that a person—
(a) has appeared or been brought before a magistrates' court charged with an offence (other than a service offence) that is alleged to be a related offence, or
(b) has been charged on an indictment with such an offence without having been sent for trial for it,
and the prosecuting authority requests the coroner to suspend the investigation.
(5) The fourth case is where the Director of Service Prosecutions informs the coroner that a person has been charged with a service offence that is alleged to be a related offence, and the Director requests the coroner to suspend the investigation.
(6) The coroner need not suspend the investigation—
(a) in the first case, if a prosecuting authority informs the coroner that it has no objection to the investigation continuing;
(b) in the second case, if the Director of Service Prosecutions informs the coroner that he or she has no objection to the investigation continuing;
(c) in any case, if the coroner thinks that there is an exceptional reason for not suspending the investigation.

A1.1 Coroners and Justice Act 2009

(7) In the case of an investigation that is already suspended under paragraph 1—
- (a) a suspension imposed by virtue of sub-paragraph (2) of that paragraph comes to an end if, in reliance of sub-paragraph (6)(a) above, the coroner decides not to suspend the investigation;
- (b) a suspension imposed by virtue of sub-paragraph (3) of that paragraph comes to an end if, in reliance on sub-paragraph (6)(b) above, the coroner decides not to suspend the investigation;
- (c) a reference above in this paragraph to suspending an investigation is to be read as a reference to continuing the suspension of an investigation;
- (d) if the suspension of the investigation is continued under this paragraph, the investigation is to be treated for the purposes of paragraphs 1(4), 7 and 8 of this Schedule as suspended under this paragraph (and not as suspended under paragraph 1).

Suspension pending inquiry under Inquiries Act 2005

3

(1) Subject to sub-paragraph (2), a senior coroner must suspend an investigation under this Part of this Act into a person's death if—
- (a) the Lord Chancellor requests the coroner to do so on the ground that the cause of death is likely to be adequately investigated by an inquiry under the Inquiries Act 2005 (c 12) that is being or is to be held,
- (b) a senior judge has been appointed under that Act as chairman of the inquiry, and
- (c) the Lord Chief Justice has indicated approval to the Lord Chancellor, for the purposes of this paragraph, of the appointment of that judge.

In paragraph (b) "senior judge" means a judge of the High Court or the Court of Appeal or a Justice of the Supreme Court.

(2) The coroner need not suspend the investigation if there appears to be an exceptional reason for not doing so.

(3) In the case of an investigation that is already suspended under paragraph 1—
- (a) a reference above in this paragraph to suspending the investigation is to be read as a reference to continuing the suspension of the investigation;
- (b) if the suspension of the investigation is continued under this paragraph, the investigation is to be treated for the purposes of paragraphs 1(4), 7 and 9 of this Schedule as suspended under this paragraph (and not as suspended under paragraph 1).

4

(1) This paragraph applies where an investigation is suspended under paragraph 3 on the basis that the cause of death is likely to be adequately investigated by an inquiry under the Inquiries Act 2005 (c 12).

(2) The terms of reference of the inquiry must be such that it has as its purpose, or among its purposes, the purpose set out in section 5(1) above (read with section 5(2) where applicable); and section 5 of the Inquiries Act 2005 has effect accordingly.

General power to suspend

5

A senior coroner may suspend an investigation under this Part of this Act into a person's death in any case if it appears to the coroner that it would be appropriate to do so.

Effect of suspension

6

(1) Where an investigation is suspended under this Schedule, the senior coroner must adjourn any inquest that is being held as part of the investigation.

(2) Where an inquest held with a jury is adjourned under this paragraph, the senior coroner may discharge the jury.

NOTES

Amendment
   Amended by the Criminal Justice and Courts Act 2015, s 29(4), Sch 6, para 12; the Domestic Violence, Crime and Victims (Amendment) Act 2012, s 3, Schedule, para 12.

PART 2
RESUMPTION OF INVESTIGATIONS

Resumption of investigation suspended under paragraph 1

7

An investigation that is suspended under paragraph 1 must be resumed once the period under sub-paragraph (4) of that paragraph, or as the case may be the extended period under sub-paragraph (5) of that paragraph, has ended.

Resumption of investigation suspended under paragraph 2

8

(1) An investigation that is suspended under paragraph 2 may not be resumed unless, but must be resumed if, the senior coroner thinks that there is sufficient reason for resuming it.

(2) Subject to sub-paragraph (3)—
   (a) an investigation that is suspended under paragraph 2 may not be resumed while proceedings are continuing before the court of trial in respect of a homicide offence, or the service equivalent of a homicide offence, involving the death of the deceased;
   (b) an investigation that is suspended by virtue of sub-paragraph (4) or (5) of that paragraph may not be resumed while proceedings are continuing before the court of trial in respect of the offence referred to in that sub-paragraph.

(3) The investigation may be resumed while the proceedings in question are continuing if—
   (a) in the case of an investigation suspended by virtue of sub-paragraph (2) or (4) of paragraph 2, the relevant prosecuting authority informs the coroner that it has no objection to the investigation being resumed;
   (b) in the case of an investigation suspended by virtue of sub-paragraph (3) or (5) of that paragraph, the Director of Service Prosecutions informs the coroner that he or she has no objection to the investigation being resumed.

(4) For the purposes of sub-paragraph (3)(a), the relevant prosecuting authority—
   (a) in the case of an investigation suspended by virtue of sub-paragraph (2) of paragraph 2, is the prosecuting authority responsible for the prosecution in question;
   (b) in the case of an investigation suspended by virtue of sub-paragraph (4) of that paragraph, is the prosecuting authority that made the request under that sub-paragraph.

A1.1 *Coroners and Justice Act 2009*

(5) In the case of an investigation resumed under this paragraph, a determination under section 10(1)(a) may not be inconsistent with the outcome of—
    (a) the proceedings in respect of the charge (or each charge) by reason of which the investigation was suspended;
    (b) any proceedings that, by reason of sub-paragraph (2), had to be concluded before the investigation could be resumed.

Resumption of investigation suspended under paragraph 3

9

(1) Where an investigation is suspended under paragraph 3—
    (a) it may not be resumed unless, but must be resumed if, the senior coroner thinks that there is sufficient reason for resuming it;
    (b) it may not be resumed before the end of the period of 28 days beginning with the relevant day;
    (c) where sub-paragraph (4), (6), (8) or (10) applies, it may be resumed only in accordance with that sub-paragraph (and not before the end of the 28-day period mentioned in paragraph (b)).

(2) In sub-paragraph (1)(b) "the relevant day" means—
    (a) if the Lord Chancellor gives the coroner notification under this paragraph, the day on which the inquiry concerned is concluded;
    (b) otherwise, the day on which the findings of that inquiry are published.

(3) Sub-paragraph (4) applies where, during the suspension of the investigation, the coroner—
    (a) becomes aware that a person has appeared or been brought before a magistrates' court charged with a homicide offence involving the death of the deceased, or
    (b) becomes aware that a person has been charged on an indictment with such an offence without having appeared or been brought before a magistrates' court charged with it.

(4) The coroner must not resume the investigation until after the conclusion of proceedings before the court of trial in respect of the offence in question, unless a prosecuting authority informs the coroner that it has no objection to the investigation being resumed before then.

(5) Sub-paragraph (6) applies where, during the suspension of the investigation, the coroner becomes aware that a person has been charged with the service equivalent of a homicide offence involving the death of the deceased.

(6) The coroner must not resume the investigation until after the conclusion of proceedings before the court of trial in respect of the offence in question, unless the Director of Service Prosecutions informs the coroner that he or she has no objection to the investigation being resumed before then.

(7) Sub-paragraph (8) applies where, during the suspension of the investigation, a prosecuting authority informs the senior coroner that a person—
    (a) has appeared or been brought before a magistrates' court charged with an offence (other than a service offence) that is alleged to be a related offence, or
    (b) has been charged on an indictment with such an offence without having been sent for trial for it.

(8) If the prosecuting authority requests the coroner not to resume the investigation until after the conclusion of proceedings before the court of trial in respect of the offence in question, the coroner must not do so.

(9) Sub-paragraph (10) applies where the Director of Service Prosecutions informs the coroner that a person has been charged with a service offence that is alleged to be a related offence.

(10) If the Director of Service Prosecutions requests the coroner not to resume the investigation until after the conclusion of proceedings before the court of trial in respect of the offence in question, the coroner must do so.

(11) In the case of an investigation resumed under this paragraph, a determination under section 10(1)(a) may not be inconsistent with the outcome of—
- (a) the inquiry under the Inquiries Act 2005 (c 12) by reason of which the investigation was suspended;
- (b) any proceedings that, by reason of sub-paragraph (4), (6), (8) or (10), had to be concluded before the investigation could be resumed.

Resumption of investigation suspended under paragraph 5

10

An investigation that is suspended under paragraph 5 may be resumed at any time if the senior coroner thinks that there is sufficient reason for resuming it.

Supplemental

11

(1) Where an investigation is resumed under this Schedule, the senior coroner must resume any inquest that was adjourned under paragraph 6.

(2) The following provisions apply, in place of section 7, to an inquest that is resumed under this paragraph.

(3) The resumed inquest may be held with a jury if the senior coroner thinks that there is sufficient reason for it to be held with one.

(4) Where the adjourned inquest was held with a jury and the senior coroner decides to hold the resumed inquest with a jury—
- (a) if at least seven persons who were members of the original jury are available to serve at the resumed inquest, the resumed inquest must be held with a jury consisting of those persons;
- (b) if not, or if the original jury was discharged under paragraph 6(2), a new jury must be summoned.

SCHEDULE 2
CORONER AREAS

Section 22

Coroner areas

1

(1) England and Wales is to be divided into areas to be known as coroner areas.

(2) Each coroner area is to consist of the area of a local authority or the combined areas of two or more local authorities.

(3) Subject to paragraph 2—
- (a) the coroner areas are to be those specified in an order made by the Lord Chancellor;
- (b) each coroner area is to be known by whatever name is specified in the order.

(4) Before making an order under this paragraph, the Lord Chancellor must consult—
- (a) every local authority,
- (b) the Welsh Ministers, and
- (c) any other persons the Lord Chancellor thinks appropriate.

Alteration of coroner areas

2

(1) The Lord Chancellor may make orders altering coroner areas.

(2) Before making an order under this paragraph the Lord Chancellor must consult—
- (a) whichever local authorities the Lord Chancellor thinks appropriate,
- (b) in the case of a coroner area in Wales, the Welsh Ministers, and
- (c) any other persons the Lord Chancellor thinks appropriate.

(3) "Altering", in relation to a coroner area, includes (as well as changing its boundaries)—
- (a) combining it with one or more other coroner areas;
- (b) dividing it between two or more other coroner areas;
- (c) changing its name.

Relevant authorities

3

(1) This paragraph sets out for the purposes of this Part what is the "relevant authority" for a given coroner area.

(2) In the case of a coroner area consisting of the area of a single local authority, that authority is the relevant authority for the coroner area.

(3) In the case of a coroner area consisting of the areas of two or more local authorities, the relevant authority for the coroner area is—
- (a) whichever one of those authorities they jointly nominate;
- (b) if they cannot agree on a nomination, whichever one of them the Lord Chancellor determines.

(4) Before making a determination under sub-paragraph (3)(b) the Lord Chancellor must consult—
- (a) the Secretary of State, in a case involving local authorities in England;
- (b) the Welsh Ministers, in a case involving local authorities in Wales.

(5) This paragraph has effect subject to paragraph 2 of Schedule 22.

Effect of body being outside coroner area etc

4

(1) This paragraph applies where—
- (a) a senior coroner is responsible for conducting an investigation under this Part into a person's death, and
- (b) the body is outside the coroner's area (whether because of its removal or otherwise).

(2) The coroner has the same functions in relation to the body and the investigation as would be the case if the body were within the coroner's area.

(3) The presence of the body at a place outside the coroner's area does not confer any functions on any other coroner.

SCHEDULE 3
APPOINTMENT ETC OF SENIOR CORONERS, AREA CORONERS AND ASSISTANT CORONERS

Section 23

PART 1
APPOINTMENT OF SENIOR, AREA AND ASSISTANT CORONERS

Appointment of senior coroners

1

(1) The relevant authority for each coroner area must appoint a coroner (the "senior coroner") for that area.

(2) In the case of a coroner area that consists of the areas of two or more local authorities, the relevant authority for the area must consult the other authorities before making an appointment under this paragraph.

(3) A person may not be appointed as a senior coroner unless the Lord Chancellor and the Chief Coroner consent to the appointment of that person.

Appointment of area and assistant coroners

2

(1) The Lord Chancellor may by order require the appointment, for any coroner area, of—
  (a) an area coroner, or a specified number of area coroners;
  (b) a minimum number of assistant coroners.

(2) Before making an order under this paragraph in relation to a particular coroner area, the Lord Chancellor must consult—
  (a) the Chief Coroner, and
  (b) every local authority whose area falls within the coroner area (or, as the case may be, the local authority whose area is the same as the coroner area).

(3) The relevant authority for a coroner area in relation to which provision is made under sub-paragraph (1)(a) must appoint an area coroner or, as the case may be, the number of area coroners specified for the area in the order.

(4) The relevant authority for a coroner area in relation to which provision is made under sub-paragraph (1)(b) must appoint at least the number of assistant coroners specified for the area in the order.

(5) A person may not be appointed as an area coroner or assistant coroner unless the Lord Chancellor and the Chief Coroner consent to the appointment of that person.

PART 2
QUALIFICATIONS OF SENIOR, AREA AND ASSISTANT CORONERS

3

To be eligible for appointment as a senior coroner, area coroner or assistant coroner, a person must—
  (a) be under the age of 70, and
  (b) satisfy the judicial-appointment eligibility condition on a 5-year basis.

4

(1) A person who is a councillor for a local authority, or has been during the previous 6 months, may not be appointed as the senior coroner, or as an area coroner or

assistant coroner, for a coroner area that is the same as or includes the area of that local authority.

(2) In the application of this paragraph to the Common Council, the reference to a councillor is to be read as a reference to an alderman of the City of London or a common councillor.

PART 3

VACANCIES; FUNCTIONS OF AREA AND ASSISTANT CORONERS

Filling of vacancies

5

(1) This paragraph applies where a vacancy occurs—
- (a) in the office of senior coroner for an area, or
- (b) in an office of area coroner for an area.

(2) The relevant authority for the area must—
- (a) give notice in writing of the vacancy to the Lord Chancellor and the Chief Coroner as soon as practicable after the vacancy occurs;
- (b) appoint a person to fill the vacancy under paragraph 1 or 2 (as the case may be) within 3 months of the vacancy occurring, or within whatever further period the Lord Chancellor allows;
- (c) give notice in writing of the appointment of a person to fill the vacancy to the Lord Chancellor and the Chief Coroner as soon as practicable after it is filled.

6

(1) This paragraph applies where—
- (a) a vacancy occurs in an office of assistant coroner for an area, and
- (b) the vacancy causes the number of assistant coroners for the area to fall below (or further below) the minimum number specified under paragraph 2(1)(b).

(2) Within 3 months of the vacancy occurring, or within whatever further period the Lord Chancellor allows, the relevant authority for the area must appoint a person to fill the vacancy.

Person to act as senior coroner in case of vacancy

7

(1) This paragraph applies where a vacancy occurs in the office of senior coroner for an area.

(2) Subject to sub-paragraph (3), the area coroner for the area (or, if there is more than one such area coroner, whichever of them is nominated by the relevant authority for the area) is to act as senior coroner for the area while the office remains vacant.

(3) Where there is no area coroner for the area, whichever assistant coroner for the area is nominated by the relevant authority for the area is to act as senior coroner for the area while the office remains vacant.

(4) In the case of a coroner area that consists of the area of two or more local authorities, the relevant authority for the area must consult the other authority or authorities before making a nomination under this paragraph.

(5) A person who acts as senior coroner for an area by virtue of this paragraph is to be treated for all purposes of this Part of this Act (except those of this paragraph and paragraphs 1 to 5 and 9 to 19 of this Schedule) as being the senior coroner for the area.

Functions of area and assistant coroners

8

(1) An area coroner or assistant coroner for an area may perform any functions of the senior coroner for the area (including functions which that senior coroner has by virtue of section 2 or 3)—
    (a)   during a period when that senior coroner is absent or unavailable;
    (b)   at any other time, with the consent of that senior coroner.

(2) Accordingly a reference in a statutory provision (whenever made) to a senior coroner is to be read, where appropriate, as including an area coroner or assistant coroner.

PART 4
TERMS OF OFFICE OF SENIOR, AREA AND ASSISTANT CORONERS

Status of office

9

The offices of senior coroner, area coroner and assistant coroner are not to be regarded as freehold offices.

Vacation or termination of office

10

A senior coroner, area coroner or assistant coroner must vacate office on reaching the age of 70.

11

(1) The senior coroner or an area coroner or assistant coroner for an area ("the relevant coroner area") must vacate office immediately if—
    (a)   he or she becomes a councillor for a local authority, and
    (b)   the area of that local authority is the same as or falls within the relevant coroner area.

(2) In the application of this paragraph to the Common Council, the reference to a councillor is to be read as a reference to an alderman of the City of London or a common councillor.

12

The senior coroner or an area coroner or assistant coroner for an area may resign office by giving notice in writing to the relevant authority for the area.

13

(1) The Lord Chancellor may, with the agreement of the Lord Chief Justice, remove a senior coroner, area coroner or assistant coroner from office for incapacity or misbehaviour.

(2) The Lord Chief Justice may nominate a judicial office holder (as defined in section 109(4) of the Constitutional Reform Act 2005 (c 4)) to exercise the functions of the Lord Chief Justice under sub-paragraph (1).

A1.1 *Coroners and Justice Act 2009*

Discipline

14

Chapter 3 of Part 4 of the Constitutional Reform Act 2005 (c 4) (discipline) applies in relation to the offices of senior coroner, area coroner and assistant coroner as it would apply if those offices were listed in Schedule 14 to that Act.

Salary of senior and area coroners

15

(1) The senior coroner for an area is entitled to a salary.

(2) The amount of the salary is to be whatever is from time to time agreed by the senior coroner and the relevant authority for the area.

(3) If the senior coroner and the relevant authority cannot agree about an alteration in the amount of the salary—
    (a) either of them may refer the matter to the Lord Chancellor;
    (b) the Lord Chancellor may determine the amount of the salary and the date on which it is to become payable.

Any alteration in the amount of salary is to take effect in accordance with the Lord Chancellor's determination.

(4) In making a determination under sub-paragraph (3), the Lord Chancellor must have regard—
    (a) to the nature and extent of the coroner's functions, and
    (b) to all the circumstances of the case.

(5) The salary to which the senior coroner for an area is entitled under this paragraph is payable by the relevant authority for the area.

(6) This paragraph applies in relation to an area coroner for an area as it applies in relation to the senior coroner for an area (references to the senior coroner being read as references to an area coroner).

Fees payable to assistants

16

(1) An assistant coroner for an area is entitled to fees.

(2) The amount of the fees is to be whatever is agreed from time to time by the assistant coroner and the relevant authority for the area.

(3) The fees to which an assistant coroner for an area is entitled under this paragraph are payable by the relevant authority for the area.

Pensions for senior and area coroners

17

A relevant authority for a coroner area must make provision for the payment of pensions, allowances or gratuities to or in respect of persons who are or have been senior coroners or area coroners for the area.

Prohibition on receipt of fees etc

18

Except as permitted by or under this or any other Act, a senior coroner, area coroner or assistant coroner may not accept any remuneration or fee in respect of anything done by that coroner in the performance of his or her functions.

Other terms of office

19

Subject to the preceding provisions of this Part, the senior coroner or an area coroner or assistant coroner for an area holds office on whatever terms are from time to time agreed by that coroner and the relevant authority for the area.

SCHEDULE 4
CORONER FOR TREASURE AND ASSISTANT CORONERS FOR TREASURE
Section 25

PART 1
APPOINTMENT, QUALIFICATIONS AND TERMS OF OFFICE OF CORONER FOR TREASURE

Appointment

1

The Lord Chancellor may appoint a person as the Coroner for Treasure.

Qualifications

2

To be eligible for appointment as the Coroner for Treasure, a person must—
  (a) be under the age of 70, and
  (b) satisfy the judicial-appointment eligibility condition on a 5-year basis.

Vacation or termination of office

3

The Coroner for Treasure must vacate office on reaching the age of 70.

4

The Coroner for Treasure may resign office by giving notice to the Lord Chancellor.

5

(1) The Lord Chancellor may, with the agreement of the Lord Chief Justice, remove the Coroner for Treasure from office for incapacity or misbehaviour.

(2) The Lord Chief Justice may nominate a judicial office holder (as defined in section 109(4) of the Constitutional Reform Act 2005 (c 4)) to exercise the functions of the Lord Chief Justice under sub-paragraph (1).

A1.1 *Coroners and Justice Act 2009*

Remuneration, allowances and expenses

6

(1) The Lord Chancellor may pay to the Coroner for Treasure amounts determined by the Lord Chancellor by way of remuneration or allowances.

(2) The Lord Chancellor may pay to the Coroner for Treasure amounts determined by the Lord Chancellor towards expenses incurred by the Coroner for Treasure in performing functions as such.

PART 2
DESIGNATION AND REMUNERATION OF ASSISTANT CORONERS FOR TREASURE

Designation

7

The Chief Coroner may designate one or more assistant coroners to act as Assistant Coroners for Treasure.

8

A person who is designated under paragraph 7 to act as an Assistant Coroner for Treasure may act as such for so long as the designation continues to have effect.

9

A person's designation under that paragraph ceases to have effect—
- (a) when the person ceases to be an assistant coroner;
- (b) if earlier, when the designation is terminated by notice given—
  - (i) by the person to the Chief Coroner, or
  - (ii) by the Chief Coroner to the person.

Remuneration, allowances and expenses

10

(1) The Lord Chancellor may pay to an Assistant Coroner for Treasure amounts determined by the Lord Chancellor by way of remuneration or allowances.

(2) The Lord Chancellor may pay to an Assistant Coroner for Treasure amounts determined by the Lord Chancellor towards expenses incurred by the Assistant Coroner for Treasure in performing functions as such.

PART 3
MISCELLANEOUS

Functions of Assistant Coroners for Treasure

11

(1) An Assistant Coroner for Treasure may perform any functions of the Coroner for Treasure—
- (a) during a period when the Coroner for Treasure is absent or unavailable;
- (b) during a vacancy in the office of Coroner for Treasure;
- (c) at any other time, with the consent of the Coroner for Treasure.

(2) Accordingly a reference in this Part of this Act to the Coroner for Treasure is to be read, where appropriate, as including an Assistant Coroner for Treasure.

Staff

12

(1) The Lord Chancellor may appoint staff to assist the Coroner for Treasure and any Assistant Coroners for Treasure in the performance of their functions.
(2) Such staff are to be appointed on whatever terms and conditions the Lord Chancellor thinks appropriate.

SCHEDULE 5
POWERS OF CORONERS

Section 32

Power to require evidence to be given or produced

1

(1) A senior coroner may by notice require a person to attend at a time and place stated in the notice and—
　(a)　to give evidence at an inquest,
　(b)　to produce any documents in the custody or under the control of the person which relate to a matter that is relevant to an inquest, or
　(c)　to produce for inspection, examination or testing any other thing in the custody or under the control of the person which relates to a matter that is relevant to an inquest.
(2) A senior coroner who is conducting an investigation under this Part may by notice require a person, within such period as the senior coroner thinks reasonable—
　(a)　to provide evidence to the senior coroner, about any matters specified in the notice, in the form of a written statement,
　(b)　to produce any documents in the custody or under the control of the person which relate to a matter that is relevant to the investigation, or
　(c)　to produce for inspection, examination or testing any other thing in the custody or under the control of the person which relates to a matter that is relevant to the investigation.
(3) A notice under sub-paragraph (1) or (2) must—
　(a)　explain the possible consequences, under paragraphs 6 and 7 of Schedule 6, of not complying with the notice;
　(b)　indicate what the recipient of the notice should do if he or she wishes to make a claim under sub-paragraph (4).
(4) A claim by a person that—
　(a)　he or she is unable to comply with a notice under this paragraph, or
　(b)　it is not reasonable in all the circumstances to require him or her to comply with such a notice,
is to be determined by the senior coroner, who may revoke or vary the notice on that ground.
(5) In deciding whether to revoke or vary a notice on the ground mentioned in sub-paragraph (4)(b), the senior coroner must consider the public interest in the information in question being obtained for the purposes of the inquest or investigation, having regard to the likely importance of the information.
(6) For the purposes of this paragraph a document or thing is under a person's control if it is in the person's possession or if he or she has a right to possession of it.
(7) The validity of a notice under sub-paragraph (1) or (2) is not limited to the coroner area for which the senior coroner issuing the notice is appointed.

(8) A reference in this paragraph to a senior coroner is to be read as including the Coroner for Treasure.

2

(1) A person may not be required to give, produce or provide any evidence or document under paragraph 1 if—
- (a) he or she could not be required to do so in civil proceedings in a court in England and Wales, or
- (b) the requirement would be incompatible with a retained EU obligation.

(2) The rules of law under which evidence or documents are permitted or required to be withheld on grounds of public interest immunity apply in relation to an investigation or inquest under this Part as they apply in relation to civil proceedings in a court in England and Wales.

Power of entry, search and seizure

3

(1) A senior coroner conducting an investigation under this Part, if authorised—
- (a) by the Chief Coroner, or
- (b) by another senior coroner nominated by the Chief Coroner to give authorisation,

may enter and search any land specified in the authorisation.

(2) An authorisation may be given only if—
- (a) the senior coroner conducting the investigation has reason to suspect that there may be anything on the land which relates to a matter that is relevant to the investigation, and
- (b) any of the conditions in sub-paragraph (3) are met.

(3) Those conditions are—
- (a) that it is not practicable to communicate with a person entitled to grant permission to enter and search the land;
- (b) that permission to enter and search the land has been refused;
- (c) that the senior coroner has reason to believe that such permission would be refused if requested;
- (d) that the purpose of a search may be frustrated or seriously prejudiced unless the senior coroner can secure immediate entry to the land on arrival.

(4) A senior coroner conducting an investigation under this Part who is lawfully on any land—
- (a) may seize anything that is on the land;
- (b) may inspect and take copies of any documents.

(5) A reference in this paragraph to land is not limited to land within the coroner area for which the senior coroner in question is appointed.

(6) A reference in this paragraph to a senior coroner is to be read as including the Coroner for Treasure.

4

(1) The person by whom an authorisation under paragraph 3(1) is given must make a record—
- (a) setting out the reasons for the suspicion referred to in paragraph 3(2)(a);
- (b) specifying which of the conditions in paragraph 3(3) is met.

(2) Where the authorisation is given by a senior coroner nominated under paragraph 3(1)(b), that coroner must give the record made under this paragraph to the Chief Coroner.

(3) The Chief Coroner must retain a record made this paragraph until the Chief Coroner has given to the Lord Chancellor the report under section 36 for the calendar year in which the authorisation in question was given.

5

(1) A power under paragraph 3(4) is not exercisable unless the person exercising the power has reasonable grounds for believing—
- (a) that its exercise may assist the investigation, and
- (b) in the case of the seizure of anything, that the seizure is necessary to prevent the thing being concealed, lost, damaged, altered or destroyed.

(2) The power under paragraph 3(4)(b) includes power to require any information that is stored in an electronic form and is on, or accessible from, the land to be produced in a form—
- (a) in which it can be taken away, and
- (b) in which it is legible or from which it can readily be produced in a legible form.

(3) A power under paragraph 3(4) does not apply to any item that the person by whom the power is exercisable has reasonable grounds for believing to be subject to legal privilege.

(4) Anything that has been seized or taken away under paragraph 3 may be retained for so long as is necessary in all the circumstances.

(5) A person on whom a power is conferred by virtue of paragraph 3 may use reasonable force, if necessary, in the exercise of the power.

(6) In this paragraph "subject to legal privilege", in relation to an item, has the meaning given by section 10 of the Police and Criminal Evidence Act 1984 (c 60).

Exhumation of body for examination

6

(1) A senior coroner may order the exhumation of a person's body if sub-paragraph (2) or (3) applies.

(2) This sub-paragraph applies if—
- (a) the body is buried in England and Wales (whether or not within the coroner area for which the coroner is appointed), and
- (b) the coroner thinks it necessary for the body to be examined under section 14.

(3) This sub-paragraph applies if—
- (a) the body is buried within the coroner area for which the coroner is appointed, and
- (b) the coroner thinks it necessary for the body to be examined for the purpose of any criminal proceedings that have been instituted or are contemplated in respect of—
  - (i) the death of the person whose body it is, or
  - (ii) the death of another person who died in circumstances connected with the death of that person.

(4) In sub-paragraph (3) "criminal proceedings" includes proceedings in respect of an offence under section 42 of the Armed Forces Act 2006 (c 52) (or section 70 of the Army Act 1955 (3 & 4 Eliz 2 c 18), section 70 of the Air Force Act 1955 (3 & 4 Eliz 2 c 19) or section 42 of the Naval Discipline Act 1957 (c 53)).

A1.1 *Coroners and Justice Act 2009*

Action to prevent other deaths

7

(1) Where—
- (a) a senior coroner has been conducting an investigation under this Part into a person's death,
- (b) anything revealed by the investigation gives rise to a concern that circumstances creating a risk of other deaths will occur, or will continue to exist, in the future, and
- (c) in the coroner's opinion, action should be taken to prevent the occurrence or continuation of such circumstances, or to eliminate or reduce the risk of death created by such circumstances,

the coroner must report the matter to a person who the coroner believes may have power to take such action.

(2) A person to whom a senior coroner makes a report under this paragraph must give the senior coroner a written response to it.

(3) A copy of a report under this paragraph, and of the response to it, must be sent to the Chief Coroner.

NOTES

Amendment
Amended by SI 2018/1252, reg 3.

SCHEDULE 6
OFFENCES

Section 33

PART 1
OFFENCES RELATING TO JURORS

1 Serving while disqualified, failure to attend etc

(1) It is an offence for a person to serve on a jury at an inquest if the person—
- (a) is disqualified from jury service (by reason of being a person listed in Part 2 of Schedule 1 to the Juries Act 1974 (c 23)), and
- (b) knows that he or she is disqualified from jury service.

(2) A person guilty of an offence under this paragraph is liable on summary conviction to a fine not exceeding level 5 on the standard scale.

2

(1) It is an offence for a person—
- (a) to refuse without reasonable excuse to answer any question put under section 8(5),
- (b) to give an answer to such a question knowing the answer to be false in a material particular, or
- (c) recklessly to give an answer to such a question that is false in a material particular.

(2) A person guilty of an offence under this paragraph is liable on summary conviction to a fine not exceeding level 3 on the standard scale.

3

(1) It is an offence for a person who is duly summoned as a juror at an inquest—
- (a) to make any false representation, or
- (b) to cause or permit to be made any false representation on his or her behalf,

with the intention of evading service as a juror at an inquest.

(2) A person guilty of an offence under this paragraph is liable on summary conviction to a fine not exceeding level 3 on the standard scale.

4

(1) It is an offence for a person to make or cause to be made, on behalf of a person who has been duly summoned as a juror at an inquest, any false representation with the intention of enabling the other person to evade service as a juror at an inquest.

(2) A person guilty of an offence under this paragraph is liable on summary conviction to a fine not exceeding level 3 on the standard scale.

5

(1) A senior coroner, or (as the case may be) the Coroner for Treasure, may impose a fine not exceeding £1000 on a person duly summoned as a juror at an inquest who—
- (a) fails without reasonable excuse to attend in accordance with the summons, or
- (b) attends in accordance with the summons but refuses without reasonable excuse to serve as a juror.

(2) But a fine may not be imposed under this paragraph unless the summons was duly served on the person in question not later than 14 days before the day on which he or she was required to attend.

5A Research by jurors

(1) It is an offence for a member of a jury at an inquest to research the case during the inquest period, subject to the exceptions in sub-paragraphs (6) and (7).

(2) A person researches a case if (and only if) the person—
- (a) intentionally seeks information, and
- (b) when doing so, knows or ought reasonably to know that the information is or may be relevant to the inquest.

(3) The ways in which a person may seek information include—
- (a) asking a question,
- (b) searching an electronic database, including by means of the internet,
- (c) visiting or inspecting a place or object,
- (d) conducting an experiment, and
- (e) asking another person to seek the information.

(4) Information relevant to the inquest includes information about—
- (a) a person involved in events relevant to the inquest,
- (b) the senior coroner dealing with the inquest,
- (c) any other person who is involved in the inquest, whether as a lawyer, a witness or otherwise,
- (d) the law relating to the case,
- (e) the law of evidence, and
- (f) procedure at inquests.

(5) "The inquest period", in relation to a member of a jury at an inquest, is the period—
- (a) beginning when the person is sworn to inquire into the case, and
- (b) ending when the senior coroner discharges the jury or, if earlier, when the senior coroner discharges the person.

(6) It is not an offence under this paragraph for a person to seek information if the person needs the information for a reason which is not connected with the case.

(7) It is not an offence under this paragraph for a person—
- (a) to attend proceedings at the inquest;
- (b) to seek information from the senior coroner dealing with the case;
- (c) to do anything which the senior coroner dealing with the case directs or authorises the person to do;

A1.1 *Coroners and Justice Act 2009*

(d) to seek information from another member of the jury, unless the person knows or ought reasonably to know that the other member of the jury contravened this paragraph in the process of obtaining the information;

(e) to do anything else which is reasonably necessary in order for the jury to make a determination or finding in the case.

(8) A person guilty of an offence under this paragraph is liable, on conviction on indictment, to imprisonment for a term not exceeding 2 years or a fine (or both).

(9) Proceedings for an offence under this paragraph may only be instituted by or with the consent of the Attorney General.

5B Sharing research with other jurors

(1) It is an offence for a member of a jury at an inquest intentionally to disclose information to another member of the jury during the inquest period if—

(a) the member contravened paragraph 5A in the process of obtaining the information, and

(b) the information has not been provided at the inquest.

(2) Information has been provided at the inquest if (and only if) it has been provided as part of—

(a) evidence presented at the inquest, or

(b) other information provided to the jury or a juror during the inquest period by, or with the permission of, the senior coroner dealing with the case.

(3) A person guilty of an offence under this paragraph is liable, on conviction on indictment, to imprisonment for a term not exceeding 2 years or a fine (or both).

(4) Proceedings for an offence under this paragraph may not be instituted except by or with the consent of the Attorney General.

(5) In this paragraph, "the inquest period" has the same meaning as in paragraph 5A.

5C Jurors engaging in other prohibited conduct

(1) It is an offence for a member of a jury at an inquest intentionally to engage in prohibited conduct during the inquest period, subject to the exceptions in sub-paragraphs (4) and (5).

(2) "Prohibited conduct" means conduct from which it may reasonably be concluded that the person intends to make a determination or finding otherwise than on the basis of the evidence presented at the inquest.

(3) An offence under this paragraph is committed whether or not the person knows that the conduct is prohibited conduct.

(4) It is not an offence under this paragraph for a member of the jury to research the case (as defined in paragraph 5A(2) to (4)).

(5) It is not an offence under this paragraph for a member of the jury to disclose information to another member of the jury.

(6) A person guilty of an offence under this paragraph is liable, on conviction on indictment, to imprisonment for a term not exceeding 2 years or a fine (or both).

(7) Proceedings for an offence under this paragraph may not be instituted except by or with the consent of the Attorney General.

(8) In this paragraph, "the inquest period" has the same meaning as in paragraph 5A.

NOTES

Amendment

Amended by the Criminal Justice and Courts Act 2015, s 75, Sch 13, paras 3, 4.

PART 1A
OFFENCE RELATING TO JURY'S DELIBERATIONS

5D Offence

(1) It is an offence for a person intentionally—
- (a) to disclose information about statements made, opinions expressed, arguments advanced or votes cast by members of a jury in the course of their deliberations in proceedings at an inquest, or
- (b) to solicit or obtain such information,

subject to the exceptions in paragraphs 5E to 5G.

(2) A person guilty of an offence under this paragraph is liable, on conviction on indictment, to imprisonment for a term not exceeding 2 years or a fine (or both).

(3) Proceedings for an offence under this paragraph may not be instituted except by or with the consent of the Attorney General.

5E Initial exceptions

(1) It is not an offence under paragraph 5D for a person to disclose information in the inquest mentioned in paragraph 5D(1) for the purposes of enabling the jury to make findings or a determination or in connection with the delivery of findings or a determination.

(2) It is not an offence under paragraph 5D for the senior coroner dealing with that inquest to disclose information—
- (a) for the purposes of dealing with the inquest, or
- (b) for the purposes of an investigation by a relevant investigator into whether an offence or contempt of court has been committed by or in relation to a juror in the inquest.

(3) It is not an offence under paragraph 5D for a person who reasonably believes that a disclosure described in sub-paragraph (2)(b) has been made to disclose information for the purposes of the investigation.

(4) It is not an offence under paragraph 5D to publish information disclosed as described in sub-paragraph (1) or (2)(a) in the inquest mentioned in paragraph 5D(1).

(5) In this paragraph—
"publish" means make available to the public or a section of the public;
"relevant investigator" means—
- (a) a police force;
- (b) the Attorney General;
- (c) any other person or class of person specified by the Lord Chancellor for the purposes of this paragraph by regulations.

(6) The Lord Chancellor must obtain the consent of the Lord Chief Justice before making regulations under this paragraph.

5F Further exceptions

(1) It is not an offence under paragraph 5D for a person to disclose information to a person listed in sub-paragraph (2) if—
- (a) the disclosure is made after the jury at the inquest mentioned in paragraph 5D(1) has been discharged, and
- (b) the person making the disclosure reasonably believes that—
  - (i) an offence or contempt of court has been, or may have been, committed by or in relation to a juror in connection with that inquest, or
  - (ii) conduct of a juror in connection with that inquest may provide grounds for an application under section 13(1)(b) of the Coroners Act 1988.

(2) Those persons are—

(a) a member of a police force;
(b) the Attorney General's Office;
(c) a judge of the High Court;
(d) the Chief Coroner;
(e) the senior coroner who dealt with the inquest mentioned in paragraph 5D(1);
(f) a coroner's officer or a member of staff assisting a senior coroner who would reasonably be expected to disclose the information only to a person mentioned in paragraphs (b) to (e).

(3) It is not an offence under paragraph 5D for a member of a police force to disclose information for the purposes of obtaining assistance in deciding whether to submit the information to a person listed in sub-paragraph (2), provided that the disclosure does not involve publishing the information.

(4) It is not an offence under paragraph 5D for the Attorney General's Office or a judge of the High Court to disclose information for the purposes of an investigation by a relevant investigator into—
(a) whether an offence or contempt of court has been committed by or in relation to a juror in connection with the inquest mentioned in paragraph 5D(1), or
(b) whether conduct of a juror in connection with that inquest may provide grounds for an application under section 13(1)(b) of the Coroners Act 1988.

(5) It is not an offence under paragraph 5D for a person who reasonably believes that a disclosure described in sub-paragraph (4) has been made to disclose information for the purposes of the investigation.

(6) It is not an offence under paragraph 5D for a person to disclose information in evidence in—
(a) proceedings for an offence or contempt of court alleged to have been committed by or in relation to a juror in connection with the inquest mentioned in paragraph 5D(1),
(b) proceedings on an application to the High Court under section 13(1)(b) of the Coroners Act 1988 in connection with the inquest mentioned in paragraph 5D(1) where an allegation relating to conduct of or in relation to a juror forms part of the grounds for the application, or
(c) proceedings on any further appeal, reference or investigation arising out of proceedings mentioned in paragraph (a) or (b).

(7) It is not an offence under paragraph 5D for a person to disclose information in the course of taking reasonable steps to prepare for proceedings described in sub-paragraph (6)(a) to (c).

(8) It is not an offence under paragraph 5D to publish information disclosed as described in sub-paragraph (6).

(9) In this paragraph—
"the Attorney General's Office" means the Attorney General, the Solicitor General or a member of staff of the Attorney General's Office;
"publish" means make available to the public or a section of the public;
"relevant investigator" means—
(a) a police force;
(b) the Attorney General;
(c) the Criminal Cases Review Commission;
(d) the Crown Prosecution Service;
(e) a senior coroner, area coroner or assistant coroner;
(f) any other person or class of person specified by the Lord Chancellor for the purposes of this paragraph by regulations.

(10) The Lord Chancellor must obtain the consent of the Lord Chief Justice before making regulations under this paragraph.

5G Exceptions for soliciting disclosures or obtaining information
(1) It is not an offence under paragraph 5D to solicit a disclosure described in paragraph 5E(1) to (4) or paragraph 5F(1) to (8).
(2) It is not an offence under paragraph 5D to obtain information—
- (a) by means of a disclosure described in paragraph 5E(1) to (4) or paragraph 5F(1) to (8), or
- (b) from a document that is available to the public or a section of the public.

NOTES

Amendment
Inserted by the Criminal Justice and Courts Act 2015, s 75, Sch 13, para 6.

PART 2
OFFENCES RELATING TO WITNESSES AND EVIDENCE

6

A senior coroner, or (as the case may be) the Coroner for Treasure, may impose a fine not exceeding £1000 on a person who fails without reasonable excuse to do anything required by a notice under paragraph 1 of Schedule 5.

7

(1) It is an offence for a person to do anything that is intended to have the effect of—
- (a) distorting or otherwise altering any evidence, document or other thing that is given, produced or provided for the purposes of an investigation under this Part of this Act, or
- (b) preventing any evidence, document or other thing from being given, produced or provided for the purposes of such an investigation,

or to do anything that the person knows or believes is likely to have that effect.
(2) It is an offence for a person—
- (a) intentionally to suppress or conceal a document that is, and that the person knows or believes to be, a relevant document, or
- (b) intentionally to alter or destroy such a document.

(3) For the purposes of sub-paragraph (2) a document is a "relevant document" if it is likely that a person conducting an investigation under this Part of this Act would (if aware of its existence) wish to be provided with it.
(4) A person does not commit an offence under sub-paragraph (1) or (2) by doing anything that is authorised or required—
- (a) by a senior coroner or the Coroner for Treasure, or
- (b) by virtue of paragraph 2 of Schedule 5 or any privilege that applies.

(5) Proceedings for an offence under sub-paragraph (1) or (2) may be instituted only by or with the consent of the Director of Public Prosecutions.
(6) A person guilty of an offence under sub-paragraph (1) or (2) is liable on summary conviction to a fine not exceeding level 3 on the standard scale, or to imprisonment for a term not exceeding 51 weeks, or to both.

8

(1) It is an offence for a person, in giving unsworn evidence at an inquest by virtue of section 45(2)(a), to give false evidence in such circumstances that, had the evidence been given on oath, he or she would have been guilty of perjury.
(2) A person guilty of an offence under this paragraph is liable on summary conviction to a fine not exceeding £1000, or to imprisonment for a term not exceeding 51 weeks, or to both.

(3) In relation to a person under the age of 14, sub-paragraph (2) has effect as if for the words following "summary conviction" there were substituted "to a fine not exceeding £250".
(4) For the purposes of sub-paragraph (3), a person's age is to be taken to be that which it appears to the court to be after considering any available evidence.

PART 3
MISCELLANEOUS

9

(1) The powers of a senior coroner or the Coroner for Treasure under paragraph 5 or 6 are additional to, and do not affect, any other power the coroner may have—
    (a)   to compel a person to appear before him or her;
    (b)   to compel a person to give evidence or produce any document or other thing;
    (c)   to punish a person for contempt of court for failure to appear or to give evidence or to produce any document or other thing.

(2) But a person may not be fined under paragraph 5 or 6 and also be punished under any such other power.

10

In relation to an offence committed before the commencement of section 281(5) of the Criminal Justice Act 2003 (c 44), a reference in this Schedule to 51 weeks is to be read as a reference to 6 months.

11

Nothing in paragraph 5A, 5B or 5C affects what constitutes contempt of court at common law.

NOTES

Amendment
    Amended by the Criminal Justice and Courts Act 2015, s 75, Sch 13, para 7.

SCHEDULE 7
ALLOWANCES, FEES AND EXPENSES

Section 34

PART 1
ALLOWANCES PAYABLE TO JURORS

1

A person who serves as a juror at an inquest is entitled, in respect of attending the inquest, to receive payments by way of allowance—
    (a)   for travelling and subsistence;
    (b)   for financial loss.

This is subject to any conditions prescribed by regulations.

2

But a person is entitled to receive payments by way of allowance for financial loss only if, in consequence of attending the inquest, the person has—
    (a)   incurred expenses (other than on travelling and subsistence) that he or she would otherwise not have incurred,
    (b)   suffered a loss of earnings that he or she would otherwise not have suffered, or
    (c)   suffered a loss of benefit under the enactments relating to social security that he or she would otherwise not have suffered.

3

Regulations may prescribe the rates of any allowances payable under paragraph 1.

4

The amount due to a person under paragraph 1 is to be calculated by the senior coroner and paid by (or on behalf of) the senior coroner or, where appropriate, the Coroner for Treasure.

PART 2
ALLOWANCES PAYABLE TO WITNESSES

5

(1) Regulations may prescribe the allowances that may be paid by (or on behalf of) senior coroners or the Coroner for Treasure—
- (a) to witnesses;
- (b) to persons who produce documents or things by virtue of paragraph 1(1) or (2) of Schedule 5;
- (c) to persons who provide evidence in the form of a written statement by virtue of paragraph 1(2)(a) of that Schedule.

(2) In this paragraph "witness" means a person properly attending before a senior coroner to give evidence at an inquest or in connection with the possibility of doing so (whether or not the person actually gives evidence), but does not include—
- (a) a police officer, or a member of a service police force, attending in his or her capacity as such;
- (b) a full-time officer of an institution to which the Prison Act 1952 (c 52) applies in his or her capacity as such;
- (c) a prisoner in respect of an occasion on which he or she is conveyed in custody to appear before a senior coroner.

PART 3
MISCELLANEOUS FEES, ALLOWANCES AND EXPENSES

6

Regulations may prescribe the fees and allowances that may be paid by (or on behalf of) senior coroners to persons who make examinations under section 14.

7

(1) A relevant authority for a coroner area may issue a schedule of the fees, allowances and expenses that may be lawfully paid or incurred by the senior coroner for the area in the performance of the coroner's functions.

(2) The power under sub-paragraph (1) includes power to amend or revoke any schedule issued.

(3) In exercising the power under sub-paragraph (1) a relevant authority must have regard to any guidance from time to time issued by the Lord Chancellor.

(4) A copy of any schedule that is issued or amended must be given to the senior coroner.

(5) The reference in sub-paragraph (1) to fees and allowances does not include fees or allowances within any of the preceding paragraphs of this Schedule.

8

Regulations may prescribe the fees payable to coroners for supplying copies of documents in their custody relating to investigations or inquests under this Part of this Act that they are conducting or have conducted.

A1.1 *Coroners and Justice Act 2009*

PART 4
MEETING OR REIMBURSING EXPENSES

9

(1) Regulations may make provision for or in connection with meeting or reimbursing—
- (a) expenses incurred by senior coroners (including expenses incurred under or by virtue of paragraph 4, 5 or 6);
- (b) expenses incurred by area coroners and assistant coroners;
- (c) expenses incurred by virtue of Schedule 10 in the conduct of an investigation by the Chief Coroner or the Coroner for Treasure or by a judge, former judge or former coroner.

(2) The regulations may make provision—
- (a) for accounts or evidence relating to expenses to be provided to relevant authorities;
- (b) for or in connection with the meeting or reimbursement by relevant authorities of expenses of a description specified in the regulations;
- (c) for or in connection with appeals relating to decisions with respect to meeting or reimbursing expenses.

This sub-paragraph is not to be read as limiting the power in sub-paragraph (1).

(3) A reference in this paragraph to meeting or reimbursing expenses incurred by a person ("P") includes a reference to indemnifying P in respect of—
- (a) costs that P reasonably incurs in or in connection with proceedings in respect of things done or omitted in the exercise (or purported exercise) by P of duties under this Part of this Act;
- (b) costs that P reasonably incurs in taking steps to dispute claims that might be made in such proceedings;
- (c) damages awarded against P, or costs ordered to be paid by P, in such proceedings;
- (d) sums payable by P in connection with a reasonable settlement of such proceedings or of claims that might be made in such proceedings.

PART 5
SUPPLEMENTAL

10

For the purposes of paragraph 1, a person who attends for service as a juror in accordance with a summons is to be treated as serving as a juror even if he or she is not sworn.

11

(1) The power to make regulations under this Schedule is exercisable by the Lord Chancellor.

(2) Regulations under this Schedule may be made only if—
- (a) the Lord Chief Justice, or
- (b) a judicial office holder (as defined in section 109(4) of the Constitutional Reform Act 2005 (c 4)) nominated for the purposes of this sub-paragraph by the Lord Chief Justice,

agrees to the making of the regulations.

SCHEDULE 8
CHIEF CORONER AND DEPUTY CHIEF CORONERS

Section 35

Appointment of Chief Coroner

1

(1) The Lord Chief Justice may appoint a person as the Chief Coroner.
(2) To be eligible for appointment as the Chief Coroner a person must be—
    (a) a judge of the High Court or a Circuit judge, and
    (b) under the age of 70.
(3) The Lord Chief Justice must consult the Lord Chancellor before making an appointment under this paragraph.
(4) The appointment of a person as the Chief Coroner is to be for a term decided by the Lord Chief Justice after consulting the Lord Chancellor.
(5) In this paragraph "appointment" includes re-appointment.

Appointment of Deputy Chief Coroners

2

(1) The Lord Chief Justice may secure the appointment as Deputy Chief Coroners of however many persons the Lord Chief Justice thinks appropriate.
(2) To be eligible for appointment as a Deputy Chief Coroner a person must be—
    (a) a judge of the High Court, a Circuit judge, the Coroner for Treasure or a senior coroner, and
    (b) under the age of 70.
(3) The Lord Chief Justice must consult the Lord Chancellor as to—
    (a) the appropriate number of persons to be appointed as Deputy Chief Coroners;
    (b) how many of them are to be persons eligible for appointment by virtue of being judges and how many are to be persons eligible for appointment by virtue of being senior coroners or the Coroner for Treasure.
(4) The function of appointing a person as a Deputy Chief Coroner is exercisable, in the case of a judge of the High Court or a Circuit judge, by the Lord Chief Justice after consulting the Lord Chancellor.
(5) The appointment by the Lord Chief Justice of a person as a Deputy Chief Coroner is to be for a term decided by the Lord Chief Justice after consulting the Lord Chancellor.
(6) The function of appointing a person as a Deputy Chief Coroner is exercisable, in the case of a senior coroner or the Coroner for Treasure, by the Lord Chancellor at the invitation of the Lord Chief Justice.
(7) The appointment by the Lord Chancellor of a person as a Deputy Chief Coroner is to be for a term decided by the Lord Chancellor after consulting the Lord Chief Justice.
(8) In this paragraph "appointment" includes re-appointment.

Resignation or removal

3

(1) The Chief Coroner, or a Deputy Chief Coroner appointed by the Lord Chief Justice, may resign from office by giving notice in writing to the Lord Chief Justice.

A1.1 *Coroners and Justice Act 2009*

(2) But the resignation does not take effect unless and until it is accepted by the Lord Chief Justice, who must consult the Lord Chancellor before accepting it.

(3) A Deputy Chief Coroner appointed by the Lord Chancellor may resign from office by giving notice in writing to the Lord Chancellor.

(4) But the resignation does not take effect unless and until it is accepted by the Lord Chancellor, who must consult the Lord Chief Justice before accepting it.

4

(1) The Lord Chief Justice may, after consulting the Lord Chancellor, remove the Chief Coroner, or a Deputy Chief Coroner appointed by the Lord Chief Justice, from office for incapacity or misbehaviour.

(2) The Lord Chancellor may, after consulting the Lord Chief Justice, remove a Deputy Chief Coroner appointed by the Lord Chancellor from office for incapacity or misbehaviour.

Remuneration, allowances and expenses

5

The Lord Chancellor may pay to the Chief Coroner—
- (a) amounts determined by the Lord Chancellor by way of remuneration or allowances;
- (b) amounts determined by the Lord Chancellor towards expenses incurred by the Chief Coroner in performing functions as such.

6

The Lord Chancellor may pay to a Deputy Chief Coroner—
- (a) amounts determined by the Lord Chancellor by way of remuneration or allowances;
- (b) amounts determined by the Lord Chancellor towards expenses incurred by that Deputy Chief Coroner in performing functions as such.

7

A reference in paragraph 5 or 6 to paying expenses incurred by a person ("P") includes a reference to indemnifying P in respect of—
- (a) costs that P reasonably incurs in or in connection with proceedings in respect of things done or omitted in the exercise (or purported exercise) by P of duties under this Part;
- (b) costs that P reasonably incurs in taking steps to dispute claims that might be made in such proceedings;
- (c) damages awarded against P, or costs ordered to be paid by P, in such proceedings;
- (d) sums payable by P in connection with a reasonable settlement of such proceedings or of claims that might be made in such proceedings.

Exercise of Chief Coroner's functions by Deputy Chief coroner

8

(1) A Deputy Chief Coroner may perform any functions of the Chief Coroner—
- (a) during a period when the Chief Coroner is absent or unavailable;
- (b) during a vacancy in the office of Chief Coroner;
- (c) at any other time, with the consent of the Chief Coroner.

(2) Accordingly a reference in this Part to the Chief Coroner is to be read, where appropriate, as including a Deputy Chief Coroner.

Staff

9

(1) The Lord Chancellor must appoint staff to assist the Chief Coroner and any Deputy Chief Coroners in the performance of their functions.
(2) Such staff are to be appointed on whatever terms and conditions the Lord Chancellor thinks appropriate.

SCHEDULE 9
MEDICAL ADVISER AND DEPUTY MEDICAL ADVISERS TO THE CHIEF CORONER

Section 38

Appointment and functions of Medical Adviser to the Chief Coroner

1

The Lord Chancellor may appoint a person as Medical Adviser to the Chief Coroner ("the Medical Adviser") to provide advice and assistance to the Chief Coroner as to medical matters in relation to the coroner system.

Appointment and functions of Deputy Medical Advisers to the Chief Coroner

2

(1) The Lord Chancellor may appoint however many Deputy Medical Advisers to the Chief Coroner ("Deputy Medical Advisers") the Lord Chancellor thinks appropriate.
(2) A Deputy Medical Adviser may perform any functions of the Medical Adviser—
  (a) during a period when the Medical Adviser is absent or unavailable;
  (b) during a vacancy in the office of Medical Adviser;
  (c) at any other time, with the consent of the Medical Adviser.

Qualification for appointment

3

A person may be appointed as the Medical Adviser or as a Deputy Medical Adviser only if, at the time of the appointment, he or she—
  (a) is a registered medical practitioner and has been throughout the previous 5 years, and
  (b) practises as such or has done within the previous 5 years.

Consultation before making appointment

4

Before appointing a person as the Medical Adviser or as a Deputy Medical Adviser, the Lord Chancellor must consult—
  (a) the Chief Coroner, and
  (b) the Welsh Ministers.

A1.1 *Coroners and Justice Act 2009*

Terms and conditions of appointment

5

The appointment of a person as the Medical Adviser or as a Deputy Medical Adviser is to be on whatever terms and conditions the Lord Chancellor thinks appropriate.

Remuneration, allowances and expenses

6

(1) The Lord Chancellor may pay to the Medical Adviser—
   (a) amounts determined by the Lord Chancellor by way of remuneration or allowances;
   (b) amounts determined by the Lord Chancellor towards expenses incurred in performing functions as such.

(2) The Lord Chancellor may pay to a Deputy Medical Adviser—
   (a) amounts determined by the Lord Chancellor by way of remuneration or allowances;
   (b) amounts determined by the Lord Chancellor towards expenses incurred by that Deputy Medical Adviser in performing functions as such.

SCHEDULE 10
INVESTIGATION BY CHIEF CORONER OR CORONER FOR TREASURE OR BY JUDGE, FORMER JUDGE OR FORMER CORONER

Section 41

Investigation by Chief Coroner

1

(1) The Chief Coroner may conduct an investigation into a person's death.

(2) Where the Chief Coroner is responsible for conducting an investigation by virtue of this paragraph—
   (a) the Chief Coroner has the same functions in relation to the body and the investigation as would be the case if he or she were a senior coroner in whose area the body was situated;
   (b) no senior coroner, area coroner or assistant coroner has any functions in relation to the body or the investigation.

(3) Accordingly a reference in a statutory provision (whenever made) to a senior coroner is to be read, where appropriate, as including the Chief Coroner exercising functions by virtue of this paragraph.

Investigation by Coroner for Treasure

2

(1) The Chief Coroner may direct the Coroner for Treasure to conduct an investigation into a person's death.

(2) Where a direction is given under this paragraph—
   (a) the Coroner for Treasure must conduct the investigation;
   (b) the Coroner for Treasure has the same functions in relation to the body and the investigation as would be the case if he or she were a senior coroner in whose area the body was situated;

(c) no senior coroner, area coroner or assistant coroner has any functions in relation to the body or the investigation.

(3) Accordingly, a reference in a statutory provision (whenever made) to a senior coroner is to be read, where appropriate, as including the Coroner for Treasure exercising functions by virtue of this paragraph.

Investigation by judge, former judge or former coroner

3

(1) If requested to do so by the Chief Coroner, the Lord Chief Justice may nominate a person within sub-paragraph (2) to conduct an investigation into a person's death.

(2) A person is within this sub-paragraph if at the time of the nomination he or she is—

    (a) a judge of the High Court,

    (b) a Circuit judge, or

    (c) a person who has held office as a judge of the Court of Appeal or of the High Court (but no longer does so),

and is under the age of 75.

(3) The Chief Coroner may request a person who at the time of the request—

    (a) has held office as a senior coroner (but no longer does so), and

    (b) is under the age of 75,

to conduct an investigation into a person's death.

(4) If a person nominated or requested under this paragraph agrees to conduct the investigation—

    (a) that person is under a duty to do so;

    (b) that person has the same functions in relation to the body and the investigation as would be the case if he or she were a senior coroner in whose area the body was situated;

    (c) no senior coroner, area coroner or assistant coroner has any functions in relation to the body or the investigation.

(5) Accordingly a reference in a statutory provision (whenever made) to a coroner is to be read, where appropriate, as including a person who has been nominated or requested under this paragraph to conduct an investigation and has agreed to do so.

(6) The Lord Chief Justice must consult the Lord Chancellor before making a nomination under this paragraph.

. . .

4

. . .

Investigations already begun

5

A reference in this Schedule to conducting an investigation, in the case of an investigation that has already begun, is to be read as a reference to continuing to conduct the investigation.

NOTES

Amendment

Amended by the Public Bodies Act 2011, s 33(2).

CORONERS (INQUESTS) RULES 2013, SI 2013/1616

PART 1
INTRODUCTION

1 Citation and commencement
These Rules may be cited as the Coroners (Inquests) Rules 2013 and shall come into force on 25th July 2013.

2 Interpretation
(1) In these Rules—
"the 2009 Act" means the Coroners and Justice Act 2009;
"bank holiday" means a day designated as a bank holiday in England and Wales under the Banking and Financial Dealings Act 1971;
"copy" means in relation to a document, anything on to which information recorded in the document has been copied, by whatever means and whether directly or indirectly;
"coroner" means—
    (a) a senior coroner, area coroner or assistant coroner;
    (b) the Chief Coroner when conducting an inquest; or
    (c) a judge, former judge or former coroner conducting an inquest in accordance with Schedule 10 to the 2009 Act;
"document" means any medium in which information of any description is recorded or stored;
"working day" means a day that is not a Saturday, a Sunday, a bank holiday, Christmas Day or Good Friday.
(2) All references to section and schedule provisions in these Rules are references to provisions in the 2009 Act, unless a rule specifically states otherwise.
(3) Any reference to a Form in these Rules is a reference to a Form in the Schedule to these Rules.

3 Application to existing inquests
(1) These Rules apply to any inquest which has not been completed before 25th July 2013.
(2) Any direction, time limit, adjournment or other decision made by the coroner in relation to an inquest made before 25th July 2013 shall stand.

PART 2
FORMALITIES

4
This Part applies where a coroner is under a duty to hold an inquest under section 6.

5 Opening of an inquest
(1) An inquest must be opened as soon as reasonably practicable after the date on which the coroner considers that the duty under section 6 applies.
(2) At the opening of the inquest, the coroner must, where possible, set the dates on which any subsequent hearings are scheduled to take place.

6 Pre-inquest review hearing
A coroner may at any time during the course of an investigation and before an inquest hearing hold a pre-inquest review hearing.

7 Days on which an inquest may be held
An inquest must be held on a working day, unless the coroner considers that there is an urgent reason for holding it on some other day.

8 Timing of an inquest
A coroner must complete an inquest within six months of the date on which the coroner is made aware of the death, or as soon as is reasonably practicable after that date.

9 Notification of inquest hearing arrangements
(1) A coroner must notify the next of kin or personal representative of the deceased of the date, time and place of the inquest hearing within one week of setting the date of the inquest hearing.
(2) A coroner must notify any other interested persons who have made themselves known to the coroner of the date, time and place of the inquest hearing within one week of setting the date of the inquest hearing.
(3) Where an inquest hearing is to be held, the coroner must make details of the date, time and place of the inquest hearing publicly available before the inquest hearing commences.

10 Coroner to notify interested persons of any alteration of arrangements for an inquest hearing
(1) Where the date, time or place of the inquest hearing is altered the coroner must notify the next of kin or personal representative of the deceased, and any other interested persons who have made themselves known to the coroner, of the alteration within one week of the decision to alter.
(2) The coroner must make the details of any alteration made under paragraph (1) publicly available within one week of the decision to alter.

11 Inquest hearings to be held in public
(1) A coroner must open an inquest in public.
(2) Where the coroner does not have immediate access to a court room or other appropriate premises, the coroner may open the inquest privately and then announce that the inquest has been opened at the next inquest hearing held in public.
(3) An inquest hearing and any pre-inquest hearing must be held in public unless paragraph (4) or (5) applies.
(4) A coroner may direct that the public be excluded from an inquest hearing, or any part of an inquest hearing if the coroner considers it would be in the interests of national security to do so.
(5) A coroner may direct that the public be excluded from a pre-inquest review hearing if the coroner considers it would be in the interests of justice or national security to do so.

PART 3
DISCLOSURE

12
This Part applies to the disclosure of documents by the coroner during or after the course of an investigation, pre-inquest review or inquest.

13 Disclosure of documents at the request of an interested person
(1) Subject to rule 15, where an interested person asks for disclosure of a document held by the coroner, the coroner must provide that document or a copy of that

document, or make the document available for inspection by that person as soon as is reasonably practicable.

(2) Documents to which this rule applies include—
- (a) any post-mortem examination report;
- (b) any other report that has been provided to the coroner during the course of the investigation;
- (c) where available, the recording of any inquest hearing held in public, but not in relation to any part of the hearing from which the public was excluded under rule 11(4) or (5);
- (d) any other document which the coroner considers relevant to the inquest.

14 Managing disclosure
A coroner may—
- (a) disclose an electronic copy of a document instead of, or in addition to, a paper copy;
- (b) disclose a redacted version of all or part of a document; or
- (c) make a document available for inspection at a particular time and place.

15 Restrictions on disclosure
A coroner may refuse to provide a document or a copy of a document requested under rule 13 where—
- (a) there is a statutory or legal prohibition on disclosure;
- (b) the consent of any author or copyright owner cannot reasonably be obtained;
- (c) the request is unreasonable;
- (d) the document relates to contemplated or commenced criminal proceedings; or
- (e) the coroner considers the document irrelevant to the investigation.

16 Costs of disclosure
A coroner may not charge a fee for any document or copy of any document, disclosed to an interested person before or during an inquest.

PART 4

MANAGEMENT OF THE INQUEST HEARING

17 Evidence by video link
(1) A coroner may direct that a witness may give evidence at an inquest hearing through a live video link.

(2) A direction may not be given under paragraph (1) unless the coroner determines that giving evidence in the way proposed would improve the quality of the evidence given by the witness or allow the inquest to proceed more expediently.

(3) Before giving a direction under paragraph (1), the coroner must consider all the circumstances of the case, including in particular—
- (a) any views expressed by the witness or any interested person;
- (b) whether it would be in the interests of justice or national security to give evidence by video link; and
- (c) whether in the opinion of the coroner, giving evidence by video link would impede the effectiveness of the questioning of the witness.

(4) A direction may be given under paragraph (1)—
- (a) on an application by the witness, or in the case of a child witness the parent or legal guardian of that witness;
- (b) on an application by an interested person; or
- (c) on the coroner's own initiative.

18 Evidence given from behind a screen

(1) A coroner may direct that a witness may give evidence at an inquest hearing from behind a screen.

(2) A direction may not be given under paragraph (1) unless the coroner determines that giving evidence in the way proposed would be likely to improve the quality of the evidence given by the witness or allow the inquest to proceed more expediently.

(3) In making that determination, the coroner must consider all the circumstances of the case, including in particular—
- (a) any views expressed by the witness or an interested person;
- (b) whether it would be in the interests of justice or national security to allow evidence to be given from behind a screen; and
- (c) whether giving evidence from behind a screen would impede the effectiveness of the questioning of the witness by an interested person or a representative of the interested person.

(4) A direction may be given under paragraph (1)—
- (a) on the application by the witness, or in the case of a child witness the parent or legal guardian of that witness;
- (b) on an application of an interested person; or
- (c) on the coroner's own initiative.

19 Entitlement to examine witnesses

(1) A coroner must allow any interested person who so requests, to examine any witness either in person or by the interested person's representative.

(2) A coroner must disallow any question put to the witness which the coroner considers irrelevant.

20 Evidence given on oath or affirmation

(1) A witness providing evidence at an inquest hearing shall be examined by the coroner on oath or affirmation subject to paragraph (2).

(2) A child under the age of 14, or a child aged 14 or over who is considered by the coroner to be unable to understand the nature of an oath or affirmation, may, on promising to tell the truth, be permitted to give unsworn evidence.

21 Examination of witnesses

Unless the coroner otherwise determines, a witness at an inquest hearing must be examined in the following order—
- (a) first by the coroner;
- (b) then by any interested person who has asked to examine the witness; and
- (c) if the witness is represented at the inquest, lastly by the witness's representative.

22 Self incrimination

(1) No witness at an inquest is obliged to answer any question tending to incriminate him or her.

(2) Where it appears to the coroner that a witness has been asked such a question, the coroner must inform the witness that he or she may refuse to answer it.

23 Written evidence

(1) Written evidence as to who the deceased was and how, when and where the deceased came by his or her death is not admissible unless the coroner is satisfied that—
- (a) it is not possible for the maker of the written evidence to give evidence at the inquest hearing at all, or within a reasonable time;
- (b) there is a good and sufficient reason why the maker of the written evidence should not attend the inquest hearing;

A1.2 Coroners (Inquests) Rules 2013, SI 2013/1616

(c) there is a good and sufficient reason to believe that the maker of the written evidence will not attend the inquest hearing; or
(d) the written evidence (including evidence in admission form) is unlikely to be disputed.

(2) Before admitting such written evidence the coroner must announce at the inquest hearing—
(a) what the nature of the written evidence to be admitted is;
(b) the full name of the maker of the written evidence to be admitted in evidence;
(c) that any interested person may object to the admission of any such written evidence; and
(d) that any interested person is entitled to see a copy of any written evidence if he or she so wishes.

(3) A coroner must admit as evidence at an inquest hearing any document made by a deceased person if the coroner is of the opinion that the contents of the document are relevant to the purposes of the inquest.

(4) A coroner may direct that all or parts only of any written evidence submitted under this rule may be read aloud at the inquest hearing.

24 Inquiry findings

(1) A coroner may admit the findings of an inquiry, including any inquiry under the Inquiries Act 2005, if the coroner considers them relevant to the purposes of the inquest.

(2) Before admitting such inquiry findings as evidence, the coroner must announce publicly that—
(a) the findings of the inquiry may be admitted as evidence;
(b) the title of the inquiry, date of publication and a brief account of the findings; and
(c) that any interested person is entitled to see a copy of the inquiry findings if he or she so wishes.

25 Adjournment and resumption of an inquest

(1) A coroner may adjourn an inquest if the coroner is of the view that it is reasonable to do so.

(2) The coroner must inform the next of kin or personal representative of the deceased and any other interested persons who have made themselves known to the coroner as soon as reasonably practicable of the decision to adjourn, the date of the decision to adjourn and the reason for the adjournment.

(3) The coroner must inform the next of kin or personal representative of the deceased and any other interested persons who have made themselves known to the coroner as soon as reasonably practicable of the date, time and place at which an adjourned inquest is to be resumed.

(4) A coroner must adjourn an inquest and notify the Director of Public Prosecutions, if during the course of the inquest, it appears to the coroner that the death of the deceased is likely to have been due to a homicide offence and that a person may be charged in relation to the offence.

26 Recording inquest hearings

A coroner must keep a recording of every inquest hearing, including any pre-inquest review hearing.

27 No address as to facts

No person may address the coroner or the jury as to the facts of who the deceased was and how, when and where the deceased came by his or her death.

PART 5
JURY INQUESTS

28

This Part applies to inquests heard or to be heard with a jury.

29 Method of summoning jurors

(1) A juror must be summoned using Form 1.

(2) Form 1 must be sent by post with a return envelope, to the juror or delivered by hand at his or her address as shown in the electoral register.

30 Summoning in exceptional circumstances

If it appears to the coroner that a jury will be, or probably will be, incomplete, the coroner may require any persons up to the number needed who are in, or in the vicinity of, the place of the inquest hearing to be summoned (without any written notice) for jury service.

31 Certificate of attendance

A person duly attending an inquest hearing to serve on a jury in compliance with a summons issued under rule 29 or rule 30 is entitled on request to the coroner to a certificate recording that fact.

32 Validity of proceedings where jury not present

Where an inquest hearing begins without a jury but a jury is subsequently summoned, the validity of anything done by the coroner before the jury was summoned is still effective.

33 Summing up and directions to the jury

Where the coroner sits with a jury, the coroner must direct the jury as to the law and provide the jury with a summary of the evidence.

PART 6
RECORD

34 Record of the inquest

A coroner or in the case of an inquest heard with a jury, the jury, must make a determination and any findings required under section 10 using Form 2.

A1.2 Coroners (Inquests) Rules 2013, SI 2013/1616

SCHEDULE

Rules 29 and 34

ANNEX A   **FORM 2: RECORD OF AN INQUEST**

Form 2
Record of an inquest

The following is the record of the inquest (including the statutory determination and, where required, findings)—

1. Name of the deceased (if known):

2. Medical cause of death:

3. How, when and where, and for investigations where section 5(2) of the Coroners and Justice Act 2009 applies, in what circumstances the deceased came by his or her death: (see note (ii)):

4. Conclusion of the coroner/ jury as to the death: (see notes (i) and (ii):

5. Further particulars required by the Births and Deaths Registration Act 1953 to be registered concerning the death:

1.	2.	3.	4.	5.	6.
Date and place of death	Name and surname of deceased	Sex	Maiden surname of woman who has married	Date and place of birth	Occupation and usual address

Signature of coroner (and jurors):

NOTES:

(i) One of the following short-form conclusions may be adopted:—

I. accident or misadventure

II. alcohol / drug related

III. industrial disease

IV. lawful/ unlawful killing

V. natural causes

VI. open

VII. road traffic collision

VIII. stillbirth

IX. suicide

(ii) As an alternative, or in addition to one of the short-form conclusions listed under NOTE (i), the coroner or where applicable the jury, may make a brief narrative conclusion.

(iii) The standard of proof required for the short form conclusions of "unlawful killing" and "suicide" is the criminal standard of proof. For all other short-form conclusions and a narrative statement the standard of proof is the civil standard of proof.

CORONERS (INVESTIGATIONS) REGULATIONS 2013, SI 2013/1629

PART 1
INTRODUCTION

A1.3

1 Citation and commencement
These Regulations may be cited as the Coroners (Investigations) Regulations 2013 and shall come into force on 25th July 2013.

2 Interpretation
(1) In these Regulations—
"2009 Act" means the Coroners and Justice Act 2009;
"bank holiday" means a day designated as a bank holiday in England and Wales under the Banking and Financial Dealings Act 1971 ;
"coroner" means—
> (a) a senior coroner, area coroner or assistant coroner;
> (b) the Chief Coroner when conducting an investigation under paragraph 1 of Schedule 10 to the 2009 Act; or
> (c) a judge, former judge or former coroner conducting an investigation under paragraph 3 of Schedule 10 to the 2009 Act;

"document" means any medium in which information of any description is recorded or stored;
"enforcing authority" has the same meaning as in section 18(7) of the Health and Safety at Work etc Act 1974;
"investigation" means an investigation into a death conducted under Part 1 of the 2009 Act;
"working day" means a day that is not a Saturday, a Sunday, a bank holiday, Christmas Day or Good Friday.
(2) All references to sections and schedule provisions in these Regulations are references to provisions in the 2009 Act, unless a regulation specifically states otherwise.
(3) A reference to a Form in these Regulations is a reference to a Form in the Schedule to these Regulations.

3 Application
(1) These Regulations shall have effect in relation to any investigation (including any inquest) which has not been completed before 25th July 2013.
(2) Any decision of the coroner made in relation to an investigation, or inquest as the case may be, including any decision relating to a post-mortem examination before 25th July 2013 shall stand.

PART 2
GENERAL

4 Coroner availability for urgent matters
A coroner must be available at all times to address matters relating to an investigation into a death which must be dealt with immediately and cannot wait until the next working day.

5 Register of reported deaths

(1) The senior coroner must keep a register of all deaths reported in his or her coroner area.

(2) The senior coroner must record in the register, the following information, when known—
- (a) the date on which a death was reported under section 1;
- (b) the deceased's full name, gender, age and full address;
- (c) any other information that aids the identification of the deceased; and
- (d) the place of death or, if that is unknown, the place where the body was found.

6 Informing the deceased's next of kin or personal representative

A coroner who is under a duty to investigate a death under section 1, must attempt to identify the deceased's next of kin or personal representative and inform that person, if identified, of the coroner's decision to begin an investigation.

7 Delegation of administrative functions

A coroner may delegate administrative, but not judicial functions, to coroner's officers and other support staff.

8 Providing information to the registrar of births and deaths

Where a coroner suspends an investigation under paragraph 1, 2, 3 or 5 of Schedule 1 the coroner must provide the registrar of births and deaths with the particulars required to register the death under the Births and Deaths Registration Act 1953.

9 Interim certificate of fact of death

(1) Where a coroner has begun but not yet completed or discontinued an investigation, he or she may, if requested to do so by the next of kin or personal representative of the deceased, provide that person with a certificate of the fact of death.

(2) A coroner must use Form 1 when issuing a certificate of the fact of death.

10 Resumption of investigation

Where a coroner resumes a suspended investigation in accordance with paragraph 7 of Schedule 1, the coroner must notify—
- (a) The next of kin or personal representative of the deceased; and
- (b) any other interested persons who have made themselves known to the coroner,

of the resumption and the reason for the resumption of the investigation.

PART 3
POST-MORTEM EXAMINATIONS

11 Delay in post-mortem examination to be avoided

A coroner who considers that a post-mortem examination should be made under section 14, shall request a suitable practitioner to make that post-mortem examination as soon as reasonably practicable.

12 Post-mortem examination where homicide offence is suspected

Where a coroner is informed by a chief officer of police that a homicide offence is suspected in connection with the death of the deceased, the coroner must consult that chief officer of police about who should make the post-mortem examination.

13 Notification of post-mortem examination

(1) Where a coroner has requested a suitable practitioner to make a post-mortem examination, the coroner must notify the persons or bodies listed in paragraph (3) of the date, time and place at which that post-mortem examination is to be made.

(2) A coroner need not give such notification, where it is impracticable or where to do so would cause the post-mortem examination to be unreasonably delayed.
(3) The persons to be notified are—
- (a) the next of kin or the personal representative of the deceased or any other interested person who has notified the coroner in advance of his or her desire to be represented at the post-mortem examination;
- (b) the deceased's regular medical practitioner, if he or she has notified the coroner of his or her desire to be represented at the post-mortem examination;
- (c) if the deceased died in hospital, that hospital;
- (d) if the death of the deceased may have been caused by an accident or disease which must be reported to an enforcing authority, to that enforcing authority or the appropriate inspector or representative of that authority;
- (e) a Government department which has notified the coroner of its desire to be represented at the examination; and
- (f) if the chief officer of police has notified the coroner of his or her desire to be represented at the examination, the chief officer of police.

(4) Any of the persons or bodies listed in paragraph (3) are entitled to be represented at a post-mortem examination by a medical practitioner, or if they are a medical practitioner, may attend themselves.
(5) The following persons may attend a post-mortem examination—
- (a) A representative of the chief officer of police from the police force of which he or she is chief officer; and
- (b) any other person including a trainee doctor, medical student or other medical practitioner but only with the consent of the coroner.

14 Preservation or retention of material from a post-mortem examination

(1) Where a suitable practitioner conducts a post-mortem examination under section 14 and preserves or retains material which in his or her opinion relates to the cause of death or identity of the deceased, he or she must provide the coroner with written notification of that fact.
(2) A suitable practitioner who preserves or retains material under paragraph (1) must provide the coroner with a written notification that—
- (a) identifies the material being preserved or retained; and
- (b) explains why that practitioner is of the opinion set out in paragraph (1).

(3) A written notification under paragraph (2) may—
- (a) specify the period of time for which the suitable practitioner believes the material should be preserved or retained; and
- (b) specify different periods of time in relation to different preserved or retained material.

(4) On receiving a notification under paragraph (1), the coroner must notify the suitable practitioner of the period of time for which he or she requires the material to be preserved or retained for the purposes of fulfilling his or her functions under the 2009 Act.
(5) On making the notification under paragraph (4) the coroner must also notify, where known—
- (a) the next of kin or personal representative of the deceased; and
- (b) any other relative of the deceased who has notified the coroner of his or her desire to be represented at the post-mortem examination,

that material is being preserved or retained, the period or periods for which it is required to be preserved or retained and the options for dealing with the material under paragraph (6) once the period or periods of preservation or retention has or have expired.

(6) The options for dealing with material are—
(a) disposal of the material by burial, cremation or other lawful disposal by the suitable practitioner;
(b) return of the material to a person listed in sub-paragraph (a) or (b) of paragraph (5); or
(c) retention of the material with the consent of a person listed in sub-paragraph (a) or (b) of paragraph (5) for medical research or other purposes in accordance with the Human Tissue Act 2004.

15 Further provisions relating to preservation or retention of material from post-mortem examinations
(1) A coroner who—
(a) receives a request from a prosecuting authority, Provost Marshal or the Director of Service Prosecutions under paragraph 1 of Schedule 1 to suspend an investigation because a person may be charged with an offence in relation to the death of the deceased; or
(b) becomes aware or is informed under paragraph 2 of Schedule 1 that a person has been charged with an offence in relation to, or connected with, the death of the deceased,

must notify the chief officer of police or prosecuting authority, of any period for which the coroner requires material to be preserved or retained under regulation 14(4).
(2) Where the coroner is informed that a public inquiry is to be held instead of an inquest, the coroner must notify the chairman of that inquiry of any period for which the coroner requires material to be preserved or retained under regulation 14(4).
(3) A coroner may from time to time vary a period notified under regulation 14(4) and must notify both the suitable practitioner and any person notified under regulation 14(5), 15(1) and 15(2) of the variation.
(4) Where a suitable practitioner has received a notification from a coroner under regulation 14(4) and the suitable practitioner believes that the material should be preserved or retained for a different period, the suitable practitioner may request that the coroner vary the time by providing a notification in accordance with regulation 14(2).
(5) Where a suitable practitioner has retained material in accordance with regulation 14 and the period notified under regulation 14(4) has expired, that suitable practitioner must record the fact that—
(a) the material has been disposed by the suitable practitioner or on behalf of the suitable practitioner;
(b) the material has been delivered into the possession of a specified person; or
(c) the material has been dealt with in accordance with regulation 14(6).
(6) Any record made by a suitable practitioner under paragraph (5) must be retained by him or her.

16 Post-mortem examination report
(1) A suitable practitioner, on completion of a post-mortem examination, must report to the coroner as soon as practicable after the examination has been made.
(2) Unless authorised in writing by the coroner, the suitable practitioner who made the post-mortem examination may not supply any other person with the post-mortem examination report or any copy of that report.

17 Discontinuance of investigation where cause of death is revealed by post-mortem examination
Where a coroner discontinues an investigation in accordance with section 4(1) because the post-mortem examination reveals the cause of death, the coroner must record the

cause of death and notify the next of kin or personal representative of the deceased using Form 2.

PART 4
TRANSFER OF INVESTIGATIONS

18 Transfer of investigations
(1) Where Coroner A and Coroner B agree to transfer an investigation under section 2, or the Chief Coroner directs Coroner B to conduct an investigation under section 3—
  (a) Coroner A must provide Coroner B with all relevant evidence, documents and information;
  (b) Coroner B must notify the next of kin or personal representative of the deceased of the transfer; and
  (c) Coroner B must notify any other interested persons who have made themselves known to the coroner of the transfer.
(2) A coroner must fulfil their obligations under this regulation within 5 working days of the date the transfer is either agreed or directed, unless there are exceptional circumstances.

19 Costs of a transferred investigation
(1) Where Coroner A and Coroner B agree to transfer an investigation in accordance with section 2, the relevant authority for Coroner B's coroner area will be responsible for all costs related to the transferred investigation and any associated inquest from the date the transfer is made.
(2) Where the Chief Coroner directs Coroner B to conduct an investigation in accordance with section 3, the relevant authority for Coroner A's coroner area shall be responsible for all costs related to the transferred investigation and any associated inquest from the date the transfer is made, unless the Chief Coroner otherwise directs.

PART 5
POWERS IN RELATION TO BODIES

20 Release of bodies
(1) A coroner must release the body for burial or cremation as soon as is reasonably practicable.
(2) Where a coroner cannot release the body within 28 days of being made aware that the body is within his or her area, the coroner must notify the next of kin or personal representative of the deceased of the reason for the delay.

21 Burial or cremation order
(1) A coroner may only issue an order authorising the burial or cremation of a body where the coroner no longer needs to retain the body for the purposes of the investigation.
(2) A coroner must use Form 3 when issuing an order to bury a body.

22 Exhumation
(1) A coroner may issue a direction to exhume a body lying within England and Wales.
(2) Where such a direction is made the coroner must use Form 4.

A1.3 Coroners (Investigations) Regulations 2013, SI 2013/1629

PART 6
DISCLOSURE AND PROVISION OF INFORMATION

23
Part 3 of the Coroners (Inquests) Rules 2013 applies to the disclosure of documents to an interested person made by the coroner at any time during the course of an investigation.

24 Providing information to a Local Safeguarding Children Board or in Wales a Safeguarding Children Board
(1) Where a coroner decides to conduct an investigation into a death under section 1 or directs that a post-mortem examination should be made under section 14, and the coroner believes the deceased was under the age of 18, the coroner must notify the appropriate Local Safeguarding Children Board or, as the case may be, the appropriate Safeguarding Children Board within 3 days of making the decision or direction.
(2) A coroner must provide all information to the appropriate Local Safeguarding Children Board or, as the case may be, the appropriate Safeguarding Children Board.
(3) In this regulation—

"the appropriate Local Safeguarding Children Board" means the Board established under section 13(1) . . . of the Children Act 2004 within whose area the deceased died or within whose area the body was found; . . .

"the appropriate Safeguarding Children Board" means the board established under section 134 of the Social Services and Well-being (Wales) Act 2014 within whose area the deceased died or within whose area the body was found; and

"information" means any information that is—
    (a) held by the coroner for the purposes of an investigation under Part 1 of the 2009 Act; and
    (b) relates to the death of a person who was or may have been under the age of 18 at the time of death.

NOTES

Amendment
Amended by SI 2016/211, reg 3, Sch 3, Pt 1, paras 160, 161.

25 Power of the Chief Coroner to require information
(1) The Chief Coroner may at any time require information from a coroner in relation to a particular investigation or investigations that have or are being conducted by that coroner.
(2) A coroner must provide the Chief Coroner with the information requested under paragraph (1).

26 Investigations lasting more than a year
(1) Where an investigation has not been completed or discontinued within a year of the date that the death was reported, the coroner must notify the Chief Coroner of that fact as soon as is reasonably practicable from the date that the investigation becomes a year old and explain why the investigation has not been completed or discontinued.
(2) A coroner who completes or discontinues an investigation that the coroner has previously notified to the Chief Coroner under paragraph (1), must notify the Chief Coroner of the date the investigation is completed or discontinued and provide a reason for any further delay in completing or discontinuing the investigation.

27 Retention and release of documents
(1) Any document in the possession of a coroner in connection with an investigation or post-mortem examination must, unless a court or the Chief Coroner otherwise

directs, be retained by or on behalf of the coroner for at least 15 years from the date that the investigation is completed.

(2) The coroner may provide any document or copy of any document to any person who in the opinion of the coroner is a proper person to have possession of it.

(3) A coroner may charge for the provision of any document or copy of any document in accordance with any regulations made under Schedule 7.

PART 7

ACTION TO PREVENT OTHER DEATHS

28 Report on action to prevent other deaths

(1) This regulation applies where a coroner is under a duty under paragraph 7(1) of Schedule 5 to make a report to prevent other deaths.

(2) In this regulation, a reference to "a report" means a report to prevent other deaths made by the coroner.

(3) A report may not be made until the coroner has considered all the documents, evidence and information that in the opinion of the coroner are relevant to the investigation.

(4) The coroner—
- (a) must send a copy of the report to the Chief Coroner and every interested person who in the coroner's opinion should receive it;
- (b) must send a copy of the report to the appropriate Local Safeguarding Children Board or as the case may be the appropriate Safeguarding Children Board (which have the same meaning as in regulation 24(3)) where the coroner believes the deceased was under the age of 18; and
- (c) may send a copy of the report to any other person who the coroner believes may find it useful or of interest.

(5) On receipt of a report the Chief Coroner may—
- (a) publish a copy of the report, or a summary of it, in such manner as the Chief Coroner thinks fit; and
- (b) send a copy of the report to any person who the Chief Coroner believes may find it useful or of interest.

NOTES

Amendment
Amended by SI 2016/211, reg 3, Sch 3, Pt 1, paras 160, 162.

29 Response to a report on action to prevent other deaths

(1) This regulation applies where a person is under a duty to give a response to a report to prevent other deaths made in accordance with paragraph 7(1) of Schedule 5.

(2) In this regulation, a reference to "a report" means a report to prevent other deaths made by the coroner.

(3) The response to a report must contain—
- (a) details of any action that has been taken or which it is proposed will be taken by the person giving the response or any other person whether in response to the report or otherwise and set out a timetable of the action taken or proposed to be taken; or
- (b) an explanation as to why no action is proposed.

(4) The response must be provided to the coroner who made the report within 56 days of the date on which the report is sent.

(5) The coroner who made the report may extend the period referred to in paragraph (4) (even if an application for extension is made after the time for compliance has expired).

(6) On receipt of a response to a report the coroner—
- (a) must send a copy of the response to the report to the Chief Coroner;

(b) must send a copy to any interested persons who in the coroner's opinion should receive it; and
(c) may send a copy of the response to any other person who the coroner believes may find it useful or of interest.

(7) On receipt of a copy under paragraph (6)(a) the Chief Coroner may—
(a) publish a copy of the response, or a summary of it, in such manner as the Chief Coroner thinks fit; and
(b) send a copy of the response to any person who the Chief Coroner believes may find it useful or of interest (other than a person who has been sent a copy of the response under paragraph (6)(b) or (c)).

(8) A person giving a response to a report may make written representations to the coroner about—
(a) the release of the response; or
(b) the publication of the response.

(9) Representations under paragraph (8) must be made to the coroner no later than the time when the response to the report to prevent other deaths is provided to the coroner under paragraph (4).

(10) The coroner must pass any representations made under paragraph (8) to the Chief Coroner who may then consider those representations and decide whether there should be any restrictions on the release or publication of the response.

SCHEDULE
FORMS

Regulations 9, 17, 21 and 22

Form 1
Coroner's certificate of fact of death
To whom it may concern,
CD (insert name):
of (insert address):
died on (insert date):
The precise cause of death, *was as follows/ *has yet to be established
*Delete as appropriate

Date:
Signature:
Coroner:

Form 2
Notice of Discontinuance
To (insert name):
The investigation into the death of CD has been discontinued under section 4 of the Coroners and Justice Act 2009.
The investigation was discontinued for the following reason(s):

Date:
Signature:
Coroner:

Form 3
Order for burial
I authorise the burial of CD (insert name)
aged, (insert age)
who died at, (insert time and place)
on, (insert date)

Date:
Signature:
Coroner:

Form 4
Direction to exhume
To
(insert the names of the Minister and churchwardens or other persons having control over the churchyard, cemetery, or other place where the body is buried).

I have been informed that the body of CD, has been buried in (insert the name of the churchyard, cemetery or other place where the body is buried), and it appears to me that it is necessary for the body to be exhumed and examined for the purposes of:
1 conducting an investigation into the death of the deceased under Part 1 of the Coroners and Justice Act 2009; or
2 discharging a coroner's function in relation to the body or death of the deceased, namely: (insert function)
I direct that you allow the body of CD to be exhumed.

Date:
Signature:
Coroner:

Index

A

Aberfan disaster 24.35
Abroad, death occurring *see* Overseas, death occurring
Absence of body
  guidance 2.47, 2.49
  reporting of 2.46–2.52
Accident or misadventure, death by
  conclusion of 6.55–6.58
  neglect, and 6.158, 6.159
  notifiable accident, poisoning or disease 4.101–4.107
  road traffic collisions, and 17.22
Adjournment
  compulsory, criminal proceedings, for 21.22, 21.23
  road traffic collision deaths 17.16
Administrative procedures
  safeguarding life for 3.70–3.107
    clinical negligence 3.83–3.87
    dangerous activities/natural hazards 3.72–3.78
    mental health patients 3.79
    military deaths 3.81, 3.82
    prisoners 3.80
Alcohol/drug-related death
  conclusion of 6.59, 6.60
  road traffic collisions, and 17.22
Allowances *see* Fees; Funding
Amenas inquests 2.98
Anonymity
  deceased child 12.19, 12.20
  witnesses 4.36–4.41, 12.14–12.16
    child 12.17, 12.18, 22.12, 22.13
Area/assistant coroners
  powers 1.25
  qualification 1.25
  role 1.23, 1.24
Armed forces *see* Military deaths
Article 2
  inquests
    causation, test for 6.186–6.197

Article 2 – *cont.*
  inquests – *cont.*
    clinical negligence 13.16–13.26
    custody/state detention deaths 14.5
    PFD report, and 7.29
    road traffic collisions, and 17.11, 17.23–17.25
    scope 3.51–3.54
  investigative duty, under 3.58, 3.98–3.107
    compliance with 3.104–3.107
    deaths in custody 14.6, 14.22
    deaths in combat 19.36–19.39
      Iraq, case law 19.47, 19.48
    deaths in mental health detention 15.15
    deprivation of liberty 15.64, 15.65
    discharge of 3.51
    engagement of 3.52–3.54, 3.102, 3.103
    judicial review, grounds for 8.58, 8.59
    narrative conclusions 6.164–6.169
    public inquiries, and 24.20
    resumption of investigation 21.49–21.51
    test for 3.6, 3.98–3.101
  negative duty, under 3.59, 3.61–3.69
    'honest belief' 3.66, 3.67
    meaning 3.61
    self-defence 3.68
  operational duty, under 3.59, 3.88–3.97
    clinical negligence, and 13.21–13.26
    medical care, and 14.18
  positive substantive duties, under 3.59, 3.70–3.107
  systemic duty, under 3.70–3.87
    clinical negligence 3.83–3.87
    dangerous activities/natural hazards 3.73–3.78
    mental health patients 3.79
    military deaths 3.81, 3.82
    prisoners 3.80
Autopsies *see* Post mortem
Avoidance of future deaths *see* PFD reports

417

Index

B

Before the event insurance 9.34, 9.35
Bias
  impartiality, coroner of 1.3
Bloody Sunday Inquiry 24.11, 24.41
Bodies *see also* Post mortem; Release of bodies
  disposal
    registrar's certificate 2.15
  release of 2.89, 2.90
    applications for 2.43
  removal from jurisdiction 2.21
  repatriation 2.19
Brecon Beacons SAS training 19.42–19.46
Burial
  release of body 2.55, 2.89

C

Cadre, coroners of
  guidance 19.7
  military deaths 19.7
Care homes
  Art 2 duty, and 3.92, 3.97, 15.11
  DoL safeguards 15.50, 15.59, 15.61, 15.70
  public authorities, as 3.44, 15.55
Care proceedings
  child, death of 22.1–22.11
Care Programme Approach 15.27–15.32
Causation 6.174–6.180
  Art 2 inquests 6.186–6.197
  Galbraith Plus test 6.198–6.203
  neglect, and 6.181–6.185
  test for 6.175
Cause of death
  certificate
    COVID-19, and 20.16–20.18
  circumstances requiring notification 2.6, 2.7
  death certificate 2.4–2.11
  family, communicating 10.67–10.70
  medical cause 6.10–6.12
  notifiable disease 2.11
  post mortem, revealed by 2.39, 2.86–2.88
Certificate *see also* Death certificate
  disposal of body, permitting 2.15
  no resumption of inquest for 2.132
Charitable assistance 9.38–9.40
Chief Coroner
  decisions, challenging 1.16
  guidance 1.17, 1.19
  information, power to request 1.16
  law sheets 1.18, 1.19
  qualifications 1.16

Chief Coroner's guidance
  cadre, coroners of 19.7
  conclusions 6.3, 6.6, 6.18, 6.21, 6.22, 6.30, 6.32, 6.36, 6.49, 6.50, 6.53, 6.56, 6.57, 6.119, 6.123–6.125, 6.135, 6.138, 6.141–6.143, 6.155, 6.161, 6.163, 6.166, 6.170, 6.171, 13.41, 24.50, 24.53, 24.54
    road traffic collision 17.21–17.23, 17.25
  conduct at post mortem 2.75, 2.78, 2.81, 2.83, 2.84
  Coronavirus Act 2020 20.16–20.21
  COVID-19 2.5, 20.6–20.14
    workplace deaths 3.30, 6.61, 6.117, 16.2, 20.22–20.32, 24.39
  documentary inquests 4.46
  expedited post mortem 2.66
  family proceedings 22.3–22.7, 22.10
  fast track inquests 2.105
  investigations without body 2.47, 2.49
  juries 5.39–5.42
  liberty, deprivation of, safeguards 4.93, 15.41, 15.49–15.52, 15.59, 15.60
  media 4.36, 4.37, 12.3–12.10, 12.12, 12.13, 12.17, 12.18, 18.14, 22.13
  PFD reports 7.1, 7.2, 7.7, 7.9, 7.12, 7.13, 7.19–7.21, 12.26
  post mortem imagery 2.71
  pre-inquest review 4.1, 4.2, 4.6, 4.8–4.10, 4.34, 4.37, 4.116
  suspension of investigations 2.113, 2.126, 2.127, 17.15, 17.16, 21.16, 21.18, 21.21, 21.44, 21.47
  transfer of jurisdiction 2.92, 2.95, 2.96
Chilcot Inquiry 24.19
Children
  anonymity 12.17–12.20, 22.12, 22.13
  death
    care proceedings, in 22.1–22.11
    post mortem, for 2.76, 2.77
  reporting restrictions, and 22.12–22.14
  witnesses as 22.12, 22.13
Civil proceedings
  inquests, and 23.1–23.10
    inadmissibility of conclusion 23.7–23.10
Client care 10.1, 10.2, 11.1
  cause of death, communicating 10.67–10.70
  clinical inquests 13.2
  conflicts of interest 11.5
  death, following 10.3–10.11
  deaths in custody 14.23
  disclosure of information 10.38–10.42
  during proceedings 10.28–10.33
  evidence, family by 10.58–10.62
  expert evidence, and 10.63–10.66
  first contact 10.19–10.27

418

Index

Client care – *cont.*
  hearing, at 10.49–10.57, 11.12–11.14
  inquest conclusions 10.71–10.77
  instructions 11.3
  media
    access, and 12.22–12.33
    adverse coverage 11.7
    statement, to 11.15
  mental health cases 15.76, 15.77
  military inquests, in 19.11–19.14
  pathologist's evidence, advance warning 10.17, 10.18
  PFD reports 10.78, 10.79, 11.15
  PIR hearing 10.34–10.37, 11.8
  post-inquest 10.80, 10.81
  post-mortem report, access to 10.12–10.16
  pre-interest preparation 11.9–11.11
  preliminary contact 11.2–11.4
  previous reports and investigations 11.6
  witnesses statements 10.43–10.48
Clinical negligence
  Art 2, and 3.83–3.87, 13.16–13.26
  disclosure 13.27–13.31
  establishing 13.3–13.5
  expert evidence 13.34–13.38
  family, representation of 13.2
  healthcare providers
    duty of candour 13.32, 13.33
  inquest conclusions, and 13.39–13.41
  jurisdiction 13.6–13.15
  scope, generally 13.1
Combat, death in *see also* Military deaths
  Art 2, and 19.36–19.39
  Crown immunity 19.40, 19.41
  Iraq, case law 19.47, 19.48
Conclusions *see also* Narrative conclusion; Short-form conclusion
  advice to family 10.71–10.77
  Art 2 inquests 6.188–6.197
  challenges to *see* Judicial review
  clinical negligence 13.39–13.41
  coroner's discretion 13.41
  fast track/documentary inquests 2.111, 2.112
  form of 6.22–6.24
  generally 6.1–6.6
  guidance 6.3, 6.6, 6.18, 6.21, 6.22, 6.30, 6.32, 6.36, 6.49, 6.50, 6.53, 6.56, 6.57, 6.119, 6.123–6.125, 6.135, 6.138, 6.141–6.143, 6.155, 6.161, 6.163, 6.166, 6.170, 6.171, 13.41, 17.21–17.23, 17.25, 24.50, 24.53, 24.54
  inadmissibility in civil proceedings 23.7, 23.8
  inquest following criminal proceedings 6.42

Conclusions *see also* Narrative conclusion; Short-form conclusion – *cont.*
  interested persons
    admissions of failings 6.43–6.48
    submissions from 6.29
  jury inquests 6.34–6.41
  public inquiries, and 24.50
  reasons, duty to provide 6.30–6.33
  suicide 15.16
Conditional fee agreements 9.29–9.33
Contractor
  interested person
    workplace deaths 16.35
Coroner *see also* Chief Coroner
  appointment 1.1
  categories 1.15–1.26
  challenging *see* Judicial review
  duty to investigate 2.22–2.30
    'reason to suspect' 2.23
  family court, co-operation with 22.10
  impartiality 1.3
  jurisdiction 1.1
  notification of death to 2.4–2.21
  notification of intention not to investigate 2.31
  power to conduct enquiries 2.29
  role of 1.1–1.14
Coroner's areas
  absence of body
    jurisdiction for investigation 2.46–2.52
  death in 2.4–2.11
  exhumation in 2.63
  register of deaths reported in 2.32
  repatriation of body in 2.19
Coroner's discretion
  clinical negligence conclusions 13.41
  disclosure 21.28, 21.29
  experts, calling of 4.114–4.124
  interested persons, naming of 4.21
  PFD reports 3.31
  scope of inquest 3.22–3.28, 3.30
  summoning of jury 4.109–4.113
Coroner's duty
  to act fairly 5.21–5.24
Coroner's officer
  role 1.26
Corporate manslaughter *see also* Homicide offences; Unlawful killing
  duty of care 6.97–6.99
  elements of offence 6.93–6.96
  gross breach 6.100–6.102
Corpses *see* Bodies
Costs
  judicial review 8.65, 8.66
  recovery 9.41–9.43, 9.52–9.55
    proportionality 9.47–9.51

419

Index

Costs – *cont.*
  recovery – *cont.*
    relevance 9.44–9.46
    transfer of proceedings 2.94
Court of Protection
  deprivation of liberty orders 15.51, 15.52
COVID-19 pandemic
  certification of death 2.5, 2.10
  coroner's guidance 20.1–20.3, 20.5
  cremations during
    documentation 20.19
  death certificates 20.16–20.18
  deaths in prison/state detention 20.14
  guidance 2.5, 3.30, 6.61, 6.117, 16.2
    workplace deaths 16.2, 24.39
  jury inquests, and 20.20, 20.21
  key workers, death of 24.39
  natural cause of death 20.6–20.12
  notifiable disease, COVID, as 20.4
  post mortems, and 20.13
  workplace, deaths at 20.22–20.32
    guidance 20.22–20.32
    PPE provision 20.26–20.32
Cremation
  documentation required, coronavirus pandemic, during 20.19
  release of body 2.55, 2.89, 2.90
Criminal proceedings *see also* Corporate manslaughter; Homicide offences; Unlawful killing 21.1
  compulsory adjournment of inquest 21.22, 21.23
  conclusions, resumed inquest, at 6.42
  disclosure 21.24, 21.25, 21.39
    coroner's discretion 21.28, 21.29
    documents publicly available 21.30–21.33
    guidance 21.37, 21.38
    'non-sensitive' material 21.35
    police records 21.34
    'relevant' material 21.36
    'sensitive' material 21.35
    statutory/legal prohibition 21.26, 21.27
  inquest, following 21.53–21.56
    trial not bound by verdict 21.58
    victim's right of review 21.57
  jurisdiction 21.2
    rules for precedence 21.3, 21.4
  resumption of investigation 21.40–21.42, 21.52
    Art 2, under 21.49–21.51
    sufficient reason 21.43–21.48
  road traffic collision deaths, and 17.14–17.20
  suspension of investigation 21.5–21.14
    discretionary 21.15, 21.16

Criminal proceedings *see also* Corporate manslaughter; Homicide offences; Unlawful killing – *cont.*
  suspension of investigation – *cont.*
    effect of 21.17, 21.18
    exceptions 21.19–21.21
Crown immunity
  combat deaths 19.40, 19.41
Custody or state detention *see also* Hospitals; Police custody; Prisons 14.1–14.7
  Art 2, and 14.5
  conclusions 14.7
  COVID-19, death by 20.14
  disclosure of records 14.19
  excessive force, use of 14.16, 14.17
  expert evidence 14.21, 14.22
  healthcare assessments 15.20
  meaning 15.53–15.56
  medical care, in 14.18
  mentally ill person, death 15.6, 15.57–15.61
    Art 2, and 15.64–15.74
    jury inquests 15.62, 15.63
  no discontinuance power 2.40
  PIR hearing 4.93–4.99
  regulatory bodies 14.17
  representation of parties 14.23
  self-inflicted deaths 14.8–14.15
  state investigations 14.20
  violent or unnatural death 14.6

D

Death certificate
  COVID-19, and 2.5, 2.10, 20.9, 20.11, 20.16–20.18
  interim 2.44, 2.45
  medical cause of death 2.4
  requirement 2.4–2.11
Deepcut *see also* Military deaths 19.49, 19.50
Detention *see* Custody or state detention, deaths in
Disclosure *see also* Evidence
  client care 10.38–10.42
  coroner's discretion 21.28, 21.29
  criminal proceedings 21.24, 21.25, 21.39
    documents publicly available 21.30–21.33
    guidance 21.37, 21.38
    'non-sensitive' material 21.35
    police records 21.34
    'relevant' material 21.36
    'sensitive' material 21.35
    statutory/legal prohibition 21.26, 21.27
  deaths in custody 14.19

Index

Disclosure *see also* Evidence – *cont.*
　family proceedings, in **22.7**
　identity of child **22.13**
　media, applications for **12.4–12.8**
　medical records **13.27–13.31, 14.19**
　mental health inquest **15.39, 15.40**
　military inquests, in **19.19–19.29**
　PIR hearing **4.48–4.85**
　　coroner, to **4.51–4.57**
　　interested person, to **4.66–4.82**
　　medical records **4.83–4.85**
　　notices for **4.61–4.63**
　　public interest immunity **4.58–4.60**
　　witness summons **4.64**
　product-related deaths **18.15–18.19**
　public inquiries, and **24.10**
　workplace deaths **16.41–16.43**
Discontinuance
　action following **2.88**
　cause of death revealed **2.86–2.88**
　criteria for **2.39**
　judicial review **2.87**
　reasons for **2.40**
Discretion of coroner
　witnesses, calling of **4.33, 4.34**
Doctor *see* Medical practitioner
Documentary evidence
　guidance **4.46**
　PIR hearing **4.42–4.47**
　public inquiries
　　access to **24.10**
Documentary inquests **2.104–2.112**
　circumstances for **2.107**
　conclusion following **2.111, 2.112**
　evidence, submission of **2.108**
　guidance **2.105**
　notification of **2.109**
Driving offences *see also* Road traffic collision
　unlawful killing conclusion **6.66**

E

Electronic communications
　disclosure of **4.71**
Employees
　interested person
　　workplace deaths **16.38**
Employers
　interested person
　　workplace deaths **16.32, 16.33**

End of life disputes **2.33, 2.34**
European Convention on Human Rights *see also* Article 2 **3.35–3.38**
　life, right to **3.55–3.69**
　protection of rights generally **1.6**
　torture or inhuman/degrading treatment **3.39**
　substantive rights under **3.39**
Evidence *see also* Disclosure; Experts; Standard of proof; Witnesses
　admissibility of **5.13**
　calling of witnesses **5.4–5.12**
　CCTV **2.100**
　deaths overseas **2.102**
　documentary **4.42–4.47**
　family proceedings in **22.1, 22.6, 22.11**
　hearsay **5.14–5.20, 23.9**
　investigation for **2.98–2.103**
　medical records **2.99**
　new
　　ground for statutory review **8.24–8.31**
　non-statutory inquiries **24.18**
　oral, family by **10.58–10.62**
　order at hearing **5.2, 5.3**
　pathologist by **10.17, 10.18**
　PFD reports, and **7.5–7.7**
　PIR, disclosure **4.48–4.85**
　　coroner, to **4.51–4.57**
　　interested person, to **4.66–4.82**
　　medical records **4.83–4.85**
　　notices for **4.61–4.63**
　　public interest immunity **4.58–4.60**
　　witness summons **4.64**
　police custody records **2.101**
　public inquiries, at **24.8, 24.9, 24.22**
　regulatory bodies, from **2.103**
　summing up of **5.33**
　witnesses by **4.33–4.41**
Excessive force
　custodial officers, by **14.16, 14.17**
Exhumation
　power for **2.61–2.64**
Expenses *see* Fees, Funding
Experts *see also* Evidence
　clinical negligence **13.34–13.38**
　death in custody **14.21, 14.22**
　duties and fees **4.125, 4.126**
　fees for time **4.61**
　instruction of **10.63–10.66**
　mental healthcare for **15.33–15.38**
　PIR hearing **4.114–4.124**
　post mortem **2.75**

421

Index

Experts *see also* **Evidence** – *cont.*
  product-related deaths, for 18.20–18.24
  workplace deaths 16.25

F

Fair trial, right to
  public inquiries 24.8
Families
  cause of death, communicating 10.67–10.70
  client care during proceedings 10.28–10.33
  death, following 10.3–10.11
  disclosure of information 10.38–10.42
  expert evidence, and 10.63–10.66
  first contact 10.19–10.27
  hearing, at 10.49–10.57
  inquest conclusions 10.71–10.77
  interested person 10.38–10.42
    workplace deaths 16.31
  mentally ill person, of 15.76, 15.77
  military inquests, in 19.11–19.14
  oral evidence 10.58–10.62
  pathologist's evidence, advance warning 10.17, 10.18
  PFD reports, family access to 10.78, 10.79
  PIR hearing 10.34–10.37
  post-mortem report, access to 10.12–10.16
  representation 10.1, 10.2
    clinical inquests 13.2
    media reporting, and 12.22–12.30
  support following inquest 10.80, 10.81
  witnesses statements 10.43–10.48
Family proceedings
  guidance 22.3–22.7, 22.10
  inquests, and 22.1–22.14
  reporting restrictions 22.12–22.14
Fast track inquests 2.104–2.112
  circumstances for 2.106
  conclusion following 2.111, 2.112
  guidance 2.105
Fees
  documents for 4.72
  experts, for 4.125, 4.126
  pathologist 2.76
Fraud
  ground for statutory review 8.32
Funding 9.1–9.8
  before the event insurance 9.34, 9.35
  charitable assistance 9.38–9.40
  conditional fee agreements 9.29–9.33
  family proceedings, in 22.1
  legal aid 9.9–9.28
  privately funded retainer 9.36, 9.37

Funding – *cont.*
  union membership 9.34, 9.35

G

Galbraith Plus test 6.112, 6.198–6.203
Grenfell Tower inquiry 24.12, 24.36
  PFD report 7.11, 7.17

H

Health and safety *see also* **Corporate manslaughter; Work, death at**
  notifiable accident, poisoning or disease, death by 4.101–4.107
  offences, workplace deaths 16.10–16.12
  PPE, provision of
    COVID-19, and 20.26–20.32
Health and Safety Executive
  interested person
    workplace deaths 16.39, 16.40
Hearing *see also* **Pre-inquest review hearings**
  admissibility of evidence 5.13
  anonymity of witnesses 12.14–12.16
  calling of witnesses 5.4–5.12
  client care 10.49–10.57, 11.12–11.14
  closing submissions 5.30–5.33
  coroner's duty to act fairly 5.21–5.24
  coroner's introduction 5.1
  evidence
    family by 10.58–10.62
    hearsay evidence, use of 5.14–5.20
    order of 5.2, 5.3
  juries 5.34–5.46
  live communication, media by 12.13
  media, attendance by 12.9
  military inquests, legal representation 19.15–19.18
  privilege, self-incrimination, against 5.25–5.29
Hearsay
  admissibility 5.14–5.20
Hillsborough disaster 8.20, 8.24, 8.29, 8.33, 24.35
  inquest location 2.97
Homicide offences *see also* **Corporate manslaughter**
  causation 6.110
  defences 6.106–6.109
  meaning 2.115, 21.6
  post mortem 2.79
    report, disclosure 2.82
  'related offence' 2.115, 17.18, 17.20, 21.6
  road traffic collision deaths 17.17, 17.18, 17.20

422

Index

Homicide offences *see also* Corporate manslaughter – *cont.*
  second post mortem, request for 2.84
  standard of proof 6.111
  suspension of investigation, requirement 2.114, 2.116–2.118, 21.5–21.14
  unlawful killing conclusion 6.65
  workplace deaths 16.7–16.9
Hospitals *see also* Custody or state detention; Liberty, deprivation of; Mental healthcare; Mentally ill person
  Art 2 duty, and 3.59, 3.92
  deaths, in
    notification of 2.4, 2.12
    post mortem 2.68
    prisoner receiving treatment 4.97
    unexpected 2.103
  DoL safeguards 15.49, 15.50, 15.55, 15.59, 15.61
  mental healthcare 15.21, 15.23, 15.30
  neglect 6.151
  PFD reports 7.6
How deceased died 3.6, 6.10–6.21
  Art 2, and 6.15–6.21
Human rights *see also* European Convention on Human Rights
  care homes, and 3.92, 3.97, 15.11, 15.50, 15.55
  public inquiries, and 24.42, 24.43
Human Rights Act 1998 3.40, 3.41
  Convention rights, protection 1.6
  inquest, relevance to 3.42–3.50
  public authorities, under 3.40–3.44, 4.93, 4.99, 8.58, 15.20, 15.54–15.56
Hutton Inquiry 24.19

I

Industrial disease
  death caused by 4.101–4.107
    conclusion of 6.61
Infanticide
  conclusion as 6.103–6.105
  unlawful killing conclusion 6.65
Information *see* Disclosure; Evidence
Inquest *see also* Investigations; Pre-inquest review
  applications for release of body 2.43
  civil proceedings 1.12
    following 23.5, 23.6
  completion, timing for 2.42
  criminal proceedings 1.12, 1.14
  determinations and findings 3.5
  duty to hold 2.39
  ECHR, and *see* Article 2

Inquest *see also* Investigations; Pre-inquest review – *cont.*
  evidence, deceased relating to 2.43
  human rights, and 3.42–3.50
  inquisitorial nature of 1.9–1.14
  matters to be ascertained 3.4
  opening, public hearing 2.41
  scope 3.1–3.9
    Art 2, and 3.29
    coroner's discretion 3.22–3.28, 3.30
    determination of 3.29–3.34
    Jamieson/Middleton inquests 3.10–3.21
    statutory provisions 3.3–3.9
Inquiries *see* Public inquiries
Interested person
  admissions of failings 6.43–6.48
  closing submissions 5.30–5.33
  coroner's discretion 4.21
  disclosure to 4.66–4.82
    electronic communications 4.71
    post-mortem report 4.80
    redacted documents 4.71
  family, as 10.38–10.42
  family proceedings 22.5
  post-mortem report, disclosure 2.82
  product-related deaths 18.3–18.13
  prohibition against addressing coroner 5.30
  resumption of inquest, notification 2.133
  rights 4.11, 4.12, 4.24–4.31
    declining 4.20
  road traffic collisions 17.6, 17.7
  status 4.13–4.23
  submissions from 6.29
  workplace deaths 16.30–16.40
Investigations *see also* Inquest; Pre-inquest review
  absence of body 2.46–2.52
  end of life disputes 2.33, 2.34
  evidence 2.98–2.103
  generally 2.1–2.3
  no requirement for 2.31, 2.32
  opening *see* Opening of investigation
  purpose of 1.5–1.8
  regulatory bodies by 2.103
  resumption *see* Resumption of investigation
  stillbirths 2.35–2.37
  suspension *see* Suspension of investigation
Investigative duty
  Article 2, under 3.58
    compliance with 3.104–3.107
    deaths in custody 14.6, 14.22
    deaths in combat 19.36–19.39
      Iraq, case law 19.47, 19.48
    deaths in mental health detention 15.15

423

Index

Investigative duty – *cont.*
  Article 2, under – *cont.*
    deprivation of liberty 15.64, 15.65
    discharge of 3.51
    engagement of 3.52–3.54, 3.102, 3.103
    how deceased died 6.15
    judicial review, grounds for 8.58, 8.59
    narrative conclusions 6.164–6.169
    resumption of investigation 21.49–21.51
    test for 3.6, 3.98–3.101

J

***Jamieson* inquests** *see also* Article 2 3.10–3.21
Judicial review *see also* Remedies
  applications 8.36–8.38
    'sufficient interest' 8.36
  claims forms 8.41–8.44
  costs 8.65, 8.66
  decisions susceptible to 8.46, 8.47
  discontinuance of investigation 2.87
  grounds 8.50
    Art 2 positive obligations 8.58, 8.59
    illegality 8.51–8.53
    irrationality or unreasonableness 8.55–8.57
    procedural unfairness 8.54
  media access decisions 12.21
  permission 8.45
  PFD report, challenges to 7.30, 7.31
  procedure 8.39–8.45
  public inquiry, failure to hold 24.5
  remedies 8.60–8.64
  statutory framework 8.1
  timing of challenge 8.48, 8.49
  transfer of jurisdiction, decisions 2.97
  use of 8.67–8.74
Juries
  closing submissions, limits on 5.32
  composition 4.88, 5.35, 5.36
  conclusions 6.34–6.41
    Art 2 inquests 6.188–6.197
  deaths in mental health detention 15.18
  discharge 5.39
  discretion to summon 4.109–4.113
  disqualification 4.88, 4.89, 5.36
  DoLS detention 15.62, 15.63
  eligibility for 4.88, 5.35
  Galbraith Plus test 6.198–6.203
  guidance 5.39–5.42
  irregularity 5.40–5.42
  jury questionnaires 5.45, 5.46
  PFD reports, and 7.8, 7.9
  PIR hearing 4.86–4.92

Juries – *cont.*
  questions posed to 5.38
  questions raised by 5.44
  refusal for service 5.37
  requirement for 4.90–4.92, 5.34
    deaths caused by notifiable accident, poisoning or disease 4.101–4.107
    deaths caused by police action/omission 4.100
    removal of, coronavirus pandemic, during 20.20, 20.21
    state detention deaths 4.93–4.99
    validity of proceedings 4.108
  submissions, consideration by 5.43
  unlawful killing conclusion 6.112–6.116
  workplace deaths 16.44
Jurisdiction
  absence of body 2.46–2.52
  clinical negligence 13.6–13.15
  criminal proceedings 21.2
  death in mental health detention 15.6–15.8
  exhumation power 2.62–2.64
  opening an investigation 2.22–2.30
  overseas deaths, and 2.19, 2.21
  rules for precedence 21.3, 21.4
  transfer of 2.91–2.97
    family's wishes 2.96, 2.97
    guidance 2.92, 2.95, 2.96
    judicial review 2.97

L

Lawful killing
  conclusion of 6.68
Legal aid 9.9
  applications 9.11
  eligibility 9.12
  legal help 9.20–9.23
  legal representation 9.24–9.28
  means test 9.13–9.15
  merits test 9.16–9.19
  types 9.10
Legal privilege
  waiver 5.29, 9.32, 10.64, 10.65
  workplace deaths 16.26, 16.27
Legal representatives
  legal aid for 9.24–9.28
  military inquests, at 19.15–19.18
  public inquiries 24.23, 24.49
  role of 9.7, 9.8
Liberty, deprivation of *see also* Mentally ill persons
  Art 2, and 15.64–15.74
  authorisations for 15.50–15.52

424

Index

Liberty, deprivation of *see also* Mentally ill persons – *cont.*
  care homes 3.92
  guidance
    safeguards 15.41, 15.49–15.52, 15.59, 15.60
    jury inquest 15.62, 15.63
    legality 15.49
    meaning 15.47, 15.48
  safeguards
    guidance 4.93
Life, right to *see also* Article 2; European Convention on Human Rights 3.55–3.69
  custody/state detention deaths 14.18
  duties arising from 3.59, 3.61–3.69
  foetuses in utero 3.57
  public inquiry 24.43
  state obligations 3.39
Limitation
  judicial review 8.41–8.44
  product-related deaths 18.13
Litvinenko Inquiry 2.120
London 7/7 Bombings
  PFD report 7.22, 7.23

M

Manchester Arena Bombing 24.22
Manslaughter
  gross negligence manslaughter 6.76, 6.81–6.92
    causation 6.90, 6.91
    mental element 6.92
    test for grossness 6.84–6.89
  unlawful act manslaughter 6.76–6.80
  unlawful killing conclusion 6.65
Manufacturer
  interested person
    workplace deaths 16.36
Material irregularities or errors
  ground for statutory review 8.33–8.35
Media and publicity 12.1–12.3
  access decisions, challenging 12.21
  adverse coverage 11.7
  anonymity of witnesses 12.14–12.16
  client care 11.7
  disclosure applications by 12.4–12.8
  families, assistance relating to 12.22–12.30
  guidance 12.3–12.10, 12.12, 12.13, 12.17, 12.18, 18.14, 22.13
  inquest, attendance by 12.9
  live communication during inquest 12.13
  organisations, assistance relating to 12.31–12.33
  product-related deaths 18.25

Media and publicity – *cont.*
  reporting restrictions 12.10–12.12
  statement, to 11.15
Medical examiners
  notification of death 2.12
Medical negligence *see also* Hospital, deaths in
  Art 2, and 3.83–3.87, 13.16–13.26
  disclosure 13.27–13.31
  establishing 13.3–13.5
  expert evidence 13.34–13.38
  family, representation of 13.2
  healthcare providers
    duty of candour 13.32, 13.33
  inquest conclusions, and 13.39–13.41
  jurisdiction 13.6–13.15
  scope, generally 13.1
Medical practitioner
  alleged negligence by 2.69
  notification of death 2.4–2.11
    workplace, at 16.3
  post mortem, attendance 2.68
Medical records
  disclosure 4.83–4.85, 13.27–13.31, 14.19
  evidence as 2.99
Memorandum of understanding
  Chief Coroner/HSE 16.13, 16.14
  generally 2.103
Mental capacity 15.41
  deprivations of liberty 15.47–15.49
    authorisations for 15.50–15.52
  lack of 15.42
  state detention, and 15.53–15.56
    Art 2, and 15.64–15.74
    deaths after 3 April 2017 15.57–15.59
    deaths before 3 April 2017 15.60, 15.61
    jury inquests 15.62, 15.63
  test for 15.43–15.46
Mental healthcare
  Care Programme Approach 15.27–15.32
  community services 15.26
  disclosure 15.39, 15.40
  experts 15.33–15.38
  inpatient care 15.21
  legal framework 15.22–15.25
  service providers 15.19, 15.20
  witnesses 15.39, 15.40
Mentally ill person *see also* Custody or state detention; Liberty, deprivation of
  Art 2 duty, and 3.79, 3.92
  detention, death in 15.6–15.8
  suicide, self-harm and self-inflicted deaths 15.1–15.18
    Art 2 operational duty 15.9–15.15
    conclusions 15.16, 15.17

425

Index

Mentally ill person *see also* **Custody or state detention; Liberty, deprivation of** – *cont.*
suicide, self-harm and self-inflicted deaths – *cont.*
jury inquests **15.18**
***Middleton* inquests** *see also* **Article 2** 3.10–3.21
Military deaths
Art 2 duty, and 3.81, 3.82, 3.92
Brecon Beacons SAS training 19.42–19.46
combat, in 19.36–19.39
Crown immunity 19.40, 19.41
Deepcut 19.49, 19.50
disclosure 19.19–19.29
families, assistance for 19.11–19.14
generally 19.1–19.3
guidance 19.7
inquest, organisation of 19.4–19.10
jurisdiction 19.8
internal investigation of 19.30–19.35
Iraq, case law 19.47, 19.48
legal representation 19.15–19.18
Multiple-death disasters
public inquiry for 24.40
Murder *see also* **Corporate manslaughter; Homicide offences**
defences 6.73–6.75
meaning 6.69
mental elements 6.71, 6.72
physical elements 6.70
unlawful killing conclusion 6.65

N

Narrative conclusion *see also* **Conclusions; Short-form conclusion**
content 6.164–6.171
Art 2 inquests 6.164–6.169, 17.23
non-Art 2 inquests 6.170, 6.171
generally 6.160–6.163
road traffic collision 17.23–17.25
Natural causes, death from
conclusion of 6.117, 6.118
COVID-19, as 20.6–20.12
Neglect *see also* **Medical negligence**
causation 6.181–6.185
conclusion of 6.142
deaths in custody 14.7
definition of 6.143–6.148
failure/'gross failure' 6.149, 6.150
multiple acts/omissions 6.151–6.157
self-harm, and 6.158, 6.159, 15.17
Notices
disclosure for 4.61–4.63
non-compliance 4.62

Notices – *cont.*
disclosure for – *cont.*
variation 4.63
Notifiable disease
death caused by 2.11
Notification of death
death abroad 2.19–2.21
family by 2.8, 2.18
medical examiner by 2.12
medical practitioner by 2.4–2.11
police by 2.17
registrar by 2.13–2.16
requirement 2.6–2.8

O

Open conclusion
standard of proof 6.119, 6.173
use of 6.119–6.125
Opening of investigation
coroner's duty 2.22–2.30
discontinuance power 2.39, 2.40
duty to hold inquest 2.39, 2.41
no requirement for 2.31, 2.32
notification of 2.38
Operational duty
Art 2 under 3.59, 3.88–3.97, 13.21–13.26
death in mental health detention 15.9–15.13
deprived of liberty 15.68–15.74
safeguarding life 3.88–3.97
Organ donation/retention
consent for 2.57, 2.58, 2.60
guidance 2.58
informing family 10.18
objections 2.59
Organisations, representation 11.1
conflicts of interest 11.5
hearing, at 11.12–11.14
instructions 11.3
media
access, and 12.31–12.33
adverse coverage 11.7
statement, to 11.15
PFD reports 11.15
PIR hearing 11.8
pre-interest preparation 11.9–11.11
preliminary contact 11.2–11.4
previous reports and investigations 11.6
Overseas, death occurring
evidence gathering 2.102
military personnel 19.5, 19.6
multiple deaths 19.6
notification of 2.19
jurisdiction 2.19

Index

Overseas, death occurring – *cont.*
  repatriation 19.5

P

Pathologist *see also* Post mortem
  cause of death 10.67–10.70
  deaths in custody 14.21, 14.22
  evidence by 4.114, 10.17, 10.18
  fees 2.76
  forensic post mortem 2.79
  instruction 2.75
  qualification 2.75
  tissue/organ retention, notification 2.80

Permission
  judicial review 8.45

Personal protective equipment (PPE)
  COVID-19, and 20.26–20.32

PFD report
  action following 7.24–7.26
  Art 2 inquest, and 7.29
  challenges to 7.30, 7.31
  concerns giving rise to 7.15–7.17
    presentation of 7.18–7.20
  content of 7.13–7.23
  coroner's duty to make 7.1, 7.3, 7.4
  family access to 10.78, 10.79
  guidance 7.1, 7.2, 7.7, 7.9, 7.12, 7.13, 7.19–7.21, 12.26
  jury cases, in 7.8, 7.9
  letter as alternative 7.27, 7.28
  matters to avoid 7.21–7.23
  road traffic collisions following 17.26, 17.27
  scope of 7.1, 7.2
  submissions/evidence 7.5–7.7
  timing of 7.10–7.12
  workplace deaths 16.54–16.59

Poisoning
  death caused by 4.101–4.107

Police
  custody records
    evidence, as 2.101
  death caused by 4.100
  interested person status 4.22, 4.23
  post mortem
    attendance 2.68
    consultation with 2.79
    report, disclosure 2.82
  records
    disclosure of 21.34
  use of force, Art 2 3.62, 3.67

Post mortem
  arrangements for 2.67–2.69
  body, release of 2.89, 2.90

Post mortem – *cont.*
  cause of death established by 2.39
  child 2.76, 2.77
  code of practice 2.78
  conduct 2.75–2.82
    guidance 2.75, 2.78, 2.81, 2.83, 2.84
  COVID-19, and 20.13
  delay, and 2.55
  discontinuance, and 2.86–2.88
  exhumation for 2.61–2.64
  expedited 2.65, 2.66
    guidance 2.66
  expert, instruction of 2.75, 2.76
  medical practitioner, attendance 2.68
  no requirement for 2.31, 2.32
  non-invasive 2.70–2.74
  notification of 2.67
  organ donation/tissue retention 2.56–2.60
  post-mortem report, access to 10.12–10.16
  removal of body for 2.54
  report 2.81
    disclosure 2.82
  requirement 2.53
  second 2.83–2.85
  tissue/organ retention 2.80

Pre-Action Protocol for Judicial Review 8.40

Pre-inquest review
  client care 10.34–10.37, 11.8
  deaths caused by notifiable accident, poisoning or disease 4.101–4.107
  deaths caused by police action/omission 4.100
  disclosure 4.48–4.85
    coroner, to 4.51–4.57
    interested person, to 4.66–4.82
    medical records 4.83–4.85
    notices for 4.61–4.63
    public interest immunity 4.58–4.60
    witness summons 4.64
  documentary evidence 4.42–4.47
  experts, use of 4.114–4.126
  guidance 4.1, 4.2, 4.6, 4.8–4.10, 4.34, 4.37, 4.116
  interested persons 4.11–4.31
  juries, and 4.86–4.108
    discretion to summon 4.109–4.113
  road traffic collisions 17.8–17.13
  scope, generally 4.1–4.10
  state detention deaths 4.93–4.99
  witnesses 4.33–4.41

Prevention of future deaths *see* PFD reports

Prison and Probation Ombudsman 14.20

Prisons
  Art 2 duty, and 3.80, 3.92
    investigative duty 3.103, 3.104

427

Index

Prisons – *cont.*
  deaths, in *see also* Suicide, self-harm and self-inflicted deaths
    COVID-19, by 20.14
    excessive force 3.103, 14.16, 14.17
    inadequate care 13.24, 14.18
    hospital, prisoner receiving treatment 3.92, 4.97
Privately funded retainer 9.36, 9.37
Privilege
  doctor/patient 4.83
  evidence 5.13
  legal 5.29, 10.65
  self-incrimination, against 5.25–5.29
  waiver 5.29, 9.32, 10.64, 10.65
Procedural duty
  deprived of liberty 15.66, 15.67
Product-related deaths 18.1
  'defect' 18.11
  defences 18.12
  disclosure 18.15–18.19
  expert evidence 18.20–18.24
  interested persons 18.3–18.13
  limitation 18.13
  'product' 18.2
  publicity 18.25
  regulatory issues 18.15–18.19
  similar cases, research into 18.14
Psychiatric detention *see* Custody or state detention
Public funding *see* Funding
Public inquiries 24.1, 24.2
  Art 2 duty, and 24.20
  chair
    appointment 24.5, 24.7
    duties 24.10
  core participants 24.23, 24.24, 24.48, 24.49
  criticism, warning letters 24.14
  determinations 24.50
  documents, access to 24.10
  establishment, minister by 24.5
  evidence 24.8, 24.9, 24.22
  halting of 24.15
  historical context 24.4
  human rights, and 24.42, 24.43
  inquests, similarities and differences 24.21–24.24
  legal representation 24.23, 24.49
  nature of 24.3–24.20
  non-statutory 24.16–24.19
  procedural matters 24.44–24.59
  public access, restriction of 24.10
  reason for holding 24.25–24.28
  report following 24.13, 24.14
  resumption of inquest, and 2.128

Public inquiries – *cont.*
  scope 24.22, 24.29–24.43
  standard of proof 24.11, 24.12, 24.22, 24.52
  statutory framework 24.5
  suspension of investigation, and 2.119–2.121
  'terms of reference' 24.6
  timescales 24.46
  transparency, presumption 24.10
Public interest immunity
  PIR hearing 4.58–4.60

R

Reasons, duty to provide
  conclusion of death 6.30–6.33
Record of Inquest
  attestation 6.27
  caption 6.28
  cause of death 6.10–6.12
  circumstances of death 6.13–6.21
  conclusion 6.22–6.24, 6.29
    reasons 6.30–6.33
  form of 6.8
  further particulars 6.25, 6.26
  generally 6.1–6.6
  name of deceased 6.9
  purpose 6.7
Redacted documents
  disclosure of 4.71
Register of reported deaths
  content 2.32
Registrar of births and deaths
  certificate permitting disposal of body 2.15
  information, power to request 2.14
  no resumption of inquest, notification 2.132
  reporting death to 2.13–2.16
  suspension of investigation, notification 2.124
Release of bodies
  post mortem following 2.89, 2.90
Remedies
  damages 8.60
  quashing orders 8.60–8.64
Removal of bodies
  permission for 2.21
Reporting restrictions
  access decisions, challenging 12.21
  child witnesses 22.12
  child, identity of 12.17, 12.18
    deceased child 12.19, 12.20
  coroner's power 12.10–12.12
  deceased child 22.13

Index

Representing families 10.1, 10.2
  cause of death, communicating 10.67–10.70
  client care during proceedings 10.28–10.33
  clinical inquests 13.2
  death, following 10.3–10.11
  disclosure of information 10.38–10.42
  expert evidence, and 10.63–10.66
  first contact 10.19–10.27
  hearing, at 10.49–10.57
  inquest conclusions 10.71–10.77
  media reporting, and 12.22–12.30
  mentally ill person, of 15.76, 15.77
  military inquests, in 19.11–19.14
  oral evidence 10.58–10.62
  pathologist's evidence, advance warning 10.17, 10.18
  PFD reports, family access to 10.78, 10.79
  PIR hearing 10.34–10.37
  post-mortem report, access to 10.12–10.16
  support following inquest 10.80, 10.81
  witnesses statements 10.43–10.48
Representing organisations 11.1
  conflicts of interest 11.5
  hearing, at 11.12–11.14
  instructions 11.3
  media
    access, and 12.31–12.33
    adverse coverage 11.7
    statement, to 11.15
  PFD reports 11.15
  PIR hearing 11.8
  pre-interest preparation 11.9–11.11
  preliminary contact 11.2–11.4
  previous reports and investigations 11.6
Resumption of investigation
  Art 2 investigative duty 21.49–21.51
  criminal proceedings 21.40–21.42, 21.52
    sufficient reason 21.43–21.48
  decision not to resume 2.132
  discretion for 2.130
  guidance 2.131
  jury, recall 2.129
  notification 2.133
  public inquiry after 2.128
  requirement for 2.126, 2.127
Road traffic collision 17.1, 17.2
  Art 2, and 17.11, 17.23–17.25
  conclusion on 6.126, 6.127
  inquest, need for 17.3–17.5
  interested person 17.6, 17.7
  PFD reports, and 17.26, 17.27
  police investigations 17.14, 17.15
  pre-inquest review 17.8–17.13
  short-form conclusion, as 17.21–17.25
    guidance 17.21–17.23, 17.25

Road traffic collision – *cont.*
  suspension of investigation 17.16–17.20

S

Self incrimination
  privilege against 5.25–5.29
Self-harm/ self-inflicted deaths *see* Suicide, self-harm or self-inflicted deaths
Senior coroner
  jurisdiction 1.20
  qualification 1.21
  register of reported deaths 2.32
  role 1.20, 1.22
Serious untoward incident reports
  healthcare providers 13.32, 13.33
Service deaths *see* Military deaths
Short-form conclusion *see also* Conclusions; Narrative conclusion
  Art 2 cases 17.23
  accident/misadventure 6.55–6.58
  alcohol/drug related 6.59, 6.60
  clinical negligence 13.40
  industrial disease 6.61
  lawful killing/unlawful killing 6.62–6.116
  natural causes, death from 6.117, 6.118
  neglect 6.142–6.159
  open conclusion 6.119–6.125
  overview 6.49–6.54
  road traffic collision 6.126, 6.127, 17.21–17.25
  standard of proof 6.172
  stillbirth 6.128–6.133
  suicide 6.134–6.141
  workplace deaths 16.51–16.53
Slavery and forced labour, prohibition
  state obligations 3.39
Standard of proof
  civil standard 1.12, 1.13
  coroner's duty to investigate, and 2.23
  criminal standard 1.12
  homicide offences 6.111
  open conclusions 6.119, 6.173
  public inquiries 24.11, 24.12, 24.22, 24.52
  short-form conclusions 6.172
  suicide conclusions 15.16
State agents 14.20
  Art 2 3.18, 3.65, 3.71
    investigative duty 3.8, 3.99
  deaths involving
    excessive force 3.103
    outside jurisdiction 24.43
    parallel investigations 14.20
    public inquiry 24.43
  slavery and forced labour 3.39

429

Index

State detention *see* Custody or state detention
Statutory review
  applications 8.4, 8.5, 8.9
  authorisation by Attorney-General 8.6–8.8
  coroner's jurisdiction 8.10
  power to order investigation 8.11–8.15
    jurisdiction 8.13
    nature of death 8.14, 8.15
  power to quash findings 8.16–8.18
    desirability 8.19–8.23
    fraud 8.32
    material irregularities or errors 8.33–8.35
    necessity 8.19–8.23
    new evidence 8.24–8.31
  statutory framework 8.1–8.3
  use of 8.67–8.74
Stillbirth
  conclusion of 6.128–6.133
  generally 2.35–2.37
Submissions 10.65
  interested persons, from 6.29
  interested persons, by 5.30–5.32
Suicide, self-harm and self-inflicted deaths
  conclusion of 6.134–6.141
    Maughan, and 6.135
  custody/state detention in 14.8–14.15
  mentally ill person 15.1–15.18
    Art 2 operational duty 15.9–15.15
    conclusions 15.16, 15.17
    jury inquests 15.18
  neglect, and 6.158, 6.159
  standard of proof 1.12, 1.13
Summing up/directions
  challenges to *see* Judicial review
Summons
  witness for 4.64
Suspension of investigation
  death of foreign military personnel 2.121
  discretionary 2.122, 21.15, 21.16
  duty to suspend 2.113–2.118
  effect of 2.123–2.125, 21.17, 21.18
  exceptions 21.19–21.21
  guidance 2.113, 2.126, 2.127, 17.15, 17.16, 21.16, 21.18, 21.21, 21.44, 21.47
  ongoing criminal proceedings 16.16
  ongoing criminal proceedings, and 21.5–21.14
  public inquiry, for 2.118–2.121
  registrar, notification 2.124
  road traffic collision deaths 17.16–17.20
Systemic duty *see also* Article 2
  death in mental health detention 15.14

Systemic duty *see also* Article 2 – *cont.*
  safeguarding life 3.70, 3.71, 3.73–3.87
    clinical negligence 3.83–3.87
    dangerous activities/natural hazards 3.72–3.78
    mental health patients 3.79
    military deaths 3.81, 3.82
    prisoners 3.80

T

Tissue retention
  consent for 2.56, 2.58, 2.60
  guidance 2.58
  informing family 10.18
  objections 2.59
Torture or inhuman/degrading treatment, prohibition *see also* Article 2; European Convention on Human Rights
  public inquiry 24.43
  state obligations 3.39
Trade union representative
  interested person
    workplace deaths 16.37

U

Unlawful killing *see also* Corporate manslaughter; Homicide offences
  causation 6.110
  conclusion of 6.62–6.67
    infanticide 6.65
    manslaughter 6.65
    Maughan, following 6.62, 6.63
    murder 6.65
  corporate manslaughter 6.93–6.102
  defences 6.106–6.109
  Galbraith Plus test 6.112–6.116
  infanticide 6.103–6.105
  jury, directions to 6.112–6.116
  lawful withdrawal of treatment 6.72
  manslaughter 6.76–6.92
  mercy killings 6.72
  murder 6.69
    defences 6.73–6.75
    mental elements 6.71, 6.72
    physical elements 6.70
  standard of proof 1.12, 1.13, 6.111
Unnatural death
  duty to investigate 2.24, 2.26
  meaning 2.27, 2.28
  no discontinuance power 2.40

V

Verdicts *see* Conclusions; Narrative conclusion; Short-form conclusion
Violent death
    duty to investigate 2.24, 2.25
    mentally ill person 15.7, 15.8
    no discontinuance power 2.40

W

When deceased died 3.6, 6.13–6.21
Where deceased died 3.6, 6.13–6.21
Who deceased was 3.6, 6.9
Witnesses
    anonymity 12.14–12.16
    calling of 4.33–4.41
        coroner's discretion 4.33, 4.34
        power to compel 4.35
        protective measures 4.36–4.41
    child as *see* Children
    examination of 5.3
    family, statements by 10.43–10.47
    hearsay evidence 5.14–5.20
    mental health inquest 15.39, 15.40
    order at hearing 5.2, 5.3
    power to compel 4.35
    questioning of 5.4–5.12
    self-incrimination, privilege against 5.25–5.29

Witnesses – *cont.*
    statements by, family disputing 10.48
    workplace deaths 16.24, 16.45–16.50
Work, death at, *see also* Corporate manslaughter
    conclusions 16.51–16.53
    COVID-19 pandemic, and 16.2, 20.22–20.32
        PPE provision 20.26–20.32
    disclosure 16.41–16.43
    documentary evidence 16.24
    expert evidence 16.25
    generally 16.1–16.4
    health and safety offences 16.10–16.12
    homicide offences 16.7–16.9
    inquest, preparation for 16.23–16.29
    interested person 16.30–16.40
    jury inquest 16.44
    legal privilege 16.26, 16.27
    medical practitioner, notification 16.3
    memorandum of understanding 16.13, 16.14
    PFD reports 16.54–16.59
    proceedings, timeline for 16.15–16.22
        HSE's discretion 16.17
    regulator, investigation by 16.5, 16.6
    statistics 16.3, 16.4
    witness statements 16.24
    witnesses 16.45–16.50
Work-related Deaths Protocol 16.6